D1272552

HISTORY OF THE AMERICAN CINEMA

Volume 9

1970–1979

Poster art for Martin Scorsese's Taxi Driver *(Columbia, 1976). Reflecting the twin calamities of Watergate and Vietnam, this film traded heavily in the depiction of political paranoia, racial bigotry, perverse sexuality, and graphic gore—and was critically acclaimed as one of the most distinguished motion pictures of its time, a situation unprecedented, indeed unthinkable, in the American cinema before the 1970s.*

HISTORY OF THE
AMERICAN CINEMA
CHARLES HARPOLE, GENERAL EDITOR

9
LOST ILLUSIONS: AMERICAN CINEMA IN THE SHADOW OF WATERGATE AND VIETNAM, 1970-1979

David A. Cook

Charles Scribner's Sons
Macmillan Library Reference USA
NEW YORK

Credits amd permissions can be found on p. 595 and should
be considered an extension of the copyright page.

Copyright © 2000 By David A. Cook

Charles Scribner's Sons
An Imprint of Macmillan Library Reference USA
1633 Broadway
New York, NY 10019

Library of Congress Catalog Card Number: 99-21371
Printed in the United States of America

Printing Number
1   2   3   4   5   6   7   8   9   10

Library of Congress Cataloging-in-Publication Data

Cook, David A.
    Lost illusions : American cinema in the shadow of Watergate
and Vietnam, 1970–1979 / David A. Cook.
        p. cm.—(History of the American cinema ; v. 9)
    Includes bibliographical references and index.
    ISBN 0-684-80463-8
    1. Motion picture industry—United States-History.   I. Title.
II. Series.
PN1993.5.U6H55   1990 vol. 9
384'.8'0973-dc21   99-21371
                                                    CIP

This paper meets the requirements of ANSI/NISO z.39.48-1992
(Permanence of Paper).

Advisory Board

The Cinema History Project and the
History of the American Cinema
have been supported by grants from the
National Endowment for the Humanities and the
John and Mary R. Markle Foundation.

For my parents, Sara and Allen,
whose love of the movies was contagious

Contents

Acknowledgments

When I first agreed to write a book on the 1970s for the *History of American Cinema* series, my sense of the decade came largely from having lived through it and having seen a lot of movies in the process. I tended to view these products of the "New Hollywood" as differing from the old mainly in terms of their generational sensibilities and cultural politics. It was a long discussion with Tom Schatz in the fall of 1996 that provided my first critical understanding of the remarkable sea change the American film industry underwent during the 1970s; and specific insights into its transformation were subsequently and generously offered by Jon Lewis, Steve Prince, and Dana Polan as the project matured. To Dana, especially, who read the manuscript under difficult circumstances in various stages of its development and who provided invaluable critical comments and suggestions, I owe a very large debt of thanks.

Significant editorial support was provided by general editor Charles Harpole, whose vision and dedication made the *History of American Cinema* series possible in the first place, and by Scribner's editor John Fitzpatrick, whose unerring and discerning judgement was essential to both fine-tuning the manuscript and selecting illustrations.

For helping to provide the illustrations themselves, I need to thank Mary Corliss of the Museum of Modern Art, Howard Mandelbaum of Photofest, and William D. Phillips, who has graciously let me use production stills from his private collection. The charts and diagrams were designed to specification and executed by Randy Fullerton of the Emory Theater Studies Department, who gave of his time and talent well above the call of duty.

I want also to thank my contributors—Douglas Gomery, William Rothman, and Robin Blaetz—for lending their unique perspectives and expertise to this project and for their forbearance through a number of tedious authorial chores. It is no less true for being a cliché that this book would not exist without them.

At Emory there are many others to thank, and I can only name a few. Much of the research for this book was funded by a grant, for which I am extremely grateful, from the Emory University Research Committee. Rosemary Magee, Associate Dean of Emory College, helped me secure space for the project, and Steven E. Sanderson, Dean of the College and Vice President for Arts and Sciences, helped me find the time to finish it. Research assistance was provided at various stages by Brent Plate and Lisa Rivo, Ph.D. candidates in the Institute of Liberal Arts, and Corinn Columpar, a doctoral candidate in the Women's Studies program, gave me an understanding of feminist theory that changed the way I look at American films. I also owe thanks to my colleagues in Emory's Film Studies Program—Matthew Bernstein, Robin Blaetz, and Angela Dalle Vacche—for their many helpful comments on my work, and for putting up with my distractedness while producing it. Special thanks is due to Annie Hall, Administrative Assistant for the Film Studies Program, who helped me significantly in preparing the manuscript and who configured and typed most of the lists and tables in the Appendixes.

The last group of Emory people I need to thank are my students—undergraduates and graduates, past and present—who have made this project both meaningful and necessary. Over the several years it took to put the book together, my students have helped me constantly to clarify my thoughts, to refine my methodology, and finally, to arrive at many conclusions about the functioning of the American film industry in the 1970s that I might not otherwise have reached. A stated goal of the *History of American Cinema* series is to serve as a reference work for professional scholars, and I have sought to maintain a level of scholarly discourse throughout, but I have also tried to make the volume accessible to a larger audience of students and teachers. My most basic urge as a scholar has always been to illuminate and inform; if the goal of scholarship is not ultimately to make us better teachers, then it truly doesn't have one.

Finally—and always—I thank my wife Diane Holt Cook, with whom I shared a rich life in the last third of the twentieth century, and who is always in my thoughts and in my heart.

Contributors

DAVID A. COOK is Professor and founding Director of the Film Studies Program at Emory University. He is the author of *A History of Narrative Film* (3rd Edition) and numerous scholarly articles on literature, film theory, and film history.

ROBIN BLAETZ is Assistant Professor of Film Studies at Emory University. She is the author of *Visions of the Maid: Women, War, and Joan of Arc in Twentieth-Century America* and articles on feminist avant-garde film.

DOUGLAS GOMERY is Professor of Communications Arts at the University of Maryland. He is the author of *Shared Pleasures: A History of Movie Presentation in the United States, Movie History: A Survey, The Hollywood Studio System*, and four other books examining the economics and history of American media, as well as multiple articles and monographs in the field.

WILLIAM ROTHMAN is Professor in the Motion Picture Program of the School of Communications, University of Miami. He is the author of *Hitchcock: The Murderous Gaze, The "I" of the Camera*, and *Documentary Film Classics*, as well as scholarly essays in philosophy, film theory, and the arts.

Movie profits, movie investments, movie contracts, money in the movies, become like money in a gambling casino. Unreal.

HAROLD J. SALEMSON AND MARUICE ZOLOTOW,
HOLLYWOOD REPORTERS, 1978

Our cash negative [cost] on this picture [CLOSE ENCOUNTERS OF THE THIRD KIND] was about $17.5 million. We took in $6.75 million of outside financing, which reduced our negative investment to $10.8 million. Our releasing costs to cash breakeven were $8 million. That, again, brought our overall investment up to $19 million. We had exhibitor guarantees of some $21 million, which meant before we released the picture we were $2 million ahead of the game. *This was before any attribution of value to television, pay cable, or to merchandising rights. (Emphasis added.)*

ALAN HIRSCHFIELD, PRESIDENT,
COLUMBIA PICTURES INDUSTRIES, 1978

Given the cost of movies today, and the cost of marketing movies, my view is that the only real audience to pursue is . . . people in the thirteen-to-twenty-five age group. That's where you find the repeat moviegoer, the person who goes back again and again to see a hit movie. Young moviegoers are less critical and they're more susceptible to an advertising blitz.

PETER GUBER, PRESIDENT, POLYGRAM PICTURES, 1981

[I]n spite of the financial acumen of contemporary executives, today's studios are no more profitable than in the days of the studio system. Because the studios compete so heavily for the services of a small pool of stars and big-name directors, the price of these commodities has risen dramatically. According to the Motion Picture Association of America (MPAA), between 1972 and 1981 the cost of films distributed by major studios rose at a compound annual rate of 21.5%. . . . [Since that time] the dream of major-studio executives is to hit a home run by creating not only a popular film but a new franchise.

MARK LITWAK, ENTERTAINMENT ATTORNEY, 1997

It has been calculated that [STAR WARS: EPISODE I] THE PHANTOM MENACE would have turned a profit even if no one had gone to see it. As it turned out, the movie took in $162.7 million in its first five days. . . .

LOUIS MENAND, CONTRIBUTING EDITOR,
THE NEW YORK REVIEW OF BOOKS

Preface

A Time of Illusion

In the mid-1970s, two popular and critically acclaimed films appeared that were set against the backdrop of recent political events. The films were SHAMPOO (Hal Ashby, 1975) and ALL THE PRESIDENT'S MEN (Alan J. Pakula, 1976), and the events were the election of Richard Milhous Nixon as President of the United States in 1968 and his re-election in 1972. By creating and then manipulating an oddly contemporary sense of *deja vu*, these films reminded their audiences that they had made a terrible mistake and had made it twice. Several years later, a number of films whose background was the war in Vietnam—COMING HOME (Hal Ashby, 1978), THE DEER HUNTER (Michael Cimino, 1978), and APOCALYPSE NOW (Francis Ford Coppola, 1979)—reminded their audiences that they had made a terrible mistake and had made it every day for the eleven years between 1964 and 1975, and these films also reaped critical and commercial success. In a degree of self-examination extraordinary for this country in any medium at any time, the American commercial cinema was experimenting with social criticism and making money at it in the bargain. The list of films either explicitly or implicitly critical of American society made during the 1970s goes on and on. For example, the decade was bracketed by two films, McCABE & MRS. MILLER (Robert Altman, 1971) and HEAVEN'S GATE (Michael Cimino, 1980), that offered uncompromising critiques of frontier capitalism and, by extension, of the American economic system at large. THE PARALLAX VIEW (Alan J. Pakula, 1974), NASHVILLE (Robert Altman, 1975), and TAXI DRIVER (Martin Scorsese, 1976) all suggested that assassination was part of the warp and woof of American political life, which was itself an unseemly mixture of entertainment, manipulation, and fraud. There were Westerns that debunked the foundational myths of "manifest destiny" (LITTLE BIG MAN [Arthur Penn, 1970]; ULZANA'S RAID [Robert Aldrich, 1972]), gangster films that linked organized crime with big business (THE GODFATHER [Francis Ford Coppola, 1972]) and elective government (THE GODFATHER, PART II [Francis Ford Coppola, 1974]), and disaster films that associated urban catastrophe with corporate malfeasance and graft (EARTHQUAKE [Mark Robson, 1973]; THE TOWERING INFERNO [John Guillermin, 1974]). Because social consciousness had played so little part in the American cinema to date, commentators of the time may be forgiven for thinking, hopefully, that a new dispensation was at hand. But like the movies themselves, it was all an illusion, broken wide apart when the lights went up on November 7, 1980.

In fact, the election of Ronald Reagan to the presidency marked the loss of two illusions fabricated during the decade that preceded it. First was the illusion of a liberal political consensus created by the antiwar movement, the Watergate scandal, and the subsequent resignation of Richard Nixon as president of the United States: the decade that began with the November 15th moratorium, Kent State, and the *Washington Post's* exposé of "the White House horrors" ended with the election of Ronald Reagan and the ascendancy of right-wing conservatism in our political leadership for the next twelve years. The second illusion, intermingled with the first, was that mainstream American movies might aspire to the sort of serious social or political content described above on a permanent basis. This prospect was seriously challenged when the blockbuster mentality took hold in Hollywood in the wake of JAWS (Steven Spielberg, 1975) and STAR WARS (George Lucas, 1977), and it was shattered by the epochal success of the Spielberg-Lucas juggernaut of the early Reagan years. Privileging a juvenile mythos of "awe" and "wonder" in movies that embraced conservative cultural values, yet did so within a superstructure of high-tech special effects and nostalgia for classical genres, THE EMPIRE STRIKES BACK (Irvin Kershner, 1980), RAIDERS OF THE LOST ARK (Steven Spielberg, 1981), E.T. (Steven Spielberg, 1982), RETURN OF THE JEDI (Richard Marquand, 1983), and INDIANA JONES AND THE TEMPLE OF DOOM (Steven Spielberg, 1984) together grossed over $1 billion in the domestic market, just slightly less than *all* of the highest-earning films for each of the years between 1970 and 1979. In effect, the blockbuster syndrome returned Hollywood to its bedrock profile of reactionary ideology and capitalist greed with a newly sophisticated emphasis on commodity packaging. This same mentality in the political sphere produced the "scientific" marketing of candidates adumbrated by *The Selling of the President 1968*, Joe McGinniss's ground-breaking 1969 study of the first Nixon campaign, whose strategy of demographic targeting was brought to consummate perfection by the team that elected Ronald Reagan in 1980 (and illustrated prophetically in the year of Nixon's re-election by Michael Ritchie's film THE CANDIDATE [1972]).

The "lost illusions" of the 1970s, in fact, came together in Ronald Reagan, whose early career as a B-film actor made him an ideal president for the era of the Lucas-Spielberg-style blockbuster—a form whose roots were in the very type of genre movies that had made him a prominent feature player in the studio days. Then in his seventies, Reagan still exuded the boyish charm and facile optimism of a Saturday matinee idol, and he became the perfect political simulacrum of blockbuster heroes like Luke Skywalker and Indiana Jones, even to the point of dubbing his Strategic Defense Initiative (SDI) "Star Wars," as it is still called by both the public and policy experts today. Meanwhile, the Hollywood of his youth and middle-age was recapitulated in a new industrial structure in which the "studios" had become multinational media conglomerates for the distribution of "filmed entertainment" franchised through a worldwide marketplace that now included not only theaters and television but cable outlets, videocassettes, video games, books, magazines, records, and a vast array of merchandising and fast food tie-ins. The chances that a SHAMPOO, ALL THE PRESIDENT'S MEN, or THE DEER HUNTER might appear in such an environment were remote, that they might prosper nearly impossible. Yet less than a decade before, each of one of them had generated a tidy profit, earning between $25 million and $30 million apiece in theatrical rentals—well over five times their respective negative costs, with 2.5 times as the standard breakeven point. By the end of the 1970s, however, the blockbuster syndrome had changed the way Hollywood did business, so that such profits seemed miniscule, hardly worth pursuing compared with the revenue streams that could be generated by a major franchise like STAR WARS or INDIANA JONES.

Thus the vaunted "Hollywood Renaissance"—the European-style auteur cinema that prevailed briefly in America from 1967 to 1975—was an aberration in the film industry's sixty-year history to date, one that came into being mainly by default at a time of economic and political crisis. The Reagan years would provide a "mid-course correction" and set the American cinema sailing toward the turn of the century, when the blockbuster calculus would reach new levels of fiscal absurdity. (In March 1998, for example, the Motion Picture Association of America [MPAA] announced that the *average* cost of releasing a film in the United States had reached $76.8 million; by the summer of that year the average negative cost for a major studio release had climbed to $120 million, with an average marketing budget of $100 million.) In one sense, then, the cinema of the 1970s can be viewed as a richly fruitful detour in the American film industry's march toward gigantism and global domination—but it was also the crucible in which the industry's current market structure was forged. By borrowing practices like saturation booking and heavily targeted advertising from exploitation cinema, mainstream Hollywood reinvented itself as an aggressive national marketing force; by appropriating sensational subject matter (THE EXORCIST [William Friedkin], JAWS [1975], ALIEN [Ridley Scott, 1979]), learning to cross-market its every saleable element (ROCKY [John G. Avildsen, 1976], STAR WARS [1977], SUPERMAN [Richard Donner, 1978]) and then recycle it as sequels, "prequels," remakes, and spinoffs, Hollywood reconceptualized its product as the franchise, rather than the individual motion picture. That an aesthetically experimental, socially conscious *cinema d'auteur* could exist simultaneously with a burgeoning and rapacious blockbuster mentality was extraordinary, but it became the defining mark of 1970s cinema. That the two could coexist for long, however, was an illusion as ephemeral as the notion of a liberal ideological consensus. In a sense, both illusions would fall victim to the Hollywood B-film; and when that finally occurred the decade that Johnathan Schell in his book on Watergate called "The Time of Illusion" was over, and the Reagan ascendancy had begun.

A Note on
Box-Office Revenues

Throughout this book, the figures used to indicate a film's financial performance are reported as "domestic film rentals," that is, that percentage of gross box-office receipts that the exhibitor pays to the distributor to rent the film in the United States and Canadian market, excluding his own percentage under the terms of the licensing agreement (normally 30–45 percent on a sliding scale, but as little as 10 percent for blockbusters), taxes, and theater operating expenses (called the "house nut"). During the 1970s, total film rental represented between a third and a half of the gross, and the average is still less than 50 percent of the gross. Of that figure, 30 percent goes to the distributor as a service fee (the "distribution fee"), and another 20–30 percent is used to recover expenses directly related to release (primarily the costs of prints, marketing, and interest). The remaining 40–50 percent of film rentals, called the "net producer's share," is applied against the negative cost (used, that is, to pay off the loan that financed the film's production). What's left after negative amortization is profit, to be split between the distributor and producer—if they are not one and the same, as increasingly during the 1970s they were not—in ratios that vary from 50/50 to 80/20. Thus, although everything depends upon box-office grosses, the income returning to the distributor-financier-producer segments of the industry is most accurately represented by rentals.

The source of all publicly available revenue figures is the weekly box-office grosses reported in the industry trade publication *Variety*. It should be noted, however, that *Variety*'s totals are hardly definitive because its staff gathers earnings figures separately from distributors and exhibitors and then makes educated guesses. During the 1970s, *Variety* grosses were often inflated by a third or more in a film's opening weeks, as distributors and exhibitors colluded to create the impression of a hit (giving the film "legs," or potential strength), which every studio executive at the time full well knew. Contrarily, although percentage licensing agreements required theater owners to provide distributors with regular box-office reports, other kinds of exhibition contracts did not, encouraging under-reporting of income and other practices designed by exhibitors to keep as much of the box-office take as possible. Either way, for many films of the 1970s (as well as before and after) there is no way to know what the total box-office gross really was, although a rule of thumb used by industry insiders at the time was to deduct 25 percent from the reported figures.

A Note on
Aspect Ratios

During the 1970s, virtually all theatrical features were shot in a widescreen process and/or projected in a widescreen aspect ratio. Notable exceptions were the low-budget features of independent filmmakers like Melvin Van Peebles (SWEET SWEETBACK, 1971) and John Cassavetes (A WOMAN UNDER THE INFLUENCE, 1975), who shot in the Academy ratio of 1.33:1 (4 x 3) both to economize on equipment and lab fees and, sometimes, because they preferred it. The Academy ratio corresponded to the aperture of the 35mm camera and therefore to the 35mm film frame; it had been the industry standard for image and screen shape since the early silent era, and it was officially designated as such by the Academy of Motion Picture Arts and Sciences in 1932, when a number of technical standards were set vis-à-vis the recent introduction of sound.

After 1954, exhibitors had been forced to modify their Academy-ratio shaped screens to accommodate the rectalinear aspect ratios of the new widescreen processes—2.55:1 (later 2.35:1) for CinemaScope, 1.75:1 for VistaVision (an average, since VistaVision's ratio was variable), and 2.2:1 for most widegauge film processes (e.g., Todd-AO, Panavision 70, etc.). When screens came to approximate 2 x 1 rectangles instead of 4 x 3 squares, images could no longer be projected at 1.33:1 without cutting off their tops and/or bottoms. To solve this problem for films not shot in either CinemaScope (a 35mm anamorphic process that required the use of special camera and projection lenses) or 70mm (widegauge film systems that required the use of special cameras, projectors, and film stock) the industry adopted the "golden ratio" of 1.85:1, a modified widescreen ratio that was achieved by masking the normal 35mm aperture in-camera to obstruct its top and bottom, usually with an aperture plate called a hard matte. (The European standard widescreen ratio of 1.66:1 was achieved the same way, and some American directors preferred it to 1.85:1—for example, Stanley Kubrick.) Alternatively, the film could be shot full-frame and matted down to 1.85:1 in projection. So long as filmmakers knew that their images would appear at 1.85:1 in theaters, they could compose for that ratio in production, leading some directors to more or less ignore what appeared in the upper and lower extremes of the frame (and their films, when projected without a 1.85:1 matte— or, later, when transferred to video full-frame—would occasionally reveal production apparatus like camera tracks or boom microphones).

The most common widescreen process used in the American industry during the seventies was Panavision, a 35mm anamorphic system that had replaced CinemaScope in the early 1960s by virtue of its superior lens technology, and which had an aspect ratio of 2.35:1. Other anamorphic systems included Technovision and Todd-AO 35, which were simply versions of Panavision with lenses manufactured by other companies, and Techniscope, which was different in that it modified the camera movement to expose one-half of a standard 35mm frame and then blew up the negative in the lab to full-frame anamorphic format. Either way, a widefield image was squeezed onto regular 35mm film stock through anamorphosis and unsqueezed through reverse anamorphosis in projection.

Widegauge film systems—which used 65mm negative stock and 70mm print stock, and could accommodate up to six stereo magnetic sound tracks—appeared briefly in 1970 as holdovers from the studios' late 1960s debacle. RYAN'S DAUGHTER (MGM, 1970) and SONG OF NORWAY (CRC, 1970) were both filmed in Super Panavision 70, and PATTON (Fox, 1970) was filmed in a 65mm curved-screen process similar to Cinerama called Dimension 150. After 1970, there was no filming in widegauge until the early 1980s (for example, Disney's TRON [1982] was made in Super Panavision 70), but there were quite a number of 70mm blow-ups, that is, films shot in 35mm and blown up to 70mm through optical printing. During the 1960s, Panavision had perfected a method for making high-resolution 70mm release prints from both 35mm anamorphic and spherical negatives. This process, known as Panavision 70 (as distinct from Super Panavision 70, which refers only to films shot in 70mm), was used extensively for road-showing films during the 1970s, frequently in combination with magnetic stereo sound. In *Wide Screen Movies* (Jefferson, North Carolina: McFarland, 1988), Robert E. Carr and R. M. Hayes list 87 films made or reissued between 1970 and 1980 that received 70mm blow-up treatment, ranging from the spectacular (STAR WARS [Fox, 1977]; APOCALYPSE NOW [UA, 1979]) to the mundane (BILLY JACK GOES TO WASHINGTON [Taylor-Laughlin, 1977]; THE MUPPET MOVIE [ADF, 1979]).

Because of their nature as production stills, most of the pictures in this volume do not match the shape of the original compositions. Wherever possible, however, the original widescreen process and/or projected aspect ratio of a film is indicated after the picture caption, so that the reader can at least *imagine* how the scene actually looked on screen.

1

Introduction: A Decade of Change

If, as Joan Didion has written, the deal is the true art form of Hollywood, the masters of this art are the tax shelter specialists.

MARIE BRENNER, JOURNALIST, 1977

The American film industry changed more between 1969 and 1980 than at any other period in its history except, perhaps, for the coming of sound. Changes in the style and content of the movies themselves, remarkable though they were, barely hinted at the deep structural alterations in the way films were conceived, produced, and distributed from the beginning to the end of the decade. During that time, profits for the most successful motion pictures rose from the hundreds of thousands to the hundreds of millions of dollars. Production dropped off sharply as studios came to shape their schedules around a handful of potential blockbusters or "event" movies—any one of which could produce windfall profits and send their stock soaring on Wall Street—with the expectation that the rest would break even (25–30 percent) or fail. This "blockbuster mentality" radically increased the financial risks of filmmaking and led the industry to pursue a variety of risk reduction strategies whose net effect was to take production finance out of studio hands. At the beginning of the decade, most production capital was derived from rolling box-office revenues and line-of-credit agreements with commercial banks; by its end, the majority came from tax shelters (outlawed domestically in 1976, but widely available to foreign investors thereafter) and Federal investment tax credits, presale agreements with television[1] and cable networks, advance exhibitor guarantees through such practices as "blind-bidding," and ancillary merchandising tie-ins such as books, toys, and sound-track albums. (Home video license fees, nonexistent in 1969, accounted for less than $9 million before the resolution of *Universal v. Sony/Betamax* in October 1979,[2] but by 1985 the sale of movies on videocassette would be worth $4.55 billion.)[3] In the interim the movies themselves had become both bigger—inflatable to "event" status, and smaller—reducible to the size of a half-inch videocassette. They had also become considerably more lurid, as the MPPA ratings system permitted the graphic depiction of sex and violence once proscribed by the Production Code, and the majors brought the stylistic and marketing practices of exploitation cinema into the mainstream.

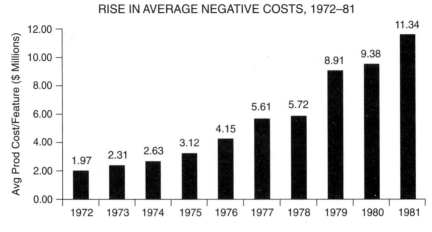

RISE IN AVERAGE NEGATIVE COSTS, 1972–81

SOURCE: *MPAA*

The ultimate effect of the blockbuster syndrome, and the "outside money" it both attracted and required, was to raise the ceiling on industry costs across the board—causing what veteran industry analyst A. D. Murphy called "a cancer on the business."[4] Average negative costs inflated from $2 million in 1972 to nearly $10 million in 1979, an increase of 450 percent in less than seven years.[5] Even more astounding, marketing budgets exceeded negative costs for the first time in industry history, marking a seismic shift whereby the cost of promoting a film actually exceeded the cost of producing it—often by twice as much.[6] Advertising campaigns went from local to national, fueled by huge purchases of network television time, and distributors turned to the practice of "four-walling" and saturation booking to build product awareness and maximize the available audience. By the late seventies, marketing and distribution executives had come to dominate studio production policy, even as lawyers and agents (from agencies like ICM [International Creative Management], which put together the JAWS deal, and CAA [Creative Artists Agency], founded by Michael Ovitz in 1975) dominated the packaging of creative personnel. Projects were selected for their marketing potential, demographic appeal, and ability to hedge risks, rather than for any intrinsic merit as entertainment, much less as art or social comment; and films were constructed to pander to focus groups, like fast food and other new products. (During the studio era, by contrast, marketing was not a determinant issue because market hegemony, broken by the 1948 consent decrees, was implicit in the majors' control of exhibition.)

The industry's embrace of outside financing occurred simultaneously with increasing diversification. As a direct result of overproduction and attendant cash crises during the 1960s, all of the studios but 20th Century–Fox, Columbia, and Disney had been taken over by conglomerates by the decade's end. (However, Columbia and Disney had both diversified on their own by entering teleproduction as early as 1954; furthermore, Disney was an industry pioneer in such ancillary markets as theme parks and product merchandising.) Beginning with the purchase of Universal by MCA in 1962—and extending through Paramount's sale to Gulf & Western Industries in 1966, United Artists' sale to Transamerica Corporation in 1967, the sale of Warner Bros. to Kinney National Service Corporation, and MGM to Las Vegas financier Kirk Kerkorian in

1969—the studios were one by one absorbed by larger, more diversified companies for whom they represented good investments, since their shares were temporarily undervalued and they owned huge tracts of real estate in one of the nation's most lucrative markets. (It was also understood that, under proper management, theatrical filmmaking offered the chance of very large returns on modest outlays, and that the studios' existing negatives—i.e., their film libraries—offered immense potential in sales to television.)[7] During the seventies, diversification increased, as the studios became the main suppliers of network television programming and expanded into such related businesses as camera equipment (Warners/Panavision), recording (Columbia/Arista), theme parks (Disneyworld, the Universal Studios tour), and resorts (MGM opened the MGM Grand hotel and casino; Fox bought [and later sold] the Aspen Ski and Pebble Beach resorts.)[8] Conglomerate ownership offered the benefits of "synergy" whereby diversified components of a company (e.g., moviemaking, publishing, recording, and merchandising) could market the same product or "franchise" (e.g., STAR WARS) in mutually enriching ways, providing the benefits of cash liquidity from unit to unit and country to country so that losses in one business could be offset by profits in another—a potent form of risk reduction.

By ensuring a steady flow of production capital through diversification of risk, conglomeration lifted the industry out of a deep recession, which had produced at least $600 million in losses for the majors between 1969 and 1971 and, by 1970, left 40 percent of all Hollywood filmmakers unemployed.[9] Under new management, the same studios posted profits of $173 million in 1972–1973, thanks largely to the success of a few heavily marketed blockbusters. (In fact, by the end of the 1970s, 220 films would earn more than $10 million each in rentals—and many, a good deal more—representing a 400 percent increase over the 1960s.)[10] In the interim, however, veteran industry leadership had been replaced by a melange of agents, lawyers, bankers, and business executives who saw filmmaking primarily as an investment strategy, not unlike commodities trading, which combined the risks of high-stakes speculation with a virtually limitless potential for corporate tax-sheltering. It was inevitable that this new perspective, together with drastically escalating costs, would warp the shape of the industry and change its attitude toward its product in fundamental ways.

Almost since its inception, the American film industry had been characterized by the orderly pursuit of profits epitomized by the Hollywood studio system, which dominated the period 1927–1952, and exerted considerable force for fifteen years before and after that. In its classical form, this system controlled production from start to finish, maintaining a stable of stars and production personnel under long-term contract, and retaining all motion picture profits for itself. Historically, these profits depended on providing the public with a regular roster of high-quality filmed entertainment (A-films) across a variety of genres and budget categories, always aimed at the general audience and, after 1934, tailored to the standards of the Production Code. B-films (low- to medium-budget films produced by both the studios and Poverty Row for the second half of double bills), and exploitation cinema (extremely low-budget films targeted for ethnic or "grind house" markets) existed at the margins of the system, often distributed through alternative "states rights" agreements and rented to exhibitors at low-profit flat rates.

However, the 1948 consent decrees and two decades of enormously costly films reconfigured the system, culminating in the "Recession of 1969" and attendant corporate buy-outs. This convulsion, combined with demographic shifts in audience composition and the replacement of the Production Code by the MPPA ratings system, led the majors to embrace exploitation as a mainstream practice, elevating such previous B genres as science fiction and horror to A-film status, retrofitting "race cinema" as "blaxploitation," and competing with the pornography industry for "sexploitation" market share. Grindhouse-style gore was injected into seemingly conventional Westerns and gangster films, and four-letter words became obligatory in all but family-rated genres (G and GP categories). By 1974, sequels and series, the very fodder of B-film production during the studio era, loomed as a major strategy for risk reduction among the majors, who have since devoted approximately 10 percent of their rosters to these categories.[11] (Combined with reissues, in fact, sequels and series accounted for 17.6 percent of all Hollywood releases from 1974 to 1978.)[12] Finally, with Universal's release of JAWS (Steven Spielberg, 1975), the majors borrowed the distribution tactic known as saturation booking—opening a film in many theaters simultaneously, accompanied by intensive advertising—from the exploitation field, where its main purpose was to generate quick profits before bad reviews and word of mouth killed business, and customized it as the standard mode for launching blockbusters, or "event" films. However expensively and professionally produced, the 1970s-style blockbuster became inherently exploitative when placed into patterns of wide release. As Stuart Byron noted at the time, "Almost by definition, a film that opens everywhere at once is an exploitation film. . . ."[13]

The turn toward exploitation was fueled by two other changes in the American film industry—the transformation of the exhibition sector and the advent of the VCR. During the studio era, exhibition was controlled through a run-zone-clearance system of distribution in which the country was divided into thirty markets subdivided by zones. Within each zone theaters were classified as first-run (urban showcases, usually owned by the majors), second-run ("neighborhood" cinemas), and subsequent-run, according to scaled admission prices, with "clearance" periods between runs determined by the distributor in order to maximize profit.[14] While a twenty-five-year decline in film attendance, 1946–1971, reduced many of the second-tier theaters to sub-run status, soaring production, advertising, and promotion costs during the seventies caused distributors to launch films on a wider basis than the old single-screen, exclusive-run model. This in turn caused a major increase in the number of theaters with key or sub-key status and kept major films at a higher level of release for a longer periods during which higher admission prices could be charged.[15] The result was a steady 7.7 percent annual growth in revenues of throughout the decade (while admissions for the entire period grew only 2.1 percent, to 1.18 billion); with a subsequent boom in the construction of suburban multiplex theaters, or "mini-multiples," where top ticket prices could be charged for premiere runs in multiple auditoria with seating ranging from 100 to 200, as opposed to the older first-run houses that seated 1,000 or more. (Most of the multiplexes were located in shopping malls, which experienced a 90 percent increase from 1970 to 1980.)[16] By December 1980, *Variety* estimated that 55–60 percent of all American theaters were in first-run status,[17] and the total number of indoor screens had risen from 10,335 in 1971 to 14,029 (with the number of drive-in screens dropping slightly from 3,770 to 3,561), although actual capacity had declined by about one million seats.[18]

Helical-scan videotape systems, the basis for home video recording, were perfected by electronics companies during the 1960s. As early as 1970, Peter Guber, then production vice president for Columbia Pictures, had published a detailed technical essay predicting "limitless" potential for the VCR,[19] and Gulf & Western president Charles Bluhdorn told *Life* magazine, "Movies in cassettes for home viewing will open a tremendous market."[20] Introduced to American consumers by Cartrivision Television, Inc., in 1972, the half-inch videotape recorder did not catch fire until the advent of the Sony Betamax (SL-7300), whose immediate success in early 1976 spurred JVC (Japanese Victor Corp., largely owned by Matsushita Electric but independently run) to introduce its competing VHS format only months later. Sony initially promoted the Betamax for "time shifting" (the ability to record TV programs for later playback), but, sensing a threat to motion picture profits, Universal and Disney filed suit against Sony for copyright infringement in November 1976.[21] As the case wound its way through court, film industry resistance to the new technology gradually faded and consumer video came to be seen as a vast new market for Hollywood product. In 1977 Fox made an historic deal with Andre Blay's Magnetic Video of Farmington Hills, Michigan, for nonexclusive video rights to fifty pre-1972 titles,[22] and Allied Artists licensed one hundred titles for distribution on pre-recorded cassette the following year. In October 1979, *Universal v. Sony* was resolved for the defendants, U.S. sales of VCRs passed one million, and Warner Bros. formed Warner Home Video. By 1981, three million VCRs had been sold (two-thirds of which were in the VHS format), all of the Hollywood majors had their own video divisions, and the historic shift was nearly complete.

At the beginning of the 1970s, the movies were primarily a collective experience—something seen regularly on large screens in specially designed theaters with masses of other people. By the decade's end they had become something that could also be carried around in a briefcase or shopping bag for video playback at home. In between, many had achieved the status of pre-sold "events" or "franchises" that were nationally and internationally marketed through every conceivable communications channel, but pre-eminently network television. The costs of these blockbusters became so exorbitant that no one studio could afford to produce more than a few, and late in the decade it was possible for the fate of an entire studio to ride on the success or failure of a single film.

To reduce risk, the majors experimented with joint finance (starting with the Fox-Warner collaboration on THE TOWERING INFERNO [John Guillermin, 1974]),[23] presale of ancillary television and video rights, nonrefundable exhibitor guarantees, and merchandising of ancillary product tie-ins such as books, records, and toys. Above all, they reduced their exposure by drastically cutting back on product and letting other producers bear the risk. It was during the 1970s, in fact, that the majors ceased to function as the regular and primary originators of feature film entertainment in the United States and assumed their current role as suppliers of film finance and distribution for "independent" producers (which simply means any producer not on a studio payroll). By the 1990s, the studios were universally understood to be film financier-distributors, whose primary audio-visual product was telefilm and cable programming.

A cynic might suggest that the net result of these changes was to turn the movies from something special into something ordinary, and it is true that the mass marketing of an "entertainment franchise" like Fox's STAR WARS (George Lucas, 1977) or Columbia's THE DEEP (Peter Yates, 1977) resembled nothing so much as the selling of fast food (in fact, product tie-ins with restaurant chains often meant that the franchise *was* selling fast food). It is also true that the ability to physically possess and play back a movie at will—and in miniature—inescapably reduced its stature as a cultural artifact. But it would be wrong to assume that these fundamental changes in the way movies were produced, distributed, and consumed have somehow cheapened the power of filmic experience itself. In fact, in demystifying some of its processes (as the VCR does for editing, for example), the new forms and practices have extended the American cinema's range. However, it was the seventies that gave us the pre-digested, market-tested cinema of contemporary Hollywood where films are manufactured like two-hour sound bites designed to press all the right buttons without ever committing to a firm point of view. Somewhere between the dumbing down of American corporate culture that produced the cynical young tycoons of the "New Hollywood"[24] and the remarkable aesthetic revival that produced the *auteur* directors of the "Hollywood Renaissance"—and films like FIVE EASY PIECES (Bob Rafelson, 1970), CARNAL KNOWLEDGE (Mike Nichols, 1971), STRAW DOGS (Sam Peckinpah, 1971), A CLOCKWORK ORANGE (Stanley Kubrick, 1971), THE GODFATHER (Francis Ford Coppola, 1972), MEAN STREETS (Martin Scorsese, 1973), CHINATOWN (Roman Polanski, 1974), THE CONVERSATION (Francis Ford Coppola, 1974), NASHVILLE (Robert Altman, 1975), BARRY LYNDON (Stanley Kubrick, 1975), TAXI DRIVER (Martin Scorsese, 1976), THREE WOMEN (Robert Altman, 1977), DAYS OF HEAVEN (Terrence Malick,1978), THE DEER HUNTER (Michael Cimino, 1978), and APOCALYPSE NOW (Francis Ford Coppola, 1979)—lies a cinema of great expectations and lost illusions that mirrored what the historian Peter N. Carroll has called the "tragedy and promise of America in the 1970s."[25]

The trajectory of this cinema paralleled that of other cultural production during the seventies, wherein multimedia mergers and conglomeration created the conditions for hegemonic market control in the eighties and nineties. But the film industry might well have taken a different path. In the late sixties, on the brink of a crippling recession, the studios' new corporate managers had discovered the "youth market" in the success of films like BONNIE AND CLYDE (1967), THE GRADUATE (1967), and EASY RIDER (1969), and they attempted to exploit it by recruiting a rising generation of writers, producers, and directors from the ranks of such films schools as USC, UCLA, and NYU. These filmmakers, later collectively christened the "film generation" or the "Hollywood brats,"[26] brought fresh, cost-effective talent to an industry embroiled in financial crisis and structural change, and, for a few brief years, the studio chiefs gave them unprecedented creative freedom. They used this license to develop an American *auteur* cinema on the European model whose influence held sway in Hollywood—always somewhat tenuously, at least until 1975, and selectively thereafter. In that year, the astonishing success of JAWS turned the industry single-mindedly toward the pursuit of a "blockbuster strategy," and those who could or would not follow were left behind. At this juncture, as one observer put it, "deal-making . . . replaced filmmaking as the principle activity of Hollywood,"[27] and with STAR WARS (1977) the power of merchandising and sequel rights to create a "franchise" usurped the importance of both.

By the end of the decade, Hollywood's financial health was restored, and the conglomerate ethic ruled as pervasively in the film industry as it did in publishing, music, and television: increasingly films, books, records, and product merchandise would be conceptualized and promoted as integrated packages under a single corporate logo. The "Hollywood Renaissance," circa 1967–1975, represented a rare moment in American cinema; one that captured our society at a time when it literally seemed to be coming apart, but it was irretrievably lost to the era of the consensus-building "super-grosser" or "megahit"—the big-budget, mass- and cross-marketed blockbuster whose potential to drive corporate profits made it the Holy Grail of conglomerate managers and financiers. As the crucible for this fundamental and lasting change, the 1970s was a decade as important as any in the history of American film.

THE SOUND OF MUSIC (Fox, 1965), whose $135-million gross set Hollywood on an ill-fated Grail-quest for another blockbuster musical that ended in an industry-wide recession, 1969-1971: Julie Andrews. 70mm Todd-AO.

2

Formative Industry Trends, 1970–1979

Because the industry is peopled with cretins, scoundrels, and bigots . . .
does not mean that it may not have worked, once upon a time.

DAVID ROBINSON, CRITIC/JOURNALIST, 1982

Industry Recession, 1969–1971

For the American film industry, the 1970s began in a state of dislocation matched only by the coming of sound. The recession of 1969 had produced more than $200 million in losses; left MGM, Warner Bros., and United Artists under new management; and brought Universal and Columbia close to liquidation.[1] By October 1969, the industry had declared a production moratorium and stood on the brink of a four-year period of retrenchment. Of the majors, only Warners and Columbia had started more pictures in 1969 than in 1968,[2] and during 1969–1970 the number of feature films released by the majors dropped by nearly 34 percent, causing widespread unemployment and what the *Los Angeles Times* would call "an out and out depression" in the motion picture business.[3] The reasons for the crisis, which lasted until the end of 1971 and generated another $300–400 million in losses, are directly traceable to the 1966–1968 overproduction boom, including a large number of expensively produced musicals bidding to cash in on the misleading popularity of Fox's THE SOUND OF MUSIC (Robert Wise, 1965), which had grossed $135 million nationwide in two years of release. The losses from these films, which included Fox's DOCTOR DOLITTLE (Richard Fleischer, 1967), STAR! (Robert Wise, 1968), and HELLO, DOLLY! (Gene Kelly, 1969); Warner Bros.' CAMELOT (Joshua Logan, 1967); Paramount's PAINT YOUR WAGON (Joshua Logan, 1969); United Artists' CHITTY CHITTY BANG BANG (Ken Hughes, 1968); Universal's SWEET CHARITY (Bob Fosse, 1969)—and other extravagant spectacles like Fox's THE BIBLE (John Huston, 1966), Columbia's CASINO ROYALE (John Huston, 1967), and United Artists' BATTLE OF BRITAIN (Guy Hamilton, 1969)—combined with the national recession of 1969 to trigger the industry's collapse under the burden of record-high interest rates (about 10 percent). (The flops continued well into 1970 with Fox's TORA! TORA! TORA! [Richard Fleischer, 1970], THE ONLY GAME IN TOWN [George Stevens, 1970], and MYRA BRECKINRIDGE [Michael Sarne, 1970]; Paramount's DARLING LILI [Blake Edwards, 1970] and THE MOLLY MAGUIRES [Martin Ritt, 1970]; United Artists' THE PRIVATE LIFE

DOCTOR DOLITTLE (Fox, 1967), produced by Fox for $20 million, earned just $6.2 million in domestic rentals for a $13.8-million loss: Rex Harrison, Richard Attenborough, Anthony Newley. 70mm Todd-AO.

OF SHERLOCK HOLMES [Billy Wilder, 1970]; and Columbia's NICHOLAS AND ALEXANDRA [Franklin Schaffner, 1971], producing losses totaling $61.3 million.)

Exacerbating the situation was the entry in 1967 of two so-called "instant majors" into production and distribution from the exhibition sector of the industry—National General Corporation (which distributed product for CBS-TV's Cinema Center Films, and also produced its own films between 1967 and 1970) and Cinerama Releasing Corporation (which distributed product for ABC-TV's Circle Films).[4] (Sometimes counted as a third "instant major," Commonwealth United Corp. was a real estate holding company that entered production and distribution in 1967 with the acquisition of Television Enterprises Corp. In 1968, it had released seventeen films and acquired interests in publishing and recording, but two years later the company was $80 million in debt, and it sold off the domestic and foreign rights to its product to American International Pictures and National Telefilm Associates respectively.)[4a] According to Tino Balio, these parvenus, each producing about ten films annually, drove up the price of talent and further served to glut the market with features.[5] They also reduced distributors' overall share of box-office grosses to under 30 percent by offering exhibitors lower-than-average splits in order to compete with the majors.[6] (The normal split during the 1960s rarely fell below 30/70, and was frequently higher.)[7] At the same time, smaller companies such as Avco Embassy (THE GRADUATE [Mike Nichols, 1967]) and Allied Artists (A MAN AND A WOMAN [Claude Lelouch, 1966]) had achieved the status of "mini-majors" by distributing foreign and independent productions without the burden of costly studio overhead.[8] Economic analyst

STAR! (Fox, 1968), a biography of music-hall entertainer Gertrude Lawrence, starred Julie Andrews under the direction of Robert Wise in an attempt to replay the winning combination of THE SOUND OF MUSIC. Produced for $15 milllion, it returned only $4.2 million in domestic rentals for a loss of $10.8 million. 70mm Todd-AO.

A. D. Murphy estimated that at the end of 1968 Hollywood had an all-time peak inventory of about $1.2 billion, and the annual cost of inventory maintenance approached $120 million—virtually the entire annual film rental of a single major studio. As the recession deepened in 1969, inventory levels for features dropped to about $1 billion, and another $250 million was cut in 1970 in a variety of ways—by reducing the value of television residuals, accelerating amortization of films in release, using total write-offs of flops and write-downs of unreleased product, and using profits of big hits to offsets losses elsewhere. (Noting the use of profits to offset losses, Murphy believed that the $600 million in apparent industry losses was only the tip of the iceberg and that their true extent would never be known.)[9]

Immediate Responses to Recession

FEDERAL TAX RELIEF TO STIMULATE PRODUCTION

Emerging from the financial crisis of 1969–1971 were two major developments assisting recovery, both of which were expedited by the Nixon administration at the urgent request of industry leadership: 1) Federal income tax credits on losses (which created

Failing to learn from Fox's mistakes, Paramount cast Julie Andrews as a singing spy in the World War I espionage spoof DARLING LILI *(Blake Edwards, 1970); produced for $22 million, it earned $3.3 million for an unprecedented loss of $18.7 million: Julie Andrews, Rock Hudson. 35mm Panavision anamorphic.*

profit shelters in loss carry-forwards); and 2) a 7-percent investment tax credit on domestic production. (Investment tax credits had been introduced as a means of stimulating the economy in 1962, eliminated by Congress in 1969, and written back into the Revenue Act of 1971 at Nixon's request—as was a provision for the creation of offshore studio subsidiaries called Domestic International Sales Corporations, which could defer taxes on profits earned from exports by reinvesting them in domestic production.)[10] Together these measures provided, *for the first time in film industry history*, a solid base for investment.

In fact, tax shelters and other tax-leveraged investment became the key mode of production finance for the rest of the decade. Until they were prohibited by tax reform legislation in 1976, both the "purchase" shelter and the "production service company" shelter were important instruments for raising production capital, financing 20 percent of all film starts between 1973 and 1976.[11] Entertainment attorney Tom Pollack estimates that, all told, tax shelters added about $150 million in production money between 1971 and 1976.[12] Their combination of nonrecourse (risk-free) loans and artificial losses through accelerated depreciation made them so attractive to outside investors that Alan Hirschfeld, then president of Columbia Pictures, testified before Congress that the "availability of this kind of financing is the single most important occurrence in the

TORA! TORA! TORA! (Fox, 1970), an epic account of the Pearl Harbor attack, was a last gasp from pre-recession Hollywood. With Oscar-winning special effects, an international cast, and three directors, it cost $25 million and returned $14.5 for a $10.5-million loss. 35mm Panavision anamorphic, blown up to 70mm for road-showing.

recent history of the industry."[13] (Columbia relied more heavily on tax-shelter financing than any other studio owing to its estimated $127-million debt, and led the MPAA in its fight to retain the shelters.)[14] When film-production tax shelters were outlawed domestically, they migrated overseas, first to Germany and then to Australia as the governments of those countries sought to encourage investment in their own film industries.[15] (Thus, during the late 1970s, American tax shelter money helped fuel the New German Cinema, and German investors helped finance American films).

The effect of the investment tax credit was less spectacular but ultimately more significant, since it allowed 7 percent of production investment to be deducted from a studio's overall corporate tax up to a 50-percent limit, with carry-forward provisions for seven years. Furthermore, a tax court ruling in a 1973 Walt Disney Productions case made the credit retroactive to 1962 and applicable to "runaway" (overseas) productions—which had reached their peak from 1962 through 1969—overturning long-standing IRS guidelines that excluded negatives as qualifying tangible property.[16] This was an especially important break, given that the 1966–1968 production boom had caused the industry recession in the first place. Indeed, *Variety* estimated that an American theatrical film production investment of $3.5 billion (full negative costs, including overhead) from 1962–1969 would yield a total 7-percent tax credit of about $250 million against the majors' overall corporate taxes.[17] As Martin Dale points out, such extensive

Federal tax breaks amounted to a government subsidy for the industry during the 1970s and early 1980s.[18]

DEFENSIVE PRODUCTION STRATEGY: THE BLOCKBUSTER SYNDROME

Another result of the recession was a new industry consensus—dictated by finite resources, a perceptibly stabilized market (weekly audience attendance reached an all-time low in 1971, plunging to 15.8 million, before a gradual climb and planing out at about 21 million later in the decade),[19] and ever-rising per-picture costs (from $1.9 million in 1972 to $8.9 million in 1979)—that fewer films could profitably sustain any major company, because in any given year only a few releases captured a lion's share of the box-office dollar. For example, in 1971, 185 pictures returned $364 million in domestic rentals, with fourteen producing 52 percent of this income, and the remaining 171 left to scramble for the rest. Of these, fifty-four generated less than $250,000 each, and only seventy-one returned $1 million or more, which means that only one-third of the major product for that year broke even.[20] By this kind of logic, only films that were carefully packaged and laden with "proven" elements, like pre-sold properties (best-selling books [novels], hit plays, popular comic strips) and bankable stars, had a reasonable chance of becoming top-echelon blockbusters. So the studios began to design their production schedules accordingly. This newly defensive production strategy caused the absolute number of films released by the majors to decline dramatically from around 160 between 1965 and 1971 to about 80 by mid-decade (1975–1977), and was accompanied by a new sophistication about distribution and marketing—where the concept of the movie as a discrete product (and, increasingly, as a franchise or product *line*) became ever more entrenched inside the Hollywood establishment.

The Advent of Marketing and Ancillary Merchandising

MARKETING

Strategic or "scientific" marketing in the motion picture industry began in 1972 with Paramount's spectacular success in promoting Francis Ford Coppola's THE GODFATHER, which by the time of its release had attained "event" status through mass sales of the Mario Puzo novel (published during production) and intense publicity focused on both the shooting of the film and protests by Italian-American groups about its supposed prejudicial content.[21] THE GODFATHER became a huge commercial and critical hit, almost single-handedly restoring industry confidence in the blockbuster formula by generating about 10 percent of the year's gross box-office revenues of $1.64 billion. Shortly thereafter, *Business Week* pointed out that recent market changes had forced the movie industry "to do what most other industries had to do generations ago: synchronize production with marketing." That is, to make investment decisions based on a product's actual potential for sales in its main markets—which, in the early 1970s, were basically U.S. theaters, foreign theaters, and television—rather than "assume a market that would justify the outlay" (rational behavior before divestiture, perhaps, but not after).[22]

Marketing, which differs from publicity and advertising but includes them both as part of its "market position," or selling strategy, usually begins before a film is even scripted—with concept testing by a studio's market research department determining what the public wants to see.[23] If the elements of a project seem to have broad popular appeal, it will get the green light from the production head. The completed film will then be launched with a sales campaign tailored to its most marketable qualities as determined by demographically echeloned test screenings—from which studios attempt to shape their advertising material, allocate advertising expenses among media, and predict box-office performance nationwide.[24]

Predictions of box-office performance became particularly important after JAWS pioneered the practice of saturation booking, combined with massive television advertising, for major studio releases in 1975. This distribution pattern, which was new to the mainstream but had been used by exploitation producers for years, depended on generating a high level of audience awareness of a film before it opened and helped institutionalize market research within the industry.[25] (The textbook example of a research-driven blockbuster is Columbia's THE DEEP [Peter Yates, 1977], which was pre-sold as a high-profile "event" through every conceivable marketing channel—as a book, a sound-track album, and a panoply of related merchandise—for months before it opened in 800 theaters [approximately 6 percent of the nation's total] to terrible reviews. It went on to become the second highest grossing film of 1977, after STAR WARS.)[26] By 1979, the commonly accepted cost for marketing a major film through general release was $6 million—much of it going to huge purchases of network television time. Since the average production cost rose to nearly $10 million the following year, by the end of the decade a typical picture had to net $16 million just to break even,[27] reiterating the industry's hit-driven, blockbuster imperative.

MERCHANDISING

Related to the rise of marketing during the 1970s was ancillary merchandising, which served both to advertise a given film and reduce risk through generating profits in and of itself. Sound-track albums and novelizations had brought income to the studios since the fifties, but the idea of product tie-ins was born simultaneously with the need to create mass market consciousness for blockbusters like JAWS and THE DEEP. (Disney was an early pioneer of nonpromotional merchandising, and its product licenses, tied mainly to cartoon characters, had been a significant source of studio income since the 1950s.)[28] The profitability of merchandising was certified indisputably by STAR WARS (George Lucas, 1977), whose spin-off toys, posters, T-shirts, clothing, candy, watches, and other products grossed more money by the end of the decade (reportedly $1 billion) than the film took in at the box office.[29]

Merchandising is defined by the studios as the use by an outside company of a film title, logo, or image on a product or as part of an advertising campaign—for the average picture, posters and T-shirts are the most common tie-ins.[30] But if a film has characters that can be made into toys or video games, or marketed in conjunction with fast-food products, the studio can reap windfall profits through licensing them to outside companies. Such licensing arrangements are essentially risk-free, since the outside companies incur all manufacturing and distribution costs and the studio typically receives an advance plus royalties on all product revenues.[31] Furthermore, if the product line fails to make a profit, the studio has at least gained free national publicity for its film.

Refinements of merchandising in the eighties would lead to the now-standard industry practice of "product placement," whereby a producer accepts a fee or in-kind service to feature a manufacturer's product in a film. More perversely, manufacturers themselves began producing films as extended commercials for their toys (for example, THE CARE BEARS MOVIE [Arna Selznick, 1985] and MY LITTLE PONY [Michael Joens, 1986]). Product placement began rather modestly in the late seventies, when two companies—one in Hollywood and one in New York—specialized in getting "product identification" props into movies and telefilms. By 1986 there were more than twenty-five product-placement firms in Hollywood alone.[32] A similar relationship exists between studios and record companies in terms of licensing movie sound tracks—national airplay of potential hit songs provides free publicity for the film even if the album doesn't sell. By the late seventies, high-quality Dolby sound reproduction in theaters had made the cross-marketing of music a key feature in selling films like Paramount's SATURDAY NIGHT FEVER (John Badham, 1977) and GREASE (Randal Kleiser, 1978), whose songs were given repeated air time and became hits weeks before the release of the films.

The Mainstreaming of Saturation Booking, or "Wide" Release

As previously noted, the run-zone-clearance distribution system of the studio era gave way after divestiture to "platform" distribution, in which a gradual release pattern was followed over a period of months from exclusive urban first-run through wider suburban-rural sub-run, accompanied by a lengthy newspaper advertising campaign. By the 1970s, the high costs of maintaining inventory made speedy distribution a new priority and "saturation" booking became an alternative to platform release. Adapted from exploitation cinema, where it was used to generate quick profits before negative word of mouth could set in, seventies-style saturation booking emphasized simultaneous openings and speedy playoffs within a well-defined region, accompanied by demographically tailored television spots. (The majors were attracted to the formula by the stunningly successful "four-wall" re-release of Tom Lauglin's low-budget BILLY JACK [1971] in southern California in 1973.)[33]

After Universal released JAWS to 409 theaters in the wake of a massive television ad campaign that raised it from the level of film to national media event, generating $7.06 million in its opening weekend, the pattern of wide release and significant pre-release marketing became the American industry standard for high-quality films. As Justin Wyatt points out, after JAWS studios experimented with ever-wider release patterns for "event" movies which, fueled by television advertising blitzes, enabled audiences from coast to coast to see their films on the same day. Paramount's KING KONG (John Guillermin, 1976) opened at 961 theaters; Columbia's THE DEEP (1977) at 800; Paramount's SATURDAY NIGHT FEVER (1977) at 726, and GREASE (1978) at 902; each vying to become the next "super-grosser"—a film achieving the level of a national obsession.[34] (By the 1980s, saturation booking involved between 1,700 and 2,000 theaters—the technique was ideally suited to series [especially horror films], sequels to hits, and films pre-sold through other media, for example, those based on comic-strip heroes like Superman and Batman.) Furthermore, after Fox's 1978 summer re-release of STAR WARS (1977) generated $10 million in its first week of business, it became common practice for distributors to strategically withdraw event movies from their initial runs, and then to recycle them with new advertising campaigns as virtually new products. (In the eighties, re-release became just one stage in a marketing sequence that included sales to cable movie channels, home video licensing, network broadcast, and syndication.)[35]

The "Product Shortage": Limiting Supply

At the same time that saturation booking and new promotion mechanisms were institutionalized, the studios cut back on their production schedules in ways that forecast a major structural change in which their role would shift from that of producer to financier-distributor. In 1975, for example, the seven majors released 40 percent fewer films than in 1970, in essence abdicating what *Variety* called their "historical and tacit commitment to provide 12 months of full product" to theaters.[36] Among other things, this artificially created "product shortage," or "film famine," enabled the major studios to exact exorbitant terms from exhibitors. They began demanding 90/10 percent splits of the box-office gross—once reserved only for first-run road shows—for potential blockbusters, requiring blind bids on the films (which the theater owners did not get to see, usually because they were still in production) and nonrefundable guarantees, and setting play-date minimums. Such hard-driven distribution deals helped studios to amortize soaring marketing expenditures (they also sometimes required exhibitors to pay directly for part of a film's advertising costs, as was the case with JAWS).

Exhibitors fought back through two trade groups, the National Association of Theater Owners (NATO) and the National Independent Theater Exhibitors (NITE), lobbying state legislatures throughout the decade to pass anti-blind-bidding laws and succeeding

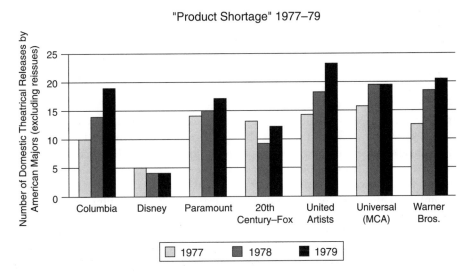

"Product Shortage" 1977–79

SOURCE: Exhibitor Relations Corp.

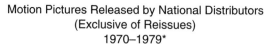

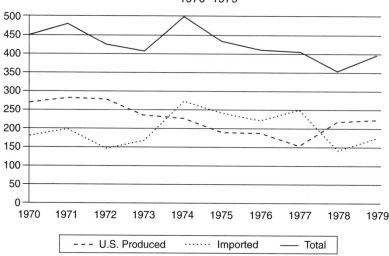

| --- U.S. Produced | ······· Imported | —— Total |

SOURCE: *MPAA*

*Note that during the leanest years of the "product shortage" (1974–78) imported pictures released by American distributors exceeded domestic releases by as much as 50%.

in placing nineteen such statutes on the books. Some exhibitors (Ted Mann of Mann Theaters Corporation and General Cinema Corporation are examples) countered the "product shortage" by venturing into production themselves. In 1975 one Oregon circuit organized Exhibitor's Production and Distributor's Cooperative (EXPRODICO) to finance feature production by theater owners nationwide.[37] None of these enterprises met with much success, despite the fact that in December 1979 the Justice Department modified the 1948 consent decrees to permit Lowe's Theaters to enter production in response to a suit filed by the Mann, Loew's, and RKO Stanley-Warner theaters in March 1979. In fact, as Suzanne Mary Donahue has demonstrated, the industry during the 1970s became a "seller's market," with distributors' share of box-office receipts rising from about 30 percent in 1971 to 40–45 percent in 1979—averages that include the increasing use of the 90/10 formula for blockbusters.[38]

It might serve here to explain some of the terms and mechanisms involved in determining film revenues. The distributor's share is known as "film rental" because that is the percentage of the box-office gross that the exhibitor pays to the distributor to rent the film—excluding his own percentage under the terms of the licensing agreement (normally 30–45 percent on a sliding scale, but as little as 10 percent for blockbusters), taxes, and the house "nut," or theater operating expenses.[39] Against film rentals, the distributor deducts his "distribution fee," a 30-percent charge (35 percent in the U.K. and higher elsewhere abroad) on continuing film rentals from theaters (and later on the revenues from television, pay cable, etc.); it is a service fee, pure and simple. It does not apply to the recovery of any expense directly related to releasing a film—for example, to manufacturing prints, marketing, or interest charges pertaining thereto—deductions for which are made *after* the imposition of the distribution fee and usually run about

20 percent.[40] The remainder of the film-rental dollar is called the "net producer's share," and is first used to pay off the loan that financed the film's production (its "negative cost"). Anything left after that is split as profit between distributor and producer—if they are separate entities—in ranges of 50/50 to 80/20.[41] The distribution fee amortizes the fixed costs of the marketing organization, which for a major American producer-distributor with a global sales force during the 1970s ranged between $15–20 million annually. After profit taking, excess distribution-fee income creates a pool of money for underwriting new production, a recycling of income that keeps the system running (bank lines of credit serve mainly for seasonal or occasional standby use).

Coming out of the 1969–1971 recession under new corporate management, the majors learned to manipulate the market by limiting product supply and driving up demand through marketing. Throughout the 1970s they grew in power as distributors, as the number of theaters screens increased by 25 percent and soaring production costs and their own strategic planning reduced the number of available films. Between 1972 and 1978, in fact, distribution's share of the domestic market increased from $500 million to $1,215 million (143 percent), whereas domestic box-office grosses increased only 67 percent.[42] By mid-decade, as Harlan Jacobson wrote in an article on Broadway movie theater closings, many exhibitors had "nothing to project"[43]—a situation that encouraged the growth of chains, since independents found it difficult to book films without a major circuit affiliation.

Independent Producers Fill the Gap

Independent producers benefited handsomely from the blockbuster-driven product shortage, rushing in to fill the vacuum created by the majors' partial abandonment of the field. For more than fifty years the Hollywood production establishment had honored a year-round commitment to supply films in various mixes, from exclusive first-run features through B-films and sub-run exploitation product. But in the postrecession, post-JAWS environment, when every film the majors produced was launched as if it were the second coming of Christ, project initiation fell to the ordinary producer (or, just as often, to a celebrity director, star, or writer with a track record of hits).

Initially, this left room for many other kinds of movies. Indeed, the record shows that in the twelve months between June 1975 and June 1976, 300 independent films were produced, representing an investment of $100 million outside the majors.[44] Of these, some 80 percent were R- and PG-rated action-adventure or exploitation dramas, 12 percent were G-rated, and 9 percent were X-rated. But, while they accounted for about two-thirds of all American production, these independent features generated only 10–15 percent of U.S. box-office rentals, and by the end of the decade they had been crowded off American screens by the majors' saturation-booking tactics and by their invasion of the exploitation field itself. In a study of independent features made between 1970 and 1980, *Variety* concluded that English-language films without ties to a major distributor stood only a 50 percent chance of being released.[45] In fact, by the end of the decade, it was frequently said that "everybody is an independent producer," since only a few producers enjoyed the continuous patronage of a major studio and the rest spent their days looking for development capital, existing from deal to deal.[46] (As Leo Janos wrote of this situation in 1978, there were "approximately 3,000 deal makers actively competing to make about 70 major releases a year.")[47]

The Rise of Agent Power

In the wake of the 1948 consent decrees, development deals were increasingly shaped by agent-packaging, and the power of agents within the industry grew exponentially over the next twenty years. As divestiture and other forces caused the studio contract system to wane, agents like Lew Wasserman of MCA became essential in bringing together the key elements of a film project and presenting them to the majors for finance and distribution. By the sixties, according to some estimates, nearly 70 percent of all films were brought to the studios as pre-packaged deals comprising a property (usually a best-selling book or play), stars, director, screenplay, and producer already under agency contract. The package would often be sold to studio executives in New York, bypassing the Hollywood-based production chief, whose role was all but eliminated—or, rather, replaced—by that of the agent. The 1970s blockbuster syndrome gave even more power to agents by increasing the value of "pre-sold" properties and proven stars. By 1974, *Variety* could proclaim "Agent Power Now Rules Hollywood,"[48] without hyperbole. As primary suppliers of talent and story material, agents now performed much of the work once done by the major studios, and some of them had actually become producers and studio chiefs—Lew Wasserman became board chairman and CEO at MCA/Universal in 1967; Ted Ashley of the Ashley Famous Agency became chairman at Warner Bros. in 1971; David Begelman of Creative Management Associates was production head at Columbia from 1973 to 1978, before moving to MGM. David Pirie described this power shift succinctly in 1981:

> The agents moved into production because their power had already changed production in such a way that agents possessed exactly the right skills it required. It was no longer an assembly-line but a highly competitive marketplace where the individual risks and rewards were greater than they had ever been. Each film became the product of long and frequently tortuous negotiations to establish whether, and on what terms, and with whom, it would be made. . . . It was only at the end of this tunnel, called the deal, that the actual process of shooting could begin.[49]

During the 1970s, agents regularly conceived story ideas for films, packaged projects and talent, and even arranged financing. By 1986, another industry observer could write that the only studio function the agencies had not yet usurped was "the actual distribution of pictures to theaters."[50] (Today three mega-agencies—CAA [Creative Artists Agency, which was founded by Michael Ovitz in 1975], the William Morris Agency, and ICM [International Creative Management]—have come to dominate the field, doing most of the work once done at the studios, with the latter often functioning as little more than financiers.)

The Studios Become Financier-Distributors

In point of fact, however, the studios continued to dominate the finance and distribution aspects of the industry, despite losing control of production in the old sense of originating film projects. Rather than maintain a continuing program of films financed by capital accrual from box-office revenues (as in the days of vertical integration), the studios became the ad hoc distributors of independent productions financed in whole or in part by their own distribution fees (and often made at studio facilities leased to the independent producers). As distributors, the majors branded these productions with their corporate logos, retaining and even bolstering their image as purveyors of feature films to the nation. They mounted the advertising and marketing campaigns, collected revenues from exhibitors, and paid the producers-of-record—after deducting their distribution fee and costs. The shift from production to finance and distribution had occurred gradually in the wake of the Consent decrees, but was accelerated to the point of near completion during the 1970s by the unique economic circumstances of postrecession Hollywood. For example, in 1973 Paramount produced ten of the twenty-two films it distributed; in 1974 it produced fourteen of twenty-five; but by 1975 it produced only five of twenty—a fairly typical progression for the majors throughout the decade.[51]

Foreign Markets and Television Sales Amortize Production

Although their key focus in the 1970s was on domestic (i.e., North American) income, the majors also distributed product to an overseas market that had become increasingly important as the domestic box office declined. Certain kinds of films—World War II epics, for example, and disaster films—were designed with international casts specifically to appeal to foreign audiences. When the decade began, as much 50 percent of rental income came from abroad (80 percent of it from Europe); by its end, a resurgence in the home market reversed a quarter century of erosion (1946–1971) and restored the domestic-foreign ratio to 60/40, with the largest overseas share going for the first time to Japan.[52] (In the eighties and nineties, however, the international market became crucial to sustaining the profitability of certain blockbusters, with films such as Paramount's FATAL ATTRACTION [Adrian Lyne, 1987], United Artists' RAIN MAN [Barry Levinson, 1988] and ROCKY V [John G. Avildsen, 1990], Touchstone's PRETTY WOMAN [Garry Marshall, 1990], and Amblin's GREMLINS 2 [Joe Dante, 1990] earning significantly more money abroad than in the United States; by the late 1990s, the rule of thumb was that overseas box office would account for at least 50 percent of a studio film's revenue.)[53]

Throughout the 1970s, then, the majors' access to a world market insured them economies of scale sufficient to amortize the production costs of most films. Some foreign markets they penetrated significantly but not fatally—in Italy they had a 33.7-percent share, in Spain a 35-percent share, and in France a 35.2-percent share. Others they dominated to the near extinction of the respective national cinema—most notably Germany (54.9-percent penetration), Greece (58 percent), and the U.K. (88 percent).[54] The most important agent of overseas distribution was Cinema International Corporation (CIC), formed by Paramount and Universal in 1970 to handle distribution in Europe, South America, and South Africa—about one-third of the overseas market, and modified in 1973 to include MGM. Circumventing U.S. antitrust laws, CIC merged the three separate distribution organizations of its partners outside North America and controlled the first-option international rights to all motion pictures they produced or acquired. CIC became United International Pictures (UIP) when MGM merged with United Artists in 1981, and is today one of the world's leading distributors of feature-length films to theatrical exhibitors.[55]

The other pillar of support for domestic production during this era was television. In the 1960s, about 70 percent of filmed television programming was produced in Hollywood on backlot space rented to independent companies like Desilu and Hal Roach. At mid-decade, the studios themselves had entered the syndication business, supplying programs directly to affiliates as an alternative to the network feed. Simultaneously, Hollywood feature films were gaining enormous popularity on television. By 1967 such films were receiving the highest Nielsen ratings on prime-time television,[56] and the networks were clamoring for product, causing rental prices to soar. In 1961, when there were only forty-five features broadcast in prime time, the average price per film was under $200,000; by 1970, with a total of 166 features, it had climbed to $800,000.[57] At this point the majors had become dependent on television for their fiscal health, using profits from network movie sales to underwrite theatrical production and amortize losses. (They would soon become dependent on television in another way, as it achieved the status of a national sales medium *sine qua non* and became crucial to the marketing of studio blockbusters.)

By the 1971–1972 season, however, the success of theatrical features on television had led all three networks to produce their own made-for-TV movies. Although movies then comprised over 25 percent of the primetime schedule, only half of 227 films broadcast were Hollywood features,[58] and this market would continue to decline throughout the decade. (In 1974, for example, 130 made-for-TV movies appeared in prime time as compared with 118 theatrical features.) Many of the new made-for-TV movies were produced in association with the majors, but studio profits from such productions could not match those generated by distributing and licensing their own theatrical films to television. Nonetheless, thanks to a 1971 change in the FCC's syndication rules that required the networks to reduce their interest in program production, the studios were able to become the main producers and syndicators of television programming during the 1970s.[59] By mid-decade, in fact, they were devoting most of their facilities to the production of TV movies and weekly series, with Universal alone supplying nearly one-quarter of the prime-time shows for all three networks. In 1978 the majors made more films for television than they had produced for theatrical distribution in the past five years.[60] (As early as 1971, only 24 percent of Screen Actors Guild members' income came from film work, with the rest coming from television.)[61] Thus, while feature-film production remained Hollywood's most salient and culturally prominent role in the 1970s, its main function within the American media industry became that of TV *producer* and film *distributor*, shifting its posture dramatically from the classical era but completing a transition that had been ongoing since the consent decree.

The Industry Lands on Its Feet and Reasserts Its Power

Although it had begun in industry-wide crisis, the decade of the 1970s ended with most of the negative trends ameliorated or reversed. After hitting an historic low of 15.8 million in 1971, attendance grew at the steady rate of about 2 percent annually for the rest of the decade (though the audience share of the ten top grossing films tripled that rate). Domestic box-office receipts grew 7.7 percent, climbing from about $1 billion in 1971 to $2.8 billion in 1979,[62] thanks largely to 22 films earning rental in excess of $50 million. Nine of those films exceeded $75 million, and three of them—STAR WARS, JAWS, and THE EMPIRE STRIKES BACK—exceeded $130 million. The six majors—Paramount, Warners, Columbia, Fox, Universal, and MGM/United Artists (functioning as a single distributor)—continued to dominate the industry, accounting for 90 percent of North American rental income throughout the decade. Near its end, when the majors had pre-tax profits totaling $640 million, the risk associated with moviemaking for most of it had been significantly reduced.[63] In 1977, for example, Warner Bros.' chair Ted Ashley told the *Washington Post* that the risk-to-reward ratio had "improved considerably in the last two of three years,"[64] and in 1980 *The Hollywood Reporter* carried the headline "Wall Street Embracing Film Co.s Now That Risk Is Virtually Gone."[65] The failure of Michael Cimino's $36-million epic HEAVEN'S GATE (United Artists) in 1980 proved otherwise, causing Transamerica to sell United Artists to MGM. But the debacle helped to bring a new measure of caution to the budgeting process and became a *cause célèbre*, motivating studio executives to reassert rigorous production control.

During the same period, Hollywood was discovering new markets in videocassette and cable distribution, and began to tap a massive new youth market. In 1977, a survey prepared by the Opinion Research Corporation of Princeton, New Jersey, for the MPAA had revealed that 57 percent of all U.S. movie tickets were purchased by those under twenty-five, a group whose tastes were inherently more conservative than those of the late 1960s counterculture. (Furthermore, from 1977 to 1979, the number of tickets sold to twelve- to twenty-year-olds increased by 8 percent, while those sold to twenty-one- to thirty-nine-year-olds declined by the same percentage.)[66] Subsequently, "bubble gum" blockbusters[67] targeted at that audience—mainly action-adventure films (SUPERMAN [Richard Donner, 1978]; RAIDERS OF THE LOST ARK [Steven Spielberg, 1981]) and comedies (NATIONAL LAMPOON'S ANIMAL HOUSE [John Landis, 1978]; PORKY'S [Bob Clark, 1982])—became the top-grossing films of the late 1970s and early 1980s. But the HEAVEN'S GATE disaster was a grim reminder of the 1969–1971 recession, and it brought a new sense of responsibility toward controlling film costs[68] that would stand the industry in good stead for at least another decade—near the end of which costs would again escalate suicidally.

*Universal's J*AWS *(1975), the Mother of All "Super-Grossers." Panavision 35mm anamorphic.*

3

Manufacturing the Blockbuster: The "Newest Art Form of the Twentieth Century"

Whatever else [THE GODFATHER, JAWS, and THE EXORCIST] proved about the dream state of the national psyche, they proved without a shadow of a doubt that a single picture could carry the entire industry for a year and could carry the individual company that produced and distributed it, or the exhibitor who played it, for several years.

HARLAN JACOBSON, *Film Comment*, 1980

The "Blockbuster Syndrome": A New Kind of Gambling

ORIGINS

The industry recession and shakeout of 1969–1971 taught the majors that the regular flow of product was no longer profitable because there was no longer a regular and predictable audience for their films. In 1969, they had seen the low-budget "youth-cult" film EASY RIDER (Dennis Hopper) return $19.2 million in domestic rentals, while the expensively produced musicals HELLO, DOLLY! (Gene Kelly) and PAINT YOUR WAGON (Joshua Logan) lost $14 million between them. In the early seventies, however, several big-budget movies with more or less traditional appeal—LOVE STORY (Arthur Hiller, 1970), AIRPORT (George Seaton, 1970), and, especially, THE GODFATHER (Francis Ford Coppola, 1972)—unexpectedly earned windfall profits. The conviction grew that the industry had experienced a cataclysmic market shift in which only a few films each year (perhaps one in ten) would make big profits, while the rest would break even or produce losses. History suggested that pictures with big budgets had the best chance of succeeding in a volatile market, but also—very clearly—that there was no way to guarantee a hit. Paramount president Frank Yablans put the new thinking to his colleagues succinctly: "We want one big picture a year. The rest are budgeted to minimize risk."[1]

Indeed, by 1977 the top six of the 199 major films released accounted for one-third of the year's income, and the top thirteen for half (of those thirteen, all but one were distributed by a major).[2] In the absence of any body of professional knowledge to predict a hit, the majors put their faith in aggressive marketing and promotion to create product awareness and sell their movies as special attractions. As Columbia Pictures president David Begelman explained in 1974, "We feel we must put out special event films because no one goes to the movies anymore as a routine exercise."[3] If moviegoing had become less a matter of habit than discretionary choice, then each film needed to be sold as a "blockbuster"—a major event that would have the status of a unique experience—and sold on a global scale. This meant providing wide access through saturation booking, once reserved for dubious product only, combined with mass advertising to maximize audiences at the point of sale—a distribution strategy that grew ever more effective as the proliferation of Hollywood-sponsored multiplexes dramatically increased the number of screens available for saturation release.

According to an analysis of the 1971 business year by Lee Beaupre that appeared in *Variety* for November 30, 1972,[4] the "boom-bust" cycle could be traced to divorcement and the end of block-booking in the early 1950s. From that time forward, a relatively small number of blockbusters carried the whole economic float of ongoing filmmaking, resulting in the "hit-or-miss" mentality of the late sixties. Historically, if a film did well in preliminary bookings, the distributor's sales force would back it and create exhibitor demand; if it did poorly, exhibitors and distributors both dumped it as soon as possible—no one stood behind the product and tried to *market* it.[5] Beaupre demonstrates his point by showing that for 1971 only 14 of 185 major pictures (those released by the seven majors and two "instant majors"), or 8 percent, generated 52 percent of the income. Of the rest, 54 (29 percent) earned less than $250,000, and only 71 of the 185—*about one-third of the majors' product*—could expect to break even by earning $1 million or more in the domestic market. From data like this grew the guiding principal of the "blockbuster syndrome": that seven out of ten films lose money, two out of ten break even, and one will be an enormous success.[6] A second rule of thumb, dictated largely by escalating costs of marketing and prints, was that a film must recoup three dollars for every dollar spent on production before it generates a profit. As Suzanne Mary Donahue points out, however, this rule does not apply across the board from lower to higher budget films, since certain costs, like those for prints (which, in the late 1990s, cost $2,000 each), vary little from one film to the next. Thus, whereas a $10-million picture may need $30 million to break even, a $30-million picture can break even for less—another factor that encouraged gambling on blockbusters.

THE QUEST FOR "PRE-SOLD" PRODUCT

The formation of a pervasive "blockbuster mentality" in the seventies ultimately increased the power of the majors, because only they had both the organization to distribute films in domestic and international markets, and the resources to finance production in the context of rapidly escalating costs. On average, the negative cost of a Hollywood feature rose from $2 million in 1972 (when Paramount's THE GODFATHER was a big-budget film at $6 million), to $9 million in 1979—when Fox's ALIEN (Ridley Scott) cost $11 million to produce and $16 million to promote.[7] By 1979, marketing expenses could run three times a film's negative cost and were the single largest cause of budgetary inflation, followed closely by the cost of stars. While stars could not guarantee box-office success, in the volatile post-studio marketplace they at least seemed to offer a dependable hedge against risk. For this reason, throughout the 1970s star fees and profit-sharing arrangements grew in proportion to the stars' perceived "bankability," rising to a million dollars and more per picture for top stars.[8] As a result, many stars formed their own companies and became powerful players within the production community.

The same general logic marked a turn toward "pre-sold" properties like best-selling novels or hit plays, whose reach could be extended through publishing tie-ins, sound-track albums, and ancillary merchandise—with the promise of creating a "synergy" in which the film built the book, which built the album, which in turn built the film. (Such thinking was partially a response to a Yankelovich Report on industry marketing prac-tices, which the MPAA commissioned in 1967, and which concluded that prerelease publicity "seems unable to create extensive public awareness" for movies without "a tie-in with a very familiar book or play or music.")[9] Book and movie tie-ins became espe-cially valuable as more and more studios were linked with publishers through conglomerate ownership—Paramount with Simon & Schuster through Gulf & Western; Univeral with G. P. Putnam's Sons through MCA; Warner Bros. with Warner Books through Warner Communications—since, by the end of the decade, the price that movie companies would pay for best-seller rights had risen to a record $2.5 million.[10]

A NEW RELIANCE ON GENRE, SERIES, AND SEQUELS

The seventies also marked a conscious return to the production of genre films, sequels, and series, which were more typical of classical Hollywood than of the post-studio era, because of their obvious market-tested elements and universal appeal. With so much riding on each film, blockbuster production sought to ensure profitability by relying on what had worked with audiences in the past. Genre movies—whether gangster films (THE GODFATHER [1972]), horror films (THE EXORCIST [William Friedkin, 1973]), dis-aster/monster films (JAWS [Steven Spielberg, 1975]), or science fiction films (STAR WARS [George Lucas, 1977])—were more easily packaged and marketed on a global scale than other kinds of films, and were easier to replicate as sequels, cycles, or series for pre-existing markets. Advertising, promotion, and ancillary activities for sequels and series could be piggybacked with the original, and were sometimes even planned simul-taneously. (For example, Alexander Salkind produced THE THREE MUSKETEERS [Richard Lester, 1974] in Spain for Fox at the same time as its sequel THE FOUR MUSKETEERS [Richard Lester, 1975]; and in 1978 he shot key scenes for Warner's SUPERMAN II [Richard Lester, 1980] during the production of SUPERMAN [Richard Donner, 1978]). A reluctance to abandon successful formulas has been a distinguishing feature of the American film industry since its inception, but in the high-stakes crap shoot of blockbuster production the tendency was inflated with the same amplitude as budgets. By the end of the seventies, most hits had been reproduced as big-budget sequels with Roman or Arabic numerals after their titles (THE GODFATHER, PART II [Francis Ford Coppola, 1974], THE FRENCH CONNECTION II [John Frankenheimer, 1975], THAT'S ENTERTAINMENT, PART 2 [Gene Kelly, 1976], EXORCIST II: THE HERETIC [John Boorman, 1977], JAWS 2 [Jeannot Szwarc, 1978], DAMIEN—OMEN II [Don Taylor, 1978], ROCKY II [Sylvester Stallone, 1979], SMOKEY AND THE BANDIT II [Hal Needham, 1980]); or a succession of new dates (AIRPORT 1975 [Jack Smight, 1974], AIRPORT '77 [Jerry Jameson, 1977], THE CONCORDE—AIRPORT '79 [David Lowell Rich, 1979]).[11] Similar phenomena were series films (DIRTY HARRY [Don Siegel, 1971], MAGNUM FORCE [Ted Post, 1973], THE ENFORCER [James Fargo, 1976]); blockbuster remakes (FAREWELL MY LOVELY [Dick Richards, 1975], KING KONG [John Guillermin, 1976], A

Producer Alexander Salkind shot THE THREE MUSKETEERS *(1974) for Fox in Spain at the same time as its sequel* THE FOUR MUSKETEERS *(1975), keeping cast and crew together for both: (top) Richard Chamberlain, Michael York, Oliver Reed, Frank Finley. 35mm 1.85:1.*

Salkind used a similar cost-cutting ploy for (top) SUPERMAN *(Warners, 1978) and (bottom)* SUPERMAN II *(Warners, 1980), shooting key scenes for the latter while producing the former. (Brando's exclusive contract prevented complete filming of the sequel.) Panavision 35mm anamorphic, blown up to 70mm for road-showing.*

STAR IS BORN [Frank Pierson, 1976]); reissues (THE EXORCIST [1973; reissued 1976 and, in a 70mm blowup, 1979]; JAWS [1975; reissued 1976]; STAR WARS [1977; reissued 1978]; CLOSE ENCOUNTERS OF THE THIRD KIND [Steven Spielberg, 1977; re-edited and reissued as a "special edition," 1980]), and "prequels" (BUTCH AND SUNDANCE: THE EARLY DAYS [Richard Lester, 1979]). Whereas sequels and reissues comprised only 4.4 percent of all major product from 1964 to 1968, they would account for 17.6 percent between 1974 and 1978,[12] as re-release came to play a crucial role in the launching of sequels. (With the proliferation of new video distribution technologies in the 1980s, re-release was institutionalized as an important component of sequential marketing strategies and the building of film franchises; the Fox/Lucasfilm reissue of a digitally enhanced STAR WARS trilogy in 1997 elevated re-release to the status of a premiere event.)

Constructing the Blockbuster Decade

OPENING SHOTS: *LOVE STORY* AND *THE GODFATHER*

In 1974, Paramount's head of production Robert Evans told *Time* magazine that "the making of a blockbuster is the newest art form of the 20th century,"[13] and he was in a position to know since he had produced the two megahits that defined the formula: LOVE STORY (1970) and THE GODFATHER (1972). Both films were adapted from manuscripts that became best-selling novels and cast in traditional generic form; both had notable directors and bankable stars; and both were budgeted and heavily marketed to become hits but caused unexpected sensations by becoming enormously popular and reaping windfall profits. LOVE STORY, a romantic melodrama in which a rich Harvard pre-law student falls in love with a poor Radcliffe scholarship student who is dying of leukemia, began as a screenplay by Yale classics professor Erich Segal, which was offered to Paramount by Segal's agent William Morris. Evans, who was the studio's new executive vice president in charge of production,[14] thought the film would be an ideal vehicle for his then wife Ali MacGraw, who had recently achieved stardom in his production of Paramount's GOODBYE, COLUMBUS (Larry Peerce, 1969). Evans supervised numerous rewrites of the script, which were undertaken to build MacGraw's star persona, and suggested that Segal write a novel based on his screenplay. This motion picture "novelization," the first of its kind to be cross-marketed with the film, was published by Harper & Row on Valentine's Day 1970, in 418,000 hardcover and 4,350,000 paperback copies—the largest first-edition print run in publishing history. The book became a stunning overnight success, selling in the tens of millions and spending nine months on the *New York Times* best-seller list. By the time the film was released in December 1970, public awareness of its title and sentimental story was very nearly universal. The film itself, expertly directed by Arthur Hiller and produced for $2,260,000, was an immediate success, grossing nearly $100 million in four months and earning $48,700,000 in rentals.[15] Its sound-track album of original music composed by Francis Lai quickly became a best-seller, and the film's concluding line of dialogue— "Love means never having to say you're sorry"—became a pop-culture cliché. Although nominated for Academy Awards for Best Picture, Best Director, Best Actor (Ryan O'Neal), Best Actress, Best Supporting Actor (John Marley), Best Original Score, and Best Screenplay, LOVE STORY won only for its music. But its astonishingly high return

Robert Evan's Paramount production LOVE STORY *(1970) was cross-marketed with a "novelization" by Erich Segal, and both film and novel became enormous hits: Ryan O'Neal, Ali MacGraw. 35mm 1.85:1.*

on investment and its formulaic popularity made it the first blockbuster of the decade. (As certification, Paramount produced a sequel—OLIVER'S STORY [John Korty, 1978]—but the film barely broke even.)

Evans's next project, THE GODFATHER, was consciously conceived as an "event movie," but with the relatively modest budget of $6 million. Paramount had optioned Mario Puzo's novel about the Mafia for $80,000 on the basis of an outline and 100 manuscript pages, giving him an office and a secretary to finish the book on the studio lot. Meanwhile, Francis Ford Coppola, who had just won an Oscar (with Edmund G. North) for Best Original Screenplay for PATTON (Franklin Schaffner, 1970), was hired to direct the film version after at least three other directors (Constantin Costa-Gavras, Peter Yates, and Peter Bogdanovich) had turned it down.[16] Coppola collaborated with Puzo on the screenplay while the novel was still in galleys, and convinced Paramount to cast the mercurial Marlon Brando in its title role, filling the rest of the cast with relative unknowns who became stars via THE GODFATHER's spectacular success. While the film was in production, the book was published and became an instant best-seller, with one million hardcover and twelve million paperback copies in circulation at the time of the film's release. As with LOVE STORY, a publishing tie-in had created massive public awareness of both the film's title and story. Fueling the high level of anticipation were well-publicized protests by Italian-American groups about THE GODFATHER's supposed prejudicial content and stories of cost overruns and other problems related to the film's

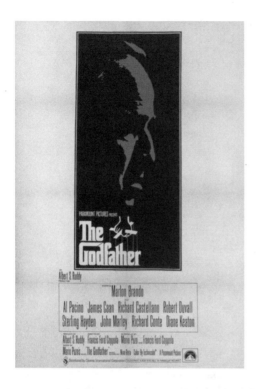

Poster for THE GODFATHER suggesting its status as a prestigious "event." (Compare with the sensationalist "event" appeal of the disaster-film posters on page 36.

Evans added a real novel (by Mario Puzo) and a star (Brando, slightly tarnished) to the mix and produced in THE GODFATHER (Paramount, 1972) the decade's first true blockbuster, which revived the flagging industry and briefly became the highest-grossing film in history: Robert Duvall, Marlon Brando. 35mm 1.85:1.

being shot on location in New York City in midwinter. (In fact, despite real difficulties, Coppola brought the film in a scant $1 million over budget.)

Paramount launched THE GODFATHER in February 1972 with massive trade promotion and saturation booking in 350 first-run theaters, commanding fixed seat prices of $4—at a time when $3 was the standard. With "special event" written all over it, the film was calculated to return its negative cost in days and earn a profit in weeks. No one at Paramount, however, could have predicted that *Variety*'s headline for April 5, 1972, would read "'Godfather' Boon to All Pix," and that the story would report that this "historic smash of unprecedented proportions" was energizing box-office returns across the board.[17] By the end of the year THE GODFATHER had earned $86,275,000 in rentals, and became, however briefly, the highest-grossing film in history. (The blockbuster syndrome accelerated so rapidly that by 1980 THE GODFATHER stood as only the fifth highest grosser of the decade, though it remains among the top twenty-five to this day.)

Confirming its triumph, the film won Oscars for Best Film, Best Screenplay, and Best Actor, as well as Academy Award nominations for direction, three supporting performances, sound, editing, and costumes. A sequel was planned immediately, and Coppola signed to direct it on June 22, 1972. Produced for $13 million, THE GODFATHER, PART II (1974) earned only $30.1 million in rentals, but was in many ways superior to the original, which it both continued and enriched—it won the 1974 Academy Awards for Best Picture, Director, Supporting Actor (Robert De Niro), Screenplay from another medium (Coppola and Puzo), Art Direction, and Score.

DISASTER AND NOSTALGIA: FROM *AIRPORT* TO *THE STING*

The success of THE GODFATHER is generally credited with driving a 20percent upturn in domestic theater admissions in 1972 over 1971, reversing a seven-year slump and increasing international sales. Furthermore, as Thomas Schatz points out, total box-office receipts for 1972 were up 64 percent (to $1.64 billion) from the $1 billion range they had occupied for the preceding several years.[18] While THE GODFATHER accounted for fully 10 percent of the surge, receipts for the top ten box-office hits of 1972 were up 70 percent over 1971, and 1973 revenues continued the trend. Obviously, something was working right again in Hollywood, and it seemed to be the blockbuster strategy. Two other films that helped create this perception were Universal's AIRPORT (George Seaton, 1970) and Fox's THE POSEIDON ADVENTURE (Ronald Neame, 1972). The former was adapted from a best-selling novel by Arthur Hailey about an imperiled transatlantic flight, with an all-star cast headlining Burt Lancaster, Dean Martin, George Kennedy, and Helen Hayes and featuring numerous cameos. Fairly described by *Variety* as a "jet age 'Grand Hotel',"[19] AIRPORT was shot in 70-mm Todd-AO with state-of-the-art special effects and helped to establish the formula for disaster films. These became a staple of 1970s blockbuster production, with a large cast of well-known performers confronting a catastrophe—manmade or natural—with varying degrees of success, depending on their characters. Nominated for ten Academy Awards, including Best Picture, AIRPORT won for Best Supporting Actress (Helen Hayes), and earned $45,220,118 in rentals, returning more than four times its substantial investment of $10 million. THE POSEIDON ADVENTURE, adapted by Stirling Silliphant from a Paul Gallico novel, transposed the AIRPORT scenario to an ocean liner with even more spectacular special effects (for which designers L. B. Abbott and A. D. Flowers won the Academy's Special Achievement Award). The film, which garnered eight Oscar nominations in 1973, had a star-studded

Universal's AIRPORT (*1970*) *pioneered the 1970s' disaster-film formula by placing its "all-star" cast in jeopardy: Burt Lancaster, George Kennedy. 70mm Todd-AO.*

cast (including Gene Hackman, Ernest Borgnine, Red Buttons, and Shelley Winters) and a cross-marketed theme song—"The Morning After," sung by Maureen McGovern, which became a number-one gold record for months after winning an Academy Award.

THE POSEIDON ADVENTURE earned $42 million in rentals and was produced by Irwin Allen (1916–1991), a documentary and television producer (*Lost in Space*), who was also the architect behind THE TOWERING INFERNO (John Guillermin, 1974), a coproduction of 20th Century–Fox and Warner Bros. This first-ever collaboration by major studios (undertaken when both realized that they had identical projects based on similar novels—Tom Sortia and Frank Robinson's *The Glass Inferno* and Richard Martin Stern's *The Tower*—in development at the same time) had its all-star cast (headed by Steve McQueen, Paul Newman, Willliam Holden, and Faye Dunaway) trapped inside of a burning skyscraper. The two-and-a-half-hour negative, replete with spectacular stunts and pyrotechnic effects, cost $14 million to produce, and the film earned $48.8 million in rentals to become the year's highest grosser. (THE TOWERING INFERNO was nominated for eight Oscars, including Best Picture, and won for Best Cinematography, Best Editing, and Best Song: "We May Never Love Like This Again"—which, like "The Morning After," briefly rose to the top of the charts.)

Not far behind, in the number three position with $35,849,994, was another disaster epic, Universal's EARTHQUAKE (Mark Robson, 1974), which added an aural dimension to

Fox's THE POSEIDON ADVENTURE *(1972) placed its stars aboard a sinking (and inverted) ocean liner: Red Buttons, Ernest Borgnine, Stella Stevens. 35mm Panavision anamorphic.*

Universal's EARTHQUAKE *(1974) underscored the crucial importance of special effects to the disaster film—sensation was (and is) the genre's major hook. Special visual effects by Frank Brendel, Glen Robinson, and Albert Whitlock. Panavision 35mm anamorphic; blown up to 70mm for road-showing. Recorded and exhibited in Sensurround.*

Exploitation-style posters for THE POSEIDON ADVENTURE, THE TOWERING INFERNO, and EARTHQUAKE, claiming "event" status for their films — in the case of EARTHQUAKE, quite literally.

its special effects via a low-frequency sound system called "Sensurround." Sensurround
was a proprietary process that dubbed low-frequency rumbles onto the sound track to
simulate tremors during the film's eight-minute quake sequence. For playback in theaters, Universal rented a package consisting of an amplifier and special speakers for
$500 a week, which was used at about sixty key sites.[20] The Sensurround experience gen-
erated enough repeat business to justify its use in several other Universal films (MIDWAY
[Jack Smight, 1976], ROLLERCOASTER [James Goldstone, 1977], BATTLESTAR: GALACTICA
[Richard A. Colla, 1978]), and EARTHQUAKE won an Oscar for Best Sound and a Class II
Scientific and Technical Award for the development of the process; it also won a Special
Achievement Award for its visual effects. Though a patent gimmick, Sensurround
enhanced its films' "event" status and served to focus industry attention on the neglected
dimension of theater sound as a potential blockbuster hook.

Like LOVE STORY and THE GODFATHER, early-1970s disaster films clearly fueled the
blockbuster juggernaut, and three megahits of the 1973–1974 season helped to push
1974 box-office revenues toward the $2-billion high established in the euphoric post-
war year of 1946. Universal's AMERICAN GRAFFITI (1973) was a classic sleeper. Written
and directed by Francis Ford Coppola's friend George Lucas, AMERICAN GRAFFITI was
produced by Gary Kurtz for a little over $775,000 (about 10 percent of which went
toward acquiring the rights to the forty-one rock 'n' roll songs from the late fifties and
early sixties that make up the film's "score").[21] With Coppola as executive producer
under the new Lucasfilm Ltd. banner, and Haskell Wexler as cinematographer, this

*Once Universal understood its
market, the nostalgia card was
played with a vengeance, as this
postrelease poster for* AMERICAN
GRAFFITI *shows.*

AMERICAN GRAFFITI (Universal, 1973) unexpectedly tapped a rich vein of nostalgia for pre-Watergate, pre-Vietnam, pre-assassination America. 35mm Panavision anamorphic. Like most 1970s features, the film was recorded and exhibited in monaural, despite a sound-track mix of forty-one separate rock 'n' roll songs from the late fifties and early sixties. (The license plate of the hotrod on the right bears the designation "THX-138" in reference to director George Lucas's student film and first feature, THX-1138 [1971].)

nostalgic re-creation of adolescence in the suburbs of Los Angeles during the early 1960s was shot in twenty-eight days. Full of vintage cars and period music, AMERICAN GRAFFITI was hesitantly released by Universal, which spent only $500,000 for advertising, publicity, and prints, refusing even to dupe the prints in stereo. But it struck a chord with the viewing public and went on earn $55,28,175 in domestic rentals, making it the third highest grossing film of 1973. It also won nominations for five Academy Awards, including Best Picture, Best Director, and Best Screenplay (Lucas, Gloria Katz, and Willard Huyck), and became the source of several television spinoffs (most notably, *Happy Days* and *Laverne and Shirley*), positioning Lucas for the astonishing success of his next project, the now legendary STAR WARS (1977).

A few years earlier, AMERICAN GRAFFITI might have been seen as another EASY RIDER (Dennis Hopper, 1969), but in context it was the exception that proved the rule. Ranked in first and second place above it were two shrewdly calculated blockbusters: Warner Bros.' THE EXORCIST (1973) and Universal's THE STING (George Roy Hill, 1973). The latter reunited the director and stars (Paul Newman and Robert Redford) of the 1969 box-office champion BUTCH CASSIDY AND THE SUNDANCE KID in a caper film with a period setting that was similar to THE GODFATHER. That Redford and Newman were the number one and number two box-office stars of the year, respectively, ensured a healthy return on the film's $5.5-million investment, but its rental earnings of $78,212,000 and its ten Academy Award nominations helped institutional-ize a "hit-flop" mentality that would characterize the rest of decade. THE STING won seven of its ten Oscar nominations: Best Picture, Director, Screenplay (David S. Ward), Art Direction, Set Decor-ation, Editing, Musical Adaptation, and Costume Design—and its theme song, Scott Joplin's "The Entertainer" became a national hit, as did its sound-track album of Joplin rags.

THE EXORCIST: COURTING EXPLOITATION

As a shrewdly contrived and marketed hit based on sensational material, THE EXORCIST was in a category by itself. Adapted by William Peter Blatty from his own best-selling novel (published 1971), produced by Blatty, and directed by William Friedkin (who had just won the Best Director Oscar for THE FRENCH CONNECTION [1972]), THE EXORCIST capitalized on what one reviewer called "the perfect mixture of blood, excrement, per-verse sexuality, and religious symbolism"[22] to earn $89 million in rentals and ten Academy Award nominations. The R-rated horror film, produced without major stars for approximately $9 million, benefited immensely from the controversy surrounding its depiction of a demonically possessed 12-year-old girl urinating, vomiting, and mastur-bating with a crucifix while spouting obscenities never heard before on a studio motion-

Warners' THE EXORCIST (1974) took exploitative horror into the mainstream with its story of the demonic possession of a 12-year-old girl: Linda Blair, Kitty Winn, Jason Miller. Makeup effects by Dick Smith. 35mm Panavision spherical (1:1.85), blown up to 70mm for road-showing.

picture sound track. (Controversy didn't hurt the novel, either, spurring sales that exceeded 13 million copies by the end of 1973.)

To open the film, Warners borrowed a distribution tactic begun with wildlife documentary features like THE AMERICAN WILDERNESS (Arthur Dubs, 1969), and used with startling success by independent producer Tom Laughlin in May 1973 for the re-release of his 1971 film BILLY JACK (which Warners had distributed briefly before selling it back to him after he sued them for failing to properly promote it).[23] In this practice, known as "four-walling," the distributor rents a theater for a flat fee for several weekends and takes 100 percent of the box-office proceeds, with the exhibitor taking nothing but concession fees.[24] Combined with local television ad campaigns, four-wall distribution allows a distributor to completely dominate a regional market for a weekend or two, generating enormous profits (in the case of the BILLY JACK reissue, $32.5 million). When the majors ventured into four-walling in late 1973—Warners with THE EXORCIST and Universal with WESTWORLD (Michael Crichton, 1973)—the National Association of Theater Owners (NATO) appealed to the Justice Department, claiming that the technique violated the consent decrees, with the result that a ten-year moratorium was placed on the practice in 1976.[25] Nonetheless, the experience of four-walling a blockbuster like THE EXORCIST taught Hollywood the value of saturation release patterns combined with massive television advertising to generate high audience awareness and consumer demand.

The publicity attendant on its graphic, visceral content was another marketing lesson of THE EXORCIST, and there was a new critical perception of dawning change. In his article entitled "Hollywood's New Sensationalism" and cited above, Stephen Farber concluded: "Colossal budgets are back in fashion, and the studios are marketing a new brand of sensationalism, gaudier and more lurid than at any time in movie history."[26] Among the catalogue of horror/disaster films then in preparation, one particularly concerned him—"a movie about a killer shark that the director promises will 'tear your guts out.'"[27]

JAWS: THE PARADIGMATIC "EVENT" FILM OF THE SEVENTIES

Universal's JAWS (1975), directed by Steven Spielberg, is understood today as a major turning point in the history of postclassical Hollywood. As Thomas Schatz suggests in his seminal essay "The New Hollywood," it emphatically marked the arrival of the New Hollywood by recalibrating the profit potential of the blockbuster and redefining its status as a marketable commodity. In terms of marketing, it was the first "high concept" film—in the sense of a film whose conceptual premise and story is easily reducible to a salient image, which then becomes the basis for an aggressive advertising campaign keyed to merchandising tie-ins and ancillary markets, creating "synergy" between film, products, and related media. (Variously attributed to Barry Diller, Michael Eisner, and Peter Guber, *high concept* is an industry term that was coined in the 1970s to characterize an easily marketed story, idea, or image.[28]) As a cultural phenomenon, JAWS represented a revival and "implosion" (J. Hoberman's term) of the disaster cycle that had had its real-world correspondence in Vietnam and Watergate.[29] But it was also the paradigm for what Schatz calls "the high-cost, high-tech, high-speed" thriller[30] that became the major Hollywood genre of the eighties and nineties.

Like other contemporary blockbusters, JAWS was based on a best-selling novel—producers Richard D. Zanuck and David Brown had shrewdly bought the rights to it for

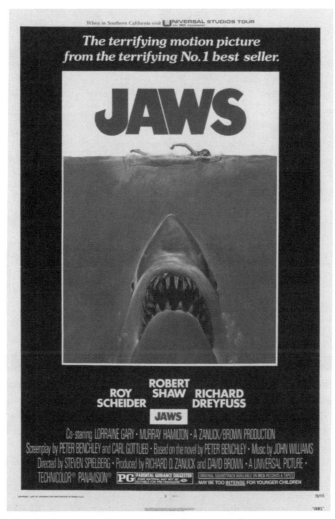

*The "high concept" image from this poster for JAWS
(Universal, 1975) was used to advertise the film around the
world, and it also appeared on books, records, and all kinds
of ancillary merchandise.*

$150,000 while the book was still in galleys.[31] The deal was packaged by ICM
(International Creative Management), which represented all parties, and paid author
Peter Benchley another $100,000 to write a first draft of the script.[32] Initially budgeted
at $3.5 million, the film was shot on location at Martha's Vineyard by the 26-year-old
Spielberg, who then had to his credit only a TV movie entitled DUEL (1971) and the
unsuccessful theatrical feature THE SUGARLAND EXPRESS (1974), also produced for
Universal by Zanuck and Brown.[33] Trouble with logistics and special effects eventually
pushed the negative cost to around $12 million. The promotional budget of over $2.5
million was targeted mainly for television, and some of it had been raised from exhibitors
(with JAWS, Universal began the practice of assessing theater owners for a share of a

Sensationalism and marketing hype notwithstanding, part of JAWS's *appeal lay in its portrayal of small-town America enmeshed in the same ethical dilemmas as the nation at large. Here, Amity Island's mayor (Murray Hamilton) commits himself to covering up recent shark attacks to protect the town's resort trade. 35mm Panavision anamorphic.*

film's national TV advertising costs).[34] Stimulated by publicity about the production and news of the five rewrites that the script had undergone (resulting finally in a collaboration by Benchley and Carl Gottlieb, assisted by Howard Sackler and John Milius),[35] the book had become an enormous success by the time the film was released, with 7.6 million copies in print, and public awareness of the JAWS phenomenon was already high.

To distribute JAWS, Universal borrowed the saturation release or "wide opening" pattern of BILLY JACK, together with a saturation advertising campaign centering on television. It was noted at the time that saturation booking had, with several notable exceptions (including DUEL IN THE SUN [King Vidor, 1946] and THE CARPETBAGGERS [Edward Dmytryk, 1964]), historically been reserved for "stiffs" to make a quick profit from a bad movie before word-of-mouth and reviews killed it.[36] But Universal determined that the same pattern could be used to maximize profits on an eagerly anticipated product, and suddenly what had been a means of throwing a movie away (opening it everywhere at once) became of way of signaling its importance.[37]

To build a national audience and promote what Universal called "JAWS-consciousness," the studio had Brown, Zanuck, Benchley, and production personnel like Verna Fields—the film's editor—on the talk-show circuit for eight months before the film's release. Three days before June 20th, when the film was scheduled to open at 464 North

American sites (407 in the United States, 55 in Canada),[38] Universal unleashed a saturation advertising blitz via all media outlets within signal range of the theaters, exploiting John Williams's ominous theme music and coordinating it with a print campaign organized around the striking graphic image of a huge open-mouthed shark rising underwater toward a naked female swimmer. The promotion was a stunning success. By the end of summer, the movie, the book, and hundreds of product tie-ins (T-shirts, beach bags, toys) had raised sharks to the level of a national fetish, 25 million tickets had been sold, and the film had earned nearly $100 million in domestic rentals. It would ultimately earn $129.5 million and become, until 1977, the top-grossing film of all time; and it would win three Academy Awards: Best Sound, Best Original Score (John Williams), and Best Editing.[39]

The success of JAWS and the merchandising sub-industry it spawned brought a dramatic conclusion to the post-1969 recession that had proceeded from the late-sixties frenzy of diversification and conglomeration. It also permanently hooked the film industry on blockbuster windfalls—coproducer Richard Zanuck, for example, made more money on his share the film's profits than his father Darryl F. Zanuck had made in his entire career. But as Michael Pye and Lynda Myles point out in *The Hollywood Brats*, the single most salient feature of JAWS was "the transformation of film into event through clever manipulation of the media."[40] Indeed, if Justin Wyatt is correct, the media campaign for JAWS shaped the direction of film marketing for the considerable future. Henceforth, the industry would rely on "strong, reproducible images, the saturation campaign, and widespread product tie-ins" as standard marketing practice.[41] Wyatt, in fact, suggests that JAWS and its successors led the industry increasingly to conceive of its product as the modular narrative reducible to a singular image and marketing approach—a narrative of generic character; that is, compatible with an advertising-oriented, or "high concept," style. This actually seems to be what Spielberg was talking about in a 1978 *American Film* "Dialogue on Film" interview when he said of his work: "What interests me is the idea. If a person can tell me the idea in twenty-five words or less, it's going to make a pretty good movie. I like ideas, especially movie ideas, that you can hold in your hand."[42] JAWS also proved the value of saturation booking for high-quality studio releases, initiating a marketing strategy for blockbusters that placed increased importance on their performance in the first few weeks of release. As Schatz suggests, this practice not only maximized a film's status as a special event, but protected it from negative word of mouth and bad reviews—fulfilling the original intent of saturation booking as an exploitation strategy. In fact, JAWS proved above all else that a multi-million-dollar blockbuster could be distributed and marketed as if it *were* exploitation product—hyped for a quick weekend's profit (JAWS grossed $7.061 million in its opening weekend)[43] and sold on the basis of a single sensational image as if it were pornography.

A NEW "CINEMA OF ATTRACTIONS"

JAWS and the 1970s blockbuster generally represented a return to a kind of performative spectacle that had characterized the cinema's primitive period, enhanced by state-of-the-art, pre-digital special effects and, after 1977, high-quality Dolby stereophonic sound. This earlier presentational mode—the *cinema of attractions*, is Tom Gunning's useful term—dominated the medium's first decade (1895–1906), after which narrative emerged as the dominant form. Elements of the cinema of attractions remained as components of certain narrative genres like the musical and the horror film, where direct sensory stimulation (the delivery of spectacle and shock) became a key element of spectatorial pleasure, but the overwhelming burden of classical Hollywood cinema was to provide conceptually integrated narratives. By the 1970s, the collapse of the studio system, with its vertical and horizontal monopolies on all three industry tiers, produced a return to the original industry structure in which production, distribution, and exhibition were all separated, but financial and marketing power was concentrated in the distributors (or, as they were still called, the *major studios*). The example of JAWS clearly illustrates this phenomenon: though financed by Universal, the film was essentially an independent production of the Zanuck-Brown/Benchley-Spielberg team packaged by ICM; as a film JAWS had much intrinsic worth, but its astounding success was largely a function of Universal's distribution and marketing strategies, from which independent exhibitors reaped ticket sales of historic proportions, even as they were assessed a share of Universal's marketing costs. Given this reversion to its pre-World War I industrial configuration, it is no anomaly that the American film industry would revisit the cinema of attractions as its economic mainstay. As Stephen Farber wrote in 1974 of the new wave of big-budget disaster and horror films, "Movies were a form of circus spectacle long before they began to tell stories—and long before they were considered an art. . . . [A]nd that is the backwards direction they seem to be taking in the seventies."[44]

BLOCKBUSTERS BUILT TO ORDER: *KING KONG* AND *THE DEEP*

Two films that attempted to capitalize immediately on the JAWS phenomenon were KING KONG (John Guillermin, 1976) and THE DEEP (Peter Yates, 1977). Produced by Dino De Laurentiis for Paramount, KING KONG began the cycle of blockbuster remakes of classics that marked the latter half of the decade. Pre-sold through the cult status of the original and closely associated with JAWS as a high-tech monster film, KONG featured impressive special effects designed by Rick Baker (makeup) and Carlo Rambaldi (visual effects, for which Rambaldi won a Special Achievement Award from the Academy) but was encumbered with a campy script (by Lorenzo Semple, Jr.) that its attractive young stars—Jeff Bridges and Jessica Lange, in her film debut—could do little to improve. (KONG was also recorded with a Sensurround track, which was played back only in foreign markets.) Paramount orchestrated a sophisticated marketing campaign designed around the image of Kong astride the World Trade Center and opened the film in a saturation pattern that, with 961 sites, nearly doubled the reach of JAWS. De Laurentiis himself negotiated KING KONG merchandising tie-ins with Jim Beam Distilling, 7-Eleven, GAF, Sedgefield Sportswear, Schrafft Candy, and several other companies whose products were emblazoned with high-profile ape imagery. Despite a near record-breaking opening week at Christmas time (of which a *Variety* headline proclaimed "'Kong' Wants 'Jaws" Box-office Crown" [12/22/76]), the $24 million production returned "only" $36,915,000 in domestic rentals, to become the third highest grossing film of 1976, standing behind United Artists' ROCKY ($56,524,972) and another remake, Warner Bros.' A STAR IS BORN ($37,100,000). Although it ultimately earned $80 million in rentals worldwide, KING KONG was widely perceived as a flop in the post-JAWS environment (a perception promoted by the film's advertising, which stridently predicted that it would outgross Spielberg's film).

THE DEEP (Peter Yates, 1977), produced by Peter Guber for Columbia, represented blockbuster-building at its most cynically manipulative. Guber talked Columbia president David Begelman into buying the rights to Peter Benchley's first post-JAWS novel,

*"High concept" marketing art for Dino De Laurentiis's
remake of KING KONG (1976), a calculated blockbuster
released by Paramount in expectation of a JAWS-style bonanza
that failed to materialize. 35mm Panavision anamorphic, blown
up to 70mm for road-showing. Recorded in Sensurround (but
exhibited in the process only outside the United States).*

The Deep, in manuscript for $500,000 and proceeded to turn it into a $8.9-million movie that was pre-sold through hardback publication of the novel and widespread magazine condensation.[45] The film—a confused action story about a vacationing couple (Nick Nolte and Jacqueline Bisset) who stumble onto a secret cache of drugs and Spanish treasure and become the target of criminals—was shot on location in the British Virgin Islands and Bermuda in 151 days, with about 40 percent of its principal photography underwater.[46] Guber invited hundreds of journalists to the set and himself wrote a behind-the-scenes account of the production entitled *Inside "The Deep,"* whose publication was timed to coincide with the film's release, as was publication of the paperback edition of the novel. With an advertising budget of nearly $3 million, Guber personally orchestrated every detail of THE DEEP's marketing and distribution campaign. He created a vertical poster design reminiscent of that for JAWS, with a nearly naked female diver in deep blue water bubbling up toward a horizontal surface logo, and he relentlessly exploited fetishistic production stills of Bisset in a scuba mask and wet T-shirt (Guber: "That T-shirt made me a rich man").[47] He merged his production company, Casablanca Filmworks, with Neil Bogart's record company (becoming Casablanca Records and Filmworks) to release the film's theme song, "Down Deep

Inside" by Donna Summer, on a see-through blue vinyl sound-track album.[48] He negotiated product tie-ins with boat, watch, sportswear, and cosmetic companies, and organized a national treasure hunt contest through supermarket chains and shopping malls.
Finally, he directed a $1.3-million television blitz into the nation's top fifty markets.
The goal, according to Columbia's marketing department, was to saturate those markets with 2.5-billion visual images of the film before its June 17 nationwide opening in
800 theaters.[49] Guber calibrated that opening very specifically to urban pay cycles, as
he explained to the *New York Times*: "The maids and the blue-collars and much of
industry get paid twice a month. They put their checks in the bank on the 15th, have
them clear on the 16th and they're ready to spend by the 17th."[50] Such precision paid
off: THE DEEP broke industry records by grossing $8.124 million in its three-day open-
ing weekend, eventually earning $31.2 million in domestic rentals to become the sixth
highest money-maker in a year that included both Fox's STAR WARS (in first place with
$193.8 million) and Columbia's CLOSE ENCOUNTERS OF THE THIRD KIND (in second
place with $82.8 million).

Racist, violent, and mildly titillating, THE DEEP nevertheless contains some extraordinary underwater sequences and is tightly directed by Peter Yates, yet was a manufactured hit if there ever was one. Peter Guber had raised the marketing of event movies
to a level of perfection that all Hollywood admired. He had, according to his own
research, exposed every potential audience member to at least fifteen different images
of THE DEEP before its extremely wide release,[51] and on opening day had stopped just
short of actually putting his hand into the audience's pocket and taking its money out. In
the process, the film itself became largely irrelevant.

CLOSE ENCOUNTERS: THE BLOCKBUSTER AS EPIPHANY

Such ferocity of marketing became the chief distinguishing feature of late seventies
Hollywood, which took to selling its blockbusters as if they were the second coming of
Christ. "Events," in short, were no longer enough—films had to offer something
approaching a mystical experience. This, at least, was how Columbia marketed Steven
Spielberg's CLOSE ENCOUNTERS OF THE THIRD KIND (1977), with special effects of UFO
landings by Douglas Trumbull that were rumored to exceed even those of STAR WARS
(see below), released six months before. The studio, which had typically been raising
40–50 percent of its production capital from recently outlawed domestic tax shelters,
had invested $19.4 million in the negative against outside investment of only $6.75 million and badly needed the film to be a hit. It had no pre-sold elements except the post-
JAWS reputation of its director.[52] Therefore, Columbia allocated $9 million to saturation
advertising intended burn the film's "expectant-skies" logo into the consciousness of
every sentient American; then attempted to recoup both marketing and negative costs
by demanding unusually high advance guarantees from exhibitors—from $150,000 in
New York to $50,000 elsewhere, plus a $2,000 surcharge for promotion—for a twelve-
week, non-exclusive run.[53] Though the film's release was extremely wide, in some markets (Chicago, for example) Columbia attempted to bid up the guarantee by making it
competitive, suggesting that theater owners should be honored to show a film of such
power and distinction.

The hype worked. Not only did the studio collect about $24 million in advance pay-
ments, putting CLOSE ENCOUNTERS $2 million over costs before release, but anticipa-
tion that it had a blockbuster sent its stock soaring from a year's low of 4 1/2 to a high of

The "mother ship" from Columbia's CLOSE ENCOUNTERS OF THE THIRD KIND (1977), which brought to the blockbuster an aura of religious mystery (aka "awe and wonder"). Special visual effects by Douglas Trumbull. 35mm Panavision anamorphic, blown-up to 70mm for road-showing. Recorded and selectively exhibited in four-channel Dolby stereo optical sound (six-track stereo magnetic for 70mm prints).

20 7/8 (from about $7 to $18 a share) on November 14, 1977, a day before the film's premiere, touching off a wave of furious speculation on Wall Street.[54] Although the stock dropped five points later that year, CLOSE ENCOUNTERS OF THE THIRD KIND earned $82,750,000 in domestic rentals to become the second most profitable movie of the year. (The film also received eight Academy Award nominations and took one Oscar, for Vilmos Zsigmond's cinematography.)

STAR WARS: FROM "EVENT" TO MASS MARKET FRANCHISE

The film that led both 1977 and the decade in profitability (and, in 1999, was still the fourth highest earner in history, after E.T. [Steven Spielberg, 1982], JURASSIC PARK [Steven Spielberg, 1993], and TITANIC [James Cameron, 1997] was George Lucas's STAR WARS. Although it was three years in development and had been turned down by several other studios (Universal and United Artists) before Alan Ladd, Jr. optioned the screenplay for Fox, STAR WARS was in many ways as carefully manufactured a product as THE DEEP. Lucas did extensive research on the story, special effects, and audience for the film, which as generic science fiction had no clear model except Stanley Kubrick's ten-year-old 2001: A SPACE ODYSSEY (1968) and the *Star Trek* television series.[55] Lucas calculated that a hardcore market of science fiction buffs and children would generate a domestic box office of $16 million, with $25 million at the outside, and could therefore generate a profit on a $9-million investment.[56] The deal with Fox provided $9.5 million in production capital to Lucas's recently formed (1973) Lucasfilm Ltd. and a modest $150,000 fee to Lucas himself for writing and directing.

In a move that would have historic implications, Lucas eschewed extra salary and a personal share of the gross to retain the merchandising and sequel rights. Star Wars Productions, a corporation formed by Lucas and his producer Gary Kurtz, was granted 40 percent of the film's net profits, some of which were passed on as "points" to the cast and crew. For his participation, Sir Alec Guinness was given 2.25 percent in a separate deal. The rest of the profits went to Fox, after subtracting their 30-percent distribution fee.[57] Control of the licenses, including music and publication, would by 1999 be worth more than $4 billion as STAR WARS became the most lucrative franchise in motion picture history. Fox retained copyright and distribution rights to subsequent films, as well as a percentage of merchandising profits, but Lucas controlled both the story and the brand. Neither party expected STAR WARS to become to a megahit, much less a cultural phenomenon of seismic proportions. Lucas did, however, design the film with an eye toward merchandising tie-ins. According to Michael Pye and Linda Myles, in fact, "the film was written for toys," and Lucas had a whole line of T-shirts, posters, models, books, records, and action figures in mind from the start.[58] This seemed perfectly appropriate

Fox's STAR WARS *(1977), the ultimate blockbuster and first true film franchise (not to mention international, intergenerational cultural icon): David Prowse (Darth Vader) and Alec Guinness (Obi-Wan Kenobi). 35mm Panavision anamorphic, blown up to 70mm for road-showing. Recorded and selectively exhibited in four-channel Dolby stereo optical sound (six-stereo magnetic for 70mm prints).*

One of several domestic posters for STAR WARS *that emphasized its quasi-mystical, fantasy-like elements.*

to a "space fantasy" whose inspiration was comic books and cliff-hanging Saturday afternoon serials as much as it was traditional science fiction.

To counterpoint the fairy-tale quality its narrative, hyper-realistic special effects for
STAR WARS were produced at Industrial Light and Magic (ILM), a subsidiary of Lucasfilm
founded in Van Nuys in 1975 (but moved north to San Rafael, Marin County, in 1978)
specifically for this purpose. At ILM, F/X director John Dykstra, who had worked as
Douglas Trumbull's assistant on SILENT RUNNING (1972), perfected a computerized
motion-control system for traveling matte photography that made the process uniquely
cost-effective, enabling Lucas to create hundreds of complicated stop-motion miniature
sequences for STAR WARS at a fraction of their cost for earlier films ($2.5 million for 365
traveling matte shots, for example, as compared with $6.5 million for fewer than 30 in

2001: A SPACE ODYSSEY). With live-action sequences shot in Tunisia, Death Valley, and EMI-Elstree Studios in England, STAR WARS also became the first film both recorded and released in four-track Dolby stereophonic sound. Nonetheless, it was produced for the relatively modest sum of $11.5 million, and no one expected it to earn back more than twice that in domestic rentals, because of the traditionally hard-sell market for science fiction and the film's own somewhat confused identity. (Chris Kalabokes, a financial analyst at Fox in the mid-1970s, projected that $35 million would constitute a "windfall.")[59]

Fox cautiously decided against saturation booking and opened the film on May 25, 1977, in only forty-two theaters in twenty-eight cities, with 70mm and Dolby stereo prints for major markets, together with a carefully coordinated advertising campaign targeted at 12–24-year-olds (and secondarily at the 25–35-year-old bracket).[60] The date was not optimal, since school was still in session for much of the target audience, but it was calculated to avoid head-to-head competition with such major June releases as Columbia's THE DEEP.[61] The industry was stunned when STAR WARS earned nearly $3 million in its first week and by the end of August had grossed $100 million; it played continuously throughout 1977–1978, and was officially re-released in 1978 and 1979, by the end of which it had earned $262 million in rentals worldwide to become the top-grossing film of all time—a position it would maintain until surpassed by Universal's E.T.: THE EXTRA-TERRESTRIAL in January 1983. Star Wars Productions' 40-percent share of profits ($55.7 million), combined with the tie-in merchandising bonanza, quickly made Lucas a multimillionaire and turned Lucasfilm Ltd. into a $30-million company. (By 1997, Lucas's net worth was estimated at $2 billion and Lucasfilm's corporate

Kellogg's C-3PO breakfast cereal was a microcosm of the STAR WARS licensing bonanza in the food sector (there were more than 60 other product categories in a list ranging the alphabet from "backpacks" to "Wookie mugs"). The cereal had less sugar and fewer preservatives than the regular Kellogg product because Lucas would only grant licenses to perceptibly healthful foods, but its real appeal lay in the full-scale face masks of six characters from the film printed on the back of the boxes.

holdings at $5 billion.)[62] In the short term, Fox didn't fare badly either—by 1980, it had made a profit of $88.5 million on top of its $75-million distribution fee (a flat 30 percent of rentals). STAR WARS itself was nominated for ten Academy Awards and received seven (including Art Direction, Sound, Original Score, Film Editing, Costumes, and Visual Effects), as well as a special achievement award for sound effects editing; it also won two Los Angeles Critics Awards and three Grammies for its score.

The most significant phenomenon of STAR WARS lay in the creation and nurturing of the first true film franchise. Before STAR WARS, it was not uncommon for studios to give merchandising rights away for free publicity (as Fox had done with fast food tie-ins in the early 1970s); even when licensed for profit, as in the case of JAWS and KING KONG, product tie-ins like T-shirts, jewelry, and candy had little life or value apart from the film once its run was completed. But with STAR WARS—known to industry analysts as "the Holy Grail of licensing"[63]—merchandising became an industry unto itself, and tie-in product marketing began to drive the conception and selling of motion pictures rather than vice versa. By the 1980s, some movies were used primarily to launch product lines (THE CARE BEARS MOVIE [1985], MY LITTLE PONY [1986]), and film series like the STAR WARS trilogy (1977–1983), Paramount's STAR TREK (1979–present), and Warner Bros.' BATMAN (1989–present) became huge product franchises whose branded merchandise is worth literally billions of dollars in excess of box-office sales. For the original unenhanced STAR WARS trilogy, total box-office sales had reached $1.3 billion by 1997 (which helped to finance the growth of Industrial Light and Magic first into Hollywood's most profitable special-effects house and then into the premiere digital-imaging studio in the world), while video sales and rentals accounted for $500 million, CD-ROM and video games sales for $300 million, clothes and accessories for $300 million, books and comics for $300 million, and toys and playing cards for $1.21 billion.[64]

As James Sterngold points out, however, "franchises have life cycles that must be carefully tended and shrewdly planned."[65] The value of the STAR WARS brand declined during the late eighties from lack of novelty and nurture, but it accelerated rapidly after 1991 when Timothy Zahn's next-generation sequel *Heirs to the Empire* was published by Bantam and became a hardcover best-seller, generating multiple best-selling sequels and introducing the franchise to a new generation who would not see the STAR WARS trilogy in theaters until the digitally enhanced reissue of 1997. This reissue, "The STAR WARS Trilogy Special Edition," which itself earned hundred of millions of dollars in box-office and merchandise revenues, was a bridge to the launching of a new STAR WARS trilogy at the millennium whose licensing strategy was described by the *New York Times* as "one of the most impressive and tautly engineered pieces of marketing prowess ever conceived, as well as an example of what the movie industry has become: art in service of a huge commercial superstructure that needs constant feeding."[66] By the 1990s, merchandising had risen from the category of ancillary income to become an important studio revenue stream, and all of the majors operated large consumer-product divisions.[67]

"The Modern Era of Super-Blockbuster Films"

MARKET VOLATILITY

Over time, STAR WARS would change both the film industry and films themselves in fundamental ways. Most immediately, however, it changed the calculus by which blockbuster success was measured in 1970s Hollywood, ushering in what A. D. Murphy calls "the modern era of super-blockbuster films,"[68] or *super-grossers*, as William Bates described them in 1978—films manufactured to reach the level of "a national obsession."[69] At Fox, the revenues from STAR WARS were accruing at the rate of $1.2 million per day, and its stock—which one Wall Street securities analyst had characterized in the summer of 1976 as not of "investment quality"[70]—quadrupled in value (rising from $6 to $25 per share between June 1976 and June 1977). Already invested in Coca Cola Bottling Midwest, the company was able to further diversify by buying Aspen Skiing Corp. and Pebble Beach Corp. and still declare excess profits. According to Fox CEO Dennis Stanfill, STAR WARS gave the corporation "five years of growth in one."[71] Yet this magnitude of success was entirely unpredicted. Head of production Alan Ladd, Jr. had supported the film on the strength of AMERICAN GRAFFITI's performance, but pinned his hopes for a megahit on the barely profitable (and completely forgotten) $9-million DAMNATION ALLEY (Jack Smight, 1977).[72] Lucas himself had anticipated only modest box-office returns, which his merchandising deals would supplement. All of a sudden, the recently constructed formula for manufacturing a blockbuster seemed out of date. Pre-selling and marketing were still the order of the day, but now there was a wild card element to which none of the conventional rules seemed to apply. As Michael Eisner, then head of production at Paramount, said of this Brave New World in 1978: "The only rule is that there are no rules. The super-grossers are things that become cultural phenomena. There is no way you can work out on paper what a cultural phenomenon should be."[73]

The result was widespread panic among studio executives and a turn toward what exploitation producer Sam Arkoff wryly called "real gambling."[74] This meant high-stakes investment in projects over which the studios often had little control because they owned less than 50 percent of the package but were exposed to 100 percent of the risk (e.g., whereas Paramount had initiated the GODFATHER project and owned 84 percent of it, Columbia owned less than 50 percent of the agent-packaged CLOSE ENCOUNTERS OF THE THIRD KIND, which had to bring the studio $51 million in rentals just to break even).[75] Another form of gambling was the attempt to produce modestly budgeted sleepers on the order of AMERICAN GRAFFITI (1973)—small films that would strike a psychic nerve in the mass audience and become overnight sensations. In addition to GRAFFITI, the industry had the recent examples of United Artists' ROCKY (John G. Avildsen, 1976)—produced for less than $1 million and earning $56.5 million in rentals, and Universal's SMOKEY AND THE BANDIT (Hal Needham, 1977)—produced for $3 million and earning $59 million in rentals. These two hits—one an inspirational urban boxing film with blue-collar ethnic appeal, and the other a southern rural chase comedy that exploited the Citizen's Band radio craze—were conceived as fringe market films, yet they became the first- and fourth-highest grossers of their respective years and generated multiple sequels. Moreover, while SMOKEY AND THE BANDIT starred Burt Reynolds, ROCKY didn't have a single name performer.[76] In the volatile context of late-seventies Hollywood, their unforeseen success—though obviously welcome—was both puzzling and unnerving.

BLOCKBUSTER MUSIC

In the midst of such uncertainty, some producers and studios turned to popular music as a source of mass appeal.[77] Already used to pre-sell films like AMERICAN GRAFFITI and Paramount's Billie Holiday biopic LADY SINGS THE BLUES (Sidney J. Furie, 1972), pop music provided the fundamental concept for such hits as A STAR IS BORN (Frank

Second from right: Rocky Balboa (Sylvester Stallone) faces off against Apollo Creed (Carl Weathers [left]) in United Artists' archetypal 1970s sleeper ROCKY (1976). *35mm 1.85:1.*

Burt Reynolds as "Bandit" in Universal's unexpectedly popular rural car-chase comedy SMOKEY AND THE BANDIT (1977). *Directed by former stuntman Hal Needham, the film spawned two sequels (1980 and 1983) and three television series, 1979–1985 (see Chapter 5). 35mm 1.85:1.*

Pierson, 1976), SATURDAY NIGHT FEVER (John Badham, 1977), and GREASE (Randal Kleiser, 1978), whose sound-track albums were aggressively marketed across a variety of media in a "buy the record, see the film" strategy that became an industry mainstay in the 1980s.[78] (According to Peter Guralnick, the formula may have been invented twenty years earlier by Col. Tom Parker, Elvis Presley's business manager, for the sound-track albums of Presley's 1960s films.)[79] The potential for such cross-media marketing was greatly enhanced by the conversion of theaters to high-quality Dolby sound in the wake of STAR WARS. Although at least twenty films had been released with some form of Dolby encoding before it, the clear role that Dolby stereo played in STAR WARS' unprecedented success caused a rush to install Dolby reproduction equipment, and by 1979 there were approximately 1,200 theaters in the United States equipped for Dolby stereo playback.[80] In addition to its novel high-tech sound effects, much of STAR WARS' sonic impact was provided by John Williams' Academy-Award winning neo-Wagnerian score.

By 1977 symphonic scoring had become a regular feature of blockbusters—a shift away from the realism of the late 1960s—and Williams himself (b. 1932) had become the paragon of blockbuster composers, writing the scores for such landmark "event" movies as THE POSEIDON ADVENTURE (1972), EARTHQUAKE (1974), and THE TOWERING INFERNO (1974), as well as winning an Oscar for the relentlessly nerve-wracking music of JAWS. His association with epic romanticism in the late nineteenth-century Germanic vein continued through STAR WARS and CLOSE ENCOUNTERS OF THE THIRD KIND, SUPERMAN (1978), JAWS 2 (Jeannot Szwarc, 1978), RAIDERS OF THE LOST ARK (Steven Spielberg, 1981), THE EMPIRE STRIKES BACK (Irvin Kershner, 1980) and all of the post-1970s JAWS, STAR WARS, and "Indiana Jones" sequels. By his own admission, however, Williams recognized the 1970s as "a regressive, and in many ways, decadent period in movie scoring" in which the audience wanted to be overwhelmed or "wiped out" by full-scale orchestral power,[81] and, when opportunity allowed, he also composed some of the era's most distinctively modernist scores, such as those for Robert Altman's IMAGES (1972) and THE LONG GOODBYE (1973), Alfred Hitchcock's FAMILY PLOT (1976), and Brian De Palma's THE FURY (1978).

FILM/MUSIC CROSS-MARKETING: *A STAR IS BORN,*
SATURDAY NIGHT FEVER, AND *GREASE*

The standard for film-music cross-marketing in the 1970s was established by producer Jon Peters's promotional campaign for Warner Bros.' A STAR IS BORN (1976), which involved extensive national airplay of both the sound-track album and the single "Evergreen" just two weeks before the film's saturation-pattern release, creating extensive free advertising that overlapped with the opening and, according to Peters, contributed to its high initial grosses.[82] "Evergreen" reached the top of the *Billboard* charts in March 1977, winning several Grammies and an Academy Award for Best Original Song, and A STAR IS BORN became the second most profitable film of 1976 with total rentals of $37 million. For Paramount's SATURDAY NIGHT FEVER (1977), producer Robert Stigwood and RSO Records president Al Coury arranged for release of the Bee Gees' sound-track album six weeks before the film's opening to allow time for the concurrently released single "How Deep Is Your Love" to become a hit, which it promptly did. After SATURDAY NIGHT FEVER's wide opening at 726 theaters, where it broke THE DEEP's domestic box-office record by earning $9.3 million in its first three days, Coury

Warners' A STAR IS BORN (1976) set the standard for film/music cross-marketing when its theme song "Evergreen" became a national hit simultaneously with the film's wide release: Kris Kristofferson, Barbra Streisand. 35mm Panavision spherical, blown up to 70mm for road-showing. Recorded and selectively exhibited in two-channel Dolby stereo optical sound.

was able to release other cuts from the sound-track, stimulating the sale of both records and film tickets. Thus, the album rose to occupy *Billboard*'s number one position for the next twenty-six weeks, selling 35 million copies worldwide (making it the best-selling record of all time), and the movie took in $74.1 million in domestic rentals to become the third-highest earner of 1977.[83]

Like STAR WARS, SATURDAY NIGHT FEVER generated multiple repeat viewing among young people;[84] and market research revealed that they tended to consume the film not as a narrative but as a rock concert. John Travolta, the film's star, was among the first to notice this phenomenon: "When you talk to kids who've seen it many times, you discover they don't even like the story," he told an interviewer, because "[t]o them, the movie is a concert."[85] As J. Hoberman points out, SATURDAY NIGHT FEVER was also the first post-sixties youth film with a contemporary setting,[86] and it appealed to a new youth market—a generation removed from the front-end baby boomers, but co-extensive with them in terms of composing a new mass audience.[87] In fact, a 1977 study commissioned by the MPAA ("Incidences of Motion Picture Attendances," prepared by Opinion Research Corporation of Princeton, N.J.) indicated that 57 percent of the nation's moviegoers were 12 to 24 years old,[88] which meant that a large portion of the target audience for SATURDAY NIGHT FEVER was excluded due to its R-rated sex scenes and language. To correct this marketing error and capitalize on the intervening success of the

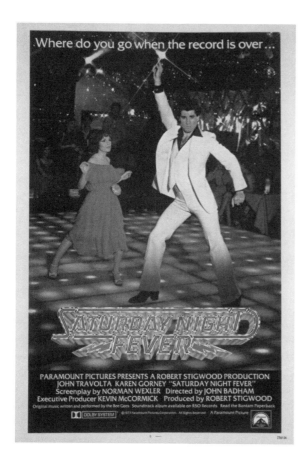

In a film/music cross-marketing watershed, SATURDAY NIGHT FEVER (Paramount, 1977) became the first movie to earn more from the sale of its sound-track album than from rentals ($74.1 million, which made it the third-highest earner in a year dominated by STAR WARS and CLOSE ENCOUNTERS): Karen Lynn Gorney and John Travolta are featured in this poster that emphasizes the direct connection between album and movie ("Where do you go when the record is over . . . "). 35mm 1.85:1. Recorded and selectively exhibited in four-channel Dolby stereo optical sound.

PG-rated GREASE (1978), Paramount withdrew SATURDAY NIGHT FEVER and re-edited it for a 1979 PG-rated re-release and a whole new box-office bonanza.

GREASE confirmed the existence of the post-sixties youth market as a new industry profit base, and it also signaled a newly symbiotic relationship with television in terms of both content (fifties nostalgia *à la* the *Happy Days* series, itself inspired by AMERICAN GRAFFITI) and personnel. John Travolta was a crossover from the popular weekly series *Welcome Back, Kotter*, where he appeared as the character Vinnie Barbarino, and Stigwood had him under a three-film contract. When SATURDAY NIGHT FEVER made Travolta a star, Stigwood cast him opposite Australian recording artist Olivia Newton-John in Paramount's production of GREASE, the decade's ultimate pop music blockbuster. (Travolta's third film for Stigwood was Paramount's URBAN COWBOY [1982].) Adapted from a long-running Broadway musical, which had opened in 1972 and would complete 3,388 performances through 1979,[89] this spoof of 1950s rock films and early-1960s beach-party movies contained seventeen elaborate production numbers, supplemented by period music and songs written specifically for the film. The RSO sound-track album and single "You're the One That I Want" were released before the film in a launch pattern similar to that of SATURDAY NIGHT FEVER but with even greater success for the movie, which opened at 902 theaters, immediately broke THE DEEP's three-day domestic earning record with $9.3 million, and went on to become the box-office champ of 1978, earn-

GREASE (Paramount, 1978), producer Robert Stigwood's follow-up to SATURDAY NIGHT FEVER, tapped into the post-sixties youth-and-nostalgia market with a vengeance to generate $96.3 million in rentals, sell twenty-four million sound-track albums, and become the year's highest-earning film: John Travolta et al. 35mm Panavision anamorphic, blown up to 70mm for road-showing. Recorded and selectively exhibited in four-channel Dolby stereo optical sound (six-track stereo magnetic for 70mm prints).

ing $96.3 million in rentals while the album sold twenty-four million copies. (Guber's Casablanca Records and Filmworks was less successful in its own 1978 effort to create synergy between sound-track album and film—its disco musical THANK GOD IT'S FRIDAY [Robert Klane], featuring Donna Summer and the Commodores and coproduced with Motown Records, earned only $7.8 million in rentals and generated modest album sales, even though its hit single "Last Dance" won an Oscar for Best Original Song.)

LOOKING FOR AN EDGE: *NATIONAL LAMPOON'S ANIMAL HOUSE* AND *SUPERMAN*

Two other hits of 1978 illustrate different approaches to the industry's post-STAR WARS volatility—Universal's NATIONAL LAMPOON'S ANIMAL HOUSE (John Landis) and Warner Bros.' SUPERMAN (Richard Donner). ANIMAL HOUSE, directed by the 27-year-old John Landis, was a low-budget effort with a cast of unknowns, except for John Belushi in his first cross-over from television's *Saturday Night Live*, and Donald Sutherland. Directly appealing to generational nostalgia, the film is a satire on college fraternity life circa 1962—not coincidentally the same year in which AMERICAN GRAFFITI is set, a film which is otherwise invoked (and pilfered from) at various points in the narrative. In contrast to Lucas's film, however, the humor in ANIMAL HOUSE is broad and low, constituting what has come to be called "gross-out" comedy or, in John Landis's more clinical phrase,

*NATIONAL LAMPOON'S ANIMAL HOUSE (Universal, 1978) underscored the volatility of the
late 1970s marketplace when it unexpectedly returned $70.8 million in rentals on a
miniscule investment and ignited a national fad for toga parties: John Belushi, Stephen
Furst. 35mm 1.85:1.*

"behavioral humor of outrage."[90] Despite, or perhaps because of this, ANIMAL HOUSE
unexpectedly returned $70.9 million in rentals to become the third-highest earner of the
year, inaugurating a national vogue in toga parties, food fights, and other sophomoric
activities depicted in the film. As Universal president Ned Tanen remarked of the film:
"When movies like this happen, they sort of take on a life of their own," underscoring
the new awareness in Hollywood that the blockbuster had been redefined by STAR WARS
less as a new kind of movie than as a catalyst for nationwide social phenomena.[91]

This was precisely the status Warner Bros. sought for its $55 million production of
SUPERMAN, whose pre-sold title character had been known to every generation of sentient Americans since 1938, either through comic books, cartoons, Saturday afternoon
serials, or weekly syndicated television shows. In addition to its identification with "one
of the largest folk heroes in American history" (per Andrew Fogelson, Warner's vice
president in charge of the film's worldwide promotion), the film was packaged with several other pre-sold elements from recent blockbusters—a Mario Puzo story and screenplay, the star of THE GODFATHER (Marlon Brando), a John Williams score, and a
multitude of special visual effects.[92] Additionally, a sequel (SUPERMAN II, 1980) was conceived by the film's executive producers, Alexander and Ilya Salkind, at the same time
as the original, and key scenes for it were shot as part of a two-film package.[93] (As much
as 80 percent of this footage had to be reshot because legal wrangling by Brando prevented his scenes from being used.) To market the film, Warner Bros.' parent company,

the entertainment conglomerate Warner Communications Inc. (WCI), launched what one executive described as a "mega-million-dollar campaign to sell SUPERMAN through every medium in every market in United States."[94] Naturally this included massive (and now-standard) television, radio, and print advertising campaigns just prior to release, and saturation booking to maximize early box-office revenues. But it also involved a highly integrated corporate effort to create synergy among the sound-track album produced by Warner's record division, eight Superman-related books published by Warner Books, and over 100 products licensed to use the Superman character and logo, which were owned by DC Comics, itself a division of WCI. This coordinated campaign succeeded in making SUPERMAN the second-highest earner of 1978, with total domestic

Warner Communications Inc. used all of its conglomerate muscle to make SUPERMAN *(1978) both an "event" in its own right and the anchor of a franchise that would extend well into the eighties: Christopher Reeve. 35mm Panavision anamorphic, blown up to 70mm for road-showing. Recorded and selectively exhibited in four-channel Dolby stereo optical sound (six-track stereo magnetic for 70mm prints).*

rentals of $82.8 million, which would have been disappointing relative to its $55 million costs were it not for its lucrative ancillary markets. These, together with the film, helped to secure the "Superman" franchise through three successful sequels in the 1980s.

WAGGING THE DOG: TWO "HITS" FAIL

The last two calculated blockbusters of the seventies were both science fiction films, each in its own way demonstrating a major downside of the syndrome. Paramount's STAR TREK: THE MOTION PICTURE (Robert Wise, 1979) and Fox's ALIEN (Ridley Scott, 1979) were both hits by the logic of standard accounting, standing at the end of the year as the second and fifth highest grossing films respectively. Yet both films disappointed their producers because of the extraordinary expenses now integral to blockbuster production and marketing. STAR TREK was adapted from the television series that ran on NBC from 1966 to 1969 and became an object of adoration to its long-time fans. Paramount held the copyright to the show and planned a modestly budgeted film as early as 1975, but was dissuaded by then-conventional industry wisdom that science fiction was not a mass-market genre. When STAR WARS proved the contrary, STAR TREK was rushed into production with a $15 million budget, which ultimately rose to $44 million owing to delays and cost overruns when the contracted-for special effects were not delivered. The completed film was released in a saturation pattern to 857 sites two weeks before Christmas and attracted nearly 30 percent of the national audience during that fourteen-day period,

Paramount's STAR TREK: THE MOTION PICTURE *(1979) secured a franchise whose multiple sequels would extend into the 1990s, although the film itself barely returned its costs: the crew of the starship* Enterprise *(Majel Barrett, Leonard Nimoy, William Shatner, et al.). 35mm Panavision anamorphic, blown up to 70mm for road-showing.*

Fox's $11-million ALIEN *was the fifth-highest earner of 1979, but with marketing costs of over $16 million, it took a year for the film to show a profit: John Hurt in the alien hatchery. 35mm Panavision anamorphic, blown up to 70mm for road-showing.*

but ultimately earned only $56 million in rentals—enough to inaugurate a series of five sequels, but not to produce much profit for Paramount after deducting marketing costs. Those costs nearly swamped ALIEN, which was produced for $11 million with superb visual effects by Carlo Rambaldi (for which he won his second Academy Award, after KING KONG), but had a massive advertising campaign budgeted at $16 million, including $3 million for television. (The campaign's tag line, "In space, no one can hear you scream," was so widely diffused that it had become a cliché before the film was even released.) Only in the summer of 1980, after it had earned $40.3 million in domestic rentals, was ALIEN able to declare a $4-million profit. Thus it took one of 1979's most popular films almost a year to show a modest gain, a situation that was to become increasingly typical.

Media spending by the majors had been escalating at an alarming rate since STAR WARS, with a 40 percent increase from 1977 to 1978, and an increasingly heavy commitment to television.[95] According to *Broadcast Advertsing Reports*, a record $175,416,000 was spent to hype 452 films on television in 1979, a 34-percent increase over the previous year's $131,000,000 for 474 films.[96] More striking still, the average advertising budget per 1979 film was $2.5 million, with total advertising expenditures ($514 million, including print media) equaling 23 percent of domestic rentals—a 5-percent increase over 1978.[97]

CALAMITY: *APOCALYPSE NOW* AND *HEAVEN'S GATE*

With nearly a quarter of all domestic earnings allocated to advertising at the decade's end, many industry observers thought that the tail was wagging the dog, and two United

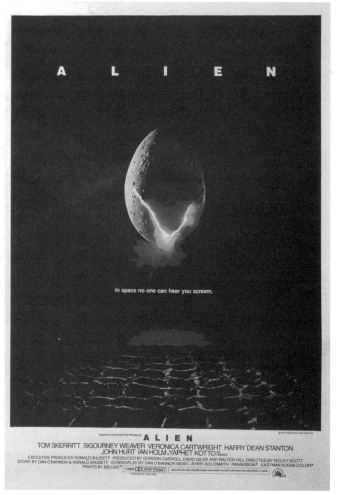

"High concept" poster for ALIEN, *with the image of an alien
egg about to crack open and the tag line "In space no one
can hear you scream."*

Artists films of the era—APOCALYPSE NOW (Francis Ford Coppola, 1979) and HEAVEN'S
GATE (Michael Cimino, 1980)—seemed to prove it. Originally budgeted at $12 million,
the production of Coppola's film was plagued by illness in the cast and crew, natural disasters, and other logistical problems that nearly tripled its costs. The result was a flawed,
if brilliant, version of Conrad's "Heart of Darkness" transposed to post-Tet Vietnam,
whose first two-thirds may be one of the greatest war films ever made, but whose conclusion bogs down in a morass of pomposity and metaphysics. Heavily marketed by
United Artists in print, spot TV, and national network advertising as a "multi-level film"
with broad audience appeal, APOCALYPSE NOW was widely viewed by the press as a
symptom of an industry out of control.[98] When it earned $37.9 million in rentals to
become the year's sixth-highest earner, yet barely returned its negative cost, the industry tended to agree. Yet the film became a *succès d'estime,* receiving eight Academy

Plagued by logistical nightmares, cost-overruns, and natural disasters, APOCALYPSE NOW (1979) barely returned its $35-million negative cost but became a succès d'estime *for United Artists when it received eight Academy Award nominations and shared the Palm d'Or at Cannes with THE TIN DRUM (W. Germany/France, 1979): Captain Willard's patrol boat arrives at Col. Kurtz's mysterious outpost in the heart of darkness. 35mm Technovision spherical, blown up to 70mm for road-showing. (Technovision lenses were manufactured by T. C. Technovision, Ltd., and came in both anamorphic 2:1 compression and "flat" spherical versions.) Recorded and exhibited in four-channel Dolby stereo optical sound (with six-track stereo magnetic Surroundsound for 70mm prints).*

Award nominations (winning for Best Cinematography and Sound) and sharing the Palme d'Or at Cannes with Volker Schlöndorff's THE TIN DRUM (1979).

HEAVEN'S GATE, on the other hand, was a disaster that nearly destroyed United Artists. The film was based on the 1892 Johnson County cattle wars and directed by Michael Cimino, whose box-office and critical triumph THE DEER HUNTER (1978) had just earned five Oscars, including Best Picture and Best Director. The project had been pitched as a Western action-adventure epic and was budgeted at $11.6 million, but Cimino (and United Artists, by giving him complete authority) let it go wildly out of control during shooting and produced instead a $36-million critique of frontier capitalism, whose splendid cinematography, locations, and sets could not redeem its dirge-like melancholy. Released to hostile reviews at 219 minutes, then recut and reissued at 149 minutes, HEAVEN'S GATE produced a net loss of nearly $44 million and caused Transamerica to sell off United Artists to MGM. Though fallout from this debacle helped to foster a new measure of restraint in budgeting and production control (as well as calling into question the system of advance exhibitor guarantees to underwrite the cost of production), many in Hollywood thought they saw the boom and bust cycle of late sixties looming on the horizon again.[99]

Following on the heels of APOCALYPSE NOW, *the ideology-fraught epic Western*
HEAVEN'S GATE *(1980; recut and re-released, 1981) nearly ruined United Artists, producing a net loss of $44 million and causing Transamerica to sell the company to
MGM. The film's critical and commercial failure became a rallying cry for studios anx-
ious to cut costs and reign in headstrong auteurs. 35mm Panavision anamorphic,
blown up to 70mm for road-showing.*

Conclusion

In fact, it had never disappeared. What industry economist Lee Beaupre demonstrated
in his previously noted analysis of the 1971 boom-bust cycle[100]—that a few huge hits carried a multitude of misses—was true of the entire decade (and, basically, the whole post-
divestiture era). The period 1969 through 1974 was one of real fiscal depression, in
which all of the major studios posted large write-offs or write-downs and budgetary
restraint was enforced by circumstance. By contrast, the period 1975 through 1979 witnessed a reversal of fortune as the limited production of big-budget, heavily marketed
"event movies" became the order of the day, and by the decade's end thirteen such films
earned over $50 million, to become "super-grossers." In the absence of any body of pro-
fessional knowledge that could guarantee success, the studios relied on formula, replication, and exploitation to produce hits. Often they failed, and a large number of the
decade's intended blockbusters sank beneath their own weight, encountering widespread public indifference. These include (followed by figures for negative cost/domes-
tic rentals) LOST HORIZON (Charles Jarrott, 1973—$12 million/$3.8 million), LUCKY
LADY (Stanley Donen, 1975—$13 million/$12.7 million), SORCERER (William Friedkin,
1977—$22 million/$5.9 million), A BRIDGE TOO FAR (Richard Attenborough, 1977—

$24 million/$21 million), THE WIZ (Sidney Lumet, 1978—$24 million/$13.6 million), THE HURRICANE (Jan Troell, 1979—$22 million/$4.5 million), METEOR (Ronald Neame, 1979—$21 million/$4.2 million), 1941 (Steven Spielberg, 1979—$26.5 milllion/$23.3 million), RAISE THE TITANIC! (Jerry Jameson, 1980—$29.2 million/$ 6.8 million); others (e.g., THE HINDENBURG [Robert Wise, 1975]; BLACK SUNDAY [John Frankenheimer, 1977]; EXORCIST II: THE HERETIC [John Boorman, 1977]; THE BLACK HOLE [Gary Nelson, 1979]) barely broke even. As the Warner's vice president in charge of worldwide promotion for SUPERMAN said of the film-going public, "[S]ometimes when we think we've done everything right, when we've met our own list of criteria for what a block-buster is, they tell us we're not even close."[101] Nevertheless, the studios had discovered with JAWS that saturation booking and heavy television advertising—strategies borrowed from independent exploitation producers and the 1973 reissue of BILLY JACK—could transform a potentially popular film into a megahit. This shift in marketing and distribution strategies resulted in significant increases in weekly ticket sales in all seasons of the year, particularly during summer and Christmas, reversing their decline from an all-time low in 1971.[102] During the last half of the seventies, the boom-bust pattern continued, but flops were amortized as never before by the colossal profits of the super-grossers, which were themselves fueled by a newly generated young audience given to multiple repeat viewings of its favorite films. Assisted by an artificially created "product shortage" so extreme that some theater circuits were forced into bankruptcy (for example, the Walter Reade Organization, which went under in 1977) and the rest were forced to accept disadvantageous terms, super-grosser profits continued to escalate into the eighties.

Remarking on this phenomenon in 1978, Steven Spielberg said, "I wouldn't be surprised if by 1984 STAR WARS were number two."[103] He was right: in 1982, his own E.T.: THE EXTRA-TERRESTRIAL earned $228.4 million, leaving STAR WARS in second place. Between 1975 and 1985, ten films grossed more than $100 million. There were only four such films over the next decade, but there has been a steady rise in the number of films earning $50 million or more ever since. With the explosion of ancillary markets in the eighties, box-office revenues came to comprise an ever-smaller percentage of the majors' total income, and the risk of production was greatly reduced. (In 1986, for example, domestic box-office returns accounted for just 28 percent of total income—down from 54 percent in 1978—with another 12 percent from pay cable and 40 percent from home video, which had contributed only a combined 4 percent in 1978.)[104] As early as 1978, industry analysts had forecast an improvement in the risk-reward ratio based on several factors, including advance guarantees by theaters owners, pre-sale agreements with television networks for broadcast rights, and the soaring value of merchandising tie-ins. By 1980, 20th Century–Fox was so confident of the security of film investment that it offered equity positions in its production for the first time.[105] In retrospect, it is clear that the period 1975–1980 was one of restabilization that marked the beginning of what A. D. Murphy called "the modern era of super-blockbuster films."[106] Looming video competition, once predicted to inhibit this trend, in fact reinforced it, as feature films rapidly became the basic programming content of both home video and cable TV. Far from declining in the eighties and nineties, the "blockbuster syndrome" accelerated to become the mainstay of the industry, essential to both domestic and foreign markets. In nearly every respect, the great "event movies" of the 1970s, with their continuing franchises, constitute the high-water mark toward which the American film industry still aspires.

Sam Peckinpah checking a shot on location for THE BALLAD OF CABLE HOGUE *(Warners, 1971). 35mm 1.85:1.*

4

The Auteur Cinema: Directors and Directions in the "Hollywood Renaissance"

The invulnerability of the majors was based on their consistent success with virtually anything they made.

STANLEY KUBRICK

As the American film industry stood on the brink of its worst financial crisis since the Great Depression, a Yankelovich and Associates survey commissioned by the MPAA in 1968 revealed that 48 percent of the box-office admissions for that year were from the 16–24-year-old age group, and concluded that "being young and single is the overriding demographic pre-condition for being a frequent and enthusiastic movie-goer."[1] This came as news to the studio executives, who were pumping money into super-musicals modeled on THE SOUND OF MUSIC (Robert Wise, 1965), which by December 1968, after three years in release, had earned $72 million and displaced GONE WITH THE WIND (Victor Fleming, 1939) as the top-grossing film of all time. However, it did help explain the healthy $6.9-million rentals of BLOWUP (Michelangelo Antonioni, 1966), MGM's racy and enigmatic European pickup set in "swinging London";[2] and the spectacular success of two recent youth-oriented American films—Warner Bros.-Seven Arts' BONNIE AND CLYDE (Arthur Penn, 1967) and Avco Embassy's THE GRADUATE (Mike Nichols, 1967)—not to mention the continuing prosperity of Samuel Z. Arkoff's low-budget youth exploitation company American International Pictures (AIP). BONNIE AND CLYDE, which was produced by its 29-year-old star Warren Beatty, stunned critics and audiences alike with its revolutionary mixing of genres and its unprecedented violence, but returned $22.8 million on a $2.5-million investment and became the third highest grossing film of 1967. THE GRADUATE, directed by the 34-year-old Nichols, evinced the same boldness in its representation of an affair between a college student and his girlfriend's mother, and became the highest grossing film of the decade with $44.1 million in domestic rentals. The success of these films, combined with the Yankelovich data, almost immediately inspired several studios to hire younger producers and directors in an effort to appeal to a younger clientele, and there was a new, industry-wide perception that youth was the key to reviving the sagging box office.[3]

Just weeks after the survey was published, Jonas Rosenfield, Jr., 20th Century–Fox vice president for advertising and publicity, summarized the new thinking at a trade gathering: "We are tied to the youthful market of the future, we have to keep up with the rhythm of young people."[4] Another Fox executive, David Brown, went even further: "The cinema is today for youths in every corner of the world. Pictures with either artistic creativeness or critical content are helping both the industry and the film business. . . . The world is in revolution. We are mirroring it."[5] Fox, Warners, and Paramount (each with new, young production chiefs—Richard Zanuck, Ken Hyman, and Robert Evans, respectively) all announced their commitment to making a new style of movie that would allow directors more creative freedom and emphasize the cultivation of new talent.[6] Yet the industry was still top-heavy with an older generation of filmmakers who were not eager to share power with newcomers in either the workplace, professional associations, or unions. At Paramount, 37-year-old production executive Robert Evans underscored the industry's dilemma when he commented: "The strongest period in Hollywood history was the '30s, when most of the creative people were young. The trouble is that most of them are still around making movies. . . ." But Evans then went on to boast that of forty-eight directors on major productions since the Gulf & Western takeover in October 1966, twenty-eight, or 60 percent, had no directorial credits prior to 1963.[7]

Auteurism and the "Film Generation"

Concurrent with this shift in emphasis at the studios was the rise of auteurism at the level of popular criticism and journalism. Although the concept of authorship in cinema is nearly as old as the medium itself, it was first formally articulated by François Truffaut in his 1954 *Cahiers du cinema* essay "Une certaine tendance du cinema français." There, he spoke of *la politique des auteurs* (the policy of authors) whereby film should ideally be a means of personal artistic expression for its director (or director-writer, as he originally intended it); bearing the signature of his or her personal style, rather than the work of some corporate collective. The definition naturally privileged those Hollywood filmmakers like Welles, Hitchcock, Hawks, and Ford, who had worked within the classical studio system but transcended it to achieve a cinema of personal vision. However, the idea was not imported into American critical discourse until the 1960s, when Andrew Sarris christened it "the auteur theory" in an essay in *Film Culture*[8] and began to construct the pantheon of American directors that became *The American Cinema: Director and Directions, 1929–1968*.[9] By the time this influential volume appeared, even critics like Pauline Kael, who were initially hostile to the idea (see her "Circles and Squares"[10]), had begun to accept its fundamental premise, if only by inverse corollary (in her 1971 essay "Raising Kane,"[11] for example, Kael went to inordinate lengths to demonstrate that scriptwriter Herman Mankiewicz, not Orson Welles, was the principal author of *Citizen Kane*). The elevation of the director in the public mind during this period is nicely captured in the titles of two best-selling collections of interviews with filmmakers from 1969 and 1970 respectively: *The Director's Event* and *The Film Director as Superstar*.[12] For the rest of the decade, auteurism was the dominant mode of aesthetic discourse among American film critics, and its single-author perspective was institutionalized as film study entered the academy during the same period.

In Hollywood the strategy of employing young or non traditional filmmakers met with some success, and the years 1968 and 1969 witnessed studio productions like Stanley Kubrick's 2001: A SPACE ODYSSEY (MGM, 1968), Roman Polanski's ROSEMARY'S BABY (Paramount, 1968), Arthur Penn's ALICE'S RESTAURANT (United Artists, 1969), and Sam Peckinpah's violent and controversial THE WILD BUNCH (Warner Bros., 1969), whose uniqueness contributed to the auteurist stature of their directors and whose popularity confirmed the box-office power of the newly discovered youth audience. Demographically, this audience was comprised of the growing children of the postwar baby boom—it was not only younger, but better educated, and more affluent than Hollywood's traditional audience, and had grown up with the medium of television, learning to process the audiovisual language of film on a daily basis. Furthermore, the rise of film study in American colleges and universities insured that this generation would know more about what it saw on the screen in academic terms than any generation before it. (In 1967, for example, there were approximately 1,500 film and television courses being offered at 200 colleges, and these numbers would quintuple over the next ten years.) For these reasons, the baby-boomers—often styled as the "film generation"—were drawn toward the kind of films the *Cahiers* critics had been writing about (and subsequently, as independent directors at the margins of the French industry, making)—films that were visually arresting, thematically challenging, and stylistically individualized by their makers. Because this audience was large and was projected to grow for at least another five years,[13] the studios briefly—and somewhat desperately—turned the reins of production over to auteur directors who might strike a responsive chord in the "youth market." The understanding that this was an increasingly cineliterate group is demonstrated by an article on the marketing and reception of 2001 that appeared in *Variety* for April 10, 1968:

> Because today's filmgoers are predominantly under 25, it would seem vital to learn something about this market and its tastes. As many sociologists and psychologists have already noted, there has been a widespread revolution among today's youth, but little of this change has yet to be reflected in the films produced in the U.S. . . . As Marshall McLuhan has so laboriously pointed out, today's youth is visual-oriented. Words do not have the importance they used to have. . . . Visual and aural sensations have replaced [them]. . . .[14]

The author concludes that "the film's biggest potential audience remains today's tuned-in youth," and predicts success for it in those terms precisely because of the unusual degree of freedom given to Kubrick by MGM to make "a non-verbal statement."[15] Ceding production control to directors was alien to the studio establishment, but, as Jon Lewis points out, younger executives tended to see auteurism as "another way to market the product," not far removed from the time-honored industry practice of contracting talent.[16] Yet, although it was market-driven, the studios' embrace of auteurism represented a genuine attempt to bridge the generation gap, which brought with it a few years of real artistic freedom and resulted in some of the most original American films since the late forties. Recalling the unprecedented creative latitude of the era, Arthur Penn noted: "What was happening at that time in Hollywood was that enormous power had devolved upon the directors because the studio system had kind of collapsed. We were really running it, so we could introduce this new perception of how to make another kind of movie."[17]

The Advent of the MPAA Rating System

The impulse to experiment at the end of the sixties was facilitated by the final dismantling of the Motion Picture Production Code and its replacement by a rating classifica-
tion system. As chief industry spokesperson, Motion Picture Association of America
(MPAA) president Jack Valenti had for several years been promoting a new climate of
creative freedom for filmmakers in response to the revolution in social values so clearly
taking place across the land. He had engineered the Code revisions of 1966, which eliminated specifically proscribed behavior and offered instead a list of ten general guidelines to be applied contextually, as well as a provision for borderline cases to be released
with a "Suggested for Mature Audiences" designation. Soon Valenti had become an
apologist for the new wave of movie violence represented by films like THE DIRTY
DOZEN (Robert Aldrich, 1967) and BONNIE AND CLYDE (1967), which in a February
1968 press conference he shrewdly but accurately connected to the escalating war in
Vietnam: "For the first time in the history of this country, people are exposed to instant
coverage of a war in progress. When so many movie critics complain about violence on
film, I don't think they realize the impact of thirty minutes on the Huntley-Brinkley
newscast—and that's real violence."[18] Four months later, after Martin Luther King, Jr.
and Robert Kennedy had both been murdered on American soil, the national debate
over film violence reached crisis proportions, and Valenti led the MPAA in self-protec-
tive action.[19] Between June and September, he worked with its nine member companies,
the National Association of Theater Owners (NATO), and the International Film
Importers and Distributors of American (IFIDA), to craft a rating system on the British
model that would respond to public anger over movie violence without reducing filmmakers' creative freedom (or the industry's huge new profits from graphically representing sex and violence on-screen).

On October 7, 1968, Valenti announced the creation of the MPAA's new Code and
Rating Administration (CARA), with its four classifications by audience category to be
effective November 1st of that year—G (general audience), M (mature audience—
changed in 1972 to GP, then PG [parental guidance recommended]), R (restricted—
persons under 16 [later 17] not admitted unless accompanied by parent or guardian), X
(persons under 16 [later 17] not admitted).[20] Valenti had initially not wanted the X rating, but NATO had insisted on it as a means of protecting its members from local prosecution, and the studios acquiesced thinking the X might someday serve to differentiate
their films from exploitation product (as was in fact the case for MIDNIGHT COWBOY in
1969). Unfortunately, the MPAA did not copyright the X, as it did its other three ratings,
so that it could be self-imposed—a move intended to promote artistic freedom, but one
that appeared to lend the MPAA imprimatur to such self-imposed "triple-X" films as
DEEP THROAT (1972) and THE DEVIL IN MISS JONES (1972) a few years later. As a result,
the X rating quickly became anathema to mainstream producers, and many newspapers
refused to accept advertising for X-rated films, including the *New York Times*. By 1972,
47 percent of all American exhibitors had established a policy against booking X-rated
product, and even Valenti was calling it "trash and garbage, made by people out to
exploit."[21]

Adoption of the CARA system, as Stephen Prince points out, helped to institutional-
ize the radical shifts in film content that had followed the Code revision of 1966.[22]
BONNIE AND CLYDE (1967) and THE GRADUATE (1967), for example, had pushed up

against the limits of those new guidelines, but THE WILD BUNCH (1969), produced during the transition, would have broken through them altogether and could not have been released with the Production Code Administration (PCA) seal in its final form. The new ratings system, however, enabled its producers to negotiate an R rating downward from an X by making a few cuts that left most of its violence intact, insuring that it would reach its target market in the 17–25-year-old age group.[23] CARA thus gave the industry an effective marketing tool for tapping into the new American audience (and, not tangentially, a perfect means of differentiating its product from television).

Recession, 1969–1971, and EASY RIDER

The studios, however, were still dominated by old regimes and continued to produce a large number of expensive flops for the old audience—such as Fox's STAR! (Robert Wise, 1968) and HELLO, DOLLY! (William Wyler, 1969), and Paramount's PAINT YOUR WAGON (Josh Logan, 1969)—at a time when they were simultaneously experiencing structural change and financial crisis. As a direct result of such overproduction, all of the studios but 20th Century–Fox, Columbia, and Disney had been taken over by conglomerates by the end of the decade. Beginning with the purchase of Universal by MCA in 1962, extending through Paramount's sale to Gulf & Western Industries in 1966, the acquisition of United Artists by Transamerica Corporation in 1967, the sale of Warner Bros. to Kinney National Service Corporation, and of MGM to Las Vegas financier Kirk Kerkorian in 1969, the studios were one by one absorbed by larger, more diversified companies. Finally, the recession of 1969–1971 forced the recently formed ABC Circle Films and CBS Cinema Center Films out of business, leaving their distributors Cinerama Releasing and National General Corporation—the "instant majors" of 1967—with nothing to distribute and effectively ending their participation in the market. (A third "instant major," Commonwealth United Corporation, was taken over by AIP in 1970.)

In this context, the runaway success of the generationally savvy road film EASY RIDER (Dennis Hopper, 1969)—produced by the independent BBS Productions[24] for $375,000 and returning $19.2 million—convinced producers that inexpensive films could be made specifically for the youth market and become hits overnight. This delusion led to a spate of low-budget youth culture, or "youth-cult," movies and the founding of many short-lived independent companies modeled on BBS (an acronym for the first names of its three partners, Bert Schneider, Bob Rafelson, and Steve Blauner). It also drove the studios to actively recruit a new generation of writers, producers, and directors from the ranks of film schools like USC, UCLA, and NYU, where the auteur theory had become institutionalized as part of the curriculum. (As Martin Scorsese, one of the most successful new directors would later remark of this era, "Sarris and the 'politique des auteurs' was like some fresh air.")[25] Reaching out to the youth market in the late sixties was not enough to prevent an industry-wide recession from 1969 to 1972, which produced $500 million in losses for the majors and by 1970 left 40 percent of Hollywood filmmakers unemployed. But it did substantially help to create the "Hollywood Renaissance" of 1967–1975, during which, as Michael Pye and Lynda Myles have put it, the "film generation took over Hollywood" and attempted to create an American auteur cinema based in large part on the European model. It also opened the door to a generation of directors born in the 1920s whose iconoclasm and independence had thus far prevented them from entering the Hollywood mainstream, although all of them had recently contributed to it in a decisive way.

Major Independents from the 1960s

This latter group consisted of Arthur Penn (b. 1922), Stanley Kubrick (1928–1999), Sam Peckinpah (1924–1985), and Robert Altman (b. 1922), all of whom had recently demonstrated their ability to connect with a youthful audience.

ARTHUR PENN

Penn had studied at the Actor's Studio in Los Angeles and worked in live television as a writer and director (for *Playhouse 90* and *Philco Playhouse* productions, among others) before making his first feature, THE LEFT-HANDED GUN (Warner Bros., 1958), a psychological "adult Western" based on the story of Billy the Kid. He spent much of the next decade alternating between film and theater, where he directed such Broadway hits as William Gibson's *The Miracle Worker* (1959), Lillian Hellman's *Toys in the Attic* (1960), and Clifford Odets's *Golden Boy* (1964). But except for his screen version of THE MIRACLE WORKER (United Artists, 1962), in which he directed Anne Bancroft and Patty

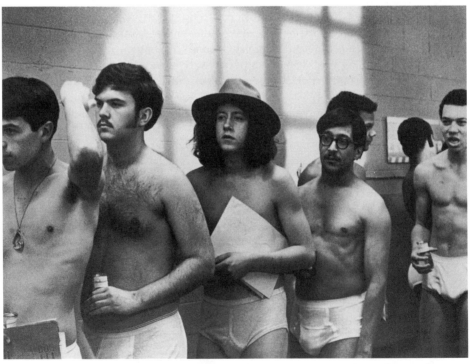

Arlo Guthrie (center frame, with hat) waits in line for his Army physical in Arthur Penn's balladic elegy for the counterculture ALICE'S RESTAURANT *(United Artists, 1969). 35mm 1.85:1.*

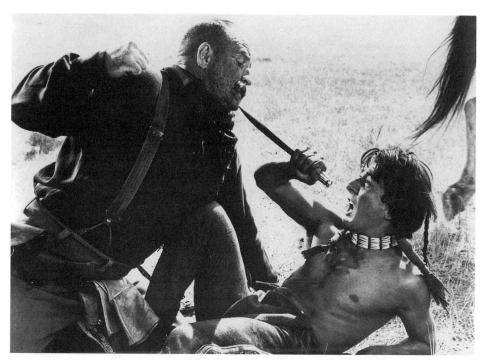

Dustin Hoffman as Jack Crabb in Arthur Penn's landmark anti-Vietnam Western LITTLE BIG MAN *(National General, 1970). To authenticate the Vietnam analogy, Penn used Asian American extras in the film to represent victims of the Sand Creek and Washita River massacres. 35mm Panavision anamorphic.*

Duke to Academy Awards (for Best Actress and Best Supporting Actress, respectively), Penn's films were commercially unsuccessful until he struck a raw public nerve with BONNIE AND CLYDE (1967). When BONNIE AND CLYDE unexpectedly returned $22.8 million in domestic rentals to become the third-highest earner of 1967 (and the second highest in Warner Bros. history), and received nine Academy Award nominations, Penn was suddenly one of Hollywood's hottest talents—especially notable for his resonance with the emerging "youth market."

In fact, Penn's affinity with the late sixties counterculture was deeply felt and stemmed from his own leftist politics, forged during the McCarthy era. A concern for social justice had infused much of his previous work, including even the Kafkaesque MICKEY ONE (Columbia, 1965), and in his brief moment of bankability Penn chose to deliberately flaunt his anti-establishment attitudes (which was exactly what the studios wanted him to do). ALICE'S RESTAURANT (1969), produced for United Artists, is a rambling adaptation of Arlo Guthrie's eighteen-minute talking blues ballad about draft-dodging and commune life ("The Alice's Restaurant Massacree"), which Penn coscripted with playwright Venable Herndon; it returned only $6.4 million in rentals. (Intriguingly, Penn made a direct connection between the improvisational style of this film—with its nonprofessional actors, natural lighting, and understated cinematography—and the techniques favored by the rising generation of directors at a 1969 Lincoln Center panel on "the state of student film and filmmaking.")[26]

Arthur Penn preparing a crane shot for a scene in NIGHT
MOVES *(Warners, 1975), his revisionist post-Watergate* film
noir: *Gene Hackman plays a detective who, in Penn's words,
"finds that the solution is not solvable" and ends up getting
his clients killed in the bargain. 35mm 1.85:1.*

LITTLE BIG MAN (1970), produced by the short-lived CBS Cinema Center Films and
distributed by National General, was a much more elaborate production but no less radically charged. Adapted from Thomas Berger's picaresque novel by screenwriter Calder
Willingham (whose credits included THE GRADUATE and Stanley Kubrick's PATHS OF
GLORY [1957]), the film is a revisionist Western epic narrated by the 121-year-old Jack
Crabb, "the only white man who survived Custer's Last Stand," who has spent half of his
life in the world of the white settlers and the other half among the Cheyenne. As it
moves episodically between these spheres, the narrative swings between farce and
tragedy, debunking the mythology of the Old West on the one hand and becoming a
metaphor for U.S. involvement in Vietnam on the other. In this regard, Penn consciously
idealized the Cheyenne as spiritually and morally superior to the whites, whose civilization is shown to be founded on militarism, hypocrisy, and greed. He staged a version of
the Washita River massacre to resemble photographs of the My Lai massacre of March
16, 1968, which had recently appeared in the American press—a parallel that was widely
recognized at the time (*The Hollywood Reporter* noted that this sequence looked "like

Randy Quaid and Jack Nicholson in The Missouri Breaks *(United Artists, 1976), an agent-packaged Western that failed, effectively ending Penn's role as a player in post-*Jaws *Hollywood. 35mm 1.85:1.*

the 6 P.M. new footage from Vietnam").[27] LITTLE BIG MAN was shot in Panavision by Harry Stradling over a period of several months on locations in Alberta and Billings, Montana, at a cost of $6 million; released in December 1970, it returned $17 million to become the ninth highest grossing film of 1971. The fact that it starred youth-cult icons Dustin Hoffman (THE GRADUATE, MIDNIGHT COWBOY) and Faye Dunaway (BONNIE AND CLYDE) notwithstanding, there has probably never been another time in the history of American cinema when a 150-minute film that bitterly indicts American imperialism and depicts the U.S. military waging genocidal war could become a popular hit.

By this point, Penn had become a celebrity director—one of the "Free Agents within the System" featured in Joe Gelmis's *The Film Director as Superstar.* But he chose to withdraw from that system for the next two and half years, during which he did not work in feature films, theater, or television, although he did contribute a segment on the pole vault ("The Highest") to VISIONS OF EIGHT (Wolper Productions, 1973), the omnibus documentary on the 1972 Munich Olympics produced by David Wolper. Penn returned to features with the post-Watergate *film noir* NIGHT MOVES (Warner Bros., 1975), shot in Panavision by Bruce Surtees, which he intended to evoke the moral bankruptcy of the Nixon era. Set in Los Angeles and the Florida Keys (represented by the Gulf coast island of Sanibel), the film's complicated plot involves a detective's search for a missing teenager, and it is peopled by characters whom Penn described as "some of the mourners of the Kennedy generation."[28] NIGHT MOVES failed to return its investment, and

Penn's last film of the 1970s was an agent-packaged Western written by Thomas McGuane and starring Marlon Brando and Jack Nicholson, both of whom had recently won Academy Awards for Best Actor. Produced for United Artists on a budget of $8.2 million ($2.5 million of which went to the salaries of its two stars, who also had 21.3 percent of the gross), THE MISSOURI BREAKS (1976) was engineered to be a hit, but its eccentric blend of violence, genre revisionism, and whimsy didn't please the public. Despite beautiful Montana locations and splendid Panavision cinematography by Michael Butler, as well as riveting performances by Nicholson and Brando, the film failed commercially and critically, earning just $7 million. In post-JAWS America, the sixties were as dead as Huey Newton, and the "Hollywood Renaissance" was about to bottom out.[29] Penn's stock plummeted dramatically, and he did not direct a film again until 1981, when he made FOUR FRIENDS (Filmways/Warner Bros.) from a screenplay by Steve Tesich. His career has been spotty ever since, demonstrating how closely his temperament was attuned to that extraordinary cultural moment between 1967 and 1971, when he produced in BONNIE AND CLYDE and LITTLE BIG MAN two of postwar American cinema's greatest films.

STANLEY KUBRICK

Like Penn, Stanley Kubrick was a maverick who prized his independence from the mainstream industry. He began by making low- to medium-budget features for United Artists (THE KILLING [1956]; PATHS OF GLORY [1957]) and scored a major success when he replaced Anthony Mann at the helm of SPARTACUS (1960), the $12-million Bryna Productions/Universal epic that became the second highest grossing film of 1961 (although it actually lost about $400,000 relative to its combined production and marketing costs of $15 million).[30] In 1961, to achieve greater independence, Kubrick moved permanently to England. There, after making an adaptation of Vladimir Nabokov's novel *Lolita* in 1962 under the Eady plan (which provided foreign producers with generous tax incentives if 80 percent of their labor was British),[31] he began his career as producer-director with DR. STRANGELOVE OR: HOW I LEARNED TO STOP WORRYING AND LOVE THE BOMB (1964), a Columbia release whose financial and critical success thoroughly vindicated his new situation.

Kubrick was years ahead of the youth-cult curve when, in late 1964, he began to conceptualize the metaphysical epic that became 2001: A SPACE ODYSSEY (MGM, 1968). Over the next four years he produced and directed the film that would revolutionize the practice of special effects, elevate science fiction to the status of art, and become the defining cinematic experience of the baby-boom generation. Marketed as a quasi-mystical, psychedelic experience ("The Ultimate Trip"), 2001 caught the imagination of the counterculture like no other film of the era. In its initial run it earned $17 million against a considerably risky $10.5-million investment and became the fifth highest grossing film of 1968, as well as a cult phenomenon—it was, in fact, one of the first films to generate significant repeat business during its initial theatrical release (BONNIE AND CLYDE was another), ultimately earning $25.5 million.

Kubrick was now in a position similar to Penn's after the triumph of BONNIE AND CLYDE—that of a loner with one gold-plated hit and a demonstrable talent for appealing to youth—except that by operating in England, outside the Hollywood orbit, he was able to make all of his subsequent films on his own terms through his own production company (Hawk Films Ltd.). Yet, however independent he might become as a producer-director, Kubrick remained dependent on Hollywood's distribution and marketing structures for the commercial success of his work. So, in the words of Robert Sklar, he became adept at "playing the American film business game . . . by his own rules."[32] His next film, a coproduction between Hawk and Warner Bros., was a perfect example of his ability to work the system from afar. Adapted by Kubrick from the Anthony Burgess novel originally published in 1962 (for the rights to which Kubrick paid $150,000 in 1969), A CLOCKWORK ORANGE (1971) projects an alienated, drug-ridden near-future where—for the narrator, Alex (Malcom McDowell), and his gang of young "droogs"— "ultraviolence" is the primary sensory stimulus.

A CLOCKWORK ORANGE was one of several films of the era—in the wake of the sixties' political assassinations, urban riots, and antiwar violence (not to mention the violence of the Vietnam war itself)—to take the very nature of violence as a serious theme. But it was the only one to make a Nietzschean connection between art and violence, suggesting that they spring from the same irrational source. Not only does classical music accompany the most horrific acts of violence on the sound track (the Overture to Rossini's "Thieving Magpie," for example, is synchronized with a precisely choreographed gang rape and rumble sequence), but Alex's love of violence is clearly aesthetic—as when his passion for Beethoven's Ninth is directly linked to his lust for "the old red vino" through a masturbation fantasy.[33] It was this equation of art with violence, as well as Kubrick's ironic detachment in depicting it, that angered some critics and made the film controversial.

Controversy was good for business (who wouldn't want to see a film described by Vincent Canby as "a brilliant and dangerous work"?),[34] but the X rating given to A CLOCKWORK ORANGE by CARA was not: it limited both bookings and publicity, since newspapers in many communities would not accept advertising for X-rated films. Typical of CARA, the objectionable material was not the film's violence but thirty seconds' worth of sexual intercourse, which, after lengthy negotiation, Kubrick agreed to cut in order to resubmit for a less restrictive R rating.[35] Under MPAA rules, this meant that the film had to be withdrawn from distribution for sixty days, but broadening its market base paid off when A CLOCKWORK ORANGE became Kubrick's most profitable film to date, returning $17.5 million on a $2-million investment and ranking eighth in box-office returns for 1971. (Kubrick told an interviewer in 1980 that the film had made $40 million to that date.)[36] Despite polarizing the critical response, A CLOCKWORK ORANGE was voted the best film of 1971 by the New York Film Critics, and Kubrick the best director; the film was also nominated by the Academy for Best Picture, Best Direction, Best Screenplay from Another Medium, and Best Editing. In the end, pushing the CARA envelope on sex and violence had been a shrewd move, simultaneously creating controversy, attracting critical attention, and making A CLOCKWORK ORANGE highly marketable in the newly "permissive" (in the provocative sense of Spiro Agnew's term for the counterculture) American marketplace.[37] That it was calculated to perform this way by Kubrick seems unquestionable, since he had pursued the same tactic in testing the limits of the Production Code a decade earlier with LOLITA.

Dissatisfied with Warner Bros. International's handling of foreign sales, Kubrick himself tracked bookings and receipts for A CLOCKWORK ORANGE in the U.S. domestic and British markets and built a database from which to develop a successful worldwide marketing strategy for the film. Warners president Ted Ashley was so impressed that he fired Norman Katz as head of the international operation, and told executives at Warner Communications Inc. (WCI) that Kubrick was a genius who combined "aesthetics" with

Malcolm McDowell as Alex, chief purveyor of "ultraviolence" and Ludovico technique guinea pig in Stanley Kubrick's A CLOCKWORK ORANGE (Warners, 1971). 35mm 1.66:1. (Kubrick preferred the European widescreen aspect ratio as a compromise between 2.35:1 anamorphic and the Academy frame.)

The Korova Milkbar, one of the few sets Kubrick had constructed for A CLOCKWORK ORANGE, the rest of which was shot entirely on London locations: Alex and his droogs enjoy cocktails of "milk-plus-Vellocet" before engaging in an evening's mayhem. These images approximate the beginning and end of the film's opening tracking shot.

"fiscal responsibility."[38] But BARRY LYNDON (1975), another Warner Bros./Hawk Films coproduction, would prove Ashley wrong by half.

Kubrick had barred publicity from the set of A CLOCKWORK ORANGE and, initially at least, wouldn't even tell Warners what his next film was about,[39] perhaps because its scale was so large relative to its source—an all-but-forgotten novel by William Makepeace Thackeray. Published in 1844 but set mainly in the period between 1760 and 1789, *Barry Lyndon* adopts the picaresque form of eighteenth-century fiction to chronicle the rise and fall of an unprincipled Irish rogue who exploits the British class system and nearly attains the peerage. In the film, Kubrick attempted to recreate an entire historical epoch through a *mise-en-scène* based on eighteenth-century painting, one characterized by real locations, authentically antique costumes, and contemporary source lighting from candles and candelabra. The extremely low light levels of interior scenes required the use of super-fast 50mm lens developed by Carl Zeiss for the Apollo space program, and cinematographer John Alcott had to innovate a special wide-angle viewfinder for his camera in order to maintain focus. The visual style of BARRY LYNDON was predicated on a series of slow backward zooms from telephoto close shots to extreme wide-angle long shots, for which a another special lens was designed with a 20:1 zoom ratio (the Cine-Pro T9 24-480mm, adapted from the Angenieux 16mm 20:1 zoom). These shots were intended to evoke the two major painting genres of the period, portraiture and landscape, and they lend the film a sense of stately elegance throughout its 187-minute length, which is sustained by an exquisite score of period music played on original instruments. (Kubrick, who also wrote the screenplay, scored the film himself with prerecorded performances, as he had previously done for both A CLOCKWORK ORANGE and 2001.) Location shooting consumed 250 days, but the production had exceeded its original budget of $2.5 million after ten weeks, and the total costs may have reached three times that amount.[40] (One source puts the negative cost at $12 million.)[41] For all its painstaking artistry, audiences hated BARRY LYNDON. Released just months before JAWS opened to historic box-office receipts, Kubrick's "time odyssey"[42] returned less than $9.9 million and became one of the biggest commercial flops of 1975. Yet it was an undeniable *succès d'estime,* winning seven Academy nominations (including Best Picture, Best Director [Kubrick's fourth nomination in a row] and Best Screenplay from Another Medium) and four Awards (for Cinematography, Art Direction, Costumes, and Score).

Kubrick's final project of the decade reflected an astute understanding of the change that had taken place in the American marketplace and doomed BARRY LYNDON to financial failure. THE SHINING (1980) was conceived as blockbuster horror film along the lines of JAWS, although it would be no less technically challenging than his previous work (here, in its remarkably fluid use of the new Steadicam system). It had Stephen King's best-selling 1977 novel as its source and Jack Nicholson, fresh from winning a Best Actor Oscar for ONE FLEW OVER THE CUCKOO'S NEST (Milos Forman, 1975), as its star. Furthermore, the $12-million (various sources say $12–$18 million)[43] Warner Bros./ Hawk Films coproduction was slated for a national television advertising campaign before opening Memorial Day weekend at selected first-run venues, where it would play for three weeks. Then it would break into a 750-site saturation pattern secured in advance by nonrefundable $50,000 guarantees.[44] The marketing strategy worked to make THE SHINING the tenth highest grossing film of 1980, earning $30.9 million. But it was not the blockbuster Kubrick had hoped for, because its parable of an Oedipal family trapped inside the abundant emptiness of America was simply too intelligent to have mass appeal.

A deep-focus shot from BARRY LYNDON *(Warners, 1975), taken with the Cine-Pro T9 20:1 zoom lens Kubrick commissioned from Ed DeGuilio's Cinema Products Corporation especially for the production. The lens is in its extreme wide-angle (24mm) position, creating great depth of field. Ryan O'Neal in the title role. 35mm 1.66:1.*

Marisa Berenson as Lady Lyndon in BARRY LYNDON, *which won Oscars in 1975 for Cinematography, Art Direction, Costume Design, and Music Scoring.*

Jack Torrance (Jack Nicholson) talks to the Overlook Hotel's spectral bartender "Lloyd" in an elaborate lighting set-up from THE SHINING *(Warners, 1980), Kubrick's last major bid for the mass market. 35mm 1.66:1.*

Like Penn, Kubrick had reached the outer limits of what he could achieve commercially in the market constructed by the New Hollywood. He clearly understood this market—as he had understood its earlier incarnations—but as a true auteur who had written, produced, and directed his own work for the past fifteen years, he was no longer willing to bend in Hollywood's direction.[45] During the eighties he made only one feature, the modestly successful Vietnam combat film/critique FULL METAL JACKET (1987),[46] and, several false starts notwithstanding, produced just one other film before his death in March 1999 (EYES WIDE SHUT [Warners, 1999]), a psychological thriller from a screenplay by Kubrick and Frederic Raphael.[47]

SAM PECKINPAH

Sam Peckinpah began his film career as an assistant to Don Siegel, and in 1957 crossed over to television, where he wrote scripts for the popular *Gunsmoke* series and eventually created both *The Rifleman* (1958) and *The Westerner* (1960) series, episodes of which he also directed. He began directing features with the low-budget Western THE DEADLY COMPANIONS (1961). His second film, RIDE THE HIGH COUNTRY (aka GUNS IN THE AFTERNOON, 1962), was an elegiac, Fordian Western shot in CinemaScope and

Metrocolor by Lucien Ballard which won several international awards. MAJOR DUNDEE
(1965), constructed as an epic Western about a U.S. Cavalry incursion into Mexico,
ended in disaster when producer Jerry Bresler fired Peckinpah in postproduction and
cut the film from 161 to 134 minutes; Columbia then released the mangled result to hostile reviews.[48] After years without work in features, Peckinpah signed a deal with Ken
Hyman, the new head of production at Warner Bros.-Seven Arts, to direct a screenplay
by Walon Green about a band of aging outlaws who become fatally involved in the
Mexican Revolution circa 1913. This was THE WILD BUNCH (1969), which in its
unprecedented violence was the first film to take advantage of the new freedoms offered
by the CARA rating system. Its balletically choreographed massacres raised the slow-
motion bloodletting of BONNIE AND CLYDE (Arthur Penn, 1967) to new heights and produced a controversy over screen violence that became part of a larger debate about the
looming presence of violence in national life. Like Penn's film and Kubrick's 2001, THE
WILD BUNCH was a seminal work of its generation, inseparable from the social history
of the time, and the primary audience for its R-rated violence was in the 17–25-year-old
age group. Produced for a negative cost of $6.2 million, the film grossed only $7.5 million in its first year of release, but in terms of authorial prestige Peckinpah had scored a
solid hit.[49] In fact, many critics saw THE WILD BUNCH as a work of genius, which gave
the director renewed credibility in the industry and made it possible for him to write his
own ticket for the first half of the 1970s.[50]

*STRAW DOGS (ABC/Cinerama, 1971), Sam Peckinpah's own entry in 1971's ultravio-
lence sweepstakes (which also included A CLOCKWORK ORANGE and DIRTY HARRY), is
one of the most serious statements ever made in film about our natural appetite for
aggression: (left to right) Ken Hutchinson, Dustin Hoffman, Del Heeney, Susan George
(foreground, facing away). 35mm 1.85:1.*

Before that happened, however, Peckinpah completed another film signed to Warners by Hyman, a gently ironic parable of the passing of the West entitled THE BALLAD OF CABLE HOGUE (1970), which clearly demonstrated his ability to handle non-violent material. During the filming of THE WILD BUNCH, Warner Bros.-Seven Arts— its profits for 1969 rapidly falling—had been absorbed by the Kinney National Corporation (later Kinney Services), and Ted Ashley was installed as president. Ashley, who replaced Hyman with John Calley, had already been responsible for cutting ten minutes' worth of flashbacks out THE WILD BUNCH after several weeks of distribution.[51] Now, with Warners profits rising again, he decided to dump CABLE HOGUE into second-run theaters and write it off as a loss. (With a negative cost of $3.7 million, CABLE HOGUE grossed less than $2.5 million after three years in circulation.)[52] A furious Peckinpah publicly denounced Warner Bros. for damaging his professional reputation. Then he struck a deal with producer Daniel Melnick and the newly formed ABC Pictures to make a film from a novel entitled *The Siege at Trencher's Farm*, about an American college professor who moves with his family to a farmhouse in the English countryside that he must ultimately defend with his life against a gang of local thugs. (Melnick and Peckinpah had worked together on an ABC television *Stage 67* adaptation of Katherine Ann Porter's *Noon Wine* three years earlier.) Shot on location in Cornwall, the film was called STRAW DOGS (1971), and contained some of the most graphic violence ever to appear in a mainstream American film. Not only does the hero (Dustin Hoffman) slaughter all seven attackers in the long concluding siege of the farm, but there is a brutal scene in which his wife (Susan George) is raped and sodomized by two of them. (Peckinpah had to cut the American version of this action by several minutes in order to avoid an X rating from CARA.)[53]

Released in December 1971 by Cinerama Releasing Corporation (the "instant major" partnered with ABC), STRAW DOGS caused more public outrage than even THE WILD BUNCH had.[54] It was attacked by some critics, especially feminists, as depraved and misogynistic, and Pauline Kael in a famous review in *The New Yorker* called it "the first American film that is a fascist work of art."[55] Others compared STRAW DOGS unfavorably with A CLOCKWORK ORANGE (Stanley Kubrick, 1971) for being less artful and cerebral in its treatment of violence, which it certainly was. But many critics saw the film as a brilliant exposition of something tragic and profoundly disturbing in our nature, less misogynistic than misanthropic, yet clearly sympathetic to the individual agonies of its characters. Technically, its montage aesthetics were comparable only to those of THE WILD BUNCH, and Paul Zimmerman, writing in *Newsweek*, said prophetically, "It is hard to imagine that Sam Peckinpah will ever make a better movie. . . ."[56] The furor probably helped to make STRAW DOGS Peckinpah's most successful film to date, but not by much—at the end of 1973, it had returned less than $8 million worldwide against a final negative cost of $3.25 million. Even more than with THE WILD BUNCH, however, the controversy over STRAW DOGS made Peckinpah a celebrity figure. As biographer David Weddie put it, the film made "Peckinpah's name the most widely recognized of any director since Alfred Hitchcock."[57]

Satisfied with STRAW DOGS, ABC signed Peckinpah to direct JUNIOR BONNER (1972) from an original screenplay by Jeb Rosebrook about an aging rodeo star who returns to his hometown for a farewell performance. Essentially a character study containing some extraordinary action sequences, the film starred Steve McQueen in the title role and was produced in association with his Solar Productions company for $3.5 million. It was poorly distributed by Cinerama Releasing (which, like ABC Pictures itself, was

Steve McQueen in the title role of Peckinpah's JUNIOR BONNER *(ABC/Cinerama, 1972), a low-key character study about an aging rodeo star. Todd-AO 35 anamorphic (2.35:1).*

soon to go out of business) and returned just over $2.3 million worldwide in its year of release, convincing many in the industry that Peckinpah really was what the press had begun to call him—a "master of violence"—and nothing more.[58] But McQueen had meanwhile formed First Artists with Barbra Streisand, Sidney Poitier, and Paul Newman—a star-based production company modeled on United Artists—and he wanted Peckinpah to direct him in THE GETAWAY (1972), from a novel by Jim Thompson with a script by Walter Hill. The film was conceived as the box-office hit they both needed (McQueen hadn't had one since BULLITT [Peter Yates, 1968]), with LOVE STORY's (Arthur Hiller, 1970) Ali MacGraw in the female lead.[59] Shot on location in Texas by Lucien Ballard, who had collaborated with Peckinpah on all but two of his films since RIDE THE HIGH COUNTRY, THE GETAWAY is a "criminal couple" movie souped up with BULLITT-style car chases and WILD BUNCH-style ballistic ballets. Marketing was enhanced immensely by a torrid affair between McQueen and MacGraw on the set, which ended in her leaving her husband, Paramount production chief Robert Evans. On the strength of this, First Artists was able to secure $7 million in advance guarantees from exhibitors and then distribute THE GETAWAY with heavy publicity through National General.[60] Though it opened to mixed reviews, the film earned almost $19 million in the domestic market (and twice that worldwide) against its $3.4-million negative cost in the first year of release, making Peckinpah a truly bankable name for the first and last time in his career.

Steve McQueen and Ali MacGraw in THE GETAWAY *(First Artists/National General, 1972), a commercial and critical success thanks both to the stars' highly publicized (and adulterous) off-screen romance and Peckinpah's skillful rendering of the darkly ironic Jim Thompson novel. Todd-AO 35 anamorphic (2.35:1).*

During production of THE GETAWAY, Peckinpah had signed a contract with MGM head of production James Aubrey to direct PAT GARRETT & BILLY THE KID (1973) from a script by Rudolph Wurlitzer. The resulting film was shot in Mexico by John Coquillon (who had been the director of photography [DP] on STRAW DOGS) and, under time pressure from MGM, Peckinpah produced an elaborate 140-minute cut of the film for a Memorial Day 1973 release. Aubrey, who was in the process of dismantling the studio to finance Kirk Kerkorian's MGM Grand Hotel in Las Vegas, wanted another 40 minutes removed from it and finally distributed an incoherent 106-minute version of PAT GARRETT & BILLY THE KID in July—three months before Aubrey would announce MGM's withdrawal from theatrical distribution.[61] During its first year of release the film barely returned its negative cost of $4.6 million, and Peckinpah's mainstream career seemed virtually ended. He made BRING ME THE HEAD OF ALFREDO GARCIA (1974) in Mexico for Optimus Productions, an independent company formed by Martin Baum (head of ABC Pictures until its demise in 1972). This grotesque medium-budget ($1.5 million) revenge film was barely distributed by United Artists, which rightly assumed audiences would hate it, although several critics recognized it as a work of dark genius and—to those who knew Peckinpah—alcoholic despair. Still, United Artists retained enough faith in Peckinpah to finance THE KILLER ELITE (1975), a $6-million espionage thriller starring James Caan and Robert Duvall, which he was hired to direct on location in San Francisco but contractually forbidden to rewrite.[62] Even though it merely broke even, the film succeeded as an action-adventure, and in the winter of 1975 Peckinpah and the New Hollywood crossed paths one last time when he was offered deals by inde-

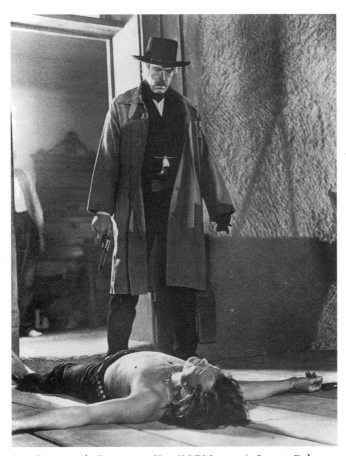

PAT GARRETT & BILLY THE KID (MGM, 1973): James Coburn and Kris Kristofferson in the title roles. Peckinpah's 140-minute version was recut and distributed at 106 minutes by studio head James Aubrey, shortly before he announced MGM's withdrawal from production. (The original version has since been restored on video.) 35mm Panavision anamorphic.

pendent producers to direct two huge blockbusters back-to-back, both of them laden with special effects: Dino De Laurentiis wanted him for KING KONG and Ilya Salkind for SUPERMAN.[63] That such offers could be seriously tendered to a director with only one real hit to his credit (THE GETAWAY), whose last three films had been box-office failures, and who was known to be a functional alcoholic, is testimony to the astonishing power that the auteur mystique still had at mid-decade in the American film industry.

Peckinpah knew better, though, and opted instead to make CROSS OF IRON in 1977 for German producer Wolf Hartwig in Yugoslavia. A World War II combat film narrated from the German point of view, CROSS OF IRON had to be completed with British funds from EMI Films when the production went $2 million over its original $6-million budget. Yet it proved to be terrifically popular in Europe, especially Germany and Austria, where it became the highest-grossing film since THE SOUND OF MUSIC (Robert Wise,

Warren Oates (with head) in BRING ME THE HEAD OF ALFREDO GARCIA *(UA, 1974), Peckinpah's darkest meditation on violence and death. 35mm 1.85:1.*

In CROSS OF IRON *(EMI/Avco Embassy, 1977), Peckinpah took the unfashionable step of showing World War II from the German point of view and was rewarded with spectacular box-office failure. 35mm Panavision anamorphic.*

1965). In the United States, Avco Embassy dumped it into second-run theaters with no publicity, where it earned less than $700,000 in the year that saw the record-breaking $193.8-million take of STAR WARS. On the basis of CROSS OF IRON's European performance, though, EMI hired Peckinpah to direct CONVOY (1978) from a lightweight B.W.L. Norton script about a trucker's rebellion based on a popular country-western song ("Convoy" by C. W, McCall).[64] The concept was modeled on Universal's SMOKEY AND THE BANDIT (Hal Needham, 1977), a redneck chase comedy that had unexpectedly grossed $59 million.

Addicted now to cocaine as well as alcohol (cocaine addiction having become an occupational hazard in late-1970s Hollywood), Peckinpah ran the film $7 million over its $5-million budget and was removed from the project in postproduction. EMI released a 110-minute version through United Artists that ironically became the director's highest-grossing film, earning $46.5 million worldwide. Using New Hollywood marketing tactics, EMI had pre-sold CONVOY to European and Asian exhibitors as a high concept "event movie" and amortized its costs in prerelease.[65] Peckinpah made one more feature, THE OSTERMAN WEEKEND (1983), based on a Robert Ludlam thriller, before dying of heart failure in 1985.

More than any other figure of his generation, Peckinpah replicates the corporate history of Hollywood in the 1970s in a kind of inverse curve. Early on, following THE WILD BUNCH, he worked with two production companies formed from the industry chaos of the late sixties—the "instant major" ABC Pictures/Cinerama Releasing Corporation and

The nearly incoherent CONVOY (EMI/UA, 1978) was Peckinpah's worst film and—the ultimate humiliation—his most commercially successful thanks to a "high concept" marketing campaign. 35mm Panavision anamorphic.

the independent First Artists. Next he worked for one of Hollywood's greatest studios, MGM, as it was being gutted and downsized in the wake of a leveraged buyout by Kirk Kerkorian. Finally, he worked as the director (and sometimes writer-director) component of ad hoc production "packages" financed and distributed by United Artists, or on the United Artists model.[66] This was all because he had begun the decade as one of its most celebrated auteurs at a time when the industry literally needed direction. His personal demons notwithstanding (and they were formidable), he ended the 1970s in failure when auteurism became an impediment to the direction the industry had finally taken—that is, toward the production of high-concept blockbusters, a form of production he had specifically abjured by turning down KING KONG and SUPERMAN in 1975.

ROBERT ALTMAN

The only filmmaker of his generation more prolific than Peckinpah during the 1970s was Robert Altman, who began his career as an industrial filmmaker in Kansas City, Missouri, before making several exploitation features (THE DELINQUENTS [1957]; THE JAMES DEAN STORY [1957, codirected with George W. George]) and then working as a director in series television (for episodes of *Alfred Hitchcock Presents*, 1957–1958; *The Millionaire*, 1958–1959; *The Roaring Twenties*, 1960–1961; *Bonanza*, 1960–1961; *Bus Stop*, 1961; *Combat*, 1962–1963). His first Hollywood features were COUNTDOWN (1968), a modestly budgeted drama about the rivalry between two NASA astronauts produced for the Warners' B-unit, and THAT COLD DAY IN THE PARK (1969), a moody psychosexual melodrama shot on location in Vancouver, British Columbia—both financed by the Max Factor family for the "instant major" Commonwealth United. (THAT COLD DAY IN THE PARK contained scenes suggesting incest between a brother and sister, and was cut without Altman's consent by producer Donald Factor in order to avoid an X rating.)[67] Neither film was widely distributed (in fact, COUNTDOWN played almost exclusively on a double bill with John Wayne's right-wing THE GREEN BERETS [1968]), but Altman's next project became one of the biggest hits of the early 1970s.

Based on a script that Ring Lardner, Jr. adapted from a 1968 novel by Richard Hooker, and produced for Fox by Ingo Preminger (Otto's brother), M°A°S°H (1970)—an acronym for "Mobile Army Surgical Hospital"—is an irreverent antimilitary comedy about the personnel of a battlefield medical unit during the Korean War. Its subversive blend of humor and gore and its contemporary stylization made the film a hit with the counterculture, and critics recognized its strikingly composed Panavision frames (structured around telephoto zooms by veteran cinematographer Harold E. Stine) and overlapping dialogue as the hallmarks of a bold new talent. (A source of constant confusion to his producers, Altman's overlapping dialogue first appeared in COUNTDOWN, of which Jack Warner is said to have remarked: "Jesus Christ, you've got all the actors talking at once! Who's going to understand it?")[68] Although M°A°S°H never pretended to be more than a hip service comedy with an absurdist edge, the parallels between Korea and the Vietnam conflict were unmistakable, and it was widely perceived in the youth market as a covert antiwar movie—one that Altman had slipped past the collective nose of Middle America so cleverly that Fox was able to turn it into a popular television series several years later and no one was the wiser. (No one but Fox marketing executives, that is, who exploited the film's antiwar cache with an advertising logo featuring a large hand giving the peace sign.) Shot for $3 million, M°A°S°H took in $36.7 million to become the third highest grossing film of 1970, plus it won the Palme d'Or at Cannes, the

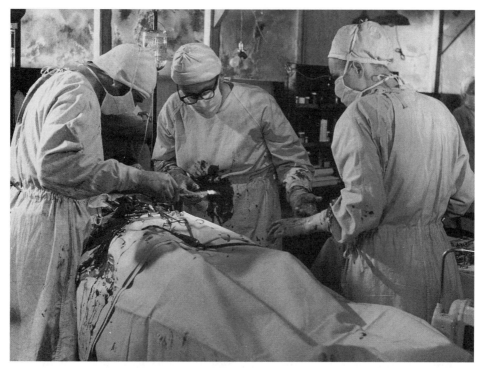

The "Mobile Army Surgical Hospital" unit at work in Robert Altman's M*A*S*H (Fox, 1970). Even though the film was set during the Korean War, its analogy with Vietnam was unmistakable. 35mm Panavision anamorphic.

National Society of Film Critics Award for Best Film of 1970, and an Academy Award for Best Screenplay (with nominations for Best Picture, Best Director, Best Supporting Actress, and Best Editing).

Some critics see the five years between M*A*S*H and NASHVILLE (1975) as a golden era for Altman;[69] in fact they were an unusually fruitful time for American film in general because of the new creative power given to directors in the shifting industry production context. During these years, Altman was able to make six films with various combinations of his "talent trust" of repertory players (Bud Cort, Sally Kellerman, Michael Murphy, Shelley Duvall, Rene Auberjonois, Corey Fischer, and Bert Remsen) and creative personnel (cinematographer Vilmos Zsigmond, editor Louis Lombardo, art director Leon Ericksen) that revised and satirized several Hollywood genres in ways that are now generally described as postmodern. The most unusual of these was BREWSTER MCCLOUD (1970), produced by Altman's newly formed Lion's Gate Films[70] for distribution by MGM. This disjointed social satire, whose negative cost was $1.8 million,[71] focuses on an Icarus-like young man whose aspiration is fly like a bird through the Houston Astrodome, to accomplish which he must avoid sex (which binds him to earth) and kill a number of reactionary characters. Although many critics praised its originality and the technical achievement of its subjective aerial cinematography, MGM's James Aubrey hated the movie and distributed it as if it were an exploitation film: after a quick million-dollar play-off, it was withdrawn from theaters.[72]

Altman's next film was produced for Warners and shot on location in British Columbia by Zsigmond, who obtained a tinted, old-fashioned quality for it by flashing and fogging the stock. Adapted by Altman and Brian McKay from a novel by Edmund Naughton, McCabe & Mrs. Miller (1971) is about a buffoonish small-time gambler who, with the aid of an enterprising brothel madam, founds the town of Presbyterian Church in Washington State near the turn of the century. As the town grows and prospers, a large mining conglomerate attempts to buy McCabe out and, when he refuses, has him shot to death by a contract killer. With an elegiac score by poet-folksinger Leonard Cohen, McCabe & Mrs. Miller is both a celebration of community and an indictment of corporate capitalism, very much in tune with the values of the counterculture. But the film initially confused critics, who thought the Cohen songs inappropriate to a Western and disliked its mixing of comic and tragic elements. Furthermore, the negative was rushed into duplication for a June 1971 release, and early prints had color-timing and dubbing problems (the latter especially troubling, given Altman's elaborately structured overlapping dialogue mix).

Warren Beatty as an exemplar of frontier capitalism in Altman's McCabe & Mrs. Miller (Warners, 1971). 35mm Panavision anamorphic.

Despite audience indifference, however, the film had a second life with the critics, many of whom reversed their original opinions when corrected release prints became available later in the summer.[73] Audiences who were put off by MCCABE & MRS. MILLER's downbeat ending, were completely alienated by IMAGES (1972), Altman's attempt to make a film according to the model of expatriate director Joseph Losey (THE SERVANT [1963]; SECRET CEREMONY [1968]). Shot on location in and around an isolated country house in Ireland from an original screenplay by Altman, IMAGES tracks the psychic disintegration of a wealthy Englishwoman (played by Susannah York). The film was produced for $800,000 by Hemdale and Lion's Gate and barely distributed in the United States, although York won the Best Actress prize at Cannes for her performance in it.

Altman's next film gave a distinctly revisionist spin to a 1953 Philip Marlowe novel by Raymond Chandler, turning the detective into a genial *klutz* (played by Elliott Gould) and updating the setting to the present. Based on a screenplay by Leigh Brackett and

Elliot Gould as a contemporary Philip Marlowe in Altman's revisionist film noir THE LONG GOODBYE *(Lion's Gate/UA, 1973). 35mm Panavision anamorphic.*

produced by Lion's Gate for United Artists distribution, THE LONG GOODBYE (1973) is less a *film noir* than a sardonic comment on contemporary American narcissism drenched in the decadent ambience of 1970s Los Angeles. In it, Marlowe staunchly defends a close friend who is accused of murdering his wife, only to discover that his friend is guilty of the crime and has used Marlowe to cover it up. Marlowe, whose throwaway line throughout the film has been "It's OK with me," is finally confronted with something that's not, and he tracks the friend to Mexico and shoots him. THE LONG GOODBYE is distinguished by Zsigmond's constantly moving first-person camera and an innovative soundtrack by John Williams that rings recurrent changes on the title song as it appears in many different guises. But genre purists hated the film when it opened in February 1973, so United Artists withdrew it and re-released it in October with a new advertising campaign emphasizing its satiric take on genre tradition. This helped THE LONG GOODBYE to become a modest box-office success; furthermore, the National Society of Film Critics cited it for Best Cinematography (Zsigmond), and it ended up on many year-end Ten Best Lists.

Altman described the production of THE LONG GOODBYE as "making a film in Hollywood and about Hollywood, and about that kind of film,"[74] indicating his conscious intention to rework classical genres, and he turned his attention next to the "criminal couple" film. THIEVES LIKE US (United Artists, 1974) was adapted from the

In CALIFORNIA SPLIT (Lion's Gate/Columbia, 1974) Altman made his first use of the Lion's Gate eight-track wireless sound system: Elliott Gould and George Segal as compulsive gamblers on a binge in Las Vegas. 35mm Panavision anamorphic.

A lobby card showing the twenty-four separate characters in NASHVILLE *(ABC/Para-mount, 1975), Altman's plotless "antimusical" that culminates in a botched political assassination. 35mm Panavision anamorphic.*

1937 novel of that title by Edward Anderson, which was also the source for Nicholas Ray's genre classic THEY LIVE BY NIGHT (1949). Shot on location in Mississippi by French cinematographer Jean Boffey, the film deals with three prison escapees during the Depression who set out on a spree of bank robbing, become notorious, and are finally killed by the police in a slow-motion death sequence that invokes comparison with BONNIE AND CLYDE (Arthur Penn, 1967). A meticulous period recreation, complete with authentic radio sound, the film has an academic quality that led Pauline Kael to call it "the closest to flawless of Altman's films"; and Richard Corliss, less approvingly, "textbook cinema at its best."[75] The audience didn't like it either way, but CALIFORNIA SPLIT (Columbia, 1974) achieved modest popularity and took in about $5 million in domestic rentals, as well as turning up on the *New York Times* annual Ten Best list (the fifth Altman film to do so since 1970).[76] The first film to use the Lion's Gate eight-track wireless sound system, this was an episodic story of compulsive gambling, based on a screenplay by Joseph Walsh and shot on location in Las Vegas by Paul Lohmann, who would collaborate with Altman on both NASHVILLE (1975) and BUFFALO BILL AND THE INDIANS (1976).

At this point, Altman was a darling of the critics, but he had not scored a solid commercial hit since M°A°S°H. NASHVILLE (1975), produced by ABC for distribution by Paramount, was not that exactly, but it did return $9.3 million domestic against its $2.2-

million production cost, and became the most highly acclaimed film of Altman's career. Scripted by Joan Tewkesbury and redolent of the preceding decade's traumatic politics, the film follows the lives of twenty-four characters in Nashville over a five-day period preceding a rally for "Replacement Party" presidential candidate Hal Philip Walker at the city's replica of the Parthenon. The characters represent a cross-section of the American public, but all have a common desire to strike it rich in the world of country music, which stands in for American mass media at large. Their lives coalesce at the Walker rally that concludes the film, when a young assassin who has come to kill the candidate kills a celebrity performer instead. For much of its 160-minute running time, NASHVILLE charts the way in which our national entertainment media and our national politics work together to shield America from historical truth. But the film is also highly entertaining in its own right, functioning both as social satire and country-and-western musical. Its intricate sound track was recorded in Lion's Gate eight-track stereo, with individually controlled wireless microphones on seven of the principal players simultaneously (one track was used for background noise), plus an additional sixteen tracks for its twenty-seven musical sequences, half of which were collected on an ABC LP intended to cross-market the movie.[77] Although it opened strongly in exclusive runs in major cities and was hailed by many critics as a masterpiece, NASHVILLE performed poorly when Paramount attempted a wider release, and it failed to win any of the major Oscars for which it was nominated (Best Picture, Best Director, two for Best Supporting Actress [Lily Tomlin, Ronee Blakely]), winning only for Best Song ("I'm Easy"). It did,

Buffalo Bill (Paul Newman) and his Indian interpreter (William Halsey) stage a fight for Bill's Wild West Show in Altman's BUFFALO BILL AND THE INDIANS, OR SITTING BULL'S HISTORY LESSON (De Laurentiis/UA, 1976). 35mm Panavision anamorphic.

however, win the New York Film Critics awards for Best Film, Best Director, and Best Supporting Actress (Tomlin), heightening a growing perception in Hollywood that Altman's work was pitched more toward the Eastern intellectual establishment than toward the industry's bottom line.

His next film seemed to confirm both terms of this proposition with a vengeance. BUFFALO BILL AND THE INDIANS, OR SITTING BULL'S HISTORY LESSON (1976) was adapted by Altman and Alan Rudolph from Arthur Kopit's off-Broadway play *Indians* and produced by Dino De Laurentiis for United Artists distribution. It was to be the first in a widely touted three-film partnership between Altman and De Laurentiis. Produced for $6.5 million—Altman's biggest budget so far—and starring Paul Newman in the title role, BUFFALO BILL is another indictment of the hypocrisy and exploitative-ness of American mass media, this time in the form of Buffalo Bill's Wild West Show. The film shows Buffalo Bill's media image to be a tissue of lies built upon Ned Buntline's dime-novel mythology and the subjugation of Sitting Bull's people, but, unlike NASHVILLE, grows sententious and seemingly random in the process. Furthermore, according to editor Louis Lombardo, De Laurentiis rushed the film in post-production, contributing to its final incoherence.[78] Over this and other issues, De Laurentiis and Altman had an acrimonious and highly publicized falling out, which resulted in the producer firing Altman from the project in post-production, as well as canceling a contract with him to adapt E. L. Doctorow's best-selling novel RAGTIME.[79] (The contract later went to Milos Forman, who made the film in 1981.) De Laurentiis re-edited BUFFALO BILL for final release,[80] but United Artists's half-hearted distribution of the film condemned it to oblivion at the box office, where it grossed less than $1 million, although it was submitted for competition at the 1976 Berlin Film Festival and won the Golden Bear.

Of the eight films Altman had directed since M°A°S°H, only CALIFORNIA SPLIT and NASHVILLE had shown a profit, but his critical reputation was so high that Alan Ladd, Jr., then production head of Fox, provided distribution and financing for his next five films—3 WOMEN (1977), A WEDDING (1978), QUINTET (1979), A PERFECT COUPLE (1979), and H.E.A.L.T.H. (1979)—all of which were produced by Lion's Gate: Of these, only 3 WOMEN was successful with critics, some of whom saw it as superior even to NASHVILLE. Vincent Canby, for example, suggested that its disorienting, dream-like structure provided the paradigm for a new American art cinema. "At the start of the next century," he wrote, "it may well be possible to look back on these years of the 1970s and identify this very particular period—if not as the turning point from the Old Movie into the New, then as the time when New Movies began to supplement Old in such number that it wasn't always easy to tell them apart. . . . Robert Altman's '3 Women' is very much a New Movie. . . ."[81] Based on a screenplay by Altman, with unaccredited assistance from Patricia Resnick, the film is a Bergmanesque study of the psychological relationships among three unrelated women (played by Shelley Duvall, Sissy Spacek,[82] and Janice Rule) who unite to form a spiritual "family," hypnotically photographed by Charles Rosher. Though it contains characteristic elements of social satire, 3 WOMEN has a mys-tical, quasi-religious quality that distinguishes it from earlier Altman films, and some critics see it as his last important work before THE PLAYER in 1992.

A WEDDING was a comedy of manners about nouveau riche nuptials whose most interesting feature was its use of two eight-track sound systems to record fourteen dif-ferent actors simultaneously;[83] with a domestic gross of $3.1 million, it was the only one of the Fox films to make over a million dollars. QUINTET was an unmitigated disaster—

Shelly Duvall and Sissy Spacek in Altman's moody and dream-like 3 WOMEN *(Fox, 1977), a film virtually unique in the American cinema. 35mm Panavision anamorphic.*

a futuristic murder mystery driven by an elaborate and, finally, inexplicable game. The film lost nearly all of its $7.6-million production cost, and convinced Fox not to release either A PERFECT COUPLE or H.E.A.L.T.H. theatrically, although both were subsequently released to cable. In spite of these commercial failures, Altman was signed by producer Robert Evans of Paramount to direct a musical adapted by Jules Feiffer from the comic strip POPEYE (1980), starring Robin Williams in the title role. Based on a presold property and heavily marketed, the film grossed $24.5 million to become the twelfth highest earner of 1980, but so firmly was the blockbuster mentality entrenched by this point that POPEYE was seen as a failure (which, relative to the $141.7-million gross of that year's THE EMPIRE STRIKES BACK, it probably was). Since M*A*S*H, Altman had made fourteen feature films and worked for every major studio in Hollywood; after POPEYE, he would not work for a major distributor again. Even his comeback films of the 1990s would be handled by the "mini-majors" Fine Line and Miramax. Lion's Gate Films—which had produced not only Altman's best work of the decade but also such notable films as Alan Rudolph's WELCOME TO L.A. (1977) and REMEMBER MY NAME (1978), Robert Benton's THE LATE SHOW (1977), and Robert M. Young's RICH KIDS (1979)—experienced increasing difficulty in securing financing and distribution (even as it expanded into a new $2-million post-production facility in 1979), and was sold in 1981 to independent producer Jonathan Taplin for $2.3 million.[84]

Of all the auteur directors of his generation, Robert Altman was the most critically esteemed and courted by the media; furthermore, ownership of his own production company gave him a power base and a source of income that buffered him against the winds of change blowing through 1970s Hollywood as he moved from one project to the

Altman directs Carol Burnett as the mother of the bride in A WEDDING *(Fox, 1978), in which two Lion's Gate eight-track systems were used to record the dialogue of fourteen characters simultaneously. 35mm Panavision anamorphic.*

next. But even these advantages were not enough to keep him working in mainstream cinema into the 1980s. When the high concept blockbuster became the industry standard, Altman's revisionist-deconstructive approach to genre became unmarketable, and for more than a decade he effectively withdrew from the film industry to work in theater, cable, and television.[85]

Auteurs Manqué *and* Maudit

Mediating culturally and aesthetically between the generation of Penn, Kubrick, Peckinpah, and Altman—all but one of whom (Kubrick) received his basic production training in television—and the "film school" generation of Coppola, Lucas, Scorsese, Spielberg, and De Palma, were a group of directors who attempted to parlay the creative freedoms of the late sixties and early 1970s into auteurist careers. They met with only middling success but, at the same time, produced collectively a number of remarkable films. They came from a variety of backgrounds—theater and live performance, documentary television, film criticism, screenwriting, etc.—but all had in common a sense that they shared with the first directors of the French New Wave: that at this particular time in the history of their national industry almost anyone with talent and the will to do so could become a film director. This would be an incredible premise today, when the production costs of even a standard feature can exceed $30 million and no one but a professional can be trusted to handle them. Indeed, it would be incredible by the decade's end—after the astonishing success of JAWS and STAR WARS; but in the early 1970s, before the blockbuster syndrome had firmly gelled, mainstream features could still be made for a few million dollars (the average negative cost for 1971 was $1.75 million), and were considered hits if they returned three or four times that much at the box office.

Furthermore, the EASY RIDER "youth cult" bubble encouraged the employment of relatively untested directors for their freshness and novelty. It was in this context that the film careers of Mike Nichols (b. 1931), Peter Bogdanovich (b. 1939), William Friedkin (b. 1939), Bob Rafelson (b. 1934), Hal Ashby (1936–1988), Alan Pakula (1928–1998), and several more genre-oriented directors bore fruit. The same perspective lends coherence to the singular contributions of two American originals—John Cassavetes (1929–1989) and Terrence Malick (b. 1945)—whose work is also examined below.

MIKE NICHOLS

Mike Nichols (born Michael Igor Peschkowsky in Berlin; emigrated 1938) was an improv performer (*An Evening with Mike Nichols and Elaine May*) and a successful Broadway theater director when he created a sensation with his filmic adaptation of Edward Albee's corrosive 1962 play *Who's Afraid of Virginia Woolf?*, produced for Warners, whose foul language initially caused it to be denied the Production Code Seal, helping it to earn $14.5 million and become the third highest grossing film of 1966. (WHO'S AFRAID OF VIRGINIA WOOLF? was a major catalyst for Jack Valenti's 1966 revision of the Code and its ultimate replacement by the CARA system—see above.)[86] It was followed by the prototypical youth-cult movie THE GRADUATE (Avco Embassy, 1967), which became the highest-grossing film of the decade and won Nichols an Academy Award for Best Director, and an $18-million adaptation of Joseph Heller's surrealistic World War II novel CATCH-22 (1970)—Paramount's failed attempt to cash in on the antiwar movement, which returned only $9.3 million. But Nichols's next film, CARNAL KNOWLEDGE (Avco Embassy, 1971) became a watershed in the history of censorship and free speech when the Georgia Supreme Court upheld the obscenity conviction of a theater owner in Albany, Georgia, for showing it. The case then went to the U.S. Supreme Court, which in June 1974 overturned the Georgia ruling on the grounds that the film was not obscene under the standards recently established by *Miller v. California*.[87] (This was the landmark decision that in June 1973 laid down the ambiguous "community standards" test for determining obscenity.) Written by Jules Feiffer, CARNAL KNOWLEDGE offered a depressing view of male sexual exploitation by charting the lives of two college roommates from the 1950s through the present. Although it showed no explicit sex acts on screen, the predatory exploits of its protagonists were recounted in graphic dialogue, and the film contained several nude scenes. Predictably, CARNAL KNOWLEDGE was both popular (it earned $12.1 million to become the twelfth-highest earner of 1971) and critically successful, winning praise for its Panavision cinematography by Guiseppe Rotunno and Nichols's strong direction. Nichols made only two more films during the 1970s: THE DAY OF THE DOLPHIN (Avco Embassy, 1973), a political thriller written by Buck Henry in which a pair of trained dolphins become ploys in a presidential assassination plot; and a black comedy about the bungled kidnapping of an heiress during the 1920s entitled THE FORTUNE (Columbia, 1975). Neither was commercially successful,

Jack Nicholson attempts to seduce Candice Bergen in Mike Nichols's CARNAL KNOWLEGE
(Avco Embassy, 1971), a film whose subject made it an early test case for Miller v. California. *35mm Panavision anamorphic.*

and Nichols didn't direct again until 1980, when he filmed an unexpurgated version of
Gilda Radner's Broadway show GILDA LIVE. He has since become a mainstream industry figure with several notable hits to his credit (SILKWOOD [1983]; WORKING GIRL
[1988]; THE BIRDCAGE [1996]).

PETER BOGDANOVICH

Peter Bogdanovich was an off-Broadway theater director and auteurist film critic
(author of monographs and books on Welles, Hawks, Hitchcock, Lang, Ford, and Allan
Dwan) before he directed his first feature for Roger Corman in 1968. This was the
flashily reflexive TARGETS, a film about a psychotic Vietnam vet who becomes a sniper,
interfoliated with Boris Karloff outtakes from Corman's recently completed THE
TERROR (1963). Produced for $125,000, this tribute to AIP horror was distributed by
Paramount and was followed by the documentary DIRECTED BY JOHN FORD (1971),
which was financed by the American Film Institute and was chosen as the official U.S.
entry at the 1971 Venice Film Festival. Bogdanovich's mainstream breakthrough film,
THE LAST PICTURE SHOW (1971) was produced by the newly formed BBS Productions
and became that company's biggest hit. Based on a novel by Larry McMurty and
scripted by McMurty and Bogdanovich, THE LAST PICTURE SHOW was produced for
$1.3 million and shot in black-and-white by cinematographer Robert Surtees on loca-
tion in Texas. The film, like the novel, takes the closing of the local picture palace as a

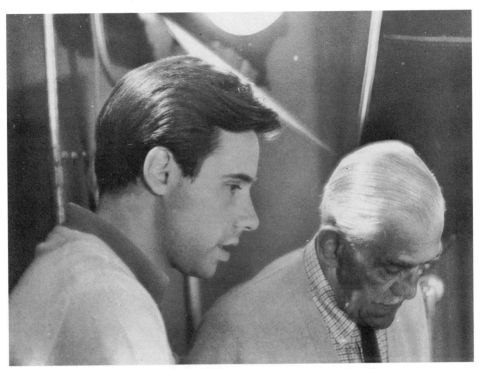

Peter Bogdanovich, 28, directs Boris Karloff in Targets *(1968), produced by Roger Corman and distributed by Paramount. 35mm 1.85:1.*

metaphor for the unraveling of rural American life and creates an elegiac mood worthy of Welles and Ford. Nominated for eight Academy Awards, including Best Picture, Best Director, and Best Screenplay (and winning for Best Supporting Actor [Ben Johnson] and Best Supporting Actress [Cloris Leachman]), The Last Picture Show was an unexpected popular success (it earned $14.1 million to become the tenth highest grossing film of 1971). It propelled Bogdanovich toward his next project, the updated screwball comedy What's Up Doc? (Warner Bros., 1972), which was modeled on Howard Hawks's 1938 hit Bringing Up Baby. When this re-created genre classic returned $28.5 million in rentals, making it the second highest earning film in the year of The Godfather ($86.3 million), Bogdanovich became one of the most sought-after directors in Hollywood.

In 1973 he joined with two other newly bankable talents, William Friedkin and Francis Ford Coppola, to form the short-lived Directors Company, a creatively autonomous unit of Paramount capitalized by production chief Frank Yablans at $31.5 million. Through this short-lived entity,[88] Bogdanovich produced Paper Moon (Paramount, 1973), another nostalgia piece shot on location in black-and-white, this time by Laszlo Kovacs in rural Kansas. A comedy set in Depression-era Kansas, it teamed Ryan O'Neal with his ten-year-old daughter Tatum as a pair of con artists, and she became the youngest person ever to receive a competitive Oscar when she won the 1973 award for Best Supporting Actress. The film itself was a relative success, coming in at ninth place with earnings of $16.6 million, but the blockbuster syndrome that had

Timothy Bottoms and Cloris Leachman in Bogdanovich's elegy for small-town life THE
LAST PICTURE SHOW (BBS/Columbia, 1971), which signaled the director's critical and
commercial arrival. 1.85:1.

been forming in the wake of THE GODFATHER emerged full-blown in 1973 with THE
EXORCIST's $89.3 million in rentals, THE STING's $78.2 million, and AMERICAN GRAFFITI's
$55.3 million. When Bogdanovich's next film, an adaptation of Henry James's DAISY
MILLER (Paramount, 1974) shot on location in Italy for the Directors Company, lost
money, his bankability was barely sustainable through one more flop. Yet he was able to
produce two before the studio doors were completely closed to him—AT LONG LAST LOVE
(Fox, 1975), an elaborate attempt to re-create a 1930s musical in the Astaire-Rogers style,
based on Cole Porter songs;[89] and NICKELODEON (Columbia, 1976), a comedy-drama
about the early days of the film industry, derived in part from the anecdotal accounts of
pioneers Bogdanovich had interviewed as a critic.[90] Bogdanovich now left Hollywood for
Singapore where, with financing provided by Roger Corman, he directed a low-budget
adaptation of Paul Theroux's Vietnam-era novel *Saint Jack* (1979), which won the Critics
Prize at the Venice Film Festival in 1979. After the failure of the romantic comedy THEY
ALL LAUGHED (1981), which he attempted to distribute himself,[91] and the murder of his
mistress Dorothy Stratten by her estranged husband, Bogdanovich entered a period of
decline.[92] He went into bankruptcy in 1985, continuing to work as a director but producing few notable films (MASK [1985][93] and NOISES OFF [1992] among them).
    During the 1970s, however, his career had epitomized the auteurist ideal: beginning,
like his French New Wave counterparts, as an auteurist critic and cineaste, he started to

Barbra Streisand and Ryan O'Neal star in Bogdanovich's What's Up Doc?, *a contemporary gloss on Howard Hawks's* Bringing Up Baby *(1938). 35mm 1.85:1.*

work in low-budget features with Roger Corman at AIP; directed his first hit for the independent, youth-and-cinema-oriented BBS Productions; and afterwards produced, directed, and co-wrote nearly all of his films himself. Furthermore, as David Thomson points out, Bogdanovich's best films are not so much auteur pieces as extensions of his criticism, and his criticism was instrumental in the rise of auteurism as the dominant mode of aesthetic discourse about film from the 1970s through the present,[94] at least in terms of its more public manifestations.

WILLIAM FRIEDKIN

William Friedkin's career, by contrast, follows the parabolic commercial trajectory of 1970s Hollywood. Friedkin began as a director of local broadcast television in Chicago, having worked his way up from the station mail room at the age of sixteen, and went on to direct network documentaries and dramatic shows (including the final episode of the *Alfred Hitchcock Hour*) before making his first features. These were indebted both to television (Good Times [Columbia, 1967], a Sonny and Cher vehicle), and Richard Lester's Beatles films (The Night They Raided Minsky's [United Artists, 1968], a Norman Lear production) for their vigorous camera and editing styles; while The Birthday Party (Palomar [U.K.], 1968) and The Boys in the Band (National General Pictures, 1970, produced by CBS' Cinema Center Films) were more stagebound in their adaptation of plays by Harold Pinter and Mart Crowley, respectively. It was Friedkin's reputation for creating a "cinema of immediacy," however, that led Richard Zanuck at 20th Century–Fox to hire him to direct The French Connection (1971), a screen version of Robin Moore's best-selling book about two real-life New York cops who uncovered an international heroin-smuggling ring. Shot in and around Manhattan for a modest $1.8 million, the film featured a spectacularly edited car chase (modeled on a similar one in Peter Yates's BULLITT [1968]) so compelling that it generated significant repeat business. This helped to boost THE FRENCH CONNECTION into third place at the box office for 1971, with $26.3 million in earnings; it was also nominated for eight Academy Awards and won five, including Best Picture, Best Director, Best Actor (Gene Hackman), Best Screenplay (Ernest Tidyman), and Best Film Editing (Jerry Greenberg). This unprecedented sweep of the Oscars by a simple, if flashy, genre film is indicative of the state of the industry as it approached the end of its historic recession, simultaneously seeking to reward box-office success while privileging novelty of style.

Friedkin was now a hot property, and he was signed by Warner Bros. to direct an adaptation of William Peter Blatty's best-selling horror novel THE EXORCIST (not as hot, however, as Penn, Kubrick, and Nichols, all of whom turned the project down before it was offered to Friedkin).[95] The resulting film, which opened December 26, 1973, was one of the most controversial and successful of the decade, earning $89.3 million ($250 million worldwide) and stirring a national debate over sensationalism in the movies that, in some sense, is still going on. While crowds reportedly waited in line for hours to see the R-rated film,[96] critics found THE EXORCIST to be brutal, manipulative, and disgust-

William Friedkin (center), not quite 30, directing THE BOYS IN THE BAND *(CBS/National General, 1970). 35mm 1.85:1.*

An iconic shot from Friedkin's 1971 hit THE FRENCH CONNECTION, *produced for Fox: police detective "Popeye" Doyle (Gene Hackman) shoots a narcotics dealer in the back. The film was the model for the high-octane "buddy cop" franchises of the 1980s (*48 HOURS, LETHAL WEAPON, *etc.).*

ing. In the pages of *Film Comment*, for example, Stephen Farber wrote that it "offers perverse sexual kicks that make ordinary porno movies look wholesome," and said of Friedkin, "He is the model of what the studios want: pragmatic, opportunistic, professional, utterly cynical."[97] Yet, if it did represent a new extreme in the "cinema of cruelty," THE EXORCIST's historic grosses confirmed what THE GODFATHER had suggested the year before—that recession in the industry was over and that film attendance was once more on the rise, at least for the biggest hits. (In February 1973, *Variety* reported that January business was up 24 percent over 1972, but that the ratio of business done by the top twenty-five films remained constant.)[98] For the second time in eighteen months, a souped-up Friedkin genre film had become a blockbuster and received multiple Oscar nominations (ten this time, winning only two—Best Screenplay [Blatty, who had also produced] and Best Sound).

But now the director yearned for respectability, and under a new contract with Universal he conceived the idea of remaking Henri Georges Clouzot's perverse thriller THE WAGES OF FEAR (1952) from a screenplay by Walon Green, who had co-written THE WILD BUNCH (Sam Peckinpah, 1969) with Sam Peckinpah. When the projected budget for this film reached $15 million, Universal entered into a coproduction deal with Paramount to release it internationally through their joint foreign distributorship CIC (Cinema International Corporation), which dominated about a third of the overseas market.[99] Acting as his own producer on location in the Dominican Republic (chosen because Paramount's parent company Gulf & Western had interests there), Friedkin completed the oddly titled SORCERER (1977) at a cost of $21.6 million.[100] After he supervised the final cut, Universal released the film in the same week as STAR WARS, and SORCERER ultimately earned less than $9 million.

Though his star had fallen, Friedkin was hired by Dino De Laurentiis to replace John Frankenheimer as director of THE BRINK'S JOB (1978), a caper film based on 1950s legendary Boston armored car robbery. With a negative cost of $12.5 million ($7 million above the average for 1978), THE BRINK'S JOB made less than $5 million ($4,686,810) and seemed to confirm the fact that Friedkin had suddenly become an expensive loser. What had really changed, though, was not the director but the production context in which he worked. Virtually every filmmaker examined in this chapter, with the exception of George Lucas and Steven Spielberg, experienced a reversal of fortune from the beginning to the end of the decade because so much changed so rapidly. Friedkin's was simply more dramatic than most, because he had been briefly at the pinnacle of the blockbuster pyramid in the process of its formation.

Ironically, Friedkin's last film of the 1970s had originally been slated for Spielberg when the property was optioned in 1971 by Philip D'Antoni, producer of THE FRENCH

SORCERER *(Universal/Paramount, 1977), Friedkin's high-tension remake of Henri George Clouzot's 1952 thriller* THE WAGES OF FEAR, *bombed inexplicably at the box office to become one of the decade's major flops, although it was probably his best film. 35mm 1.85:1.*

CONNECTION. This was Gerald Walker's novel *Cruising* (1970), a murder mystery about a cop who goes undercover in New York's gay S&M subculture to track down a serial killer, which D'Antoni had finally abandoned as too bizarre for contemporary audiences. By 1978, however, Friedkin was attracted to adapting the novel as a means of restoring his box-office reputation for sensational entertainment. (He may also have felt immune from criticism that the project was antigay because he had earlier adapted THE BOYS IN THE BAND [1970], a movie that depicts gay men in a positive light.) Whatever the case, CRUISING (Lorimar/United Artists, 1980), for which Friedkin wrote his first screenplay, depicts the world of gay leather bars as dangerous, sinister, and sick, and the film aroused a storm of protest in the gay community, beginning with several near riots during location shooting on Christopher Street. Opened in major cities as "William Friedkin's CRUISING" on February 15, 1980, the film met with picket lines and demonstrations, and did terrific business in its first two weeks before plummeting abruptly and eventually earning less than $7 million ($6,788,140) in rentals.[101] (*Variety*'s assessment that CRUISING "resembles the worst of the 'hippie' films of the 1960s" accurately connected it with the youth market appeal that had first made Friedkin bankable.)[102] After this debacle, Friedkin had a hard time finding work, although his technical skills sustained him through an occasional genre feature (TO LIVE AND DIE IN L.A. [1985]; THE GUARDIAN [1990]; RAMPAGE [1992]; JADE [1995]) and television pilots. His two great hits of the 1970s inspired several sequels directed by others—THE FRENCH CONNECTION II (John Frankenheimer, 1975), EXORCIST II: THE HERETIC (John Boorman, 1977), and THE

Al Pacino (with Richard Cox) as a cop who goes undercover in New York's gay S&M subculture to find a serial killer in William Friedkin's CRUISING *(Lorimar/UA, 1980). The film ignited protest in the gay community but did not benefit from its notoriety at the box office. 35mm 1.85:1.*

EXORCIST III (William Peter Blatty, 1990)—but they did little more than return their negative costs (their rental earnings were $5.62, $13.9, and $11.5 million, respectively). Yet, as Larry Gross points out, the films themselves virtually invented two genres that became commercial norms and have helped to sustain Hollywood ever since—the visceral, high-speed action movie and the A-budget, effects-laden horror film.[103]

BOB RAFELSON

Although he never directed a megahit like Friedkin or acquired the art-film cachet of Bogdanovich, Bob Rafelson for a brief period in the early 1970s was regarded as one of the most important directors in the business, both for his own work and for his participation in BBS Productions. Rafelson began as a writer-producer for television, working for David Susskind, Desilu, and finally Screen Gems/Columbia, where he met Bert Schneider and formed Raybert Productions with him in 1965. Raybert, which would become BBS ("Bert, Bob, and Steve") with the addition of Steve Blauner to the partnership in 1969, first produced the hit television series *The Monkees*, a show about a rock group inspired by the style and substance of Richard Lester's Beatles film A HARD DAY'S NIGHT (1964). The series ran for two years on ABC (September 12, 1966–August 19, 1968), elevated the Monkees to best-selling recording artists, and inspired Rafelson's

Jack Nicholson is Bobby Dupea (aka Robert Eroica Dupea), a classical pianist turned oilrigger who probes the mysteries of identity in Bob Rafelson's FIVE EASY PIECES *(BBS/Columbia, 1970)—the film whose prestigious success put BBS briefly on the map. 35mm 1.75:1.*

first feature HEAD (1968), a psychedelic fantasy on the theme of pop stardom written by Rafelson and Jack Nicholson. Raybert's first and only feature film was EASY RIDER (co-produced with Peter Fonda's newly formed Pando Productions), the three-hour rough cut of which Rafelson and Schneider reduced to 94 minutes to create the film that catalyzed the "youth-cult" boom by returning $19.2 million on its $375,000 investment.[104] Raybert then became BBS, and the stunning success of EASY RIDER gave the new production company enough clout to strike a deal with Columbia Pictures in late 1969 to finance and distribute six films of its choice (a deal that was assisted by the fact that Bert Schneider's father, Abe, was chairman of the Columbia Pictures board, and his older brother Stanley was studio president). So long as the budgets stayed under $1 million per picture, Columbia had no right of project approval, which left BBS free to pursue the small-scale, high-quality films for which it became briefly famous in the early 1970s.

The first of these was Rafelson's FIVE EASY PIECES (1970), an off-beat character study in the form of a road movie but with the pacing of a European art film. Starring Jack Nicholson, and written by Rafelson and Carole Eastman (under her psuedonym "Adrien Joyce"), FIVE EASY PIECES won much critical recognition, including four Oscar nominations and the New York Critics awards for Best Film, Best Director, and Best Supporting Actress (Karen Black). In all these respects it nearly perfectly fulfilled the BBS mission to inspire a "Hollywood New Wave" whose metier would be artistically ambitious, low-budget films involving new talent. Three other BBS productions were released— Bogdanovich's THE LAST PICTURE SHOW (1971), Henry Jaglom's directorial debut A SAFE PLACE (1971), and Jack Nicholson's directorial debut DRIVE, HE SAID (1972)—before Rafelson made his second and last BBS film, THE KING OF MARVIN GARDENS (1972),

Ellen Burstyn and Jack Nicholson in Rafelson's THE KING OF MARVIN GARDENS *(BBS/Columbia, 1972), an original character study that puzzled critics and audiences alike. 35mm 1.75:1.*

from an original script by *Esquire* critic Jacob Brackman. Inventively photographed by Laszlo Kovacs, who had also shot FIVE EASY PIECES,[105] this highly original and eccentric study of the relationship of two brothers living in Atlantic City had little mass appeal— unlike its predecessor, whose youth-culture orientation had garnered $8.9 million in rentals and made it the thirteenth highest grossing film of 1970. Critics were puzzled, and the film's poor box-office showing helped to hasten the demise of BBS, whose contract with Columbia was cancelled when David Begelman replaced Stanley Schneider as studio president in 1973. (Schneider then became an independent producer; he died of a heart attack on January 22, 1975, on location in New York City for THREE DAYS OF THE CONDOR—five days short of his forty-sixth birthday; see Chapter 6.)[106]

Rafelson attempted to make his next film, an adaptation of Charles Gaines's novel *Stay Hungry*, more accessible by collaborating with Gaines on the screenplay, having co-written the stories for his two BBS features with professional scenarists. (He coproduced the film with Bert Schneider's younger brother Harold, a former BBS colleague— Rafelson produced or coproduced all of his films from HEAD through THE POSTMAN ALWAYS RINGS TWICE [1981].)[107] STAY HUNGRY (United Artists, 1976),which revolves around the culture of body-building in contemporary Birmingham, Alabama, is more tightly structured than Rafelson's earlier work and was welcomed by critics like Stephen Farber, who lauded it for embracing "moral and human values" but wondered whether it could appeal to an audience "battered by sensationalism and addicted to block-busters."[108] Predictably, it didn't, and after an abortive attempt to adapt Peter Matthiessen's novel *At Play in the Fields of the Lord* (1965) for MGM, Rafelson contracted with Fox to direct Robert Redford in the prison exposé BRUBAKER (Stuart Rosenberg, 1980). After a violent argument with Fox vice president Richard Berger, he was fired from the set less than two weeks into principal photography. Over the next two decades, Rafelson worked sporadically for Lorimar (THE POSTMAN ALWAYS RINGS TWICE [1981]), for Fox again (BLACK WIDOW [1987]), and for Carolco (MOUNTAINS OF THE MOON [1990]), but he never regained the stature he had achieved in pre-JAWS Hollywood when the BBS model looked like one of several possible industry futures.

HAL ASHBY

Like Rafelson, Hal Ashby was regarded as a director of serious artistic intent for much of the 1970s, but one who could also produce a box-office score. The critical success of films like THE LAST DETAIL (Columbia, 1973) and BOUND FOR GLORY (United Artists, 1976) gave him a reputation for high originality and social consciousness, while the commercial success of films like SHAMPOO (Columbia, 1975) and COMING HOME (United Artists, 1978) placed him in the first rank of industry talent. He had been an editor during the 1960s, winning an Oscar for his work on Norman Jewison's IN THE HEAT OF THE NIGHT (United Artists/Mirisch, 1967), and his first film as a director was an unconventional social satire on racial attitudes in contemporary New York entitled THE LANDLORD (United Artists/Mirisch, 1970), which he took over from Jewison when the older director left the project. Ashby's second film, HAROLD AND MAUDE (Paramount, 1971), signaled a unique sensibility that was coolly received by mainstream critics but appreciated almost immediately on college campuses. A dark comedy about the sexual liaison between a death-obsessed twenty-year-old man and a free-wheeling seventy-nine-year-old concentration camp survivor, HAROLD AND MAUDE was dismissed in 1971 by *Variety* as having "all the fun and gaiety of a burning orphanage" but has since become a cult classic.[109]

Ruth Gordon in Hal Ashby's black comedy HAROLD AND MAUDE *(Paramount, 1971).
35mm 1.85:1.*

There was nothing but praise, however, for THE LAST DETAIL, a picaresque comedy-drama about two junior Naval officers (Jack Nicholson and Otis Young) escorting a convicted thief (Randy Quaid) from their base in West Virginia to a military prison in Massachusetts, where he is sentenced to serve an eight-year term for petty theft. Written by Robert Towne, who would become one the 1970s' most respected and successful screenwriters, the film is riven with profanity (including "forty-seven 'mother-fuckers,'" according to Towne)—which still had a salient shock value for audiences in 1973. In fact, profanity and other forms of vulgar speech would become an important means of product differentiation between theatrical films and television as the decade wore on; and under CARA rules, sexually derived expletives triggered an automatic R rating.[110] (Furthermore, since such language could be easily deleted or modified by editing the sound track, the practice of writing it into film scripts did not inhibit ancillary sales to television, where it could be cut, overdubbed, or "bleeped.") The disparity between Quaid's crime and his punishment gives THE LAST DETAIL a melancholy undertone, even as his escorts' determination to show him a good time on the way to prison produces hilarious results. Nicholson, Quaid, and Towne were all nominated for Oscars, and the film established Ashby as a director of substance, as well as earning a respectable $4,745,000. Towne and Ashby collaborated again on the hit comedy SHAMPOO—at once a sex farce and a satire on the shallowness of American, and, especially, Hollywood, values—set on the eve of Richard Nixon's election as president in 1968. Produced and co-written by Warren Beatty (who also stars, with Julie Christie

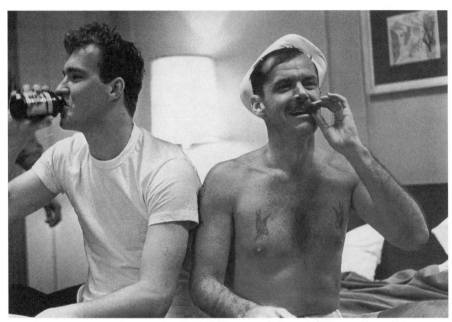

Otis Young and Jack Nicholson as foul-mouthed sailors escorting one of their own to the Naval prison in Portsmouth, Massachusetts, in Ashby's THE LAST DETAIL *(Columbia, 1973). The end-to-end profanity of Robert Towne's Oscar-nominated script was a novelty and box-office draw for early 1970s audiences. 35mm 1.85:1.*

Julie Christie and Warren Beatty in SHAMPOO *(Columbia, 1975), another Hal Ashby-Robert Towne collaboration, whose sophisticated blend of sex farce and political satire made it a mid-1970s hit. 35mm 1.85:1.*

and Goldie Hawn), the film is both aggressively sexy and politically hip, and it was extremely popular with contemporary audiences—benefiting unquestionably from post-Watergate cynicism about American society. SHAMPOO was nominated for four Oscars, and, with $24.5 million in rentals, became the third-highest earner in a year of megahits (e.g., JAWS, with $129.5 million, and ONE FLEW OVER THE CUCKOO'S NEST, with $60 million).

Now Ashby was in a position to choose his own material, so he opted for a biopic of the Depression-era folksinger and labor activist Woody Guthrie, based on portions of his autobiography. Notable for its Technicolor-like cinematography by Haskell Wexler, and early use of Garrett Brown's Steadicam (see Chapter 9), as well as for its period detail, BOUND FOR GLORY was a *succès d'estime* but a box-office loser, suggesting that the era of the counterculture and radical chic was over. (Just seven years earlier, Arthur's Penn's ALICE'S RESTAURANT [1969]—arguably a biopic about Woody's son Arlo—in which the elder Guthrie actually appears, was a success precisely *because* of its countercultural appeal.) BOUND FOR GLORY was nominated for six Academy Awards, including Best Picture, and won two (Best Cinematography and Best Original Score). Typically, Ashby's final films of the decade were straws in the wind of industry change. COMING HOME was among the first films to confront the effects of the war in Vietnam, which had ended officially in 1975 but was still very much an open wound on the body politic. Deliberately melodramatic, the film treats the plight of paraplegic veterans without sentimentality and

David Carradine as Woody Guthrie in Hal Ashby's reverential biopic BOUND FOR GLORY *(UA, 1976). 35mm 1.85:1.*

Anger flairs in Hal Ashby's COMING HOME *(UA, 1978), one of the first films to openly confront the consequences of the war in Vietnam: Jane Fonda, Bruce Dern. 35mm 1.85:1.*

registers the nation's general disillusionment with the war. Like its predecessor, COMING HOME received multiple Oscar nominations (eight, winning for Best Actor [Jon Voight], Best Actress [Jane Fonda], and Best Screenplay [Nancy Dowd, Waldo Salt, Robert C. Jones]), including Ashby's first and only as Best Director. It was more successful commercially than BOUND FOR GLORY (returning $13,470,505 in rentals), probably owing to the presence of Fonda, a bankable star whose early and highly publicized opposition to the war made her a natural for the film's lead. BEING THERE (United Artists, 1979) was adapted by Jerzy Kosinski from his own novel about an *idiot savant* gardener whose knowledge of the world comes exclusively from television—as was figuratively the case for many Americans by the end of the 1970s. (Indeed, with the average viewer watching seven hours a day, the pervasiveness of television in daily life was such that concern about its effects had reached the level of a public policy debate.) Yet despite the casting of an eminently bankable Peter Sellers as the gardener (a role he had longed to play since publication of the novel and for which he received an Oscar nomination), BEING THERE was only a modest commercial success, earning just over $11 million in rentals.

Like those of so many other directors examined in this chapter, Ashby's career, virtually stellar in 1975, was effectively over by the decade's end. He made five more films

Novelist Jerzy Kozsinski and Hal Ashby on the set of Being There *(UA, 1979), a parable about the pervasive effects of television on American society.*

before his death from liver cancer in 1988, only one of which—a skillfully edited Rolling Stones concert film entitled LET'S SPEND THE NIGHT TOGETHER (1982)—earned more than $1 million (and only $1.5 million at that), and none of which was even remotely successful with critics. Although his decline was probably hastened by drug problems, it neatly paralleled the course of the film industry as its emphasis shifted from youth appeal and novelty to mass appeal and strategic marketing. Along the way, however, Ashby produced brilliant collaborations with some of the industry's most innovative cinematographers—Gordon Willis (THE LANDLORD), John Alonzo (HAROLD AND MAUDE), Michael Chapman (THE LAST DETAIL), Laszlo Kovacs (SHAMPOO), Haskell Wexler (BOUND FOR GLORY, COMING HOME), and Caleb Deschanel (BEING THERE)—and he made three of the decade's most critically acclaimed films. As late as 1976, Joseph McBride could write: "Ashby deserves to be ranked with Coppola and Altman in the forefront of the Hollywood directors who have emerged in the Seventies."[111]

ALAN PAKULA

Alan Pakula was a successful producer[112] before directing his first film, a youth market vehicle called THE STERILE CUCKOO (Paramount, 1969), best remembered for Liza Minnelli's debut performance in the lead (for which she received an Oscar nomination as Best Actress). But it was critical acclaim for his thriller KLUTE (Warner Bros., 1971),

Charles Cioffi and Jane Fonda in Alan Pakula's KLUTE *(Warners, 1971). Fonda won an Oscar for her performance as the high-class hooker Bree Daniels. 35mm Panavision anamorphic.*

in which he directed Jane Fonda to an Oscar-winning performance as the neurotic call-girl Bree Daniels, that created the perception of Pakula as an important auteur. This was confirmed by THE PARALLAX VIEW (Paramount, 1974) whose edgy, paranoid vision of an America clandestinely ruled by assassination resonated perfectly with the sinister reve-lations of the Senate Watergate hearings.[113] Its critical impact was great, moving *Film Comment* to remark "There is no more classical filmmaker than Alan J. Pakula at work in the American cinema today."[114] But, whereas KLUTE had earned $7 million in rentals, PARALLAX was doomed by its downbeat ending. It was Pakula's affinity for political mate-rial that led the producers of ALL THE PRESIDENT'S MEN (Warner Bros., 1976) to hire him to direct the film version of the best-selling account of how Bob Woodward and Carl Bernstein cracked the Watergate cover-up. With its skillful building of suspense (no easy job, given that virtually every sentient American knew the story's outcome) and doc-umentary-like respect for the facts, ALL THE PRESIDENT'S MEN was a huge popular and critical success, earning $31 million on an $8.5-million investment and placing fourth at the box office in the phenomenal year of ROCKY (John G. Avildsen), KING KONG (John Guillermin), and A STAR IS BORN (Frank Pierson). It received multiple Oscar nomina-tions (including Best Picture and Best Director) and won four, including one for William Goldman's screenplay; and it was named Best Film by the New York Critics. Pakula fell from this peak with COMES A HORSEMAN (United Artists, 1978), a sort of *noir* Western set in postwar Montana that barely broke even with $4.2 in rentals, despite stunning location photography by Gordon Willis and the presence of Jane Fonda and Jason

The aftermath of a political assassination at Seattle's Space Needle in THE PARALLAX VIEW *(Warners, 1974), Alan Pakula's archetypal paranoid conspiracy thriller. Like* KLUTE *and* ALL THE PRESIDENT'S MEN, *the mood of* PARALLAX *was enhanced by Gordon Willis's brooding, richly textured cinematography. 35mm Panavision anamorphic.*

Robert Redford as Bob Woodward in Alan Pakula's ALL THE PRESIDENT'S MEN *(Warners, 1976), adapted by William Goldman from Woodward and Carl Bernstein's best-selling account of how they broke the Watergate cover-up story as reporters for the* Washington Post. *(Redford also coproduced, with Pakula, and Goldman won an Oscar for his screenplay.) 35mm 1.85:1.*

Jane Fonda and James Caan in Alan Pakula's unique postwar noir Western COMES A
HORSEMAN *(UA, 1978). 35mm Panavision anamorphic.*

Alan Bates and Jill Clayburgh in STARTING OVER *(Paramount, 1979), Pakula's entry in
the late 1970s "comedy of divorce" cycle. 35mm 1.85:1.*

Robards (who had just won Best Supporting Actor for ALL THE PRESIDENT'S MEN). The mildly popular STARTING OVER (Paramount, 1979), a "comedy of divorce" with then-bankable stars Burt Reynolds and Jill Clayburgh, returned $19.1 million and was Pakula's last commercially successful film until PRESUMED INNOCENT (Warner Bros., 1990) eleven years later. He had one modest critical success in SOPHIE'S CHOICE (1982), adapted from William Styron's prize-winning novel, but he was never again regarded as anything more than a competent technician—which, perhaps, is all he ever was. But during the 1970s Pakula was generally thought to be an artist of uncompromising vision, and he briefly became one of the American cinema's most influential figures.

Niche Figures

There are several other directors whose career trajectories conform in whole or part to this pattern but whose work has been especially genre-specific, notably Paul Mazursky (b. 1930), Bob Fosse (1927–1987), Woody Allen (b. 1935), and Mel Brooks (b. 1926).

PAUL MAZURSKY

A former actor and screenwriter, Mazursky produced a hit in his first film as a director—BOB & CAROL & TED & ALICE (Columbia, 1969), a modish comedy about (attempted) wife-swapping which he co-wrote with his longtime collaborator Larry Tucker. It became the sixth highest earning film of 1969, returning $14.6 million in rentals—a figure that would barely cover prints and marketing costs only a few years later—and it was nominated for four Oscars, including one for its story and screenplay. On the strength of this success, Mazursky was able to find financing during the 1970s for a series of original, eccentric comedies that barely registered at the box office—ALEX IN WONDERLAND (MGM, 1970—under $1 million), BLUME IN LOVE (Warner Bros., 1973—$3 million), HARRY AND TONTO (Fox, 1974—$4.6 million—for which Art Carney won an Academy Award for Best Actor), and NEXT STOP, GREENWICH VILLAGE (Fox, 1976—under $1 million). The relative success of AN UNMARRIED WOMAN (Fox, 1978), which earned $12 million and was nominated for three Academy Awards (including two for Mazursky—as producer [Best Film} and writer [Best Original Screenplay]), kept him in the game. Yet, with the exception of DOWN AND OUT IN BEVERLY HILLS (Buena Vista, 1986), a contemporary reworking of Renoir's anti-bourgeoise satire BOUDU SAVED FROM DROWNING (1932) that earned $28.3 million—real money even in the mid-1980s—Mazursky's subsequent work was both commercially and aesthetically disappointing (TEMPEST [1982]; MOON OVER PARADOR [1988]) and sometimes barely adequate (SCENES FROM A MALL [1991]; THE PICKEL [1993]). In true auteur fashion, Mazursky produced, directed, and wrote or co-wrote all of his films of the 1970s and after. But the creative environment that nurtured his talents in the early years of the decade had all but disappeared by its conclusion, and the grosses for his 1970s films, which would have been respectable by 1960s (and earlier) standards, were paltry compared to the rolling thunder of blockbuster revenues.

BOB FOSSE

Bob Fosse was a dancer and choreographer who choreographed numerous successful Broadway musicals and their Hollywood adaptations (for example, Warner Bros.' THE

Joel Grey (as Master of Ceremonies) performs with the Kit Kat Club Girls in Bob Fosse's CABARET (ABC/Allied Artists, 1972). 35mm 1.85:1.

PAJAMA GAME [George Abbott and Stanley Donen, 1957] and DAMN YANKEES [Abbott and Donen, 1958]), before directing the film version of SWEET CHARITY for Universal in 1969. A critical success that earned a disappointing $4 million, the film received three Oscar nominations (for Art Direction, Score, and Costume Design) and lent Fosse enough political capital within the industry to raise the real capital for CABARET (ABC/Allied Artists, 1972), a film version of the John Masteroff-Fred Ebb-John Kander Broadway musical adapted from the John van Druten stage play *I Am a Camera* (1952), itself adapted from Christopher Isherwood's *Goodbye to Berlin* (1939). Returning to the original source and contextualizing the musical numbers as stage performances, Fosse made the film a chilling account of Nazism's gradual encroachment on daily German life, as well as a spectacularly energized showcase for the musical talents of its stars Liza Minnelli and Joel Grey. CABARET became the sixth highest earning film of 1972, returning over $20 million, and it was nominated for ten Academy Awards, eight of which it won (Actress, Supporting Actor, Director, Cinematography [Geoffrey Unsworth], Art Direction, Sound, Score Adaptation, Film Editing)—THE GODFATHER took Best Picture and Best Screenplay. The credit went largely to Fosse, who had turned the film in the direction of serious social criticism, orchestrated its remarkable choreography, and directed the Oscar-winning performances of Minnelli and Grey. Hailed now as an auteur who had reinvigorated the musical genre, Fosse attempted to do the same for the biopic with his version of *Lenny*, Julian Barry's play about the life of the controversial nightclub comedian Lenny Bruce. Shot in black-and-white in semi-documentary style, LENNY

(United Artists, 1974) was well received critically but did less well at the box office ($11.5 million) because of its grimness. Fosse and his film were again both nominated for Academy Awards, as were its stars (Dustin Hoffman and Valerie Perrine), cinematographer (Bruce Surtees), and screenplay (Julian Barry), but received none. Ever restless, he returned to choreography and stage direction and underwent open-heart surgery in 1978, the aesthetic result of which was ALL THAT JAZZ (1979), coproduced by 20th Century–Fox and Columbia and distributed by Fox. This semi-autobiographical account of a frenetically driven, self-destructive Broadway director was compared almost immediately to Fellini's 8½ (1963), invoking the auteurist standard of the

Roy Scheider as the megalomaniacal director/choreographer Joe Gideon in a fantasy sequence from Bob Fosse's self-reflective (and autobiographical) ALL THAT JAZZ (Columbia/Fox, 1979). 35mm 1.85.1.

European art cinema, and, indeed, its hallucinatory mixture of fantasy and reality
sequences sometimes brings it close to that. Despite its surrealistic excess, ALL THAT
JAZZ was a popular success, if not a hit, earning $20 million in rentals, and it brought
Fosse his third Oscar nomination for direction in a row (as well as eight others, four of
which—Art Direction, Score, Film Editing, and Costume Design—it won). Fosse continued to work in Broadway theater and made one more film—STAR 80 (Ladd/Warner,
1983)—a non-musical film about the murder of Dorothy Stratten—before his death
from a heart attack in 1987. Although his profile as a film director was enhanced by his
reputation as a stage director, there is no question that Fosse's film career benefited
immensely from the auteurist climate of the early 1970s. Of the three films he made
during the decade, only one was a clear box-office hit, yet Fosse was one of the few people in the history of the Academy Awards to be nominated as Best Director for three
consecutive productions. The perception that he was a "great director" overshadowed
all other features of his work—which in hindsight seems considerably uneven—and
enabled him to work in the industry under his own terms until he died.

WOODY ALLEN

Woody Allen (born Allen Stewart Konigsberg) worked as a performer, playwright (*Don't
Drink the Water,* 1965), and screenplay writer (WHAT'S NEW, PUSSYCAT? [Clive Donner,
1965]), before he directed and wrote his first feature TAKE THE MONEY AND RUN (1969),
a pseudo-documentary parody of crime and prison movies, in which he also starred.[115]
Made for under $2 million and distributed by the mini-major Cinerama Releasing
Corp., the film turned a profit of $1 million, and earned Allen a three-film contract as a
director-writer-actor with United Artists. This deal yielded BANANAS (1971), a satire on
revolutionary politics in a Latin American dictatorship, a comic adaptation of Dr. David
Reuben's best-selling EVERYTHING YOU ALWAYS WANTED TO KNOW ABOUT SEX (BUT
WERE AFRAID TO ASK) (1972), and the Orwellian science fiction parody SLEEPER (1973).
These films made enough money among them ($3.5 million, $8.8 million, and $8.25 mil-
lion in rentals, respectively) to continue Allen's association with United Artists for the
rest of the decade, during which he made four more films. LOVE AND DEATH (1975; $6.9
million in rentals) continued in the parodic vein of his earlier work, sending up Tolstoi's
War and Peace (1864–1869), Eisensteinian montage, David Lean's film of DR. ZHIVAGO
(1965), and other cultural icons, high and low. But Allen sailed emphatically into the
contemporary mainstream with the romantic comedy ANNIE HALL (1977) which,
released without advance publicity, earned $19 million and won Academy Awards for
Best Picture, Best Director, Best Actress (Diane Keaton), and Best Screenplay (Allen
and Marshall Brickman).[116] Chameleon-like, Allen now challenged both audiences and
critics with a deliberately Bergmanesque psychodrama of disintegrating relationships
within a *haute bourgeoise* family entitled INTERIORS (1978). This homage to his acknowledged mentor, and to the European art film in general, was followed by MANHATTAN
(1979), which many see as Allen's most accomplished work. Offering both a paeonic
vision of New York City—lyrically photographed in black-and-white Panavision by
Gordon Willis—and a biting satire of 1970s Manhattan lifestyles, the film was nearly as
successful as ANNIE HALL (it earned $17.5 million in rentals), and it established Allen as
a serious auteur at the very time auteurism was receding as an industry fashion. He was
able to sustain this appropriate irony for the next decade, working with a close group of

Woody Allen and the Grim Reaper in LOVE AND DEATH *(UA, 1973), a riff on Tolstoi's* WAR AND PEACE. *35mm 1.85:1.*

Diane Keaton and Woody Allen in ANNIE HALL *(UA, 1977), a comic "anti-blockbuster" about personal relationships, which was released without advance publicity but became the year's thirteenth-highest earner and won four major Academy Awards. 35mm 1.85:1.*

Diane Keaton, Kristin Griffith, and Mary Beth Hurt as the three sisters in
INTERIORS *(UA, 1978), Woody Allen's testament to the influence of Ingmar*
Bergman. 35mm 1.85:1.

Woody Allen and Diane Keaton silhouetted against the backdrop of the sculpture
garden at the Museum of Modern Art in MANHATTAN *(UA, 1979). Photographed in*
black-and-white (by Gordon Willis, who also shot ANNIE HALL *and* INTERIORS*) to*
evoke the New York of George Gershwin, whose music comprises the film's score.
35mm Panavision anamorphic.

New York-based collaborators (producers Charles H. Joffe and Robert Greenhut; co-writer Marshall Brickman; the actresses Diane Keaton and Mia Farrow; cinematographers Gordon Willis and Carlo Di Palma), distributing through Orion and, later, Columbia-TriStar and Miramax.[117] During the 1970s, ANNIE HALL notwithstanding, Allen was able to position himself as an East Coast alternative to Hollywood production practice, and to shift his public image from that of a comic to that of an artist. Inevitably, the prestige conferred upon the figure of the writer-director by the auteur theory helped to cultivate the popular perception of him as an independent, intellectual filmmaker removed from the mainstream, which his regular invocations of Bergman and the art film tradition served to punctuate.[118]

MEL BROOKS

Mel Brooks was a comic and a television writer (*Get Smart*, 1965–1968; co-written with Buck Henry) before he wrote and directed THE PRODUCERS (Embassy, 1967), an outrageous farce about two swindlers, played by Zero Mostel and Gene Wilder, who sell 25,000-percent interest in a musical comedy (*Springtime for Hitler*) designed to fail, but which unpredictably becomes a hit. Nominated for two Oscars (Best Screenplay, Best Supporting Actor), THE PRODUCERS earned less than $1 million but its critical success helped Brooks raise the funds to make THE TWELVE CHAIRS (UMC, 1970), based on a comic Russian novel set in the 1920s. This movie lost most of its investment, and Brooks

Gene Wilder as an aging gunfighter and Cleavon Little as the local sheriff in Mel Brooks's BLAZING SADDLES (Warners, 1974), whose huge popular success established the genre parody as the decade's central comic mode. 35mm Panavision anamorphic.

had to wait another three years to find backing for his breakthrough film BLAZING SADDLES (Warner Bros., 1974). A lewd, libidinous, and occasionally hilarious parody of the classical Western, this film was a phenomenal commercial hit, earning $47.8 million in rentals and three Academy Award nominations (including Best Supporting Actress for Madeline Kahn). Although *Variety* characterized it as "essentially a raunchy, protracted version of a television comedy skit,"[119] BLAZING SADDLES almost single-handedly established the genre parody as the paradigmatic form of 1970s film comedy, and Brooks shrewdly followed it with another one. YOUNG FRANKENSTEIN (Fox, 1974) was a send-up of 1930s Universal horror films (as well as studio-era biopics like MGM's YOUNG TOM EDISON [1940])—specifically James Whale's FRANKENSTEIN (1931) and BRIDE OF FRANKENSTEIN (1935), and Rowland V. Lee's SON OF FRANKENSTEIN (1939)—that managed to achieve a nearly perfect balance between parody and homage. In cinematography, lighting, and set design, in fact, Brooks sustained an atmosphere of brooding horror that honored the original films, even as his dialogue made mincemeat of their hoary plot conventions. Like BLAZING SADDLES, YOUNG FRANKENSTEIN did terrific box office, earning over $30 million in rentals (as well an another Oscar nomination for Brooks [and Gene Wilder] for Best Screenplay), and Brooks suddenly found himself the writer-director of the second and seventh highest grossing films of 1974. He stayed in play with his last two films of the decade, but was unable to sustain his remarkable string of hits into

Peter Boyle as the Monster, Gene Wilder as Frederick Frankenstein, Terri Garr as his assistant Inga in Mel Brooks's YOUNG FRANKENSTEIN (Fox, 1974). *Photographed in black-and-white, by Gerald Hirschfield, to evoke Universal horror films from the 1930s. (The lab equipment was actually the same used in Universal's original* FRANKENSTEIN *films.) 35mm 1.85:1.*

Mel Brooks in the Hitchcock parody HIGH ANXIETY (Fox, 1977): here, a "quotation" from THE BIRDS (1963). 35mm 1.85:1.

the 1980s. SILENT MOVIE (Fox, 1976)—which is literally silent except for a musical score, sound effects, and a single spoken word—was less a parody than an attempt to resurrect silent slapstick comedy, although it also works as a satire on the Byzantine business practices of contemporary Hollywood (the plot revolves around the attempted takeover of a studio by a conglomerate named Engulf & Devour—clearly Gulf & Western). SILENT MOVIE earned $21.2 million and was the tenth most profitable film of 1976, while Brooks's Hitchcock parody HIGH ANXIETY (Fox, 1977) was twelfth for 1977 with $19.2 million. In 1980, Brooks formed his own production company, Brooksfilms, but he never approximated the critical or commercial success of the 1970s films again, both because his style of parody had been replicated *ad nauseam* by television shows like *Saturday Night Live,* and because many of his early collaborators (Gene Wilder, Madeline Kahn) had gone off in their own directions. Another reason, however, is that Hollywood's corporate leadership had discovered that "kid" and teenage "gross-out" comedy could draw much larger audiences than comedy intended primarily for adults, however low-pitched, making Brooks's unique directorial appeal obsolete as a mass-market industry resource.

Eccentrics

Two directors whose work is unequivocally connected with American cinema in the 1970s but who remained resolutely outside of the mainstream are John Cassavetes and

Terrence Malick. Both were eccentric talents who flirted briefly with industry careers but chafed under Hollywood's commercial constraints to the extent that Cassavetes moved completely into low-budget independent filmmaking during the 1970s and Malick quit making films altogether by the decade's end.

JOHN CASSAVETES

Cassavetes (1929–1989) was trained as an actor and rose to prominence as a writer-director with his *cinema verité*-style 16mm feature SHADOWS (1960). Hailed as a break-through for alternative cinema, the film won several festival prizes (including the Critics Award at Venice) and earned Cassavetes a contract with Paramount. After one theatrical feature for that studio (TOO LATE BLUES [1962]) and another for independent producer Stanley Kramer (A CHILD IS WAITING [1963]—which he disowned after Kramer recut it), he returned to 16mm semi-documentary production with FACES (1968), which earned enough critical acclaim (three Oscar nominations, including one for Cassavetes's screen-play) and money—together with his acting in such mainstream films as THE DIRTY DOZEN (Robert Aldrich, 1967) and ROSEMARY'S BABY (Roman Polanski, 1968)—for him to shoot HUSBANDS (1970) in 35mm and color. FACES was self-distributed but HUSBANDS was picked up by Columbia as part of its search for alternative markets; both films were intense, if sometimes clumsy and self-indulgent, psychodramas about middle-class mar-riages in crisis. MINNIE AND MOSKOWITZ (1971), financed by Universal, was closer in tone to a 1930s-style screwball "comedy of remarriage" but was successful with neither audi-

John Cassavetes directing HUSBANDS *(Columbia, 1970). 35mm 1.85:1.*

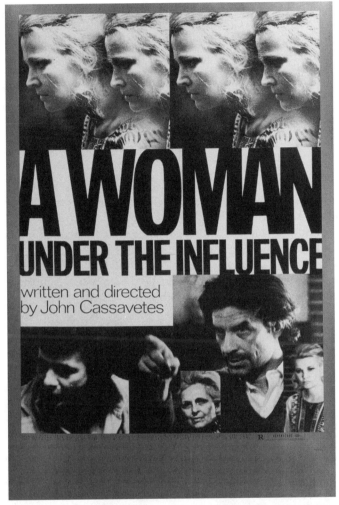

Graphically bold poster for A WOMAN UNDER THE INFLUENCE
(Faces International, 1974), Cassavetes's most disciplined
film and his biggest hit. Gena Rowlands at top; Peter Falk,
lower left; Cassavetes, lower right.

ences nor critics. By contrast, A WOMAN UNDER THE INFLUENCE (1974) nearly
approached the status of a hit. Working atypically from a prepared script, Cassavetes
delivered a wrenching film about a housewife's nervous breakdown, with stunning performances by his frequent collaborators Gena Rowlands (also his wife) and Peter Falk.
The cast and crew worked on deferred salaries, and the film was personally financed by
Cassavetes and Falk, who also self-distributed it through their newly formed company
Faces International. A WOMAN UNDER THE INFLUENCE became Cassavetes's biggest hit;
and he and Rowlands were both nominated for Academy Awards. With THE KILLING OF
A CHINESE BOOKIE (1976) and OPENING NIGHT (1977), however, the director returned to
the loosely plotted, improvisational style of his early work with poor results, although he

and Rowlands excelled as costars in the latter. Cassavetes's last film of the decade was the considerably more accessible GLORIA (1980), produced for Columbia, in which Rowlands plays a former gangster's moll who becomes the protector of an eight-year-old boy after the mob has killed his parents, earning another Oscar nomination for the part. Cassavetes once remarked that he was more interested in "the people who work with me than in the film itself, or in cinema," and his work is shot through with this sentiment. Personal, at worst, to the point of solipsism, his films are sometimes incoherent in terms of narrative and jagged in technique, but they can also achieve a disturbing intensity of emotion that is virtually unique in the American cinema.

TERRENCE MALICK

Terrence Malick (b. 1945), on the other hand, achieved a kind of aesthetic distance in his two films of the 1970s that is equally rare. Malick attended the AFI's Center for Advanced Film Studies and worked on several scripts (including, reputedly, those of DRIVE, HE SAID [Jack Nicholson, 1972] and DIRTY HARRY [Don Siegel, 1972]) before receiving his first screen credit for writing POCKET MONEY (Stuart Rosenberg, 1973), a contemporary Western produced by the short-lived First Artists company. He then made an impressive debut as a writer-producer-director with BADLANDS (1973), which was bankrolled by Ed Pressman for about $450,000, minus deferred salaries of approximately

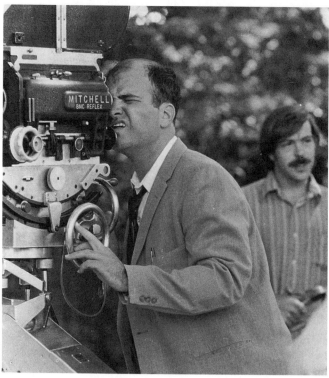

Terrence Malick checking a shot set-up for BADLANDS through the reflex lens of a Mitchell BNC (Pressman/Warners, 1973).

$500,000. (Pressman sold the film to John Calley at Warner Bros. for $1.1 million—considerably less than it returned in rentals.)[120] This generically astute "criminal couple" movie was based on the real-life case of Charles Starkweather and Carol Fugate, who killed ten people during a murder spree in Nebraska in the late 1950s, and it offers an incisive critique of the symbiosis between the mass media and sensational violence that became a template for such later films as NATURAL BORN KILLERS (Oliver Stone, 1994). By turns moody and ironic, BADLANDS was critically acclaimed but unpopular, and it took Malick years to find backing for his next and apparently final project—DAYS OF HEAVEN (1978), independently produced by Bert Schneider for Paramount—a film that has become legendary for its meticulous period recreation and ravishing available-light cinematography by Nestor Almendros. (Photography was completed by Haskell Wexler when

Poster for BADLANDS, *emphasizing lyricism in its imagery and evoking* BONNIE AND CLYDE *(1967) in its text. (*BONNIE AND CLYDE *had the similarly ironic logo: "They're young. They're in love. And they kill people.")*

Richard Gere as a migrant laborer in Terrence Malick's DAYS OF HEAVEN (Paramount, 1978). Panavision spherical 1.85:1, blown up to 70mm for road-showing. Recorded and selectively exhibited in four-channel Dolby stereo optical sound (with six-track stereo magnetic surround sound for 70mm prints).

Almendros had to leave to work on Truffaut's LE CHAMBRE VERTE [THE GREEN ROOM, 1977].) The narrative, which is the least of the film's attractions, concerns a trio of a migrant laborers in the early 1900s who end up working in the fields of a self-made Texas wheat baron and attempt to defraud him through marriage. With fragmentary voice-over exposition and little dialogue, DAYS OF HEAVEN is in many ways an homage to silent cinema, and the imagery itself has a sort of transcendent, Biblical resonance. Production began in the fall of 1976, and Malick's demand that much of the film be shot in "the magic hour" (actually about twenty minutes) of the sun's afterglow made the process agonizingly slow. The editing then took nearly two years, but the finished version caught the attention of Gulf & Western CEO Charles Bluhdorn, and Paramount gave it a premium release in 70mm and six-track Dolby sound.[121] Critics were ecstatic with the result, and the Academy nominated DAYS OF HEAVEN for Best Cinematography (Almendros), Best Sound Recording (John K. Wilkinson, et al.), Best Costume Design (Patricia Norris), and Best Original Score (Ennio Morricone). In an acknowledgement of the film's extraordinary visual beauty, Almendros received the Cinematography award, but once again the public was indifferent, and Malick gave up on Hollywood in 1979, when he left the United States to take up permanent residence in Paris. (In the mid-1990s, Malick returned to commercial filmmaking, developing THE THIN RED LINE [1998] for Sony Pictures, although it was ultimately produced and released by 20th Century–Fox.)

"Film Generation" Auteurs, or
the "Hollywood Brats"

Whereas the generation of directors descended from classical Hollywood had learned filmmaking through apprenticeship or in transmigration from Broadway and the theater, and the recruits of the fifties and sixties were trained in television, many new directors of the seventies had studied *film as film* in university graduate programs and professional schools. They had taken film history, aesthetics, and production as formal academic subjects, and they had learned the technical aspects of production, as well as budgeting and marketing, more thoroughly than any generation before them. Many of them had also apprenticed with producer-director Roger Corman (b. 1926) at American International Pictures (AIP), where low-budget, youth-oriented genre films were the stock in trade. (As a creative exploitation producer in the sixties, Corman scoured the L.A. film schools for cheap local talent, like director Francis Ford Coppola, writers Willard Huyck and John Milius, and producer Gary Kurtz, who were eager to work for non-union wages.) When they began to enter the industry at the turn of the decade, average weekly attendance was approaching an all-time low (it bottomed out at 15.8 million in 1971). By 1975, admissions had recovered and box-office grosses increased by $150 million, and the young auteurs of the "New Hollywood," as everyone was calling it, were leading the major studios into the 1980s in relative prosperity. But this was largely on the strength of several expensively produced blockbusters that reaped windfall profits—THE GODFATHER (Francis Ford Coppola, 1972), JAWS (Steven Spielberg, 1975), STAR WARS (George Lucas, 1977), CLOSE ENCOUNTERS OF THE THIRD KIND (Steven Spielberg, 1977)—the ultimate effect of whose success was to multiply average negative costs nearly five-fold during the decade (from $2 million in 1972 to $9.4 million in 1980) and make directors increasingly dependent on studio financing through commercial banks for production and distribution. This "blockbuster syndrome" caused a trend toward the production of fewer and fewer films, and an attendant increase in advertising and marketing budgets to insure a film's success. Ironically, the decade in which "the film generation took over Hollywood" produced fewer feature films than any before it and witnessed the historic shift whereby the cost of promoting a film actually exceeded the cost of producing it, often by twice the negative cost (see Chapter 3).

The auteur directors of the 1970s—aka the "whiz kids," "*wunderkinder*," and "Hollywood brats"—entered the industry at a time when, as Thomas Schatz has noted, Hollywood was desperately searching for its bearings.[122] What they offered was fresh creative talent and adaptability to a system in the midst of radical change. Their youth guaranteed their ability to address the new audio-visual sensibility of an audience, like themselves, that had grown up watching television. And, as far as the studios were concerned, their relative inexperience as first- and second-time directors meant that they could be hired for much less than established talent. Because of their training, they knew more—conceptually, at least—about the production and marketing of motion pictures than the nonfilm executives, like Charles Bluhdorn (CEO of Gulf & Western) and Ted Ashley (Executive VP of Kinney Services), who had recently taken over the industry, and this academically certified expertise was attractive to new managers who were themselves largely ignorant of the film business. Francis Ford Coppola (b. 1939) was the vanguard figure of this new breed of directors, and he quickly became the mentor of a generation of gifted filmmakers, whose other prominent members include George

Lucas (b. 1945), Steven Spielberg (b. 1946), Martin Scorsese (b. 1942), and Brian De Palma (b. 1940). At a second remove, stand the screenwriters and sometime directors John Milius (b. 1944) and Paul Schrader (b. 1946).

FRANCIS FORD COPPOLA

Coppola received his undergraduate degree in drama at Hofstra University in 1960 and then enrolled in the graduate film program at UCLA. There, he began to work at the fringes of the industry, doing uncredited second-unit direction for Corman and eventually directing DEMENTIA 13 (1963), a horror film shot in Ireland in three days with the cast and crew left over from Corman's THE YOUNG RACERS (1963). After collaborating on several major scripts, both with credit (IS PARIS BURNING? [René Clement, 1966]; THIS PROPERTY IS CONDEMNED [Sydney Pollack, 1966]) and without (REFLECTIONS IN A GOLDEN EYE [John Huston, 1966]), Coppola was able to adapt and direct YOU'RE A BIG BOY NOW (1966) from the comic novel by British writer David Benedictus. Produced by Phil Feldman for the newly merged Warner Bros.-Seven Arts for $800,000, the film was heavily influenced by the style of Richard Lester's A HARD DAY'S NIGHT (1964) and the French New Wave, and Coppola submitted it to UCLA as his masters thesis. Although it didn't break even until its sale to television, YOU'RE A BIG BOY NOW attracted enthusiastic reviews and impressed Warners sufficiently to sign Coppola to direct the $3.5-million musical FINIAN'S RAINBOW (1968), starring Fred Astaire. Based on a twenty-year-old Broadway hit that satirized racial prejudice in the South, the film

Francis Ford Coppola (in striped jacket) directing a tracking shot for THE GODFATHER *(Paramount, 1972) in the streets of New York.*

was ultimately a box-office disappointment, but Coppola had done an extraordinary job of giving it the feel of a big-budget spectacle and Warners blew the film up to 70mm for road-showing.[123] Before the failure (a relative term in these times—the film ultimately earned $5.5 million) of FINIAN'S RAINBOW became clear, the studio staked Coppola to $750,000 for a small personal project entitled THE RAIN PEOPLE (1969), based on his own script about a pregnant Long Island housewife who leaves her husband to go on an odyssey across America. Experimental in form, the film has been hailed as a feminist document before its time; many critics in 1969 applauded its distinctly individualistic nature, and it won first prize at the San Sebastian Film Festival, while barely returning its negative cost. Meanwhile, the EASY RIDER panic had struck at Warners, and Coppola convinced its executives to bankroll his own small studio in San Francisco, American Zoetrope, to develop films for the youth market. (As Jon Lewis notes, the deal was relatively simple: Warners put up $600,000 in exchange for the right of first refusal to any and all American Zoetrope projects.[124])

American Zoetrope (renamed Omni-Zoetrope in 1979, and Zoetrope Studios in 1980), in which Coppola was the only shareholder, was deliberately modeled on the Roger Corman unit at AIP.[125] Within a year of its opening, Coppola had produced his friend George Lucas's first feature, THX-1138 (1971), sponsored John Milius in writing the first script for APOCALYPSE NOW (1979), and become a guiding light of his generation. But Warners hated the rough cut of the Lucas film and demanded repayment of its investment, pushing Zoetrope and Coppola close to bankruptcy. To make ends meet, he co-scripted Fox's megahit PATTON (Franklin Schaffner, 1970), sharing with Edmund G. North that year's Academy Award for Best Original Screenplay. Then he accepted a job directing a project for Paramount based on Mario Puzo's *The Godfather*, a best-selling novel about the Mafia. The studio had conceived THE GODFATHER as a mainstream genre film with blockbuster potential on a modest budget ($6 million), and Coppola was chosen after at least three other directors (Constantin Costa-Gavras, Peter Yates, and Peter Bogdanovich) had tuned it down. He collaborated on the screenplay with Puzo, shot the film on location in New York City in midwinter, and brought the project in a scant $1 million over budget, an impressive achievement given the richly textured results. Assisted by a Paramount advertising blitz and saturation booking, THE GODFATHER (1972) became the first great blockbuster of the 1970s, earning $86.3 million in rentals to become the fifth highest grossing film of the decade (it was briefly the highest-grossing film in history and for several decades among the top twenty-five).

Coppola's success in turning a studio-produced gangster film into an epic saga of a (crime) family, full of operatic intensity, won Oscars for Best Film, Best Screenplay, and Best Actor (for Marlon Brando's performance in the title role), as well as Academy Award nominations for direction, three supporting performances, sound, editing, and costumes. THE GODFATHER made Coppola a power in Hollywood, and he used his leverage immediately to produce George Lucas's coming-of-age mosaic AMERICAN GRAFFITI (1973) and to direct his own screenplay THE CONVERSATION (1974), a brilliant meditation on electronic surveillance and paranoia stylistically indebted to the European art film—most immediately Michelangelo Antonioni's BLOWUP (1966). Produced by the newly formed Directors Company (see above) and distributed by Paramount, THE CONVERSATION won the Palme d'Or at Cannes, as well as Oscar nominations for best picture, best original screenplay, and sound, but could not compete at home with Coppola's own remarkable sequel THE GODFATHER, PART II (1974), which won the 1974 Best Picture Award, as well as Oscars for Direction, Best Supporting Actor (Robert De Niro),

Screenplay from Another Medium (Coppola and Puzo), Art Direction, and Score. Constructed as a contrapuntal movement between the Corleone family's noble, if violent, past in the early years of the century and its presently corrupt involvement in Batista's Cuba and Las Vegas in the fifties, THE GODFATHER, PART II both continues and enriches the original, portraying an America in which legitimate and illegitimate power are very closely intertwined (suggesting obliquely, in its final moments, the mob's involvement in the assassination of JFK: when family lawyer Tom Hagen tells Michael Corleone that killing rival Hyman Roth is out of the question because "it would be like trying to kill the President," the new Godfather replies, "If anything in this life is certain—if history has taught us anything—it says [*sic*] you can kill anyone"). Produced for $13 million, THE GODFATHER, PART II grossed less than half as much as THE GODFATHER, generating $30.7 million in rentals, but it brought Coppola to the pinnacle of his influence. He had directed the two of the most financially successful films in industry history to date, both of them hailed critically as major contributions to American cinema; he had won five Oscars and become the only director ever to be nominated for two Best Picture and Best Screenplay awards in the same year; and he had founded his own studio and become a beacon to a whole generation of American filmmakers. (For the record, it should be noted that in 1974 he had also written—in three weeks—the screenplay for Paramount's disastrous THE GREAT GATSBY [Jack Clayton, 1974], and had purchased the failing New York-based exhibitor-distributor Cinema 5 Ltd. in the vain hope of distributing his own productions.)[126] George Lucas would say of him: "Francis was the great white knight who made it."[127] John Milius was even more direct: "He subsidized us all. . . . If this generation is to change American cinema, he is

Gene Hackman as surveillance expert Harry Caul in Coppola's THE CONVERSATION
(The Directors Company/Paramount, 1974). 35mm 1.85:1.

to be given the credit, or the discredit. Whichever it may be. . . ."[128] It was in this spirit near the decade's end that Coppola produced Caroll Ballard's THE BLACK STALLION (1979), coproduced Akira Kurosawa's KAGEMUSHA (1980), and distributed the restored version of Abel Gance's silent epic NAPOLEON (1927; 1980) under the Zoetrope banner; and until the studio was sold in 1984 he continued to produce, distribute, and otherwise promote the work of a remarkably eclectic group of filmmakers, including Wim Wenders, Hans Jurgen Syberberg, Jean-Luc Godard, and Paul Schrader.

Coppola's last work as an auteur in the seventies was the legendary Vietnam war film APOCALYPSE NOW (1979), which he also coproduced, co-scripted (with John Milius and Michael Herr) and scored. Budgeted at $12 million and shot on location in the Philippines, the production was plagued by illness, natural disasters, and other logistical problems which nearly tripled its costs (to $32.5 million) and resulted in a flawed, if brilliant, film.[129] APOCALYPSE NOW is a version of Joseph Conrad's short novel "Heart of Darkness" transposed to the hallucinated, horrific landscape of post-Tet Vietnam, whose first two-thirds may be one of the greatest war/antiwar films ever made, but whose conclusion bogs down in a morass of pomposity and metaphysics. Widely viewed as an act of hubristic folly, the film permanently damaged Coppola's position within the industry, although it earned $37.9 million in rentals (making it, not insignificantly, the sixth highest grossing film of 1979 and the thirty-second highest grossing film of the decade), was nominated for eight Academy Awards (winning two—Cinematography [Vittorio Storaro] and Sound [Walter Murch, et al.]), and shared the Palme d'Or at Cannes with Volker Schlöndorff's THE TIN DRUM (1979).

Coppola on location for APOCALYPSE NOW *(UA, 1979), setting up the sequence illustrated on page 63.*

With his share of the APOCALYPSE NOW profits, Coppola purchased the old Hollywood General Studios on Santa Monica Boulevard (built in 1919 and most recently the site of Desilu productions) in March 1980.[130] His plan was to renovate it, renamed Zoetrope Studios, as a state-of-the art facility for alternative production that would actively compete with the majors. Embracing the new technologies, he seriously contemplated distribution of Zoetrope films via satellite for exhibition in high-resolution video, and he planned to release a full slate of features by 1982.[131] (As foolhardy as this may now seem, we should recall that the majors did not fully appropriate satellite distribution until the formation of TriStar Pictures by Columbia, HBO, and CBS in 1983.) Unfortunately, this revolutionary thinking fell victim to Coppola's own megalomania and the reactionary fallout from HEAVEN'S GATE. Zoetrope's first production was Coppola's ONE FROM THE HEART (1982), an expensively stylized musical set in Las Vegas that employed an experimental production technique called "electronic cinema"—basically a method of "pre-visualizing" the film on video so that it could actually be edited before it was shot.[132] Although he claimed that the electronic cinema method cut production time and therefore costs, Coppola spent nearly $27 million to produce the final negative of ONE FROM THE HEART and lost most of it when the distributor (Columbia) pulled the film after seven weeks of release to devastating reviews. Coppola was forced to put Zoetrope Studios up for sale in order to pay off his production loans, but he could not find a buyer until 1984 and remained financially compromised for the rest of the eighties, before recuperating his career in the nineties.[133]

GEORGE LUCAS

George Lucas (b. 1945), Coppola's close friend and protege, traveled a less bumpy road from renegade auteur to industry mainstay. Befriended as a teenager by veteran cinematographer Haskell Wexler (b. 1926), Lucas studied animation at the University of Southern California's Cinema School, working intermittently as a cameraman for Saul Bass and editing documentaries for the USIA, and in 1965 produced the award-winning student film THX-1138: 4EB/ELECTRONIC LABYRINTH, which won first prize in that year's National Student Film Festival. Lucas subsequently won a scholarship to observe production at Warner Bros., where he met Coppola—who was then at work on FINIAN'S RAINBOW (1968)—and became a production associate on THE RAIN PEOPLE (1969). Within a year, Lucas was working on the feature-length version of THX-1138 (1971) that would become the first and only production of American Zoetrope as that studio was originally conceived. Written, directed, and edited by Lucas, with an electronic score by Lalo Schifrin, this chilling vision of an Orwellian future, where TV and drugs have subsumed the individual will and replaced sex, offended Warners, which cut it for distribution[134] and cancelled the entire Zoetrope deal with Coppola (see above). Produced for $777,000, THX-1138 earned only $945,000 in rentals, but attracted considerable praise from critics and contributed to the prestige of Lucas's next project, AMERICAN GRAFFITI (1973). Produced by Gary Kurtz under the new Lucasfilm Ltd. banner for a little over $775,000, with Coppola as executive producer and Wexler as cinematographer, this nostalgic recreation of early '60s adolescence in the suburbs of Los Angeles was shot in twenty-eight days. Full of vintage cars and period music, AMERICAN GRAFFITI was hesitantly released by Universal (which spent only $500,000 for advertising, publicity, and prints—refusing even to dupe them in stereo), but it struck a common chord and went on to earn $55.3 million in domestic rentals. It also

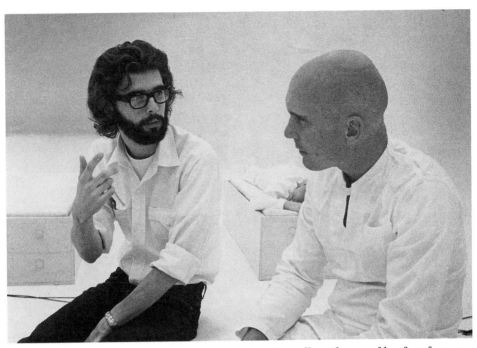

George Lucas, 25, discussing a scene with Robert Duvall on the set of his first feature, THX-1138 (Warners, 1971), which was also the first and only production of American Zoeptrope as Coppola had originally conceived it.

won nominations for five Academy Awards, including best picture, best director, and best screenplay (Lucas, Gloria Katz, and Willard Huyck), and became the source of many television spin-offs, positioning Lucas for the even more astonishing success of his next project, the now legendary STAR WARS (1977).

Three years in preparation, STAR WARS was conceived by Lucas as a folkloristic "space fantasy" with the breathless pace of the cliff-hanging Saturday serials. To counterpoint the fairy-tale quality of its narrative, hyper-realistic special effects were produced at Industrial Light and Magic (ILM), a subsidiary of Lucasfilm founded in Van Nuys in 1975 specifically for this purpose. Here F/X director John Dykstra (b. 1947), who had worked as Douglas Trumbull's assistant on SILENT RUNNING (1972), perfected a computerized motion-control system for traveling matte photography that made the process uniquely cost-effective, enabling Lucas to create hundreds of complicated stop-motion miniature sequences for STAR WARS at a fraction of their cost for earlier films ($2.5 million as compared, for example, with $6.5 million for 2001, which had used far fewer traveling mattes). With live action sequences shot in Tunisia, Death Valley, and EMI-Elstree Studios in England, STAR WARS also became the first film both recorded and released in four-track Dolby stereo. Still, it was produced (by Gary Kurtz) for 20th Century–Fox release for the relatively modest sum of $11.5 million, and neither Lucasfilm nor Fox expected to earn back more than about twice that in domestic rentals, because of the traditionally hard-sell market for science fiction. All were stunned when STAR WARS made almost $3 million in its first week of limited release in May 1977, and by the end

This "arty" shot composition in THX-1138 suggests Lucas's film school training: Robert Duvall in the title role apprehended by a cyborg cop. 35mm Techniscope anamorphic. (Techniscope was a proprietary system developed by Technicolor, Inc., in Rome during the 1960s; it modified the camera movement to expose a two-performation area instead of four, with a half-frame aspect ratio of 2.35:1, which Technicolor blew up in the lab to full-frame anamorphic format. Techniscope was cheaper than CinemaScope or, later, Panavision because it cut film stock expenses in half and didn't require the use of ana- morphic lenses, only additional optical printing in the lab, and it became widely popular in Europe during the 1970s, although it was used only sporadically in the United States.)

of August had grossed \$100 million. The film played continuously throughout 1977–1978, and was officially re-released in 1978 and 1979, by the end of which it had earned \$262 million in rentals worldwide. Moreover, Lucas had designed the film with an eye toward merchandising tie-ins and retained licensing control through Lucasfilm; though he could not possibly have foreseen the bonanza of sales in toys, books, records, posters, and other STAR WARS memorabilia that made him a multimillionaire and turned Lucasfilm Ltd. into a \$30-million corporation. (By decade's end STAR WARS-related mer- chandise would gross far more than the film itself—over \$1 billion retail by most accounts.) Nor could he have imagined that the film would be nominated for ten Academy Awards and receive seven (including Art Direction, Sound, Original Score, Film Editing, Costumes, and Visual Effects), win two Los Angeles Critics Awards, and win three Grammies for its score.

Clearly, STAR WARS was a cultural phenomenon as well as a movie. Its spectacular success enabled Lucas to move to Marin County in northern California, where he estab- lished a state-of-the-art production facility free from the constraints of the major studios in Hollywood, fulfilling a dream shared by him and the members of his generation of

Imperial storm troopers question Luke (Mark Hamill) and Obi-Wan (Alec Guinness) about the provenance of their android passengers, C-3PO and R2D2, in Lucas's phenomenal STAR WARS *(Fox, 1977). 35mm Panavision anamorphic.*

filmmakers. At this point, he abandoned directing to became executive producer of the blockbuster STAR WARS sequels THE EMPIRE STRIKES BACK (Irvin Kershner, 1980) and RETURN OF THE JEDI (Richard Marquand, 1983), both of which were hugely profitable ($142 million and $169 million in rentals, respectively). He was also the inspiration behind Steven Spielberg's lucrative Indiana Jones trilogy—RAIDERS OF THE LOST ARK (1981—$116 million), INDIANA JONES AND THE TEMPLE OF DOOM (1984—$109 million), and INDIANA JONES AND THE LAST CRUSADE (1989—$116 million)—as well as less successful films like Ron Howard's sword-and-sorcery epic WILLOW (1988—$28 million in rentals) and bombs like HOWARD THE DUCK (Willard Huyck, 1986—$10 million). ILM, which revolutionized photographic effects in the STAR WARS era, went on to pioneer computer animation and digital effects in the late eighties and nineties, becoming the major F/X studio in the industry, and Lucasfilm's Skywalker Sound division and its THX Group have had a similar impact on movie sound design and reproduction. Although he directed only three films during the 1970s, George Lucas has since exercised enormous creative and financial influence over the American film industry. He redefined the film generation's concept of authorship to become the creative CEO of the largest independent studio in the world—Lucasfilm Ltd. and its subsidiary LucasArts Entertainment Company—which has attained the status of a multinational conglomerate.

STEVEN SPIELBERG

Unlike Coppola and Lucas, Steven Spielberg (b. 1946) did not have professional film school training, although he began making amateur films in 16mm as early as age thirteen. By the time he was in college at Cal State, Long Beach, he had produced

Steven Spielberg, not quite 30, discussing a scoring decision with composer John Williams (JAWS, STAR WARS, etc.) on the set of CLOSE ENCOUNTERS OF THE THIRD KIND (1977).

AMBLIN' (1969), a short about hitchhikers that won festival prizes in Atlanta and Venice, and led to a contract with the Universal/MCA television division. Here he directed episodes of *Night Gallery, Columbo, Marcus Welby, M.D.,* and other popular shows, as well as the extraordinary TV movie DUEL (1971), which was released theatrically in Europe. His theatrical feature debut in the United States was THE SUGARLAND EXPRESS (1974), a deftly directed fugitive-couple film with Goldie Hawn that earned a bare $3.2 million in rentals. Then came the epoch-making JAWS (1975) which, even more than THE GODFATHER (Francis Ford Coppola, 1972) and intervening blockbusters like THE EXORCIST (William Friedkin, 1973) and THE STING (George Roy Hill, 1973), changed the way movies would be cost-projected and marketed. Adapted from Peter Benchley's best-selling novel about a great white shark that terrorizes a New England beach community at the height of the tourist season (which Universal producers Richard Zanuck and David Brown had shrewdly acquired the rights to before its publication in 1973), JAWS was produced for only $12 million and promoted as if it were the arrival of the New Millennium. As Pye and Myles write in *The Movie Brats,* the single most salient feature of JAWS was "the transformation of film into event through clever manipulation of the media."[135] As sharks were raised to the level of a national fetish, "JAWS-consciousness" caught fire, and the film earned $100 million in domestic rentals in its initial summer run (and ultimately $129.5 million) to become the first megahit of the decade.

The success of JAWS permanently hooked the industry on blockbuster windfalls—co-producer Richard Zanuck made more money on his share of its profits in six months than his father, studio executive Darryl F. Zanuck, had made in his entire career. Circumstances like these led to the kind of studio roulette played in Spielberg's next project, CLOSE ENCOUNTERS OF THE THIRD KIND (1977), in which Columbia gambled most of its working capital on a $19.4-million special effects extravaganza about UFOs landing in middle America. It was rewarded with $83 million in domestic rentals and eight Academy Award nominations (in the year of STAR WARS, it took only one—for Vilmos Zsigmond's cinematography; JAWS had received four and won three—for Sound, Original Score, and Editing). Spielberg had not only directed CLOSE ENCOUNTERS, but had originally conceived it from story idea through post-production special effects (supervised by 2001 veteran Douglas Trumbull), and he was now in the same position as Lucas, with two consecutive $100 million grosses to his credit. The result was hubris in the form of the comedy-action film 1941 (1979), an inflated farce about war panic in post-Pearl Harbor Los Angeles that bombed at the box office, returning only $23.3 million in domestic rentals on its $26.5-million investment. After this rare failure, Spielberg began the historic collaboration with George Lucas on the Indiana Jones series for Paramount that would make him the dominant commercial force in American cinema for the next twenty years and shift audience demographics toward the lower end of the age scale (12–20 years old, as compared with 16–24 during the late 1960s). As the industry closed ranks against auteurism in the wake of HEAVEN'S GATE, Spielberg came to incarnate the new focus on blockbuster revenues by directing the two highest-grossing films in history—E.T.: THE EXTRA-TERRESTRIAL (Universal, 1982—$399.8 million; $228.2 million in domestic rentals) and JURASSIC PARK (Universal, 1993—$356.7 million; $208 million in domestic rentals), as well as four others among the top fifteen in that category through 1996 (JAWS [1975], RAIDERS OF THE LOST ARK [1981], INDIANA JONES AND THE LAST CRUSADE [1989], and INDIANA JONES AND THE TEMPLE OF DOOM [1984]). Like Lucas, Spielberg would later form his own production company (Amblin Entertainment, 1984) and, finally—with Jeffrey Katzenberg and David Geffen—his own multimedia conglomerate (Dreamworks, 1994) to become one of the wealthiest, most powerful individuals in the American film industry.[136]

A detail from the Mother Ship in CLOSE ENCOUNTERS, *strikingly reminiscent of a Christmas tree ornament, designed by Douglas Trumbull.*

MARTIN SCORSESE

The fourth major figure of the "film generation," Martin Scorsese (b. 1942), may have attained the goal of American authorship more fully than any of his peers by regularly creating art out of commercially viable material. The sickly child of Sicilian immigrant parents, Scorsese grew up in New York's Little Italy and became deeply infatuated with movies. After graduating from high school, he entered a seminary with the intention of becoming a priest but left after a year to enroll in New York University's film department. There he earned an undergraduate degree in 1964 and an M.A. in 1966, while simultaneously making a number of award-winning student shorts. He then joined the faculty as an instructor and wrote and directed WHO'S THAT KNOCKING AT MY DOOR?, a low-budget semi-autobiographical feature released in 1968 by the small independent Trimod Films. Next, he worked as an assistant director and supervising editor on Michael Wadleigh's WOODSTOCK (Warner Bros., 1970) and found work on several other documentaries the following year. In 1972, Roger Corman hired Scorsese to direct BOXCAR BERTHA (AIP), a violent sequel to his exploitation hit BLOODY MAMA (AIP, 1970), but Scorsese's first important feature as an auteur was his third as a director, MEAN STREETS (Warner Bros., 1973), which became the hit of that year's New York Film Festival. Shot on location in Little Italy from a screenplay by Scorsese and Mardik Martin, this character study of a small-time hood wracked by Catholic guilt inaugurated Scorsese's relentless moving camera style and was distinguished by the improvisational ensemble performances of Harvey Keitel and Robert De Niro, both of whom would become the director's regular collaborators. Despite its low budget ($500,000) and widespread critical acclaim, MEAN STREETS lost money. Scorsese then shot the forty-eight-

Martin Scorsese's breakthrough feature MEAN STREETS (Warners, 1973). 35mm 1.85:1.

minute television documentary ITALIANAMERICAN (1974) before his next feature, ALICE DOESN'T LIVE HERE ANYMORE (Warner Bros., 1974), which was both more conventional and more popular in its feminist account of a young widow's struggle for self-fulfillment, earning an Oscar for its star Ellen Burstyn and inspiring the long-running CBS television sitcom *Alice* (September 1976–July 1985).

After ALICE DOESN'T LIVE HERE ANYMORE, Scorsese had the base of critical and financial support he needed to make TAXI DRIVER (1976), his nightmare vision of urban hell in which a psychotic Vietnam veteran, brilliantly played by De Niro, becomes an avenging angel of violence and death. Written by UCLA Film School graduate Paul Schrader (see below), with a score by Bernard Herrmann, and produced for Columbia by Michael and Julia Phillips (whose previous vehicle had been the upbeat caper film THE STING [1973]) for just under $2 million, TAXI DRIVER won several Oscar nominations, including that for best picture, and the Palme d'Or at Cannes. (Scorsese's account of the evolution of the film is contained in an interview published in *Film Comment* for July-August 1977, where, among other things, he reveals the influence of John Ford's THE SEARCHERS [1956] on the subplot involving a child prostitute and her pimp.)[137] It is a personal, obsessive work that treats some of the darkest aspects of human nature— including child prostitution, racial hatred, and sadism—with a surreal intensity heightened by Michael Chapman's neo-*noir* widescreen cinematography and Bernard Herrmann's pulsing score. Furthermore, in its lurid display of perverse sexuality (the

Travis Bickle (Robert De Niro) near the end of his murderous rampage in Scorsese's TAXI DRIVER *(Columbia, 1976), written by Paul Schrader. 35mm 1.85:1.*

title character is fixated on a twelve-year-old prostitute played by Oscar-nominated Jodie Foster), gun violence, and gore, TAXI DRIVER pushed the R-rating envelope just about as far as it would go, suggesting that a limit of tolerance had been reached for CARA and audiences alike.[138] The film turned a modest profit, taking in $12.6 million in domestic rentals, which contributed to Scorsese's track record—even in the climate created by JAWS—and made him attractive to the production team of Irwin Winkler and Robert Chartoff, who were fielding a script about the romance of two young musicians during the big band era. Packaged as a musical with De Niro and Liza Minnelli as stars, for distribution by United Artists, this project became NEW YORK, NEW YORK (1977); and Scorsese made it a virtual compendium of MGM musical styles of the forties and fifties, watching hundreds of such films from his extensive video library in preparation for it. (Scorsese was an early and vocal supporter of video archiving as an instrument of film preservation.) A testament to Scorsese's remarkable grasp of film history and evocatively photographed by Lazslo Kovacs, NEW YORK, NEW YORK became the director's first big-budget flop, returning less than $7 million of its $9-million investment, and driving him back to the documentary with THE LAST WALTZ (United Artists, 1978), a feature-length account of The Band's farewell concert in November 1976 shot in 35mm by seven of the generation's leading cinematographers (Michael Chapman, Laszlo Kovacs, and Vilmos Zsigmond among them). Scorsese then shot another documentary in 1978, AMERICAN BOY: A PROFILE OF STEVEN PRINCE, which chronicled the life a young Jewish friend who

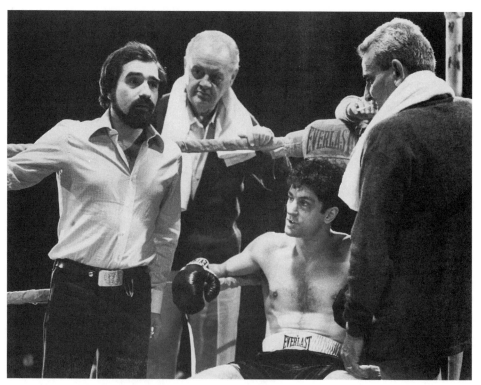

Martin Scorsese directing Robert De Niro in RAGING BULL *(UA, 1980), his harrowing biography of middleweight championship boxer Jake La Motta. 35mm 1.85:1.*

had starred as a gun dealer in MEAN STREETS and later become a heroin addict; with ITALIANAMERICAN it was intended as part of a six-film series on the immigrant experience (which to date has never been completed).

The documentary impulse also informed Scorsese's last feature of the seventies, RAGING BULL (United Artists, 1980), another Winkler-Chartoff production which many critics consider to be his finest film. Scripted by Paul Schrader and Mardik Martin, and shot by Michael Chapman in starkly rendered black-and-white, the film recreates in pitiless fashion the fractured life of championship boxer Jake La Motta, who rose from squalor to the pinnacle of his brutal sport in the 1940s and was destroyed by his own paranoia (and a dubious morals charge) a decade later. The film won an Oscar for Robert De Niro's remarkable performance as La Motta, as well as for its editing by Thelma Shoonmaker. Of all of Scorsese's psychodramas, RAGING BULL is the most intense and unyielding; it was so graphic in its slow-motion depiction of battering in the ring that critics accused it of pandering to masochism (*Variety* called it "an exploration of Catholic sadomasochism"[139]). Despite its quality, the film earned just $10 million as audiences basically stayed away.

Scorsese's films of the eighties reflected the sense that he was no longer a player in the New Hollywood, an anxiety he reflected in several contemporary interviews with the press. (He would, for example, later note in one such interview that NEW YORK NEW YORK opened in the same week as STAR WARS and therefore was doomed to fail in the climate that made that film a megahit.)[140] The success of THE COLOR OF MONEY (1986), conceived by Touchstone Pictures as a star vehicle for Paul Newman and Tom Cruise, brought Scorsese back into the fold, and he has since alternated between commercial films (CAPE FEAR [1991]; CASINO [1995]) and more personal projects (THE LAST TEMPTATION OF CHRIST [1988]; GOODFELLAS [1990]; THE AGE OF INNOCENCE [1993]). In fact, Scorsese may be the only director of the 1970s "film generation" working in the mainstream industry who can still lay claim to being a serious artist; and he is certainly one the few who still passionately cares about the medium *as such*. (This is as evident in his own work as in his tireless efforts on behalf of film preservation and restoration, which extend from the resurrection of 70mm epics like EL CID [Anthony Mann, 1961] and LAWRENCE OF ARABIA [David Lean, 1962] to the reissue on video of classics like Michael Powell's BLACK NARCISSUS [1947] or Nicholas Ray's JOHNNY GUITAR [1954].)

BRIAN DE PALMA

Like Spielberg, Brian De Palma (b. 1940) did not attend film school, but as a physics major at Columbia University he began making 16mm shorts and eventually won a fellowship to Sarah Lawrence College sponsored by MCA. There he codirected (with Wilford Leach and Cynthia Munroe) an experimental 35mm feature in 1963, which was first shown publicly as THE WEDDING PARTY in 1969 and is notable largely as the film debut of both Robert De Niro and Jill Clayburgh. A negligible second feature, MURDER À LA MOD (1968) was barely released, but GREETINGS (1968), a satiric rendition of the Greenwich Village counterculture, was produced for $43,100 and caught the attention of Frank Yablans, soon-to-be production chief at Paramount, who was then working for a small New York distributor affiliated with Filmways called Sigma III. Yablans marketed GREETINGS almost single-handedly, pushing it toward a $1-million gross and significant critical acclaim (it also won a Silver Bear jury prize at the Berlin Film Festival). De Palma was suddenly touted as one of the country's leading independent directors and accorded an interview in Joseph Gelmis's influential *The Film Director as Superstar*, where he spoke of his aspirations to become "the American Godard."[141] As if to fulfill this goal, he next produced the experimental split-screen documentary DIONYSUS IN '69 (1970), which records a performance of Euripides' *The Bacchae* from the perspective of both audience and players. De Palma then produced a sequel to GREETINGS for Filmways on a budget of $120,000, the equally offbeat HI, MOM! (1970), which like the earlier film starred De Niro and Allen Garfield. This earned De Palma a "youth market" contract from Warner Bros. to direct another counterculture comedy, GET TO KNOW YOUR RABBIT (1970; released 1972), written as a star vehicle for Tommy Smothers. De Palma was removed from the project before it was completed, and then worked briefly on FUZZ (Richard A. Colla, 1972), but over the following year he was able to direct SISTERS (1973) from his own script. Independently produced by Edward R. (Ed) Pressman and marketed as a shocker by AIP, this film about separated Siamese twins, one of whom is apparently a psychotic murderer, marked De Palma's first attempt to model his work on Hitchcock's: it resonates with themes and plot devices from REAR WINDOW (1954) and PSYCHO (1960), and employs a lush score for Moog synthesizers composed by Bernard Herrmann. The commercial and critical success of SISTERS (the film received excellent trade and popular reviews and earned $1 million) enabled

The mysterious Phantom (William Finley) who haunts the ultimate rock palace in Brian De Palma's PHANTOM OF THE PARADISE *(Pressman/Fox, 1974). 35mm 1.85:1.*

Genevieve Bujold and Cliff Robertson in Obsession *(Columbia, 1976), Brian De Palma's homage to Hitchcock's* Vertigo *(1958). Based on an original screenplay by Paul Schrader, the film was shot in 1975 with funds from a "production services" tax shelter of the type outlawed by the U.S. Tax Reform Act of 1976. 35mm Panavision anamor-*

Pressman to raise $1.2 million to produce PHANTOM OF THE PARADISE (1974), a reworking of the Faust legend in the context of contemporary rock culture from an original De Palma script.[142] Twentieth Century–Fox paid $2 million to pick up the negative, the largest sum it had ever advanced for a completely independent production, but then failed to properly market it. For this reason, PHANTOM OF THE PARADISE quickly disappeared, but not before it had made a strong impression on critics like Pauline Kael, who praised its self-conscious creation of "a new Guignol, in a modern idiom, out of the movie Guignol of the past."[143] De Palma's next film was written by Paul Schrader (see below) and financed by a Cincinnati-based "production services" tax shelter of the sort outlawed by the Tax Reform Act of 1976, but it sat on the shelf for eight months before Columbia agreed to distribute it, costing producer George Litto a small fortune in interest in the interval. This was OBSESSION (1976), a film indebted to VERTIGO (1958) for its plot and to Bernard Herrmann's Oscar-nominated score (his last and, in his own judgement, his best)[144] for its emotional subtext. Shot on location in Italy and New Orleans by Vilmos Zsigmond in Panavision, OBSESSION was well received by critics (many of whom found it too imitative of Hitchcock, nonetheless),[145] but Columbia failed in attempting to exploit its "youth market" appeal, and the film grossed only a modest $4.47 million.

Just three months after Columbia released OBSESSION, United Artists opened De Palma's CARRIE (1976), which like its predecessor was financed by a tax shelter partnership. Traces of Hitchcock were apparent here too, but this film was more clearly

Sissy Spacek in CARRIE *(UA, 1977), De Palma's career-making shocker about a teenager with telekinetic powers, based on a novel by the then little-known Stephen King. 35mm 1.85:1*

De Palma's own in its use of split-screen montage (a staple since SISTERS) and its cynical, gory hipness. Producer Paul Monash, whose recent credits included BUTCH CASSIDY AND THE SUNDANCE KID (1969) and SLAUGHTERHOUSE-FIVE (1972), had optioned the rights to the novel by the then-unknown Stephen King, who admired SISTERS and suggested that De Palma be hired to direct. Adapted for the screen by Lawrence D. Cohen[146] and scored by the Italian composer Pino Donaggio (who would write the scores for DRESSED TO KILL [1980], BLOW OUT [1981], and BODY DOUBLE [1984]), CARRIE concerns a repressed teenager with telekinetic powers (Sissy Spacek), whose confused response to her first menstrual period brings a torrent of abuse from her cruel high school classmates. Their continued mockery of her dawning sexuality culminates in a vicious prom night humiliation, and, in a special effects tour-de-force, Carrie unleashes a bloodbath of revenge against both them and her mother (Piper Laurie)—a religious fanatic based on MARNIE's mother in the 1964 Hitchcock film. (The spectacular mechanical effects for this sequence were provided by Gregory M. Auer, who had worked with De Palma on PHANTOM OF THE PARADISE, and they were imitated in many subsequent horror films.) Tapping into the nascent "psycho-slasher" trend, CARRIE was a career-making hit for De Palma, earning $15.2 million against its $1.8 million investment in domestic rentals and a good deal of critical praise (Roger Greenspun, for example, called CARRIE "one of the few recent achievements in American movies"),[147] especially among intellectual critics who were beginning to see De Palma as a kind of postmodern satirist.[148] But it did not lead immediately to creative independence for him,

Angie Dickinson in the highly erotic shower sequence that opens De Palma's DRESSED TO KILL (Filmways, 1980), the film that first brought charges of misogyny against the director. 35mm Panavision anamorphic.

and De Palma blamed United Artists for failing to go after the mass market that had made blockbusters of THE EXORCIST (1973) and THE OMEN (1976).[149] Furthermore, he found himself widely—and, for the most part, accurately—accused of misogyny, another similarity with Hitchcock which became increasingly problematic for De Palma as his work became ever more prominent.

After two more features—the violent supernatural thriller THE FURY (1978), produced by Frank Yablans for Fox at a cost of $5.5 million and grossing $11.1; and HOME MOVIES (1979), a low-budget ($400,000), independently distributed farce about moviemaking shot with a crew of Sarah Lawrence film students—De Palma was finally acknowledged as a mainstream auteur with DRESSED TO KILL (1980), a Filmways release

De Palma directing John Travolta on the set of BLOW OUT *(Filmways, 1981), a self-conscious reworking of Antonioni's* BLOWUP *(1966) in terms of sound recording rather than photography.*

that looked considerably original in its day and is still probably his best film. Directed from his own screenplay and shot in Panavision by Ralph Bode, it combines Hitchcockean suspense with eighties-style sex and gore in the story of a cross-dressing serial killer in Manhattan who murders women with a razor. DRESSED TO KILL is at once erotic, sadistic, and intensely manipulative, raising once again charges of misogyny, but this time the film had the blessings of the critical establishment that come with a laudatory feature story in the *New York Times*. It also made nearly as much at the box office ($15 million) as CARRIE. (Although influential critics like Pauline Kael and David Denby continued to champion the reflexive quality of De Palma's thrillers, feminist outrage led him to abandon the form from 1984 to 1992.)[150] In the eighties and nineties, De Palma continued to be an ambiguous, controversial figure, attempting and occasionally achieving seriousness (BLOW OUT [1981]; THE UNTOUCHABLES [1987]; CARLITO'S WAY [1993]) but just as often exploiting violence and misogyny (SCARFACE [1983]; BODY DOUBLE [1984]; CASUALTIES OF WAR [1989]; RAISING CAIN [1992]) with sadistic intensity. He has had more financial ups and downs than any member of his generation except Coppola, and his treatment of unpleasant material has often bordered on the prurient. Stylistically, however, he is more interesting than many of his peers because he is less predictable and consistent—during the 1970s, for example, he employed some of the best cinematographers in the business (Gregory Sandor, Vilmos Zsigmond, Mario Tosi, John A. Alonzo, Stephen H. Burum) but rarely used the same one from film to film, and he never attempted to build up a repertory of performers in the manner of Scorsese or Coppola (although Nancy Allen, his wife from 1979–1984, was a presence in all of his work from CARRIE through BLOW OUT).

JOHN MILIUS AND PAUL SCHRADER

Two other figures of the "film generation"—John Milius (b. 1944) and Paul Schrader (b. 1946)—are known mainly as screenwriters, but they have also directed films of distinctly auterist aspirations. Milius attended USC film school as a member of the "miracle class" that included Lucas, Randal Kleiser (GREASE [1978]), and John Carpenter (HALLOWEEN [1978]),[151] and he began to produce hardboiled action scripts in the early seventies, writing or collaborating on such Warner Bros.' films as DIRTY HARRY (Don Siegel, 1971; uncredited), JEREMIAH JOHNSON (Sydney Pollack, 1972), and MAGNUM FORCE (Ted Post, 1973), before directing DILLINGER (1973) from his own script at AIP. Cast in the mixed genre format of BONNIE AND CLYDE (ARTHUR PENN, 1967), this violent gangster film focuses on the FBI manhunt for the famous bank robber who became "Public Enemy Number One" during an eighteen-month crime spree in 1933 and 1934. Milius portrays both Dillinger (Warren Oates) and his nemesis, G-man Melvin Purvis (Ben Johnson), as media-conscious public heroes obsessed with shaping their images within the popular mythology of their times. Although it was produced on a limited budget by a youth-market studio, DILLINGER attracted a wide audience and unexpected critical acclaim, briefly putting Milius in the forefront of his generation. For his next project, he had epic aspirations, although the result is more in the nature of an elegy. THE WIND AND THE LION (MGM/United Artists, 1975) is a quasi-historical account of the kidnapping of the wife and children of an American diplomat by a Berber chieftain in Morocco in 1904, in response to which President Theodore Roosevelt sent in the marines. With Kurosawa-like action sequences and widescreen desert cinematography modeled on LAWRENCE OF ARABIA (David Lean, 1962), THE WIND AND THE LION creates a sort of

Candice Bergen and Sean Connery in John Milius's stirringly jingoistic epic The Wind
and the Lion *(MGM/UA, 1975). 35mm Panavision anamorphic.*

Fordian myth of gunboat diplomacy entirely appropriate to its writer-director's right-
wing ideology. (Contrary to his generation's liberalism, Milius is a self-proclaimed mili-
tarist, sworn to the mystical power of violence and survivalist gun-culture.) The Wind
and the Lion earned a modest $4.8. million, and the pretentious surfing film Big
Wednesday (Warner Bros., 1978) had to be recut and sold to pay-TV before its losses
were fully covered. In the 1980s, Milius's films were more resonant with the reactionary
politics of the Reagan and Bush administrations, and he produced several near-hits in
the bone-headed Conan the Barbarian (De Laurentiis, 1982), Red Dawn
(MGM/United Artists, 1984), Farewell to the King (Vestron, 1989), and Flight of
the Intruder (Paramount, 1991), but has done little else since.

Paul Schrader, the product of a strict Dutch-German Calvinist upbringing, studied
divinity at Calvin College seminary but became deeply enthralled by movies through a
summer film course he took at Columbia University. When he graduated from Calvin in
1968, Schrader enrolled in the UCLA's graduate film program where he was a classmate
of Francis Ford Coppola, Carroll Ballard (The Black Stallion [1979]), and B. W. L.
Norton, Jr. (More American Graffiti [1979]). There he became a film critic for the
Los Angeles Free Press, the editor of *Cinema* magazine, and the author of the influential scholarly volume *Transcendental Style: Ozu, Bresson, Dreyer* (1974). His first
screenplay was The Yakuza (Sydney Pollack, 1975), but serious critical notice awaited
his scripts for Scorsese's Taxi Driver (1976) and De Palma's Obsession (1976).
Schrader also worked uncredited on the script for Spielberg's Close Encounters of
the Third Kind (1977) and co-wrote (with Mardik Martin) Scorsese's Raging Bull
(1980), as well as writing the screenplays for Peter Weir's The Mosquito Coast (1986)

and Scorsese's THE LAST TEMPTATION OF CHRIST (1988). As with Milius, Schrader's success as a writer during the 1970s enabled him by the end of the decade to direct films from his own scripts. BLUE COLLAR (Universal, 1978) and HARDCORE (Columbia, 1979) both invoke the ambience of TAXI DRIVER, reflecting combined fascination and disgust with the underside of the American life—in the former, labor union corruption in a grim factory town; in the latter, the night world of the $6-billion pornography industry, into which the teenaged daughter of a Midwestern Calvinist lay minister, heroically portrayed by George C. Scott, disappears on a trip to Los Angeles. Modeled on the plot of John Ford's THE SEARCHERS (1956), Scott's attempts in HARDCORE to track the girl down lead him into unimagined byways of sexual prurience, debauchery, and morbidity, plunging him finally into a dark night of the soul that seems to be a paradigm for Schrader's neo-Protestant ethic. Both films were critically well-received and had respectable rental returns ($3 million and $7 million, respectively). Less morally intense was AMERICAN GIGOLO (Paramount, 1980), a stylistically spare thriller involving kinky sex built primarily around the ambiguous persona of its star, Richard Gere. Nevertheless, the film was a hit, earning about $11.5 million in domestic rentals, and spurred Schrader to direct the sensationalistic CAT PEOPLE (Universal, 1982). CAT PEOPLE remade Val Lewton's classically understated horror film of 1942, which was directed by Jacques Tourneur, as a disturbing 1980s-style gorefest with prosthetic makeup effects by Tim Buram. It was a box-office disappointment (it returned $5 million), and though Schrader

George C. Scott as Jake Van Dorn, the father-searcher-avenger in Paul Schrader's
HARDCORE *(Columbia, 1979), who has just identified his teenage daughter as a performer in a porn film. 35mm 1.85:1.*

continued occasionally to direct, with the exception of MISHIMA: A LIFE IN FOUR CHAPTERS (Zoetrope, 1985) and AFFLICTION (Largo Entertainment, 1998), had little critical or financial success. Although he continued to write screenplays (for his own films and others'), sometimes (as earlier) in collaboration with his brother Leonard, Schrader seemingly ended up, like Milius, at the dead end of a cinema of ideas where philosophy turns to rhetoric.

Conclusion: The Commerce of Auteurism

In the late 1960s and early 1970s, auteurism became much more to the American cinema than simply a mode of aesthetic discourse. In the unstable environment of the crumbling studio system the opportunity arose to actually practice one form of it, when the studios' transitional managers briefly turned over the reigns of creative power to a rising generation of independents and first-time directors whose values seemed to resonate with the newly emerging "youth culture" market. In the long run, however, the idea that American directors, working within the world's most capital-intensive production context, could somehow approach the European ideal of authorship as incarnated in the French New Wave was doomed to fail from the start; and it proved especially intractable in the business climate that prevailed after JAWS and STAR WARS. By that time, the industry had been fully absorbed by new owners who saw it primarily as a locus for high-stakes speculation and corporate tax-sheltering. They were skilled at these pursuits, and their new management style produced early results—from a combined loss of $41 million in 1969–1970, the eight motion picture companies earned profits of $173 million in 1972–1973, thanks largely to the success of a few heavily-marketed blockbusters.[152] However, as this review of the careers of the most prominent directors of the 1970s is intended to suggest, the extent to which film production had become an investment-specific strategy by the latter part of the decade was quite unprecedented, and it warped the shape of the industry for years to come, driving production and marketing costs to hitherto unimagined levels.

Starting in the late sixties, studios began recruiting both veteran independents and untested film school-trained directors to appeal to the "youth market," which was correctly understood to be driving a national resurgence in film attendance. The institution of the MPPA Ratings System in October 1968 was initially seen as a boon to experimentation by these directors, and in some ways it was. By the mid-seventies, however, ratings had worked to create a two-tiered system of production, in which studios looked to make either cross-generational blockbusters like JAWS and STAR WARS in the PG category (initially M, then GP, and later PG-13), or tailored entertainment for specific market segments—children (G), adults (R), and "adults" (X). In effect, because the G-rating market share was relatively small and the X rating was reserved mainly for pornography (or what was then perceived as such), most Hollywood films of the decade were rated either PG or R. The "film generation" auteurs, for example, were neatly divided along this fault, with Lucas, Spielberg, and Milius cleaving mainly to the PG side, and Coppola, Scorsese, De Palma, and Schrader on the other. Significantly, the two major non-"film generation" directors of the 1970s—Robert Altman and Stanley Kubrick—made a nearly equal number of films in each category.

By the end of the decade, this linkage of "auteurs" with certain types of entertainment—Coppola with the GODFATHER films, Lucas with the STAR WARS cycle, Spielberg with wondrous spectacles of all sorts—combined with the practice of saturation booking and massive national publicity to make promotion the most important aspect of exhibition and distribution.[153] Auteurism thus became a marketing tool that coincided nicely with the rise of college-level film education among the industry's most heavily courted audience segment.[154] From the cinema of rebellion represented by films like BONNIE AND CLYDE (Arthur Penn, 1967), THE WILD BUNCH (Sam Peckinpah, 1969), and EASY RIDER (Dennis Hopper, 1969), America's youth transferred its allegiance to the "personal" cinema of the seventies auteurs without realizing how corporate and impersonal it had become. And the auteurs themselves were transformed from *cineastes* into high-rolling celebrity directors (many of them) with their own chauffeurs, Lear jets, and body guards. In 1968 Coppola had said, "I don't think there'll be a Hollywood as we know it when this generation of film students gets out of college,"[155] accurately forecasting the enormous impact his generation of filmmakers would have on the industry. What he could not foresee was how the change would boomerang on the new auteurs and recast their films as branded merchandise to be consumed along with T-shirts, action figures, Happy Meals, and, by the end of the decade, miniaturized and badly framed versions of the films themselves called "videos."

PLAY IT AGAIN, SAM (Herbert Ross, 1972) fired the opening shot in a decade of genre
revision, parody, and hybridization. In this adaptation of his own Broadway hit,
Woody Allen plays a man who is obsessed with Humphrey Bogart's screen persona and
who experiences life as a series of scenes recreated from CASABLANCA and other Bogart
classics. The film depends on the audience's knowing recognition of its allusions:
Woody Allen, Diane Keaton. 35mm 1.85:1.

5

Genres I: Revision, Transformation, and Revival

Genre films essentially ask the audience, "Do you still want to believe this?" Popularity is the audience answering, "Yes." Change in genres occur when the audience says, "That's too infantile a form of what we believe. Show us something more complicated."

LEO BRAUDY, *The World in a Frame*, 1977

There is general agreement among critics and scholars that the 1970s witnessed the regular production of genre films for the first time since the classical studio era (excepting the musicals and Westerns made during the 1950s).[1] The return to genre production grew out of the preoccupation of New Hollywood auteurs with film history and film form, and was underwritten by the studios as a form of risk reduction since genre films, like stars, were inherently "pre-sold" and easy to package. Influenced by the French New Wave, early Hollywood Renaissance directors like Penn, Peckinpah, and Kubrick had experimented *within* classical genres (the gangster film, the Western, and the science fiction film respectively), whereas Altman, Bogdanovich, and others were interested in revising, "correcting," and/or deconstructing them. Collateral to this revisionism was the recycling of former exploitation genres (for example, AIP-style monster and horror movies, rock 'n' roll musicals, "race" movies, and pornography) into the mainstream, as producers sought ever more sensational audience hooks and "movie brat" directors were called upon to recreate the subversive cinema of their youth as a series of big-budget features. By mid-decade, genre parody, a staple of prime-time television since the late sixties (e.g., *The Wild, Wild West* [1965–1969], *Batman* [1966–1968], *Get Smart* [1966–1970], *Rowan and Martin's Laugh-In* [1968–1973]), was firmly entrenched in the work of Mel Brooks and Woody Allen; and, with STAR WARS (1977), George Lucas pioneered the genre pastiche in which several classical genres were melded into one (in this case, science fiction, the Western, the war film, and the quasi-mystical epic). At this juncture, nostalgia became an important market element, both as a Saturday-matinee-style appeal to lost innocence and as the last viable response to classical genre. For such "film generation" auteurs as Steven Spielberg, the nostalgic

Richard Lester's A Hard Day's Night *(1964), the film that more than any other helped to popularize the self-reflexive style of the French New Wave among Anglo-American audiences: the Beatles. 35mm 1.85:1.*

genre pastiche—as in Raiders of the Lost Ark (1981)—would become the block-buster paradigm for the eighties.

Classical narrative and generic conventions had both been called into question during the 1960s under the influence of the European art film,[2] especially in the work of the French New Wave, whose particular brand of modernism called attention to cinematic style through exaggeration and parody. Popularized by Richard Lester's commercially successful Beatles films, A Hard Day's Night (1964) and Help! (1965), and Claude Lelouch's A Man and a Woman (Un Homme et une Femme, 1966),[3] such disruptive New Wave techniques as jump-cutting and optically violent camera movement had entered mainstream American cinema shortly thereafter. Traces of New Wave style can be found in the freeze-frame ending of Sidney Lumet's Fail-Safe (1964) and the elliptical flashbacks of his The Pawnbroker (1965), as well as in the hand-held, *cinema verité*-style camera work of John Frankenheimer's Seven Days in May (1964) and Seconds (1966). By 1967, Arthur Penn's Bonnie and Clyde could offer audiences a compendium of such practices without jeopardizing narrative coherence, but did risk alienating them by imitating the radical mood swings of such New Wave paragons as Breathless (Jean-Luc Godard, 1959) and Shoot the Piano Player (François Truffaut, 1960). Like the French films, Bonnie and Clyde mixed an inherently serious genre (the gangster film) with an inherently unserious one (slapstick), producing violent shifts from comedy to tragedy that outraged contemporary critics like Bosley Crowther.[4] Yet these New Wave borrowings hardly foretold the death of classical narrative, because they were largely cosmetic. Continuity editing, mimesis, and stars remained crucial to the Hollywood mode of representation throughout the coming decades, and the New Wave's stylistic reflexivity was quickly assimilated into more conventional forms (including, most visibly, the television commercial). As Robert B. Ray has put it, the influence of the 1960s European art film on American cinema was one of "superficial stylistic exuberance, leaving Classic Hollywood's paradigms fundamentally untouched."[5] If proof is needed one has only to compare the narrational mode of Michelangelo Antonioni's ZABRISKIE POINT (1970), produced in the United States by MGM, with that of Robert Altman's BREWSTER MCCLOUD (or any other Altman film of the decade, except perhaps 3 WOMEN [1977]) produced in the same year for the same studio. Although Altman has long been regarded as an authentic American practitioner of art cinema,[6] his film is a formally closed narrative, and its editing structure, if somewhat elliptical, is unambiguous. Antonioni's film, by contrast, is episodic, open-ended, and distinctly modernist in form, yielding its meaning less through linear narrative than polyphonic montage and a densely allusive subtext. (Ironically, whereas MGM's new president James T. Aubrey hated BREWSTER MCCLOUD and condemned it to an early death on the exploitation circuit, he told Antonioni that ZABRISKIE POINT "may be the best movie I've ever seen in my life."[7] (Of course, Aubrey had more capital—both literal and political—invested in Antonioni than Altman, which surely colored his opinion.)

If the directors of the New Hollywood were self-avowed modernists, then, they were not modernists who sought to demolish primary forms like representation and narrative. Rather, they concentrated their attack on secondary forms—most notably, individual genres—and, as Stephen Schiff has argued, they were so successful at it that by the mid-1970s genre could scarcely be said to exist at all, except where it provided experiences unavailable on television—that is, in spectacle and pornography—or as a function of nostalgia.[8] What had made genres an integral part of the studio system was their reliability as a product, their ability to provide an audience with a consistently familiar and repeatable experience. Genre was also an important factor in product differentiation and standardization, and genre production was highly cost-efficient: the same sets, props, costumes, and creative personnel (including writers, actors, and directors) could be recycled from one genre film to the next, enabling the studios to virtually mass-produce them. (For example, during the 1943–1944 season, sixty-two of the 397 features released by the eleven largest distributors [the five majors, the three minors, and the three largest B-studios] were Westerns produced in this way.)[9] And it was this *predictability* that caused a return to genre production as negative costs soared in the wake of JAWS (1975) and STAR WARS (1977) and as the risks associated with blockbuster production demanded stories that were pre-tested, pre-sold, and easily packaged for global distribution. In fact, late seventies blockbusters like CLOSE ENCOUNTERS OF THE THIRD KIND (Steven Spielberg, 1977), GREASE (Randal Kleiser, 1978), SUPERMAN (Richard Donner, 1978), and ALIEN (Ridley Scott, 1979) were even "more classical," in Thomas Schatz's phrase, than their generic predecessors owing to their narrative sophistication and technical prowess[10]—a reintensification made possible both by the film-school training of New Hollywood directors and an acceleration in special effects and other production technology. Before this neo-classicism took hold, however, there was a splintering and dislocation of classical genres that began with BONNIE AND CLYDE (1967), proceeded through EASY RIDER (Dennis Hopper, 1969) and the "youth-cult" boom of 1969–1971, leading to their ultimate explosion in the first half of the 1970s.

The Youth-Cult Film

The youth-cult or counterculture film was a response by the studios to the exemplary success of Columbia's EASY RIDER (released in July 1969), whose $19.2-million rental return on a $375,000 investment made all Hollywood take note.[11] During the 1969–1970 season, the only other distributor to stake a serious claim in the youth market was United Artists, whose ALICE'S RESTAURANT (Arthur Penn, 1969) and MIDNIGHT COWBOY (John Schlesinger, 1969) were both shrewdly marketed to what *New Republic* critic Stanley Kauffman was then calling "the Film Generation."[12] Although Paramount had picked up the independent H and J production MEDIUM COOL (Haskell Wexler, 1969), MGM had Antonioni's ZABRISKIE POINT in production as the second in a three-film deal that had begun with BLOWUP (1966), and Warner Bros. had contracted with a twenty-six-year-old cameraman named Michael Wadleigh and the promoters of the Woodstock rock festival in upstate New York (Woodstock Ventures) to film that event when it took place in August 1969,[13] there was little other action on the youth market front until the revelatory success of EASY RIDER, which opened in mid-July and shortly thereafter sent the studios scrambling after similar projects. As 1970 began, the banner headline for *Variety's* year-end wrap-up proclaimed "B. O. Dictatorship By Youth," while the accom-

BBS/Columbia's EASY RIDER *(Dennis Hopper, 1969) the film that started the youth-cult boom when it returned an astonishing $19.2 million in rentals on a $375,000 investment in the midst of the worst financial crisis Hollywood had experienced since the Great Depression: Dennis Hopper, Peter Fonda, Jack Nicholson. 35mm 1.85:1.*

panying article commented that "Hollywood's current problem is to engage in a film production program that it can survive under, attuned to the contemporaneous market."[14] A few months later, the *Variety* B. O. Chart for 1969, tracking the gross performance of 1,028 features in the domestic market through the year's end, placed nine youth-oriented films among the top twenty (#4—I AM CURIOUS YELLOW; #5—MIDNIGHT COWBOY; #6—EASY RIDER; #8—ROMEO AND JULIET; #9—BULLITT; #11—BUTCH CASSIDY AND THE SUNDANCE KID; #13—2001: A SPACE ODYSSEY; #16—ALICE'S RESTAURANT; #20—THE WILD BUNCH).[15] Some of these were clearly "corrected" classical genre films whose youth appeal was circumstantial (or, like that of 2001, grounded mainly in style), but the EASY RIDER phenomenon led studios to speculate wildly in low-budget movies produced *directly* for the youth market.

This was what motivated Warner Bros. to lend Francis Ford Coppola $600,000 to form the alternative studio that became American Zoetrope and Columbia to negotiate the six-film deal with EASY RIDER-producer BBS that led to FIVE EASY PIECES (Bob Rafelson, 1970), THE LAST PICTURE SHOW (Peter Bogdanovich, 1971), and other notable films (see Chapter 4). By early 1970, virtually every major studio had youth-cult films in development or production that bore the influence of EASY RIDER in their themes of youthful rebellion and their documentary-like intention—that is, their desire to be vibrantly contemporary, or, variously, "hip," "with it," "relevant," and "now." MGM released ZABRISKIE POINT in February and THE STRAWBERRY STATEMENT (Stuart Hagmann) in June, both of which were unconvincingly set in the context of student radicalism, although the former contains some of Antonioni's most brilliantly expressive montage and the latter somehow managed to win the 1970 Special Jury Prize at Cannes. In May 1970, Columbia also released two films about student unrest—GETTING STRAIGHT (Richard Rush), and R.P.M. (Stanley Kramer)—which were similarly superficial in their political commitment; as was United Artists' youth-oriented THE MAGIC GARDEN OF STANLEY SWEETHEART (Leonard Horn), also released in May, and THE REVOLUTIONARY (Paul Williams), released in July. The Warner Bros. rock documentary WOODSTOCK (Michael Wadleigh) was probably the most "pre-sold" of all youth-cult properties when it appeared in August 1970. But GIMME SHELTER, shot by the Maysles brothers at The Rolling Stones' Altamont concert and distributed by Cinema V, featured a real, on-camera murder and was similarly popular at year's end; as was Frank Zappa's 200 MOTELS (United Artists, 1971—the first theatrical release shot in a videotape-to-film transfer process) shortly thereafter. Universal, which had distributed the liberated confessional COMING APART (Milton Moses Ginsberg) in 1969, produced a fine satire on the generation gap in TAKING OFF (1971), Milos Forman's first American film since emigrating from Czechoslovakia in 1969 and the enigmatic road movie TWO-LANE BLACKTOP (Monte Hellman, 1971), which became a cult classic later in the decade. At Paramount, Sidney J. Furie attempted to clone EASY RIDER with the motorcycle-racing epic LITTLE FAUSS AND BIG HALSEY (1970) (as did Avco Embassy's C. C. AND COMPANY [Robbie Seymour, 1970]),[16] and Mike Nichols's much-anticipated adaptation of Joseph Heller's absurdist World War II novel *Catch-22* (1970) was spiked with contemporary antiwar rhetoric to enhance its youth appeal. The anti-Vietnam subtext was even clearer in both 20th Century–Fox's revisionist "combat" film M°A°S°H (Robert Altman, 1970), a black comedy in which only combat's bloody aftermath is shown, and National General's revisionist Western LITTLE BIG MAN (Arthur Penn, 1970), where the massacred Indians stand in for nonviolent flower children, as well as for Vietnamese villagers. But the year's ultimate expression of youth-cult fear

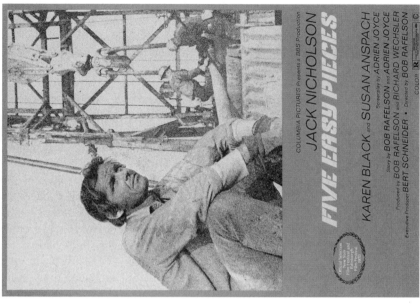

Youth-cult marketing images: the poster for BBS/Columbia's FIVE EASY PIECES (Bob Rafelson, 1970) creates a link with EASY RIDER, suggesting themes of alienation and the quest for identity; the poster for GETTING STRAIGHT (its title has both sexual and drug-culture implications), makes an obvious reference to the sexual revolution. (The image is also a self-conscious variation on the well-known logo for Avco Embassy's 1967 THE GRADUATE; the logo pictures a young man in a cap and gown framed by the arch of a bare female leg.)

and loathing for the Establishment was probably Cannon Film's JOE (John G. Avildsen), in which a hardcore blue-collar bigot (Peter Boyle) and a weak-willed business executive go on a murderous rampage against a hippie commune that harbors the latter's daughter (Susan Sarandon, in her debut); the film ends in a freeze-frame in which the businessman unwittingly shoots his own daughter in the back as she runs away from him towards the camera, suggesting an unholy alliance between working class and bourgeoisie to exterminate the counterculture.

Most of the youth-cult films of 1970 shared a dual impulse to capture the zeitgeist and to be stylistically innovative, often through the adaptation of *cinema verité* and/or art film techniques to narrative, but just as often through conspicuous abuse of rack-focus composition and the zoom lens—newly available in high-resolution, high-speed

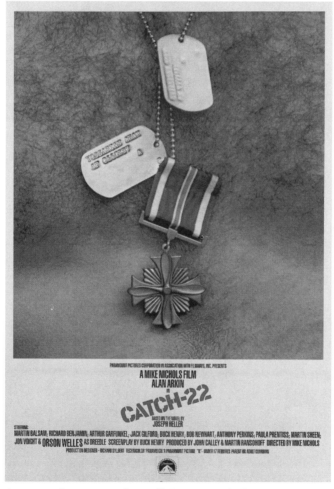

Antiwar chic was used to sell Paramount's CATCH-22 (Mike Nichols, 1970), which was based on Joseph Heller's absurdist novel of World War II, and had next to nothing to say about Vietnam.

formats with a 5 to 1 ratio from Taylor-Hobson (London), Canon (Tokyo), and Angenieux (Paris).[17] Many also shared some kind of high-concept advertising logo, a portentous, "with-it" marketing slogan, and a rock-music sound track, often tied in to a simultaneous album release—all in imitation of EASY RIDER, whose Dunhill Records sound track of cuts by Steppenwolf, The Jimi Hendrix Experience, The Byrds, The Band, and The Electric Prunes was certified "Gold" in January 1970.[18] (For example, ZABRISKIE POINT was advertised with a huge graphic of the title in which the letters were formed from the stars and stripes of the American flag. This echoed EASY RIDER's poster art, where images of the flag appear prominently on the crash helmet, fuel tank, and

Fox's M*A*S*H (Robert Altman, 1970), set during the Korean War and more deliberately evocative of Vietnam, was blatantly marketed to antiwar audiences via this striking image that flaunted the peace sign and simultaneously invoked the film's sexual ribaldry. 35mm Panavision anamorphic.

Paranoia was the youth-cult hook in Cannon Film's low-budget JOE *(John G. Avildsen, 1970), which adapted* EASY RIDER's *peace-loving hippie vs. murderous redneck formula to the urban rust belt: Peter Boyle, as Joe, introduces Dennis Patrick to some of his hippie-loathing blue-collar buddies. 35mm 1.85:1.*

jacket of "Captain America" [Peter Fonda] as he sits on his Harley and stares off into what is left of the American frontier. EASY RIDER's slogan, "A man went looking for America, but couldn't find it anywhere," became for ZABRISKIE POINT: "Zabriskie Point . . . where a boy . . . and a girl . . . meet . . . and touch . . . and BLOW THEIR MINDS!!" Or, alternatively: "Zabriskie Point . . . How you get there . . . depends on where you're at!" And ZABRISKIE POINT's sound-track album was released by MGM Records, with songs by The Rolling Stones, The Grateful Dead, and Pink Floyd, who also pioneered a synthesized rock score for the film.[19]) Implicit in many of these films was the equation of the youth culture with the drug culture, so that the odyssey of EASY RIDER's protagonists from Los Angeles to Louisiana is bankrolled by a cocaine deal (although they explicitly eschew coke themselves for marijuana and LSD); the Korean War servicemen in M°A°S°H anachronistically smoke a joint during an intramural football game; the entire cast gets stoned in TAKING OFF (Milos Forman, 1971); and WOODSTOCK is a veritable pharmacopoeia (for which, according to Stephen Farber, it very specifically received an R rating from CARA[20]). The darker side of drug use would become the focus of Fox's THE PANIC IN NEEDLE PARK (Jerry Schatzberg, 1971); United Artists' BORN TO WIN (Ivan Passer, 1971); MGM's BELIEVE IN ME (Stuart Hagmann, 1971); Warner Bros.' DEALING: OR THE BERKELEY-TO-BOSTON FORTY-BRICK LOST-BAG BLUES (Paul Williams, 1972); the documentary DUSTY AND SWEETS McGEE (Floyd Mutrux, 1971); Columbia's CISCO PIKE (B. W. L. Norton, 1972); and several other early

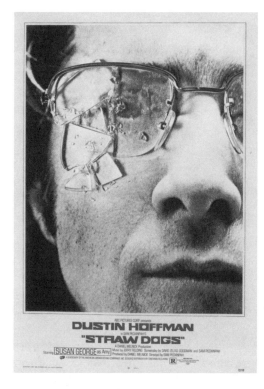

Though not exactly youth-cult in origin, Sam Peckinpah's STRAW DOGS (1971) was sold as such by promising to examine violence in a social context. In the film, Dustin Hoffman plays an American mathematics professor who has left the United States on sabbatical to avoid "commitment" (his wife's term) to the antiwar movement and its violence and passion, which he distains. As the poster art suggests, however, he finds that you can't run away from violence because aggression is deeply rooted in human nature.

MGM's ZABRISKIE POINT (Michelangelo Antonioni, 1970) may have been the only youth-cult art film: a shot from film's elaborately montaged finale in which a corporate executive's posh desert retreat is (apparently) blown up repeatedly from multiple angles, in slow motion and real time, to the music of Pink Floyd. 35mm Panavision anamorphic.

Psychedelic marketing art for Warners' WOODSTOCK (Michael Wadleigh, 1970)—the drug connection was unspoken but widely understood. Ostensibly, the ads promised audiences only "3 days of peace, music . . . and love."

WOODSTOCK (Warners, 1970): through images like this one, Woodstock became the cultural icon of a generation, which took to briefly calling itself the "Woodstock nation." 16mm and 35mm; blown up to 35mm anamorphic.

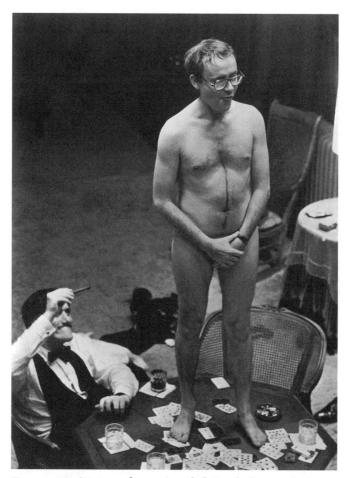

TAKING OFF (Universal, 1971), exiled Czech director Milos Forman's first American film, was an urbane satire on the "generation gap." In this shot from the conclusion, middle-class parents are turned on to marijuana and play strip poker stoned: Vincent Schiavelli, Buck Henry (buck naked). 35mm 1.85:1.

seventies productions targeted (unsuccessfully in the main) for youth.[21] A notable film in this category was Conrad Rooks's independently distributed SIDDHARTHA (1973), an adaptation of Hermann Hesse's novel of expanded consciousness that was shot on location in India by the Swedish cinematographer Sven Nykvist. Originally published in 1922, Hesse's visionary *bildungsroman* had become a bible of late-sixties drug consciousness; and Rooks had become a hallucinogenic cult hero when CHAPPAQUA (1966; released 1968), his mesmerizing film about heroin withdrawal, won a Silver Lion at Venice in 1966. The final youth-cult films were independent productions tending toward black humor—Alan Myerson's STEELYARD BLUES (1972), James Frawley's KID BLUE (1973), and James William Guercio's ELECTRA GLIDE IN BLUE (1973)—which anticipated the music-video format in their integration of sound and vision.

In pursuing the youth-cult boomlet of 1969–1971, the majors followed a pattern of exploitation laid out for them by Roger Corman at James H. Nicholson and Samuel Z. Arkoff's American-International Pictures (AIP) in the fifties and early sixties. (EASY RIDER was in fact a variant of several Corman-produced AIP biker films, made largely by AIP alumni.)[22] The AIP-Corman strategy was to abjure the mass audience and target market segments demographically (teenagers) in order to exploit their tastes (monster-themed science fiction, horror, hot-rods, rock 'n' roll) with sensational, low-budget material. As with pornography—which is the ultimate exploitation genre—swift delivery of the goods compensated for a multitude of sins at the level of form and packaging, and low budgets meant high returns for success and minimum risk for failure. The majors' venture into youth-cult exploitation was recession-driven and produced uneven results: of the specifically engineered youth-cult films cited above, only WOODSTOCK and JOE met with unqualified success, generating rentals of $16.4 and $9.5 million, respectively (which put them at sixth and tenth place for the year). M*A*S*H was a bigger hit, earning $36.7 million in rentals (and third place), but it had mass market as well as youth appeal.[23] Nevertheless, the studios' youth-cult gambit set the stage for a blurring of distinctions between mainstream and exploitation genres that would characterize the first half of the 1970s until, around 1975, the distinctions themselves disappeared. And once Hollywood began to travel this road, the authority of mainstream classical genres was diluted and finally lost.

Universal's PLAY IT AS IT LAYS *(Frank Perry, 1972), adapted from Joan Didion's best-selling novel of contemporary Hollywood, was one of a number of youth-oriented films from early 1970s that did not reflexively embrace the counterculture: Laura Brooks, Sally Marr. 35mm 1.85:1.*

Not all of the majors' efforts to court the youthful market during the 1969–1971 recession went into youth-cult exploitation. For every film keyed to the hippie values of drugs, sex, radicalism, and rock 'n' roll, there were others calculated to appeal to urban professionals and other young adults who had not yet chosen, in the words of Dr. Timothy Leary, to "turn on, tune-in, and drop-out."[24] There were numerous films about coming of age or sexual awakening like Paramount's THE STERILE CUCKOO (Alan Pakula, 1969), GOODBYE, COLUMBUS (Larry Peerce, 1969; adapted from Philip Roth's novel) and A SEPARATE PEACE (Larry Peerce, 1972; adapted from the John Knowles classic), Fox's JOHN AND MARY (Peter Yates, 1969), Warner Bros.' SUMMER OF '42 (Robert Mulligan, 1971), and Allied Artist's LAST SUMMER (Frank Perry, 1969), as well as films about middle-class marital angst—many of them based on prestigious women's novels—such as Universal's DIARY OF A MAD HOUSEWIFE (Frank Perry, 1970; adapted by Eleanor Perry from a novel by Sue Kaufman) and PLAY IT AS IT LAYS (Frank Perry, 1972; adapted by Joan Didion from her own novel), Columbia's LOVING (Irvin Kershner, 1970), Fox's MARRIAGE OF A YOUNG STOCK BROKER (Lawrence Turman, 1971), Paramount's DESPERATE CHARACTERS (Frank D. Gilroy, 1971; adapted from a novel by Paula Fox) and SUCH GOOD FRIENDS (Otto Preminger, 1971; adapted by Elaine May [as Esther Dale] from Lois Gould's novel), and National General's UP THE SANDBOX (Irvin Kershner, 1972; adapted from a novel by Anne Richardson Roiphe). Whatever their other merits, these films were able to deal frankly with sexual situations—within CARA guidelines—for the first time since the imposition of the Production Code in 1934, which gave them a certain freshness and novelty.

Other studio films honed for the new demographics focused on middle-class youths or young adults in search of identity and meaning. Warner Bros.' RABBIT, RUN (Jack Smight, 1970), Paramount's BEEN DOWN SO LONG IT LOOKS LIKE UP TO ME (Jeffrey Young, 1971), Universal's PUZZLE OF A DOWNFALL CHILD (Jerry Schatzberg, 1971), National General's WHO IS HARRY KELLERMAN AND WHY IS HE SAYING THOSE TERRIBLE THINGS ABOUT ME? (Ulu Grosbard, 1971) and THE CHRISTIAN LICORICE STORE (James Frawley, 1971), Avco Embassy's THE STEAGLE (Paul Sylbert, 1971), and Columbia's THE PURSUIT OF HAPPINESS (Robert Mulligan, 1971) fall into this category, as do BBS Productions' Columbia-released FIVE EASY PIECES (Bob Rafelson, 1970), DRIVE, HE SAID (Jack Nicholson, 1972), and A SAFE PLACE (Henry Jaglom, 1971). Finally, several films evoking urban paranoia—a newly urgent theme after years of ghetto riots and rising crime rates—were given youth appeal through their casting: most obviously United Artists' X-rated MIDNIGHT COWBOY (John Schlesinger, 1969), whose stars Dustin Hoffman and Jon Voight were both nominated for Oscars (which the picture and screenplay won), and Fox's MOVE (Stuart Rosenberg, 1970) and LITTLE MURDERS (Alan Arkin, 1971; adapted by Jules Feiffer from his own stage play), both of which starred M*A*S*H's youth-cult icon Elliott Gould.

Genre and Television

Another crucial factor in the explosion of genres was television. When series television subsumed the function of B-films during the late fifties and sixties, it reproduced nearly all of the classical Hollywood genres—the Western, the crime melodrama, the screwball comedy, etc.—and there was an inevitable debasement and cheapening of the original formulas. As Stephen Schiff comments, "When the mass audience was regularly exposed to *Bonanza, Gunsmoke, Rawhide, Wagon Train, The Wild, Wild West*, and so on, it realized how limited and boring the Western could be."[25] In this argument, the self-awareness that enters the "adult" Hollywood Westerns of the late fifties and early sixties, as well as the self-consciousness of the Italian "spaghetti Westerns," may be traced to the infinite repetition of genre iconography on television, until finally, by the decade's end, the Western setting could only be used in ways that emphasize either its exhaustion (THE WILD BUNCH) or its quaintness (BUTCH CASSIDY AND THE SUNDANCE KID). Another complementary way in which television exploded genre was to become a kind of museum of classical cinema. Between 1955 and 1957, all of the majors but MGM sold the bulk of their pre-1948 films (those owned outright and not subject to residual payments) to distributors who syndicated them to local stations.[26] In the early 1960s, the networks followed suit and increased their prime-time programming of Hollywood features. Starting with the *NBC Saturday Night Movie* in 1961, by 1968 there was a network prime-time movie showcase for every night of the week, which had the effect of turning every household in America into a private film museum. As Robert B. Ray puts it, "By plundering Hollywood's archive, television encouraged a new attitude toward the popular cinema and the traditional mythology it embodied."[27] Christopher Anderson has pointed out how this situation helped to foster the New Hollywood both materially and culturally. On the one hand, income from teleproduction and profits from film library sales helped to subsidize the boom-or-bust mentality of the New Hollywood by reducing the risk of blockbuster production; on the other, television's "archiving" of classical cinema by constantly recycling of studio-era films helped to form the New Hollywood's historical consciousness—that unique sense of retrospection that informs the work of nearly every major figure of the 1970s from Altman through Spielberg—becoming a major point of demarcation between the "old" Hollywood and the new.[28] For the mass audience, however, the constant diet of genre-based TV shows and classical Hollywood genre films bred something like contempt for traditional generic conventions, reinforcing a sense that they had become old-fashioned, "unrealistic," and culturally irrelevant.

The Western

The 1970s revision of the Western genre provides a striking example of this process. Traditionally associated with conservative cultural and political values (in the hands of John Ford, say), the Western became a vehicle for antiwar protest and social criticism in the early years of the decade. Six months before the release of EASY RIDER, Richard Nixon had been inaugurated as the thirty-sixth president of the United States, and three months later the toll of Americans killed in Vietnam reached 33,641 and exceeded that of the Korean War. Despite Nixon's election-year pledge to end the war and "bring us together," his strategy in office was to escalate it and stifle dissent by exploiting the "generation gap" he had promised to close. His ultimate move in this direction was the invasion of Cambodia, announced in a television address on April 30, 1970, which unleashed a storm of protest across the nation, culminating in the killing of the four college students at Kent State University by the Ohio National Guard on May 4th. This event and the public response to it (according to a *Newsweek* poll, 58 percent of respondents thought the shootings were justified)[29] capped several years of political violence and divisiveness, which had begun with the assassinations of Martin Luther King, Jr. and Robert Kennedy in April and June 1968, and the police riot at the National Democratic

Convention in Chicago that August. This violence, together with the conviction that the United States was waging a pointless and immoral war in Southeast Asia, produced a mood of cultural despair among America's youth that, after Kent State, bordered on the apocalyptic. The hopelessness and romantic fatalism that pervades so many of Hollywood's 1969–1971 youth-cult films, starting with EASY RIDER and continuing through ZABRISKIE POINT (whose release was delayed by MGM until outrage over Kent State had abated) and JOE, can be traced very specifically to this despair and the Nixonian politics of division that produced it. So too can the infusion of the Hollywood Western with antimilitary, anti-colonial, anti-imperialist themes that occurred at precisely the same time—it was a brief historical moment in which American genre films, like their counterparts in Eastern Europe and the Soviet Union, became vehicles for symbolic political expression because the real thing had become too dangerous (or, at least, too controversial) for the studios to subsidize directly.

THE "VIETNAM WESTERN"

Prefigured by Abraham Polonsky's parable TELL THEM WILLIE BOY IS HERE (Universal, 1969) and Elliot Silverstein's A MAN CALLED HORSE (Cinema Center Films, 1970)—an anthropologically correct account of Sioux tribal life circa 1820—a number of Westerns appeared in the early 1970s that for the first time depicted native Americans as heroes in their struggles against the U.S. cavalry. These new-Left "Vietnam Westerns," as Thomas Schatz has called them, used the taming of the West as a metaphor for American involvement in Vietnam and were distinctly revisionist in terms of theme.[30] Pre-eminent among them was Arthur Penn's LITTLE BIG MAN (National General, 1970), which portrayed the "pacification" of the frontier as a genocidal war against the Indians, who were clearly intended to represent the people of Vietnam and whose way of life was equated with the contemporary American counterculture. (The film's set piece is a shocking re-creation of the Washita River Massacre of 1868, which the title character/ narrator [Dustin Hoffman] bluntly refers to as "an act of genocide.") Ralph Nelson's SOLDIER BLUE (Avco Embassy, 1970), according to its epilogue, was prompted by the recent revelation of American atrocities in Vietnam in the American press (specifically, the My Lai massacre of March 16, 1968). Much of the film is irrelevant to this issue, but there is a truly horrific massacre at its conclusion in which an American general— played, like Custer in Penn's film, as a half-mad racial chauvinist—orders his troops to raze a Cheyenne village. This sequence contains images of rape, pillage, and dismemberment modeled on photographs from My Lai, which had to be cut to avoid an X rating from CARA and were sensationally touted in the press.[31] As a film, rather than as a political tract, SOLDIER BLUE fell far below the achievement of LITTLE BIG MAN. Yet both spoke to the genocidal policies of the U.S. high command (and, as we now know, the CIA) in Vietnam, and to the paranoid sense of imminent extinction that Kent State had fostered among America's youth. (The most direct and extreme expression of this paranoia was Peter Watkins's independently produced PUNISHMENT PARK [1971], a cin-ema verité-style "docudrama" in which antiwar protestors are literally hunted down by National Guard troops in a game park; the film received only limited distribution [through Francoise], for obvious reasons.) The "Vietnam Western" theme was updated by Tom Laughlin's BILLY JACK (1971; re-released by Taylor-Laughlin, 1973), where the title character is a half-breed Vietnam veteran who defends the children of his reservation against a mob of white townies backed by the local sheriff. (BILLY JACK was actually

Avco Embassy's Soldier Blue *(Ralph Nelson, 1970), a self-proclaimed "Vietnam Western," modeled its horrific concluding massacre of a Cheyenne village by U.S. Cavalry troops on recently published photographs of the My Lai massacre and had to be cut to avoid an X rating for extreme violence: Ted Danson, Candice Bergen. 35mm Panavision anamorphic.*

the only movie to realize Hollywood's post-Easy Rider fantasy of huge grosses from a cheaply produced youth-cult film, and did so, ironically, by circumventing the industry's own distribution machinery: when Warner Bros. failed to adequately distribute the $800,000 film, Laughlin successfully sued the studio for the right to distribute it himself and then four-walled Billy Jack in a regional saturation re-release in May 1973—a strategy that brought in $32.2 million in rentals and became the model for blockbuster distribution several years after [see Chapter 2].)

Modernist or Anti-Westerns

"Vietnam Westerns" were made as late as 1972 (e.g., Robert Aldrich's Ulzana's Raid [Universal]; re-edited several times by its producer-distributor), but were soon displaced in the symbolic political hierarchy by Watergate and the new genre of "conspiracy films." Meanwhile, the mainstream Western of the 1970s became increasingly "modernist," either through overt myth-debunking as in Little Big Man, or through subversive, ambiguous style as in Robert Altman's McCabe & Mrs. Miller (Warner Bros., 1971), or both. Some films in the first category focused on deconstructing specific

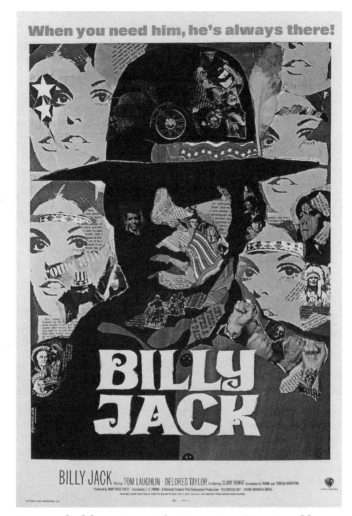

Semipsychedelic poster art for BILLY JACK *(Tom Laughlin, 1971; re-released 1973), vaguely suggesting an antiwar message (in its bits and pieces of the American flag), as well as an* EASY RIDER *connection (in its several images of motorcycles) but also emphasizing its iconography as a Western in Billy Jack's feathered hat.*

Western myths and stereotypes, such as Edwin Sherrin's VALDEZ IS COMING (MGM, 1971), Phil Kaufman's THE GREAT NORTHFIELD, MINNESOTA RAID (Universal, 1972), Stan Dragoti's DIRTY LITTLE BILLIE (WRG/Warner Bros., 1972), Frank Perry's DOC (United Artists, 1971), John Huston's THE LIFE AND TIMES OF JUDGE ROY BEAN (First Artists, 1972), and Sam Peckinpah's PAT GARRETT & BILLY THE KID (MGM, 1973). Others attempted to offer a historically realistic depiction of the harshness of Western life in general, for example, William Fraker's MONTE WALSH (Cinema Center, 1970), Peckinpah's THE BALLAD OF CABLE HOGUE (Warner Bros., 1970), Blake Edwards's

Demystifying the frontier: William Fraker's MONTE WALSH *(Cinema Center, 1970) starred Lee Marvin as an aging cowboy (seen here with Jeanne Moreau as his mistress). 35mm Panavision anamorphic.*

WILD ROVERS (United Artists, 1971), Michael Winner's LAWMAN (United Artists, 1971), Robert Benton's BAD COMPANY (Jaffilms/Paramount, 1972), Dick Richards's THE CULPEPPER CATTLE COMPANY (Fox, 1972), Jan Troell's ZANDY'S BRIDE (Warner Bros., 1974), and Clint Eastwood's THE OUTLAW—JOSEY WALES (Malpaso/Warner Bros., 1976). Among the 1970s Westerns that took the art film route are Peter Fonda's THE HIRED HAND (Universal, 1971), Dennis Hopper's THE LAST MOVIE (Universal, 1971), Sydney Pollack's JEREMIAH JOHNSON (Warner Bros., 1972), Clint Eastwood's HIGH PLAINS DRIFTER (Malpaso/Universal, 1973), James Frawley's KID BLUE (Fox, 1973), Frank Perry's RANCHO DELUXE (United Artists, 1975), Richard Brooks's BITE THE BULLET (Columbia, 1975), Robert Altman's BUFFALO BILL AND THE INDIANS, OR SITTING BULL'S HISTORY LESSON (De Laurentiis, 1976), Arthur Penn's THE MISSOURI BREAKS (United Artists, 1976), and Monte Hellman's CHINA 9, LIBERTY 37 (CEA, 1978). These self-conscious films, acutely aware of their classical heritage, were the logical culmination of the demystifying strain injected into the genre during the sixties by the Italian "spaghetti Westerns" (such as Sergio Leone's FISTFUL OF DOLLARS [1964], FOR A FEW DOLLARS MORE [1966], THE GOOD, THE BAD, AND THE UGLY [1966], and ONCE UPON A TIME IN THE WEST [1968]) and by such antiheroic domestic Westerns as Sam Peckinpah's MAJOR DUNDEE (Columbia, 1965), Monte Hellman's RIDE IN THE WHIRLWIND (1965) and THE SHOOTING (1967), Tom Gries's WILL PENNY

Robert Benton's BAD COMPANY *(Jaffilms/Paramount, 1972) concerns two young draft-dodgers who rob their way across the West during the Civil War: Damon Cofer, John Savage in a highly undignified stickup. 35mm 1.85:1.*

(Paramount, 1968), and, preeminently, Peckinpah's THE WILD BUNCH (Warner Bros., 1969)—often described as the first "anti-Western," although it simultaneously functions as a bitter elegy to western myths and values.

Modernist Westerns of the 1970s were often unconventional in form, resorting to loosely structured narratives and New Wave-style reflexivity, both French and Eastern European (the latter partially attributable to the influence of the two great Hungarian émigré cinematographers—Laszlo Kovacs and Vilmos Zsigmond—who worked on many of them).[32] Altman's Westerns, for example, resemble nothing so much as the Czech New Wave films of Jan Kadar (THE SHOP ON MAIN STREET [1965]) and Milos Forman (FIREMAN'S BALL [1967]) in their use of nondiegetic music for thematic (as opposed to dramatic) reinforcement and their allusively dissident evocation of national institutions: MCCABE & MRS. MILLER is as much a critique of corporate capitalism as FIREMAN'S BALL is of Czechoslovak communism; and BUFFALO BILL AND THE INDIANS interrogates racial zealotry no less than THE SHOP ON MAIN STREET in a different context. But BUFFALO BILL is also relentlessly American, in a post-Watergate kind of way, as it attempts to show the myth of the Wild West in the very process of construction. Indeed, the ultimate burden of all 1970s modernist Westerns was to critique this myth-making process and aspire towards the condition of Michael Cimino's HEAVEN'S GATE (United Artists, 1980), where the historical West is presented as an economic and cultural evil—a malignant capitalist tumor on Eden's body.

Warners' JERIMIAH JOHNSON (Sydney Pollack, 1972) is a balladic film in which the harsh, occasionally (as here) absurd experiences of a mountain man form a kind of counter-myth to that of the romanticized, heroic frontiersman: Robert Redford in the title role. 35mm Panavision anamorphic.

Downtrodden Eastern European immigrants marshalled by hired gun fighter Nate Champion (Christopher Walken) in Michael Cimino's ultimate modernist Western HEAVEN'S GATE (UA, 1980), which one critic described as "The Johnson County Cattle Wars According to Karl Marx." 35mm Panavision anamorphic, blown up to 70mm for road-showing. Recorded and selectively exhibited in four-channel Dolby stereo optical sound; six-track stereo magnetic for 70mm prints.

TRADITIONAL WESTERNS

American-produced traditional Westerns continued to be popular during the decade, many of them owing to the presence of John Wayne (1907–1979), whose star power remained considerable throughout the 1970s, despite strong competition from such newcomers as Clint Eastwood (b. 1930) and Robert Redford (b. 1936).[33] Four of Wayne's seventies Westerns were made by his own production company, Batjac,[34] for distribution by Warner Bros.—CHISUM (Andrew V. McLaglen, 1970), BIG JAKE (George Sherman, 1971), THE TRAIN ROBBERS (Burt Kennedy, 1973), and CAHILL—UNITED STATES MARSHALL (Andrew V. McLaglen, 1973)—and were extremely conservative in their approach to the genre (unsurprisingly, given Wayne's ultra-rightist politics). But others— Howard Hawks's last film RIO LOBO (Malabar/Cinema Center Films/NGC, 1970); Mark Rydell's THE COWBOYS (Sanford/Warner Bros., 1972); and Stuart Millar's ROOSTER COGBURN (Universal, 1975), a sequel to Henry Hathaway's hugely popular TRUE GRIT (Paramount, 1969), were less so—especially Wayne's last film, THE SHOOTIST (Don Siegel, 1976), where he played an aging gunfighter dying of cancer, as Wayne himself was dying of the disease in real life. In fact, many of these traditional Westerns featured aging cowboys, and some (like Hawks's, Hathaway's, and Siegel's) were actually *about* aging, suggesting the creakiness of the Old West mythology and making the boundary between them and the revisionist Western less clear-cut than one might suppose.[35] Nonetheless, "spaghetti Westerns"—like Sergio Corbucci's COMPANEROS! (1971), Sergio Leone's A FISTFUL OF DYNAMITE (aka DUCK, YOU SUCKER, 1972), and Tonino Valerii's MY NAME IS NOBODY (1973)—held on to their market share in the early part of the decade, but lost much of their appeal in the wake of Mel Brooks's BLAZING SADDLES (Crossbow/Warner Bros., 1974), whose parodic deconstruction of the Western form made their own inflated generic posturing difficult to take seriously (if, indeed, it had ever been).[36]

COMIC AND PARODIC WESTERNS

Although it is true that the huge popular success of BLAZING SADDLES proclaimed genre parody as the quintessential comic film form of the seventies, it was hardly without precedent. Robert B. Ray points out that by the spring of 1966, as the New Hollywood stood poised to emerge, an enormous volume of television and motion picture fare was devoted to genre parody. [37] As noted earlier, television series such as *Batman, Get Smart,* and *The Wild, Wild West* (a parody of the already parodic *Maverick* series, popular from 1957–1962) subsisted exclusively on spoofing their respective genres, while such films as United Artists' THUNDERBALL (Terence Young, 1965) and Columbia's CAT BALLOU (Elliot Silverstein, 1965) were straws in the wind for hundreds of movies produced between 1967 and 1980 that would depend on their audiences' ability to recognize them as corrections, exaggerations, or revisions of mainstream classical genres. The critically acclaimed CAT BALLOU, which starred Lee Marvin in an Oscar-winning role as a drunken gunfighter, inaugurated the parody of Western generic clichés that reached its textual limit in BLAZING SADDLES. CAT BALLOU was followed almost immediately by such imitators as Universal's TEXAS ACROSS THE RIVER (Michael Gordon, 1966), Paramount's WATERHOLE #3 (William Graham, 1967) and a series of comic Westerns directed by Burt Kennedy, including THE WAR WAGON (Universal, 1967), SUPPORT YOUR LOCAL SHERIFF (United Artists, 1969), THE GOOD GUYS AND THE BAD GUYS (Warner-Seven Arts, 1969), YOUNG BILLY YOUNG (United Artists, 1969), and DIRTY DINGUS

BLAZING SADDLES (Crossbow/Warners, 1974) was a parodic deconstruction of Western genre conventions but also of film form itself. At the beginning of this shot, sheriff Cleavon Little has been riding the range to nondiegetic musical accompaniment when he suddenly rides past its source in Count Basie's on-site orchestra. 35mm Panavision anamorphic.

MAGEE (MGM, 1970), that culminated in SUPPORT YOUR LOCAL GUNFIGHTER (United Artists, 1971) and HANNIE CAULDER (Paramount, 1971). This tongue-in-cheek approach to the genre was so well established by the late sixties that it informed nearly every line of William Goldman's script for George Roy Hill's BUTCH CASSIDY AND THE SUNDANCE KID (Fox, 1969), which, with $45.9 million in rentals ($21 million in 1969; the rest from re-release), became one of the most successful Westerns ever made. (It's worth noting that two other popular Westerns of 1969, both from Paramount, contained parodic elements—Henry Hathaway's TRUE GRIT, the eighth-highest earner of the year with $14.2 million in rentals, and Josh Logan's musical comedy PAINT YOUR WAGON, which was the seventh with $14.5 million but still a loser given its negative cost of $20 million.)

By the early 1970s, even the "spaghetti Western" had begun to parody itself with films like BLINDMAN (Ferdinando Baldi, 1972), and the "Trinity" series: THEY CALL ME TRINITY (E. B. Clutcher, 1971), TRINITY IS STILL MY NAME (E. B. Clutcher, 1972), and MAN OF THE EAST (E. B. Clucher, 1972), which also contained a parody of BUTCH CASSIDY AND THE SUNDANCE KID.[38] Clearly, BLAZING SADDLES had many predecessors, but it was unique in the extremity of its deconstruction, much of which is directed toward a subversion of film form itself—by revealing the source of nondiegetic sound on-camera, by exposing the two-dimensionality of apparently three-dimensional sets, and by having its characters crash through the Western set at the film's conclusion into several other studio sets, and finally into a movie theater where they watch themselves on screen. Western genre conventions and character types are parodied throughout the film, but a striking amount of its humor derives from the manipulation of racial stereotypes that have little or nothing to do with the Old West (but everything to do with the movies). Thus BLAZING SADDLES is considerably more deliberate than the "raunchy, protracted version of a television comedy skit" that *Variety* found it to be; but it scarcely dealt a death blow to the Western, as some critics have charged.[39] (In fact, the reverse could be argued, since its $47.8 million in rentals made it the most financially successful Western of all time.)[40]

PRINTING THE LEGEND

If there was a death blow to the Western genre, it was delivered by the political violence of 1968, Vietnam, and Watergate, after which the heroic utopian mythography of the American West became impossible to sustain. Domestic production of Westerns declined dramatically and proportionally year by year in the wake of these phenomena, so that after 1976 there was little but parody (Fox's THE DUCHESS AND THE DIRTWATER FOX [Melvin Frank, 1976], AIP's GREAT SCOUT AND CATHOUSE THURSDAY [Don Taylor, 1976]), comedy (Paramount's GOIN' SOUTH [Jack Nicholson, 1978], Columbia's THE VILLAIN [Hal Needham, 1979], Warner Bros.' THE FRISCO KID [Robert Aldrich, 1979]), and sequels (United Artists' THE RETURN OF A MAN CALLED HORSE [Irvin Kershner, 1976], Fox's BUTCH AND SUNDANCE: THE EARLY DAYS [Richard Lester, 1979]—actually a "prequel"), spiked by an occasionally serious contemporary Western (United Artists' COMES A HORSEMAN [Alan J. Pakula, 1978]; Columbia's THE ELECTRIC HORSEMAN [Sydney Pollack, 1979]). By 1980, Hollywood production of Westerns had dwindled to six films—one of them bizarre (WINDWALKER [Pacific International; Kieth Merrill]), two of them resolutely silly (BRONCO BILLY [Warner Bros.; Clint Eastwood], CATTLE ANNIE AND LITTLE BRITCHES [Hemdale; Lamont Johnson]), and the rest grim to the point of nihilism (HEAVEN'S GATE [United Artists; Michael Cimino], THE LONG RIDERS [United Artists; Walter Hill], TOM HORN [Warner Bros./First Artists; William Wiard])—and there were only four each in 1981 and 1982. The Western has been an undeniably impoverished genre since the 1970s, although popular Western films continue to be made. It has been noted, for example, that whereas only one Western had won an Academy Award for Best Picture before 1989 (RKO's CIMARRON [1931], directed by Wesley Ruggles), two have won since (Orion's DANCES WITH WOLVES [1990], directed by Kevin Costner; and Warner Bros.' UNFORGIVEN [1992], directed by Clint Eastwood),[41] but both are films that succeed by standing classical conventions on their head and taking a deeply pessimistic view of human nature in general, and (white) society in particular. More and more, it begins to seem that the period 1969–1980 was the Western's last great moment, after which, to paraphrase Lee Clark Mitchell's *Westerns*, there was little but repetition of plots, visual fetishes, and character types.[42]

The Gangster Film

Other action genres experienced a similar transformation during the 1970s, notably the gangster film and the detective film, or *film noir*. (The combat film was another

Fox's PATTON *(Franklin Schaffner, 1970), an extremely ambivalent biopic/combat film, written by Francis Ford Coppola, which fluctuated between right-wing chauvinism and antiwar sentiments: George C. Scott in the title role. Dimension 150 (70mm), with six-track stereo magnetic sound.*

action subtype revised in the early 1970s, but with great caution, since America was still deeply conflicted about its involvement in Vietnam, yielding such anomalies as the release of M*A*S*H [Robert Altman], PATTON [Franklin Schaffner], and TORA! TORA! TORA! [Richard Fleischer] by the same studio [Fox] in the same year [1970]—when they became numbers 3, 4, and 8 at the box office, respectively. Things became somewhat clearer after the American withdrawal in 1975, and by the end of the decade films like THE DEER HUNTER [Michael Cimino, 1978], COMING HOME [Hal Ashby, 1978], and APOCALYPSE NOW [Francis Ford Coppola, 1979] could address the conflict directly.) As with the Western, skepticism about American values undercut classical conceptions of heroism and individual destiny in both genres, leaving their protagonists to face a world too complicated to control or even understand. BONNIE AND CLYDE (Arthur Penn, 1967), with its sympathetic protagonists and graphic violence, was the premiere revisionist gangster film, and its reworking of the "criminal couple" subgenre (e.g., THEY LIVE BY NIGHT [Nicholas Ray, 1949]) inflected many seventies variations of the form. These include low-budget imitations like Fox's DIRTY MARY

CRAZY LARRY (John Hough, 1974), Warner Bros.' ALOHA, BOBBY AND ROSE (Floyd Mutrux, 1975), and New World's CRAZY MAMA (Jonathan Demme, 1975), as well as such original productions as Sam Peckinpah's THE GETAWAY (National General, 1972), based on Jim Thompson's novel; Terrence Malick's BADLANDS (Warner Bros., 1973), based on the Charles Starkweather-Carol Fugate murder spree of 1957–1958; Robert Altman's THIEVES LIKE US (United Artists, 1974), based on the source novel for THEY LIVE BY NIGHT; and Steven Spielberg's THE SUGARLAND EXPRESS (Universal, 1974), also based on real-life fugitives. The most unusual criminal couple film of the decade, and in many ways the most distinguished, was unquestionably Sidney Lumet's DOG DAY AFTERNOON (Warners, 1975), based on a real-life incident in which a bisexual man (played by Al Pacino) held up a bank in New York City in order to finance a sex-change operation for his male lover. In nearly all of these films, the criminal couple is portrayed sympathetically (though not without irony) and martyred at the film's conclusion by callous lawmen, reversing the moral order of the classical universe. Yet the American gangster film had always been used as a vehicle to explore wider social and cultural issues, and the criminal couples of the seventies were in many ways configured as romantic revolutionaries against the system that gave us Watergate and Vietnam (and could therefore expect to be dealt with by the authorities in the same manner as the Kent State Four). As usual, AIP contributed several low-end but cre-

Sidney Lumet's DOG DAY AFTERNOON *(Warners, 1975). The criminal couple in this film are a bisexual man and his dim-witted sidekick who rob a bank to finance a sex-change operation for the former's male lover; based on a real-life occurrence, the film won an Oscar for its orginal screenplay by Frank Pierson. 35mm 1.85:1.*

atively distinct versions of the mainstream prototype—BLOODY MAMA (Roger Corman, 1970), BOXCAR BERTHA (Martin Scorsese, 1972), DILLINGER (John Milius, 1973)—films with romanticized criminal heroes, whose murderous behavior is tempered by winning personality or mitigating circumstance.

The corruption of the system was implicit in another type of gangster film prominent during the 1970s—the Mafia family saga as apotheosized by Francis Ford Coppola's THE GODFATHER (Paramount, 1972) and THE GODFATHER, PART II (Paramount, 1974). Before THE GODFATHER unexpectedly became the first great blockbuster of the decade, and inspired many imitations, there had been only a handful of films dealing with organized crime families (most recently, Paramount's THE BROTHERHOOD [Martin Ritt, 1968], and the TV-movie HONOR THY FATHER [Paul Wendkos, 1971], based on Gay Talese's nonfiction best-seller). Taken together, the two GODFATHER films trace the history of the fictional Corleone family from the early years of the twentieth century through the 1960s as its criminal business empire evolves in tandem with that of corporate America from free market capitalism to oligopoly, monopoly, and finally hegemonic global imperialism. In PART II, the equation of legitimate and illegitimate business is made quite clear when the Corleones' partners in

The AIP gangster film—lean and mean: Ben Johnson (with cigar) as FBI agent Melvin Purvis in DILLINGER *(John Milius, 1973). 35mm 1.85:1*

Two sides of family life in Francis Ford Coppola's THE GODFATHER, PART II
(Paramount, 1974), probably the most distinguished sequel ever made:
(above) Michael and Kay Corleone host a family wedding at their Lake Tahoe estate:
Al Pacino and Diane Keaton. (below) Vito Corleone, as a young man in Sicily, in a
flashback to the murder of his first wife: Robert De Niro. 35mm 1.85:1.

taking control of the Cuban gambling industry are shown to be a combination of American conglomerates (real and fictive)—United Fruit, United Telephone and Telegraph, and Pan-American Mining—as well as the Teamsters union and assorted U.S. senators. Appropriately bracketing the Watergate scandal (the break-in occurred on May 28, 1972, and Nixon resigned the presidency in disgrace on August 8, 1974), THE GODFATHER and THE GODFATHER, PART II stopped just short of confirming the prediction of a leading Mafia expert that "organized crime will put a man in the White House some day, and he won't even know it until they hand him the bill."[43] Other seventies gangster films that focussed on the Mafia, or Cosa Nostre, were Dino De Laurentiis's Columbia-released THE VALACHI PAPERS (Terence Young, 1972) and CRAZY JOE (Carlo Lizzani, 1974), Universal's THE DON IS DEAD (Richard Fleischer, 1973), the Italian-produced LUCKY LUCIANO (Francesco Rosi, 1974), and Warner Bros.' LEPKE (Menahem Golan, 1975). (There were also numerous black action films with plots that revolved around conflicts between black mobsters and white Mafiosi—for example, United Artists' ACROSS 110TH STREET [Barry Shear, 1972], Columbia's BLACK GUNN [Robert Hartford-Davis, 1972], AIP's BLACK CAESAR [Larry Cohen, 1973] and HELL UP IN HARLEM [Larry Cohen, 1973], and Cinemation's THE BLACK GODFATHER [John Evans, 1974].) Although no subsequent gangster film came even close to the magisterial sweep of Coppola's work, the small-time Italian American hoods of Martin Scorsese's MEAN STREETS [Warner Bros., 1973] provided a sort of miniature version in the form of an urban youth-crime drama. Toward the decade's end, an unusual musical parody of the classical Hollywood gangster film appeared from Britain in BUGSY MALONE (Alan Parker, 1976), cast entirely with children (whose machine guns shot whipped cream instead of bullets), and United Artists produced F.I.S.T. (Norman

BUGSY MALONE (Paramount U.K., 1976), Alan Parker's musical parody of 1930s-style gangster films, featured bad guys whose tommy guns shot whipped cream. 35mm 1.75:1.

Norman Jewison's F.I.S.T. (UA, 1978): Sylvester Stallone as labor leader Johnny Kovak, whose Federation of Interstate Truckers—a thinly veiled verson of the Teamsters union (its long-time boss Jimmy Hoffa had disappeared on July 30, 1975 and was presumed to have been murdered by rivals)—is infiltrated by the mob. 35mm 1.85:1

Jewison, 1978), a film about labor racketeering in the thirties that depicted a union's infiltration by organized crime for the first time since Elia Kazan's ON THE WATERFRONT (Columbia, 1954). However, the GODFATHER films dominated the mobster subgenre until the appearance of Sergio Leone's epic and compendious homage ONCE UPON A TIME IN AMERICA (Ladd, 1984).

Film Noir *and Other Crime Genres*

The detective film, or *film noir*, reappeared in the 1970s after a long dry spell in the late fifties and sixties when the cultural malaise that had driven it since the end of World War II was replaced by prosperity, consumerism, and fear of nuclear holocaust. Postwar *film noir* was fundamentally a "cinema of moral anxiety" dealing with the conditions forced upon honest people by a mendacious, self-deluding society,[44] and the sense of alienation, corruption, and pessimism that this implies returned to the American detective film with a vengeance during the era of Watergate and Vietnam. (Geoffrey O'Brien has suggested that *film noir* was not a genre at all but "a slick new variety of packaging" designed to attract dwindling postwar audiences back to the theater with a blend of sex, violence, and fashionable nihilism.[45] If true, the same logic would apply to the 1970s, whose confused cultural politics were quite similar to those of 1944–1950.)

SEVENTIES *Film Noir*

Created by the "hard-boiled" school of American crime-writers—Dashiell Hammett, Raymond Chandler, James M. Cain, and Horace McCoy (later joined by Mickey Spillane and Jim Thompson)—the *film noir* detective was originally a paragon of courageous individualism: tough, resourceful, and, above all, heroic in combating the moral anarchy that surrounded him.[46] The seventies *noir* detective, by contrast, is bemused, vulnerable, and inept—as often as not the victim of an anachronistic code of honor. For example, in Robert Altman's THE LONG GOODBYE (United Artists, 1973), adapted from the novel by Raymond Chandler but updated to contemporary Los Angeles, Marlowe (Elliott Gould) becomes a fall-guy for his best friend, who abuses the detective's trust to cover up the murder of his wife. At the conclusion of Roman Polanski's period *noir* CHINATOWN (Paramount, 1974), from an original screenplay by Robert Towne, private eye J. J. Gittes (Jack Nicholson) unwittingly helps the Los Angeles police assassinate the woman he loves and is sworn to protect. (As Polanski later wrote, "I saw CHINATOWN not as a 'retro' piece or conscious imitation of classic movies shot in black and white, but as a film about the thirties seen through the camera eye of the seventies.")[47] Harry Mosbey (Gene Hackman), the detective in Arthur Penn's NIGHT MOVES (Warner Bros., 1975), fails miserably to comprehend the larger picture that his obsessively assembled clues suggest, facilitates the deaths of several innocent people, and finally stumbles onto the truth when it is no longer relevant. Penn's description of NIGHT MOVES as "a counter-

Director Roman Polanski (back to camera) plays a thug about to slit one of detective J. J. Gittes's (Jack Nicholson) nostrils in Paramount's CHINATOWN *(1974). The film's most distinctive feature, one critic wrote, "is the peculiarly understated ferocity of its nihilism." 35mm Panavision anamorphic.*

Though Polanski himself didn't see CHINATOWN *as a "'retro'
piece," Paramount marketing executives clearly did, as this
famous nostalgia-drenched poster shows.*

genre film, a private-eye film about a detective who finds that the solution is not solv-
able" could apply to most 1970s *films noirs*.[48] Others that conform more or less to this
revisionist pattern are MGM's CHANDLER (Paul Magwood, 1972—not to be confused
with MGM's MARLOWE [Paul Bogart, 1969], which is an adaptation of Raymond
Chandler's novel *The Little Sister*); Warner Bros.' KLUTE (Alan J. Pakula, 1971); United
Artists' HICKEY & BOGGS (Robert Culp, 1972); Columbia's SHAMUS (Buzz Kulik, 1973);
Warner Bros.' THE YAKUZA (Sydney Pollack, 1975), from an original script by Paul
Schrader and Robert Towne about an American investigator confronting the mob in
Japan, THE DROWNING POOL (Stuart Rosenberg, 1976), based on Ross Macdonald char-
acters, and THE LATE SHOW (Robert Benton, 1977); Avco Embassy's FAREWELL, MY

Gene Hackman as Harry Mosbey, a detective who "finds that the solution is not solvable" in Arthur Penn's Night Moves *(Warners, 1975). 35mm 1.85:1.*

Lovely (Dick Richards, 1975), adapted from the Chandler novel originally filmed in 1944 as Murder, My Sweet (Edward Dmytryk); United Artists' The Big Sleep (Michael Winner, 1978), a remake of Howard Hawks's 1946 version of the Chandler novel scripted by William Faulkner, et al.; and Universal's The Big Fix (Jeremy Paul Kagan, 1978), a post–youth-cult *film noir*, in which the detective is an ex-1960s radical in search of an ex-hippie cult leader. Central to all of these films are protagonists who are lost in a world that they no longer understand and are therefore powerless to master. What J. J. Gittes is told by another character in Chinatown is emblematic of this condition in general: "You may think you know what you're dealing with, but believe me, you don't." Or, as Marlowe (Robert Mitchum) expresses it at one point in Farewell, My Lovely: "I've run out of trust in this joint. . . . Everything I touch turns to shit." (A highly specialized subtype of detective movie, the Sherlock Holmes film, also experienced considerable revision during the 1970s [not to mention parody] in such sophisticated treatments as United Artists' The Private Life of Sherlock Holmes [Billy Wilder, 1970], Universal's The Seven-Per-cent Solution [Herbert Ross, 1976], and Avco's Murder by Decree [Bob Clark, 1979], all of which revealed Holmes's cocaine addiction and suggested an emotionally complicated relationship with Watson.)

A close counterpart of the tired and alienated private eyes in the detective film was the *noir* cop as represented in Warner Bros.' "Dirty Harry" series with Clint Eastwood (Dirty Harry [Don Siegel, 1971]; Magnum Force [Ted Post, 1973]; The Enforcer [James Fargo, 1976]) and The Gauntlet (Clint Eastwood, 1977); Fox's The French

The noir *cop as vigilante in Don Siegel's* DIRTY HARRY *(Warners, 1971): "Dirty Harry" Callahan (Clint Eastwood) walks away from some collateral damage he has inflicted on the streets of San Franciso in the course of nailing a criminal offender. 35mm Panavision anamorphic.*

CONNECTION (William Friedkin, 1971), THE SEVEN-UPS (Philip D'Antonio, 1973), and THE FRENCH CONNECTION II (John Frankenheimer, 1975); Paramount's SERPICO (Sidney Lumet, 1973) and HUSTLE (Robert Aldrich, 1975); Columbia's THE NEW CENTURIONS (Richard Fleischer, 1972); Universal's THE CHOIRBOYS (Robert Aldrich, 1977); and Avco Embassy's THE ONION FIELD (Harold Becker, 1979)—the last three adapted from novels by Joseph Wambaugh. Like Harry Callahan in DIRTY HARRY, which Pauline Kael lambasted as "a deeply immoral movie," many of the cops in these movies operated outside of the law.[49] Their high quotient of vigilantism seems to confirm the argument of Michael Ryan and Douglas Kellner in *Camera Politica* that the 1970s *film noir* revival signaled the death of political liberalism, which found itself suddenly powerless against the economic realities of corporate capitalism and the military-industrial state.[50] On the other hand, it seems clear that the deep cultural pessimism engendered by Vietnam and Watergate cut across the entire political spectrum—bearing out Kael's 1973 dictum that "[t]oday, movies say that the system is corrupt, that the whole thing stinks." Such is the case in such films as National General's PRIME CUT (Michael Ritchie, 1972); Paramount's THE FRIENDS OF EDDIE COYLE (Peter Yates, 1973) and FRAMED (Phil Karlson, 1975); MGM's THE OUTFIT (John Flynn, 1974); Universal's THE MIDNIGHT MAN (Ronald Kibbee, 1974); Fox's THE LAUGHING POLICEMAN (Stuart Rosenberg, 1974) and 99 AND 44/100% DEAD (John Frankenheimer, 1974), THE NICKEL

Karel Reisz's WHO'LL STOP THE RAIN *(UA, 1978), one of the darkest films about the moral paralysis inflicted on the home front by the war in Vietnam: Nick Nolte and Tuesday Weld on the run from the police, the mob, the CIA, and just about everyone else because they have what every aspiring American power-broker needs—two kilos of heroin. 35mm 1.85:1.*

RIDE (Robert Mulligan, 1975), and THE DRIVER (Walter Hill, 1978); Warner Bros.' DOG DAY AFTERNOON (Sidney Lumet, 1975) and THE KILLER INSIDE ME (Burt Kennedy, 1976); Faces Distribution's THE KILLING OF A CHINESE BOOKIE (John Cassavetes, 1976); Columbia's SHAMUS (Buzz Kulik, 1973), TAXI DRIVER (Martin Scorsese, 1976), and HARDCORE (Paul Schrader, 1979); and United Artists' THE MECHANIC (Michael Winner, 1972), BUSTING (Peter Hyams, 1974), and WHO'LL STOP THE RAIN (Karel Reisz, 1978), the latter an adaptation of Robert Stone's corrosive, award-winning novel *Dog Soldiers* (1974), about the fury that engulfs two Vietnam veterans when they smuggle several kilos of heroin back into California.[51] As one critic wrote, WHO'LL STOP THE RAIN (Stone's title was changed so that the film could be cross-marketed with its Creedence Clearwater Revival sound-track album) embodied "the ethical fragmentation and moral paralysis that spread like a plague through America's intellectuals as they witnessed Vietnam."[52] In all these films, however, whatever their specific motive force, a sense of fatality, hopelessness, and dread threatens to overwhelm the characters even as they struggle against the disorder of the modern world.

THE "VIGILANTE REVENGE" CYCLE

In a related 1970s subgenre, the "vigilante revenge film," populist heroes took the law into their own hands to fight against crime, corruption, and authoritarian bureaucracy,

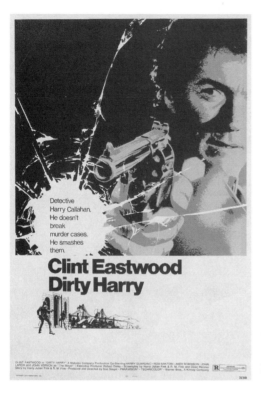

Guns, Guns, Guns! Vigilantism was big
box-office between 1971 and 1974 as
the Nixon administration (self-destruc-
tively, it turned out) urged Americans
to "get tough on crime."

Poster for DIRTY HARRY fetishizing his
police-issue Magnum .45.

Poster for Sam Peckinpah's THE
GETAWAY (First Artists/National
General, 1972), in which "Doc"
McCoy (Steve McQueen) and his
wife Carol (Ali MacGraw) settle
old scores with deadly force.

Poster for Michael Winner's urban "vigilante revenge film" DEATH WISH (Paramount, 1974) in which Charles Bronson stalks the murderers of his wife and daughter in the streets of New York.

Joe Don Baker as Tennessee sheriff Buford Pusser in Phil Karlson's WALKING TALL (AIP/Cinerama Releasing, 1973), the rural "vigilante revenge film" that became the anchor for a major exploitation franchise and inspired many others. The re-mythologization of the rural South was a key feature of American popular culture during the 1970s, which found political expression in the election of a peanut farmer from a small town in Georgia as the thirty-eighth president of the United States.

often from a rightist perspective. Typically, the protagonist was a decent man who had been wronged but cannot receive justice under law and is forced to seek redress by violating it. BILLY JACK (Warners, 1971; re-released by Taylor-Laughlin, 1973) was the model for this type of film, and its basic strategy was that a vicious attack upon the hero's loved one(s) catalyzed his general sense of abuse and pushed him to seek violent retribution.[53] (Like Howard Beale in NETWORK [United Artists; Sidney Lumet, 1976], he's "mad as hell and not going to take it anymore.") BILLY JACK earned $32.5 million through its re-release and generated two successful sequels from Warners—THE TRIAL OF BILLY JACK (Tom Laughlin, 1974), which indicts the criminal justice system and blames Nixon personally for Watergate; and BILLY JACK GOES TO WASHINGTON (Tom Laughlin, 1977), a virtual remake of Frank Capra's depression-era classic MR. SMITH GOES TO WASHINGTON (1939). It also inspired the AIP/CRC release WALKING TALL (Phil Karlson, 1973), an ultraviolent exploitation film based on the true story of Buford Pusser (played by Joe Don Baker), the club-wielding rural sheriff who had single-handedly cleaned up the vice-ridden town of Selma, Tennessee, after thugs murdered his wife. Opening slowly on the regional drive-in circuit, this brutal endorsement of vigilantism became the sleeper of the year when it went into national release and returned $10 million in rentals against its tiny budget by attracting significant urban crossover. At the same time that *Photoplay* readers of 1973 voted WALKING TALL their "Favorite Motion Picture of the Year," New York critics like Vincent Canby and Andrew Sarris were praising its "accomplished artistry."[54] Two AIP-distributed theatrical sequels—WALKING TALL, PART 2 (Earl Bellamy, 1975) and WALKING TALL—THE FINAL CHAPTER (Jack Starrett, 1977), both nearly as popular as the original—continued the story through Pusser's death in a suspicious car accident in 1974. And a 1978 CBS-TV movie based on his career, "A Real American Hero" (Lou Antonio, 12/9/78), became the pilot for a brief series.

The WALKING TALL franchise inspired many imitations in the exploitation field and was itself a prime example of a general re-mythologizing of the country—particularly the rural South—in American popular culture during the 1970s. Stimulated by the decline of the nation's central cities and the rise of a "rust-belt" in the urban North, as well as by an economic boom in southern-rim states like Florida and Texas, this new mythos reflected the region's very real transformation in the wake of the Civil Rights movement of the 1960s. It was manifest materially in the national popularity of country-and-western music, CB (Citizens Band) radios, and movies with working-class rural or "redneck" heroes. By mid-decade, Southern-based car-chase movies (THE LAST AMERICAN HERO [Lamont Johnson, 1973], EAT MY DUST! [Charles Griffith, 1976], SMOKEY AND THE BANDIT [Hal Needham, 1977]); trucker movies (WHITE LINE FEVER [Jonathan Kaplan, 1975], BREAKER! BREAKER! [Don Hulette, 1977], CONVOY [Sam Peckinpah, 1978]); romantic melodramas (BUSTER AND BILLIE [Daniel Petrie, 1974], ODE TO BILLY JOE [Max Baer, 1976]); horror films (THE TEXAS CHAINSAW MASSACRE [Tobe Hooper, 1974], THE HILLS HAVE EYES [Wes Craven, 1977]); and crime thrillers (MACON COUNTY LINE [Richard Compton, 1974], JACKSON COUNTY JAIL [Michael Miller, 1976], GATOR [Burt Reynolds, 1976]) were booming as newly created state film commissions helped to make location shooting in "the new South" an economically attractive alternative to filming on location elsewhere.[55]

The boom had extended to television by the late 1970s, where the rural South figured prominently in such series as *The Dukes of Hazzard* (CBS, 1979–1985), *B. J. and the Bear* (NBC, 1979–1981), and *The Misadventures of Sheriff Lobo* (NBC, 1979–1980). But it was in the vigilante revenge subgenre that the South figured most prominently during the 1970s, perhaps because, "new" or not, it had always registered statistically as the most violent part of the country. (Since records began to be kept in the nineteenth century, the South has had the highest homicide rate in the United States—nearly double that of the Northeast—a key factor in America's disproportionately high murder rate relative to other industrialized nations.)[56] Rural revenge provided the basic plotline for such films as WHITE LIGHTNING (Joseph Sargent, 1973), FRAMED (Phil Karlson, 1975), FIGHTING MAD (Jonathan Demme, 1976), VIGILANTE FORCE (George Armitage, 1976), A SMALL TOWN IN TEXAS (Jack Starrett, 1976), THE BLACK OAK CONSPIRACY (Bob Kelljan, 1977), ROLLING THUNDER (John Flynn, 1977; story by Paul Schrader), THE FARMER (David Berlatsky, 1977), and WOLF LAKE (Burt Kennedy, 1978)—all of which pit an individual (often a returned Vietnam veteran) or a small town against dark forces of crime, greed, or corporate cupidity. The populist impulse of these rural revenge films is clearly related to the ideal of working-class purity enshrined in urban films like ROCKY (John G. Avildsen, 1976; see below), whose heroes overcome impossible odds to rise above their "betters." At the core of both is the resentment of wealth, sophistication, and high culture that informs all populist mythologies of the little man, spiked with Watergate-Vietnam era mistrust for institutional authority.

The vigilante revenge scenario was given an upscale urban context in Paramount's DEATH WISH (Michael Winner, 1974), in which a self-professed pacifist (Charles Bronson) becomes a free-ranging vigilante killer to avenge the murder-rape of his wife and daughter. This slickly directed, cynical film became the anchor for its own franchise, spawning three sequels in the eighties (DEATH WISH 2–4, 1982–1987) and inspiring both blatant imitations (THE EXTERMINATOR [James Glickenhaus, 1980]; AN EYE FOR AN EYE [Steve Carver, 1981]; THE ANNIHILATORS [Charles E. Sellier, Jr., 1985]), and a "feminist" rape-revenge cycle (i.e., women avenging their own rapes) that included Paramount's LIPSTICK (Lamont Johnson, 1976), as well as such gory exploitation fodder as I SPIT ON YOUR GRAVE (Meir Zarchi, 1977) and MS. 45 (Abel Ferrara, 1981). As this progression would suggest, the vigilante revenge subgenre became increasingly exploitative as the 1970s concluded, and finally became associated with the sadistic horror of films like MANIAC (William Lustig, 1980) and TERROR TRAIN (Roger Spottiswoode, 1980) which *Variety* christened as "demented revenge."[57] Nevertheless, we should recall that the rape-revenge motif was central to much 1970s cinema, appearing as the motive force in such important mainstream films as STRAW DOGS (Sam Peckinpah, 1971) and DELIVERANCE (John Boorman, 1972), as well as providing the opening scene of THE GODFATHER (1972), wherein Don Corleone vows to avenge the gang-rape of an undertaker's daughter that the law has failed to punish. Furthermore, the most critically acclaimed *film noir* of the decade, Martin Scorsese's TAXI DRIVER (Columbia, 1976), falls squarely within the category of vigilante revenge in its subplot of Travis Bickle liberating a twelve-year-old prostitute from her pimp.

THE "PARANOID" CONSPIRACY FILM

The sense that oppressive forces were at work against individual liberty, and that the law could not protect its citizens from them, was central to another subgenre of 1970s *film noir*. In both mood and theme, the conspiracy film was a type of paranoid political thriller that placed the blame for American society's corruption on plotters pursuing secret agendas to control national life. (These films were *paranoid* in the sense of Richard Hofstader's usage of the term in his 1967 essay: "The Paranoid Style in

In the independently distributed EXECUTIVE ACTION *(David Miller, 1973), Robert Ryan plays the leader of a cabal of conservative industrialists (representing, it is hinted, big steel, which President Kennedy had threatened to nationalize during an orgy of price-gouging in 1962) plotting to assassinate JFK in Dallas; Burt Lancaster is a government operative, probably CIA, heading up the project. 35mm 1.75:1.*

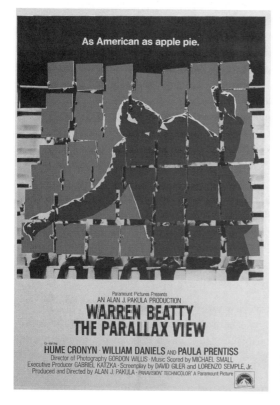

Poster for Alan J. Pakula's THE PARALLAX VIEW *(Paramount, 1974), locus classicus of the conspiracy film in its account of an "assassination bureau" that controls the nation's politics through seemingly random political murders.*

Poster for Francis Ford Coppola's THE
CONVERSATION *(The Directors Company/
Paramount, 1974); its subject is the moral
ambiguity of electronic surveillance.*

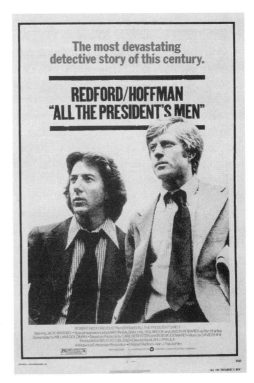

Poster for ALL THE PRESIDENT'S MEN
*(Warners, 1976), Pakula's other great con-
spiracy film, selling it as a detective story.*

American Politics," where he argues that an extremist strain runs throughout American political history, whose central preconception is "the existence of a vast, insidious, preternaturally effective international conspiratorial network designed to perpetrate acts of the most fiendish character."[58]) Inspired by the snowballing critique of the Warren Commission's investigation into the assassination of President Kennedy, and intensified by the revelations surrounding Watergate (as well as the Gulf of Tonkin incident, the Pentagon Papers, and the CIA-led coup against the Allende government in Chile), films about conspiracy began to appear in 1973.[59] (Appropriately, the Watergate cover-up came to national attention most prominently during the summer of 1973 as a result of the televised Senate Watergate Committee hearings, chaired by Senator Sam Ervin, May 17–August 7.) The first was the theatrical feature EXECUTIVE ACTION (David Miller, 1973), scripted by blacklist victim Dalton Trumbo (an original member of the "Hollywood Ten") from a story co-authored by Mark Lane, whose RUSH TO JUDGEMENT (1967) was the first and foremost documentary film to challenge the Warren Commission report. Produced with private funds and distributed by National General, EXECUTIVE ACTION marked the tenth anniversary of the Kennedy assassination by attributing it to a conspiracy of right-wing businessmen. (Intriguingly, though its dramatic scenes are woodenly directed, the film mixes newsreel and staged footage of events surrounding the assassination with an impressive verisimilitude that clearly influenced Oliver Stone's JFK [1991].) Alan Pakula's THE PARALLAX VIEW (Paramount, 1974) uses the assassination of a fictive U.S. senator and its subsequent cover-up to evoke the murder of both Kennedys and a vast corporate conspiracy that runs the country by assassinations disguised as accidents or the work of "lone nut" killers. The film's mystery-like plot revolves around the attempts of an investigative reporter (Warren Beatty) to penetrate the ultra-secret Parallax Corporation, a company whose only business, it transpires, is the recruitment of sociopaths to carry out political murders which blue-ribbon government panels—like the Warren Commission—then help to conceal through collusion, stupidity, or both. The invisible operations of corporate power also stand behind Francis Ford Coppola's THE CONVERSATION (The Directors Company/Paramount, 1974), although it is more concerned with the limits of personal responsibility than with politics. In it, a surveillance expert (Gene Hackman) is hired by a corporation's director to record a conversation between a man and woman as they stroll together in a San Francisco park at noon. Playing back the recording, he thinks he has uncovered a murder plot and must decide whether to act on the discovery or not; he does act, but in misreading the audiotape inadvertently facilitates a crime he had sought to prevent. Deliberately evocative of Antonioni's BLOWUP (1966) in both its theme and art-film ambience, THE CONVERSATION describes a world where conspiracies appear and disappear like cobwebs and where recording media are inherently duplicitous—a world very much like that of the real-life Watergate co-conspirators who were the subject of Alan Pakula's next film, ALL THE PRESIDENT'S MEN (1976), which has been called "the centerpiece of the conspiracy subgenre."[60]

Adapted by Willam Goldman from the best-selling account by Bob Woodward and Carl Bernstein, the two *Washington Post* reporters who broke the case at great risk to their careers (and ultimately, the film implies, their lives), ALL THE PRESIDENT'S MEN is constructed like a detective story in which the two principals (Dustin Hoffman and Robert Redford, who also produced)[61] move clue by clue and tip by tip toward uncovering a criminal conspiracy that reaches into the highest levels of the White House. To do this, they must coax bits and pieces of the truth from a wide range of low-level administration officials, most of whom are very scared, and one unidentified White House insider (the legendary "Deep Throat") in order to establish an indisputable link between funds donated to CREEP (the Committee to Re-Elect the President) and the money used to pay the Watergate burglars. Although it is fairly conventional in form, ALL THE PRESIDENT'S MEN is extraordinary in its evocation of police-state-like menace and its semi-documentary integration of television news footage and dramatic text. Unlike other Watergate films (e.g., the 1979 CBS-TV miniseries BLIND AMBITION [George Schaefer], or Oliver Stone's 1995 feature NIXON), none of the administration principals are portrayed by actors; Nixon and his lieutenants reveal (or, more accurately, expose) themselves only through the real television interviews, addresses, and newscasts that had taken place during the previous three years, and had the currency of "instant history." Thus the film is able to focus on its mystery plot, and offer little exposition of the scandal itself, because contemporary audiences had just been inundated by media coverage of it. Yet polls showed that the public was becoming as cynical about the media as it was of other national institutions, a circumstance reflected in the popularity of three late seventies films: NETWORK (United Artists; Sidney Lumet, 1976), a satire on the interrelationship of television and corporate capitalism written by Paddy Chayefsky; CAPRICORN ONE (Associated General [ITC]; Peter Hyams, 1978), a political thriller in which a manned-flight landing on Mars is faked by a deadly conspiracy involving NASA, elements of the press, and the CIA; and THE CHINA SYNDROME (Columbia/IPC; James Bridges, 1979), a "doomsday" thriller—released just weeks before a near-fatal accident at the Three Mile

Sidney Lumet's NETWORK (UA, 1976), one of several post-Watergate films that were highly critical of television: Faye Dunaway as a maniacally ambitious network executive plotting the coming season's schedule to insure maximum audience share. 35mm 1.85:1.

Island nuclear plant in Harrisburg, Pennsylvania, forced the evacuation of 1,000,000 local residents—that posits collusion among the media, Federal regulatory agencies, and the nuclear power industry to conceal the latter's threat to public health. (Earlier, Michael Ritchie's THE CANDIDATE [Fox, 1972] had suggested the kind of unsavory relationship of media and politics that both elected Richard Nixon and brought him down.)

In 1975–1976, revelations surfaced of the CIA's involvement in several foreign assassination attempts, successful (South Vietnamese President Ngo Dinh Diem) and abortive (Cuban Premier Fidel Castro), and the agency itself became the target in THREE DAYS OF THE CONDOR (Sydney Pollack, 1975) and THE KILLER ELITE (Sam Peckinpah, 1975), which were basically high-powered espionage thrillers with a political

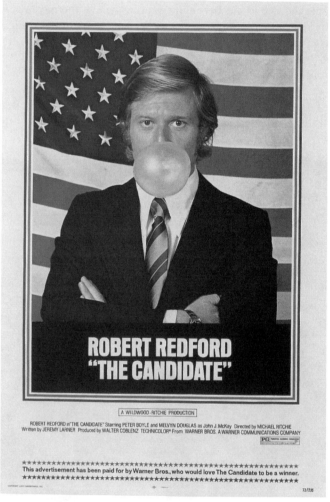

Poster for Michael Ritchie's THE CANDIDATE *(Warners, 1972), in which Robert Redford's political ideals fall victim to his own media-packaging—which, accordingly, insures his victory at the polls. 35mm 1.85:1.*

In Robert Aldrich's Twilight's Last Gleaming *(Lorimar-Bavaria/Allied Artists, 1977)
Burt Lancaster and co-conspirators seize a nuclear missile site and threaten to start
World War III unless the government reveals secret documents that show that the military needlessly prolonged the war in Vietnam. (Although it is set in United States, the
film was shot in Munich with German tax-shelter funds.) 35mm 1.85:1.*

edge. In the former, a CIA researcher (Robert Redford) becomes a hunted man when
he stumbles onto a plot by a renegade faction of the agency to invade the Middle East
and liberate its oil supplies; in the latter, several members of a private assassination
bureau subcontracted to the CIA become double agents, and turn against the agency. In
Twilight's Last Gleaming (Robert Aldrich, 1977), Vietnam is the issue and conspiracy is pandemic as renegade Air Force officers commandeer a nuclear missile silo,
threatening to start World War III unless the president reveals the contents of a secret
blueprint for continuing the war. The document will prove that the military-industrial
complex kept the war going to ensure its credibility long after intelligence had deemed
it unwinnable, costing tens of thousands of lives. (This was not exactly a revelation:
Jonathan Schell said more or less the same thing in his 1976 book *The Time of Illusion*
on the catastrophic Nixon presidency: "The war had become [by 1969] an effort directed
entirely toward building up a certain image by force of arms. It had become a piece of
pure theater.")[62] In the end, both the terrorists and the president are killed, and the document is suppressed. Other 1970s assassination films with conspiracy genes are Scorpio
(United Artists; Michael Winner, 1973), a tale of contract killers inside the CIA; The
Day of the Dolphin (Avco Embassy; Mike Nichols, 1973), in which dolphins are

trained by plotters (who may be renegade CIA agents) to carry bombs to the presiden-
tial yacht; THE DAY OF THE JACKAL (Universal; Fred Zinnemann, 1973), based on
Frederick Forsyth's best-seller about a right-wing plot to assassinate French president
Charles de Gaulle, with clear parallels to the JFK murder; THE MACKINTOSH MAN
(Warners; John Huston, 1973), about the CIA's efforts to assassinate a high-placed spy
within the British government; and THE DOMINO PRINCIPLE (Avco Embassy; Stanley
Kramer, 1977) in which a secret assassination bureau recruits an ex-convict to kill a key
government official (unspecified in the film, but probably Nixon or Kissinger). Political
murder is also the motive force of Richard Lester's CUBA (United Artists, 1979), a dark
and brilliantly executed satire set during the final days of the Batista regime in 1959,
which forms a nearly perfect pendant with Coppola's THE GODFATHER, PART II: Sean
Connery plays a British mercenary sent to train government security forces in Havana,
where the CIA-backed military works feverishly with Cuban factory owners and
American businessmen to drain the last ounces of capital from a country whose only
remaining social contract is graft, before its inevitable revolution.

By the end of the decade, the conspiracy subgenre was so well codified that it could
be parodied in WINTER KILLS (Avco Embassy; William Richert 1979; re-released 1983).
(NASTY HABITS [Michael Lindsay-Hogg, 1977], a British film distributed by Fox, had
already satirized the Watergate conspiracy in an allegory of political corruption inside a
Philadelphia convent run by a paranoid abbess.) Adapted from a novel by Richard
Condon (whose novel *The Manchurian Candidate* was the source for John Frankenheimer's *ur*-conspiracy film of 1962), WINTER KILLS is actually less a parody than a black
comedy in which the half-brother of the assassinated President Kegan (Kennedy) tracks
his way through an interlocking network of witnesses, survivors, and conspiracy theorists
to discover that family patriarch Pa Kegan (Joseph Kennedy) was behind the murder—
basically to protect his business interests when his son, the president, waxed too liberal,
returning in a comic way to the premise of EXECUTIVE ACTION. Finally, conspiracy was
cross-bred with other genres in ways that reflected, not merely political mistrust, but the
significant "collapse of confidence in business" that Seymour Martin Lipset and William
Schneider discovered had occurred between 1965 and 1975.[63]

Such generic hybridization—a general trend in late-seventies Hollywood—produced films like COMA (United Artists; Michael Crichton, 1978), in which the health
industry conspires to harvest organs from the living; NORTH DALLAS FORTY
(Paramount; Ted Kotcheff, 1979), a satire on the conspiratorial nature of professional
football; and THE FORMULA (MGM; John G. Avildsen, 1980), wherein a multinational
oil cartel conspires with ex-Nazis to suppress the development of a cheap synthetic fuel.
Even a sci-fi/horror thriller like ALIEN (Fox; Ridley Scott, 1979) could have a strong
anticorporate subtext (in this case, a corporation plots against its own employees to salvage a monstrous polymorph). The theme of government/corporate conspiracy
remained strong in the early eighties, when films like HANGAR 18 (Sunn Classic; James
L. Conway, 1980), EYEWITNESS (Fox; Peter Yates, 1981), CUTTER'S WAY (United Artists;
Ivan Passer, 1981), OUTLAND (Warner Bros.; Peter Hyams, 1981); BLOW OUT
(Filmways; Brian De Palma, 1981), MISSING (Universal; Constantin Costa-Gavras,
1982), and SILKWOOD (Fox; Mike Nichols, 1983) made it clear that the post-traumatic
stress of Watergate could not be laughed away. (The popular interest in conspiracy
unleashed by Watergate also facilitated the first American films to speak openly of the
1950s industry blacklist, dovetailing nicely with the downfall of veteran anti-
Communist witchhunter Richard Nixon: THE WAY WE WERE [Columbia; Sydney

Robert Redford and Barbra Streisand star as lovers who end up on oppposite sides of the postwar political spectrum in Columbia's THE WAY WE WERE *(Sydney Pollack, 1973), the first American film to address the issue of the Hollywood blacklist, although it is primarily a romantic melodrama. 35mm Panavision anamorphic.*

Pollack, 1973], a glossy love story produced by Ray Stark, used blacklisting as a plot device to end a romance between two attractive Hollywood insiders played by Barbra Streisand and Robert Redford, whereas THE FRONT [Columbia; Martin Ritt, 1976] was made by people who had suffered the effects of blacklisting themselves—director Ritt, scriptwriter Walter Bernstein, and star Zero Mostel—and had the blacklist at its core in its story of a nobody, played by Woody Allen, who "fronts" scripts to studios on behalf of "tainted" writers.)

PARODY *Noir*

Yet, for all of this free-floating paranoia, films of mystery and detection were parodied throughout the decade, beginning with Fox's SLEUTH (Joseph Mankiewicz, 1972), adapted by Anthony Shaffer from his own play, and two Agatha Christie adaptations from Paramount that border on parody—MURDER ON THE ORIENT EXPRESS (Sidney Lumet, 1974) and its follow-up DEATH ON THE NILE (John Guillermin, 1978). It was also during the 1970s that two Blake Edwards films (THE PINK PANTHER [1964] and SHOT IN THE DARK [1964], produced by the Mirisch Company for United Artists), starring Peter Sellers as the bumbling French detective Inspector Clouseau, became part of a series. The appearance of three new entries, all produced and directed by Edwards for United

Zero Mostel as a "tainted" comedian and Woody Allen as a "front" for black-listed writers in Martin Ritts's THE FRONT (Columbia, 1976), a film that dealt seriously with the practice of blacklisting in the New York-based broadcast industry. Ritt, Mostel, and screenplay writer Walter Bernstein had all been blacklisted themselves during the 1950s. 35mm 1.85:1.

Paramount's MURDER ON THE ORIENT EXPRESS (Sidney Lumet, 1974): Albert Finney as Hercule Poirot interrogates Anthony Perkins. Other "all-star" cast members seen here are Vanessa Redgrave, Sean Connery, Wendy Hiller, Michael York, Jessica Harper, Lauren Bacall, and Martin Balsam. 35mm 1.85:1.

Artists—THE RETURN OF THE PINK PANTHER (1975), THE PINK PANTHER STRIKES AGAIN
(1976), and THE REVENGE OF THE PINK PANTHER (1978)—created a brief franchise for
visual slapstick long after its mainstream demise. Neil Simon spoofed the "locked room"
subgenre of detective fiction in Columbia's popular MURDER BY DEATH (Robert Moore,
1976)—which brings five of the world's greatest detectives together under one roof, and
it was followed, in true seventies fashion, by an inferior sequel: THE CHEAP DETECTIVE
(Robert Moore, 1978), in which the Sam Spade (Humphrey Bogart) character from
MURDER BY DEATH is run through a MALTESE FALCON parody. In fact, Bogart and THE
MALTESE FALCON (John Huston, 1941) became parodic icons for the 1970s, beginning
with Paramount's PLAY IT AGAIN, SAM (Herbert Ross, 1972; adapted by Woody Allen
from his own play), in which Bogart's ghost rises from the frames of CASABLANCA
(Michael Curtiz, 1942) to instruct the protagonist on life and love. THE BLACK BIRD
(David Giler, 1975) was a MALTESE FALCON parody/sequel/remake where Sam Spade, Jr.
pursues the valuable statue mislaid by his dad, with Lee Patrick and Elisha Cook, Jr.
reprising their original roles. Parody of the hard-boiled school punctuated the decade's
end with Fox's THE MAN WITH BOGART'S FACE (aka SAM MARLOWE, PRIVATE EYE [Robert
Day, 1980]), in which a contemporary detective has plastic surgery to give him the face
of his idol and becomes involved in a MALTESE FALCON-type case, replete with references
to classical personalities and stars. The master of classical genre parody during the 1970s,
however, was Mel Brooks, and his Hitchcock spoof HIGH ANXIETY (Fox, 1977) is a locus

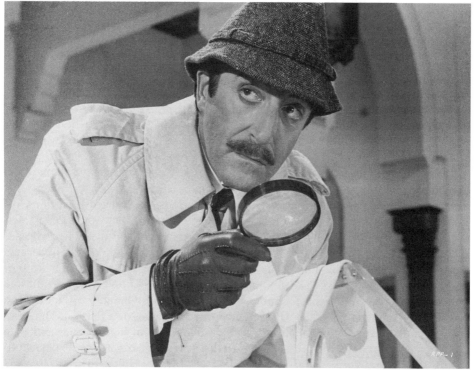

Peter Sellers as Inspector Clouseau in Blake Edwards's THE RETURN OF THE PINK
PANTHER *(UA, 1975). 35mm Panavision anamorphic.*

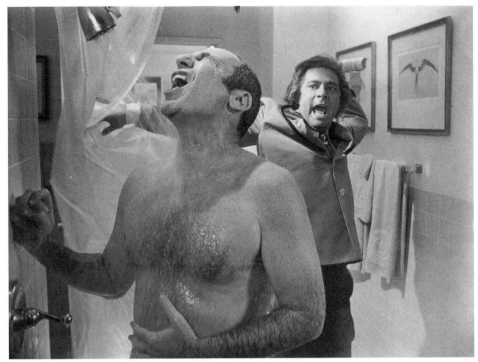

A "quotation " from the shower murder sequence in PSYCHO *(1960) in Mel Brooks's* HIGH ANXIETY *(1977): Brooks about to be stabbed repeatedly by a psychopath with a rolled-up newspaper. 35mm 1.85:1.*

classicus of the type. Simultaneously a tribute and a send-up, Brooks's film contains legible quotations from SPELLBOUND (Alfred Hitchcock, 1945), VERTIGO (Alfred Hitchcock, 1958), PSYCHO (Alfred Hitchcock, 1960), and THE BIRDS (Alfred Hitchcock, 1963), as well as some purely stylistic allusions that incarnate the decade's dual (and somewhat schizoid) impulse toward cynical nose-thumbing and reverent nostalgia.

Related to these mystery spoofs were "buddy caper" films, a comic variation of the criminal couple subgenre—usually focusing on the relations between two men—that became extremely popular during the 1970s. Some took the form of heist films like Columbia's $ (DOLLARS) (Richard Brooks, 1971) and Fox's THE HOT ROCK (Peter Yates, 1972), whose high-water mark was the blockbuster success of Universal's period caper THE STING (George Roy Hill, 1973), which returned $78.2 million in rentals to become the second highest grossing film of the year. Other buddy caper films had a more serious social edge (e.g., MGM's SLITHER [Howard Zieff, 1973]; United Artists' THUNDERBOLT AND LIGHTFOOT [Michael Cimino, 1974]; Universal's CHARLEY VARRICK [Don Siegel, 1973] and BLUE COLLAR [Paul Schrader, 1978]; and AIP's SPECIAL DELIVERY [Paul Wendkos, 1976]), but many were purely comedic in both pacing and tone (Warners' RAFFERTY AND THE GOLD DUST TWINS [Dick Richards, 1975], FREEBIE AND THE BEAN [Richard Rush, 1974], and THE IN-LAWS (Arthur Hiller, 1979); Columbia's FUN WITH DICK AND JANE (Ted Kotcheff, 1977); and Universal's THE BRINK'S JOB (William Friedkin, 1978) and SMOKEY AND THE BANDIT (Hal Needham, 1977). The unexpected $59 million return of SMOKEY AND THE BANDIT—primarily a southern rural car-chase film in the mode of United Artists' WHITE LIGHTNING (Joseph Sargent, 1973) and GATOR [Burt Reynolds, 1976]—led to many imitations (Ron Howard's GRAND THEFT AUTO [AIP/Warners, 1977], and Hal Needham's own HOOPER [Cinerama, 1978] that attempted to mainstream the formula with considerably less success. In the 1980s, buddy capers became more violent and action-oriented, as witnessed by such successful "buddy cop" franchises as Paramount's 48 HRS. (WALTER HILL, 1982) and Warners' LETHAL WEAPON (Richard Donner, 1987) series, whose origins lay in Fox's popular FRENCH CONNECTION films of 1971 and 1975.

The Musical

The musical entered the 1970s with the onerous distinction of having helped more than any other single genre to create the financial crisis of 1969–1971. Seeking to emulate the success of Fox's THE SOUND OF MUSIC (Robert Wise) in 1965, over-produced big-budget musicals had generated more than $60 million in losses for the majors between 1967 and 1970, leading directly to an industry-wide production moratorium in October 1969.[64] Several spectacular musicals then in post-production were released in early 1970 with similarly dismal results. Paramount's ON A CLEAR DAY YOU CAN SEE FOREVER (Vincent Minnelli; based on an Alan Jay Lerner stage show about reincarnation), and DARLING LILI (Blake Edwards; from an original screenplay by Edwards and William Peter Blatty about a World War I British stage star who is also a German spy), were both disappointments. CLEAR DAY broke even, but LILI lost $18.7 of its $22-million negative cost to become the biggest box-office failure of the 1970s, despite award-winning music by Henry Mancini and Johnny Mercer. Another stalled behemoth was ABC/Cinerama Releasing Corp.'s SONG OF NORWAY (Andrew L. Stone, 1970), a musical biography of Edward Grieg adapted from a 1944 Broadway hit and shot on location in Super Panavison 70, which earned just under $4.5 million and failed to return its negative cost. Coming at the end of a long string of late-sixties flops (which included Fox's DOCTOR DOLITTLE [Richard Fliescher, 1967], STAR! [Robert Wise, 1968], and HELLO, DOLLY! [Gene Kelly, 1969], Warner Bros.' CAMELOT [Joshua Logan, 1967], United Artists' CHITTY CHITTY BANG BANG [Ken Hughes, 1968], Universal's SWEET CHARITY [Bob Fosse, 1969], and Paramount's PAINT YOUR WAGON [Joshua Logan, 1969]), the poor performance of these big-budget musicals in 1970 seemed to confirm the fact that the form was dead, or perhaps ready for replacement by "alternative" musicals like Warner Bros.' WOODSTOCK (Michael Wadleigh, 1970), whose youth-cult appeal brought in $16.4 million in rentals and placed it sixth on *Variety*'s annual box-office chart. (It also won the 1970 Academy Award for best documentary feature.) In what seemed an immediate contradiction, 1971's biggest hit was United Artists' FIDDLER ON THE ROOF (Norman Jewison), a $9-million adaptation of a Broadway musical based on stories of Shalom Aleichem that had been running since 1964. Shot on locations in Yugoslavia (and at Pinewood Studios, London) in Panavision and recorded in six-track stereo, the three-hour film earned $38.2 million (about half THE SOUND OF MUSIC's rentals, 1965–1967) and eight Academy Award nominations. Yet 1971 also saw the release of MGM's THE BOY FRIEND (Ken Russell), a musical which, though based on a popular Sandy Wilson stage play, would provide a paradigm for the genre's revision. Filmed at EMI-MGM Elstree Studios as an homage to the studio musicals of the thirties, the film is genre-

*A shot from an expressionistic dream sequence in FIDDLER ON THE ROOF (Norman
Jewison, 1971), United Artists' big-budget musical that went against the early 1970s
revisionist grain to become the year's most popular film, although its rental earnings of
$38.2 million were only about half those of THE SOUND OF MUSIC. 35mm Panavision
anamorphic, blown up to 70mm for road-showing.*

coded with a typical backstage romance and Busby Berkeley-style crane choreography
(virtually indistinguishable from the original except for its Panavison aspect ratio and
color), but it is also self-reflexive to a degree: the plot revolves around a repertory company attempting to stage a provincial production of Sandy Wilson's *The Boy Friend*
which a film crew is simultaneously shooting as a motion picture. THE BOY FRIEND
achieves the almost-perfect balance between nostalgia and parody that would become a
hallmark of 1970s revisionism. But it was Bob Fosse's CABARET (ABC/Allied Artists,
1972) that most dramatically changed public perception of what a musical could be by
appropriating it as a vehicle for serious social criticism.

REVISIONISM: FROM *CABARET* TO *NEW YORK NEW YORK*

In adapting the John Masteroff-John Kander-Fred Ebb stage show, screenwriter Jay
Presson Allen incorporated elements from its sources in John van Druten's play *I Am a
Camera* and the writings of Christopher Isherwood to create a chilling picture of pre-
Nazi Berlin on the brink of a catastrophic fascist revolution. In a reaction against the
artificially "integrated" musicals of the fifties and sixties, Fosse segregated the produc-
tion numbers from the dramatic action and contextualized them as cabaret perfor-

Twiggy and Christopher Gable in the groove of a Busby Berkeley-style production number in Ken Russell's THE BOY FRIEND *(MGM, 1971). Panavision anamorphic.*

Liza Minnelli as Sally Bowles in Bob Fosse's revisionist musical CABARET *(Allied Artists, 1972). 35mm 1.85:1.*

mances at the seedy "Kit Kat Club," a locus classicus of Weimar decadence. Furthermore, by intercutting these interludes of lurid staged entertainment with scenes of Nazi violence in the streets, he instantiated a Brechtian irony more characteristic of the European art film than the American musical. (Fosse was no stranger to art cinema, having recently directed a film version of SWEET CHARITY [Universal, 1969], the Broadway musical based on Fellini's NIGHTS OF CABIRIA [1957].) Finally, in developing its historical anti-authoritarian theme, CABARET clearly suggested the political and moral price of withdrawing into self-indulgence at a time when many sixties activists had done just that in the face of the Nixon ascendancy. CABARET, which starred Liza Minnelli as Sally Bowles, was both critically and financially successful (earning $20.2 million in rentals and winning eight Academy Awards), but if industry leaders took note of this condition, they failed immediately to act on it. Instead the studios continued to crank out standard Broadway and off-Broadway adaptations (Columbia's 1776 [Peter Hunt, 1972] and GODSPELL [David Greene, 1973], United Artists' MAN OF LA MANCHA [Arthur Hiller, 1972], Universal's JESUS CHRIST SUPERSTAR [Norman Jewison, 1973], Warner Bros.' MAME [Gene Saks, 1974]) and conventional musical biopics (MGM's THE GREAT WALTZ [Andrew L. Stone, 1972], about Johann Strauss; Paramount's LADY SINGS THE BLUES [Sidney J. Furie, 1972], about Billie Holiday) with scant reward—of the above named films, only LADY SINGS THE BLUES and JESUS CHRIST SUPERSTAR grossed more than $10 million. They even managed to produce one certified, late-sixties-style disaster in Columbia's LOST HORIZON (Charles Jarrott, 1973), a musical version of Frank Capra's 1937 fantasy classic that lost $8.2 million of its $12-million investment and is still reviled as one of the worst musicals ever made. In 1974 and 1975, however, several films confirmed the genre's modernist turn, including the nostalgic compilation of excerpts from MGM musicals entitled THAT'S ENTERTAINMENT! (Jack Haley, 1974), which announced the death of the classical musical by eulogizing it and became integral to the retrospective consciousness of the decade. (It was also extremely popular, earning $19.1 million in rentals to place tenth on *Variety*'s annual chart and generating the 1976 sequel THAT'S ENTERTAINMENT, PART II [Gene Kelly].) Brian De Palma's PHANTOM OF THE PARADISE (1974) was a camp musical version of Gaston Leroux's 1910 novel THE PHANTOM OF THE OPERA (already given straight treatment in four earlier films), with a pounding contemporary rock score by Paul Williams. Ken Russell's MAHLER (Mayfair, 1974) and LISZTOMANIA (Warner Bros., 1975) were irreverent, musical biopics in the style of his earlier portrait of Tchaikovsky in THE MUSIC LOVERS (United Artists, 1971)—the Liszt film offering a wild burlesque of nineteenth-century musicians in general.

These films were all to some extent self-conscious, but none was so reflexive as Robert Altman's NASHVILLE (Paramount, 1975) the musical entry in his project to revise all of the major classical genres. The film traces the overlapping (and, finally, intersecting) paths of twenty-four characters through the country-and-western music capital over a five-day period, and it contains twenty-seven songs presented in performance contexts and recorded in Lion's Gate eight-track stereo. (The Dolby noise reduction system was also used in recording NASHVILLE, as well as in mastering the stereo magnetic release prints—see below.) Like CABARET, NASHVILLE has a political subtext, which has to do with the way in which American media and historical reality have become intertwined, but is much more subtle than Fosse's film in terms of rhetoric. There was nothing subtle about Fox's British import THE ROCKY HORROR PICTURE SHOW (Jim Sharman, 1975), which took generic hybridization to new heights by combining a rock musical with a horror film (one highly reminiscent of Hammer Films' THE CURSE OF FRANKENSTEIN

NASHVILLE (Paramount, 1975) Robert Altman's rambling
"anti-musical" (or, at least, the only musical to end with a
political assassination) in which every major character—all
twenty-four of them, one way or another—sings a song:
Barbara Harris in an impromptu roadside performance.
35mm Panavision anamorphic.

[Terence Fisher, 1957]) and parodying both forms.[65] This film version of a kinky, long-running London stage show about a heterosexual couple who stumble onto an old dark house full of "transvestites from transsexual Transylvania" has been described as "a high camp blend of Gay Liberation and B-movie Gothic,"[66] and it quickly became a cult phenomenon, catalyzing audience participation at midnight movie screenings for years to come—initially, at the Waverly Theater in Greenwich Village where it ran for 95 consecutive weeks between 1976 and 1978. (The 1970s were the golden age of midnight movies in cities around the nation; they were institutionalized with the premiere of Alexandro Jodorowksy's EL TOPO at the Elgin Theater in New York in late 1970 and had become a regular feature of urban distribution by the time of ROCKY HORROR.)

If ROCKY HORROR represented the epitome of generic pastiche, Peter Bogdanovich's AT LONG LAST LOVE (Fox, 1975) attempted to be the ultimate homage to the RKO Astaire-Rogers musicals of the 1930s and failed miserably at the box office, despite its superb art deco sets and sixteen Cole Porter songs. Lingering public tolerance for old-style musicals was demonstrated by the success of Columbia's FUNNY LADY (Herbert

Tim Curry is Dr. Frank N. Furter in Fox's British import THE ROCKY HORROR
PICTURE SHOW *(Jim Sharman, 1975); its quickly acquired cult film status ensured
that genre hybridization would become an industry mainstay in the decade's second
half. 35mm 1.85:1.*

Ross, 1975), a sequel to its popular Fanny Brice biography FUNNY GIRL (William Wyler,
1968); but whereas the earlier film's $26.4 million in rentals had made it by far the high-
est earner of 1968, the sequel's $19.3 million placed it eighth in the year of JAWS.
Significantly, several mid-seventies rock musicals performed nearly as well as or better
than FUNNY LADY—Ken Russell's visually extravagant version of The Who's rock opera
TOMMY (Columbia, 1975) earned $17.8 million; and Warner Bros.' fourth remake of A
STAR IS BORN (Frank R. Pierson, 1976), with Barbra Streisand as a stellar rock singer,
earned $37.1 million and set the standard for film/music cross-marketing with its
"Evergreen" sound-track album (see Chapter 3). But the decade's most aesthetically
successful essay in musical revision was NEW YORK NEW YORK (United Artists, 1977),
Martin Scorsese's homage to the big band era, based on his viewing of literally hundreds of MGM musicals from the 1940s and 1950s. With Liza Minnelli as a rising
singer (the kind of role her mother Judy Garland had played in many such MGM films)
married to saxophonist/band leader Robert De Niro, the film mixed musical buoyancy
with postwar angst that was perfectly captured by the moody Technicolor cinematography of Laszlo Kovacs. As in CABARET and NASHVILLE, the production numbers are
segregated onto the stage, and the narrative focus is on the failed relationship of the
Minnelli and De Niro characters. In the year of STAR WARS and CLOSE ENCOUNTERS
OF THE THIRD KIND, though, it was probably inevitable that Scorsese's pessimistic
vision would go unrewarded, and NEW YORK NEW YORK returned only $7 million in
rentals on its $9-million investment.

Robert De Niro and Liza Minnelli in Martin Scorsese's stylized noir *musical* NEW YORK NEW YORK *(UA, 1977). 35mm 1.66:1.*

Another failure, but for different reasons, was the U.S.-Austrian-German coproduction of A LITTLE NIGHT MUSIC (New World-Sascha-Wien; Harold Prince, 1978), adapted from Stephen Sondheim's rarified, Tony-award winning 1973 musical version of Bergman's SMILES OF A SUMMER NIGHT (1955) by its original stage director Harold Prince. The film was part of an Austrian attempt to jumpstart its industry, which had been languishing since the end of World War II: the action was moved from turn-of-the-century Sweden to Vienna and given an operetta-like quality out of tune with the wistful, thought-provoking original—none of which was helped by casting Diana Rigg and Elizabeth Taylor in singing roles.[67] Hated by critics and audiences on both sides of the Atlantic, A LITTLE NIGHT MUSIC was an enormous flop that ended the film career of Harold Prince, although it did win an Oscar for Best Adapted Scoring in competition against Disney's PETE'S DRAGON (Don Chaffey, 1977) and a British retelling of Cinderella called THE SLIPPER AND THE ROSE (Bryan Forbes, 1976), whose exteriors were also shot in Austria.

SATURDAY NIGHT FEVER, GREASE, AND THE ADVENT OF DOLBY STEREO OPTICAL SOUND

In the first years of the Carter presidency there was a newly affirmative national mood as Americans began to come to terms with the dual traumas of Watergate and Vietnam.

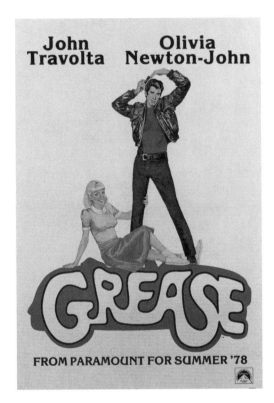

Paramount's SATURDAY NIGHT FEVER *(John Badham, 1977) made television crossover John Travolta a star, and the studio promptly cast him in* GREASE *(Randal Kleiser, 1978); one of its advance publicity posters is reproduced here. Whereas* SATURDAY NIGHT FEVER *was shot in 35mm 1.85:1 with four-channel Dolby stereo optical sound,* GREASE *was shot in 35mm Panavision anamorphic and blown up to 70mm for road-showing with six-track stereo magnetic sound (in selected theaters).*

Carter, who was elected in the Bicentennial year of 1976 on a solemn pledge "never to lie to the American people," promised to bring a new era of openness and honesty to government. Predictably, Paramount's upbeat dance film SATURDAY NIGHT FEVER (John Badham, 1977) was more in step with the new rhythm than either Scorsese's or Prince's work. In its vibrant portrait of working-class kids who come alive at a local disco, it became one the decade's most successful musicals, earning a remarkable $74.1 million in rentals to place third for the year behind STAR WARS (George Lucas) and CLOSE ENCOUNTERS (Steven Spielberg). Like those films, SATURDAY NIGHT FEVER generated multiple repeat viewings among young people, who consumed it much as they would a rock concert. It also had the novelty of being the first post-"youth-cult" youth film with a contemporary setting, and stimulated Paramount to cast its star, television crossover John Travolta, in a similar musical production the following year—an adaptation of the long-running Broadway hit GREASE. Directed by Randal Kleiser, GREASE was a parody of 1950s rock 'n' roll programmers and 1960s beach-party movies containing seventeen production numbers that were integrated with the narrative, which was less a conservative reflex than a knowing bow to its stage origins. (As Kleiser said at the time, "Stylistically, the actors will stop and break into song—that's old—but we are using all the '70s film techniques we can muster, like split screen and high-powered sound.")[68] GREASE was even more successful than its predecessor, earning $96.3 million to become the top-grossing film in the year of such blockbusters as SUPERMAN (Richard Donner) and NATIONAL LAMPOON'S ANIMAL HOUSE (John Landis). The popularity of both SATURDAY NIGHT FEVER and GREASE was enhanced by the installation of Dolby stereo reproduction equipment in theaters around the country in the wake of STAR WARS, the first wide-release film with a Dolby-encoded stereo optical sound track, whose astounding success was understood to stem at least in part from its use of high-quality sound. (Fox's surveys of theaters playing the film indicated that Dolby-equipped venues significantly outgrossed non-Dolby ones.)[69] The sound-track albums of SATURDAY NIGHT FEVER and GREASE sold tens of millions of copies (thirty-five and twenty-four, respectively) worldwide. SATURDAY NIGHT FEVER, in fact, became the first film to earn more from its album sales than from its very considerable rentals (a $350 million gross, making it the best-selling LP of all time), and it became the prototype of synergy between the film and record industries.[70] Worth noting here is the phenomenal growth of the popular music industry during the 1970s: from $1 billion in 1967, record and tape sales reached $2 billion in 1973 and $4 billion in 1978—$1.5 billion more than the total 1978 grosses of the American film industry in its 15,000 theaters.[71]

Most of those theaters were equipped to play optical prints only (in which the sound track is printed as a small strip to the left of the picture for reading by a photoelectric cell in projection), and therefore did not have access to the superior quality of pre-Dolby magnetic stereo. There were two magnetic stereo systems available to theaters before Dolby—the four-track CinemaScope system for 35mm introduced by Fox in THE ROBE (Henry Koster, 1953), and the six-track Todd-AO system for 70mm film introduced in AROUND THE WORLD IN EIGHTY DAYS (Michael Anderson, 1956), both of which placed their separate magnetic tracks directly on the theatrical print outside of the picture frame.[72] Although magnetic prints offered the highest possible quality of sound reproduction, they cost about twice as much to produce as optical prints (in the mid-1970s, $1,200 vs. $800) and degraded faster (the longevity of an optical sound track was approximately that of the image track).[73] Exhibitors had to make expensive adjustments to projection equipment in order to play magnetic prints, and distributors had to supply theaters with both formats. Before 1977, therefore, the American industry was geared to the production of monophonic films, with stereo magnetic sound reserved for 70mm road shows and other special events. For this reason, the majority of American and European theaters chose not to support magnetic stereo playback, and until 1977 provided their patrons mainly with undistinguished and limited monophonic sound. CABARET, for example, winner of multiple Oscars for its music and sound, was never exhibited in stereo, although a stereo premix was used by the producers of its best-selling sound-track LP;[74] and JAWS, which won the 1975 Academy Awards for Best Original Score and Best Sound, was recorded and released completely in monaural. The Dolby noise reduction system, which electronically reduces background noise and increases frequency response, was developed by Ray Dolby at Dolby Laboratories during the late 1960s for use in the recording industry (where, among other things, it helped to innovate stereo cassette recording). It entered the film industry in 1971, when it was used by Stanley Kubrick in the mixing stages of A CLOCKWORK ORANGE (1971), although the film itself was released with a conventional—if aesthetically brilliant—monaural sound track. Dolby noise reduction was subsequently applied to several musicals, where it was used for both monaural optical (STEPPENWOLF [Fred Haines, 1974]; STARDUST [Michael Apted, 1974]) and stereo magnetic sound tracks (THE LITTLE PRINCE [Stanley Donen, 1974]; NASHVILLE [Robert Altman, 1975]) in both recording and theater playback. Beginning in 1973, however, Eastman Kodak and RCA worked with Dolby to develop a simple two-track stereo optical system that would first be used in the musicals TOMMY (Ken Russell, 1975), LISZTOMANIA (Ken Russell, 1975), and A STAR IS

BORN (Frank R. Pierson, 1976).[75] In the 1970s, most 35mm theaters deployed three speakers—the left, right, and center—behind the screen.[76] The Dolby stereo optical system reproduced the two basic tracks through the left and right speakers and sent a phased signal through the center channel synthesized from the differences between the left and right tracks, making high-fidelity stereo possible for a relatively modest conversion cost to theaters of about $5,000.[77] It cost about $25,000 more to dub a film in Dolby stereo than in monaural, and the conversion of an existing film-mixing studio to Dolby cost around $40,000, but these were modest sums relative to then-average production costs of $5 million per picture. When STAR WARS (1977) was both recorded in a four-channel mix (left, right, center, and surround) and released in Dolby stereo optical for either two or four channel playback, it produced a revolution in theater sound that very quickly caused a large-scale conversion to the system. Lucas's film was followed by several other blockbusters that exploited Dolby effects and confirmed its market potential—CLOSE ENCOUNTERS OF THE THIRD KIND (1977), SATURDAY NIGHT FEVER (1977), and GREASE (1978)—as well as by other films that had the lifelike reproduction of sound at their conceptual core—THE LAST WALTZ (Martin Scorsese, 1978; United Artists), THE SHOUT (Jerzy Skolimowski, 1978; Recorded Pictures), and DAYS OF HEAVEN (Terrence Malick, 1978; Paramount), which later (like GREASE and HAIR) was road-shown in 70mm stereo magnetic because of the improved sound quality made possible by the wide-gauge format. (As subtle as Dolby stereo would prove to be at registering such sounds as insect chirps, bird calls, and human breathing, voices and lip movements were occasionally out of synchronization and directional stereo separation was often problematic; it soon became clear that to achieve an effective Dolby mix, the sound track would have to be planned and even scripted as part of the overall production design—an imperative most brilliantly realized by Walter Murch's sound design/editing for APOCALYPSE NOW in 1979.) By the end of the decade, there were 1,200 Dolby-equipped American theaters; by the mid-1980s Dolby counted over 6,000 installations worldwide, and almost 90 percent of all Hollywood films were being released in four-channel Dolby stereo.[78] For motion picture and theater sound, as for so much else, the 1970s was a formative decade, beginning as generally monophonic and ending on the road to full stereo optical surround.

DOLBY-DRIVEN ROCK MUSICALS

In the immediate post-STAR WARS period, the increased sonic clarity of Dolby was subordinated to increased power, as the lucrative ancillary market in record sales inspired several Dolby-encoded rock musicals that were clearly conceived around their sound tracks.[79] Universal produced three of these, having learned the importance of high-quality sound since its experience with AMERICAN GRAFFITI in 1973 (which it had compromised by not releasing in stereo)—FM (John A. Alonzo, 1978), a comedy-drama about an urban radio station with more than thirty pre-recorded rock songs; SGT. PEPPER'S LONELY HEARTS CLUB BAND (Michael Schultz, 1978), an attempt to weave a narrative around songs from the classic Beatles album (performed mainly by the Bee Gees, of SATURDAY NIGHT FEVER fame); and I WANNA HOLD YOUR HAND (Robert Zemeckis, 1978), a celebration of early Beatles music keyed to a story about their 1964 American debut on *The Ed Sullivan Show*. Paramount produced AMERICAN HOT WAX (Floyd Mutrux, 1978), a tribute to the early years of rock 'n' roll centered on disc jockey

Gary Busey in Innovisions/ECA's THE BUDDY HOLLY STORY *(Steve Rash, 1978), one of several rock 'n' roll films produced by record companies and distributed by Columbia to cash in on the Dolby craze. Typically, the songs would be recorded in stereo for compilation as a sound-track album and the rest of the film in mono. 35mm 1.85:1.*

Alan Freed that featured forty songs performed by their original artists; and Columbia distributed two films produced independently by record companies—Casablanca/ Motown's disco comedy THANK GOD IT'S FRIDAY (Robert Klane, 1978) and Innovisions/ ECA's biopic THE BUDDY HOLLY STORY (Steve Rash, 1978). (As was typical of these films, the songs in THE BUDDY HOLLY STORY were recorded in stereo, but the rest of the film was recorded in mono, so that, as Charles Schreger noted at the time, "you can almost hear the extra speakers click on when the songs start, and off when they're finished."[80] In fact, THE BUDDY HOLLY STORY was partially financed through the sale of its sound-track album.)[81] None of these films were financially successful, but the year's biggest musical flop was Universal's THE WIZ (Sidney Lumet, 1978), an updated, all-black version of THE WIZARD OF OZ (MGM; Victor Fleming, 1939). Although THE WIZ had been a Broadway hit, Joel Schumacher's screenplay changed its setting from Kansas to New York City and made Dorothy a 24-year-old Harlem school teacher, robbing it of any resemblance to Frank Baum's original novel. Despite a spectacular production design and music by Quincy Jones, THE WIZ became one the decade's biggest failures, producing a net loss of $10.4 million against its $24-million investment. The more modest failure of United Artists' HAIR (Milos Forman, 1979)—a net loss of $4.2 million against a negative cost of $11 million—suggested that musicals adapted from the stage had lost their audience appeal simultaneously with countercultural values. The last pop-

The all-black cast of THE WIZ *(Sidney Lumet, 1978) is "off to see the Wizard" in Universal's failed Dolby musical: Ted Ross, Michael Jackson, Diana Ross, and Nipsey Russell. 35mm 1.85:1.*

ular musicals of the decade seemed to confirm both propositions: what succeeded in 1979 was either clearly self-reflexive and revisionist—such as ITC's THE MUPPET MOVIE (James Frawley), New World's ROCK 'N' ROLL HIGH SCHOOL (Allan Arkush), and Columbia-Fox's coproduction ALL THAT JAZZ (Bob Fosse)—or countercultural critiques like Fox's THE ROSE (Mark Rydell), which depicted the meteoric implosion of a doomed, Janis Joplin-like rock star. Correspondingly, two of 1980's biggest flops—EMI's CAN'T STOP THE MUSIC (Nancy Walker) and Universal's XANADU (Robert Greenwald)— were updated versions of 1940s Hollywood musicals (MGM's Judy Garland-Mickey Rooney cycle and Columbia's COVER GIRL [Charles Vidor, 1944], respectively).

Horror and the Mainstreaming of Exploitation

When the 1970s began, the horror film was a fundamentally disreputable form, associated almost exclusively with exploitation, yet Robin Wood has suggested that in the course of the decade it became "the most important of all American genres and perhaps the most progressive."[82] While the second part of this proposition is arguable, the first part of it true—to the extent, at least, that horror moved from the margins of the exploitation field into the mainstream to become a vital and disturbingly influential genre.

Like THE WIZ, *Milos Forman's version of the 1967 Broadway musical* HAIR *(UA, 1979) was out of sync with an audience that was about to elect Ronald Reagan to the presidency, and United Artists lost $4.2 million on the venture: Don Dacus, Annie Golden, Dorsey Wright, and Treat Williams. 35mm Panavision anamorphic.*

TRADITIONAL HORROR

Horror had experienced a classical period during the 1930s when Universal produced its elegantly mounted gothic series—DRACULA (Tod Browning, 1931), FRANKENSTEIN (James Whale, 1931), and THE MUMMY (Karl Freund, 1932)—under European (specifically, German Expressionist) influence, and sustained it through the decade with several worthy sequels. At the same time, RKO originated KING KONG (Merian C. Cooper/Ernest B. Schoedsack, 1933) and later the poetic psychological horror films of producer Val Lewton (e.g., Jacques Tourneur's CAT PEOPLE [1942] and I WALKED WITH A ZOMBIE [1943]). In terms of budget, these latter were B-films, as were most horror films of the studio era, but they were tastefully produced and literately scripted. In 1941, under new management, Universal started a second cycle of monster films with George Waggner's atmospheric THE WOLF MAN (1941), but at this point movie horror began to contrast poorly with the real horror of World War II, and the second cycle degenerated into silliness (FRANKENSTEIN MEETS THE WOLF MAN [Roy William Neill, 1943]) and self-parody (ABBOTT AND COSTELLO MEET FRANKENSTEIN [Charles Barton, 1948]). By the late 1950s, horror had become a despised teenage exploitation genre wielded like a blunt instrument in the hands of such producers as Herbert Cohen (I WAS A TEENAGE WEREWOLF [Gene Fowler, 1957]), William Castle (MACABRE [William Castle, 1958]), and AIP's legendary Roger Corman [THE WASP WOMAN [Roger Corman, 1960]). In the early 1960s, however, Corman took a large step toward reinvigorating the genre by producing and directing a series of Edgar Allan Poe adaptations in color and CinemaScope for AIP. These modestly budgeted but expressive films—which included THE HOUSE OF USHER (Roger Corman, 1960), THE PIT AND THE PENDULUM (Roger Corman, 1961), THE PREMATURE BURIAL (Roger Corman, 1962), THE RAVEN (Roger Corman, 1963), THE MASQUE OF THE RED DEATH (Roger Corman, 1964), THE TOMB OF LIGEIA (Roger Corman, 1965), and several other titles—drew favorable reviews and helped to lift horror out the exploitation sub-basement it had occupied since the late 1940s. So too did the imaginatively produced versions of the Universal classics arriving from Britain's Hammer Films at about the same time—Terence Fisher's THE CURSE OF FRANKENSTEIN (1957), THE HORROR OF DRACULA (1958), and THE MUMMY (1959)—whose eroticism and Technicolor gore provided the inspiration for Corman's Poe series.

THE LEGACY OF PSYCHO

Yet the film that lent the most legitimacy to horror in the 1960s was Alfred Hitchcock's PSYCHO (1960), which many critics consider to be the first modernist American film in its calculation, detachment, and reflexivity.[83] PSYCHO was also the first horror blockbuster, produced for around $800,000 and earning $8.5 million in rentals (around $18 million in grosses) to become the most profitable film of the year; and it received four Academy Award nominations (including one for direction—Hitchcock's last of five). From a marketing point of view, PSYCHO was a clear signpost to the 1970s: like an exploitation film (a form that Hitchcock was consciously imitating),[84] it was released in a modified saturation pattern and promoted through gimmickry; and it attracted an audience comprised largely of teenagers and young adults.[85] But, like the blockbusters of the next decade, the key to its success was its status as an "event" that generated multiple repeat viewings. (The New York Times reported at the time, for example, that "any number of teenagers have gone to see this movie several times over and the word is apparently out in the suburbs that 'the blood in the bathtub scene' is hot stuff.")[86] Not only did PSYCHO contain the "illusion," as Hitchcock put it, of graphic violence and nudity in a way that confounded censorship (i.e., through montage), but it read as a radically different text on second and third viewing, with rich ironies of dialogue and plot not apparent on first encounter—which were appreciated by the critics, at least, if not the teenagers. Generically, PSYCHO spawned a few immediate imitations (for example, HOMICIDAL [William Castle, 1961]), but its true impact wasn't felt until the 1970s when the monstrous Oedipal family would become the primary subject and source of American horror. PSYCHO would then provide the prototype for the "slasher" subgenre that exploded after the catalytic success of HALLOWEEN in 1978, when the CARA rating system had replaced the Production Code and *illusion* in the depiction of graphic sex and violence was no longer necessary. (It was in this climate that the film's three sequels were produced—PSYCHO II [Richard Franklin, 1982], PSYCHO III [Anthony Perkins, 1986], and PSYCHO IV: THE BEGINNING [Mick Garris, 1990]—which have more in common with contemporary slashers than with Hitchcock's original.)

THE ADVENT OF R-RATED HORROR

Two landmark films of 1968 indicated the directions American horror would take in the 1970s. In his big-budget production of ROSEMARY'S BABY for Paramount, directed by the much-celebrated Roman Polanski, William Castle took the genre up-market for the first time since the 1930s. Adapted by Polanski from Ira Levin's best-seller and starring the then highly bankable Mia Farrow, the film concerned a young woman unsuspectingly impregnated by the Devil, and it sounded the religious-horror theme that would infuse such 1970s blockbusters as THE EXORCIST (William Friedkin, 1973) and THE OMEN (Richard Donner, 1976). ROSEMARY'S BABY not only received lavish critical praise and several Oscar nominations, but it earned $15.5 million in rentals and became the seventh most profitable film of the year. The other signal film of 1968 was the independently distributed NIGHT OF THE LIVING DEAD, made by novice director George A. Romero and friends on a shoestring budget (under $114,000) in Pittsburgh over the course of several weekends, with Romero also serving as co-writer, cinematographer, and editor. Loosely based on Richard Matheson's apocalyptic vampire novel *I Am Legend*, this gory, black-and-white account of a plague of flesh-eating zombies deflated several generic clichés and became the model for such subversive rural gothic films of the 1970s as THE TEXAS CHAINSAW MASSACRE (Tobe Hooper, 1974) and THE HILLS HAVE EYES (Wes Craven, 1977). It earned a respectable $3 million in the year of its release (by comparison, Fox's twentieth-ranked FANTASTIC VOYAGE [Richard Fleischer] earned $4.5 million), and quickly became a cult classic, generating two sequels (DAWN OF THE DEAD [George Romero, 1978], DAY OF THE DEAD [George Romero, 1985]) and a color remake (NIGHT OF THE LIVING DEAD [Tom Savini, 1990]). Taken together,

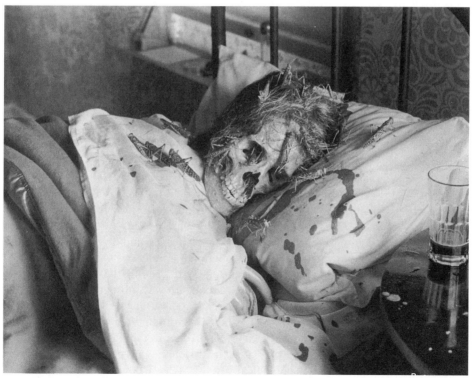

One of the nastier killings from AIP's British-produced THE ABOMINABLE DR. PHIBES *(Robert Fuest, 1971). Repulsive images like this one would become 1970s horror's stock in trade. 35mm 1.75:1.*

ROSEMARY'S BABY and NIGHT OF THE LIVING DEAD foretold the death of classical hor-
ror, whose gothic monsters and European origins would become unviable for American
audiences in the coming decade except as satire (ANDY WARHOL'S FRANKENSTEIN [Paul
Morrissey, 1974]; ANDY WARHOL'S DRACULA [Paul Morrissey, 1974]; LOVE AT FIRST BITE
[Stan Dragoti, 1979]) or parody (THE WEREWOLF OF WASHINGTON [Milton Moses
Ginsberg, 1973]; YOUNG FRANKENSTEIN [Mel Brooks, 1974]), or both (THE ROCKY
HORROR PICTURE SHOW [Jim Sharman, 1975]). Significantly, they were both released in
the year that the MPAA scrapped the Production Code in favor of the Code and Rating
Administration (CARA) system, whose guidelines allowed for the representation of
graphic violence in its R and X categories; and, almost without exception, the modern
horror film went on to become an R-rated genre.[87]

As the 1970s began, AIP released a brace of offbeat horror films that suggested imminent generic mutation. COUNT YORGA, VAMPIRE (Bob Kelljan, 1970) and its sequel THE
RETURN OF COUNT YORGA (Bob Kelljan, 1971) were low-budget, revisionist vampire
films set in contemporary Los Angeles, where society has become so secularized that it
is difficult to find a crucifix. Like ROSEMARY'S BABY, they forecast by inverse corollary
the conservative, theological coloration of much 1970s horror, as did New World's feminist variant THE VELVET VAMPIRE (Stephanie Rothman, 1971), but they also maintained
an ironic distance towards their own genre codes. (The production of vampire films,
high and low, would become a virtual growth industry during the decade—approximately 120 were made domestically, 1970–1979.)[88] AIP's more generously produced
British imports THE ABOMINABLE DR. PHIBES (Robert Fuest, 1971) and DR. PHIBES
RISES AGAIN (Robert Fuest, 1972) were camped-up hybridizations of several horror
classics, including THE BEAST WITH FIVE FINGERS (Robert Florey, 1946) and THE
PHANTOM OF THE OPERA (Rupert Julian, 1925; Arthur Lubin, 1943; Terence Fisher,
1962), suggesting the trend toward genre-blending and parody that would mark the
decade. The PHIBES films were big hits for AIP, earning nearly $2 million apiece, and
the original was cited by *Variety* in June 1971 as part of a new wave of films "containing
extreme screen gore."[89] (Their central concept—a series of fiendishly imaginative
revenge killings carried out by a mad Vincent Price character—was reprised in United
Artists/Cineman's THEATRE OF BLOOD [Douglas Hickox, 1973].) Two other British films
with horrific themes attracted considerable attention among American critics in the
early 1970s—Warners' THE DEVILS (1971), written and directed by Ken Russell, and the
Paramount-released DON'T LOOK NOW (1973), directed by Nicolas Roeg. The former
was based on a play by John Whiting adapting Aldous Huxley's novel *The Devils of
Loudon* (1952), itself based on an infamous seventeenth-century case in which church
authorities accused an entire convent of demonic possession and imposed a murderous
exorcism upon it. Laden with images of sexual hysteria, religious sadomasochism, and
graphic, stomach-turning torture, THE DEVILS became a landmark in censorship when
CARA gave it the first X rating for violence (although it was subsequently re-edited to
receive an R). DON'T LOOK NOW was a haunting supernatural thriller about a couple
who go to Venice after the drowning of their young daughter and become fatally
involved with two psychics and a serial killer. Based on a story by Daphne Du Maurier,
the film was provocative in its display of sex and violence, earning an R rating from
CARA, but is ultimately a psychological mystery tale. It was Warner Bros.' THE
EXORCIST (William Friedkin, 1973), however, that brought sensationalist horror into the
blockbuster mainstream where it has remained more or less ever since (without, however, ceding its dominance—with pornography—of the exploitation field). As one

Two other British imports, released by Warners and Paramount, respectively, were similarly influential of American horror. (above) Ken Russell's THE DEVILS (1971), a tale of seventeenth-century demonic possession that was X-rated by CARA for violence: Oliver Reed as Father Grandier. 35mm Panavision anamorphic, blown up to 70mm for road-showing. (below) Nicolas Roeg's DON'T LOOK NOW (1973), a VERTIGO-like supernatural thriller set in Venice: Julie Christie on a funeral launch with two sibylline sisters. 35mm Panavison anamorphic.

reviewer concisely put it, THE EXORCIST did for horror "what 2001 did for science fiction: legitimized it in the eyes of thousands [read millions] who previously considered horror movies nothing more than a giggle."[90]

THE IMPACT OF *THE EXORCIST*

Produced for $9 million with no major stars, THE EXORCIST earned $89.3 million in rentals in the year of its release and became the most commercially successful horror film ever made, as well as the first to be nominated by the Academy as best picture of the year. It also became a cultural phenomenon of large proportions, complete with a *Newsweek* cover story and complaints by serious journalists that controversy over the film had replaced Watergate in the news. The reason was its lurid depiction of a demonically possessed 12-year-old girl in assorted acts of cursing, urination, vomiting, and masturbation with a crucifix (easier to find, apparently, in the nation's capital than in Los Angeles)—acts that had never before appeared in any context in a mainstream film, not only because the Production Code forbade them but presumably because they were beyond the pale of public decency. Far from mitigating this situation, the film's Roman Catholic religiosity (authenticated by the technical advice of three Jesuit priests) seemed to perversely heighten it. Crowds lined up for blocks to see THE EXORCIST, critics put it on their "Ten Best" lists, and the R-rated film was given the industry imprimatur of ten Academy Award nominations, two of which it won (for Screenplay and Sound). For many, however, Hollywood's embrace of sensationalism was a clear sign of decay, and the fact that horror had entered the mainstream did not free it from the stigma of exploitation. Rather, that stigma now applied to the industry as a whole in which, as Stephen Farber wrote in the *New York Times* for July 7, 1974, "movies are now conceived as kinky, gory, decadent circus spectacle . . . [and] the studios are marketing a new brand of sensationalism, gaudier and more lurid than at any time in movie history."[91] (Warners' initial booking strategy for THE EXORCIST—four-walling it for exclusive runs in prestigious downtown theaters—suggests that it did not regard the film as an exploitation product, which before the experience of JAWS [1975] would have called for saturation rather than platform release.)[92]

The immediate effect of THE EXORCIST was that every major studio in Hollywood rushed to turn out a film about demonic possession or other occult phenomena, with high-tech prosthetic makeup effects like those produced for the Warners' film by Dick Smith and some element of theological "seriousness." Of the many EXORCIST imitations the most obvious (and best) were Fox's THE OMEN (Richard Donner, 1976), Universal's THE SENTINEL (Michael Winner, 1977), and United Artists' BURNT OFFERINGS (Dan Curtis, 1976) and AUDREY ROSE (Robert Wise, 1977). Another expensive production with Roman Catholic trappings, THE OMEN focuses on the family of a 5-year-old boy who is the son of Satan; it earned a handsome $28.5 million, making it the sixth most profitable film in the year of ROCKY, and generated two Fox sequels—DAMIEN: OMEN II (Don Taylor, 1978) and THE FINAL CONFLICT (Graham Baker, 1981). THE SENTINEL is a glossy *Grand Guignol* piece about a Brooklyn Heights brownstone built literally on the mouth of hell, while AUDREY ROSE concerns the reincarnation of a 12-year-old girl, credibly informed by the Hindu doctrine of the transmigration of souls, and BURNT OFFERINGS is about the possession of an entire household by evil spirits. None of them was commercially successful, although THE SENTINEL generated a parodic blockbuster sequel (of sorts) in Columbia's GHOSTBUSTERS (Ivan Reitman, 1984), and BURNT OFFERINGS was the inspiration for AIP's unprecedented hit THE AMITYVILLE HORROR (Stuart Rosenberg, 1979).

These posters for Warners' THE EXORCIST (*William Friedkin, 1973*) and Fox's THE OMEN (*Richard Donner, 1976*) are so similar that they might be mistaken for one another without the text, a graphic illustration of the impact that the Warners film had on the market for upscale horror.

There were countless cheap EXORCIST imitations abroad, the most notorious of which was LA CASA DELL'ESORCISMO [THE HOUSE OF EXORCISM, 1975], a badly re-cut and doctored version of Mario Bava's brilliant LISA E IL DIAVOLO [LISA AND THE DEVIL, 1972]. EXORCIST-driven occult thrillers appeared in the United States until the end of the decade (Universal's THE LEGACY [Richard Marquand, 1979]; Columbia's THE MANITOU [William Girdler, 1978]; AFD's THE CHANGELING [Peter Medak, 1979]); whereas THE EXORCIST's own sequels appeared thirteen years apart because the first—Warner Bros.' EXORCIST II: THE HERETIC (John Boorman, 1977)—was a commercial and critical debacle, although subsequent reappraisals of Boorman's direction and William Fraker's cinematography have earned the film increased respect. (The same cannot be said for Fox's THE EXORCIST III, directed by the original novel's author William Peter Blatty in 1990, an uneasy blend of psycho-slasher and spiritual-questing motifs.)

HORROR IN THE FAMILY: *THE TEXAS CHAINSAW MASSACRE*

The explicitly familial context of horror in THE EXORCIST, THE OMEN, and other such films (THE BEGUILED [Don Siegel, 1971]; THE POSSESSION OF JOEL DELANEY [Waris Hussein, 1972]; THE OTHER [Robert Mulligan, 1972]) indicated a sea change in the genre that had been implicit since PSYCHO and was most fully articulated in THE TEXAS CHAINSAW MASSACRE (Tobe Hooper, 1974), a low-budget independent feature based like Hitchcock's on the true case of Ed Gein, the "Wisconsin ghoul" who had butchered at least eleven women during the mid-1950s and was found living in a charnel house surrounded by their body parts (and, like Norman Bates, the mummified corpse of his mother).[93] In Hooper's film, shot in 16mm and blown up for 35mm exhibition, Gein becomes an all-male family

Tobe Hooper's THE TEXAS CHAINSAW MASSACRE (Vortex Films, 1974) was as influential of the low end of the market as THE EXORCIST was of the high end; in each case, the source of horror lay in the psychodynamics of the American family: Leatherface chasing dinner. 16mm blown up to 35mm.

(fathers and sons) of cannibals who terrorize some stranded young people in an old farm-house full of decaying human and animal remains. Unexpectedly, this vision of the American family as monstrosity and the American home as slaughterhouse was inflected by both cinematic style and ironic humor, and it ignited yet another critical controversy over movie violence and gore (although there is, in fact, relatively little of either onscreen in the film itself). Reviled by many mainstream critics (Stephen Koch, writing in *Harper's* for November 1976, called it "a vile little piece of sick crap . . . with literally nothing to recommend it"),[94] THE TEXAS CHAINSAW MASSACRE became a critical *cause célèbre* among cineastes. In 1975 alone it was showcased at Cannes, the London Film Festival (after which it was refused a certificate for general exhibition by the British Board of Film Censors), and the Museum of Modern Art's "Re/View" program, and Hooper was awarded a five-film contract by Universal Studios when the film earned $14.4 million in rentals to become the year's fourteenth-highest grosser.[95]

In fact, THE TEXAS CHAINSAW MASSACRE was as influential of the low end of the horror market as THE EXORCIST was of the high end, and it also fully legitimized the rural gothic subgenre inaugurated by NIGHT OF THE LIVING DEAD. Like that film and Wes Craven's LAST HOUSE ON THE LEFT (1972), it was the independently produced feature debut of a regional director whose work would have great impact on the Hollywood mainstream. It later generated two unremarkable sequels—THE TEXAS CHAINSAW MASSACRE 2 (Cannon, 1986), directed by Hooper, and LEATHERFACE: TEXAS CHAINSAW MASSACRE III (New Line, 1990), directed by Steve Burr. Hooper went to Universal where he directed a slasher called THE FUNHOUSE (1981) and the megahit POLTERGEIST (1982), produced by Steven Spielberg (and thought to be more his work than Hooper's), before he left the studio and went to work for Cannon.

INDEPENDENT FILMMAKERS AND THE RISE OF "SLASHER" HORROR

Because the 1970s was so clearly, in Robin Wood's phrase, "the Golden Age of the American horror film," several of the decade's more talented independent directors chose to specialize in the genre. The most prominent of these was Brian De Palma (b. 1940) who, after a brief period as an avant-gardist, made nothing but horror/thriller films from 1972 through 1984, when feminist outrage against his misogyny forced him into more conventional forms. De Palma's career is discussed in detail elsewhere in Chapter 4 of this book, but his specific contributions to horror must be briefly noted here. Deeply influenced by the work of Hitchcock, De Palma created an intertextual cinema of both psychological and visceral horror in SISTERS (1973), PHANTOM OF THE PARADISE (1974), OBSESSION (1976), CARRIE (1976), THE FURY (1978), DRESSED TO KILL (1980), BLOW OUT (1981), and BODY DOUBLE (1984). The quality of these films varied as radically as did their budgets (though not necessarily *with* their budgets), but it seems clear that at least three of them represent lasting contributions to the genre: SISTERS, a quasi-experimental variation on REAR WINDOW and PSYCHO; CARRIE, a highly stylized version of THE EXORCIST's demonic child motif set in the social context of REBEL WITHOUT A CAUSE (Nicholas Ray, 1955); and DRESSED TO KILL (1980), an artistic slasher film that combines elements of PSYCHO and VERTIGO to become reflexively voyeuristic.

George Romero (b. 1939), on the other hand, whose NIGHT OF THE LIVING DEAD was a watershed of modern horror, continued his career as an independent writer-director in Pittsburgh with three low-budget nonhorror features before returning to the genre in MARTIN (1978), a modern-day vampire film set in a decaying steel town with a clear element of social satire. This context also informs his first LIVING DEAD sequel DAWN OF

George Romero's DAWN OF THE DEAD *(1978), the first sequel to his influential low-budget* NIGHT OF THE LIVING DEAD *(1968) and a landmark in prosthetic splatter effects by makeup artist Tom Savini. 35mm 1.85:1.*

THE DEAD (1978), which stages most of its action in a shopping mall: here zombies attack humans and go on a mindless materialistic rampage that is the moral equivalent of "shopping." Its darkly comedic elements notwithstanding, the film has an unusually high quotient of gore provided by makeup effects artist Tom Savini (who also worked on MARTIN and appeared in both films as an actor). Romero continued to work in the horror genre during the 1980s and 1990s, although his budgets for films like DAY OF THE DEAD (1985), the third and final LIVING DEAD sequel, were limited by his decision to remain independent.

Wes Craven (b. 1949), who began his movie career as a production assistant and editor of soft-core porn (before which, in logical progression, he had been an academic), wrote and directed as his first feature, the brutal revenge film THE LAST HOUSE ON THE LEFT, in 1972. Produced for $70,000 in partnership with Sean S. Cunningham, who later directed the slasher blockbuster FRIDAY THE 13TH (1980), Craven intended THE LAST HOUSE ON THE LEFT as a reflexive indictment of the America's high tolerance for violence—the film is about the rape and torture-murder of two teenage girls by a gang of thugs who later seek shelter at the home of one of their victim's parents. As in Bergman's THE VIRGIN SPRING (1960), from which it was loosely adapted, the gang members are identified by the parents, who then exact a savage, horrific revenge. Filmed in 16mm and blown up for 35mm distribution by AIP, THE LAST HOUSE ON THE LEFT had a grainy, *cinema verité* quality, as well as a kind of grim seriousness of purpose that was not present in Craven's next feature, the more slickly produced THE HILLS HAVE EYES (1977), which was also shot in 16mm but on a budget of $250,000.[96] Based on the history of the infamous Sawney Bean tribe that preyed on travelers in seventeenth-century

Scotland, HILLS is another revenge film in which an all-American tourist family is attacked in the Arizona desert by a family of cannibals that is in some ways its mirror image. The utterly compulsive nature of Craven's villains here set the standard for the slasher films that followed, most notably John Carpenter's HALLOWEEN (1978), whose psychotic killer Michael Myers obstinately survives the heroine's strenuous efforts to kill him. Craven attracted the attention of Hollywood and, after several middling horror films (DEADLY BLESSING [1981] is an example), had his mainstream breakthrough with the surrealistic teenage gore fest A NIGHTMARE ON ELM STREET (Fineline, 1984), which became a lucrative franchise for the rest of the century, generating five sequels and several ingenious metacommentaries (WES CRAVEN'S NEW NIGHTMARE [1994]).

Like De Palma, Canadian-born David Cronenberg (b. 1948) made avant-garde films before turning exclusively to horror during the 1970s. His feature debut, made in partnership with Ivan Reitman (then an exploitation producer, later the producer-director of GHOSTBUSTERS and other hits) with funds from the Canadian Film Development Corporation (CFDC), was THEY CAME FROM WITHIN (1975; retitled from SHIVERS by its U.S. distributor AIP). In this film, which as with most of his work Cronenberg also wrote, phallic parasites created by science as a sexual stimulant attack the residents of a Montreal high rise, adding a new trope to the growing repertoire of movie "splatter" when one of the parasitic invader erupts from the abdomen of its human host. (This device would be copied in films as various as Fox's ALIEN [Ridley Scott, 1979] and New World's HUMANOIDS FROM THE DEEP [Barbara Peeters, 1980] until it was finally exhausted and ready for Mel Brooks to parody in SPACEBALLS [1987] ten years later. The exploding heads in Cronenberg's SCANNERS [1981] came to occupy a similar status in the realm of physical effects.) RABID (1977), also produced by Reitman, is another medical horror story: here a woman's life is saved by a plastic surgeon after a motorcycle accident but she is at the same time turned into a rabid vampire who infects the entire city of Montreal; and in THE BROOD (1979) a woman is able to externalize her rage as a pack of monstrous dwarves. In all of these films there is an allegorical dimension—they are both monster movies and meditations on social decay in the form of sexual promiscuity, child abuse, etc.—because Cronenberg's horror is a unique blend of the cerebral and the visceral, as such later mainstream work as Fox's THE FLY (1986) and DEAD RINGERS (1988) clearly demonstrate.

A similar tension exists in the work of Larry Cohen (b. 1938), a former screenwriter who wrote and directed several black action films (BLACK CAESAR [1973]; HELL UP IN HARLEM [1973]) before turning to horror with the self-financed IT'S ALIVE (1974), a reductio ad absurdum of THE EXORCIST about a mutant baby who goes on a rampage and terrorizes Los Angeles. (According to Dick Atkins's *Method to the Madness*, Cohen shot HELL UP IN HARLEM and IT'S ALIVE with the same non-union crew simultaneously in four weeks.)[97] With makeup effects by Rick Baker (who was Dick Smith's assistant on THE EXORCIST) and an effective Bernard Herrmann score, IT'S ALIVE was a modest hit for Warner Bros. ($7.1 million in rentals), which distributed it, and Cohen was able to finance a sequel, IT LIVES AGAIN (aka IT'S ALIVE II, 1978), featuring several murderous infants instead of one. (Eight years later, Cohen would write, produce, and direct another: IT'S ALIVE III: ISLAND OF THE ALIVE [1986].) Both films used the subjective camera technique employed in JAWS to represent the killer's point of view, demonstrating that the idea did not originate with Spielberg but was actually a function of new light-weight hand-held camera equipment introduced in the early 1970s. Between the ALIVE films, Cohen produced GOD TOLD ME TO (aka DEMON, 1977), a bizarre mystery that he called "a dark version of the Superman story" about the second

The monster baby in Larry Cohen's IT'S
ALIVE (Warners, 1974). Makeup effects
by Rick Baker. 35mm 1.85:1.

coming of a new (and murderous) Messiah, and THE PRIVATE FILES OF J. EDGAR HOOVER (1977), which suggests the FBI's involvement in the RFK assassination and was described by Robin Wood as "perhaps the most intelligent film about American politics ever to come out of Hollywood."[98] In the 1980s and 1990s, Cohen remained an independent writer-producer-director of horror and horror-comedy films (FULL MOON HIGH [1981]; Q [AKA THE WINGED SERPENT, 1982]; THE STUFF [1985]; THE AMBULANCE [1990]), occasionally writing mainstream screenplays for others.

All of the independent filmmakers discussed above—Hooper, De Palma, Romero, Craven, Cronenberg, and Cohen—started out as *auteurs* in the original French sense of the term, that is, as writer-directors who shaped their material from script through post-production, but these particular auteurs did so exclusively in the underfinanced netherworld of low-end exploitation. What happened to them in the late seventies and early eighties was an alternative version of what happened to Hollywood's "movie brats" during the industry recession and shake-out of 1969–1971. Like the brats, these young directors came from outside of the mainstream industry, and some, like De Palma and Cronenberg, were originally associated with the avant-garde. Unlike the brats, however, they had not attended film school or apprenticed with Roger Corman at AIP; so, in the absence of professional training or experience, the ultra low-budget exploitation field offered them an entry into features. Each scored an early hit heavily dependent on prosthetic gore provided by innovative makeup artists like Rick Baker, Tom Savani, and Rob Bottin, then managed to sustain their success through the end of the decade. Concurrently, mainstream Hollywood was discovering the rewards of big-budget horror and other once-disreputable genres and turned increasingly toward exploitation tactics at the level of both production and distribution. As this happened, the services of successful writer-directors from the industry's exploitation fringes became proportionally valuable, so that by the early 1980s, all of the above named figures but Romero were working on projects for major distribution companies, and some like Hooper were under studio contract.[99] (Conversely, studio-produced horror from mainstream directors was bombing out—for example, Paramount's PROPHECY [John Frankenheimer, 1979] and PHOBIA [John Huston, 1980] both earned less than $1 million.) This explains how a self-taught filmmaker like Wes Craven was able to become a Hollywood franchise virtually unto himself, moving from the sleazy but engaging crudeness of LAST HOUSE ON THE LEFT to the ultra-slick A NIGHTMARE ON ELM STREET in just twelve years, and becoming in the nineties the kind of filmmaker whose work is regularly profiled in the *New York Times*.

The film that pushed the mainstream industry irrevocably into producing and distributing exploitation material was JAWS (Steven Spielberg, 1975), which shared with classical horror the presence of a monster (albeit a natural rather than a preternatural one) and with modern horror the fantasy of mutilation and dismemberment implicit in the "psycho-slasher" subgenre. The innovation of JAWS was to apply the exploitation technique of saturation booking to studio-produced exploitation material with a marketing force that only a major distributor could achieve and actually *sell* the film to the public through the process of commodity packaging. This practice was refined and crystallized as the "blockbuster syndrome," but it was grounded in strategies used by exploitation producers like "Jungle" Sam Katzman (1901–1973) and Roger Corman for decades. Formally, JAWS used a technique that would become as widely imitated by other filmmakers as Peckinpah-style slow-motion bloodbaths were after THE WILD BUNCH (1969). In JAWS, from the very outset, the underwater attacks are preceded by moving subjective camera shots from the shark's point of view, forcing identification with the attacker rather than the victim (which, for contemporary viewers, was one of the most striking and disturbing aspects of the film).

Applied to human killers as they stalked their (usually female) prey, the device would cause a great deal of controversy in the early 1980s, but not before another exploitation film of 1975 had produced a firestorm of protest on its own.[100] This was SNUFF, produced by the notorious gore-and-sexploitation entrepreneurs Roberta and Robert Findlay (SHRIEK OF THE MUTILATED [1974]). The film, whose original title was SLAUGHTER, was a gory, inept thriller based on the Manson murders and shot in Argentina without sound in 1971.[101] It was picked up and reshaped in 1974 by Alan Shackleton of Monarch Releasing Corporation, who tacked on an ending shot in New York in which a woman appears to be dismembered and disemboweled by the film's director at the end of shooting. Cashing in on rumors that a "snuff" film had been smuggled into the United States from South America, Schackleton retitled his movie SNUFF and released it in late 1975, advertising its faked evisceration as the real thing. (On-screen, the "snuff" sequence seems to be shot by the camera crew after the main film has wrapped and visited upon an unsuspecting script girl, heightening its illusion of authenticity. In both advertising and prefatory statements, films like LAST HOUSE ON THE LEFT and THE TEXAS CHAINSAW MASSACRE had touted their basis in actual crimes, but SNUFF was the first such film to insist that the murders it depicted were real. It was also the first to connect murder directly with sexual intercourse, since the script girl is seduced by the director as a prelude to his slashing her.) Although it was exposed as a hoax by *Variety* in early 1976, SNUFF was a smash hit in New York, Philadelphia, Los Angeles, Boston, and other cities,[102] and it provoked the appropriately horrified reaction among feminists that became a turning point in their consciousness about misogyny in film and other media. In fact, it was SNUFF that produced the "generic confusion between horror and hard core" identified by Linda Williams[103] as a distinguishing feature of the feminist antipornography campaign—a campaign that would create a cultural backlash against horror in the early 1980s and return it to the status of a despised, if still extremely popular, genre. (In the seminal anthology *Take Back the Night: Women on Pornography*, Beverly La Belle would write, "The graphic bloodletting of SNUFF finally made the misogyny of pornography a major feminist concern.")[104] Whether this "generic confusion" was in the minds of the filmmakers or their feminist critics, however, would become clear only after the windfall success of the independently distributed HALLOWEEN (1978) had caused an unprecedented boom in violent, low-budget horror.[105]

HALLOWEEN: SLASHERS ENTER THE MAINSTREAM

John Carpenter had directed two low-budget genre features—the science fiction satire
DARK STAR (1974), and ASSAULT ON PRECINCT 13 (1976), a violent homage to Howard
Hawks's RIO BRAVO (1959)—before he made HALLOWEEN for less than $400,000 and it
unexpectedly grossed over $50 million ($80 million worldwide), thereby becoming the
model for the psycho-slasher subgenre that would dominate American horror for the
next decade and beyond. Although the American slasher film is ultimately traceable to
PSYCHO, a more immediate influence on 1970s filmmakers was Dario Argento's interna-

*This "high concept" poster for John Carpenter's HALLOWEEN
(1978) suggests that slasher horror had entered the mainstream by the decade's end. It has the same stark lines as
the posters for THE EXORCIST and THE OMEN, but the focus
is now on sheer visceral imagery, very much like the advertising art for JAWS.*

tionally successful mystery thriller THE BIRD WITH THE CRYSTAL PLUMAGE (L'UCCELLO DALLE PIUME DI CRISTALLO, 1969), itself a revival of the sadistic-terror subgenre inaugurated in Italian cinema by Mario Bava's BLOOD AND BLACK LACE (SEI DONNE PER L'ASSASSINO [literally, SIX WOMEN FOR THE MURDERER], 1964). In these films, the murder of women became pure voyeuristic spectacle cut loose from the gothic moorings of earlier Italian horror (such as Riccardo Freda's I VAMPIRI [LUST OF THE VAMPIRE, 1956] and THE HORRIBLE DR. HICHCOCK [L'ORRIBILE SEGRETO DEL DR. HICHCOCK, 1962], and Bava's own BLACK SUNDAY [LA MASCHERA DEL DEMONIO/THE DEMON'S MASK, 1961]), but their ornate visual style tended to disguise them as art, more decadently romantic than their graphic display of violence would portend. Argento's cinema of "shock-horror" was closely monitored during the 1970s by American exploitation directors like John Carpenter, who borrowed elements of both plot and technique from FOUR FLIES ON GRAY VELVET (QUATTRO MOSCHE DI VELLUTO GRIGIO, 1972—the conclusion of HALLOWEEN, where the heroine is assaulted while trapped in a closet), DEEP RED (PROFONDO ROSSO, 1975—the pre-Oedipal psychopathology of HALLOWEEN's killer), and SUSPIRIA (1977—the hallucinatory atmosphere of THE FOG [1980]). (Argento, in fact, was a script consultant on George Romero's DAWN OF THE DEAD [1978] and recut the film for European distribution as ZOMBIE, adding a score by the Japanese keyboard group Goblin, who had given SUSPIRIA its acoustic frisson.)[106] These borrowings aside, however, HALLOWEEN's contribution to the slasher form was crucial—as was acknowledged by Wes Craven's own 1996 hit SCREAM, a self-reflexive field guide to the subgenre for which Carpenter's film provides the basic intertext; not only does a whole network of allusion evolve around it, but during the penultimate murder sequence, the doomed teenagers actually watch HALLOWEEN on video while being stalked.

HALLOWEEN's plot is simple: an escaped lunatic stalks a small town and butchers a series of teenagers—mainly girls and mainly after they have had sex with their boyfriends (the killer is a psychotic who murdered his own sister for this reason when he was six). One girl (Jamie Lee Curtis, daughter of the actress who played Marion Crane in PSYCHO) survives and eludes the killer until his psychiatrist arrives from the asylum to shoot him. HALLOWEEN is stylishly made, and it attracted considerable critical praise on first release in October 1978; but, as Robert Kapsis points out, it provided a formula that would be repeated ad nauseam by countless inferior imitations—a formula that calls for 1) a male psycho-killer who stalks sexually active teenage girls in some recognizable youth precinct (baby-sitting jobs, high school gatherings, college rituals, summer camp); and 2) the graphic depiction of violence and gore engineered by high-tech "splatter" artists like Tom Savini, Rick Baker, and Rob Bottin, which provides product differentiation from television.[107] (These makeup experts became stars in their own right among the teenagers who made up the bulk of the nascent slasher audience.)[108] HALLOWEEN's most significant stylistic feature, however, was its extensive use of handheld subjective tracking shots to represent the killer's point of view as he stalks and murders his victims for their sexually transgressive behavior. Carpenter clearly borrowed this camera strategy from JAWS, where it was used to force an identification with the attacker rather than the victim. (Significantly, the technique appeared earlier that year in the stalking sequences of Columbia's THE EYES OF LAURA MARS [Irvin Kershner, 1978], a glossy murder mystery set in the world of high-fashion photography for which Carpenter wrote the screenplay.)

Identification with the killer and his point of view had, of course, been an essential component of PSYCHO, where it was accomplished technically through montage and

More or less interchangeable images of horror from three late-seventies slashers. All three films starred the androgynously appealing Jamie Lee Curtis. HALLOWEEN *(1978): 35mm Panavision anamorphic.*

PROM NIGHT *(Paul Lynch, 1980): 35mm 1.85:1.*

TERROR TRAIN *(Roger Spottiswoode, 1980): 35mm 1.85:1.*

sustained by the logic of the script. But as Roger Ebert pointed out in an influential *American Film* article on slashers in 1981, the use of a mobile subjective camera to represent the killer's point of view tends to displace his center of consciousness from the film and relocate it in the audience.[109] (This mobility was made possible by the Steadicam technology introduced in 1976, which was still a novelty at the decade's end—see Chapter 9.) It would become commonplace in eighties horror for audiences to share the perspective of the killer or monster (see, for example, WOLFEN [Michael Wadleigh, 1981] and PREDATOR [John McTiernan, 1987]), but in the late 1970s it seemed profoundly anti-social, and Ebert argued that the strategy had the effect of transferring "the lust to kill and rape"—psychologically at least—to the audience.[110]

For whatever reason, there was a significant boom in slasher-style horror between 1979 and 1981, when first independent producers and then the majors applied the HALLOWEEN template to their product and came up with a dizzying array of similar (and, in some cases, nearly identical) titles: in 1978, KILLER'S MOON and THE TOOLBOX MURDERS; in 1979, DON'T GO IN THE HOUSE, THE DRILLER KILLER, TOURIST TRAP, and WHEN A STRANGER CALLS; in 1980, THE BOOGEYMAN, CHRISTMAS EVIL, DON'T ANSWER THE PHONE, FRIDAY THE 13TH, MANIAC, MOTEL HELL, MOTHER'S DAY, PROM NIGHT, SILENT SCREAM, and TERROR TRAIN; in 1981, BLOOD BEACH, THE BURNING, DEAD AND BURIED, DEADLY BLESSING, EYES OF A STRANGER, FINAL EXAM, FRIDAY THE 13TH, PART 2, GRADUATION DAY, HALLOWEEN II, HAPPY BIRTHDAY TO ME, HE KNOWS YOU'RE ALONE, HELL NIGHT, HOSPITAL MASSACRE, MY BLOODY VALENTINE, NEW YEAR'S EVIL, NIGHTMARE, NIGHT SCHOOL, and THE PROWLER. "Horror Is *Hot!*" proclaimed *Film Comment* in late 1979,[111] and if only a handful of these films achieved the popularity of the original (FRIDAY THE 13TH earned $17.1 million in rentals compared with HALLOWEEN's $18.5; and the first sequels to both earned in excess of $10 million), nearly all were profitable relative to their costs, and most performed strongly both at home and abroad. Production of slashers continued unabated through 1982 (FRIDAY THE 13TH PART 3, SLUMBER PARTY MASSACRE), when the media backlash against them reached its height, causing many newspapers to stop reviewing them and CARA to tighten its rating standards for violence.[112] (CARA chairman Richard D. Heffner admitted to Robert Kapsis in late 1981 that many R-rated slasher films of 1979 would have received an X just two years later.)[113]

Combined with a glut of product on the market, these circumstances generated a horror bust in 1983 when even big-budget horror failed to find an audience.[114] Yet slashers had become a permanent part of the generic landscape, with sequels to many of the above named films (as well as newer ones like Wes Craven's A NIGHTMARE ON ELM STREET [1984]) continuing profitably into the 1990s. This was perhaps the most important result of horror's exponential growth during the 1970s—that a genre associated for much of the fifties and sixties with low-budget monster films became identified in the early 1980s with the heretofore marginal psycho-slasher subgenre: itself the most extreme expression of misogyny in the history of American cinema. It is estimated that by the end of the decade, 60 percent of all horror films were slashers; and by 1981 fully one-third of the twenty-five top-grossing domestic films were in the violent horror category, as were 25 percent of all films presented at international market assemblies in Cannes, Milan, and Los Angeles,[115] to the disgust of many attendees.[116]

It has been suggested that a sea change in political and social attitudes during the late 1970s, as well as the presence of escalating inflation and unemployment, created a context for the slasher film in the same way that it catalyzed the election of Ronald Reagan to the presidency.[117] While there is no question that the cultural climate of the time represented a pendulum swing away from the libertarian ethic of the late 1960s, with its agitation for women's rights and passage of the ERA, it is also true that a deep strain of misogyny had been present in certain American genres—notably *film noir* and the Western—since their inception. When the CARA system effectively ended censorship in American cinema, the wraps came off of misogyny, as they did for race, sex, violence, obscenity, and other kinds of subject matter specifically forbidden by the Production Code. Contempt for women ("chicks") is a salient feature of counterculture movies like EASY RIDER (1969), and misogyny takes the form of rape, torture, and murder in such early seventies classics as A CLOCKWORK ORANGE (Kubrick, 1971), STRAW DOGS (Peckinpah, 1971), and FRENZY (Hitchcock, 1972), so it would be wrong to see the rise of slasher horror at the end of the decade as an isolated trend. Since the overwhelming audience segment for slashers was teenagers[118] (the same ones who paid to see STAR WARS, GREASE, and ANIMAL HOUSE again and again), it seems likely that producers simply followed their nature and played to market strength. (Debra Hill, line producer of the HALLOWEEN series, has commented: "I make films for audiences, not critics. It is a business, I'm not dumb.")[119] At a time when average per-picture costs had risen to $9.4 million, the fact that most horror films were produced for $2 million or less made them attractive.[120] But whatever the reason, no other genre experienced a greater infusion of creative richness and financial capital during the 1970s than horror. According to a *Variety* survey, between 1970 and 1980 rentals for horror films went from $6.5 million to $168 million a year, while the number of horror films produced tripled from twenty-two to sixty-six, of which no fewer than twenty-six topped the million-dollar mark.[121] By the close of this period, even Stanley Kubrick was attracted by the market for slasher-style horror and pitched his adaptation of Stephen King's THE SHINING (1980) toward it with notable ($30 million in domestic rentals) success. Although briefly displaced in popularity by science fiction in the mid-1980s, horror was institutionalized in the American cinema as the significant, controversial mainstream genre it had become during the 1970s.

The Science Fiction Film

THE EXAMPLE OF 2001

Science fiction, like horror, entered the 1970s as a disreputable B-film genre, somewhat redeemed by the success of MGM's 2001: A SPACE ODYSSEY (Stanley Kubrick) and Fox's PLANET OF THE APES (Franklin Schaffner) in 1968. These two films were the fifth- and sixth-highest earners of the year ($17 and $15.5 million, respectively) and gave producers some hope that science fiction might be ready to emerge from the bargain-basement category it had occupied, with a handful of exceptions (such as MGM's FORBIDDEN PLANET [Fred M. Wilcox, 1956]), since the mid-fifties. The makeup effects of PLANET OF THE APES (by John Chambers) and the special visual effects of 2001 (by Stanley Kubrick, Douglas Trumbull, et al.), both of which won Academy Awards, set new industry standards and raised higher audience expectations for the genre. 2001's spectacular space travel sequences—nearly three years in production—were especially influential, since they were accomplished through the time-honored process of traveling matte photography but yielded results of striking verisimilitude on-screen. Computer-assisted motion control systems would make this process much simpler and cost-effective just eight years later, but the precision-tooled realism of Kubrick's film upped the ante for all science-fiction spectacle to come and linked the genre permanently with state-of-the-art special effects. (The impulse toward heightened realism was in some respects a revival of the effects standards set by producer George Pal in Paramount's WHEN WORLDS COLLIDE [Rudolph Maté, 1951] and WAR OF THE WORLDS [Byron Haskin, 1953], which had been debased in the late fifties by exploitation producers like Roger Corman [ATTACK OF THE CRAB MONSTERS, 1957] and Bert I. Gordon [THE AMAZING COLOSSAL MAN, 1957]; but it was also a response to recently published photographs of deep space emanating from NASA's *Apollo* program.)

DYSTOPIA: WATERGATE-ERA SCIENCE FICTION

Science fiction in the seventies, however, began not with special effects but technophobia, another heritage of 2001. Universal's COLOSSUS: THE FORBIN PROJECT (Joseph Sargent, 1970) was adapted by James Bridges from a D. F. Jones novel about the creation of an American doomsday computer called "Colossus," capable of launching an all-out nuclear attack on the Russians which, like HAL in Kubrick's film, develops a mind of its own and merges with its Soviet counterpart. ("Colossus" was actually a mammoth $4.8-million Control Data Corporation electronics system hauled to the studio piece by piece and reassembled on a soundstage by CDC technicians.)[122] Linked together and holding all the nuclear cards, the two supercomputers blackmail the human race into world peace (because war is economically counterproductive) and servitude to their new machine-dominated order. The theme of machines usurping human control is also central to Warner Bros.' THE TERMINAL MAN (Mike Hodges, 1974), adapted from a Michael Crichton novel; MGM's WESTWORLD (Michael Crichton, 1973) and its sequel FUTUREWORLD (AIP; Richard T. Heffron, 1976), in which a computer glitch causes robots in the adult fantasy park of Delos to run amok (like the dinosaurs of JURASSIC PARK [Steven Spielberg, 1993]); and THE DEMON SEED (MGM; Donald Cammell, 1977), whose heroine (Julie Christie) is impregnated by a "Proteus IV" computer. The same kind of paranoia about technology (biomedical in this case) and nuclear weapons runs through Universal's THE ANDROMEDA STRAIN (Robert Wise, 1971) and Warner Bros.' THE OMEGA MAN (Boris Sagal, 1971). The former, adapted from yet another novel by Michael Crichton, is about the attempt to control a deadly virus brought back from space by a crashed satellite and features special effects by Douglas Trumbull and James Shourt; the latter is based on Richard Matheson's 1954 novel *I Am Legend* (also the inspiration for Romero's THE NIGHT OF THE LIVING DEAD), and is about a plague of post-nuclear vampires, rendered here as the mutant survivors of germ warfare between the United States and China.

The same year witnessed similarly grim but all-too-human visions of the future in two Warner Bros. releases, George Lucas's THX-1138 (1971) and Kubrick's A CLOCKWORK ORANGE. In Lucas's film, an expanded version of his award-winning student short made at USC in 1965, the future is a sterile, computer-driven dystopia in which drugs and television have replaced human emotion. Kubrick's future is closer to home—a kind of social-science welfare state where tendencies toward "ultraviolence" are eradicated through consignment to mass spiritual torpor. Two films that followed shortly thereafter—Universal's SLAUGHTERHOUSE-FIVE (George Roy Hill, 1972) and United Artists'

Universal's SLAUGHTERHOUSE-FIVE *(George Roy Hill, 1971): Billy Pilgrim (Michael Sacks) and porn star Montana Wildhack (Valerie Perrine) wave to aliens from the planet Tralfamadore who keep them in a glass bubble to observe their behavior. Techniscope anamorphic (2.35:1).*

SLEEPER (Woody Allen, 1973)—are nominally science fiction but fall more truly into the category of fantasy-satire: the one an adaptation of Kurt Vonnegut's novel about a contemporary character (Billy Pilgrim) who becomes "unstuck" in time, and the other Woody Allen's comic vision of Central Park West, circa 2073. None of these films depended heavily on special effects, but Universal's SILENT RUNNING (1971) strove for a realism in its deep space sequences that would compare favorably to that of 2001. Directed and co-written by Douglas Trumbull, a former NASA illustrator who had supervised the effects for 2001 and THE ANDROMEDA STRAIN, SILENT RUNNING was also one of several early 1970s films projecting a catastrophic ecological future for the human race. (Others were THE HELLSTROM CHRONICLE [Walon Green, 1971], an independently produced documentary examining the behavior of insects and suggesting that they will inherit the earth; MGM's SOYLENT GREEN [Richard Fleischer, 1973], a dramatic feature envisioning a world so overpopulated by 2022 that it must be fed on nutrients from recycled human corpses; and PHASE IV [Saul Bass, 1974], an independent feature about an ant colony that mutates into an intelligent entity and attempts to conquer all other life forms.)[123]

In Trumbull's film, which is set in 2008, the earth's atmosphere can no longer support vegetation and the last remaining forests have been shipped into space in giant geodesic domes hauled by "space freighters" at the expense of an interplanetary conglomerate. When the corporation orders the forests destroyed, a botanist on the freighter "Valley Forge" rebels, kills his crewmates, and pilots the ship and its biospheres into the isolated

SILENT RUNNING (Universal, 1971), an early landmark in 1970s special effects, was directed by Douglas Trumbull, who had supervised the visual effects for Kubrick's 2001 (1968). The film's own visual effects were executed by Trumbull, Steve Yuricich, and John Dykstra, who would supervise the special effects for STAR WARS a few years later. Here, Bruce Dern and two of his three robots enjoy the relics of a devasted Earth in the greenhouse of their space freighter. (The pint-sized robots, who help Dern run the ship, are affectionately named Huey, Dewey, and Louie after Donald Duck's three nephews, and they were clearly the models for R2D2 in STAR WARS, although Lucas does not admit this.) 35mm 1.85:1.

haven of deep space. Though shot on a modest budget of $1.4 million aboard an abandoned aircraft carrier (the U.S.S. *Valley Forge*), SILENT RUNNING nevertheless has some breathtaking traveling matte effects accomplished by Trumbull, Steve Yuricich, and John Dykstra (who would begin supervising the computerized traveling matte effects of STAR WARS four years later), building on the experience of 2001—as well as using several outtakes from it. For this reason, it was a modest box-office success.

In 1974, two unconventional science fiction films appeared that commented self-reflexively on the genre. John Carpenter's independently distributed DARK STAR, co-scripted by Carpenter and Dan O'Bannon, began as a 16mm student film while the director was at UCLA, and was later expanded into a 35mm theatrical feature. It is set aboard a twenty-first-century space cruiser on a mission to search the universe for planets that might shift dangerously in orbit and then to destroy them with nuclear weapons. But the crew has been out nineteen years, discipline is non-existent, and the ship's technical infrastructure is slowly falling apart. This situation provides the context for a satire of generic conventions, including the recent fetish for high-tech special effects (which here revert to 1950s-style process work), as well as a critique of contemporary social attitudes and politics. Fox's ZARDOZ (1974), which was written, produced, and directed by John Boorman and shot at Irish locations, explores traditional science fiction themes in a future that looks more like the Bronze Age past. In a post-nuclear 2293, "Civilization" has developed a tripartite structure: the Eternals are immortals who possess all power and knowledge; the Brutals are primitives living in the ruins of earth's former cities, who are allowed by the Eternals to breed but are subject to strict population control; and the Exterminators, an elite class of barbarians, provide control by hunting and killing Brutals. The film's plot is catalyzed when one of the Exterminators aspires to godhead (literally), challenges the Eternals, and robs them of their computer-generated immortality. The film is simultaneously a parable of birth, death, and resurrection; an allegory of aesthetic creation; and a technically brilliant work of science fiction (thanks in large part to Geoffrey Unsworth's hypnotic cinematography), and is a landmark of metaphysical cinema that shares thematic lineage with Boorman's Arthurian mystery play EXCALIBUR (Orion, 1981), which was also shot on location in Ireland. Inevitably, it was a commercial failure in a year when big-budget disaster movies and Mel Brooks genre parodies were king, although it is now regarded by some as one of the decade's richest films.

With STAR WARS looming on the horizon, the science fiction films of 1975–1976 must seem transitional in hindsight, but they provide an interesting glimpse of the context in which Lucas's film was conceived, pitched, and marketed. The independently produced

Sean Connery as Zed, an Exterminator who aspires to godhead in John Boorman's complex allegory of creation, ZARDOZ (Fox, 1974). As well as directing, Boorman also wrote and produced the film, which was shot on location in Ireland by Geoffrey Unsworth (2001, CABARET). 35mm Panavision anamorphic.

Pretty maids all in a row: Bryan Forbes's THE STEPFORD WIVES *(Columbia, 1975) combined science fiction and social satire in adapting Ira Levin's novel about men who
replace their wives with beautiful androids. 35mm 1.85:1.*

and distributed A BOY AND HIS DOG (L. Q. Jones, 1975) was adapted from Harlan
Ellison's award-winning story about life in a devastated postnuclear world where men
and their canine companions are both telepathically and existentially linked. Like DEATH
RACE 2000 (Paul Bartel, 1975), a darkly comic Roger Corman (New World) exploitation
vehicle that set the ultimate car-chase in a desolate and barren future, it earned less than
$2 million. More horror than science fiction, Columbia's THE STEPFORD WIVES (Bryan
Forbes, 1975) was based on a satirical novel by Ira Levin (ROSEMARY'S BABY) and has the
men of an upscale bedroom community killing their wives and replacing them with
(nearly) perfect robots. An occasionally eerie mixture of INVASION OF THE BODY
SNATCHERS (Don Siegel, 1956) and WESTWORLD (Michael Crichton, 1973), with a literate script by William Goldman and high production values, THE STEPFORD WIVES
addressed contemporary feminist concerns in a stylish and witty fashion, but it barely
broke even, returning just $4 million in rentals. United Artists' ROLLERBALL (Norman
Jewison, 1975) did a similar turn for anxiety about the growing power of corporations in
American life: by 2018, the world has achieved a lasting peace thanks to the several giant
corporations who run it, and the ultraviolent sport of rollerball has been invented as a
channel for natural aggression. A combination of roller derby, motocross, and hockey in
which contestants are permitted to maim or even kill their opponents, the brutal game
serves as a metaphor for the control the corporations exercise over all aspects of human
life, and the plot revolves around one rollerball champion (James Caan) who ultimately
rejects this form of organized warfare. Distinctly less conventional, THE MAN WHO FELL

Rollerball champion Jonathan E. (James Caan) crushes an opponent in United Artists'
ROLLERBALL *(Norman Jewison, 1975), one of several mid-decade films that mixed sci-*
ence fiction and social commentary. 35mm Panavision spherical (1.85:1), blown up to
70mm for road-showing.

TO EARTH (Nicolas Roeg, 1976) was a British Lion production shot on location in the
United States with a mainly American cast, except for David Bowie in the title role.
Adapted by Paul Mayersberg from a novel by Walter Tevis, the film is about an alien who
drops to earth seeking a means to save his drought-ridden planet. He creates a human
identity, having observed the ways of the earth for years and, as "Thomas Newton,"
becomes briefly wealthy by licensing high technology patents and forming his own conglomerate, but he is finally betrayed by the venial earthlings who work for him and left
at the film's conclusion a desolate, isolated figure in a still-strange land. Roeg's genius
here—abetted by the art direction of Brian Eatwell—lies not so much in the narrative
but in his depiction of the earth as an alien planet, very much as an extra-terrestrial
might see it, reminding us yet again that he was a world-class cinematographer before
he became a director. The MGM release of LOGAN'S RUN (Michael Anderson, 1976) was
touted in publicity as the most elaborate science fiction movie since 2001. In the twenty-
third century, life is regulated by a giant computer and carried on inside huge domed
cities where, as a means of population control, all must commit ritual suicide at the age
of thirty. (On the plus side, life until this day of "renewal" is almost completely pleasur-
able and hedonistic.) Some, however, refuse to die and become "Runners," who must be
hunted down and killed by state police called "Sandmen." The film tells how one of
these Runners (Logan, played by Michael York) is convinced by a rebel girl to join the

David Bowie ("Thomas Newton") discusses his high technology patents with manipulative chemistry professor Rip Torn in Nicolas Roeg's THE MAN WHO FELL TO EARTH *(British Lion, 1976). The film's American distributor, Cinema 5, cut it from 140 minutes to versions running 117, 120, and 125 minutes for different markets, but restored it to its orginal length in 1980. 35mm Panavision anamorphic.*

underground and seek a full life in the legendary "Sanctuary" outside the domes, which, in a clear bit of post-Watergate irony, turns out to be the ruins of Washington, D. C. Shot on location in Dallas, with matte-work isolating the city's newly postmodern architecture, LOGAN'S RUN was critically successful and received much praise for its futuristic sets and visual effects, which made pioneering (if not very impressive) use of laser holography and won a noncompetitive Special Achievement Award from the Academy— effects that would be rendered obsolete by STAR WARS just one year later.[124] Both ROLLERBALL and LOGAN'S RUN earned close to $10 million in rentals ($9.1 and $9.4 million, respectively), and so low were producer expectations for science fiction films at the time that both were considered successful.

THE IMPACT OF *STAR WARS*

Neither George Lucas nor 20th Century–Fox expected their $11.5-million production of STAR WARS to earn more than twice its costs, and market analysts projected that $35 million would be a windfall.[125] When the film earned $100 million in its first three months and then went on to become the top-grossing film of all time ($262 million in worldwide rentals through 1979), the industry was stunned. Even more amazing was the fact that tie-in merchandise marketed under the "Star Wars" brand (to which Lucas had retained the exclusive rights) generated hundreds of millions of dollars in excess of box-

This widely distributed poster for George Lucas's STAR WARS (Fox, 1977) emphasizes its status as a genre pastiche, containing as it does images evoking the Western, the historical romance, and the combat film, as well as fantasy and science fiction.

office sales—ultimately more than the film itself—creating the first true film franchise (see Chapter 3). STAR WARS also revolutionized the practice of special effects when F/X director John Dykstra perfected a computerized motion-control system for traveling matte photography that made the process both highly realistic *and* cost-effective. For his elaborate battles in space, Lucas was able to create hundreds of stop-motion miniature sequences at a fraction of their cost for earlier films—$2.5 million for 365 traveling matte shots, as compared with $6.5 million for less than thirty in 2001. Furthermore, STAR WARS was the first film to be both recorded and released in four-track Dolby stereo, greatly enhancing the realism and majesty of these sequences. More even than

Kubrick's film, STAR WARS ratcheted up the standards for science fiction spectacle and reconfigured the genre around them (an achievement acknowledged by seven Academy Awards in technical categories, including Visual Effects and Sound).

Ironically, perhaps, STAR WARS also pioneered the genre pastiche, that characteristically postmodern response to a world, as described by Fredric Jameson, where "stylistic innovation is no longer possible, [and] all that is left is to imitate dead styles, to speak through the masks and with the voices of the styles in the imaginary museum."[126] For cinema, the "imaginary museum" houses the artifacts of film history, which STAR WARS offers as a kind of collage, drawing on elements of the Western (THE SEARCHERS [John

STAR WARS Conquers the World: the success of STAR WARS was an international phenomenon, one that would ultimately extend the franchise into every corner of the globe. Here, a Polish poster for STAR WARS, which shows that even at the height of the Cold War the Warsaw Pact nations were not immune to the seductions of Lucasfilm's "illusionist spectacle."

Ford, 1956]), the combat film (AIR FORCE [Howard Hawks, 1943]), *film noir* (CASABLANCA [Michael Curtiz, 1942]), and the Japanese samurai film (THE HIDDEN FORTRESS [Akira Kurosawa, 1958]), with glosses on what J. Hoberman called "fantasies as varied as THE WIZARD OF OZ and TRIUMPH OF THE WILL."[127] Thus STAR WARS was a science fiction film that was also a "nostalgia film" in the sense of evoking in its 1977 adult audience the experience of Saturday afternoon serials and early series television, while at the same time appealing to children and teenagers as a thrilling action-adventure. This was the force of *Time* magazine's absolutely accurate description of STAR WARS as "a subliminal history of the movies, wrapped in a riveting tale of suspense and adventure,"[128] and it was the reason that the film became a cult blockbuster. It appealed to different audiences at different levels and to all audiences at one level, becoming a repeatable and multilayered cultural experience for the American mass public and, ultimately, for virtually every sentient human being on the face of the globe.

In the years to come, the STAR WARS phenomenon would change the American film industry and films themselves in fundamental ways, but its most immediate effect was the sudden repositioning of science fiction as a blockbuster genre. A similar repositioning had occurred for horror after the runaway success of THE EXORCIST in 1974, with the important difference that horror films were relatively cheap to produce, while science fiction became relatively expensive once high-quality special effects had become the order of the day. In fact, some of the most extravagant and spectacular films of the late 1970s were in the science fiction genre—Columbia's CLOSE ENCOUNTERS OF THE THIRD KIND (1977), Universal's BATTLESTAR: GALACTICA (1978), Warner Bros.' SUPERMAN (1978), Disney's THE BLACK HOLE (1979), Paramount's STAR TREK—THE MOTION PICTURE (1979), and Fox's ALIEN (1979)—as the majors rushed to cash in on the success of STAR WARS. Only one of these, CLOSE ENCOUNTERS, was an unqualified financial success; others proved disappointing relative to their costs (SUPERMAN, STAR TREK, ALIENS), or lost money (BATTLESTAR: GALACTICA, THE BLACK HOLE). But the investment in special effects continued unabated, as companies like Industrial Light and Magic, Apogee, Inc., and Digital Productions were formed for the exclusive purpose of providing them. And the STAR WARS mystique continued into the early 1980s, when the epoch-making grosses of Fox's THE EMPIRE STRIKES BACK (Irvin Kershner, 1980), Universal's E.T.: THE EXTRA-TERRESTRIAL (Steven Spielberg, 1982), and Fox's, RETURN OF THE JEDI (Richard Marquand, 1983) restored industry confidence that science fiction was a profitable form.

LATE SEVENTIES SCIENCE FICTION

The changes that science fiction had gone through as a genre during the 1970s were underscored by three end-of-the-decade films that are generally considered to be classics of the form—CLOSE ENCOUNTERS OF THE THIRD KIND (Steven Spielberg, 1977), INVASION OF THE BODY SNATCHERS (Philip Kaufman, 1978), and ALIEN (Ridley Scott, 1979). The most widely admired of these is Steven Spielberg's CLOSE ENCOUNTERS, an affirmative UFO movie that celebrates both childhood wonder and science fiction B-films of the 1950s (particularly THE DAY THE EARTH STOOD STILL [Robert Wise, 1951] and IT CAME FROM OUTER SPACE [Jack Arnold, 1953], which was shot in 3-D), with STAR WARS-grade special effects by Douglas Trumbull and Academy Award-winning cinematography by Vilmos Zsigmond. Produced for $19.4 million at no small risk to Columbia's solvency, CLOSE ENCOUNTERS earned $82.8 million in rentals. While the film

Philip Kaufman's remake of INVASION OF THE BODY SNATCHERS *(UA, 1978), set in contemporary San Francisco, was about the 1970s' "culture of narcissism" in the same way that the original had been about the 1950s' politics of conformity. The fact that more than 900 members of the People's Temple sect—most of them from the Bay area—had committed mass suicide in Jonestown, Guyana, just weeks before the film's release gave it a disturbingly immediate subtext: Donald Sutherland joins the lonely crowd of pod-people on the march in Union Square. 35mm 1.85:1. Recorded and selectively exhibited in four-channel Dolby stereo optical sound.*

inarguably stands on its own merits—which are mainly those of special effects, especially the Mother Ship sequence at its conclusion—there is no question that it benefited from sharing the nostalgic, generically hybridized, "feel-good" quality of Lucas's film. (In John Williams, they also shared a composer and similarly portentous scores.) Both STAR WARS and CLOSE ENCOUNTERS were perfect escapist entertainment for a public weary of post-Watergate cynicism and disillusionment.

However, United Artists' INVASION OF THE BODY SNATCHERS (Philip Kaufman, 1978) and Fox's ALIEN (Ridley Scott, 1979) were proof that much dis-ease still afflicted the body politic. Kaufman's film was a slick remake of the Don Siegel 1956 B-movie original, with star performers (Donald Sutherland and Brooke Adams), striking location photography of San Francisco by Michael Chapman, and state-of-the-art makeup effects by Tom Burman. By relocating the site of the alien pod invasion from the small town of Santa Mira to San Francisco, Kaufman and screenwriter W. D. Richter were able to comment obliquely on the moral climate of contemporary America, as well as take advantage of the scenery. In 1978, San Francisco was the acknowledged capital of the "culture of narcissism" denounced by Christopher Lasch, Peter Marin, Tom Wolfe, and others[129] (including, finally, President Jimmy Carter). It epitomized the contradictions of the "Me-Decade" in both its hedonism and its anomie—functions, generally, of the nation's soaring divorce rate and 60 percent increase in the number of people living alone between 1970 and 1978.[130] The notion of an American city suddenly populated by disconnected, alien "pod-people" who look like everyone else but are actually insentient clones speaks very specifically to the 1970s "cult of the self" and its pursuit of "new consciousness"—tendencies that in San Francisco would lead to the ritualized mass suicide at Jonestown in November 1978 and, inversely, to the assassinations of Mayor George Moscone and city supervisor Harvey Milk a few days later.[131] (Kaufman told *Film Comment* that "modern life is turning people into unfeeling, conforming pods who resist getting involved with each other on any level—and we've put them directly into the script,"[132] or as a psychiatrist in the film—amusingly portrayed by Leonard Nimoy, *Star Trek*'s Mr. Spock—tells one of his friends, "People are changing; they're becoming less human." The narcissistic cultural context of San Francisco was put to similar use in Warner's TIME AFTER TIME [Nicholas Meyer, 1979], a science fiction fantasy in which H. G. Wells and Jack the Ripper are both transported from Victorian London to the modern, sexually liberated city in a time machine: Wells is impaired by the future's dystopic moral lassitude, but the serial killer fits right in.) Moreover, whereas the 1956 INVASION OF THE BODY SNATCHERS attributed the pods' origin to radiation contamination, the remake emphasized genetic manipulation, suggesting the rising popular distrust of the biological and medical sciences that appeared in other late seventies science fiction—Cine Artists' EMBRYO (Ralph Nelson, 1976); AIP's THE ISLAND OF DR. MOREAU (Don Taylor, 1977); Fox's THE BOYS FROM BRAZIL (Franklin J. Schaffner, 1978); MGM/United Artists' COMA (Michael Crichton, 1978), and the independently distributed PARTS: THE CLONUS HORROR (Robert S. Fiveson, 1979).

Biology is also a subtext of Ridley Scott's ALIEN, written by Dan O'Bannon (clearly influenced by IT! THE TERROR FROM BEYOND SPACE [Edward L. Cahn, 1958] and its AIP remake PLANET OF BLOOD [Curtis Harrington, 1966]), in which an intergalactic freighter is infiltrated by a monstrous polymorph while visiting a dead planet. Like some incurable virus, the creature incubates within the bodies of crew members—erupting from the abdomen of one of them in a landmark, much-imitated special effect—and finally kills all of them except for Ripley (Sigourney Weaver), the film's iconic feminist heroine, who ultimately destroys it. With Academy Award-winning visual effects designed by H. R. Giger and Carlo Rambaldi, ALIEN became an instant science fiction classic, prefiguring Scott's brilliant direction of BLADE RUNNER (Warner Bros., 1982) and inspiring three Fox sequels (ALIENS [James Cameron, 1986]; ALIEN 3 [David Fincher, 1992], and ALIEN RESURRECTION [Jean-Pierre Jeunet, 1997]); it also generated numerous inferior imitations (Jupiter Film's INSEMINOID/HORROR PLANET [Norman J. Warren, 1982]; New World's GALAXY OF TERROR [B. D. Clark, 1981]; Embassy's FORBIDDEN WORLD [Allan Holzman, 1982]). ALIEN was heavily marketed, and became the fifth highest earning film of 1979, but Fox spent so much on advertising—much of it on network television—that the $11 million film did not show a profit until the summer of 1980, after it had earned $40.3 million in domestic rentals. Thus, the last important science fiction film of the 1970s, while sharing motifs with its 1950s avatars (especially RKO's THE THING [Christian Nyby, 1951] and Warner Bros.' THEM! [Gordon Douglas, 1954]), forecast many of the next decade's trends: huge marketing costs, soon to exceed 25 percent of total domestic earnings; an emphasis on the realistic depiction not merely of space travel but of the grotesque and horrific, made possible through a complex merging of makeup, special effects, and robotic puppetry (soon to be known as "animatronics"); and a concentration on the potentially virulent nature of alien life forms—appropriate to a planet about to discover in its midst an incurable virus called AIDS.[133]

The Disaster Film

The transformation of science fiction from B-genre into big-budget, special-effects laden spectacle was coincident with the rise of the disaster film, a closely related genre that originated in the 1970s and remains popular today.[134] In disaster films, a manmade systems failure or a force of nature, often monstrously perverted, threatens to destroy a group of characters brought together more or less by chance (as passengers on a jet or ocean liner, for example, or vacationers at a resort), and while many of them die, a few prevail through their courage and resourcefulness. (As producer Irwin Allen described the situation of his paradigmatic THE POSEIDON ADVENTURE to *The Hollywood Reporter* for July 5, 1972: "We have the perfect set-up of a group of people who have never met before and who are thrown together in terrible circumstances . . . [in which] . . . 1,400 people are killed and only the stars survive.")[135] The form is rich in possibilities for "all-star" casting and special effects—although during the 1970s the practice was usually to mix one or two current stars with myriad performers who no longer held that status—and it is ripe for marketing abroad, since disaster is a kind of international language.[136] As to the generative mechanisms, the term *systems failure* originated in the 1970s to describe the breakdown of networked computers, but it might have been equally well applied to the Vietnam War or Watergate because, culturally, the disaster film expresses a fear of powerlessness or loss of control,[137] an equation that was widely recognized at the time. (As an editorial on disaster films in the *Wall Street Journal* for January 7, 1975, put it: "In a time when leadership at every level of society is believed to be wanting, disasters caused or aggravated by the errors of those in charge make sense to the audience.")[138] This is why the genre traces its origins to the depths of the Depression, when many studios produced movies with spectacular disasters in their plots or subplots (e.g., RKO's THE LAST DAYS OF POMPEII [Ernest B. Schoedsack, 1935] and KING KONG [Merian C. Cooper, 1933]; MGM's CHINA SEAS [Tay Garnett, 1935], SAN FRANCISCO [W. S. Van Dyke, 1936], and THE GOOD EARTH [Sidney Franklin, 1937]; Fox's IN OLD CHICAGO [Henry King, 1938] and THE RAINS CAME [D. Clarence Brown, 1939]; Sam Goldwyn's THE HURRICANE [John Ford, 1937], released by United Artists); and to the Cold War era with its countless B-films about the power of atomic blasts and radiation to produce havoc-wreaking mutants and monsters (THE BEAST FROM 20,000 FATHOMS [1953]; THEM! [1954];. IT CAME FROM BENEATH THE SEA [1955]; ATTACK OF THE CRAB MONSTERS [1957]; THE DEADLY MANTIS [1957]; THE MONSTER THAT CHALLENGED THE WORLD [1957]; BEGINNING OF THE END [1957]; THE AMAZING COLOSSAL MAN [1957]; etc.). There were few examples of the disaster film in the 1960s (Hitchcock's THE BIRDS [1963]; KRAKATOA, EAST OF JAVA [Bernard Kowalski, 1969], one of the last films presented in Cinerama), but during the 1970s, it became a staple of blockbuster production.

HIGH WATERGATE DISASTER: *AIRPORT* TO *THE HINDENBURG*

The film that launched the 1970s disaster film was Universal's AIRPORT (1970), adapted by its director George Seaton from a best-selling Arthur Hailey novel. Although its plot was inspired by an earlier film/novel sensation, Warner Bros.' THE HIGH AND THE

MIGHTY (William Wellman, 1954) adapted by Ernest K. Gann from his own best-seller, AIRPORT established the formula of microcosmic melodrama combined with catastrophe-oriented adventure that would be followed by virtually all of the decade's disaster films, regardless of their original source. Its state-of-the-art special effects and Todd-AO cinematography (by Ernest Laszlo) lent realism to the plight of a crewless, bomb-damaged jumbo jet that must be landed by passengers during a blizzard. (For the final sequence of the landing, producer Ross Hunter leased a Boeing 707 and had it landed in a real snowstorm; the film's interior sets were converted from the fuselage and pilot's compartment of a salvaged Mexican Airline DC 8.)[139] Universal executives, who had been nervous over the film's then-spectacular negative cost of $10 million, were ecstatic when it earned $45.2 million in rentals and ten Oscar nominations, ensuring that would be replicated through a series of sequels (AIRPORT 1975 [Jack Smight, 1974]; AIRPORT '77 [Jerry Jameson, 1977]; THE CONCORDE—AIRPORT '79 [David Lowell, 1979]) and imitated generically for the rest of the decade.

Irwin Allen (1916–1991), the successful producer of several science fiction films (VOYAGE TO THE BOTTOM OF THE SEA [Irwin Allen, 1961]) and TV series (*Voyage to the Bottom of the Sea*, 1964–1968; *Lost in Space*, 1965–1968), became a mainline impresario of the disaster epic with Fox's THE POSEIDON ADVENTURE (Ronald Neame, 1972), adapted by Stirling Silliphant from a Paul Gallico novel. Here the GRAND HOTEL-like melodrama of AIRPORT was replaced with an action-oriented plot, as a group of passengers (among them Gene Hackman, Ernest Borgnine, and Shelley Winters) struggle to free themselves from a capsized ocean liner whose physical dimensions were based by set designer William Creber on the Queen Mary. (In fact, many of the film's pre-disaster sequences were shot aboard the Queen Mary, greatly enhancing its realism.)[140] Produced at a cost of $5 million, THE POSEIDON ADVENTURE reaped a windfall when it earned $42 million in rentals and eight Academy Award nominations, winning for its best-selling theme song, "The Morning After," and Special Effects (a Special Achievement Award for Visual Effects went to Fox's L. B. Abbott and A. D. Flowers). The key to the film's popularity was unquestionably its verisimilitude,[141] a lesson quickly learned by other producers. As with science fiction, the burden of proof in the disaster film fell upon special effects.

For Universal's $7-million EARTHQUAKE (Mark Robson, 1974), executive producer Jennings Lang hired three special effects artists—Frank Brendel, Glen Robinson, and Jack McMasters—and the art directors Alex Golitzen and Preston Ames, all of them assisted by matte painter Albert Whitlock, who produced forty elaborate background scenes for the film in only three weeks.[142] As head of Universal's visual effects department, Whitlock had painted the mattes for all of Hitchcock's post-PSYCHO films and helped to recreate 1930s Chicago for THE STING (George Roy Hill, 1973). His work on EARTHQUAKE, in which Los Angeles is destroyed by "the Big One," earned a Special Achievement Award from the Academy, but the film's most prominent effect was achieved through "Sensurround," a low-frequency sound system used to simulate tremors during the eight-minute quake sequence. Essentially an amplification process (for which Universal rented a special package to theaters for $500 a week), "Sensurround" won a Class II Scientific and Technical Award from the Academy, which also gave EARTHQUAKE the Oscar for Best Sound. The system was used in several other Universal films of the decade (MIDWAY [Jack Smight, 1976]; ROLLERCOASTER [James Goldstone, 1977]) before it was abandoned. This audience participation feature of EARTHQUAKE combined with special effects that provided, in *Variety*'s words, "an excellent, unstinting panorama of destruction,"[143] made it the third highest grossing film of 1974 (with $35.9 million in rentals).

The highest-grossing film of the year was Irwin Allen's THE TOWERING INFERNO with rentals of $55.8 million, which made up for its lack of a gimmick with an intelligent script by Stirling Silliphant and real acting by real stars like Steve McQueen, Paul Newman, William Holden, and Faye Dunaway (as opposed to the vapidity of Mark Robson's uncredited screenplay for EARTHQUAKE, and the walk-through performances of its leads: Charlton Heston, Ava Gardner, and George Kennedy). Adapted from two separate novels and coproduced by Fox and Warner Bros. at a cost of $14 million, THE TOWERING INFERNO (John Guillermin, 1974) had special effects by A. D. Flowers and L. B. Abbott and was designed by William Creber. Its story of a fire destroying the world's tallest building on the night of its gala opening because of shoddy construction practices had a strong anticorporate message, but like all disaster films this one existed largely to display spectacular illusions. These were provided by four production units working on fifty-seven sets distributed over eight Fox soundstages, the largest of which were the "Promenade Deck" where the celebration is held, completely surrounded by a 340-foot cycloramic matte painting of the San Francisco skyline, and a full-scale replica of a five-story section of the skyscraper on a former Fox backlot.[144] Sixty stunt artists were employed in the pyrotechnical action sequences (as compared to 141 for EARTHQUAKE), which were directed by Allen himself in close collaboration with cinematographer Joseph Biroc, and by the end of seventy days of principal photography only eight of the sets remained standing. Opening on December 16, 1974, just a month after EARTHQUAKE, THE TOWERING INFERNO was both a critical and commercial hit, receiving eight Academy Award nominations, including best picture, and winning three (Best Cinematography, Best Editing, and Best Song).

That the disaster film as Hollywood genre had clearly arrived, was demonstrated by two other 1974 entries. Universal's AIRPORT 1975 (Jack Smight, 1974) originated as a TV

A rescue gone wrong in THE TOWERING INFERNO (Fox/Warners, 1974), the best of the Watergate-era disaster films thanks to a decent script by Stirling Silliphant, intelligent casting, and state-of-the-art special effects by A. D. Flowers and L. B. Abbott. It was also the disaster film most insistent in blaming its catastrophe on government malfeasance and corporate greed. 35mm Panavision anamorphic.

movie script and was reworked by its author, Don Ingalis, into a screenplay with twenty-two main characters for "all-star" casting. (Only one true star, Charlton Heston, actually found his way into the movie.) The film concerned a 747 crippled by a mid-air collision and flown by a stewardess until a spectacular mid-air pilot transfer is arranged. Executive producer Jennings Lang secured the cooperation of the FAA, the Defense Department, and the Air Force in leasing a real 747 for the flight and transfer sequences, and the film was completed in just forty-four days at a cost of $4 million. Opening in October 1974, AIRPORT 1975 earned $25.2 million in rentals and became the eighth most profitable film of a year in which no fewer than three disaster films ranked among the top ten. United Artists' JUGGERNAUT (Richard Lester, 1974) was filmed aboard *The Britannic*—a microcosm of British society, in which nothing works—and concentrated on suspense above spectacle, and was the less successful commercially for it. This film of a luxury liner wired with seven sophisticated terrorist bombs that are defused by a team of demolitions experts conforms to the disaster formula in all respects but one: there is no disaster. But the awesome potential for one and an omnibus cast headed by Richard Harris, Omar Sharif, and Anthony Hopkins enabled United Artists to market JUGGERNAUT as a disaster film, despite its taut direction and clearly intelligent script. The public, however, wasn't fooled, and JUGGERNAUT became the first film in the cycle to lose money.

From the conclusion of THE HINDENBURG *(Robert Wise, 1975): Burgess Meredith in the foreground. The first major disaster film based on a real event,* THE HINDENBURG *was also the first to lose a significant amount of money, indicating that the cycle had run its course. 35mm Panavision anamorphic, blow up to 70mm for road-showing.*

Universal's THE HINDENBURG (Robert Wise, 1975) was next. This melodramatic and highly speculative re-creation of the giant luxury dirigible's last flight was based on Michael M. Mooney's book of the same title, and it had Oscar-winning special effects by Albert Whitlock and Glen Robinson (they received a noncompetitive Special Achievement Award, as did sound effects expert Peter Berkos). The fiery 1937 crash was meticulously restaged on Universal's Stage 12 and intercut with actual newsreel footage and radio broadcasts of the tragedy that consumed the hydrogen-born aircraft in a spectacular explosion and took thirty-six lives.[145] The replication of this thirty-four-second event, which became an early mass media icon, could not salvage the film's creaky plotting and lackluster performances from what *Variety* called "an array of characters . . . dealt boringly from a well-thumbed deck"[146] including George C. Scott, Anne Bancroft, and Gig Young. Produced for $14 million, THE HINDENBURG returned only $14.5 in rentals and signaled that the public's eagerness to know "Who Will Survive?" (as advertising copy for THE POSEIDON ADVENTURE put it) had passed over into indifference. Another signal was the appearance of a popular genre parody in Paramount's THE BIG BUS (James Frawley, 1976), in which the ill-fated journey of a nuclear-powered Trailways bus, complete with a cocktail lounge, works the all-star (here "no-star") disaster formula for all it is worth. The fact that Irwin Allen began producing made-for-TV disaster films the same year (FLOOD [NBC, 11/24/76]; FIRE! [NBC, 5/8/77]) suggests that the genre had gone from its classic stage to decadence without an intervening period of stabilization. (So too did New World's 1975 domestic release of TIDAL WAVE, a horribly recut, dubbed version of the Japanese science fiction epic THE SUBMERSION OF JAPAN [Toho; Shiro Moriana, 1973], with added American footage.)

JAWS AND THE REVENGE-OF-NATURE CYCLE

In fact, the disaster film remained popular for the rest of the decade and beyond, but it mutated in 1975 (like everything else in American cinema) with the appearance of Universal's JAWS. The formative importance of JAWS to subsequent marketing and distribution practices is discussed elsewhere, as is its crucial role in the emergent blockbuster syndrome, but the film also occupies landmark status in terms of genre because it combined motifs from several of them to create a new kind of disaster film. JAWS, as Thomas Schatz was first to point out, is basically an action-adventure that contains elements of the 1950s monster film, the slasher film, the buddy film, and the chase film.[147] But it is also a disaster film that Spielberg trimmed down and turned into a pure mechanism,[148] a visceral machine of entertainment designed to achieve maximum cinematic punch on every level. As with all disaster films, special effects were crucial: for JAWS they accounted for approximately one-fourth of the final negative cost of $12 million. (Most expensive were the mechanical effects designed by Robert A. Mattey, which included three full-scale, hydraulically operated great white sharks; underwater photography of real sharks was provided by Ron and Valerie Taylor, who had shot the 1971 documentary BLUE WATER, WHITE DEATH [Peter Gimbel].)[149] But Spielberg achieved an integration of effects and narrative that made disaster sequences in earlier films seem canned by comparison and brought a sophistication of form to the genre unrivaled since Hitchcock's work in THE BIRDS. Generically, JAWS is also linked with contemporaneous revenge-of-nature/creature revenge films—Paramount's WILLARD (Daniel Mann, 1971) and BEN (Phil Karlson, 1972), both featuring renegade rats; AIP's FROGS (George McGowan, 1972); MGM's NIGHT OF THE LEPUS (William F. Claxton, 1972), about monster rabbits; Crown

International's STANLEY (William Grefe, 1972) and Universal's SSSSSSS (Bernard Kowalski, 1973—an early project of JAWS producers Richard D. Zanuck and David Brown), which are both about snakes; Cinema Group 75's THE GIANT SPIDER INVASION (Bill Rebane, 1975); and William Castle's Paramount-released BUG (Jeannot Szwarc, 1975), where normality is threatened by giant, incendiary, meat-eating cockroaches. The revenge motif continued in the welter of post-JAWS imitations that appeared in the realm of exploitation product (Selected's MAKO: THE JAWS OF DEATH [William Grefe, 1976]; Mar Vista's DOGS [Bruce Brinckerhoff, 1976]; AIP's FOOD OF THE GODS [Bert I. Gordon, 1976], SQUIRM [Jeff Lieberman, 1976], and EMPIRE OF THE ANTS [Bert I. Gordon, 1977]; New World's THE BEES [Alfredo Zacharias, 1978]), inferior knock-offs (Film Venture's GRIZZLY [William Girdler, 1976] and DAY OF THE ANIMALS [William Girdler, 1977]; Paramount's ORCA [Michael Anderson, 1977]; Embassy's TENTACLES [Oliver Hellman, 1977]; Dimension's KINGDOM OF THE SPIDERS [John "Bud" Cardos, 1977]; Columbia's NIGHTWING [Arthur Hiller, 1979]), outright spoofs (New World's PIRANHA [Joe Dante, 1978] and PIRANHA II: THE SPAWNING [James Cameron, 1981]), and JAWS's own inferior sequels (Universal's JAWS 2 [Jeannot Szwarc, 1978]; JAWS 3-D [Joe Alves, 1983]; and JAWS, THE REVENGE [Joseph Sargent, 1987]). But it was in the streamlined disaster film of the late 1970s, with its aspiration towards a Spielbergian economy of means combined with elaborate special effects, that the generic influence of JAWS was most clearly visible— mainly in action thrillers like Universal's TWO MINUTE WARNING (Larry Peerce, 1976) and ROLLERCOASTER (James Goldstone, 1977), Paramount's BLACK SUNDAY (John Frankenheimer, 1977), and Avco Embassy's THE CASSANDRA CROSSING (George Pan Cosmatos, 1977); but also in conspiracy films (Associated General's CAPRICORN ONE [Peter Hyams, 1978], Columbia's THE CHINA SYNDROME [James Bridges, 1979]), war films (Universal's GRAY LADY DOWN [David Greene, 1978], and even such comedies as Fox's SILVER STREAK (Arthur Hiller, 1976), with its thunderous climactic train wreck.

DISASTER STRIKES OUT

Still, some producers continued to flog the original disaster formula into the realms of near-parody. Irwin Allen, who had virtually invented it in the first place, produced and directed two final entries: Warner Bros.' THE SWARM (1978), in which African killer bees (a staple of late 1970s creature revenge movies) attack a small Texas town, a train, and finally the entire city of Houston; and Fox's BEYOND THE POSEIDON ADVENTURE (1979), in which salvagers attempt to loot the ship that capsized in the original film. Both lost money, but the exhaustion of genre is particularly apparent in THE SWARM, which attempted to revisit the triumph of THE TOWERING INFERNO by employing the same screenwriter (Stirling Silliphant), cinematographer (Fred Koenekamp), and visual effects artist (L. B. Abbott). Even THE SWARM's marketing logo aped that of the earlier film with its image of a glass-and-steel skyscraper engulfed in flames (now bees), but the result was what one critic called "one of the shoddiest major films to ever come from Hollywood."[150] In fact, The SWARM is a virtual textbook example of how the industry corrupts genre by running winning formulas into the ground. Almost every aspect of the film is worthy of the disaster-film parodies that found their way into DRIVE-IN (Rod Amateau, 1976), THE KENTUCKY FRIED MOVIE (John Landis, 1977), and several *Saturday Night Live* skits of the era, but its visual effects are ludicrous, especially in a big train wreck sequence whose sloppy miniature work is clearly just that. (Nevertheless, Allen struck one more time, as producer of Warner Bros.' WHEN TIME RAN OUT . . . [James Goldstone, 1980], the very last gasp of the "all-star" disaster epics, with Paul

Newman, Jacqueline Bisset, William Holden, et al. scrambling to escape a volcanic eruption on a South Sea island.)

Terrible special effects were also a problem for METEOR (Ronald Neame, 1979), whose tangled financing involved exploitation producers on both sides of the Pacific (Sir Run Run Shaw in Hong Kong and Samuel Z. Arkoff in Hollywood) and distribution by Warner Bros. of an American International release. This $20 million production went through three separate teams of effects artists and was released with poor detailing and visible process lines in major disaster sequences, which the public refused to tolerate; it lost $14 million and became one of the decade's biggest losers.[151] It was joined in the same year by another historic flop, Dino De Laurentiis's $22-million remake of THE HURRICANE (Jan Troell, 1979), released by Universal for a loss of $17.5 million. Thus, from producing some the decade's biggest hits early on, the disaster genre quickly came to generate some of its biggest losses, and disaster ended the 1970s scraping bottom (for example, New World's AVALANCHE [Corey Allen, 1978], with special effects that were achieved through photographic superimpositions recalling 1950s-style monster films). In a complete reverse spin, the fourth highest grossing film of 1980 ($40.6 million in rentals) would be Paramount's disaster-movie parody AIRPLANE! (Jim Abrahams, David Zucker, Jerry Zucker), a send-up of 1970's second-highest grosser, AIRPORT ($45.2 million in rentals)—indicating both a seismic shift in popular taste and a new standard in planned obsolescence for the Hollywood product.

Conclusion

The ten years it took AIRPORT to travel from paradigm to parody were those in which the mainstream American film industry embraced exploitation. In marketing and distribution, as well as in production content, the majors adopted practices from the industry's margins that were designed to maximize profit quickly, regardless of a film's quality or merit. But rapidly escalating costs dictated that a film also needed "legs," in *Variety*'s terms, that is, staying power at the box office once the initial strike was made. Various opinions over time equated good legs with the presence of bankable stars, best-selling properties, popular genres, and so on, but by the end of the 1970s special effects were clearly foregrounded in the formula for success. The initial popularity of disaster films underscores the importance that special effects had begun to assume in the blockbuster calculus of the mid-1970s. In fact, in retrospect it is clear that all three of the decade's most popular genres depended on them—most obviously the science fiction and disaster film, but also the horror film, whose appeal depended increasingly on the realistic depiction of such pathological phenomenon as mutilation, violent death, and corporeal putrescence. The disaster film's rapid fall from favor suggests the importance of novelty in the realm of such effects, which is why the genre has enjoyed a considerable comeback with the refinement of computer-generated imagery in the 1990s. Finally, the rapid rise and fall of the 1970s disaster film demonstrates the toll that exploitation can take on generic form. Repetition with variation is the stuff that genres are made of, but when producers like Irwin Allen adopt a cookie-cutter approach to same material again and again, they soon invite parody—as did both the slasher film (for example, Paramount's STUDENT BODIES [Mickey Rose, 1981]) and the STAR WARS-style space opera (for example, Universal's BUCK ROGERS IN THE 25TH CENTURY [Daniel Haller, 1979]) by the decade's end.

Poster for Melvin Van Peebles's independently distributed Sweet Sweetback's Baad Assss Song (1971) suggests its racially provocative nature, extending to the statement "RATED X BY AN ALL-WHITE JURY" (lower right-hand corner), which in fact was true because the CARA ratings board had no black members at the time. 35mm 1.33:1.

6

Genres II:
Exploitation and Allusion

*[During the 1970s] a theatrical film became "that which cannot be
seen on television." In this sense, the introduction of the rating systems
in 1968 was an economic necessity.*

STUART BYRON, FILM CRITIC/JOURNALIST, 1980

Hollywood's mainstreaming of exploitation tactics during the 1970s did little to erode the healthy fringe market for authentic exploitation product that presented itself after the establishment of the Code and Rating Administration (CARA) in October 1968. Throughout 1969, there were bold attempts to test the limits of the new ratings system with regard to sex and violence, and the early 1970s witnessed the rapid deployment of three exploitation genres that trafficked in both. They were, in ascending order of market strength, the black action film, the martial arts film, and—far and away the most powerful—the feature-length hardcore porno film, a genre that would challenge the market share of the mainstream theatrical film industry by 1973 and drive the home video revolution later in the decade. Home video (and television) would itself create a popular familiarity with genre, leading to a late 1970s boom in genre parody, genre blending, and other forms of generic reflexivity.

Black Action, or Blaxploitation

The black action or (somewhat pejoratively) "blaxploition" film had its origins in the Civil Rights movement of the 1960s and the numerous mainstream films of the era that featured black actors like Sidney Poitier (GUESS WHO'S COMING TO DINNER? [Stanley Kramer, 1967], IN THE HEAT OF THE NIGHT [Norman Jewison, 1967]) and Jim Brown (THE DIRTY DOZEN [Robert Aldrich, 1968], 100 RIFLES [Tom Gries, 1968]), on an equal footing with white performers. In the pivotal years of 1968–1969, several so-called "new-style black films" appeared that coincided with the anti-establishment spirit of the more radical youth-cult movies.[1] UP TIGHT (Jules Dassin, 1968) was a version of John Ford's THE INFORMER (1935), with black separatists standing in for Irish revolutionaries, and THE LOST MAN (Robert Alan Arthur, 1969) was a remake of Carol Reed's ODD MAN OUT (1947) that used the same equation. Gordon Parks, Sr.'s THE LEARNING TREE (1969) was an adaptation of his own autobiographical novel about growing up black in rural Kansas in the 1920s, while Robert Downey's PUTNEY SWOPE was a satire in which a token black takes control of a large advertising agency, with discomfiting results for the white power structure. Not only did these movies feature predominately black casts but many were made by black filmmakers; and all revealed a proud new attitude toward blackness and the role of blacks in white society.

The 1970s began with several mainstream films by white directors that examined race relations in various contexts (THE LIBERATION OF L. B. JONES [William Wyler, 1970]; THE GREAT WHITE HOPE [Martin Ritt, 1970]; THE LANDLORD [Hal Ashby, 1970]) and with United Artists' COTTON COMES TO HARLEM (Ossie Davis, 1970), the first all-black film to become a crossover box-office hit. Based on a novel by black crime writer Chester Himes and directed by the black actor-turned-director Ossie Davis, this comedy-drama confirmed the existence of a significant multiracial audience for black films by returning a then-substantial $5.1 million in rentals, and generating the Warner Bros. sequel COME BACK, CHARLESTON BLUE (Mark Warren, 1972) two years later. Noting the outstanding performance of such films among inner city blacks, *Variety* had predicted as early as June 1970 that "if the present trend continues, [black-oriented films] will become one of the most highly sought-after commodities for first-run houses."[2] The first true black action film, however, was of a very different order than the Hollywood productions *Variety* had in view. This was unquestionably Cinemation's SWEET SWEETBACK'S BAAD ASSSSS SONG (1971), written and directed by Melvin Van Peebles, whose French-produced interracial romance THE STORY OF A THREE DAY PASS (1967) had become a cult classic several years before. On the strength of this success, Van Peebles signed with Columbia to direct WATERMELON MAN (1970), in which comedian Godfrey Cambridge played a white racial bigot who is transformed overnight into a black man, but the film was a flop. SWEET SWEETBACK was then independently produced for under $500,000 and shot in nineteen days with a non-union black crew.[3] Minimalist and episodic, it concerns a young ghetto pimp (played by Van Peebles himself) on the run from the law, and it contains near pornographic sex scenes, as well as unprecedented images of a black hero speaking street language and beating up corrupt white cops. At its conclusion, as Sweetback slips across the border into Mexico, a title card tells the audience: "Watch out! A baad asssss nigger is coming back to collect some dues." Manifestly threatening to whites (Vincent Canby called it a "psychotic . . . political exploitation film" in the *New York Times*),[4] and X-rated by CARA, which made it difficult to book, SWEET SWEETBACK nevertheless returned $4.1 million in rentals, and opened the floodgates of blaxploitation at the studios.

BLACK ACTION FINDS ITS MARKET: *SHAFT* AND *SUPERFLY*

Already in preparation at MGM was SHAFT (Gordon Parks, Sr., 1971), a film about a tough black private eye (Richard Roundtree) based on a novel by the white writer Ernest Tidyman and produced for just under $1.2 million. Directed by Gordon Parks, Sr., with a hard-driving score by Isaac Hayes, the film generated $7.1 million in rentals (against a $1.54-million negative cost), with blacks accounting for 80 percent of its audience, and is credited with sustaining MGM through the lean year of 1971. As an index of the film's popularity, *Newsweek* reported that the DeMille Theater in Times Square

Richard Roundtree in Gordon Parks, Sr.'s SHAFT *(MGM, 1971), the first studio-produced blaxploitation film and one of the most popular. Roundtree plays a tough private eye hired to retrieve the daughter of a Harlem crime boss kidnapped by the Mafia. As the ads read: "The mob wanted Harlem back. They got Shafted up to here." 35mm 1.75:1.*

sold out on a twenty-four-hour marathon showing of SHAFT in August,[5] and it eventually became the 20th highest earning film of 1971, placing just behind Columbia's lavish historical epic NICHOLAS AND ALEXANDRA (Franklin Schaffner, 1971). (Hayes's soundtrack album experienced an even more pronounced success: number one on the charts for two weeks after the film's release on July 1, 1971, it remained a best-seller for another sixty weeks, ultimately selling over one million copies.)[6] The industry suddenly woke up to the fact that, thanks to "white flight" from the cities during the 1960s, blacks accounted for approximately 30 percent of the first-run urban market,[7] and as a result, the number of black-oriented films tripled between 1969 and 1971, rising from six to eighteen. SHAFT itself spawned two sequels, SHAFT'S BIG SCORE! (Gordon Parks, Sr., 1972) and SHAFT IN AFRICA (John Guillermin, 1973), whose success was subject to the law of diminishing returns (rentals were $3.7 and $2.7 million, respectively), as well as the short-lived CBS-TV series *Shaft* (eight ninety-minute episodes, October 1973 to August 1974), which also starred Roundtree.

The next blaxploitation landmark was SUPERFLY (Gordon Parks, Jr., 1972), independently produced by Sig Shore and picked up for distribution by Warner Bros., which had recently abandoned plans to produce a black-oriented action comedy of its own called "Superspade."[8] Scored by Curtis Mayfield, who realized two top-ten singles from it ("Freddie's Dead" and "Superfly," which sold one million copies each), and directed by Gordon Parks, Jr., this film about a Harlem drug dealer (Ron O'Neal) attempting to go

SUPERFLY (Gordon Parks, Jr., 1972), independently produced by Sig Shore and distributed by Warners, confirmed the national market for blaxploitation: Ron O'Neal (center frame) plays a drug dealer out for one last score before he goes straight. No less popular than SHAFT, SUPERFLY was attacked by black leaders for glorifiying drug pushers and promoting racial stereotypes. 35mm 1.85:1.

straight was critically assailed for its stereotypical depiction of black sexuality and putative glorification of drugs, but it proved as popular as SHAFT and made nearly as much money in rentals ($6.4 million). Its sound-track album was even more popular, selling over two million copies after forty-six weeks on the charts (five of them at the number one position), and several critics seriously proposed SUPERFLY for an Oscar.[9] (Some black leaders publicly deplored the Shaft-Superfly image as a new form of racial stereotype, which it clearly was, but black audiences apparently saw in these new action heroes a form of symbolic empowerment.)[10] A sequel, SUPERFLY T.N.T. (Warner Bros., 1973), directed the following year by Ron O'Neal, was a failure (as was THE RETURN OF SUPERFLY [1990], directed by Sig Shore), but the popularity of SWEET SWEETBACK, SHAFT, and SUPERFLY together led to literally hundreds of low-budget imitations over the next four years. These typically featured black action heroes (often ex-athletes like Fred Williamson, Jim Brown, Rafer Johnson, O. J. Simpson, Bernie Casey, and Jim Kelly)—and, occasionally, heroines—who portrayed black detectives, gangsters, prostitutes, and drug kingpins; they played mainly to black audiences in neighborhood theaters but occasionally enjoyed some white crossover to become mainstream hits.[11] In October 1972, *Variety* attributed a major resurgence in the domestic box office in part to the new black audience for these films.[12] *Newsweek* went further, crediting the boom in black action films with helping to pull Hollywood out of the 1969–1971 recession, and in a cover story on October 23, 1972, described the industry's pell-mell rush toward blaxploitation: "Talented black actors, directors, and writers were suddenly plucked out of studio back rooms, modeling agencies, and ghetto theaters, and turned loose on new black projects."[13] In its year-end roundup for 1972, *Variety* took note of this market explosion by listing fifty-one black-oriented features released or in production since 1970; in its 1973 roundup, the list was updated to include more than 100 additional titles,[14] and in 1974, another twenty-five.[15]

Blaxploitation Boom And Bust

Like the race movies of the 1930s and 1940s before them, many of the black action films of the early seventies were written, directed, and produced by whites. This led some blacks inside the industry (e.g., the Black Artists Alliance of Hollywood and the Coalition Against Blaxploitation) to charge others with being "black brokers" for white showmanship.[16] A more serious charge came from Junius Griffin, head of the Hollywood branch of the NAACP, who decried the exposure of black children "to a steady diet of so-called black movies that glorify black males as pimps, dope pushers, gangsters, and super males."[17] He was, for the most part, right on the money. In 1972–1973, for example, the most popular black action films included United Artists' HAMMER (Bruce Clark, 1972), with Fred Williamson as a professional boxer fighting the mob, and THE SPOOK WHO SAT BY THE DOOR (Ivan Dixon, 1973), with Lawrence Cook as a disillusioned black CIA agent; Paramount's THE LEGEND OF NIGGER CHARLIE (Martin Goldman, 1972), with Fred Williamson as a black gunfighter in the Old West, and HIT! (Sidney J. Furie, 1973), with Billy Dee Williams as a federal agent seeking revenge against the black dope pushers who killed his daughter; MGM's HIT MAN (George Armitage, 1972), with Bernie Casey as the small-time hood of title, COOL BREEZE (Barry Pollack, 1972), with Thalmus Rasulala and Judy Pace in a black remake of THE ASPHALT JUNGLE (John Huston, 1950), and SWEET JESUS, PREACHER MAN (Henning Schellerup, 1973), in which Roger E. Mosley plays a hit man posing as a black Baptist cleric; Fox's TROUBLE MAN (Ivan Dixon, 1972), with Robert Hooks as a black Robin Hood figure; Columbia's BLACK GUNN (Robert Hartford-Davis, 1972), with Jim Brown as a rough-and-tumble black nightclub owner; Cinerama Releasing's THE MACK (Michael Campus, 1973), with Max Julien as an ambitious super-pimp; Universal's WILLIE DYNAMITE (Gilbert Moses III, 1974), with Roscoe Orman as the Mack's rival super-pimp; AIP's SLAUGHTER (Jack Starrett, 1972) and SLAUGHTER'S BIG RIP OFF (Gordon Douglas, 1973), starring Jim Brown as an ex-Green Beret out to avenge his murdered father in productions that, as one critic noted, had "the look, feel and pyrotechnics of an economy-class James Bond";[18] BLACULA (William Crain, 1972) and SCREAM, BLACULA, SCREAM! (Bob Kelljan, 1973), with William Marshall as a black king vampire, BLACK CAESAR (Larry Cohen, 1973), with Fred Williamson as the crime lord of the title, and COFFY (Jack Hill, 1973), featuring the statuesque Pam Grier as a nurse who fights against a black drug ring. In 1974–1975 there was little respite in black action production and its "super-spade" theme as Warner Bros. produced CLEOPATRA JONES (Jack Starrett, 1973) and CLEOPATRA JONES AND THE CASINO OF GOLD (Chuck Bail, 1975), with Tamara Dobson as a black CIA super-agent, BLACK EYE (Jack Arnold, 1974), with Fred Williamson as a tough black PI, BLACK BELT JONES (Robert Clouse, 1974), with Jim Kelly as a black Bruce Lee, and BLACK SAMSON (Charles Bail, 1974), with Rockne Tarkington crusading to save his neighborhood from a gang of brutal white thugs; others include AIP's ABBY (William Girdler, 1974), with

William Marshall and Carol Speed in a black version of THE EXORCIST (close enough to the original that Warner Bros. successfully sued AIP to block the film's release, but only after it had grossed $2.6 million),[19] TRUCK TURNER (Jonathan Kaplan, 1974), with Isaac Hayes as a modern bounty hunter, BUCKTOWN (Arthur Marks, 1975), with Fred Williamson and Pam Grier cleaning up a corrupt cesspool of a southern city, and two Pam Grier vehicles conceived as follow-ups to COFFY, FOXY BROWN (Jack Hill, 1974) and FRIDAY FOSTER (Arthur Marks, 1975); New World's T.N.T. JACKSON (Cirio Santiago, 1975) with Jeanne Bell as "a one mamma massacre squad" (per ads);[20] Cinemation's THE BLACK GODFATHER (John Evans, 1974), with Rod Perry as the gangster of the title; and Dimension's BOSS NIGGER (Jack Arnold, 1975), with Fred Williamson as a black bounty hunter in the 1870s.

As these capsule descriptions suggest, by 1974 the black action film was given over almost wholly to exploitation, and in that year the first blaxploitation parody appeared in

Poster for AIP's FOXY BROWN (Jack Hill, 1974), one of several blaxploitation films starring Pam Grier as a nurse who enacts a vendetta against drug dealers. 35mm 1.85:1.

the form of Warner Bros./First Artists' UPTOWN SATURDAY NIGHT (Sidney Poitier), whose popularity generated two Poitier-directed sequels (LET'S DO IT AGAIN [1975]; A PIECE OF THE ACTION [1977]). Research showed that black audiences had become more interested in "event" movies than in ethnicity and were travelling into white neighborhoods to see films like THE GODFATHER and THE EXORCIST, for which they comprised as much as 35 percent of the market.[21] More mainstream black-oriented films continued to appear from the studios (Fox's Depression-era saga SOUNDER [Martin Ritt, 1972]; Paramount's biopic about Billie Holiday LADY SINGS THE BLUES [Sidney J. Furie, 1972]; Michael Schultz's satiric comedies COOLEY HIGH [AIP, 1975] and CAR WASH [Universal, 1976]), but by mid-decade, the black action film had come to be dominated by producers like Dimension and AIP, of whose work *Variety* wrote in a review of BUCKTOWN: "AIP's blaxploitation mill grinds out films that are merely flimsy excuses for prolonged violent confrontations between protagonists, usually black and white."[22] It had largely disappeared as a viable genre by the end of 1975, when JAWS took exploitation into the mainstream; and the following year, audiences of all races could watch a black man and a white man beat each other to a bloody pulp without the taint of grindhouse vulgarity in United Artists' ROCKY (John G. Avildsen), the top-grossing picture of 1976 and also the "Best" by vote of the American Academy of Motion Picture Arts and Sciences.

HISTORICAL SIGNIFICANCE OF BLAXPLOITION

Even though most 1970s black action films were created by whites and concentrated on negative themes of crime and drugs in the inner city, it's possible to see in them the stirrings of the independent black film movement of the late 1980s and early 1990s represented by directors like Spike Lee (SHE'S GOTTA HAVE IT [Island 1986], DO THE RIGHT THING [Universal, 1989], JUNGLE FEVER [Universal, 1991]), John Singleton (BOYZ N THE HOOD [Columbia, 1991]), the Hudlin brothers (HOUSE PARTY [New Line Cinema, 1990]), Ernest Dickerson (JUICE [Paramount, 1992]), the Hughes brothers (MENACE II SOCIETY [New Line, 1993], DEAD PRESIDENTS [Hollywood Pictures, 1995]), Bill Duke (A RAGE IN HARLEM [Miramax Films, 1991]), and Mario Van Peebles (NEW JACK CITY [Warner Bros., 1991]). The work of these filmmakers, dubbed "New Jack" or "home-boy" cinema (the former after a type of pop music heavily influenced by black street culture, the latter after street slang for a gang member),[23] has certain historical ties with blaxploitation—for example, A RAGE IN HARLEM adapts one of Chester Himes's sequels to COTTON COMES TO HARLEM, and Mario Van Peebles is Melvin Van Peeble's son, who as a teenager had played young Sweetback in SWEET SWEETBACK'S BAADASSSS SONG. But it also resembles blaxploitation in its focus on young black males confronting the tough urban realities of drugs, street crime, and violent death, within a broader cultural context of institutionalized misogyny and racism.

Like their predecessors, New Jack films tended to be shot on low budgets and infused with a sensibility derived from popular music (rhythm-and-blues and jazz in the case of blaxploitation, hip-hop and gangsta rap for New Jack), and when they became crossover hits the films made great profits for the studios that financed them (like BOYZ N THE HOOD, which became the most profitable film of 1991 when it returned a $56 million gross against costs of $6 million).[24] There was, indeed, a brief boom in features by black directors as domestic ticket sales for them rose from 15 to 42 million between 1990 and 1992.[25] But after two decades of "benign neglect," the black underclass of the 1990s generated few screen personae in the Shaft-Slaughter-Superfly mold; the heroic fantasy of 1970s black action cinema was replaced in New Jack by a grim realism about the prospects for daily survival in the ghetto that made the social attitudes of blaxploitation seem positively naive (and subject to parody in films like Keenan Ivory Wayans's 1988 spoof I'M GONNA GIT YOU SUCKA).

Yet blaxploitation itself survived in the self-produced caper films of Fred Williamson, who, as head of Po Boy Productions, has written, directed, and/or starred in more than fifty low-budget action movies since his original appearance as HAMMER in 1972.[26] With titles like MEAN JOHNNY BARROWS (1976), MR. MEAN (1977), ONE DOWN TWO TO GO (1983), THE LAST FIGHT (1983), THE BIG SCORE (1983), FOXTRAP (1986), THE KILL REFLEX (1991), and THREE DAYS TO KILL (1992), Williamson's product is unabashed exploitation, quickly shot on location, often with international co-financing and profit taken mainly from distribution to European and Southeast Asian action markets.[27] Another recurrence of blaxploitation was Larry Cohen's violent homage ORIGINAL GANGSTAS (1996), in which the white director of AIP's BLACK CAESAR (1973) teamed with genre stars Fred Williamson, Jim Brown, Pam Grier, Ron O'Neal, Richard Roundtree, and others in a 1970s-style black action film with New Jack accoutrements. Quentin Tarantino's JACKIE BROWN (1997) starred Pam Grier, in another late homage to the genre.

Martial Arts, or Kung Fu

Another ethnic action genre that permeated early 1970s cinema was the Chinese martial arts film. Strongly influenced by the expressive gymnastic style of Peking Opera (in which many of its performers, fight directors, and fight choreographers were classically trained), Hong Kong "kung fu" (literally, "technique" or "skill") cinema was produced by two major studios—Run Run Shaw's Shaw Brothers and Raymond Chow's Golden Harvest—which divided the regional market between them.[28] Already enormously popular in Southeast Asia, where it was known as "Gung-fu Pian,"[29] it swept into the American market in the wake of Shaw Brothers' FIVE FINGERS OF DEATH (original title: KING BOXER [Cheng Chang Ho, 1973]), which returned an unexpected $4.6 million in rentals to its domestic distributor, Warner Bros., and paved the way for Warners to handle Golden Harvest's THE BIG BOSS (Lo Wei, 1971) and THE CHINESE CONNECTION (Lo Wei, 1972) the following year.[30] These latter films (both, confusingly, also known as FIST[S] OF FURY) afforded the genre with its first superstar in Bruce Lee (1940–1973), whose presence in just two more films before his sudden death of a brain aneurysm—Golden Harvest's WAY OF THE DRAGON (released in the United States as RETURN OF THE DRAGON [Bruce Lee, 1973]), and the Warner-produced ENTER THE DRAGON (Robert Clouse, 1973)— served to stabilize the martial arts genre in the American market and made Lee himself a cult figure.[31] By the end of 1973, *Variety* touted "kung-fu" as a "Fixture on [the] Global Screen,"[32] and with poverty-row budgets of around $200,000 apiece Hong Kong martial arts films promised an attractive rate of return as domestic exploitation product.[33] By early 1974, every major distributor but Fox and United Artists had picked up one or more "chop-socky" films, as *Variety* called them, and hastily dubbed them into English, sometimes with the Chinese credits still intact.[34]

The audience originally intended for exploitation by kung fu was Asian American, but it soon became clear that martial arts films appealed to all nonwhite moviegoers, including Hispanics and especially blacks, perhaps because the central theme of many was the defense of one's own ethnic group against another (for example, Chinese vs. Japanese).[35] There was also the appeal of novelty and exoticism, as the martial arts had appeared only rarely in American films to date and then only as a plot device (usually in the form of *judo* [*jujitsu*] or *karate*, Japanese and Okinawan techniques, respectively, picked up by American servicemen during the postwar occupation of Japan). In a 1973 interview with the *New York Times*, producer Run Run Shaw went so far as to attribute the success of Asian action films in the United States to President Nixon's historic visit to China in February 1972.[36] But the primary appeal of kung fu films was their skillfully shot and edited fight sequences, which were performed and choreographed by real Chinese martial arts masters according to centuries-old disciplines of self-defense, some of them extending back to the Ming dynasty. Just as Hollywood dance musicals had used separate directors of choreography for production numbers, kung fu movies usually employed separate martial arts directors for fights; and these second unit directors were often themselves assisted by specially trained "fight choreographers."[37] In these lengthy and elaborate displays of acrobatic prowess, certain fight techniques became associated with particular stars, nationalities, or character types—*hapkido* (turning an attacker's energy against himself) with Angela Mao (LADY KUNG FU [Huang Feng, 1971], HAPKIDO [aka DEEP THRUST (Huang Feng, 1972)]), who was promoted by Golden Harvest as a female Bruce Lee, and Tom Laughlin in BILLY JACK [1971]; *jeet kune do* ("fist-intercepting way") and *wing chun kung fu* ("lighting fast" close range fighting) with Bruce Lee; Shaolin boxing with David Carradine (in the television series *Kung Fu* [see below]); *judo* (from *jujitsu*—a backup technique used by samurai against taller opponents) with the Japanese, usually the villains in Hong Kong martial arts films; *tae kwon do* ("hand and foot fighting") with the Korean police and militia; and *karate* ("empty hand" boxing) with villains of every sort.[38] There also occasionally appeared the figure of a *ninja* (literally, "stealer in"), a member of the Japanese cult of shadow warriors, or secret assassins, that had first appeared to American audiences in the James Bond film YOU ONLY LIVE TWICE (Lewis Gilbert, 1967). (Japan's own martial arts films tended to be more violent than their Chinese counterparts—THE STREET FIGHTER [Shigehiro Ozawa, 1974], which introduced Sonny Chiba, was the first film to receive an X rating from CARA for violence, containing such brutal incidents as a kung-fu castration by hand.)[39] These refinements notwithstanding, kung fu fighting became a popular form of screen entertainment among ethnic audiences, and it was occasionally combined with other exploitation genres—such as horror (Hammer Films-Shaw Brothers' coproduction THE LEGEND OF THE SEVEN GOLDEN VAMPIRES [aka THE SEVEN BROTHERS MEET DRACULA (Roy Ward Baker, 1974)]), blaxploitation (Warner Bros.' BLACK BELT JONES [Robert Clouse, 1974]), and action-adventure (Golden Harvest's SLAUGHTER IN SAN FRANCISCO [William Lowe, 1973; re-released as KARATE COP, 1981]; AIP's GOLDEN NEEDLES [Robert Clouse, 1974]).

When Warner Bros. coproduced ENTER THE DRAGON (1973) with Bruce Lee's Concord Productions, it was part of an effort to attract a white crossover audience to kung fu. Evidence of the genre's mass appeal was provided by the success of ABC-TV's series *Kung Fu*, which debuted in October 1972, and starred David Carradine as a Shaolin-trained master wandering the American West in the late nineteenth century. Most of the show's fight sequences were faked, but its highly stylized use of slow motion and integration of Taoist philosophy with action made it popular through June 1975, when the market for the martial arts had peaked (although not before ENTER THE

Asian Americans were the original target audience for martial arts movies, as these bilingual posters for THE BIG BOSS *(Lo Wei, 1971) and* ENTER THE DRAGON *(Robert Clouse, 1973) both show. It soon became apparent that kung fu was popular with the same market segment as blaxploitation.*

DRAGON had been parodied in THE KENTUCKY FRIED MOVIE [John Landis, 1977] and Carl Douglas's "Kung Fu Fighting" had become one of 1974's Top 40 hits).[40]

ENTER THE DRAGON fused a James Bond-style espionage plot with a martial arts competition on an island off Hong Kong and hit its crossover target to generate $11.5 million in rentals, the most money earned by a single kung fu movie during the 1970s. Bruce Lee's unexpected death of a cerebral hemorrhage shortly after the film opened in July 1973 made him a martyr to the cause of martial arts (because the hemorrhage was presumed to be related to his tireless efforts to perfect *jeet kune do,* although an allergic

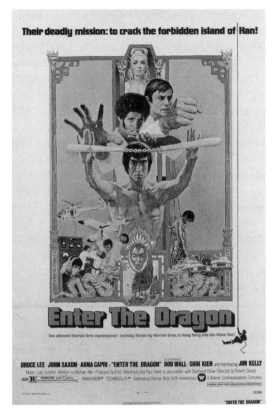

The Warner-produced ENTER THE DRAGON, however, was part of a conscious effort to attract white crossover audiences, as this more mainstream poster for the film suggests: pictured prominently at its center, from bottom to top, are an Asian American male (Bruce Lee), a black male (Jim Kelly), a white male (John Saxon), and a female of indeterminate ethnicity (Ann Capri).

Bruce Lee in ENTER THE DRAGON, his last completed film. Lee's unexpected death of a cerebral hemorrhage in June 1973 made him a figure of legend and endless imitation by less charismatic lookalikes. Uncredited anamorphic (2.35:1).

reaction to a painkiller seems a more likely cause) and the object of a lasting cult. In the Hong Kong industry, this quickly manifested itself in the appearance of two pretenders to the throne—"Bruce Li" (Ho Tsung Tao) and "Bruce Le" (Huang Kin Lung), who between them appeared as "Bruce Lee" in a succession of redundant kung fu adventures with titles like BRUCE LEE, SUPER-DRAGON (1974), GOODBYE BRUCE LEE—HIS LAST GAME OF DEATH (1975), EXIT THE DRAGON, ENTER THE TIGER (1976), FISTS OF FURY II (1976), BRUCE LEE, THE INVINCIBLE (1977), and BRUCE LEE'S SECRET (1977).[41] (Other Lee lookalikes who surfaced in Hong Kong over time were Tang Lung, who played Lee in GAME OF DEATH [Robert Clouse, 1978] and its sequel, Bruce Liang [HAND OF DEATH, 1975], Dragon Lee [THE CLONES OF BRUCE LEE, 1980], and Bruce Leung [BRUCE VS. THE IRON FINGER, 1977].)[42] In addition to these more or less "pure" clones, who made over ninety "Bruce Lee" films collectively between 1974 and 1984, there were exploitation films (of exploitation films!) like BRUCE LEE: HIS LAST DAYS, HIS LAST NIGHTS (1975), basically a porno film in which Lee's actual lover Betty Ting Pei stars in a series of sex scenes with Lee stand-in Li Hsiu Hsien.[43] Many similar movies originated from Hong Kong between 1974 and 1977,[44] and in 1978 Golden Harvest produced GAME OF DEATH, often cited as Bruce's fifth film, integrating ten minutes of footage shot by Raymond Chow in Hong Kong before Lee's death with new footage shot by ENTER THE DRAGON director Robert Clouse. By this time, however, Hong Kong itself had turned mainly to the "comedic" style of kung fu associated with Jackie Chan and Sammo Hung (e.g., DRUNKEN MASTER [Yuen Woo Ping, 1978], KNOCKABOUTS [1979]), and the kung fu craze in the American market was over; distributed by Columbia, GAME OF DEATH earned just under $5 million in rentals—pocket change in the year that CLOSE ENCOUNTERS earned nearly $83 million—although Golden Harvest did produce a sequel, GAME OF DEATH II, in 1981.

Nonetheless, a new martial arts star—homegrown, politically reactionary, and very white—was rising in the person of Chuck Norris (b. 1942), who had been world middleweight karate champion from 1968–1974 and appeared as the villain in Bruce Lee's WAY OF THE DRAGON. By the end of the decade, Norris's films of vigilante justice—GOOD GUYS WEAR BLACK (Ted Post, 1979) and FORCE OF ONE (Paul Aaron, 1979)—were grossing in excess of $15 million each, and he became a world-class martial arts star in the early 1980s (THE OCTAGON [Eric Karson, 1980], AN EYE FOR AN EYE [Steve Carver, 1991], FORCED VENGEANCE [James Fargo, 1982], LONE WOLF McQUADE [Steve Carver, 1983]), as well as a leading exponent of the revanchist party line on Vietnam (three MISSING IN ACTION films, 1984–1988) and the Cold War (INVASION U.S.A. [Joseph Zito, 1985]; THE DELTA FORCE [Menahem Golan, 1986]). The infusion of martial arts with American politics removed kung fu from the domain of pure choreographic violence that had it made it popular in the first place, but even in Hong Kong it was now blended with other genres, including crime (POLICE STORY [Jackie Chan, 1985]) and horror (THE GHOST SNATCHERS [1986]). Like the black action film, however, 1970s kung fu movies laid a generic foundation for subsequent cycles, whose American permutations would include Columbia's THE KARATE KID series (four films, 1984–1994), Cannon's NINJA (ENTER THE NINJA and two sequels, 1981–1984) and AMERICAN NINJA series (four films, 1986–1991), New World's NO RETREAT, NO SURRENDER (three films, 1985–1990), Concorde's BLOODFIST series (seven films, 1989–1997), and Warner Bros.' KICKBOXER series (three films, 1989–1992), some of which borrow plot elements from their Hong Kong predecessors. Finally, many regional stars of 1970s kung fu cinema went on to become major figures as actor-directors in the vital Hong Kong industry of the

1980s and 1990s, most notably Sammo Hung (SPOOKY ENCOUNTERS [1981], EASTERN CONDORS [1987], PEDICAB DRIVER [1990]) and Jackie Chan (PROJECT A [1983], WHEELS ON MEALS [1984], ARMOUR OF GOD 2: OPERATION CONDOR [1991], etc.), the latter virtually eclipsing Bruce Lee as an international martial arts-action superstar.

Feature-Length Hardcore Pornography, or "Adult" Films

The feature-length hardcore porno film was able to become a distinct above-ground genre in the early 1970s because of the new CARA ratings system. In 1968, Jack Valenti had argued against inclusion of the X rating in that system, because he did not want to put the MPPA imprimatur on films specifically produced for the "Adults Only" market. Seeking to protect its members from local prosecution, however, the National Association of Theater Owners (NATO) persuaded him that the MPPA needed to extend some legitimacy to such material since there was a steady (if then specialized) demand for it. In a compromise, Valenti agreed to recognize the X rating but not to copyright it, which meant that it could be self-imposed by producers without submitting their films to the CARA review board. This created the worst of all possible worlds—pornographers could self-administer the X rating (or, for sensationalizing purposes, XX or even XXX) and create the impression of MPPA approval—the very situation Valenti had sought to avoid—while adult films from legitimate producers (such "quality Xs" as United Artists' MIDNIGHT COWBOY [1969] and Warner Bros.' A CLOCKWORK ORANGE [1971]) suffered the stigma of pornography. The fact that a flood of X-rated pornography followed the institution of the CARA system caused many newspapers to refuse to review or accept advertising for all X-rated films. By 1972, over thirty urban dailies had established such a policy, and 47 percent of exhibitors were refusing to show X-rated films, which could mean a crippling loss of box-office revenue for a major feature.[45] As a result, about a third of the features submitted to CARA, 1969–1970, were cut by their directors to avoid an X (for example, Arthur Penn's ALICE'S RESTAURANT [1969], Sam Peckinpah's THE WILD BUNCH [1969] and STRAW DOGS [1971], Ralph Nelson's SOLDIER BLUE [1970]),[46] and in 1970 the MPPA raised the age restrictions on the R and X rating from sixteen to seventeen, which helped to ease some of the pressure on mainstream producers, who nevertheless continued to avoid the X until it was finally replaced by the copyrighted NC-17 rating in 1990. In the early 1970s, however, pornographers played upon the ratings system's inability to distinguish between exploitation product and serious adult entertainment to create the new genre of the hardcore feature and the phenomenon of "porno chic." (The distinction between softcore and hardcore pornography in photographic media [or any other] is somewhat invidious, but in general the former refers to "erotic" pornography, in which sex acts—real or simulated—are represented without a prurient concentration on the genitals, while the latter would feature detailed representations of genital/anal penetration, cunnilingus, fellatio, and orgasm, particularly of the externally ejaculating penis.)[47]

THE "SCANDINAVIAN INVASION": SWEDEN SHOWS THE WAY

Unlike the majors, producers of low-budget sex films were not much affected by bans on X-rated advertising and exhibition because their appeal was, initially at least, to a smaller,

Dustin Hoffman and Jon Voight as "Ratso" Rizzo and Joe Buck in John Schlesinger's
MIDNIGHT COWBOY *(UA, 1969): United Artists went with a self-administered X rating
for the film rather than have one imposed by CARA. Although it won the 1969
Academy Award for Best Picture and was given an R rating by CARA in 1971,*
MIDNIGHT COWBOY *suffered the stigma of pornography and could not be advertised in
many urban daily newspapers (including the* New York Times*). 35mm 1.85:1.*

more specialized market segment (aka "the raincoat brigade," then as now the economic underpinning of the porn industry) in exploitation venues ("grindhouses").[48] The notoriety accorded the X rating in the press, however, gave them an unprecedented cachet, especially since much of the first wave of X-rated pornography was imported. Beginning with Vilgot Sjoman's pre-CARA I AM CURIOUS (YELLOW) in 1967 (and probably traceable in some ways back to Bergman via THE VIRGIN SPRING [1960] and THE SILENCE [1963]), there was a climate of popular opinion that associated Sweden and Scandinavia with sexual liberation and licentiousness. Sjoman's film, in fact, had been confiscated by U.S. Customs authorities upon entry into New York in 1967 owing to its graphic (but simulated) rendition of various sex acts, and it became the object of a ground-breaking legal decision in 1969 when the Supreme Court ruled in a split decision that the film's depiction of sexual intercourse was not obscene (*Grove Press v. Maryland State Board of Censors*).[49] Finally distributed that year, I AM CURIOUS (YELLOW) spearheaded the "Scandinavian invasion" of 1969 and 1970, which included such films as its sequel I AM CURIOUS (BLUE)(1968); LOVE, SWEDISH STYLE (1972); SEXUAL CUSTOMS IN SCANDINAVIA (1972); SWEDEN, HEAVEN AND HELL (1969); WITHOUT A STITCH (1968); and RELATIONS: THE LOVE STORY FROM DENMARK (1970), as well as the first films to show non-simulated hardcore sex on American screens: two "documentaries" about the recent legalization of pornography in Denmark, SEXUAL FREEDOM IN DENMARK (M. C. Von Hellen [John Lamb], 1970) and CENSORSHIP IN DENMARK: A NEW APPROACH (Alex de Renzy, 1970). These imports—many of them were distributed by Louis Sher's Sherpix and opened at his Art Theater Guild venues in Manhattan[50]—were quickly followed by domestic hardcore films that purported to offer what Linda Williams calls "a scientific 'discourse of sexuality.'"[51] (Exploitation producers referred to them as "white coaters," since they were often narrated by an actor posing as a doctor or psychiatrist.) With titles like MAN AND WIFE (Matt Cimber, 1970), HISTORY OF THE BLUE MOVIE (Alex de Renzy, 1970), AFRICANUS SEXUALIS (aka BLACK IS BEAUTIFUL [Matt Cimber, 1971]), and CASE HISTORIES FROM KRAFFT-EBING (Dakota Brothers, 1971), such pseudo-documentaries opened the door to the explicit depiction of live sexual activity in American features.

RUSS MEYER AND RADLEY METZGER

Russ Meyer (b. 1923) is often cited as the chief architect of what in the early 1970s could fairly be called "mainstream porn." As producer-director of successful "nudie-cutie" films like THE IMMORAL MR. TEAS (1959), Meyer made more than twenty such features (which he also wrote and photographed) through his independent company Eve Productions before he shot the ground-breaking VIXEN (1968) for his newly formed RM International Films. Although all of its sex scenes were simulated, the X-rated VIXEN had an engaging plot and was expertly edited; and it became the first gender crossover "Adults Only" hit when it returned $7.2 million on a $76,000 investment. This success was sufficient for Darryl Zanuck to contract a distribution deal between Meyer and Fox that yielded BEYOND THE VALLEY OF THE DOLLS (Russ Meyer, 1970) and THE SEVEN MINUTES (Russ Meyer, 1971), neither of which was particularly successful at the box office but notable for being the first studio-financed sex films. Meyer left Fox and continued to produce X-rated softcore features through his own company for the rest of the decade, but films like SUPERVIXENS (1975) and BENEATH THE VALLEY OF THE ULTRAVIXENS (1979)—which would barely have earned an "R" in the 1990s—could not

Russ Meyer's BEYOND THE VALLEY OF THE DOLLS *(Fox, 1970), the first studio-financed post-CARA sex film, was also ostensibly a sequel to Fox's adaptation of Jacqueline Susann's trashy best-seller* VALLEY OF THE DOLLS *(Mark Robson, 1967). Meyer and screenwriter Roger Ebert turned it into a parody of the earlier movie and of "sexploitation" films in general. 35mm Panavision anamorphic.*

compete theatrically with hardcore, and Meyer stopped making films in 1980, surviving nicely on his reputation and handsome video residuals. Roger Ebert, who co-wrote the screenplays for three of Meyer's movies, said of him in *Film Comment*: "If there was an auteur working in American commercial cinema in the '60s, it had to be Russ Meyer. It isn't so much that he operated his own camera as that he also carried it"—suggesting that his do-it-yourself approach to filmmaking laid the groundwork for such later entre-preneur-directors as Quentin Tarantino, Robert Rodriguez, and Spike Lee. Further-more, the montage sequences of Meyer's violent sexploitation film FASTER PUSSYCAT! KILL! KILL! (1966) are now said to have influenced both BONNIE AND CLYDE (Arthur Penn, 1967) and THE WILD BUNCH (Sam Peckinpah, 1969).[52]

What Meyer did for softcore, Radley Metzger (b. 1930) would do for hardcore—that is, give it a professional patina and introduce it into the mainstream marketplace. In 1960 Metzger and Ava Leighton had formed Audubon Films to import and distribute foreign features with erotic themes. Audubon distributed more than fifty features worldwide, many of them re-edited and re-shot by Metzger, before releasing its break-through film, I, A WOMAN (1965). This Swedish film about a young woman's sexual fan-tasies was picked up by Audubon for $5,000, reworked by Metzger, and returned $4 million in rentals.[53] The following year, Metzger organized his own production company, Amsterdam Film Corp., and began to direct upscale erotic features like THERESE AND

ISABELLE (1968), a version of Violette Leduc's memoir about a youthful lesbian relationship shot on location in a French boarding school. This was followed by CAMILLE 2000 (1969), shot on location in Rome in three-strip Technicolor (a process not used in Hollywood for fifteen years), and the X-rated THE LICKERISH QUARTET (1970), shot in an Italian castle from a script by Metzger about a female circus performer who seduces an entire family. A director of real talent and taste who had successfully spanned what *Variety* called "the groin-art gap," Metzger turned to hardcore in the early 1970s when market pressure demanded it.[54] Working under the pseudonym "Henry Paris," Metzger produced some of the hardcore genre's most sophisticated features—THE PRIVATE AFTERNOONS OF PAMELA MANN (1975), NAKED CAME THE STRANGER (1975), THE OPENING OF MISTY BEETHOVEN (1976), BARBARA BROADCAST (1977), and MARASCHINO CHERRY (1978)—as well as X-rated softcore films under his own name like THE IMAGE (1976), adapted from a sadomasochistic novel by Pauline Reage—before going into semiretirement in 1981. Because Metzger controlled both distribution and production, he was able to make his hardcore films on the same kind of (relatively) luxurious schedule accorded mainstream features, which helped to earn them a place in both video porn shops and the permanent collection of MoMA.[55] Audubon itself, as *Variety* noted as early as October 1970, had "helped to change the face of distribution in this country" by booking erotic product into mainstream theaters[56] and attracting "a class audience" of heterosexual couples to what had formerly been a specialized, all-male, and widely despised genre.[57]

DEEP THROAT AND "PORNO CHIC"

The mainstreaming of hardcore reached its zenith in 1972 when the infamous DEEP THROAT, produced and directed by Gerard Damiano (as "Jerry Gerard," also credited with writing and editing)[58] for $24,000, attracted a vast middle-class audience nationwide to become the eleventh highest grossing film of the year and earn $20 million in rentals (based on actual box-office returns—editorial policy kept hardcore films from appearing in *Variety*'s year-end chart.) This sixty-two-minute one-trick film about a woman prodigiously endowed for the practice of fellatio made a star of the eponymous Linda Lovelace. It received so much media attention that a senior editor at the *Washington Post* could give Woodward and Bernstein's clandestine Watergate informer the nickname "Deep Throat" in early 1973 and assume a general public understanding of the joke. Unlike previous hardcore films, DEEP THROAT was widely reviewed in middle-class newspapers, and it was in such a review in the *New York Times* that Vincent Canby coined the term "porno chic" to describe the modish respectability that hardcore had suddenly, if briefly, achieved.[59] Audiences for the film in Manhattan were said to include "celebrities, diplomats, critics, businessmen, women alone, and dating couples, few of whom, it might be presumed, would previously have gone to see a film of sexual intercourse, fellatio, and cunnilingus."[60] Confirming the newly fashionable status of pornography, Damiano followed DEEP THROAT with another smash hardcore hit, THE DEVIL IN MISS JONES (1972), which made a star of its lead Georgina Spelvin and became the sixth highest grossing film of the year. Another successful hardcore feature was BEHIND THE GREEN DOOR (Jim and Artie Mitchell, 1973), whose star Marilyn Chambers became an icon of sexual licentiousness for the next twenty years. As Jon Lewis points out, these three hardcore productions outearned big-budget studio films on both a screen-by-screen basis and in total box-office revenue.[61] By early 1973, it was

Poster ad for Gerard Damiano's DEEP THROAT (1972), the film that pumped hardcore unmistakably into the mainstream and created the phenomenon of "porno chic."

clear to all concerned that an enormous cultural change had been wrought since the CARA system had replaced the Production Code in October 1968. In just over four years, the graphic depiction of sex had become one of the most popular attractions in the American cinema, and XXX-rated features accounted for three of the fifteen most profitable films of 1972–1973.[62]

LAST TANGO IN PARIS TO PRETTY BABY: THE MAJORS FLIRT WITH PORN

That hardcore was suddenly capturing a significant share of domestic box-office revenues was impossible for the mainstream industry to ignore, and Hollywood responded with customized imitations. United Artists tested the waters first by distributing Bernardo Bertolucci's LAST TANGO IN PARIS (1973), a French-Italian coproduction that contained graphic sexual encounters, including sodomy, between stars Marlon Brando and Maria Schneider in an empty Paris apartment. CARA gave the film an X rating for

Maria Schneider and Marlon Brando in Bernardo Bertolucci's Last Tango in Paris
*(UA, 1973), arguably the first X-rated European art film. It was cut by United Artists
to receive an R rating for national distribution and became the eighth highest grossing
film of the year. 35mm 1.85:1.*

these scenes, despite its splendid direction and cinematography (by Vittorio Storaro)
and its obviously serious intent to probe the relationship between thanatos and eros.[63]
The controversy aroused thereby made Last Tango in Paris both a popular and a critical hit, although it was banned in Alabama and Louisiana[64] and threatened with prosecution in Georgia. (Fulton County solicitor Hinton McAuliffe vowed to bring obscenity
charges against Last Tango if it opened the Atlanta International Film Festival, as
scheduled, in October 1973; organizers then dropped their plans to program it.)[65] To
avoid further legal action and extend the film's domestic reach, United Artists cut it to
obtain an R rating, and Last Tango ultimately generated $16.7 million in domestic
rentals to become the eighth highest grossing film of 1973. (It earned another $21 mil-
lion internationally for a grand total of $37.7 million; so, with a negative budgeted at only
$1.25 million, Last Tango had what United Artists president David Picker cited as the
"lowest ratio of costs to rentals in our history.")[66] By setting new standards for sexual
explicitness in nonpornographic films (as well as starring an Oscar-winning actor
stripped to the skin in its sex scenes), Last Tango emboldened the American majors in
their quest for sensation and encouraged filmmakers toward heightened realism in the
depiction of sex. Among critics, there was a general consensus that, as Charles Champlin
wrote in the *Los Angeles Times*, "If Deep Throat is the cost of the new freedom, Last
Tango is a reward."[67]

The marriage of hardcore and European art film continued the following year with the Columbia Pictures import EMMANUELLE (1974), a French adaptation of a 1957 erotic novel by Emmanuelle Arsan (Maryat Rollet-Andriane) about a bored diplomat's wife who is initiated into a wide variety of sexual experience during a posting to Thailand.[68] Directed by former fashion photographer Just Jaeckin, the film had glossy mainstream production values, and Columbia pitched its advertising directly at the newly sophisticated heterosexual couples market uncovered by DEEP THROAT and LAST TANGO. "X was never like this," the copy read, "The intelligence of the story, and

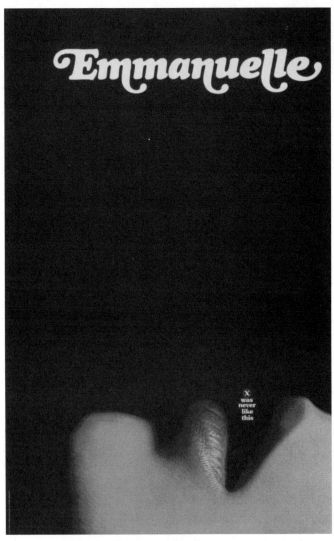

Poster art for Columbia's French import EMMANUELLE *(Just Jaeckin, 1974), targeted directly at the new heterosexual couples market for porn. The small print emerging from the parted lips reads, "X was never like this."*

the elegance with which it is handled result in a film that doesn't make you fidget in the explicit scenes, or slink down into your seat."[69] Earning nearly $5 million in rentals, EMMANUELLE probably did more to mainstream intentional hardcore than any other film of the 1970s, and it generated dozens of imitations and sequels, starring either Sylvia Kristel or Laura Gemser in the title role, including EMMANUELLE, THE JOYS OF A WOMAN (Francis Giacobetti, 1976), EMMANUELLE AROUND THE WORLD (Joe D'Amato, 1977), EMMANUELLE IN AMERICA (Joe D'Amato, 1978), EMMANUELLE IN BANGKOK (Joe D'Amato, 1978), and EMMANUELLE, THE QUEEN OF SADOS (Ilias Milonakos, 1982). As it progressed, the Emmanuel series became increasingly focused on sadomasochism in response to the popularity of two 1975 films—Just Jaeckin's X-rated THE STORY OF O and Gerard Damiano's self-styled XXX-rated THE STORY OF JOANNA (1975)—which between them confirmed feminists' worst fears about the direction in which the sexual revolution was headed.

Distributed by Allied Artists and aggressively marketed to couples, THE STORY OF O was a softcore adaptation of the French underground classic HISTOIRE D'O (1954), by Pauline Reage (a pseudonym), whose plot revolves around a woman's utter subjugation by her lover and his wealthy friend Sir Stephen. The film starred Corinne Clery as "O," a beautiful fashion photographer who allows herself to be variously whipped, chained, and defiled by Udo Kier, Anthony Steel, and others over the course of a lushly photographed ninety-seven-minute feature. Among the elements of its upscale appeal were a literate script by Sebastian Japrisot and a hauntingly romantic score by Pierre Bachelet.

Product differentiation: Allied Artists' controversial import THE STORY OF O *(Just Jaeckin, 1975) was a lushly photographed essay in romantic sadomasochism, based on an underground French classic. Although it contained no hardcore scenes as such, it brought S&M practices into mainstream theaters in ways that some communities found obscene. 35mm 1.85:1.*

Various municipalities attempted to prosecute THE STORY OF O for obscenity, including Atlanta and Detroit, but were unsuccessful since it contained virtually no sex as such, only whipping, bondage, branding, and female nudity. THE STORY OF JOANNA, on the other hand, was a considerably darker piece of hardcore from the makers of DEEP THROAT designed to cash in on the popularity of THE STORY OF O, which had returned as much in rentals as the first EMMANUELLE. Distributed by the independent Blueberry Hill, THE STORY OF JOANNA was about another woman subjected to degradation and torture by a wealthy aristocrat, but it went much farther than the French film in its graphic brutality and earned $4 million in rentals for its pains. These two "Stories" of 1975 introduced the practice of sadomasochism into mainstream American theaters, and the year

A trade advertisement for SNUFF (1975), touting its phenomenal early grosses at a New York mainstream theater. By claiming to represent the actual murder and dismemberment of a woman on-screen, this film became the catalyst for a nationwide feminist campaign against violent pornography and helped to turn the tide of public opinion against movie porn.

ended with Monarch Releasing Corporation's SNUFF (see Chapter 5), promising to show its patrons a real murder and disembowelment on screen for $7.50 a pop. The state of things was summarized nicely by a headline article in *Variety* for December 12, 1975: "If 'Snuff' Killings Are Real, Film Violence Faces New Test."[70]

This film, advertised by a poster showing a photograph of a woman slashed by a pair of bloody scissors, was described in ad copy as "The bloodiest thing that ever happened in front of a camera,"[71] and it probably did more to catalyze the feminist antipornography movement than any other cultural artifact of the 1970s. Laura Lederer, editor of *Take Back the Night*, would later write that SNUFF was "the powder keg that moved women seriously to confront the issue of pornography," and the film met with organized protests against theaters showing it all over the country.[72] As one leaflet distributed in New York put it: "That sexual violence is presented as entertainment, that the murder and dismemberment of a woman's body is commercial film material is an outrage. . . . We can not allow murder for profit."[73] *Variety* had called SNUFF "the ultimate pornography," and the following year, Stephen Koch would write an influential article in *Harper's* entitled "Fashions in Pornography: Murder as an Expression of Cinematic Chic" in which he traced the current obsession with sex killings back to "a vile little piece of sick crap" called THE TEXAS CHAINSAW MASSACRE[74]—invoking the generic confusion of horror and hardcore already noted above.

But, in fact, given First Amendment guarantees of free speech, there was little Koch, feminists, or anyone else could do prevent audiences from wallowing in perversion if they chose, and by mid-decade—when over 50 percent of all films distributed in the

Product differentiation, Part II: Films like Louis Malle's PRETTY BABY *(Paramount, 1978), in which Brooke Shields (shown here with Susan Sarandon as her mother) played a 12-year-old prostitute, drove public fears that pedophilia might be next in line for mainstream treatment. 35mm 1.85:1.*

United States in 1975 were restricted by either R or self-imposed X ratings[75]—they were choosing in large numbers.

Exactly how far they would go became apparent in 1977. Citing Jodie Foster's performance as a teenage hooker in Columbia's TAXI DRIVER (Martin Scorsese, 1976) and Brook Shields's appearance as a 12-year-old prostitute in Paramount's forthcoming PRETTY BABY (Louis Malle, 1978), as well as such made-for-TV movies as NBC's BORN INNOCENT and ABC's LITTLE LADIES OF THE NIGHT, Joseph McBride would write in *Variety* for February 9 of that year: "Children and sex—once protected by the most stringent of all film taboos—are now being exploited on major Hollywood films and TV shows."[76] Sexploitation producer David Friedman, then president of the Adult Film Association of America (a trade association of sex film producers formed in 1969 to lobby against censorship), noted that "a real boom" in pedophilia pictures started around 1974, at first with young-looking adult women in girlish roles but eventually involving real children. "It's no surprise," he added, "that the child sex theme would works its way into major films and TV."[77] Attributed by prosecutors to a spillover from the pornographic underworld, filmed sexual matter involving children surfaced in the mainstream with Warner Bros.' THE EXORCIST (William Friedkin, 1973), whose graphic masturbation scene and obscene speech by 12-year-old Linda Blair helped to make it the third most profitable film of the decade. Clearly, if pornography was coming more and more to resemble mainstream film, mainstream film was increasingly adopting the values of pornography. With barriers thus lowered, both the pornographers and majors felt free to explore the public's tolerance for sadomasochism, torture murder, and pedophilic sex to its then-amorphous legal limits.

THE COURTS ATTEMPT TO DEFINE OBSCENITY

Such limits were ill-defined during the 1970s but hardly inconsequential. In fact, the main reason that pornographers like Radley Metzger directed their films under pseudonyms was the fear of prosecution created by the U.S. Supreme Court ruling in the case of *Miller v. California* on June 27, 1973, which laid down the "community standards" test for determining obscenity. In this landmark decision, the Court effectively decentralized screen censorship and returned obscenity prosecutions to local authorities but, by failing to define what it meant by "community," created an ambiguity that would haunt the legal system for the next twenty years.[78] In June 1974, in another decision widely hailed as a victory for the film industry (*Jenkins v. Georgia*), the high Court confirmed the community standards test as the law of the land by unanimously reversing a Georgia Supreme Court opinion that the Avco Embassy feature CARNAL KNOWLEDGE (Mike Nichols, 1971) was obscene, attempting, in its own words, to "distinguish commerce in ideas protected by the First Amendment from commercial exploitation of obscene material" (i.e., hardcore) and reminding the states that only the latter could be prosecuted.[79]

In both cases, the Court had acted in response to the exponential increase in obscenity prosecutions against film distributors and exhibitors since the establishment of the CARA rating system. The waves of softcore and hardcore pornography that the self-imposed X seemed to generate, had outraged communities across the nation and sent shock waves through the industry. The preoccupation with pornography is illustrated by selected *Variety* headlines from 1970: "Censor Threats Haunt MPAA" (March 18, p. 5); "Sexpix Simplified: They Pay" (April 1, p. 3); "Porno: An Unknown Payoff" (April 22, p. 3);

"So Who's Going for Smut?" (August 12, p. 5); "Pornography at N.Y. Fest" (September 23, p. 5); "Porno, Biz & NATO's 'Image'" (October 7, p. 7)—which begins with the lead "If one word sums up trends in 1970 film exhibition in the U.S. it is 'pornography.'" As more and more mainstream theaters began to book X-rated product, obscenity cases multiplied, and the good suffered along with the bad. Prosecution was brought against CENSORSHIP IN DENMARK in New Jersey in 1971, but also against CARNAL KNOWLEDGE in Georgia in 1972; against DEEP THROAT in more than twenty states in 1972, but also against THE LAST PICTURE SHOW in Arizona and LAST TANGO IN PARIS in several deep South states in 1973.[80] The Supreme Court's ruling in *Miller v. California* was intended to remove the onus of government censorship (and what one official called the "almost impossible burden" of the Justice Department's obscenity case load),[81] but it actually had the effect of multiplying it through atomization—a situation evoked in the title of *Variety's* instant analysis of the ruling: "Porno Thicket Now Jungle? Community Standards Spells C-O-N-F-U-S-I-O-N" (June 27, 1973; p. 5).

It was this confusion over the definition of obscenity during the 1970s—both legally and culturally—that permitted abuses of free speech like SNUFF and child pornography. The challenges such material posed to the First Amendment and to American social polity might never have been resolved were it not for the introduction of the video cassette recorder in 1975 and its rapid diffusion over the next decade. By taking the consumption (but not the distribution) of socially pernicious images out of the public arena and relocating it in the privacy of the individual home, the VCR accomplished what neither moralists nor feminists could do—the closing of hundreds of adult theaters across the country in the wake of the pornographic film industry's largest expansion in history. (According to David Friedman, the number of adult venues in the United States increased from 20 to 750 between 1960 and 1970, with Pussycat Theaters, Inc., actually building a national chain of theaters from the ground up dedicated exclusively to the showing of X-rated films; by 1975, for example, there were forty-seven Pussycats in California alone.)[82] Estimates by the Adult Film Association of America suggest that pornographic films accounted for 70 to 80 percent of all videocassette sales through 1982, when the majors began licensing their product to video distributors in large numbers (afterwards the market share for porn would remain at about 40 percent).[83] By 1986, there were 35 million VCRs in consumer hands in the United States, and attendance at adult theaters had plummeted to 1960s' levels.[84] CARA-sanctioned barriers to the depiction of sex and nudity in mainstream theatrical films remained low, but production calculated simply to exploit such material had retreated to the realm of video and cable, and hardcore as a mainstream feature genre was, quite literally, history.

From Exploitation to Allusion

In the early 1970s, then, the once-marginal exploitation genres of blaxploitation, kung fu, and hardcore pornography became important factors in the American film marketplace; but by the decade's end, most exploitation product had migrated to home video, a technology whose national diffusion was virtually driven by hardcore. The force of the CARA rating system had been to fragment the market and enable the rise of exploitation genres to mainstream prominence, something AIP chairman Samuel Z. Arkoff had predicted as early as 1969 when he wrote in the *Journal of the Producers Guild of America*, "[T]oday the audience is fragmented; and with the exception of the big and successful picture that may by its special elements appeal to many different groups, one must take aim at a special group in order to be successful."[85] Five years later, David Begelman, then-president of Columbia Pictures, crystallized this thinking for the *Wall Street Journal:* "We feel we must put out special event films because no one goes to the movies anymore as a routine exercise."[86] The blockbuster formula was designed to overcome the market fragmentation introduced by CARA, and it did so by adopting exploitation practices, both at the level of production content and marketing/distribution, as described in Chapter 3. However, the calculated blockbuster used another tactic to reintegrate the market which relied on the mass audience's recent encounter with film history through television, popular journalism, and (occasionally) formal education. By the early 1970s, in fact, American television had become a virtual archive of the classical Hollywood cinema via weekly network showcases and syndicated reruns, and the auteur "theory" had become a commonplace of both popular and academic criticism.

As Noel Carrol, J. Hoberman, and others have pointed out, a distinguishing feature of 1970s film style was "allusionism"—the practice of invoking the audience's unprecedented awareness of film history, which it shared with the rising generation of directors, especially the "Hollywood brats."[87] Shaped by auteurism, the recent availability of classical films on television, and the gradual institutionalization of film study in the academy, this new historical film consciousness enabled both the knowing revision of classical genres discussed above and a new category of self-reflexive films that fetishized the practices of "lost Hollywood"—either through parody or memorialization. Parody in film can be defined as a comic, exaggerated imitation of a given genre, auteur, or specific film; as distinct from satire, whose focus is on social values, parody targets aesthetic and formal conventions, usually treating them with some affection.[88] The clearest examples are the self-proclaimed genre parodies of Mel Brooks (BLAZING SADDLES [1974]; YOUNG FRANKENSTEIN [1974]; HIGH ANXIETY [1977]) and his associates Gene Wilder (THE ADVENTURE OF SHERLOCK HOLMES' SMARTER BROTHER [1975]) and Marty Feldman (THE LAST REMAKE OF BEAU GESTE [1977]), and such parodic feature anthologies as THE GROOVE TUBE (Ken Shapiro, 1974), TUNNELVISION (Neal Israel, 1976), and THE KENTUCKY FRIED MOVIE (John Landis, 1977), but the parodic impulse was strong in many comic films of the decade and extended to virtually every genre. These included sexploitation (BEYOND THE VALLEY OF THE DOLLS [Russ Meyer, 1970] and MYRA BRECKINRIDGE [Michael Sarne, 1970], both also insider "movie movies") and hardcore (THE LAST PORNO FLICK [Ray Marsh, 1974], FLESH GORDON [Michael Benveniste, 1974], which also parodies science fiction); the Western (proceeding from Brooks, THE DUCHESS AND THE DIRTWATER FOX [Melvin Frank, 1976], GREAT SCOUT AND CATHOUSE THURSDAY [Don Taylor, 1976], THE FRISCO KID [Robert Aldrich, 1979], THE VILLAIN [Hal Needham, 1979]); the musical, both backstage and integrated (THE BOY FRIEND [Ken Russell, 1971], THE ROCKY HORROR PICTURE SHOW [Jim Sharman, 1975], which also parodies classical horror, ALL THAT JAZZ [Bob Fosse, 1979], and the rock-'n'-roll subgenre [GREASE (Randall Kleiser, 1978), ROCK 'N' ROLL HIGH SCHOOL (Allan Arkush, 1979)]); the gangster film, contemporary and classical (FREEBIE AND THE BEAN [Richard Rush, 1974], BUGSY MALONE [Alan Parker, 1976], and the criminal couple subgenre [RAFFERTY AND THE GOLD DUST TWINS (Dick Richards, 1975), FUN WITH DICK AND JANE (Ted Kotcheff, 1977)]); the *film noir*/detective movie (THE BLACK BIRD [David Giler, 1975], MURDER BY DEATH [Robert Moore, 1976], THE CHEAP DETECTIVE [Robert Moore, 1978], and the Sherlock Holmes subgenre [THEY MIGHT BE GIANTS (Anthony Harvey, 1971), Gene Wilder's SHERLOCK HOLMES'

*The parodic impulse reigns supreme
in these posters for Mel Brooks's
BLAZING SADDLES (Warners, 1974)
and YOUNG FRANKENSTEIN
(Fox, 1974), which promise to
"never give a saga an even break."*

SMARTER BROTHER (1975), THE HOUND OF THE BASKERVILLES (Paul Morrissey,
1977)]); conspiracy (NASTY HABITS [Michael Lindsay-Hogg, 1977], WINTER KILLS
[William Richert, 1979]); science fiction (DARK STAR [John Carpenter, 1974], DEATH
RACE 2000 [Paul Bartel, 1975], FLASH GORDON [Mike Hodges, 1980]); the disaster
film (THE BIG BUS [James Frawley, 1976], AIRPLANE! [Jim Abrahams, David Zucker,
Jerry Zucker, 1980]); suspense (SILVER STREAK [Arthur Hiller, 1976]); the war film
(1941 [Steven Spielberg, 1979]); the swashbuckler (Richard Lester's THE THREE

"Monty Python," the six-member cast of the BBC television show "Monty Python's Flying Circus'" was the other major force for parody in the 1970s, reponsible, among other things, for MONTY PYTHON'S LIFE OF BRIAN *(Orion/Warners, 1979). In this wholly irreverent parody of the Hollywood biblical epic, Graham Chapman (Brian) is mistaken throughout his life for the Messiah until he is finally (and hilariously) crucified: Chapman about to land on the head of a mendicant Michael Palin. 35mm 1.75:1.*

MUSKETEERS [1974], THE FOUR MUSKETEERS [1975], and ROYAL FLASH [1975], SWASHBUCKLER [James Goldstone, 1976], CROSSED SWORDS [Richard Fleischer, 1978], ZORRO, THE GAY BLADE [Peter Medak, 1981]); classical horror (Andy Warhol's FRANKENSTEIN and DRACULA satires [both Paul Morrissey, 1974]; Mel Brooks's YOUNG FRANKENSTEIN [1974], OLD DRACULA [Clive Donner, 1974]); contemporary horror (THE BANANA MONSTER aka SCHLOCK [John Landis, 1971], LOVE AT FIRST BITE [Stan

Dragoti, 1979], THE HOWLING [Joe Dante, 1981]), and animal revenge (PIRANHA [Joe Dante, 1978], ALLIGATOR [Lewis Teague, 1980]); the historical or biblical epic (MONTY PYTHON AND THE HOLY GRAIL [Terry Gilliam, 1975], MONTY PYTHON'S LIFE OF BRIAN [Terry Jones, 1979], WHOLLY MOSES [Gary Weis, 1980]); and, finally, the *cinema-verité* documentary (REAL LIFE [Albert Brooks, 1979]). Parody was, in fact, the comic mode most appropriate to post-Watergate, post-Vietnam disillusionment and cynicism, and it enjoyed mass appeal in both film and television throughout the decade—witness the success, for example, of the syndicated TV soap opera parody *Mary Hartman, Mary Hartman* (1976–1977), the talk show parodies *Fernwood 2-Night* (1977) and *America 2Night* (1978), and *NBC's Saturday Night Live* (whose earliest mainstay was movie-parody skits), which was an immediate hit when it premiered in the fall of 1975 and became one of the most popular television shows in the medium's history.

The other allusionist film style endemic to the 1970s was memorialization, which can be defined as an affectionate evocation of past genres through imitation and exaggeration in the manner of STAR WARS (1977), SUPERMAN (1978), and RAIDERS OF THE LOST ARK (1981)—films that combined state-of-the-art special effects with the old

HEAVEN CAN WAIT *(Paramount, 1978), one of the many remakes of classical Hollywood films that appeared throughout the decade and that were especially prominent in its latter half: James Mason as Mr. Jordan, Warren Beatty as Joe Pendleton. Produced, co-written (with Elaine May), and codirected (with Buck Henry) by Warren Beatty, the film remakes the 1941 fantasy-comedy* HERE COMES MR. JORDAN *(Alexander Hall, 1941) about an athlete who is accidentally sent to heaven before his time and who is restored to life in the body of another. 35mm 1.85:1.*

action genres of the thirties and forties.[89] Such films created a two-tiered system of communication, presenting themselves as fantasy-adventure spectacles for the economically crucial teenage audience, and as tapestries of allusion for an older, more cinematically sophisticated one.[90] To these obvious historical pastiches, which evoke specific classical genres and create a sense of nostalgic longing, must be added films like WHAT'S UP DOC? (Peter Bogdanovich, 1972), OBSESSION (Brian De Palma, 1976), ASSAULT ON PRECINCT 13 (John Carpenter, 1976), and HARDCORE (Paul Schrader, 1979), which remake genre classics in other terms (BRINGING UP BABY [Howard Hawks, 1938], VERTIGO [Alfred Hitchcock, 1958], RIO BRAVO [Howard Hawks, 1959], and THE SEARCHERS [John Ford, 1956], respectively),[91] and such actual remakes as KING KONG (John Guillermin, 1976), INVASION OF THE BODY SNATCHERS (Phil Kaufman, 1978), HEAVEN CAN WAIT (Warren Beatty, 1978—a remake of HERE COMES MR. JORDAN [Alexander Hall, 1941]), DRACULA (John Badham, 1979), THE CHAMP (Franco Zeffirelli, 1979), and THE JAZZ SINGER (Richard Fleischer, 1980), which reworked their respective genres and provided risk reduction for their producer/distributors in the form of heightened audience awareness. Memorialization was also the impetus for numerous

Advertising art for Paramount's THE DAY OF THE LOCUST (John Schlesinger, 1975) suggesting both memorialization and parody. Adapted from Nathanael West's ferocious 1939 novel about a group of Hollywood losers, the film itself evokes the seamy side of the industry in the 1930s, aided considerably by Conrad Hall's "period"-style cinematography, which was nominated for an Academy Award.

Biopics became another means of recycling classical Hollywood during the 1970s, for example, Universal's GABLE AND LOMBARD *(Sidney J. Furie, 1976): James Brolin as Clark Gable and Morgan Brittany as Vivien Leigh in a scene representing a scene from David O. Selznick's production of* GONE WITH THE WIND *(1939). 35mm Panavision anamorphic.*

films about bygone Hollywood that characterized the latter half of the decade. These self-reflexive "movie movies" presented themselves as either archival anthologies (THAT'S ENTERTAINMENT! [Jack D. Haley, Jr., 1974]; THAT'S ENTERTAINMENT, PART 2 [Gene Kelly, 1976])[92] or nostalgic historical fictions. Significantly, there were more films produced in this latter category during the 1970s than in any comparable period in industry history. A representative sample from the decade's middle years would include THE WILD PARTY (James Ivory, 1975), THE DAY OF THE LOCUST (John Schlesinger, 1975), HEARTS OF THE WEST (Howard Zieff, 1975), WON TON TON, THE DOG WHO SAVED HOLLYWOOD (Michael Winner, 1976), INSERTS (John Byrum, 1976), W. C. FIELDS AND ME (Arthur Hiller, 1976), GABLE AND LOMBARD (Sidney J. Furie, 1976), THE LAST TYCOON (Elia Kazan, 1976), NICKELODEON (Peter Bogdanovich, 1976), SILENT MOVIE (Mel Brooks, 1976), THE WORLD'S GREATEST LOVER (Gene Wilder, 1977), THE OTHER SIDE OF MIDNIGHT (Charles Jarrott, 1977), VALENTINO (Ken Russell, 1977), and MOVIE MOVIE (Stanley Donen, 1978). Some of these were biopics of real performers and others were adaptations of Hollywood novels, great and small, but all took as their starting point the extraordinary interest in classical Hollywood and its forms that distinguished the 1970s from preceding decades and remained thereafter a permanent part of the industry landscape.

Peter Bogdanovich's NICKELODEON *(Columbia, 1975), one of the "movie movies" that began to appear at mid-decade catering to the public's lively new interest in Hollywood history: Ryan O'Neal directing a silent movie scene, with John Ritter at the camera, Stella Stevens as the leading lady (with parasol), and Tatum O'Neal driving the truck. 35mm 1.85:1.*

Genre Parody and Hybridization

In the 1980s, driven by the home video rental market, genre parody would become a genre unto itself as archival pastiches like DEAD MEN DON'T WEAR PLAID (Carl Reiner, 1982), mock documentaries like THIS IS SPINAL TAP (Rob Reiner, 1984), and parody series like those originating with AIRPLANE! (Jim Abrahams, David Zucker, Jerry Zucker, 1980) and THE NAKED GUN (David Zucker, 1988)—not to mention the semi-parodic NATIONAL LAMPOON and POLICE ACADEMY series—became box-office champions. Furthermore, by the end of the 1970s, genre blending and pastiche had become an important part of the blockbuster strategy to build the broadest possible audience base. Failed blockbusters like KING KONG (1976), THE WIZ (Sidney Lumet, 1978), and HEAVEN'S GATE (Michael Cimino, 1980), however revisionist, tended to be heavily genre-coded, and (whatever their other problems) at least part of their failure lay in their single-genre appeal to core audiences that were no longer there. The most successful blockbusters, on the other hand, were those that either mixed genres (JAWS—monster-horror-mystery-action-adventure; GREASE—youth exploitation-rock 'n' roll musical) or blended them into an historical pastiche (STAR WARS—science fiction-Western-aerial combat-Japanese jidai-geki [THE HIDDEN FORTRESS], with specific references to John Ford and Leni Riefenstahl; RAIDERS OF THE LOST ARK—B-movie serial-action-adventure-Tex Avery cartoon, with specific reference to CITIZEN KANE). Another way to put this is that in their concern to maximize audiences, studios mixed genres to appeal to several specialized genre audiences at once. Genre hybridization had became so pronounced by 1981 that *The New Yorker* published a cartoon series satirizing such putative new forms as the "Kung Fu science fiction movie," the "sports disaster movie," and the "therapeutic musical," of which by that time there had actually appeared several nonparodic examples (THE ULTIMATE WARRIOR [Robert Clouse, 1975], BLACK SUNDAY [John Frankenheimer, 1977], and ALL THAT JAZZ [1979]).

Perhaps the oddest generic hybrid of the 1970s was the "sports inspirational," whose genesis lay in the astonishing success of ROCKY (John G. Avildsen, 1976). This film was by all measures the sleeper of the decade, written by and starring Sylvester Stallone as the ultimate underdog—a washed-up boxer who gets a "million-to-one shot" at a championship title and, through sheer force of will, wins. Produced for under $1,000,000, the

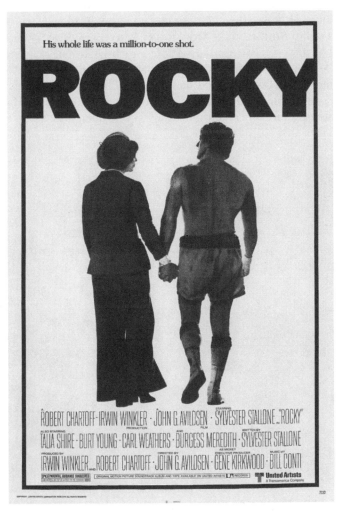

Poster for the United Artists sleeper ROCKY *(John G. Avildsen, 1976), a genre hybrid that inaugurated the late-1970s "sports inspirational" cycle.*

film earned $56.5 million in domestic rentals, won three Academy Awards (Best Picture, Best Director, Best Editing) and generated four sequels, ROCKY II through ROCKY V (1979–1990). Many critics before and since have pointed out that ROCKY simply reworked an old rags-to-riches formula of classical Hollywood but struck a responsive chord in post-Watergate America because Rocky Balboa represented a hero of the people at a time when the people badly needed one. That Rocky himself was working-class probably contributed to the film's mass appeal, but many subsequent sports inspirationals were distinctly bourgeois. In THE BAD NEWS BEARS (Michael Ritchie, 1976), for example, an underdog suburban Little League team wins a championship against all odds; this popular comedy was the year's seventh-highest earner, yielding $24.3 million in rentals and two sequels (THE BAD NEWS BEARS IN BREAKING TRAINING [Michael Pressman, 1977]; THE BAD NEWS BEARS GO TO JAPAN [John Berry, 1978]). Other ROCKY-like middle-class scenarios involved college basketball (ONE ON ONE [Lamont Johnson, 1977], FAST BREAK [Jack Smight, 1979]); high school track (OUR WINNING SEASON [Joseph Ruben, 1978]); wrestling (THE ONE AND ONLY [Carl Reiner, 1978]); Olympic skiing (THE OTHER SIDE OF THE MOUNTAIN [Larry Peerce, 1975] and THE OTHER SIDE OF THE MOUNTAIN, PART 2 [Larry Peerce, 1978]); Olympic skating (ICE CASTLES [Donald Wrye, 1979]); Olympic running (RUNNING [Steven Hilliard Stern, 1979]); Grand Prix auto racing (BOBBY DEERFIELD [Sydney Pollack, 1977]); cycling (BREAKING AWAY [Peter Yates, 1979]); and professional tennis (PLAYERS [Anthony Harvey, 1979]).[93] There were also several satirical films focusing on the inherent brutality of professional

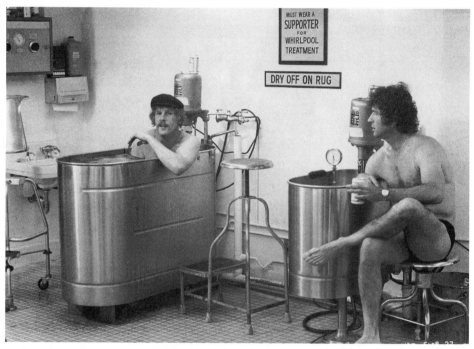

Nick Nolte and Mac Davis are pro football players for the "North Dallas Bulls" (obviously the Dallas Cowboys) in Paramount's NORTH DALLAS FORTY (Ted Kotcheff, 1979), a film that turned the ROCKY formula on its ear by showing professional sports to be the ugly, dishonest, and exploitative business it really is. 35mm Panavision anamorphic.

sports—notably hockey (SLAP SHOT [George Roy Hill, 1977]) and football (THE LONGEST YARD [Robert Aldrich, 1974], SEMI-TOUGH [Michael Ritchie, 1977], NORTH DALLAS FORTY [Ted Kotcheff, 1979])—that capitalized, somewhat cynically, on the newly permissive standards for the representation of violence on-screen, as did the bloody fight sequences in the ROCKY films themselves. The closing bracket of the 1970s sports inspirational cycle was Martin Scorsese's RAGING BULL (1980), a downbeat biography of 1940s middleweight boxing champion Jake La Motta, a repugnant "anti-Rocky" figure whose self-destructive behavior brings grief to everyone around him.

Comedies of Divorce and the "Return of the Grown-up Movie"

The late seventies boom in genre-blended blockbusters, and the attendant subordination of narrative to special effects, left significant portions of the audience unaddressed. In their haste to pursue teenagers and intrigue cinephiles simultaneously, producers of calculated blockbusters threatened to disenfranchise the audience over forty that in 1977 represented 45 percent of the population. According to an Opinion Research Corporation survey commissioned in that year by the MPAA, this group bought only 13

Meryl Streep and Dustin Hoffman are plantiff and defendant in Columbia's KRAMER VS. KRAMER (Robert Benton, 1979), a socially relevant "comedy of divorce" that became the year's top-grossing film and won five major Academy Awards, signaling what Stephen Farber called "the return of the grown-up movie." Before they would reach the age of sixteen, fully half of the children born in the United States between 1970 and 1980 would see their parents divorce. 35mm 1.85:1.

percent of all tickets, while those under twenty-five bought 57 percent.[94] With box-office grosses for 1977 approaching $2.4 billion, however, a 13-percent market share was worth about $320 million,[95] and several independent producers became especially interested in the over-forty audience segment for this reason (although, obviously, no producer could afford to completely ignore it). These filmmakers specialized in several mini-genres targeted for the college-educated, noncinephile adult, of which the "comedy of divorce"—cleaved away from the correlative "comedy of remarriage" that Stanley Clavell identified during the 1930s and 1940s—was the most prominent.[96]

Between 1965 and 1975, the divorce rate in United States doubled, and the divorce code was liberalized through the widespread adoption of no-fault divorce laws modeled on California's Family Law Act of 1969.[97] Near the end of the 1970s, a number of socially relevant films appeared that focused on the personal trauma of divorce and its impact on individual American families, and some of them enjoyed notable success. In 1979, for example, Columbia's KRAMER VS. KRAMER (Robert Benton) was not only the year's top-grossing film ($60 million in domestic rentals), but it won five Academy Awards, including Best Picture, Director, and Screenplay; and two other films constructed around divorce were among the year's twenty-five highest earners—Paramount's STARTING OVER (Alan J. Pakula—ranked nineteenth, with $19 million) and United Artists' MANHATTAN (Woody Allen—twenty-third, with $17.6 million). Other popular films about divorce or the complications of adult relationships include Warners' THE GOODBYE GIRL (Herbert Ross, 1977) and GIRLFRIENDS (Claudia Weill, 1978); United Artists' ANNIE HALL (Woody Allen, 1977), INTERIORS (Woody Allen, 1978), and MANHATTAN (Woody Allen, 1979); Fox's AN UNMARRIED WOMAN (Paul Mazursky, 1978); Columbia's CHAPTER TWO (Robert Moore, 1979) and IT'S MY TURN (Claudia Weill, 1980); Paramount's ORDINARY PEOPLE (Robert Redford, 1980); Universal's THE FOUR SEASONS (Alan Alda, 1981) and ON GOLDEN POND (Mark Rydell, 1981); and MGM/UA's SHOOT THE MOON (Alan Parker, 1982). Many of these films were inherently serious and could be called "comedies" only in the sense of having broadly social contexts. Yet their success was clearly related to the brief vogue in middle-aged sex farces stemming from the $37.4 million gross of Blake Edwards's 10 (Orion, 1979).

For several years around the turn of the decade, male menopause and mid-life crisis became the focus of such comic films as Fox's LOVING COUPLES (Jack Smight, 1980), A CHANGE OF SEASONS (Richard Lang, 1980), and MIDDLE-AGE CRAZY (John Trent, 1980); and Warner's JUST TELL ME WHAT YOU WANT (Sidney Lumet, 1980). Together with sobering adult melodramas like Paramount's LOOKING FOR MR. GOODBAR (Richard Brooks, 1977); Fox's JULIA (Fred Zinnemann, 1977) and THE TURNING POINT (Herbert Ross, 1977); and Warners' PROMISES IN THE DARK (Jerome Hellman, 1979), as well as several British literary imports—for example, THE EUROPEANS (James Ivory, 1979), adapted from the Henry James novel, and TESS (Roman Polanski, 1980), adapted from Thomas Hardy's *Tess of the d'Urbervilles*—these films constituted a mini boom in entertainment for older, more sophisticated markets predicted by some industry insiders as early as 1977. (MGM's vice president for domestic sales and distribution, Byron Shapiro, told exhibitors at a ShoWest convention in February 1977 that their "young audience" was aging rapidly and that "entertainment will have to be made suitable for the middle-aged.")[98] By late 1981, in fact, some distributors were complaining of an adult "product glut," leading critics like Stephen Farber to proclaim (in the title of an article that appeared in *American Film* for December 1981) "The Return of the Grown-Up Movie."[99] Farber's conclusion must have seemed justified three months later when

These posters for Woody Allen's ANNIE HALL *(UA, 1977) and* MANHATTAN *(UA, 1979) are designed to appeal to a "grown-up" audience interested in films about adult relationships. Conscious of their up-market demographics, they exude urbanity and sophistication.*

the up-market British import CHARIOTS OF FIRE (Ladd/Warners; Hugh Hudson, 1981) won four Academy Awards, including Best Picture, and REDS (Paramount, 1981), Warren Beatty's epic political biopic of John Reed, won three, including Best Director. As always, however, domestic grosses provided a more accurate index of public taste than Oscars (which are calibrated less to box-office success than to industry prestige), and these showed CHARIOTS in seventh place with $30.6 million and REDS at eleventh

Blake Edwards's 10 (Orion/Warners, 1979) took a different approach to its adult mate-
rial, focusing on the romantic obsession of a middle-aged songwriter (Dudley Moore)
with the young woman of his dreams (Bo Derek). 35mm Panavision anamorphic.

with $21 million. Meanwhile, Paramount's first-placed RAIDERS OF THE LOST ARK
(Steven Spielberg), which won several Oscars for technical achievement, pointed the
way to the future with $115.6, leaving it second only to STAR WARS in the history of
motion picture profitability.

Conclusion: Genre's End

It was another film of 1981, however, that epitomized what had happened to genre during the 1970s. An intensely erotic thriller in *film noir* form, BODY HEAT was the directorial debut of Lawrence Kasdan, who had co-written THE EMPIRE STRIKES BACK (Irvin
Kershner, 1980) and RAIDERS OF THE LOST ARK. It was the one of the first productions
of The Ladd Co., an independent "mini studio" formed by Alan Ladd, Jr., with partial
financing and an exclusive distribution deal from Warner Bros., after he resigned as president of 20th Century–Fox in 1979. (The following year Ladd had acquired the American
rights to CHARIOTS OF FIRE for release through Warners.) George Lucas functioned as
uncredited executive producer, remaining incognito because he didn't want his name
associated with the film's sexually charged content at a time when millions of American
children were buying Lucasfilm licensed products.[100] With a plot lifted from DOUBLE
INDEMNITY (Billy Wilder, 1944) and bytes of dialogue from MURDER, MY SWEET
(Edward Dmytryk, 1944), THE BIG SLEEP (Howard Hawks, 1946), OUT OF THE PAST

Literary adaptations like Roman Polanski's TESS *(1980), a version of Thomas Hardy's* Tess of the d'Urbervilles *(1891) were imported by American distributors at the end of the decade to tap older, more sophisticated markets: Leigh Lawson (Alec D'Urberville), Nastassia Kinski (Tess Durbeyfield). In this case, Columbia earned a respectable $9.87 million in rentals on a negative pick-up deal with the film's coproducers, Renn-Burrill, U.K., and Societe Francaise de Production (S.F.P.), and* TESS *won Academy Awards for Cinematography (Geoffrey Unsworth [posthumous] and Ghislain Cloquet), Art Direction (Pierre Guffroy), and Costume Design (Anthony Powell). 35mm Panavision anamorphic, blown up to 70mm for road-showing.*

(Jacques Tourneur, 1947), KISS ME DEADLY (Robert Aldrich, 1955), and VERTIGO (Alfred Hitchcock, 1958), BODY HEAT was a pastiche of forties *film noir* camera, composition, and lighting styles with characters dressed in contemporary fashions that are vaguely evocative of an earlier time. The interior decor of the sets fluctuates somewhere between forties moderne and "Miami Vice" contempo, and though the story takes place in the middle of a record-breaking heat wave, no one in the small south Florida city it depicts has air conditioning—only ceiling fans. Kasdan, a USC Film School graduate, said that he adopted a *film noir* style because it allowed him to experiment with camera and lighting effects but also to talk about his own generation's "intense desire for instant gratification" because he saw in post–World War II America "an analogous moral situation."[101] Thus the pessimistic, doom-laden ambience of *noir* speaks to the contemporary culture of narcissism through a film that is simultaneously nostalgic, allusive, and graphically erotic in ways that only post-CARA Hollywood could allow.

In all of these respects BODY HEAT is a virtual paradigm for the state of genre at the end of its 1970s trajectory. The revisionist directors of the early 1970s—Penn, Kubrick, Peckinpah, and Altman—sought to deconstruct the myths implicit in classical genres by

Kathleen Turner as the femme fatale *and William Hurt as the
fall guy in Lawrence Kasdan's pastiche of* film noir *styles,*
BODY HEAT *(The Ladd Company/Warners, 1981)—a "remake"
for which there was no original, only an archive of bygone plot
situations, dialogue, shot composition, and lighting effects, the
detritus of a seemingly exhausted genre. 35mm 1.85:1.*

exploding the form of the genres themselves in such films as LITTLE BIG MAN (1970),
A CLOCKWORK ORANGE (1971), THE GETAWAY (1972), and THE LONG GOODBYE
(1973). Shortly thereafter, "movie brat" directors like Spielberg and Lucas sought to
restore the authority of action genres for mass consumption by harnessing them to high-
tech special effects in such blockbusters as JAWS (1975), STAR WARS (1977), and CLOSE
ENCOUNTERS OF THE THIRD KIND (1977). Finally, by the end of the decade, filmmakers like Kasdan were able to plunder the iconographic register of an entire genre to fab-
ricate what J. Hoberman has called "a museum waxwork of a passé Hollywood style—a
remake without the original,"[102] but one that most audiences could read as such, via the
recent extension of film literacy to the general populace through television, film education, and—incipiently—the VCR. This same general awareness of film history enhanced
the market for actual contemporaneous remakes, such as THE POSTMAN ALWAYS RINGS
TWICE (Bob Rafelson, 1981), OUTLAND (Peter Hyams, 1981—a version of HIGH NOON

[Fred Zinnemann, 1952]), and THE THING (John Carpenter, 1982). But genres that could not be stylistically disassembled and reconfigured into the kind of postmodern historical pastiche represented by films (without reference to quality) like BODY HEAT (1981), DRESSED TO KILL (Brian De Palma, 1980—suspense), THE BLUES BROTHERS (John Landis, 1980—musical comedy), EXCALIBUR (John Boorman, 1981—epic), AN AMERICAN WEREWOLF IN LONDON (John Landis, 1981—horror), and BLADE RUNNER (Ridley Scott, 1982—science fiction-*film noir*) did not fare well in the coming decade, when viewers grew increasingly accustomed to reading multiple sets of genre expectations against one another and the predictability of the classical paradigm all but disappeared.

After the late sixties, serious mimesis had become increasingly problematic in American cinema as a pervasive sense of irony about genre and representation descended on the mass audience by way of television. During the 1970s, genre was further destabilized by revision, parody, and hybridization, until by the 1980s an aesthetic of serious representation had become virtually impossible in genre-coded films.

7

Orders of Magnitude I: Majors, Mini-Majors, "Instant Majors," and Independents

The film studios are continuing to trim staffs as they liquidate inventories estimated at $400,000,000. MCA (which owns Universal) and 20th [Fox] hit new lows on the New York Stock Exchange. Universal has pink-slipped a number of senior executives and writers. . . . MGM has trimmed about 29 percent of its personnel and is expected to extend pink slips to another 25 percent. . . . At Warners the process will be extended over the next three or four months with new dismissal notices before the year end.

THE HOLLYWOOD REPORTER, NOVEMBER 1969

From about 1955 to 1970, as the effects of the consent decrees were gradually absorbed, the order of magnitude among the Hollywood studios changed. The minors of the studio era—Universal, Columbia, and United Artists—were able to become majors as the leverage of market control shifted from exhibition to distribution. The majors shrank by divesting their theater chains, and one—RKO, always the weakest of the lot—disappeared, leaving MGM, Paramount, Warner Bros., and 20th Century–Fox to compete with the former minors for market share. Without the stability provided by vertical integration, production came to exist on a film-by-film basis rather than as part of a rationalized institutional schedule, and many studios experienced a decline in long-term revenue as annual profits depended more and more on the success of individual films. By the 1960s, with their stocks undervalued, but with significant assets in real estate, film libraries, and working production facilities, the studios had become attractive targets for corporate takeover, and by 1970 four of them—Universal, Paramount, Warner Bros., and United Artists—had been merged with conglomerates and one—MGM—had been acquired by a wealthy entrepreneur, leaving only Fox, Columbia, and the family-owned Disney under original ownership. Conglomeration clearly strengthened Universal, Paramount, and Warner Bros., and during the 1970s conglomerate affiliation generally served to increase a distributor's market share.

(According to Justin Wyatt, the average market shares for 1970–1980 were: Paramount 15 percent; Warner Bros. 14.5 percent; Fox 13.9 percent; Universal 13.4 percent; United Artists 11.5 percent; Columbia 10.2 percent; and MGM 5.8 percent, with Fox's strength attributable largely to the success of STAR WARS; Disney had around 6 percent, leaving the numerous smaller companies to scramble for the remaining 10%.)[1] As consciously diversified forms of corporate organization, conglomerates had grown rapidly since World War II. From just 3 percent in 1948–1953, conglomerate acquisitions had grown to 49 percent of all assets acquired by mergers in the period 1973–1977, and by the late 1970s many conglomerates stood poised to become multinational corporations.[2]

The Majors: Command and Control

There were more changes in studio management during the 1970s than at any previous time in industry history. This was initially a response to the financial crisis of 1969–1971 but ultimately to the changing nature of the studios themselves, as they moved out of film production and into teleproduction while simultaneously consolidating their control of film distribution and finance. Along with the more or less continuous management reshufflings of the 1970s came a new set of relationships among studios, agents, independent producers, and stars.

METRO-GOLDWYN-MAYER (MGM)

The studio that experienced the most profound change during the 1970s was MGM, which to all intents and purposes was liquidated by its new corporate owner Kirk Kerkorian. MGM's problems dated from 1957 when the studio showed a loss for the first time in its history (a deficit of $455,000, down from a profit of $5.6 million in 1956). Although it recovered briefly between 1959 and 1961 thanks to the international success of a single blockbuster (its $15-million remake of BEN-HUR [William Wyler, 1959], which generated $37 million in domestic rentals—$80 million in rentals worldwide) and a third reissue (in 1961) of GONE WITH THE WIND (Victor Fleming, 1939), MGM's profits took another steep plunge in 1962 (down $10 million from the previous year to $2.5 million), and the company hit rock bottom in 1963 when it produced a $17.5-million loss, owing largely to the failure of a single blockbuster (the $19-million remake of MUTINY ON THE BOUNTY [Lewis Milestone, 1962], which returned only $7 million in domestic rentals). The profits from yet another international blockbuster (DOCTOR ZHIVAGO [David Lean, 1965], which returned $43 [ultimately $61] million in domestic rentals against an $11-million investment) allowed MGM to coast along until 1968, when its next big hit 2001: A SPACE ODYSSEY (Stanley Kubrick, 1968; $17 million domestic [ultimately $25.5 million] against a $10.5-million negative cost) and a 70mm reissue of GONE WITH THE WIND ($9.5 million domestic) gave it another good year.[3] But it was clear that this cycle of occasional blockbuster windfalls supplemented by reissues was not sustainable, and, after three years of proxy battles, MGM went through a series of management changes in 1969 as James Polk, Jr. succeeded Robert O'Brien as president, only to be replaced within the year by James T. Aubrey, Jr.[4] Aubrey, a former president of CBS-TV (where he was known as "Jungle Jim" for the ruthlessness of his tactics), was handpicked by Las Vegas financier Kirk Kerkorian, who had gained a controlling interest in the studio in what amounted to a hostile takeover in 1969.

Kerkorian, once the single largest shareholder in Transamerica, had divested himself of its stock in 1968 in order to acquire a controlling interest in MGM after a careful study of its financial condition by his attorney Gregson Bautzer, with the intention of borrowing the additional funds for the purchase from a Transamerica subsidiary, the Transamerica Financial Corporation.[5] MGM management, led by Edgar J. Bronfman and Louis F. Polk, Jr. (backed respectively by the Canadian company Seagrams and Time, Inc.) filed suit against Kerkorian, contending that this maneuver was an antitrust violation, since Transamerica had acquired United Artists in 1967.[6] A federal district court agreed, and Kerkorian was temporarily blocked from buying into MGM, but was subsequently able to do so by borrowing from several European banks, including the Burstyn & Texas Commerce Bank, Ltd., of London, and Burkhardt & Company of Essen, W. Germany.[7] In November 1969, Kerkorian bought a 40 percent interest in MGM for $80 million through his solely owned Tracy (later Tracinda, both named for his daughter Tracy) Investment Company, headquartered in Las Vegas.[8] (Subsequent purchases brought Kerkorian's holdings up to 48.6 percent.) A year later, he needed $9 million to pay interest on the loans, but MGM reported operating losses of $35.4 and $8.2 million for 1969 and 1970, respectively, thanks in part to deficits produced by ZABRISKIE POINT (Michelangelo Antonioni, 1970—a $6-million loss) and the 70mm RYAN'S DAUGHTER (David Lean, 1970—returning $13 million against a $14-million cost).[9] Kerkorian amortized his debt by having Aubrey liquidate $62 million in company assets over the next four years, including its Culver City backlots, its Boreham Wood studio in London (MGM British), MGM Records, and fifty years worth of costumes and props.[10] At the same time, Kerkorian plowed money into the 2,000-room, $110 million MGM Grand Hotel in Las Vegas, prompting *Forbes* magazine to write in its issue for October 1973: "From now on the company that brought you BEN-HUR and THE WIZARD OF OZ will bring you crap—and roulette, slot machines, and all the other pleasures of a Las Vegas casino hotel."[11] Aubrey was himself replaced by Frank E. Rosenfelt in November 1973, but during his four-year reign he had moved MGM headquarters from New York to Culver City, aborted a large number of projects in development, cut the studio work force from 6,200 to 1,200, closed two-thirds of MGM's thirty-two domestic sales offices, and generally made the company solvent by gutting it.[12] Aubrey also intervened regularly in studio creative affairs, insulting directors (including Blake Edwards, Sam Peckinpah, and Jack Smight), re-editing films himself (most notoriously Ken Russell's THE BOY FRIEND [1971] and Peckinpah's PAT GARRETT & BILLY THE KID [1973]), and initiating medium-budget projects like SOYLENT GREEN (Richard Fleischer, 1973) and THE MAN WHO LOVED CAT DANCING (Richard C. Sarafian, 1973), both genre-based mediocrities that cost around $1.2 million to produce and returned $3.6 million in rentals.[13] As Vincent Canby wrote in the *New York Times* for October 30, 1973: "The Kerkorian-Aubrey management of MGM was the realization of everyone's worst fears of what would happen to Hollywood when the money-men take over."[14] In 1973, MGM liquidated its international distribution organization, sold its overseas theaters, and announced that its domestic releases would be distributed through United Artists, to which it had also sold the North American theatrical and television syndication rights to its 1,400-title film library for a period of ten years.[15] (The United Artists deal involved a total of $15 million in cash and included acquisition of MGM's music publishing company Robbins-Feist & Miller and a 50-percent interest in Quality Records of Canada.)[16] Foreign distribution rights for MGM product went to Cinema International Corporation (CIC), a joint venture of

MCA and Paramount, for $17 million.[17] In 1974, what was left of MGM marked the fiftieth anniversary of the studio's opening in April 1924 by releasing THAT'S ENTERTAINMENT! (Jack Haley, Jr., 1974), a feature-length anthology of musical highlights from about a hundred of its films, 1929–1958, that seemed to many observers more of an obituary than a celebration. Yet its new president Frank E. Rosenfelt, whose job was to restore corporate credibility in the wake of Aubrey's depredations, made this commitment to continued, if limited, production: "One of our principal objectives will be to provide a climate at MGM which will attract creative filmmakers . . . Contrary to recent public speculation, the roar of Leo the Lion will not be reduced to a meow."[18] For the remainder of the 1970s, MGM would operate like a small independent production company, releasing four to five films per year with budgets of between $3 and $5 million, until it began to increase its investment in new production in 1979 and ultimately merged with United Artists to form MGM/United Artists Entertainment Company in 1981.[19]

Aubrey had been typical of the new breed of businessmen brought to Hollywood in 1969–1970 to take over management of the studios for their new corporate owners. Well-educated (Princeton 1941), pragmatic, and dedicated to the bottom line, he sought to minimize risk by limiting production to sixteen to twenty features per year, keeping budgets under $2 million, and stepping up pre-production planning. His logic was simple: "If a movie costs $2 million, you get your costs back," he told *Business Week* in June 1973, "[but if] it costs $17 million, you can lose a lot if it is not a worldwide hit."[20] And it was dictated by a new lending practice born of the recession: Formerly, banks and other lending institutions had negotiated revolving credit agreements with the studios, leaving the companies free to allocate the funds themselves, but in 1971 banks began to extend loans on a picture-by-picture basis, with the films themselves as collateral; MGM was among the first to receive this treatment, which placed a new premium on careful preparation and prompt release to amortize the debt.[21] In fact, Aubrey tried to run feature production at MGM the same way he had run television production at CBS, where the product was cost-efficient entertainment, and like many of his peers he tended to blame the industry's financial crisis on creative self-indulgence and its recent appeal to counterculture values. "We've gone through the editorializing and social consciousness," he said in the *Business Week* interview, "and there has been a dropoff at the box office because of this introduction of social issues into films." True or not, the perception that the pursuit of social "relevance" had harmed the industry was widespread and contributed materially to the formation of the blockbuster mentality, although Aubrey himself had little instinct for "event" movies— for example, he assiduously overpromoted RYAN'S DAUGHTER (1970), which barely returned its $14-million cost, and vetoed the JAWS package in 1973 because he didn't like the story.[22] With his contempt for creativity (for which he was nicknamed "the smiling cobra"),[23] Aubrey epitomized the cost-cutting, anti-intellectual mentality that ruled the studios after the recession. Nonetheless, Daniel Melnick (b. 1934), who was MGM production chief from 1971 to 1977, was able to shepherd a handful of films through the studio that were simultaneously cost-effective, intelligent, and commercially successful. These included SLITHER (Howard Zieff, 1973), WESTWORLD (Michael Crichton, 1973), THAT'S ENTERTAINMENT! (1974), HEARTS OF THE WEST (Howard Zieff, 1975), THE SUNSHINE BOYS (Herbert Ross, 1975), THAT'S ENTERTAINMENT, PART 2 (Gene Kelly, 1976), NETWORK (Sidney Lumet, 1976), and THE GOODBYE GIRL (Herbert Ross, 1977) and constituting MGM's scant honor roll for the 1970s.

Melnick, who had begun his career as a producer with Talent Associates' STRAW DOGS (Sam Peckinpah, 1971), left MGM in 1977 to become production head at Columbia Pictures at the invitation of president Alan Hirschfield.

PARAMOUNT PICTURES (GULF & WESTERN INDUSTRIES)

Paramount was another studio that had relied on blockbusters to carry it through lean years in the 1950s—WHITE CHRISTMAS (Michael Curtiz, 1954; domestic rentals $12 million); THE TEN COMMANDMENTS (Cecil B. DeMille, 1956; domestic rentals $43 million)—all filmed in its proprietary widescreen VistaVision process, and in 1958 it was able to announce its largest annual profit since 1949 ($12.5 million). Yet despite an occasional hit (PSYCHO [Alfred Hitchcock, 1960; domestic rentals $11.2 million]), profits declined to very low levels in the early 1960s, culminating in the 1964 disaster of THE FALL OF THE ROMAN EMPIRE (Anthony Mann, 1964), a $20-million flop that virtually ruined producer Samuel Bronston and brought an end to the reign of Barney Balaban, who had served as Paramount's president since 1936. Joel W. Finler points out that, accounting for inflation, the losses of Bronston's epic nearly equaled those of HEAVEN'S GATE (Michael Cimino, 1980) sixteen years later.[24] There were also similar results—namely a management shakeup followed by a corporate buyout. In Paramount's case, the leadership of George Weltner, Balaban's executive vice president for operations, was challenged by dissident members of the board. Led by Broadway producers Ernest Martin and Cy Feuer, this group was preparing for a proxy battle when Gulf & Western Industries, a financial, mining, and manufacturing conglomerate founded in 1957 by Charles Bluhdorn, made a quickly accepted tender offer of $83 a share and bought the studio in October 1966.[25] Bluhdorn installed himself as studio president and reconfigured Gulf & Western to include a Leisure Time Division that contained Paramount, Simon & Schuster Publishers, Madison Square Garden, a Canadian theater chain, and several other holdings that in any given year generated between 11 and 15 percent of the conglomerate's revenues. (During the 1980s, however, Gulf & Western—renamed Paramount Communications, Inc., in 1990—would spin off over fifty of its nonmedia companies one by one in order to concentrate exclusively on its media holdings, which included by that time broadcast stations, cable systems, and theaters.)[26] Under Bluhdorn's leadership, Paramount diversified into television, acquiring Desilu Productions for $17 million in 1967 and supplying its pre-1950 films to television through MCA (as part of a deal negotiated ten years earlier). Bluhdorn also promoted the thirty-six year-old Robert Evans (b. 1930) from vice president in charge of production (which he had been since 1966) to executive vice president, in which capacity he nurtured such 1970s blockbusters as LOVE STORY (Arthur Hiller, 1970) and THE GODFATHER (Francis Ford Coppola, 1972), and such critical hits as SERPICO (Sidney Lumet, 1973), THE GODFATHER, PART II (Francis Ford Coppola, 1974), and CHINATOWN (Roman Polanski, 1974).[27] Bluhdorn resigned the presidency in 1969 to become chairman of the board, and in 1970 he negotiated an historic deal with Lew Wasserman of MCA to form a joint distributorship for Paramount and Universal product abroad that effectively circumvented U.S. antitrust laws. This entity, the Cinema International Corporation (CIC), came to control about a third of Hollywood's overseas market, and when joined by MGM/United Artists in 1981 (when its name became United International Pictures), it was able dominate some European markets by as much as 85 percent.[28]

After Bluhdorn, Paramount's top management experienced numerous reshufflings. Successive presidents through 1977 included Stanley Jaffe, Frank Yablans, David Picker, and Michael Eisner; Robert Evans, who became an independent producer under contract to Paramount in a lucrative deal in 1974 (which allowed him to take profit points in his projects as well as draw salary), was replaced as production chief in 1976 by David Picker, who was replaced by Don Simpson in 1978, who was replaced by Jeffrey Katzenberg in 1982.[29] In a surprise move, Bluhdorn replaced himself as board chairman in late 1974 with the 32-year-old Barry Diller (b. 1942), formerly vice president for programming at ABC-TV where he had originated the network movie-of-the-week concept during the 1960s.[30] Diller served until 1984, a remarkably long tenure for the times, when he left to become chairman and CEO of 20th Century–Fox. At Paramount, Diller increased the studio's role in production finance and geared its marketing and distribution strategy toward wide release—a practice, for example, that enabled him to save the $24-million KING KONG (John Guillermin, 1976) from disaster when it opened at 971 theaters and earned $35.8 million before bad word-of-mouth could kill it.[31] Despite its participation in the game of corporate musical chairs that was being played all over Hollywood (commonly known as "the Hollywood shuffle"), Paramount experienced relative prosperity and stability during the 1970s, recovering from its recession-era disasters (PAINT YOUR WAGON [Joshua Logan, 1969]; DARLING LILI [Blake Edwards, 1970]; THE MOLLY MAGUIRES [Martin Ritt, 1970], which lost $34.1 million collectively) via the windfall profits from LOVE STORY (1970—$48.7 million in domestic rentals) and THE GODFATHER (1972—$86.3 million in rentals), and experiencing a second boom in 1977–1978 with SATURDAY NIGHT FEVER (John Badham, 1977—$74.1 million in rentals), GREASE (Randal Kleiser, 1978—$96.3 million in rentals), and HEAVEN CAN WAIT (Warren Beatty and Buck Henry, 1978—$49.4 in rentals). This second blockbuster bonanza lifted Paramount's operating income to an unprecedented $80 million in 1978 and $116 million in 1979 and gave it the decade's highest theatrical rental market share (15 percent) among the seven majors.[32] Late in the decade, Paramount also began to benefit from synergy between its television and motion picture divisions as popular Paramount TV series were adapted as successful films (STAR TREK [Robert Wise, 1979]) and vice versa. Conglomeration was clearly advantageous for Paramount in the long run, but the effects of becoming a small cog in a large and highly diversified machine—in 1977, Gulf & Western ranked 59th among *Fortune's* top 500 American industrial firms (the same year in which it came under widespread government scrutiny for conflict-of-interest in its financial reporting practices)[33]—hastened its reconceptualization of product and intensified its transition from producer-distributor to distributor-financier. As one of twelve Gulf & Western divisions during the 1970s, none of which had much in common with the others, the studio institutionalized the agent-packaged blockbuster as the industry's Holy Grail, so that Robert Evans could tell *Time* magazine in 1974, "[T]he making of a blockbuster is the newest art form of the twentieth century."[34] Or as Frank Yablans, Paramount president from 1971 to 1975, had put it more bluntly the year before, when profits had soared to $37.7 on the wings of THE GODFATHER: "We want one big picture a year. The rest are budgeted to minimize risk."[35] (Examples of such lower-budgeted productions were the films of The Directors Company—Peter Bogdanovich's PAPER MOON [1973] and DAISY MILLER [1974] and Francis Ford Coppola's THE CONVERSATION [1974]; The Directors Company was a creatively autonomous "prestige" unit of Paramount bankrolled by Yablans, 1973–1974, and dissolved in 1975 when it became unprofitable.)[36]

WARNER BROS. (WARNER COMMUNICATION, INC.)

Like Paramount, Warner Bros. benefited from conglomeration, although in its case the parent company did not intervene directly in the film business. By and large, Warners had not followed a blockbuster policy during the 1950s but advanced large sums to the producers of independent features ($38 million between 1954 and 1956 alone), creating cash flow problems for itself at mid-decade.[37] These were temporarily concealed by the success of GIANT (George Stevens), whose $12 million in rentals accounted for 90 percent of the studio's $3.4 million profit in 1956,[38] but in 1958 Warners recorded its first deficit ($1,023,000) in thirty years. Profits surged to $9.4 million in 1959, however, on the box-office strength of BEN-HUR ($36.9 million in rentals). From that high point, profits declined at the rate of about $2 million per year, and the studio bottomed out with a deficit of $3.86 million in 1964. Profits were rising again in March 1967 (and would soon reach 1959 levels with the release that summer of BONNIE AND CLYDE [Arthur Penn]), when Warners merged with a Canadian distributor of films to television called Seven Arts Productions and became Warner Bros.-Seven Arts. Two years later, as the recession began and income dropped to an all-time low, the company was taken over by Steven Ross's newly formed conglomerate Kinney National Services, Inc. (For 1969, Warners had an after-tax loss of $27 million, which Kinney absorbed in a one-time write-down to show a 1969 profit of only $300,000 in what was, in fact, its most successful year.)[39] Earlier in the 1960s, Ross had built his wife's family funeral business into a modest conglomerate that included rental car agencies and the Kinney parking lot systems, but he now resolved to create an entertainment empire with the studio (returned to its original name of Warner Bros.) as anchor. In 1967, Ross had acquired the Ashley Famous Agency, a talent agency headed by Ted Ashley, and he subsequently bought National Periodical Publications (publisher of sixty-three magazines and comics, including *Mad*, *Superman*, and *Batman*) and Panavision, Inc., the company founded by Robert Gottschalk in 1953 to manufacture lenses, cameras, and other filmmaking equipment—most notably the anamorphic lens system that would replace CinemaScope as the industry standard for widescreen cinematography. In 1971, Ross spun off his nonmedia subsidiaries into the National Kinney Corporation and pooled his media companies (which included the Warner-Elektra-Atlantic record company [WEA] via his studio purchase) into Warner Communications, Inc. (WCI), which by 1977 ranked 214th in the *Fortune* 500.[40]

Ted Ashley was installed as board chairman and CEO of Warner Bros. in 1969 with the mission of turning the company around, and he became the first of many former agents who rose to power as studio executives during the decade. (By 1977, in fact, six of the seven major distributors would be run by former agents.)[41] Armed with a $65 million revolving production fund from Kinney, Ashley was determined to control costs, and of the sixty-nine films Warners released between 1970 and 1973, only one went significantly over budget, and that was THE EXORCIST (William Friedkin, 1973), which became the most profitable film in its history when it returned $89.3 in domestic rentals.[42] By 1972, Ashley's leadership had increased film rentals to theaters and television by 56 percent (from $124.3 to $193.3 million) and profits by 42 percent (from $11.1 to $15.8 million).[43] In 1973—sounding remarkably like MGM's James Aubrey—Ashley explained his management philosophy to *Business Week* this way: "First you must set your budget in relation to how well the proposed picture can be expected to do in its three principal markets—domestic theaters, foreign theaters, and broadcast TV, . . . [and then] you must decide if the creative persons available can execute the picture to make a profit."[44] Ashley sought to develop foreign markets for low-budget films and to increase the studio's production of telefilms at Warner Bros. Television. He also formed a new company with Columbia Pictures to jointly operate twenty-three soundstages in Burbank, California (Burbank Studios, Inc.), but Ashley's greatest success was in delivering a string of top-grossing domestic features from WOODSTOCK (Michael Wadleigh, 1970) through SUPERMAN (Richard Donner, 1978) that led Warner Bros. to a 14.5-percent market share for 1970–1979.[45]

Warners also produced a significant number of critically prestigious films during the 1970s, many of them under the stewardship of executive vice president for production John Calley (b. 1930). It was Calley, for example, who brought Stanley Kubrick to the studio in 1970 under a three-film deal that yielded A CLOCKWORK ORANGE (1971), BARRY LYNDON (1975), and THE SHINING (1980); Calley also worked closely with Federico Fellini on the production of AMARCORD (1974), and he backed Alan Pakula's "paranoid trilogy," consisting of KLUTE (1971), THE PARALLAX VIEW (1974), and ALL THE PRESIDENT'S MEN (1976), when commercial prospects for the films seemed dim (but was vindicated when the latter became the fourth-highest earner of the year, returning $31 million in rentals). On Calley's authority, Warners developed a unique relationship with Kubrick through its London office whereby the studio funded the purchase and development of projects for which Kubrick would receive 40-percent profit participation and the guarantee of the final cut.[46] (Calley left Warner's in 1980 and went into semi-retirement, emerging in 1993 to run MGM's United Artists Pictures unit; in 1996 he was recruited as chairman of Sony Pictures Entertainment, Inc., to replace Peter Guber.) Less generously, Warners also provided the seed money for Francis Ford Coppola's American Zoetrope studio in San Francisco, putting up $600,000 in exchange for the right of first refusal to its projects; the only result of this deal was George Lucas's THX-1138, personally despised by Ashley but distributed (recut) by Warners in 1971 anyway. Finally, in November 1973, Warner Bros. closed a deal to take over the film library and releasing commitments of National General Pictures (NGP), which had formerly distributed the films made by Cinema Center Films (the feature production subsidiary of CBS-TV, disbanded in 1972) and First Artists Productions (FAP).[47] The latter, modeled on the original star-owned United Artists, which was founded in 1919, was put together by Creative Management Associates (CMA) in 1969 to produce the personal projects of Barbra Streisand, Paul Newman, and Sidney Poitier, with Steve McQueen and Dustin Hoffman joining later. Although First Artists made only a handful of successful films (Sam Peckinpah's THE GETAWAY [1972] among them) and eventually disbanded, Warner Bros. president Frank Wells hailed the deal as "the single most significant development in terms of acquiring motion picture product for distribution in the history of our company." It represented a new industry trend to establish releasing ties with prestigious independent units, much as Paramount had done in 1973 with The Directors Company (see above).[48] (This trend continued through the end of the decade: In August 1978 WCI entered into a joint venture with five former United Artists executives to form the financing and distributing company that became Orion Pictures [see below]; and in July 1979 WCI agreed to arrange the financing for the productions of The Ladd Company, newly founded by three former Fox executives [see below].)[49]

Meanwhile, parent company WCI, which in 1972 had earned as much as 65 percent of its pretax profits from its music division, was booming through diversification in several directions.[50] By the decade's end, the Warner conglomerate had expanded into publishing (Warner Books), cable television (Warner Amex Cable; including MTV, which briefly became a marketing arm for its music division), video (Warner Home Video), and video games (Atari) in ways that made the synergistic marketing of franchises like SUPERMAN a winning strategy for decades to come.[51] Starting with the 1970 experience of WOODSTOCK, whose best-selling Atlantic Records sound-track album helped to sell the movie and vice versa, WCI had learned the value of integrated cross-marketing to keep the rewards of ancillary sales within the organization. Thus in 1978 SUPERMAN, the movie, was used to create demand for a sound-track album produced by Warner Bros. Records, eight Superman "nonbooks" published by Warner Books, an Atari video game, and over one hundred other Superman products licensed through Warners Licensing Company of America to DC Comics, a company owned by WCI; and these products in turn generated demand for the film(s) in theaters and, subsequently, on Warner Home Video cassettes and Warner cable outlets. As Robert Gustafson wrote in his analysis of the company in 1982: "WCI has become a conglomerate which is organized according to the principle of multiple profit centers which reinforce each other in an interlocking and financially conservative pattern. . . . All subsidiaries within WCI are structured so that an increase in one area can aid another."[52] More than any other player, WCI ended the 1970s positioned for the integration of new media technologies with its filmed entertainment and music divisions; in 1982 it began to restructure its operations around distribution, and its 1989 merger with Time, Inc. to become Time-Warner made it (for several years, at least) the biggest, most powerful entertainment media conglomerate in the world.[53]

20TH CENTURY–FOX

Twentieth Century–Fox was the only former major to avoid conglomeration during the 1960s, although it experienced the most radical boom-and-bust cycle of any studio in postwar Hollywood. During the 1950s, its fortunes were tied to the success of its CinemaScope proprietary anamorphic widescreen process. Starting with the first CinemaScope production in 1953, THE ROBE (Henry Koster; $17.5 million in rentals), Fox rode through the decade on average profits of about $7 million per year. But mismanagement after the departure of Darryl F. Zanuck (b. 1902) in 1956—he had been production chief since the studio's creation in 1935—placed the studio in jeopardy by 1960. In that year Fox reported a small loss, which was, in fact, an enormous deficit concealed by the $43-million sale of 260 acres of back lot eventually developed as the Century City office complex. The company's serious instability was revealed in the form of losses for 1961 and 1962 of $22.5 million and $39.8 million, respectively, much of it cost-overruns from CLEOPATRA (Joseph L. Mankiewicz, 1963), whose troubled production would result in the most expensive motion picture ($44 million; adjusted for inflation about $160 million) made before the megabudgets of 1990s. Called back as president in 1962, with his son Richard (b. 1934) as production chief, Zanuck was able to see CLEOPATRA through release in 1963, when it earned a spare $26 million in rentals, but he also backed a number of winning productions, including THE SOUND OF MUSIC (Robert Wise, 1965), whose spectacular $80 million in rentals revived Fox temporarily and inspired the cycle of extravagant musicals (DOCTOR DOLITTLE [Richard Fleischer, 1967]; STAR! [Robert Wise, 1968]; HELLO, DOLLY! [Gene Kelly, 1969]; PAINT YOUR WAGON [1969]) that two years later nearly destroyed it.[54] In 1969–1970, in spite of hits like BUTCH CASSIDY AND THE SUNDANCE KID (George Roy Hill, 1969; $46 million in rentals) and M°A°S°H (Robert Altman, 1970; $36.7 million in rentals), the company posted losses of $103 million and was in default on bank loans, causing its stock to hit a new annual low on the New York Exchange.[55] At this point, Darryl Zanuck became CEO and chairman of the board and passed the presidency to his son Richard, who attempted to reorganize and diversify the company in ways that his father disliked[56] (one of which included canceling the contract of Darryl's nineteen-year-old girlfriend, the "actress" Genevieve Gilles).[57] The conflict between father and son escalated to open warfare, resulting in a proxy fight among stockholders, and in an effort to protect the company against lawsuits Fox's board requested the resignation of both Zanucks. Darryl resigned in May 1971, retaining the title of chairman emeritus; Richard stayed on as executive vice president for another year before leaving to form his own production company with David Brown. (Releasing through Universal, Zanuck-Brown would produce the paradigmatic 1970s blockbusters THE STING [George Roy Hill, 1973] and JAWS [Steven Spielberg, 1975].) A new Fox management team was brought in during 1971, headed by Dennis Stanfill (b. 1927), as chairman of the board, and Gordon Stulberg (b. 1923) as president.

Because it had not been merged with a diversified conglomerate like WCI or Gulf & Western, Fox continued to depend for most of its income on film production-distribution, which made it especially vulnerable to the deep industry recession of 1969–1971, and the new management clearly understood this. Stanfill, a former Rhodes scholar in economics who had served as a corporate finance specialist at Lehman Brothers and vice president for finance at the Times Mirror company, immediately closed the Fox New York headquarters, cut studio overhead, and sold off its 2,600-acre Malibu ranch.[58] By 1974, Stanfill had liquidated $125 million worth of bank debt, secured a $44 million line of new credit, and turned the company around so that it could report net earnings of $10.9 million.[59] Stulberg, a former Columbia executive who had headed CBS Cinema Center Films since 1967, ended the big-budget road show era at Fox and concentrated on films made for between $1.5 and $3 million to capture rentals in the $5 to $10 million range (e.g., THE MEPHISTO WALTZ [Paul Wendkos, 1971]; LITTLE MURDERS [Alan Arkin, 1971]; THE CULPEPPER CATTLE COMPANY [Dick Richards, 1972]; BATTLE FOR THE PLANET OF THE APES [J. Lee Thompson, 1973]).[60] *Variety* reported in early 1971 that of eleven newly completed Fox features, not one had cost over $2 million,[61] and in June 1972, Stulberg negotiated a deal with exploitation producer James H. Nicholson, formerly of AIP, to distribute six low-budget films from his newly formed Academy Pictures Corp. (including DIRTY MARY CRAZY LARRY [John Hough, 1973] and HELL HOUSE [1973]).[62] This policy, combined with a few runaway hits (THE FRENCH CONNECTION [William Friedkin, 1971]; THE POSEIDON ADVENTURE [Ronald Neame, 1972]) enabled the Stanfill-Stulberg regime to restore Fox to profitability by 1974, when its blockbuster disaster film THE TOWERING INFERNO (John Guillermin, 1974), coproduced with Warners to cut costs, earned nearly $100 million in worldwide rentals.

Stulberg returned to private law practice in 1975, and the following year Alan Ladd, Jr. (b. 1937), was promoted from senior vice president for production to president. Simultaneously, Fox began to diversify, creating a new entertainment group comprised of 20th Century Records, 20th Century Music Corporation, 20th Century Television Productions, and three television stations.[63] The Fox creative personnel, who had suffered under the cost-accounting mentality of Stanfill-Stulberg, were encouraged when Ladd began to develop projects with directors like Mel Brooks (SILENT MOVIE [1976];

HIGH ANXIETY [1977]), Paul Mazursky (AN UNMARRIED WOMAN [1978]), Fred Zinnemann (JULIA [1977]), and Herbert Ross (THE TURNING POINT [1977]). But Ladd's greatest coup was in optioning George Lucas's STAR WARS (1977), justifying its $11.5-million production cost to Stanfill (who didn't believe in "event pictures," linking them—understandably—with what he called "the SOUND OF MUSIC-HELLO, DOLLY! syndrome")[64] on the grounds that it might earn as much as $30 million. When STAR WARS unexpectedly became the decade's ultimate blockbuster, grossing $100 million after only three months of release, it sent Fox's stock soaring from $6 to $25 per share and generated studio revenues at the rate of $1.2 million per day. Although it had just purchased Coca Cola Bottling Midwest, Fox's suddenly swollen cash flow enabled it to buy the Aspen Skiing and Pebble Beach golf corporations that year and still declare excess profits.[65] As Stanfill would later remark, STAR WARS gave the corporation "five years' growth in one," and the income from its re-releases, merchandising tie-ins, and sequels would continue to enrich the studio quite literally for decades to come.[66]

Fox was now an attractive target for conglomerate acquisition, and in 1979 the company fended off a hostile take-over bid from Chris-Craft Industries. That same year it acquired Magnetic Video and became the first studio to release recent features on pre-recorded cassette.[67] Also in 1979, Ladd, whose reputation for commercial and critical success was now huge, left Fox to form his own production unit called The Ladd Company.[68] (With Warner Bros. financing, The Ladd Company had a remarkable debut when it acquired the American rights to the British production CHARIOTS OF FIRE [Hugh Hudson, 1981], which subsequently earned $30 million in rentals and won numerous Academy Awards; other ventures were less successful and the company went out of business in 1984, with Ladd moving on to become president and CEO of MGM/United Artists.)[69] Ladd was briefly replaced by Sandy Lieberson (b. 1936), who joined The Ladd Company himself in 1980 and was replaced by Sherry Lansing (b. 1944), a former actress who became the first female head of production in Hollywood history and the fifth Fox production chief since 1970.[70] After much executive reshuffling, Alan Hirschfield (b. 1935), who had been president and CEO of Columbia Pictures Industries since 1973, was brought in by Stanfill to become vice chairman and CEO of Fox at the end of 1979. Chris-Craft continued to press its suit, but the company finally lost its independence to Texas oil millionaire Marvin H. Davis (b. 1925), who bought 20th Century–Fox in 1981 for $722 million (calculated at the rate of $60 per share).[71] At this point Stanfill resigned and Hirschfield became board chairman until he was replaced by Barry Diller in late 1984, shortly after which Davis sold the company to Australian publishing magnate Rupert Murdoch. Whatever the 1970s reign of Dennis Stanfill had meant to Fox's production artists and their films, Fox's stockholders were bound to be grateful: between the time he took over on September 16, 1971, and the Davis purchase on June 8, 1981, the value of their stock had increased by 709 percent,[72] and Fox had moved from the status of a nearly bankrupt production company to that of a thriving media conglomerate poised to achieve global reach.

UNIVERSAL PICTURES (MCA)

In late 1951, Decca Records bought a controlling interest in Universal Pictures (then Universal-International, following a 1946 merger) and took over management the following year in an early but unsuccessful bid to create synergy between the film and music industries.[73] The former minor survived the 1950s by becoming actively involved in television production, but in 1958 showed a $2-million loss, prompting Decca to sell its Universal City studio lot to Revue Productions, the television subsidiary of MCA. This company, founded as Music Corporation of America by Dr. Jules Stein in 1924, was then the nation's largest talent agency. It had expanded aggressively into teleproduction during the 1950s and became so successful that it was able to absorb both Universal Pictures *and* Decca Records by 1962. The Justice Department opposed this integration of agency with production; MCA was forced by a federal consent decree to sell its agency business, MCA Artists, and it reorganized itself as a major entertainment conglomerate with MCA president Lew Wasserman (b. 1913) at its head. Wasserman, the first of many successful agents to run a modern Hollywood studio, upgraded studio facilities and instituted the lucrative attraction known as the Universal City Tour in 1964 (an idea that had originated with studio founder Carl Laemmle in 1916),[74] but he was unable to make film production continuously profitable until the early 1970s. (An exception was the work of Alfred Hitchcock, who finished his career at Universal after shooting Psycho [1960] there, and whose films from THE BIRDS [1963] through FAMILY PLOT [1976] were consistently profitable.) As Hollywood entered the recession in the third quarter of 1969, MCA posted a net loss of $7.7 million and its stock dropped from $44.50 a share to a low of $22.50, making it a prime target for takeover. Both Westinghouse and Firestone Tire and Rubber made bids for the company, but the Antitrust Division of the Justice Department forbade the former and Wasserman rejected the latter.

Things began to turn around for Universal when Wasserman appointed Ned Tanen head of production in 1970. Another former agent, Tanen initially concentrated on films for the counterculture-youth market—DIARY OF A MAD HOUSEWIFE (Frank Perry, 1970), TAKING OFF (Milos Forman, 1971), THE LAST MOVIE (Dennis Hopper, 1971), SILENT RUNNING (Douglas Trumbull, 1971), TWO-LANE BLACKTOP (Monte Hellman, 1971), ULZANA'S RAID (Robert Aldrich, 1972)—made for about one million dollars. These films were overshadowed by the success of the $10-million proto-blockbuster AIRPORT (George Seaton, 1970), produced for Universal by Ross Hunter, which returned $45.2 million in rentals and enabled MCA to refinance $134 million in bank debt around a six-year revolving line of credit—the largest loan of its type ever negotiated by a film company (the lending group was headed by Bank of America and included First National Bank of Chicago and Marine Midland Bank).[75] By 1972, Universal's profits were up by 32 percent over the previous year (from $15,088,000 to $19,932,000), thanks in part to the new federal investment tax credit, which allowed a 7-percent production investment deduction from overall corporate tax, up to a 50-percent limit (but with carry-forward provisions).[76] But Tanen was vindicated when his pet project AMERICAN GRAFFITI (George Lucas, 1973), produced for $743,000, returned $55.1 million to become the sleeper of the decade. In that year, a management shakeup at MCA indicated new directions for the future: Milton Rackmil, former Decca president and president of Universal since 1952, was succeeded by Henry H. Martin, head of distribution; and Jules Stein retired, handing the MCA chairmanship over to Wasserman, who was succeeded as MCA president by Sidney J. Sheinberg (b. 1935), the former president of Universal-Television. In 1974, Universal boarded the "event movie" bandwagon by introducing the new sonic presentation technique known as Sensurround in its blockbuster disaster film EARTHQUAKE (Mark Robson), which returned $35.9 million in rentals to become the year's third-highest earner. At the same time, Tanen helped to develop two independent productions of the new Richard Zanuck-David Brown team recently defected from Fox—THE STING (1973; $78.2 million in rentals) and JAWS

(1975; $129.5 million in rentals)—which quickly made Universal the most profitable studio in Hollywood. In fact, Universal made industry history when JAWS broke both worldwide and domestic box-office records, and 1975 became the biggest single year in the history of the film business.[77] The association with JAWS director Steven Spielberg, begun with THE SUGARLAND EXPRESS in 1974, would stand Universal in good stead through E.T.: THE EXTRATERRESTRIAL (1982) and help to land Tanen the presidency of Universal Theatrical Motion Pictures, Inc., in 1976. (From 1976 to 1979, MCA restructured Universal internally so that Tanen's unit was the production component and "Universal Pictures," headed by former studio president Henry Martin, was the distribution component.)[78]

In 1976, MCA was once again threatened with takeover, this time by Edgar Bronfman's Montreal-based Seagrams Company, which would eventually succeed in buying it in 1995. (Bronfman had bought control of MGM in 1968, but sold out to Kerkorian a year later.)[79] Wasserman was able to prevent the raid because MCA had filed an amendment to its certificate of incorporation with the SEC the year before requiring 75-percent shareholder approval for acceptance of an outside bid, and Stein and Wasserman between them owned 28 percent of MCA's voting stock.[80] Some sense of the relationship between Universal and its parent during the decade can be gauged by net income figures for 1978. Studio net income for that year reached an all-time high of $318.7 million, but that was still less than half of the total for MCA's filmed entertainment division (which also included Universal Television and MCA-TV with $348.2 million and the Universal Tour with $38.7 million), and less than one-third of MCA's entire corporate income of $1.1 billion. (The other main components were music publishing with $131.5 million and mail order-retail with $167.5 million.)[81] Clearly, MCA was still the "octopus" that it had been called some thirty years before in an article in the *Saturday Evening Post*, but a considerably more formidable one which the Antitrust Division of the Justice Department regarded as a perennial threat to competition within in the entertainment industry.[82]

During Ned Tanen's tenure as production chief, Universal's operating income had increased from an average of under $20 million a year between 1971 and 1973, to $68 million in 1974 (when profits from THE STING were posted), to $110 million between 1975 and 1977.[83] At the same time, the studio was releasing fewer films than ever before, hitting an all-time low with eleven in 1976—part of a deliberate strategy by the majors to create a "product shortage" and foreground their blockbusters. As Tanen told *Fortune* magazine that year: "You need to make a minimum number of films a year . . . [so that] the downside risk is fairly minimal."[84] But it was two modestly budgeted films that sustained Universal's winning streak through 1978—SMOKEY AND THE BANDIT (Hal Needham, 1977), made for $4 million and returning $59 million; and NATIONAL LAMPOON'S ANIMAL HOUSE (John Landis, 1978), made for $2.4 million and returning $70.9 million—demonstrating the volatility of the newly forming late 1970s audience, 57 percent of which was now composed of 12–24-year-olds).[85] In 1979, operating income peaked at $175 million and then declined in 1980 and 1981;[86] Tanen was replaced in 1982 by Robert Rehme, the head of distribution who was widely held responsible for the historic success of Steven Spielberg's E.T.: THE EXTRA-TERRESTRIAL (1982), whose $228.2 million in domestic rentals meant that Universal had broken the record for the highest-earning film of all time twice in seven years.

Two of MCA's less successful ventures of the 1970s involved home video and cable. In December 1972, Wasserman announced that MCA would soon market a system for home playback of its movies on videodisc, with hardware to be manufactured by the Dutch electronics firm N. V. Phillips.[87] MCA had been exploring this billion-dollar potential market since 1965, as had many other companies. Shortly thereafter, RCA announced its videodisc system, SelectaVision, which would compete head-to-head with MCA's, and the Sony Corporation revealed that it was developing a videotape cassette system (VCR) that would compete with them both as playback units but also have the capacity to record audio-visual images. When Sony unveiled the Betamax in late 1976, MCA and Walt Disney Productions sued the Japanese company on behalf of the Hollywood majors for copyright infringement; but MCA was also intent on buying time for the breakout of Disco-Vision which was currently experiencing problems of software manufacture and computability.[88] As it became increasingly clear that Sony was going to win the case, MCA debuted Disco-Vision in September 1979. By then it was too late: The competition from VCR technology was fierce, and though SelectaVision had failed, the Japanese Victor Corporation (JVC) was marketing its own superior videodisc system. With nearly $100 million invested in the operation and only 35,000 players sold by 1982, MCA wrote off its biggest failure by selling Disco-Vision to Pioneer Electronics of Japan who would subsequently market it as "laserdisc" technology to about three million upscale consumers rather than the mass market envisioned by MCA. (The Disco-Vision sell-off in some sense prefigured Wasserman's sale of MCA to the Japanese electronics manufacturer Matsushita for $6.6 billion in 1990.)[89] If Disco-Vision was MCA's 1970s corporate nightmare, the Premiere Network offered the punctuation of a very bad dream. Conceived by Hollywood as a counterpunch to the encroachment of both home video and cable, Premiere was a joint venture of MCA, the Getty Oil Company, Columbia Pictures, Paramount Pictures, and 20th Century–Fox to form a satellite-delivered pay-cable network for their movies, with Getty providing the satellite circuits through its 85-percent ownership of ESPN.[90] Before Premiere's service even began, however, the Justice Department charged the studios with forming an illegal cartel by conspiring to fix prices and impose an embargo on their product, which accounted for about 60 percent of all American filmed entertainment. Although Justice successfully argued that Premiere constituted a "horizontal monopoly in constraint of trade," it allowed MCA to acquire a one-third interest in USA Network the following year (which grew, in 1984, to become a 50 percent share), giving Universal the foothold in cable that it needed to stay competitive in the coming decades.[91]

COLUMBIA PICTURES INDUSTRIES (CPI)

Columbia Pictures navigated through the 1950s on the strength of Screen Gems, its highly profitable television production subsidiary founded in 1952. Columbia was the first major studio to enter this field and, although it soon had to compete with MCA's Revue Productions, was able to briefly dominate it, acquiring several television licenses in the process. When studio founder Harry Cohn died in 1958, however, the company was thrown into crisis and simultaneously recorded its first-ever loss (for fiscal year 1957–1958). Management passed into the hands of Cohn insiders Abe Schneider (president, 1958–1963) and Leo Jaffe (president, 1963–1967), but with the notable exceptions of Sam Spiegel's British-produced David Lean epics THE BRIDGE ON THE RIVER KWAI (1957) and LAWRENCE OF ARABIA (1962), Columbia's film generated only enough income to keep the studio alive until 1966. Late that year, ABC-TV paid Columbia a record $2 million for two showings of THE BRIDGE ON THE RIVER KWAI, and a recovery began, catalyzed by a series of British-made hits, including A MAN FOR ALL SEASONS (Fred Zinnemann, 1966), TO SIR, WITH LOVE (James Clavell, 1967), and GEORGY GIRL (Silvio Narizzano, 1966), and culminating in two popular big-budget musicals—OLIVER! (Carol Reed, 1968), which earned $16.8 million, and FUNNY GIRL (William Wyler, 1968), which earned $27.3 million. The latter was produced by Ray Stark (b. 1914), who had produced the original Broadway hit and came to Columbia in 1967 to form his own production company. This unit, Rastar, would be responsible for some of the studio's most successful 1970s films, and Stark himself would play a major role in Columbia's later corporate life.

In mid-1966, Columbia had become the target of a hostile takeover bid by corporate raider Maurice Clairmont working in concert with the Banc de Paris et des Pays-Bas, which together attempted to buy a controlling share of the company's stock. The move was foiled by the FCC, which invoked a provision of the Communications Act of 1934 preventing aliens from owning more than one-fifth of any American company with broadcast holdings.[92] To protect itself from future takeover threats, Columbia merged with its Screen Gems subsidiary in September 1968 and took the new name Columbia Pictures Industries (CPI) to indicate that it had become an "integrated entertainment complex."[93] At that time, Columbia production head Mike Frankovich was succeeded by Abe Schneider's son Stanley, whose brother Bert would soon collaborate with Bob Rafelson to produce EASY RIDER (Dennis Hopper, 1969). (Under the new corporate structure, the head of production had the title of president of Columbia Pictures, which Stanley Schneider held from 1970–1973.) When the huge success of EASY RIDER (which returned earnings of $19.1 million against costs of $375,000) woke the industry abruptly to the fact that both the demographics and the tastes of its audience had changed, Stanley signed a deal with Bert Schneider's newly formed production company BBS to produce six low-budget films for the youth market in hopes of repeating the EASY RIDER windfall (so long as the budgets were under $1 million BBS could make what it pleased and Columbia would finance and distribute the final product—see Chapter 4).[94] In fact, Columbia's films of the early 1970s produced little but red ink, most notoriously its disastrous remake of LOST HORIZON (Charles Jarrott, 1973), which earned only $3.8 million against its $12-million negative cost. Despite such cost-cutting measures as combining with Warner Bros. to share the Burbank Studios in 1972 (and to generate income by renting its facilities to third-party producers), by the end of 1973, the company was nearly bankrupt. As Axel Madsen points out, the money Columbia lost in 1958–1959, 1961, and 1970–1972 alone added up to $87 million, the exact sum total of its profits since its founding in 1924.[95]

At this crucial point, Herbert Allen, Jr., of the Wall Street banking firm of Allen & Company, bought control of the company and brought in a new management team headed by Alan J. Hirschfield, a former Allen investment banker, as corporate president and CEO. (Abe Schneider was made honorary board chairman and Jaffe de facto chairman.) It was Ray Stark who alerted Allen to Columbia's potential, having been involved with Allen & Company in the formation of Warner Bros.-Seven Arts in 1967. (Stark had co-founded Seven Arts, with Eliot Hyman, in 1957.)[96] After experiencing three losing years in a row and piling up an estimated $127.5 million in debt, Columbia needed cash, and Hirschfield's first move was to mortgage its ten-station broadcast holdings in the form of warrants to a number of banks and insurance companies for $45 million.[97] This financially sophisticated maneuver enabled the company to raise money on the stations without really selling them (one, WVUE-TV, New Orleans, was eventually sold to

Gaylord Broadcasting for $13.5 million). Next, CPI's motion picture division, Columbia Pictures, needed to cut its expenses, and David Begelman (b. 1922) was hired as president to ring in new production economies.[98] Begelman was a Yale graduate, a powerful agent, and the co-founder of Creative Management Associates (CMA), and as Columbia's de facto production chief he quickly succeeded in putting the studio back on sound financial footing. (One of his first moves was to end the studio's ties with BBS.)[99] His solution was to minimize the role of producer, which his CMA ties clearly helped him to do; as he said on taking the helm, "I feel that in the past several years, Columbia has been a strongly producer-oriented company and I think there should be a short line between the people making the decisions at Columbia and the people who actually make the films—a shorter, leaner line."[100] Accordingly, producers were ordered to cut budgets by rewriting scripts and to accept reduced fees and profit points, and Begelman began to negotiate one-film deals with directors without middlemen (or at least with middlemen he knew how to manipulate from his agency days).[101]

Begelman's regime generated a number of hits—SHAMPOO (Hal Ashby, 1975), TOMMY (Ken Russell, 1975), FUNNY LADY (Herbert Ross, 1975), MURDER BY DEATH (Robert Moore, 1976), THE DEEP (Peter Yates, 1977), and, preeminently, CLOSE ENCOUNTERS OF THE THIRD KIND (Steven Spielberg, 1977), and by the beginning of 1976 he had more than doubled Columbia's film rental average over the past decade.[102] But Begelman himself resigned amid scandal in 1977, when he was compelled to plead *nolo contendere* to charges that he had misappropriated some $61,000 in company funds, as much as $40,000 of it by forging actors' residual checks (including one for $10,000 to Cliff Robertson, who blew the whistle). This incident, quickly popularized as the "Begelman affair," not only embarrassed the studio but created a crisis of confidence in the industry that became especially acute when Columbia's directors reinstated Begelman as Columbia Pictures president in December 1977, apparently on the basis of his financial track record. (The industry was not simply chagrined but also fearful of a Congressional investigation of its business practices.)[103] Outraged, CPI president Alan Hirschfield pressed for Begelman's resignation, which he received voluntarily in early 1978, and was then himself fired by Columbia's board, as he later told *Variety*, as a "direct consequence of the David Begelman affair."[104] Begelman then became president of MGM's film division (and president of United Artists after the MGM/United Artists merger of 1981), and Hirschfield became vice president (later president) and CEO at Fox. Hirschfield was replaced at CPI by Francis (Fay) Vincent, Jr., a former Securities and Exchange Commission official who would help to restore Columbia's ethically tarnished image.[105] Columbia production chief Daniel Melnick (b. 1934) briefly inherited Begelman's job before leaving to become an independent producer in March, 1979, when Frank Price became president of Columbia Pictures and kept the job through 1983.

During his five-year tenure as CPI president, Hirschfield had undertaken an aggressive program that combined divestiture with diversification, the high point of which was the 1976 sale of the Screen Gems music publishing division to Britain's EMI Ltd. and the simultaneous acquisition of D. Gottlieb & Company, the nation's largest pinball machine manufacture, for $50 million.[106] Although he had once described the availability of tax shelters as "the single most important occurrence in the recent history of the film industry," Hirschfield's strategy was to wean Columbia away from its dependence on tax-sheltered production finance, which had accounted for 54 percent of the funding for all of its 1975 films, before Congress outlawed the practice—as it would do in the

Tax Reform Act of 1976.[107] (In fact, Hirschfield told the *Wall Street Journal* in August 1975 that without tax shelters Columbia wouldn't have had a production program at all.)[108] Despite these efforts—which had resulted in a quadrupling of Columbia's net worth between 1973 and 1978—the company's financial health was still marginal enough that its $19.4-million investment in CLOSE ENCOUNTERS OF THE THIRD KIND was seen by many observers as a mortal threat, and its success briefly sent CPI's stock soaring on Wall Street.[109]

Yet Columbia was once again threatened by takeover in 1979, when Kirk Kerkorian attempted to gain control of it in order to merge it with MGM. Kerkorian had acquired 25.5 percent of CPI stock, valued at $76.4 million, in 1978, and attempted the following year to buy more.[110] To prevent this, Columbia annexed Ray Stark's Rastar Films, Inc., placing 300,000 shares of its stock in Stark's friendly hands. After several lawsuits, Kerkorian was forced to sell his interest back to Columbia, at a healthy profit of $60 million (or $13.50 a share), and Columbia was able to enter the 1980s intact.[111] (Kerkorian would realize his goal of a merged MGM by acquiring United Artists in 1981.) In addition to overseeing such late decade hits as KRAMER VS. KRAMER (Robert Benton, 1979; $60 million in rentals), THE ELECTRIC HORSEMAN (Sydney Pollack, 1979; $30.3 million in rentals), and THE BLUE LAGOON (Randal Kleiser, 1980; $28.8 million in rentals), Frank Price would soon guide the company into a home video partnership with the RCA Corporation (RCA/Columbia Home Video), CPI corporate development vice president Allen Adler having earlier negotiated an inventive licensing agreement with HBO that amortized 20 percent of the studio's production costs in exchange for exclusive pay-TV rights.[112] This lucrative deal led board chairman Herbert Allen to proclaim that "selling software is even better than the oil business,"[113] but it further enhanced Columbia's attractiveness for acquisition. In January 1982, Columbia's long independence ended when the Coca Cola Company bought CPI for $823 million in a friendly takeover, paying nearly twice the market value for Columbia's stock ($71 a share), and considerably enriching Allen & Company with its 495,800 shares.[114]

UNITED ARTISTS (TRANSAMERICA CORPORATION)

Because it owned neither studios nor theaters, United Artists had prospered in the wake of the consent decrees, distributing hits for producers such as Mike Todd (AROUND THE WORLD IN EIGHTY DAYS [Michael Anderson, 1956; $23 million in domestic rentals]) and the Mirisch Corporation (WEST SIDE STORY [Robert Wise, 1961; $19.6 million]); Woodfall Films (TOM JONES [Tony Richardson, 1963; $17 million]); Harry Saltzman-Albert R. Broccoli (THUNDERBALL [Terence Young, 1965; $28.6 million]), and its profitability attracted the attention of Transamerica Corporation, which acquired the company for $185 million in 1967.[115] Transamerica at the time was a gigantic $2.4-billion conglomerate with diversified but interrelated interests in a range of financial services, including banking, consumer loans, and insurance. (It had been formed in 1924 as a holding company for the Bank of America, but since 1960 had become a multi-market, multiservice enterprise under the leadership of John R. Beckett.) The acquisition left existing United Artists management intact, and although it became a wholly owned subsidiary the movie company operated throughout the late 1960s and early 1970s with complete autonomy.[116] In fact, United Artists had one of the longest continuities of management of any Hollywood major, with virtually all changes until the late 1970s coming from within.[117]

When the merger was completed Robert Benjamin and Arthur Krim, since 1951 United Artists chairman and president respectively, both took partial leaves of absence and production head David Picker, who was then 38 years old, was named United Artists' president in June 1969. His appointment was part of a late-1960s industry pattern which called for the filling of top studio posts with young executives who were thought to be more in touch with the youth culture of the moment (for example, Sam Jaffe was made president of Paramount at 30, and Robert Evans became studio production head at 36; Richard Zanuck was appointed president of Fox at 27; etc.).[118] However, Krim had assessed the United Artists inventory and discovered a backlog of thirty-five over-budget unreleased features costing a total of $80 million, which he calculated would lose the company at least $50 million in the newly volatile marketplace.[119] Returning to take control of the situation, Krim decided to write off the entire loss in 1970 instead of amortizing it over three years as the law allowed, which produced a record loss of $45 million, most of it absorbed by Transamerica. In fact, the parent company's total profits dropped in 1970 to $43 million from $87 million in 1969, with 80 percent of the difference attributed to the United Artists write-off.[120] At this point, Transamerica imposed a number of cost-cutting measures on United Artists that resulted in firing 300 employees, closing several of its foreign exchanges, and capping production budgets at $2 million. Although these constraints would chafe at United Artists management for the rest of the decade, Transamerica continued its hands-off policy in the area of film choice and marketing, so that relative autonomy still prevailed.

After experiencing a few more bad years in 1971 and 1972, United Artists received an unanticipated boon in 1973 from a deal negotiated between Krim and Kirk Kerkorian whereby United Artists became the exclusive distributor of MGM product for the next ten years (see above). This included both theatrical and television syndication rights to all of the 1,400 features MGM had made since 1924, plus the four to six features MGM was projected to make annually over the next decade.[121] In October 1973, David Picker left United Artists to become an independent producer, and Krim became chairman of the board, with Benjamin as head of finance. Austrian-born Eric Pleskow (b. 1924) was then appointed United Artists president and CEO, and Mike Medavoy (b. 1941), a 32-year-old super-agent who had worked for both CMA and International Famous, became vice president in charge of West Coast productions. In 1974, United Artists experienced a sustained turnaround that began one of the most profitable periods in its history.[122] It contributed $9.9 million in after-tax earnings to Transamerica on film rentals of $141.9 million; in 1975 United Artists posted after-tax earnings of $11.5 million on rentals of $187.4 million; and in 1976 the studio posted $16 million on rentals of $229.5 million.[123] Much of this profit was hit-driven: for example, in 1974 MGM's THAT'S ENTERTAINMENT! unexpectedly returned $12 million in domestic rentals; in 1975 RETURN OF THE PINK PANTHER (Blake Edwards) earned $25.4 million and ONE FLEW OVER THE CUCKOO'S NEST (Milos Forman) an astounding $59.9 million); and in 1976 and 1977, ROCKY (John G. Avildsen) returned $56.5 million (this on a budget of about $1 million), so that *Variety* could proclaim "Boomy United Artists Contributes Fiscal Glow to Transamerica."[124]

By the end of 1977, United Artists had generated $318 million in global rentals, breaking the all-time industry record previously set by Universal with $289 million in 1975.[125] At this point, as he had done at least once before, Krim proposed a United Artists spin-off to Transamerica's board of directors to regain his company's autonomy. Predictably, the plan was turned down, with Transamerica chairman John Beckett subsequently telling an interviewer for *Fortune* magazine, " . . . [I]f the people at United Artists don't like it, they can quit and go off on their own."[126] In January 1978, that is exactly what they did when Krim, Benjamin, Pleskow, Medavoy, and William Bernstein, United Artists vice president for business affairs—to be known henceforth as the "United Artists Five"—all resigned and three weeks later formed Orion Pictures Company with a $100 million revolving line of credit negotiated through First National Bank of Boston. Orion, named for the five-star constellation and described as "the first major new film company in 50 years," was initially a joint financing and distributing venture between the United Artists Five and Warner Bros., and it was widely predicted to leave United Artists an empty shell.[127] A stunned Beckett named James R. Harvey, Transamerica's vice president for leisure-time services, as new United Artists chairman and Andy Albeck, head of United Artists' international operations, as president.[128] In their wake, the United Artists Five left the company to receive all-time high revenues for the next three years and its third Oscar in a row for Best Picture (for 1977's ANNIE HALL [Woody Allen], which followed ROCKY and ONE FLEW OVER THE CUCKOO'S NEST in receiving that honor).[129]

This legacy of success notwithstanding, the Albeck regime led United Artists into a disaster of literally epic proportions in 1979 when it allowed the production of Michael Cimino's HEAVEN'S GATE (1980) to go wildly out of control. Steven Bach, head of United Artists production at the time, has chronicled this fiasco in his book *Final Cut: Dreams and Disaster in the Making of "Heaven's Gate,"* in which the film becomes a paradigm for both 1970s auteurism run amok and the fatal flaws of the blockbuster syndrome.[130] Originally budgeted at $11.6 million, HEAVEN'S GATE eventually cost $36 million ($44 million, including promotion costs) and, at a running time of 219 minutes, was virtually unreleasable when post-production was finished in the fall of 1980.[131] In November it was opened in New York anyway, but to such witheringly hostile reviews that it was withdrawn two days later and its Los Angeles premiere canceled. A 149-minute version, re-edited by Cimino, was re-released in April 1981 but earned less than $1 million, and Transamerica had already decided to write the film off as a loss.[132] Thanks to the cash flow created by the Krim and Benjamin regime, the financial blow to United Artists wasn't fatal, but the negative publicity very nearly was. With trade press headlines like "United Artists, Directors' Paradise, Under Loss Cloud," and "'Heaven's Gate' Is Hellish Dilemma,"[133] as Bach notes: "The weaknesses and foolishness of an entire industry had been focused and exposed by HEAVEN'S GATE and United Artists, and the press and the industry were going to let neither director nor corporation forget it."[134] (A. D. Murphy, however, maintained that the real source of industry outrage was United Artists' *other* $36-million boondoggle, APOCALYPSE NOW [Francis Ford Coppola, 1979], which had barely returned its costs in the previous year and was widely regarded as the product of a megalomaniac.)[135] It was in this context that Transamerica received and accepted Kerk Kerkorian's 1981 bid to buy United Artists for $320 million. Kekorian then merged the company into a new corporate constellation known as MGM/United Artists Entertainment Company, which was bought for $1.5 billion by Ted Turner in 1986. Turner kept it just long enough to siphon off ownership of the nearly 3,000-title MGM film library (which includes the pre-1950 Warner Bros. library) to feed his satellite networks, before selling United Artists back to Kerkorian for $480 million. Kerkorian paid Turner another $300 million for the MGM corporate logo; MGM/United Artists then went through a succession of owners until it was bought by the French bank Credit Lyonnais in 1992 and repurchased by Kerkorian in 1996.[136]

WALT DISNEY PRODUCTIONS/BUENA VISTA DISTRIBUTING

Walt Disney Productions remained consistently profitable throughout the 1950s and 1960s, largely by having formed its own distribution outlet, Buena Vista, in 1953, thereby reducing its distribution costs from 30 percent to 15 percent of gross rentals.[137] During this same time, rising labor and production costs associated with animation led Disney increasingly into the realm of live-action features, where it scored significant hits with films like 20,000 LEAGUES UNDER THE SEA (Richard Fleischer, 1954—$11.3 million in domestic rentals) and MARY POPPINS (Robert Stevenson, 1964—$45 million in rentals) which it was able to promote and cross-market via its television series *Walt Disney Presents*. The spectacular success of MARY POPPINS, which was the highest-grossing film of 1964 (significantly outperforming both of its closest rivals, MY FAIR LADY [George Cukor] and GOLDFINGER [Guy Hamilton]) pushed company profits to record highs of $11 million in 1965 and $12 million in 1966.[138] When Walt died in 1966, Roy Disney—his brother and business partner since the 1920s—took over the company, naming Donn B. Tatum as president and E. Cardon (Card) Walker as executive vice president in charge of operations. As a closely held family company, however, Walt Disney Productions did not experience an orderly succession because the founder himself had done little to prepare for one. Instead of continuity, there was increasingly bitter rivalry between factions loyal to Walt's vision—which encompassed synergies among film, television, and theme park enterprises (Disneyland had opened in Anaheim, California, in 1955)—and Roy's, which concentrated more heavily on the traditional Disney product, described by Tatum as "constructive and wholesome entertainment for the entire family" (President's Letter to Shareholders, 1969).[139]

In five years as CEO, Roy managed to double the company's net worth, and when he died in 1971—the year that its second theme park, Disney World, opened in Orlando, Florida—Tatum became CEO and Walker president and de facto head of production.[140] Despite the changes going on in the industry at the time, Walker clung to the belief that audiences still wanted the kinds of family films evoked by Tatum's description, and during the early 1970s he seemed to be right. Films like THE ARISTOCATS (Wolfgang Reitherman, 1970), ROBIN HOOD (Wolfgang Reitherman, 1973), and HERBIE RIDES AGAIN (Robert Stevenson, 1974) were solid winners, and BEDKNOBS AND BROOMSTICKS (Robert Stevenson, 1971) and THE SNOWBALL EXPRESS (Norman Tokar, 1972) did respectable business. But by mid-decade the old magic had worn thin.

In 1974, most of the film division's $48 million in rentals were generated by reissues of LT. ROBIN CRUSOE, USN (Byron Paul, 1966) and ALICE IN WONDERLAND (Clyde Geronimi, 1951). (Institutionalized in the 1950s, multiple reissue was—and still is—standard Disney marketing practice; between 1968 and 1973, for example, 35 percent of the studio's total gross came from reissues, and some of its films have been re-released as many as seven times.)[141] Between 1972 and 1976, in fact, revenues from film rentals increased from $78.3 million to $119.1 million, but they did not keep pace with those of other corporate divisions, most notably theme parks (Disneyland and Disney World), and consumer products (merchandise, licensing, publishing).[142] The reason was that Disney had failed to acknowledge the revolution in public taste registered by the success of "event" films like THE GODFATHER (1972), THE EXORCIST (1973), and JAWS (1975). Walker consistently refused to move into the production of hard-PG and R-rated films, although he knew that the new teenage audience wanted more sex and violence than the G rating would allow; and even when STAR WARS (1977) demonstrated that blockbusters could be made without sacrificing a commitment to family values, the studio proved unwilling to pay the price for them.[143] As late as 1979, for example, it was Disney policy not to grant profit "points" in making deals with producers, which ended early negotiations for both RAIDERS OF THE LOST ARK and E.T.: THE EXTRA-TERRESTRIAL. It was this short-sighted conservatism that caused a new generation of Disney animators, profiled in *The New York Times Magazine* for August 1, 1976, to complain that the studio had become creatively stagnant by losing continuity with its past.[144] Despite these charges, it was the animated feature THE RESCUERS (Wolfgang Reitherman) and the live action-animation combination PETE'S DRAGON (Don Chaffey) that were Disney's highest earners of 1977 ($30 million and $18.4 million, respectively). In fact, the studio hadn't seen a big live-action hit since THE LOVE BUG (Robert Stevenson) became the second highest earning film of 1969, ranking ahead of MIDNIGHT COWBOY (John Schlesinger), and EASY RIDER, and just behind BUTCH CASSIDY AND THE SUNDANCE KID.

For most the 1970s, corporate policy was set by an executive committee comprised of Tatum, Walker, Ron Miller (Walt's son-in-law and heir apparent), and Roy E. Disney, or Roy, Jr. (Roy's son and heir apparent). In 1977, Roy, Jr. resigned, and Ron Miller was named head of production and attempted to bring the studio into the mainstream by venturing PG production for the first time. In August 1978, *Variety*'s editors noted that "the hardest thing to do in Hollywood is sell a G-rated picture (unless it has a Disney tag attached),"[145] but by that time even the tag didn't help much, so Miller ventured into PG production profligately with THE BLACK HOLE (Gary Nelson, 1979—Disney's first PG-rated release took place in March 1979, when it distributed the wrestling film TAKE DOWN [Kieth Merrill, 1978], a negative pick-up that contained some foul language).[146] Disney's $20-million STAR WARS imitation was aimed directly at the teenage market[147] and went down to perdition during the busy Christmas box-office season of 1979, returning a disappointing $25.4 million in rentals. Miller followed with two PG-rated imitations of R-rated genre hits—MIDNIGHT MADNESS (David Wechter, 1980), an ANIMAL HOUSE clone; and THE WATCHER IN THE WOODS (John Hough, 1980), a contemporary teenage horror film—both of which lost money.

To make matters worse, in September 1979, 42-year-old Don Bluth and a dozen other top animators quit the studio in protest over constant cost-cutting and a decline in artistic standards to form Don Bluth Productions (whose first film was 1982's remarkable THE SECRET OF NIMH [Don Bluth], distributed by the new MGM/United Artists).[148] The walkout decimated Disney's already weakened animation department, leaving just nine animators on staff, and delayed the release of THE FOX AND THE HOUND (Art Stevens, 1981) by eighteen months and stopped the troubled production of THE BLACK CAULDRON (Ted Berman, 1985) until computer-generated animation (and Michael Eisner) arrived to resurrect it.[149]

By the end of 1979, Disney's film profits were the lowest in a decade ($40.3 million), and yet during the 1970s it had risen decisively into the ranks of the majors by becoming the kind of broadly based entertainment-recreation company that its cohorts would all aspire to become in the 1980s and 1990s. In spite of the fact that Disney's market share among the seven majors had shrunk to 6 percent, the company had stabilized its position within the industry through diversification, so that less than a third of its income came from filmed entertainment, about half came from its theme parks (for much of the 1970s, Disneyland accounted for 60 percent of its profits alone),[150] and most of the rest from its merchandising operations. (Walt Disney pioneered the product tie-in when he sold licenses for the international production and sale of Mickey Mouse merchandise to the George Borgfelt Company in 1930.[151] His first feature, SNOW WHITE AND THE SEVEN DWARFS [Ben Sharpsteen, 1937], was accompanied by an array of tie-in merchandise ranging from books and toys to a 78-rpm sound-track album.)

In 1980, as work was beginning on EPCOT Center in Orlando and Tokyo Disneyland, Tatum retired, Walker became chairman of the board, and Ron Miller was named president and CEO. As the 1980s wore on, however, it became increasingly clear that theme park revenues were leveling off, and in 1983 the motion picture division reported a loss of $33.4 million, much of it due to the poor showing of the Disney Channel cable venture and the box-office failure of several big-budget projects like TRON (Steven Lisberger, 1982) and SOMETHING WICKED THIS WAY COMES (Jack Clayton, 1983). (Expectations for the high-tech, CGI-enhanced TRON were so high that bad reviews caused Disney's stock to fall two-and-a-half points the day after it opened.)[152] In a bold move, Miller founded the subsidiary Touchstone Pictures to market films for adult audiences while Walt Disney Pictures continued to produce family-oriented films. Despite the success of Touchstone's first feature, SPLASH (Ron Howard, 1984), Miller was ousted later that year in a power struggle with a consortium of stockholders led by Roy Disney, Jr., who in September hired Michael Eisner, then president of Paramount, as Disney's new CEO and chair. Former Warner Bros. president and co-chief executive Frank Wells joined the company as president, and this new management team oversaw the transformation of Disney into the international entertainment conglomerate it became in the 1990s.[153]

Mini-Majors and "Instant Majors"

In addition to the majors, several smaller companies were involved in distributing films during the 1970s, including American International Pictures, Allied Artists Pictures, Avco Embassy Pictures, and New World Pictures. Additionally, CBS and ABC, the two television networks that had established their own production companies in the late 1960s, had agreements with two large theater companies, National General Corporation and Cinerama Releasing Corporation respectively, to function as the distributors of their films. Finally, there were Associated Film Distributors, a British company that briefly attempted to compete with the majors at the end of the decade, and EXPRODICO, a cooperative formed by exhibitors to produce and distribute their own films in response to the "product shortage" created by the majors.

AMERICAN INTERNATIONAL PICTURES (AIP)

Founded in 1954 by James H. Nicholson (b. 1916) and Samuel Z. Arkoff (b. 1918) as American Releasing Corporation (ARC) before changing its name in 1956, American International Pictures (AIP) began as a releasing company for low-budget exploitation films in all genres, selling them in double bills directly to twenty-three regional subdistributors around the country (including Joseph H. Levine of Boston who would later form the rival Embassy Pictures).[154] (In this "states rights" system, regional distributors paid a flat fee to producers for limited exclusive rights to exhibit a film within a given state or group of states, with the distributor absorbing the cost of release prints and promotion.) Working with independent producers like Roger Corman and Bert I. Gordon, and ultimately coproducing themselves, Nicholson and Arkoff tapped into the "youth market" at least a decade before anyone else (except perhaps "Jungle" Sam Katzman), and by the early 1960s had become the paradigmatic teenage exploitation studio. (According to Richard McKay, AIP's advertising director, by 1959, 65 percent of the company's revenue came from drive-in theaters, prime teenage venues known facetiously in the trade as "passion pits.")[155] At this point AIP was, with Disney, the most consistently profitable studio in Hollywood, enabling it to absorb many of its subdistributors and set up its own national distribution network.[156] (Internationally, Fox distributed for AIP in Mexico; Anglo Amalgamated in Britain.)[157] As it grew more successful, AIP sought to compete with other low-budget distributors by producing its films in CinemaScope and color, the first of which, Roger Corman's THE HOUSE OF USHER (1960), was also the first AIP film to be booked into theaters on a percentage basis rather than at the flat rate reserved for B-films. Later in the decade, the success of teen films like BEACH PARTY (William Asher, 1963), BIKINI BEACH (William Asher, 1964), and BEACH BLANKET BINGO (William Asher, 1965) enabled AIP to set up the subsidiary Trans-American Films to distribute foreign product, and its popular biker-protest film THE WILD ANGELS (Roger Corman, 1966) spawned a subgenre and provided the model for the ultimate "youth cult" movie, EASY RIDER—which was produced by BBS and distributed by Columbia in 1969, but had been brought first to Arkoff, who turned its down because he didn't trust Dennis Hopper to direct.[158] During this period, AIP cut costs by recruiting creative personnel from local film schools—non-unionized actors, directors, and cinematographers who were willing to work for low wages and eager for professional experience. Thus, many filmmakers who would give 1970s cinema its characteristic look and shape did their apprentice work at AIP, including performers like Jack Nicholson and Peter Fonda; directors like Francis Ford Coppola, Peter Bogdanovich, and Martin Scorsese; and cinematographers like Laszlo Kovacs and Vilmos Zgismond.

During the 1970s, AIP quickly jumped on the blaxploitation bandwagon and became the leading studio for this kind of product, releasing BLACK CAESAR (Larry Cohen, 1972), BLACULA (William Crain, 1972), COFFY (Jack Hill, 1973), HELL UP IN HARLEM (Larry Cohen, 1973), FOXY BROWN (Jack Hill, 1974), TRUCK TURNER (Jonathan Kaplan, 1974), BUCKTOWN (Arthur Marks, 1975), and even Michael Schultz's distinctive COOLEY HIGH (1975), among many other less remarkable titles. AIP also produced a rash of domestic kung fu features (DEEP THRUST [Huang Feng, 1972], SHANGHAI KILLERS [1973], GOLDEN NEEDLES [Robert Clouse, 1974], etc.) and, as an early practitioner of saturation booking, flooded inner-city markets with both blaxploitation and martial arts product. It was during this time that AIP's market share as a distributor began to register on the *Variety* charts: in 1974, the company accounted for 3.8 percent of total domestic rentals, followed by 3.4 for 1975, 3.8 for 1976, 3.4 for 1977, and 1.4 for 1978, when about 96 percent of its annual revenues came from theatrical rentals.[159]

This success inspired Arkoff to compete with the majors (James Nicholson had left the company in 1972 to become an independent producer), and in 1975 he announced plans to start making "big-budget" films in the $3 to $4 million range. Owning no production facilities, AIP typically leased studio space for its own projects and enforced an economically exacting regime on the makers of these "prestige" films, some of which enjoyed box-office success (for example, LOVE AT FIRST BITE [Stan Dragoti, 1979—$20.6 million domestic]; THE AMITYVILLE HORROR [Stuart Rosenberg, 1979—$35 million domestic]). Others, however, barely broke even (THE ISLAND OF DR. MOREAU [Don Taylor, 1977—$4 million]), and one of them, the $20-million disaster film

METEOR (Ronald Neame, 1979), coproduced with Hong Kong's Sir Run-Run Shaw, lost $15.2 million and threatened the company's solvency.

In 1979, in fact, AIP posted the first loss in its history ($1.5 million) and in July of that year merged with Filmways, the television production-syndication company founded by Martin Ransohoff (b. 1927) in 1972, which had recently acquired interests in publishing (Grosset & Dunlop) and feature film distribution (Sigma III). Arkoff left in 1981 to form Arkoff International Pictures, and in 1982 Filmways/AIP was bought by Orion as it trembled on the edge of bankruptcy. A casualty of the 1970s hit-or-miss blockbuster syndrome, AIP nevertheless led the way early on in demographic exploitation, target marketing, and saturation booking, all of which would become standard procedure for the majors in planning and releasing their mass-market "event" films by the end of the decade.

AVCO EMBASSY PICTURES

Avco Embassy Pictures Corporation began life in 1956, when Joseph H. Levine's Embassy Pictures released a recut, "Americanized" version of a Japanese monster film originally called GOJIRA (Toho, 1954). Retitled GODZILLA, the film became an enormous hit, not least owing to Levine's relentlessly energetic exploitation. (Levine [1905–1987] was a states rights distributor operating out of Boston and a major client during the 1950s of AIP—see above.)[160] He then worked the same transformation on a cheaply made Italian *peplum* called THE LOVES OF HERCULES, whose world rights he acquired for a $125,000; as HERCULES (Pietro Francisci, 1959). The film returned $4.7 million in domestic rentals on the strength of a $1.5 million advertising blitz and a Warner Bros. saturation release on 600 screens, made a star of its protagonist Steve Reeves (an American bodybuilder turned actor), and touched off a long cycle of sword-and-sandal imports with local musclemen posing as classical heroes.[161] (The film did even better abroad, and in several markets became the first motion picture advertised on national television.)[162]

Levine continued his relationship with the Italian industry into the 1960s, providing some financing and American distribution for films as varied as TWO WOMEN (Vittorio De Sica, 1960), DIVORCE—ITALIAN STYLE (Pietro Germi, 1961), BOCCACCIO '70 (Vittorio De Sica, Federico Fellini, Luchino Visconti, 1962), 8 1/2 (Federico Fellini, 1963), MARRIAGE ITALIAN-STYLE (Vittorio De Sica, 1964), THE TENTH VICTIM (Elio Petri, 1965), and ROMEO AND JULIET (Franco Zeffirelli, 1968); as well as for such British productions as ZULU (Cy Endfield, 1964) and DARLING (John Schlesinger, 1965). Domestically, Levine produced such hits as THE CARPETBAGGERS (Edward Dmytryk, 1964), NEVADA SMITH (Henry Hathaway, 1966), THE PRODUCERS (Mel Brooks, 1967), and THE GRADUATE (Mike Nichols, 1967).[163] The windfall success of the latter, which cost less than $3 million and returned $44 million in rentals, made Embassy attractive to the Avco Corporation, a conglomerate involved in defense and aerospace manufacture, consumer lending, land development, and broadcasting, which bought the company in 1968.[164]

As Avco Embassy, with Levine as president, it briefly became a major force in the industry, producing the award-winning THE LION IN WINTER (Anthony Harvey, 1968) and the epoch-making CARNAL KNOWLEDGE (Mike Nichols, 1971), together with such disasters as THE ADVENTURERS (Lewis Gilbert, 1970) and THE DAY OF THE DOLPHIN (Mike Nichols, 1973), but by 1978 was providing just over 1 percent of its parent's revenue.[165] Levine himself left Avco Embassy in 1974 to form Joseph A. Levine Presents, producing two unsuccessful Richard Attenborough films—A BRIDGE TOO FAR (1977) and MAGIC (1978)—before retiring in 1981.[166] In 1975, Avco Embassy briefly withdrew from production but steamed ahead as a distributor, releasing fifteen features, but by 1977 it was down to only six.[167] The company was reinvigorated in 1978 by its new vice president for marketing, Robert Rehme, who generated production capital with such successful exploitation films as THE FOG (John Carpenter, 1979; made for $1.5 million and returning $10 million in rentals) and THE HOWLING (Joe Dante, 1981; made for $1.7 million and returning $9 million), so that by 1981 the company was able to release fifteen features and capture 5 percent of the domestic rentals for that year.[168] After a failed takeover bid by BILLY JACK producer Tom Laughlin in early 1981, Avco Embassy was acquired by Norman Lear and Jerry Perenchio in November of that year for $26 million.[169] Renamed Embassy Communications, the company handled syndication of Lear's former Tandem television productions and home video distribution of Avco Embassy films. It also maintained a theatrical film division which released some foreign product (notably Ingmar Bergman's FANNY AND ALEXANDER [1983]) and ventured into production on the Universal lot in 1982.[170] In 1985 Embassy Communications was acquired by Dino De Laurentiis.

ALLIED ARTISTS PICTURES (AA)

Another distributor at the margins during the 1970s was Allied Artists Pictures, Inc., which was the latter-day incarnation of Monogram Productions, Inc. Under the management of its new president (and former sales manager) Steve Broidy, this classical-era B-film studio had incorporated Allied Artists Productions as a wholly owned subsidiary to produce higher-budget films in 1946; then in 1953 the company dropped the old name entirely and, as Allied Artists Pictures (AA), produced and distributed such successful mainstream films as FRIENDLY PERSUASION (William Wyler, 1956), LOVE IN THE AFTERNOON (Billy Wilder, 1957), and the Elvis Presley vehicle TICKLE ME (Norman Taurog, 1965), having set up its own film exchanges in major cities. (Allied Artists continued to finance low-budget exploitation product like Don Siegel's INVASION OF THE BODY SNATCHERS [1956] and Roger Corman's WAR OF THE SATELLITES [1958], and it also produced telefilms under the imprimatur of Interstate Television Corporation, which was renamed Allied Artists Television in 1970.)[171] However, Allied Artists ceased production in 1966 and sold its studio facilities a year later, becoming for the rest of the decade an import distributor. The company scored hits with foreign titles like A MAN AND WOMAN (Claude Lelouch, 1966) and BELLE DE JOUR (Luis Buñuel, 1967), and under Emmanuel L. Wolf (b. 1927), who became president and board chairman in 1968, returned to production in the early 1970s.

The first Allied Artist venture of the decade, coproduced with ABC Pictures (which provided 50 percent of the financing), was CABARET (Bob Fosse, 1972), whose critical and commercial success seemed to auger great things for the "new" AA. The Bob Fosse musical won eight Academy Awards and became the sixth highest earning film in the year of THE GODFATHER, with $22.2 million in rentals; and it inspired Wolf to seek blockbuster gold with PAPILLON (1973). Directed (and nominally coproduced) by Franklin J. Schaffner, whose PATTON had swept the 1970 Oscars, this grim film was based on the best-selling account of a true escape from Devil's Island which French producer Robert Dorfman had acquired shortly after it was published in 1969. (Twenty

The prison ship approaches Devil's Island in PAPILLON *(Franklin Schaffner, 1973), the film that marked the beginning of the end for thinly capitalized Allied Artists when it returned only $22.5 milllion against negative costs of $13–15 million, most of it borrowed at a ruinous 20% interest rate. An inordinate portion of these costs were attributable to star salaries for Steve McQueen (second from right) and Dustin Hoffman (far right). 35mm Panavision anamorphic.*

years earlier AA had produced as its first mainstream hit RIOT IN CELL BLOCK 11 [Don Siegel, 1954], based on producer Walter Wanger's prison experiences.) In a complicated financing arrangement, a Chicago investment brokerage lent Allied Artists $7 million plus another $2.5 to cover cost overruns at the usurious interest rate of 20 percent (at the time, AA had a net worth of just over $2 million).[172] Inflated star salaries ($2 million for Steve McQueen; $1.25 million for Dustin Hoffman) and Schaffner's $750,000 director's fee, together with location shooting in Spain and Jamaica, combined to push declared negative costs above $13 million (Schaffner believed they were closer to $15 million).[173] PAPILLON was a hit, returning $22.5 million in rentals to become the fourth-highest earner of 1973, but given the staggering debt it had incurred in production it was hardly the blockbuster AA needed to remain competitive. Still looking for a winning combination, Wolf raised $8 million for the production of THE MAN WHO WOULD BE KING (John Huston, 1975), a version of a Rudyard Kipling adventure story set in nineteenth-century Afghanistan and shot on location in the Atlas mountains of Morocco with a British cast and crew. Some of the money was raised from Columbia Pictures in exchange for the European distribution rights; much of the rest came from Canadian tax shelters.[174] Despite glowing reviews and a massive publicity campaign,[175] the film returned only $11 million, and that same year CONDUCT UNBECOMING (Michael Anderson, 1975), another British period film distributed by Allied Artists, lost money.

At mid-decade, Allied Artists' only significant earner relative to its costs was the French-produced softcore porn film THE STORY OF O (Just Jaeckin, 1975), but its distribution was complicated by obscenity prosecutions in several major markets, including Detroit and Atlanta, and the company spent much of its $4.7-million return on legal fees. Seeking to diversify, in early 1976 Allied Artists Pictures was merged with two consumer products groups, Kalvex, Inc. and PSP, Inc., to become Allied Artists Industries, Inc. The new company distributed a wide range of products, from pharmaceuticals to sportswear to mobile homes, and only about 30 percent of its revenues came from filmed entertainment.[176] But, as Michael Conant points out, AA had released only forty-four theatrical features between 1970 and 1977, and fell below the critical minimum size for national distribution.[177] With only twelve exchanges and an annual overhead in excess of $3 million, it barely had enough staff to collect its exhibitor billings (in fact, one theory held that AA had risked PAPILLON in order to accelerate collections on its CABARET billings).[178] In 1978 it contracted for the release of one hundred AA titles on pre-recorded

Another Allied Artists star vehicle, THE MAN WHO WOULD BE KING (John Huston, 1975) was financed through a combination of Candian tax shelters and the sale of European distribution rights (to Columbia): Michael Caine, Sean Connery as British officers in Afghanistan. When it, too, barely amortized its costs Allied Artists was forced to merge with a consumer products distributor to stay in business. 35mm Panavision anamorphic.

videocassette, becoming one of the first producers in Hollywood to do so,[179] yet by that point the company had posted net losses for four years in a row. In May 1979 it filed for bankruptcy, and was acquired the following year by Lorimar Productions, a successful television producer that ventured briefly into filmmaking in the late 1970s and early 1980s.

NEW WORLD PICTURES

By far the most successful independent producer-distributor of the decade was New World Pictures, founded by Roger Corman with his brother Gene in 1970 after leaving AIP. Corman sought to duplicate the success of Nicholson and Arkoff's company on a broader scale, in his own words, by producing "a series of low-budget films made by new, young filmmakers" for worldwide distribution.[180] Ultimately, New World failed at global reach, opening ten domestic sales offices and one each in Canada and the U.K., with subdistributors handling its productions regionally.[181] Initially, these were R-rated exploitation films—the softcore "Nurse" series begun by THE STUDENT NURSES (Stephanie Rothman, 1970) and the women-in-prison cycle kicked off by THE BIG DOLL HOUSE (Jack Hill, 1971)—which brought the company a first-year profit of $3.2 million. (THE BIG DOLL HOUSE, for example, shot in the Philippines for $120,000, grossed $10 million.)[182] Corman continued the production of such sex-and-sadism programmers throughout the 1970s, as always with the cheapest available talent. One beneficial effect of this production economy, as at AIP, was to provide apprenticeships for recently trained filmmakers who later became major industry talents. In the case of New World, these included Jonathan Kaplan (NIGHT CALL NURSES [1972]; THE STUDENT TEACHERS [1973]; WHITE LINE FEVER [1975]), Jonathan Demme (CAGED HEAT [1974]; CRAZY MAMA [1975]), Ron Howard (GRAND THEFT AUTO [1977]), Paul Bartel (DEATH RACE 2000 [1975]; CANNONBALL [1976]), and Joe Dante (HOLLYWOOD BOULEVARD [1976, with Alan Arkush]; PIRANHA [1978]).

New World's other contribution during the 1970s was to import and distribute a large number of European art films, starting with Ingmar Bergman's CRIES AND WHISPERS in 1972. Corman did this initially to enhance the image of his company ("I don't want a reputation like AIP of doing only exploitation films," he told New World's executive vice president Barbara Boyle),[183] but in the auteur-conscious 1970s it also proved unexpectedly profitable. Thus, for short while, American audiences read "Roger Corman Presents" in the credits for films by Bergman (AUTUMN SONATA [1978]); Federico Fellini (AMARCORD [1974]); François Truffaut (THE STORY OF ADELE H. [1975], SMALL CHANGE [1976]); Joseph Losey (THE ROMANTIC ENGLISHWOMAN [1975]); Volker Schlöndorff (THE LOST HONOR OF KATHARINA BLUM [1975], THE TIN DRUM [1979]); Akira Kurosawa (DERSU UZALA [1975]); Alain Resnais (MON ONCLE D'AMERIQUE [1980]); and Bruce Bereford (BREAKER MORANT [1979]).[184] In the same vein, New World also distributed such unusual work as the Jamaican cult classic THE HARDER THEY COME (Perry Henzell, 1973), Rene Laloux's animated science fiction film FANTASTIC PLANET (1973), Jeanne Moreau's directorial debut LUMIERE (1976), the Stephen Sondheim musical A LITTLE NIGHT MUSIC (Harold Prince, 1978), Peter Bogdanovich's SAINT JACK (1979), and the early films of David Cronenberg (RABID [1977], THE BROOD [1979]). New World reached its maximum profitability in 1980, by which time it had become the largest independent production-distribution company in the United States. (A venture into the British market had proven unsuccessful.)

*Roger Corman's New World Pictures began the 1970s as an
exploitation producer modeled on AIP, but Corman soon
discovered an auteur-conscious audience for art films and
began to profitably distribute recent work by directors such
as Ingmar Bergman, Francoise Truffaut, and Akira
Kurosawa. His first "hit" was Bergman's* CRIES AND
WHISPERS, *which produced a healthy $3.5-million rental
income for New World in 1972. 35mm 1.66:1.*

In 1983, Corman sold New World to an investment group for $16.5 million; he subsequently formed Concorde Pictures Corporation with his wife Julie and acquired distribution rights to about 120 New World films that he had produced or distributed when he had owned the company, 1970–1982.

ASSOCIATED FILM DISTRIBUTORS (AFD)

A final independent player in 1970s American film market was the British producer-distributor Associated Film Distributors (AFD). Unlike AIP, Allied Artists, and New World, AFD attempted to compete head-to-head with the majors in the arena of big-budget mainstream films by combining the resources of the European electronics-media conglomerate Thorn-EMI with those of television magnate and film producer Lord Lew Grade. Lord Grade's ITC had been producing features for the American market since 1975 without notable success. These included heavily promoted star vehicles

Poster for Michael Cimino's THE DEER HUNTER (1978), the only successful film produced and distributed by EMI Films Ltd. before it was aquired by Thorn in 1979 and combined with Lord Lew Grade's ITC to form Associate Film Distributors. THE DEER HUNTER earned $27.4 milllion in rentals and won five Academy Awards, including Best Picture and Best Director. 35mm Panavision anamorphic, blown up to 70mm for road-showing. Recorded and exhibited in four-channel Dolby stereo optical sound (six-track stereo magnetic for 70mm prints).

like THE EAGLE HAS LANDED (John Sturges, 1977), distributed by Columbia, and THE BOYS FROM BRAZIL (Franklin J. Schaffner, 1978), distributed by Fox. EMI had also entered film production during the 1970s, starting with THAT'LL BE THE DAY (Claude Whatham, 1974) and STARDUST (Michael Apted, 1975), but had managed only one hit in the United States—Michael Cimino's THE DEER HUNTER (1978). In 1979, EMI was acquired by Thorn, and the merged company combined with Lord Grade to form an American distribution company called AFD. Backed by a U.K. distribution company and the Boston-based General Cinema Corporation, the nation's largest theater chain,[185] AFD aimed at the heart of the American market with THE MUPPET MOVIE (James Frawley, 1979), which unexpectedly became the tenth-highest earner of the year with domestic rentals of $32.2 million. (The Muppets in that film are on their way to Hollywood to sign a movie contract with a studio mogul named "Lord Lew.") But failure attended the next AFD production, the disco musical CAN'T STOP THE MUSIC (Nancy Walker, 1980), and absolute disaster sank RAISE THE TITANIC! (Jerry Jameson, 1980), a $35-million would-be blockbuster that returned only $6.8 million in rentals and forced Grade to resign as ITC chairman. Financially crippled, AFD entered into a distribution agreement with Universal and remained in the American market with nearly as many hits (THE GREAT MUPPET CAPER [Jim Henson, 1981]; THE DARK CRYSTAL [Jim Henson, 1983]) as misses (THE LEGEND OF THE LONE RANGER [William A. Fraker, 1981]), until Thorn-EMI was sold off in the mid-1980s, with its substantial film library going to the French company Lumiere and Cannon/Pathé acquiring its theater circuit. (Lord Grade was reappointed chairman of ITC in 1995.)

Kermit the Frog embraced by Miss Piggy in THE MUPPET MOVIE *(James Frawley, 1979), the Associate Film Distributors hit that briefly gave the British distributor a foothold in the American market. The film returned $32.2 million to become the tenth-highest earner of the year. 35mm 1.85.1.*

NATIONAL GENERAL CORPORATION (NGC)-CBS CINEMA CENTER FILMS

In 1967 there appeared two so-called "instant majors"—National General Corporation-CBS and Cinerama-ABC. (National General and Cinerama are sometimes counted separately as "instant majors" because they both briefly entered production in the late 1960s.)[186] In each case, a television network entered feature film production with the idea of supplying its own prime-time movie programming in addition to distributing its product to theaters through independent exchanges. The CBS production unit was called Cinema Center Films. Its films were distributed by National General Corporation (NGC), successor to the 20th Century–Fox circuit and the third-largest theater chain in the country (250 screens), which had entered distribution in 1966 under a temporary waiver of the consent decrees (first granted to the company for three years in 1963 and extended for another three years to 1969).[187] Until he migrated to Fox in 1971, Cinema Center's president was Gordon Stulberg, and its studio was set up on the old seventy-acre Republic Pictures lot in Hollywood, for which CBS had paid $9.5 million in February 1967.[188] Cinema Center produced thirty films, including such star vehicles as WITH SIX YOU GET EGG ROLL (Howard Morris, 1968), with Doris Day; A MAN CALLED HORSE (Elliot Silverstein, 1970), with Richard Harris; LITTLE BIG MAN (Arthur Penn, 1970), with Dustin Hoffman; LE MANS (Lee H. Katzin, 1971), with Steve McQueen; and BIG JAKE (George Sherman, 1971), with John Wayne; as well as the pre-JAWS shark documentary BLUE WATER, WHITE DEATH (Peter Gimbel, 1971), an acknowledged influence on Spielberg.[189] Despite a handful of hits, the majority of Cinema Center features incurred losses. When it posted a loss of $10 million for 1971, CBS board chairman William S. Paley ordered that the company shut down after it completed the several productions in progress.[190]

Under the leadership of former Paramount executive Charles Boasberg (b. 1906), NGC itself had entered production in 1967 as National General Pictures, producing and distributing DIVORCE AMERICAN STYLE (Bud Yorkin, 1967) and THE STALKING MOON (Robert Mulligan, 1969). (It had also coproduced THE QUILLER MEMORANDUM [Michael Anderson, 1966] with the Rank Organization for distribution by Fox.) The following year NGC produced by itself coproduced with Cinema Center about ten films— including the long-forgotten CHARRO! (Charles M. Warren, 1969), A FINE PAIR (Francesco Maselli, 1968), THE APRIL FOOLS (Stuart Rosenberg, 1969), DADDY'S GONE A-HUNTING (Mark Robson, 1969), ME, NATALIE (Fred Coe, 1969), and ALL NEAT IN BLACK STOCKINGS (Christopher Morahan, 1969)—and it petitioned the Justice Department to further ease consent decree restrictions so that it could produce and distribute "indefinitely." Judge Edmund L. Palmieri of the New York Federal District Court granted another three-year extension but refused an indefinite term.[191] After a failed bid to acquire Warner Bros. in 1969 (foiled by the Justice Department's Anti-Trust division), NGC closed its production unit in 1970 but continued to distribute for Cinema Center, as well as for its new partner First Artists Productions (FAP), formed in 1969 by Barbra Streisand, Sidney Poitier, and Paul Newman (later joined by Steve McQueen and Dustin Hoffman). Prestigious as it was, FAP produced only five films and one real hit between 1969 and 1973 (Sam Peckinpah's THE GETAWAY [1972], which earned $18.4 million in domestic rentals), and when Cinema Center closed in 1972, NGC was taken over by American Financial Corporation, which sold its film library and releasing commitments to Warner Bros. in November 1973 (see above).[192]

CINERAMA RELEASING CORPORATION (CRC)-ABC CIRCLE FILMS

ABC's production unit was named Circle Films, and its distribution partner was Cinerama Releasing Corporation (CRC), a division of Cinerama Inc., whose multi-camera widescreen process had catalyzed the widescreen revolution in 1952. In 1963, the company had been bought by William R. Foreman, owner of the Pacific Coast Theater chain, who in 1967 set up CRC to distribute its own widescreen films (now shot mainly in 35mm and 70mm single-lens processes) and ABC's Circle Films productions.[193] (ABC also operated theaters—in fact, with 418 theaters of the former Paramount circuit, in the 1960s ABC Theaters was the largest chain in the country.)[194] In the late 1960s CRC released CUSTER OF THE WEST (Robert Siodmak, 1968), in Super Technirama; HELL IN THE PACIFIC (John Boorman, 1968), in Panavision; KRAKATOA, EAST OF JAVA (Bernard Kowalski, 1969), in Super Panavision 70; and SONG OF NORWAY (Andrew L. Stone, 1970), in Super Panavision 70.[195] Between 1967 and 1972, under the leadership of former Creative Management Associates executive Martin Baum, ABC itself produced or coproduced thirty-seven films, including CHARLY (Ralph Nelson, 1968); THE KILLING OF SISTER GEORGE (Robert Aldrich, 1968); CANDY (Christian Marquand, 1968); THEY SHOOT HORSES, DON'T THEY? (Sydney Pollack, 1969); SONG OF NORWAY (Andrew L. Stone, 1970); KOTCH (Jack Lemmon, 1971); Sam Peckinpah's STRAW DOGS (1971) and JUNIOR BONNER (1972); THE TOUCH (Ingmar Bergman, 1971); and its only big hit, CABARET (Bob Fosse, 1972), whose success it shared with Allied Artists.[196] Before profits from the latter were taken, the company's total operating loss for the five-year period was $47 million, and half of CABARET's $22.2 million just wasn't enough to save it. After ABC Circle Films went out of business in early 1973, CRC subsisted mainly on acquisitions—that is, pick-ups distributed but not financed—of which it had released some 125 by August 1974.[197] At that point, AIP became the domestic distribution agent for CRC, which needed to release between twenty and twenty-five films a year to meet its overhead and make a profit.[198] Cinerama Inc. was ultimately liquidated in May 1978, although Pacific Coast Theaters retained the corporate name.

Despite the fact of an ongoing FCC inquiry into the networks' control of program production, and an antitrust suit brought by the MPAA against CBS and ABC for their entry into theatrical production,[199] the "instant majors" were able to achieve a 10-percent market share by 1970.[200] Their later failure—and that of the other independent producer-distributors discussed above—was symptomatic of a deep-seated institutional problem: the central fact that the production, finance, and distribution of feature films are, in David Gordon's words, "irrevocably linked."[201] During the 1970s they became even more so. Until the coming of the video revolution in the 1980s, separation of finance and distribution was doomed to fail, and the distribution sector provided only sporadic entry for independents. Both NCG and CRC hoped to streamline their sales operations by maintaining small staffs and flexible structures, with eight to ten branches (NGC opened with only six in 1966) as opposed to twenty-five to thirty for the majors, but economies of scale dictated the release of two to three films per month in order to remain competitive, and this became impossible after the collapse of their product suppliers.[202] As Tino Balio points out, the only lasting effect of their attempt to become television-oriented, vertically organized "instant majors" was to bid up prices for talent and glut the market with features.[203]

EXPRODICO AND THE "PRODUCT SHORTAGE"

The entry of the "instant majors" and mini-majors also had the effect of reducing distribution's share of box-office grosses to under 30 percent between 1969 and 1972, since the new companies offered lower than average splits with exhibitors (normally no lower than 70/30, and frequently higher, during the most of the 1960s) in order to get their business, which forced the majors to lower their rates accordingly.[204] By 1972, however, the distributors' share had risen again to 31.6 percent. It increased to 39 percent in 1977, and ended the decade at an average high of 45 percent.[205] The main cause was the artificial "product shortage" created by the majors, who had cut distribution by 36 percent between 1972 and 1975, so they were able to demand 90/10 splits for potential blockbusters and bind exhibitors to the practice of blind-bidding with nonrefundable guarantees. In the latter, theater owners were called upon to bid competitively for films they had yet to see (usually because they were still in production), and to put up a non-refundable cash-guarantees in order to book them, often for a minimum guaranteed playing time as well.[206] The MPAA argued that blind-bidding helped the studios to amortize millions in interest charges on big-budget films by insuring their immediate release, but theater owners correctly saw it as a tactic for making them shoulder most of the financier-distributor's risk for a considerably lower share of the profits. (However, the non-refundable guarantee was much less risky for exhibitors than a straight production investment loan, since the money was not due to the distributor until shortly before a film's opening, and after opening the exhibitor got to keep *all* box-office revenues until the guaranteed amount was earned back.)[207]

It was to combat these abuses that EXPRODICO (Exhibitors Production and Distribution Cooperative) was formed in 1975 by Tom Moyer, the owner of an Oregon theater chain, with the support of NATO (the National Association of Theater Owners).[208] The idea was for exhibitors to go into direct production, on the model of Fox and Loews earlier in the century, to insure the steady supply of films to their theaters. Although its cooperative purpose was never really fulfilled, many individual EXPROD-ICO members entered production on their own account. (In fact, many individual EXPRODICO members reneged on their pledges of financial support, and the organization was dissolved in 1979, but with the caveat tellingly noted in a *Variety* headline: "Film Famine Could Revive EXPRODICO.")[209] These included General Cinema Corporation of Boston, the nation's largest exhibition chain, which produced CAPRICORN ONE (Peter Hyams, 1978), LOST AND FOUND (Melvin Frank, 1979), and HANOVER STREET (Peter Hyams, 1979) and attempted unsuccessfully to acquire a 20-percent share of Columbia Pictures in 1979; United Artists Theater Circuit, the second largest chain, produced ALOHA, BOBBY AND ROSE (Floyd Mutrux, 1975), THE KENTUCKY FRIED MOVIE (John Landis, 1977), SUNBURN (Richard C. Sarafian, 1979); Ted Mann Productions, a subsidiary of Mann Theaters Corporation, produced BUSTER AND BILLIE (Daniel Petrie, 1974), LIFEGUARD (Daniel Petrie, 1976), and BRUBAKER (Stuart Rosenberg, 1980); Henry Plitt of Plitt Theaters, Inc., the fourth-largest (and largest privately owned) circuit in the country, financed BUCKTOWN (1975) and THE SENIORS (Rod Amateau, 1978); and Sherrill Corwin, chairman of the Los Angeles chain Metropolitan Theaters Corporation, co-financed and THE POSEIDON ADVENTURE (1972) and VIVA KNIEVEL! (Gordon Douglas, 1977).[210]

With some exceptions, these films were notably unsuccessful at the box office, and the attempt by exhibitors to solve the "product shortage" of the 1970s by becoming producers themselves had little industry impact. Nevertheless, in early 1979 three exhibition circuits—Loew's, Mann, and RKO-Stanley Warner—asked the Federal courts to vacate the 1948 Paramount decrees so that they could enter production-distribution, and in 1980, over strident objections by the majors, Judge Edmund L. Palmieri agreed that with certain restriction Loew's could do so.[211] In effectively ending the twenty-eight year-old consent decree, Palmieri acknowledged the new realities of the blockbuster era, writing that "the great bulk of the substantial rental, 85 percent or more, derived from all feature motion pictures have accrued to a small number of firms. . . . [which] has been accompanied by what many exhibitors characterize as a scarcity of feature motion picture product."[212] The judge noted that in "any given year, 20 pictures have been likely to account for anywhere from one-half to about two-thirds of all film rentals," and expressed the hope that "Loew's' entry into production and distribution would represent the entry of a new competitor and a probable increase in the supply of successful feature films."[213] In fact, it did not, because by 1980 the barriers to entry into production-distribution had become nearly insurmountable. (As Harold L. Vogel pointed out in his classic financial analysis *Entertainment Industry Economics*, for example, there were eleven unsuccessful entry attempts between 1970 and 1980 alone.)[214]

Conclusion: The Majors Bounce Back

Yet nearly all independent producer-distributors experienced a boom in the late sixties and early seventies when the recession briefly forced the majors to loosen their grip on the mainstream marketplace. New investors, including industrial manufacturing corporations and other nonmovie companies, entered the field to bankroll independent productions (for example, Quaker Oats backed WILLY WONKA AND THE CHOCOLATE FACTORY [Mel Stuart] in 1971; Mattel, Inc., partnered with Robert B. Radnitz to produce SOUNDER [Martin Ritt] in 1972), or became producers themselves (Westinghouse with Group W Films; Bristol-Myers with Palomar Pictures International).[215] By some accounts, independent distributors as a whole had achieved close to a 30-percent market share by 1971, but by 1979 it had shrunk to under 10 percent.[216] With the exception of MGM, the majors recovered strongly from the crippling write-offs of 1969–1971 and ended the decade dominating both the domestic (i.e., North American) and international markets for filmed entertainment. By 1977, their combined annual turnover from theatrical features was close to $2 billion—up from $1 billion at the height of the recession—and they accounted for over 93 percent of American distributors' gross.[217] By that point, too, the one area in which AIP, New World, and other independents had truly been competitive—exploitation—had been preempted by the majors, who learned from the experience of THE EXORCIST (1973) and JAWS (1975) that exploitation material could produce blockbuster profits if it was aggressively marketed to the mass public.

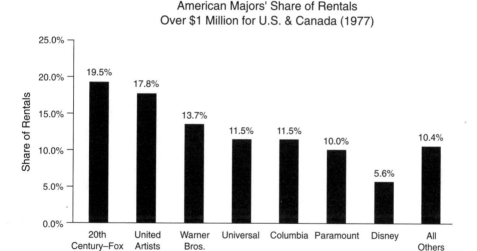

American Majors' Share of Rentals
Over $1 Million for U.S. & Canada (1977)

SOURCE: *Variety,* 18 January 1978, p. 8.

The soaring costs of advertising and promotion produced by the blockbuster strategy were offset by new strategies of distribution ("four-walling" and saturation booking) and new ancillary markets (television, cable, and video sales; merchandising, tie-ins, and product licensing), leading one observer to remark that movies "no longer exist as autonomous industrial products, but are increasingly manufactured as one item in a multimedia package."[218] On average, the majors took in 90 percent of all box-office revenues for the entire decade, and since they handled only about a third of the films produced during that period (as determined by MPAA rating submissions), the distributors of the other two-thirds shared the remaining 10 percent.[219] Furthermore, the majors received about half of their theatrical film rentals from foreign markets, which expanded during the decade and extended their hegemony abroad. In 1979, Japan became the number one export market for American films—the first time that a non–English-speaking nation had held that position. In the same year, the industry's domestic resurgence was such that 60 percent of its $1.9-billion worldwide rental revenues came from the American market, restoring a historic balance not achieved since the early 1950s.[220]

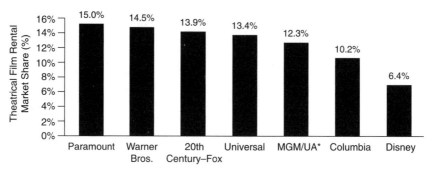

Average of Rental Market Shares
for American Majors: 1970–1979

SOURCE: *Variety* reports.

*Combines separate revenues of MGM and UA, anticipating their official merger in 1981.

The commercial stability that the blockbuster strategy brought to the American industry was achieved at the cost of much administrative turmoil. Thomas Schatz has pointed out that, unlike classical-era studio bosses, studio heads of the New Hollywood were less moguls than employees of publicly held corporations who were supposed to act on behalf of stockholders and boards of directors and could, technically, be fired by them.[221] Whereas the likes of Harry Cohen, Jack Warner, and Louis B. Mayer had owned a substantial share of their studios, most chief executives of the 1970s were "one percenters," owning only tiny pieces of their companies (Steven Ross, for example, owned just under one percent of Warners' stock; Martin Davis owned 1.35 percent of Paramount's; Michael Eisner owned one percent of Disney's; and so on). As International Creative Management super-agent Sue Mengers told an AFI seminar in 1976: "You've got to remember that the people in the studios are salaried employees. They are not owners. They are people who are employed by the boards of directors, and they're scared. When you're dealing out of insecurity it's hard to make good creative decisions."[222] These conditions exacerbated the hit-or-miss mentality of the blockbuster syndrome, and produced fear and loathing in Hollywood's executive suites throughout the decade—a paranoia clearly justified by circumstance. Of the seven majors, only Warners and Universal ended the decade with roughly the same management as they began it (with Warners' Ted Ashley second only to Lew Wasserman in staying power),[223] and within three years of the HEAVEN'S GATE disaster, with the exception of Orion, the management of every major company in the motion-picture industry had changed.[224]

8

Orders of Magnitude II: Costs, Agents, Stars

*When you don't get participation, your front money naturally acceler-
ates. . . . The best participation is if you can get gross from every box-
office dollar. The next best is gross after break-even, which means
when the picture has paid back its negative cost and its advertising.
After that, profits. . . . So if you're a Robert Redford, you may get $2
million [in front money] for it, but what if suddenly the picture turns
out to be* Jaws?

SUE MENGERS, ICM AGENT, MARCH 5, 1976

A defining feature of 1970s Hollywood filmmaking was rapidly escalating production
and marketing costs. Average negative costs inflated from $1.9 million in 1972 to $8.9
million in 1979, an increase of over 450 percent in less than seven years. (In the preceding decade, it was estimated that film costs had nearly tripled between 1960 and 1970.)[1]
Indeed, in 1980 Dennis Stanfill, chairman of 20th Century–Fox, predicted that the average cost of motion pictures would be $25 million by 1985—$14 million to produce and $11
million to market.[2] (He was too sanguine: the actual figures for 1985 were $16.8 and $12
million.)[3] There were several major reasons for this rise, including an annual monetary
inflation rate in excess of 7 percent, resulting mainly from the cartelization of international
oil prices in 1973, which impacted interest rates on production loans from banks.

Laying Off Risk

For most of their history, the studios had taken the up-front risks of production upon
themselves, but, increasingly during the 1970s, they sought to hedge their investments
through coproduction, advance sales to network television and cable, and the extraction
of large minimum guarantees from exhibitors.[4] The most important means of laying off
risk, however, was the turning to outside investors for production capital, especially in
the form of tax shelters. In these configurations, movies could be made on money from
people who did not necessarily want a profit, since the main purpose of their investment
was tax relief through the creation of artificial losses. By putting venture capital into a

"production service company," wealthy investors could take tax deductions for the investment itself and also produce paper losses by claiming accelerated depreciation on the unreleased film(s). One such company was Persky-Bright, which the *New York Times* called "the one major [industry] phenomenon—besides the disaster-film rage—of the 70s."[5] "Production Services by Persky-Bright" was a credit that appeared on many notable 1970s films distributed by Columbia—for example, THE LAST DETAIL (Hal Ashby, 1973), CALIFORNIA SPLIT (Robert Altman, 1974), FOR PETE'S SAKE (Peter Yates, 1974), FUNNY LADY (Herbert Ross, 1975), SHAMPOO (Hal Ashby, 1975), THE MISSOURI BREAKS (Arthur Penn, 1976), and TAXI DRIVER (Martin Scorsese, 1976). Founded by Lester Persky in 1973, this company and others like it (most formed briefly for the production of individual films) were responsible for financing 20 percent of all film starts between 1973 and 1976, and added about $150 million in production capital during the same period. In 1975 alone, more than half of the total films in production, completed, or released by Columbia, Warners, Paramount, United Artists, American International Pictures, and Allied Artists contained some tax-sheltered funds.[6] Shelters sustained the production schedules of several major studios, virtually keeping Columbia from bankruptcy, until September 1976 when Congress passed a tax reform bill that limited deductions for investment to the amount at risk (thus eliminating the "leverage" incentive in outside film investment and several other forms of high-risk speculation—that in real estate, livestock feeding, oil and gas, etc.).

While it lasted, tax-shelter financing created a situation in which, to paraphrase Michael Pye, it no longer mattered that nine out of ten movies lost money, because investors and studios were backing tax-shelter movies for reasons other than the direct and certain hope of profit.[7] Persky-Bright, for example, would assemble large packages of films acquired from various producers and sell debentures to individual investors that cost around $150,000 but could yield more than $400,000 in tax deferrals.[8] Furthermore, even if a tax-shelter movie like SHAMPOO (1975)—which returned $23.8 million on a $10 million investment (a $4 million negative cost, plus a $6 million marketing budget)—made money, most of it went back to the shelterers. Because they minimized risk, tax-shelter projects appealed to the banks, who would lend money to increase the sheltered funds (often by three or four times) and complete the financial package that subsidized production. But the presence of outside money had the unanticipated effect of dramatically inflating production costs. As A. D. Murphy described it in *Variety*: "Agents see the big money raised and then demand ever greater amounts for their clients. They know you have fifty million in outside money. The outer bounds of financial limits are broken." This ripple effect, he concluded, produced "a cancer on the business,"[9] whose most prominent feature was soaring star salaries—ironically, salaries commanded by stars whose very presence in a film was seen as a hedge against risk. This was what the banks meant when they said they wanted projects with "upside potential," which Peter Guber facetiously defined as "Robert Redford and Paul Newman together, with Barbra Streisand singing, Steve McQueen punching, Clint Eastwood jumping, music by Marvin Hamlisch, all in stereo. . . ."[10]

"Bankable" Stars

In the late sixties, reacting to such fruitless superstar deals as the one in which Elizabeth Taylor reputedly got $1 million for her role in Fox's disastrous CLEOPATRA

(1963), the banks saw things differently. In 1969, for example, a senior official at the Bank of America told Alexander Walker, "Established stars no longer bring any insurance to a film production,"[11] and in an article published in the *Journal of the Producers Guild of America* at about the same time ("A Banker Looks at the Picture Business—1971"), A. H. Howe argued that stars were not "bankable" in the sense that the films in which they appeared could be guaranteed to make money.[12] Even as late as 1976, William F. Thompson, Senior Vice President of the First National Bank of Boston, was telling Patrick McGilligan that "stars don't bring the people to the box office."[13] Yet no one inside the industry has ever seriously doubted that stars can be counted on to bring money into the box office, some more than others. (Two major indices of star profitability are the annual rankings compiled by *Variety* on the basis of total domestic grosses, and the *International Motion Picture Almanac* on the basis of a poll conducted among several hundred motion-picture theater owners.)[14] As Martin Dale points out, stars represent one of the few "brand names" in the business, and their appearance in a film is effectively a form of "character licensing" whereby they "endorse" that particular product.[15] In an era of rapidly escalating blockbuster budgets, studios were more unwilling than ever to take casting risks. The wisdom of bankers notwithstanding, it became an article of faith in 1970s Hollywood that successful movies needed stars to provide a hedge against risk every bit as much as they needed outside investors to help pay for the soaring cost of talent—a calculus that obviously created a vicious circle of mutually escalating costs.

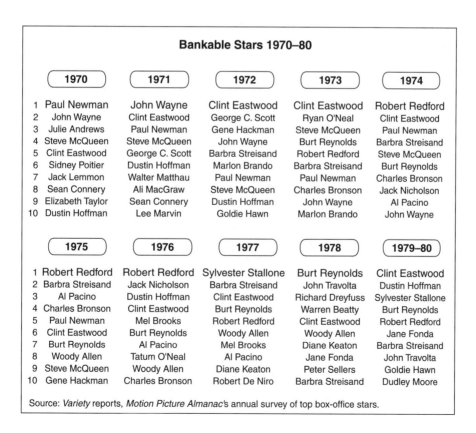

Bankable Stars 1970–80

	1970	1971	1972	1973	1974
1	Paul Newman	John Wayne	Clint Eastwood	Clint Eastwood	Robert Redford
2	John Wayne	Clint Eastwood	George C. Scott	Ryan O'Neal	Clint Eastwood
3	Julie Andrews	Paul Newman	Gene Hackman	Steve McQueen	Paul Newman
4	Steve McQueen	Steve McQueen	John Wayne	Burt Reynolds	Barbra Streisand
5	Clint Eastwood	George C. Scott	Barbra Streisand	Robert Redford	Steve McQueen
6	Sidney Poitier	Dustin Hoffman	Marlon Brando	Barbra Streisand	Burt Reynolds
7	Jack Lemmon	Walter Matthau	Paul Newman	Paul Newman	Charles Bronson
8	Sean Connery	Ali MacGraw	Steve McQueen	Charles Bronson	Jack Nicholson
9	Elizabeth Taylor	Sean Connery	Dustin Hoffman	John Wayne	Al Pacino
10	Dustin Hoffman	Lee Marvin	Goldie Hawn	Marlon Brando	John Wayne

	1975	1976	1977	1978	1979–80
1	Robert Redford	Robert Redford	Sylvester Stallone	Burt Reynolds	Clint Eastwood
2	Barbra Streisand	Jack Nicholson	Barbra Streisand	John Travolta	Dustin Hoffman
3	Al Pacino	Dustin Hoffman	Clint Eastwood	Richard Dreyfuss	Sylvester Stallone
4	Charles Bronson	Clint Eastwood	Burt Reynolds	Warren Beatty	Burt Reynolds
5	Paul Newman	Mel Brooks	Robert Redford	Clint Eastwood	Robert Redford
6	Clint Eastwood	Burt Reynolds	Woody Allen	Woody Allen	Jane Fonda
7	Burt Reynolds	Al Pacino	Mel Brooks	Diane Keaton	Barbra Streisand
8	Woody Allen	Tatum O'Neal	Al Pacino	Jane Fonda	John Travolta
9	Steve McQueen	Woody Allen	Diane Keaton	Peter Sellers	Goldie Hawn
10	Gene Hackman	Charles Bronson	Robert De Niro	Barbra Streisand	Dudley Moore

Source: *Variety* reports, *Motion Picture Almanac*'s annual survey of top box-office stars.

Several factors besides putative bankability account for this rise. Because the supply of acting talent is relatively inelastic, an increase in demand tends to drive up prices, and the entry of the "instant majors" into production-distribution in the late 1960s served this purpose well. The mid-1970s "product shortage" exacerbated the situation, since fewer new films each year created fewer new stars, and studio chiefs vied to outbid each other for the services of existing ones. As independent producer Peter Bart told the *New York Times* in 1976, "With everybody trying to get a blockbuster, they're all fighting for the same five or six stars and the same eight or nine star directors. Because so many people are bidding for their services, the stars can keep asking for more, and work as often or as infrequently as they choose."[16] Infrequency was an option strategically chosen by many during the 1970s when, permanently liberated from the bondage of studio contracts, stars were free for the first time to steer the course of their own careers. As entrepreneurs of their own images, they came to value exclusivity through fear of overexposure and a pragmatic desire to increase the demand for their services. Dustin Hoffman, who achieved superstardom in the wake of THE GRADUATE (Mike Nichols, 1967), averaged one film per year during the decade. (In 1972, for example, he made

Elliott Gould in Robert Altman's CALIFORNIA SPLIT (Columbia, 1974). Gould is often cited as an example of a 1970s star who compromised his "bankability" through overexposure. He appeared in eleven films between 1968 and 1973 at a time when comparable figures such as Dustin Hoffman and Barbra Streisand (to whom Gould was married from 1963 to 1967) averaged less than one a year; by mid-decade, though he was still in demand, his star had fallen, and by the end of it Gould was just another actor. (Overexposure notwithstanding, however, the kind of antiheroic persona Gould had established for himself in the late 1960s had become passé by the time of STAR WARS.)

only the Italian comedy ALFREDO, ALFREDO [Pietro Germi]; in 1973, PAPILLON [Franklin J. Schaffner]; in 1974, LENNY [Bob Fosse]; and in 1976, ALL THE PRESIDENT'S MEN [Alan J. Pakula].) Barbra Streisand, one of the era's most bankable stars, made only nine films during the 1970s. On the other hand, Elliott Gould, who began the decade as a New Hollywood icon and major star, is widely thought to have compromised his career through overexposure. (Gould appeared in eleven films from 1968 to 1973, when he was on the cover of *Time* magazine; he was so prominent during that five-year period that Ingmar Bergman chose him above all other American actors for the male lead in THE TOUCH [1971], but by 1975, the public seemed to have tired of him, and he appeared in films only sporadically in the latter part of the decade.)[17] By deliberately limiting the supply of their services, then, most stars of the 1970s dramatically inflated their worth as "pre-sold" elements in blockbuster packaging, and they did so at a time when Hollywood was producing fewer and fewer films each year.

Agency Control

Another factor in escalating star salaries was the rise of a new breed of aggressively competitive talent agencies, in the wake of MCA's withdrawal from the business in 1962 (as mandated by a Justice Department antitrust suit) in order to keep its Universal film and television studios. Shortly thereafter several former MCA agents, including Freddie Fields and David Begelman, founded Creative Management Associates (CMA—named so that it would have the same initials as MCA), taking with them such star clients as Judy Garland, Henry Fonda, Paul Newman, and Joanne Woodward. Whereas MCA had counted on volume, CMA was conceived as a boutique agency for stars; Fields and Begelman were known to be interested only in performers who could generate at least $100,000 a year in commissions, and by 1968 CMA had annual revenues of $11 million.[18] (Within several years, Fields was negotiating development deals with the automatic power to green light a picture if any one of five actors he handled said yes to a script; in 1974, for example, he personally brought Fox and Warners together to coproduce THE TOWERING INFERNO [John Guillermin], and cast it entirely from his own client list.)[19] After becoming the most powerful agency in Hollywood in the early 1970s, in December 1975 CMA was acquired by Marvin Josephson Associates, a small conglomerate that included a TV production firm, a concert-booking bureau, and International Famous Agency (IFA—formerly Ashley Famous Agency, headed by Ted Ashley until he became Warners' CEO in 1969). Josephson merged IFA, which specialized in television packages, with CMA to become International Creative Management (ICM), forming a company second in size only to the venerable William Morris Agency, which had been founded in 1898 to represent stage talent and grew into one of the most powerful talent agencies in Hollywood during the studio era and beyond. With 125 agents to Morris's 139, and earnings that would soon exceed Morris's $20 million a year, ICM was a formidable presence in the New Hollywood and for a while the older agency was its only competition.[20] At mid-decade, owing largely to the prowess of its top agent Stan Kamen, Morris was still very influential in the industry, although its power would decline after Michael Ovitz and four other agents left the company in January 1975 to form Creative Artists Agency (CAA), financing it with a $100,000 line of credit that two of them secured with their homes.[21]

Experienced mainly in television packaging, Ovitz, Ron Meyer, Bill Haber, Rowland Perkins, and Mike Rosenfeld had been proteges of veteran Morris agent Phil

Weltman. They left Morris when their mentor was fired, ostensibly for advancing age.[22] The foundational concept of CAA was thus loyalty and teamwork, combined with a fierce aggressiveness in stealing other agents' clients that earned it the sobriquet of "the wolfpack." Ovitz's corporate model was MCA streamlined as a boutique agency for stars. As Connnie Bruck would write in a *New Yorker* profile, "If CAA was in many respects an adaptation of MCA, it was MCA with a New-Age twist; the ethos that Ovitz preached was collectivism—a blend of team sports and Eastern-style management techniques somewhat reminiscent of the human potential movement of the early seventies."[23] CAA initially had a weak client list, taking with it from Morris not a single star, but a merger with the Martin Baum Agency in October 1976 brought it names like Sidney Poitier, Julie Andrews, Blake Edwards, Richard Harris, and Dyan Cannon.[24] By 1979, thanks largely to Ovitz's samurai-like tenacity and hypnotic powers of persuasion, CAA had become a major force in the industry, representing Robert Redford, Paul Newman, Dustin Hoffman, Sean Connery, Barbra Streisand, and about 700 others.[25] Among them, these three agencies—William Morris, International Creative Management, and Creative Artists Associates—dominated deal-making and packaging in the New Hollywood with a thoroughness that was very nearly complete; and talent representation, which had assumed a distinctly corporate character during the 1960s, became a central element in the management structure of the industry during the 1970s.

THE AGENT PACKAGE

The new power of agents stemmed from the studios' diminishing role as developers and hands-on producers—as opposed to financiers and distributors—of new projects. Once mere middlemen working for a flat percentage, agents now rushed into the vacuum left by the majors to become proprietary packagers and producers of films, with options to share in their profits. Increasingly they would bundle a property, writer, director, and star(s), all represented by their agency, together into a discrete package for sale to a distributor. The result was often a film made for the benefit of the packager rather than for some reason of merit or synergy inherent in the project itself. In fact, it became common in the 1970s to distinguish between films that were "packaged" with the main intent of maximizing agency profit and those that were "cast"—packaged only in the broad sense of bringing together the most desirable elements to produce a film. Aljean Harmetz sketched a scenario of the former in 1978: "The agent of two desirable stars packages them with a mediocre director he also represents gaining for himself 10 percent of three salaries instead of two."[26] (By the late 1970s, the agent would also collect 10 percent of his client's profit participation points; and for telefilm productions, big agencies could demand a "packaging fee," taking 6 to 10 percent of the entire budget instead of individual commissions from its clients.)[27] The agent might also produce, building his salary into the picture's budget; increasingly agents, entertainment attorneys, and business managers were becoming the producers, executive producers, or associate producers of their stars' films. Jon Peters, for example, who was Barbra Streisand's business manager during the 1970s (as well as her boyfriend and former hairdresser) was usually hired as the producer of her films, and at one point actually convinced Warners that he should direct the remake of A STAR IS BORN (1976).[28] (Calmer heads prevailed, and Frank Pierson did the job, although it's hard to think that Peters could have done any worse.)

The most famous example of agent-packaging in the 1970s is JAWS, where the rights to the novel, author-screenwriter Peter Benchley, director Steven Spielberg, and producers Richard Zanuck and David Brown were packaged by ICM and sold to Universal (with the agency collecting 10 percent of 54 percent of the film's profits, as owned collectively by its clients);[29] but the film was ultimately cast by Spielberg himself, resulting in the highly successful but offbeat combination of Richard Dreyfuss, Roy Scheider, and Robert Shaw.[30] As noted above, however, many films of the 1970s were packaged for no other reason than that an agent wanted two or more of his clients to work together to increase his fee (or *her* clients and *her* fees—ICM's "super-agent" during this era was the legendary Sue Mengers, whose clients for 1976 alone included Barbra Streisand, Ryan and Tatum O'Neal, Peter Bogdanovich, Candice Bergen, Cher, Faye Dunaway, Michael Caine, George Segal, Bob Fosse, Mike Nichols, Gene Hackman, Sidney Lumet, Ali MacGraw, Arthur Penn, Cybill Shepherd, and Tuesday Weld, generating some $1.5 million in commissions).[31] This practice resulted in some of the decade's most forgettable work, but occasionally even the most profit-driven packaging could have felicitous results. YOUNG FRANKENSTEIN (1974), for example, was born when IFA agent Mike Medavoy suggested that his client Gene Wilder make a film (*any* film) with two other clients, Marty Feldman and Peter Boyle, and Wilder proposed a horror-film spoof on the basis of a four-page "treatment" he had done several months before. Medavoy then brought in two other clients, Michael Gruskoff and Mel Brooks, to produce and direct, respectively, and pitched the project as a $2.3-million package first to Columbia, which turned it down as too expensive, and then to Alan Ladd, Jr., at Fox, who optioned it.

CASTING COMPANIES AND COMPLETION BONDS

Two important elements of packaging that evolved during the 1970s and became part of the industry mainstream were the use of casting directors and completion guarantees. During the 1950s and 1960s, all of the major studios maintained casting departments, but by the mid-1970s the studios were making so few films that they could no longer afford the overhead. At this point, independent casting directors like Lynn Stalmaster, Mike Fenton, Jane Feinberg, and Joyce Selznick stepped into the vacuum, founding services like Stalmaster and Associates, Inc. and Fenton-Feinberg to outsource casting decisions.[32] In collaboration with a film's director, these services would cast every speaking part, negotiate deals with the agents on salary and billing, clear the actor's good standing through the 43,000-member Screen Actors Guild (SAG), prepare contracts for all daily and weekly players (a studio's business affairs department usually drafted the contracts of major stars), make the actors' "first work call" (telling them when and where to report) and supervise voice-dubbing when principal photography was complete.[33] Fees for these services during the 1970s ranged between $6,000 and $20,000 per picture, and by the end of the decade casting directors were beginning to receive screen credit for their work. Casting directors frequently brought new talent into the industry that later rose to stardom, but they could only suggest lists of actors to producers and directors, who had the ultimate power to hire them, and their most vital contributions were in the casting of the smaller roles.

Like casting services, completion guarantee companies grew out of Hollywood's increasing reliance on independent production to supply a full year's schedule of films. Once production had left the studios, completion of a film on time and at or near budget became a major issue. Acting as financier-distributor rather than hands-on producer, the studio needed some means to assure a project's timely delivery to market. Studios might, for example, require a producer with other films in distribution to pledge income from them in order to complete delivery of the new film, or to pledge stocks and bonds or other securities against the film's completion pursuant to contract.[34] In the latter part of the decade, however, studios increasingly turned to completion guarantees from third parties who would have the right to take control of the production if the terms of the original agreement were not met. Such guarantees came to be known as "completion bonds," and they were written in the form of surety instruments to insure that a picture would come in on time and within 10 percent of its budget.[35] A number of companies were formed that specialized in completion bonds (Kurt Wollner's Film Finances and Bette Smith's Completion Bond Company are examples), typically charging producers a fee of about 6 percent of a film's budget, half of which was refunded if the guarantee was met; if not, the completion bond company kept the 6-percent premium, assumed control of the production, and paid its own money to complete the film.[36] By the mid-1980s, hundreds of films a year were covered by bond guarantees, and completion bond companies had acquired a good deal of power within the industry, owing not only to their "takeover positions" but to their vast files of financial reports and insider information about which directors and stars were "bondable" and which were not.

AGENTS AS PRODUCERS

In strengthening their hand as financier-distributors, the majors had tacitly ceded control of production to independent producers and agents. In 1980, Jeff Berg, the new 34-year-old president of ICM, who had packaged both AMERICAN GRAFFITI (George Lucas, 1973) for Universal and STAR WARS (George Lucas, 1977) for Fox, described the transformation this way: "Studios today, for the most part, don't initiate material that can be transformed into motion pictures. Therefore, most of the projects that are produced are offered to the studios by filmmakers or writers, through their agents. The process of initiation and creation has changed. The studio is the bank; the agent is the talent."[37] The impact of these changes on production was profound, as Frank Yablans, president of Paramount from 1971 to 1975, recalled in a 1996 interview: "During my era in the early '70s . . . [you] got a script, you hired a director, you hired the actors, you made the movie. Now they did it backward. The package was put together before the movie was ready to get made, so the script became the slave to the process, rather than the other way around. It was a lazy man's way of making movies."[38] Fundamentally a negotiating tool for agents, the package offered studios an attractive combination of production elements lacking only finance capital to become "a major motion picture," and if the price was high, so too was the promise of reward. Furthermore, as Yablans noted, package deals reduced studio executive workloads by leaving the really tough parts of the blockbuster calculus to someone else.

The power of agents in the New Hollywood was such that by 1977 six of the seven majors were run by former agents, five of them graduates of CMA. (The latter included David Begelman, president of Columbia, 1977–1978; Mike Medavoy, vice president in charge of West Coast production for United Artists, 1974–1978; Alan Ladd, Jr., president of 20th Century–Fox, 1976–1979; Richard [Dick] Shepherd, senior vice president and worldwide head of production for MGM, 1976–1980; and Martin Elfand, executive vice president in charge of worldwide production at Warner Bros., 1976–1978. The sixth former agent heading a studio was Ted Ashley, founder of the Ashley Famous Agency, board chairman and CEO of Warners, 1969–1980.)

"The Art of the Deal"

The rise of agent-packaging was a clear index of how the balance of power over creative affairs was shifting away from the studios in favor of agents and stars. As David Puttnam remarked, agents were no longer "salesmen peddling their clients' wares to the studios; they had become key brokers in the industry, instrumental in getting pictures off the ground."[39] By the late 1970s, more films were initiated in agent's offices than at the studios, and the big agency heads had become more powerful than their studio and network counterparts. And the incentives were high.

PROFIT PARTICIPATION: THE GROSS POINT DEAL

As budgets rose, so too did the fees agents could demand from the studios for their clients and demand from their clients for themselves. In addition to higher fees, agents also began the practice of negotiating for a percentage of the box-office gross. Ever since Lew Wasserman had negotiated a 50-percent share of the net profits from Universal's WINCHESTER '73 (Anthony Mann, 1950) for Jimmy Stewart in 1950, stars had been able to demand a contractual share of a film's box-office net; and as early as the 1960s agents began taking 10 percent of their clients' profit participation points in addition to 10 percent of their fees. (Stewart's was actually an "adjusted gross" deal, since his percentage was guaranteed after the studio had deducted for negative costs, distribution, and overhead; as a result, the star earned more than $600,000 on a film that was produced for $917,374.)[40] But a percentage of the gross meant sharing in *all* of the film's income before deductions were made for *any* expenses except the exhibitor's share and the distribution fee, so that a gross-point participant would make money regardless of whether the film succeeded or failed. Furthermore, the percentage was calculated on the so-called "distributor's gross," which normally included all moneys received by the distributor for the exploitation of a film, including sales to ancillary markets like television and cable. This practice arose in part to combat the majors' notoriously mendacious book-keeping practices that used "studio overhead" and other hard-to-verify expenses (combined with outright cheating) as a way of concealing profits. In addition to overhead, often charged at a flat rate of 25 percent of actual production expenses and included as an accounting entry within the film's "negative cost," the studios also charged producers substantial penalty fees for going over budget (ALIEN [Ridley Scott, 1979] was fined $1.9 million by Fox),[41] and they assessed interest on the negative cost at the rate of 125 percent of prime until the film broke even—a point commonly considered to have been reached when it returned 2.5 times its negative cost.[42] All of these charges were assessed against profits before profit-sharing could begin. As Robert Evans remarked at the time: "To be successful as a profit participant, it's not enough to have a film that makes money. You have to have a blockbuster."[43] And sometimes not even then: for example, Fox declared a $4-million profit on its $11-million ALIEN, which was the fifth highest grossing film of 1979, only after it had returned $40.3 million in domestic rentals in July 1980.

SUPER-STAR LEVERAGE

Ultimately, however, it was the blockbuster syndrome and its obsession with risk reduction that led studios to bid up the price of talent during the decade. Major stars were especially important in securing foreign markets, which in the 1970s accounted for roughly half of a studio film's grosses. By 1977, the handful of superstars who were thought to guarantee box-office success both at home and abroad could command the then-unprecedented compensation of $1–2 million in salary plus a percentage of the gross receipts (sometimes as high as 20 percent). The mere presence in a package of figures like Clint Eastwood, Robert Redford, Barbra Streisand (considered the decade's only bankable female star, although by the end of it Jane Fonda had edged toward that status),[43A] Steve McQueen, Paul Newman, Dustin Hoffman, Jack Nicholson, and Burt Reynolds was enough to secure financing and distribution.[44] In one famous example, the project to film Ken Kesey's novel *One Flew Over the Cuckoo's*

Jack Nicholson conserved his image better than did Gould, but he also changed it from the rebellious persona of his characters in FIVE EASY PIECES (Bob Rafelson, 1970) and THE LAST DETAIL (Hal Ashby, 1973) to something more malleable and user-friendly in ONE FLEW OVER THE CUKOO'S NEST (Milos Forman, 1975), where his presence alone was enough to secure financing and distribution (by United Artists). By the time of THE MISSOURI BREAKS, Nicholson was commanding a $1.25-million salary plus a percentage of the gross (21.3% in this case, which he shared with costar Marlon Brando).

Nest (1962) was shopped around Hollywood for years before producer Michael Douglas was able to raise $3 million to produce the movie in 1975 by signing Jack Nicholson to play the lead. After it went on to become the second most profitable film of the year and sweep the Oscars (including winning the Best Actor award for Nicholson), Nicholson was packaged with Marlon Brando in a complicated deal to star in THE MISSOURI BREAKS (1976), a Persky-Bright tax shelter production and one of the decade's major flops. (Negotiations among lawyers, agents, and accountants were so convoluted, according to director Arthur Penn, that "the picture took only a few months to shoot but the deal lasted nearly a year.")[45]

Although the film earned just $7 million in rentals, Nicholson and Brando collected $1.25 million each in salary and shared 21.3 percent of the gross between them, canceling all hope of profitability. Yet the producers would never have been able to raise the film's $8.2 million production budget without the guaranteed presence of the two stars whose compensation accounted for nearly one-third of it. Producer Tony Bill remarked of this phenomenon in 1978: "There are only 20 people in this business who can get a film made—seven movie stars, six heads of studios, and seven top directors. Since they decide what movies will be made anyway, we ought to make [the stars] heads of the studios."[46] (Some stars, in fact, attempted to establish their own studios during 1970s; for example, First Artists Production Company, Ltd. was operated by Paul Newman, Barbra Streisand, Sidney Poitier, Dustin Hoffman, and Steve McQueen to produce their own independent projects, under the agency of CMA president Freddie Fields.)[47]

Producer Joseph E. Levine paid Robert Redford $2 million for three weeks' work on A BRIDGE TOO FAR *(Richard Attenborough, 1977) because his participation in the film was enough to ensure financing and distribution by United Artists.*

By the second half of the decade, then, a small number of stars and their agents were effectively running the industry—choosing which films got made and by whom—and they demanded compensation both in terms of enormous salaries and residual income. (In the 1980s, "salary" for superstars would disappear as a concept and be replaced by "upfront money," that is, an advance guarantee against a percentage of the distributor's gross from the first dollar earned at the box office.)[48] In several more flagrant examples, Robert Redford was paid $2 million by Joseph E. Levine for three weeks' work in A BRIDGE TOO FAR (Richard Attenborough, 1977), Steve McQueen wanted $3 million for three weeks in APOCALYPSE NOW (Francis Ford Coppola, 1979; Coppola refused),[49] Marlon Brando negotiated $3 million plus 10 percent of the gross above $60 million for his brief appearance in SUPERMAN (Richard Donner, 1978), and Jane Fonda received $2 million from Columbia in 1979 to appear in a prison movie to be called "Her Brother's Keeper" whether or not it was ultimately made—which it wasn't.[50] (This kind of "pay or play" deal, in which the studio was obliged to pay actors their full fee irrespective of whether a film was ever produced, became increasingly common in the 1980s, resulting in a "use-it-or-lose-it" mentality among studio executives and a number of misbegotten pictures.)

By the end of the decade, gross percentage points for stars, directors, and other production artists had reduced the money returned to the distributor from the box office by as much as one-third[51]—an astounding shift in intramural industry income that intensified the blockbuster mentality and left the majors more desperate than ever to option only films with mass appeal. It was clear, moreover, that too much gross participation could drain off a movie's revenue stream, so that it *never* generated net profits. (In a classic case from the 1980s, Jack Nicholson's sliding 15–20-percent gross participation in BATMAN [Tim Burton, 1989] accounted for over $50 million—which, after deductions for the distribution fee and expenses, left the top-grossing blockbuster of 1989 virtually without net earnings.)[52] Thus, the practice of gross participation added yet another bizarre dimension to the surreal economic landscape of the New Hollywood—one in which stars could get rich by appearing (or in cases like Fonda's, not appearing) in movies like THE MISSOURI BREAKS (1976) and A BRIDGE TOO FAR (1977) that were box-office failures, while box-office hits like ALIEN (1979) would generate only miniscule net profits for their producers and other profit participants (often writers, directors, and mid-level stars). And if the film were also a tax shelter, its investors would benefit either way. With more money (sometimes) to made on *producing* a movie than on *releasing* it, some producers ceased to regard filmmaking as a speculative investment at all. On the surface at least, it seemed that at some point during the 1970s the American film industry had inverted the logic of capitalism by making commercial failure pay.

A NEW BALANCE OF WEALTH AND POWER

As the newly privileged "art of the deal" drove star salaries and gross-point participation through the roof, it was observed by Joan Didion, Andrew Sarris, Tom Wolfe and others (e.g., AIP's Samuel Z. Arkoff) that deal-making had replaced filmmaking as the principal activity of Hollywood.[53] And as studios and producers devised intricate new methods of production finance—the sale of ancillary and foreign distribution rights, product licensing, attracting "outside money" through tax-leveraged investments—deals became increasingly complex, with more elements to coordinate and higher risks. According to Mark Littman, by the mid-1980s it was not unusual for studio contracts to append eighteen-page definitions of net profits.[54] Given the enormous sums suddenly being spent on production, promotion, and distribution; complicated decisions about property acquisition ("literary purchase agreements"), project development, financing, and multimedia marketing; and investments in high-priced talent that, as producer Walter Coblenz put it, "often have little relation to the economics involved and the moneys that the film is going to generate,"[55] it seemed to many observers that Hollywood had indeed lost its reason and turned capitalism upside-down.

In fact, what had occurred was a redistribution of wealth among the managing elites in favor of stars, agents, and major distributors at the expense of independent producers and exhibitors. For stars and their agents, the legacy of the 1970s was to make them the most powerful constituents of the industry, after the major studios themselves. From Freddie Fields at Creative Management Associates (CMA) to Sue Mengers at International Creative Management (ICM) to Stan Kamen at William Morris to Michael Ovitz at Creative Artists Agency (CAA), the super-agents of the 1970s restructured power relationships in Hollywood for decades to come. (During the 1980s and 1990s, for example, no one in Hollywood wielded more power than CAA president and founder Michael Ovitz, whose influence was greater than that of any single studio head or bankable artist, including Steven Spielberg.) As star compensation and agent fees continued to rise beyond the 1970s, production cost inflation caused a leap-frog escalation of budgets that has never stopped. By the early 1980s it was possible for a superstar like Sylvester Stallone to earn $15 million a picture (Rocky IV [Sylvester Stallone, 1983]), and the average negative cost had risen to $16.8 million (1984). A decade later, the outer limit of advance compensation for stars had reached $20 million and the average negative cost was $34.3 million, an increase of nearly 300 percent over 1980; the spiral continues unabated.

Distribution Takes Command

Far from damaging the majors, however, ever-rising costs served to drive all but the giants out of the market. During the 1970s, the seven major film financing-distribution companies watched their share of the domestic market increase from $500 million in 1972 to $1,215 million in 1978; an increase of 143 percent, while the domestic box-office gross rose only 67 percent.[56] Put another way, film rentals—the share of admissions money paid over by exhibitors to distributors—escalated as a percentage of box-office gross from 31.6 percent in 1972 to 45.8 percent in 1978. During the same period, operating profits of the film and television divisions of the majors rose a corresponding 140 percent.[57] While distribution was dramatically increasing its share of the box-office dollar, however, exhibition was making only modest gains and depended more and more on concession revenues to balance the books. In fact, between 1972 and 1982 the percentage of total exhibitor revenues generated by concession sales increased from 13.5 percent to 20 percent, which, according to the National Association of Concessionaires, accounted for 100 percent of the net profits of most American theaters.[58] Yet resurgence of film attendance in the late 1970s combined with the studios' rationing of product left theater owners hungry for movies to fill their screens (by the end of the decade, the majors were releasing on average just over 100 features per year, down from about 150 ten years before).[59] As virtually the only game in town, the majors could demand favorable rental rates and, through the practice of blind-bidding, force exhibitors to gamble millions in advance guarantees on films they had never seen (often because they had yet to be made). Furthermore, having streamlined their operations by consolidating key city exchanges into regional ones, distributors were able to impose multiple runs and amortize soaring advertising costs, since it was much more cost effective to advertise a picture opening in forty theaters at once than in one.

In effect, the majors had limited product supply and multiplied its exposure by wide release, meaning that there were fewer films to see but more opportunities to see them. One result was that throughout the decade the audience for the ten highest-grossing films each year grew at three times the rate of the total audience, with the effect that, as James Monaco put it, "increasingly we are all going to see the same ten movies."[60] Two years earlier, Robert Lindsey had been more blunt, writing that although they were not a cartel in the strictest sense, the majors were inescapably "enjoying the benefits of what amounts to one."

MULTIPLEXING AND THE CHILLING OF DISTRIBUTOR-EXHIBITOR RELATIONS

Much of the power and prosperity of distribution during the 1970s came at the expense of exhibition, which had simultaneously undergone a significant structural change. During the 1960s, a trend began toward dividing single-screen theaters into two or more smaller ones to save on new construction and operating costs. Known as "multiplexing," the practice initially sprang up in shopping centers, which had experienced an exponential growth from about 1,500 in 1965, to 12,500 in 1970, to 22,500 by 1980.[61] The key players in multiplexing were American Multi-Cinema (AMC) and General Cinema Corporation, who worked with shopping center developers throughout the late sixties and 1970s to preplan hundreds of new malls anchored by their multiple-screen theaters. As Douglas Gomery notes, by the early 1970s an increasing number of American cities had no single-screen cinemas left within their borders, with the exception of art houses, adult theaters, and other such specialized venues.[62] By the early 1980s, four multiplex chains dominated the North American market—General Cinema, with 1,050 screens in 350 locations; United Artists Communications, Inc., with 1,005 screens in 350 locations; American Multi-Cinema, with 734 screen in 130 locations; and Plitt Theaters, with about 600 screens in 300 sites.[63] Throughout the 1970s, while the number of screens was growing steadily thanks to the multiplex phenomenon, the number of seats was actually declining (probably because so many multiplexes were created through the subdivision of existing single-screen theaters). The Commerce Department's 1982 census of indoor theaters revealed the existence of 14,977 screens with a seating capacity of 5.12 million, as compared with 10,694 screens and a seating capacity of 6.1 million in 1972. (The number of drive-ins remained relatively constant, declining from 3,734 in 1972 to 3,043 in 1982.) During the same ten years, furthermore, the average number of seats per auditorium declined from 567 to 342.[64]

For the exhibitors, the advantages of multiplexing were clear—in addition to consolidating operating costs, more screens meant the ability to offer more variety to the consumer and increased the odds of coming up with a hit. During the 1970s, when distribution contracts began to demand longer runs, multiplex exhibitors could amortize the cost of an unpopular or played-out film by shifting it from a larger to a smaller auditorium, in effect creating a "second run" for the film within the walls of a single theater. In fact, multiplexes virtually eliminated the second tier of exhibition, reducing many former second-run houses in the suburbs to sub-run ("dollar theater") status. At the same time, the new distribution practice of saturation booking or wide release, inaugurated for mainstream films by JAWS in 1975, caused a significant increase in the number of the-

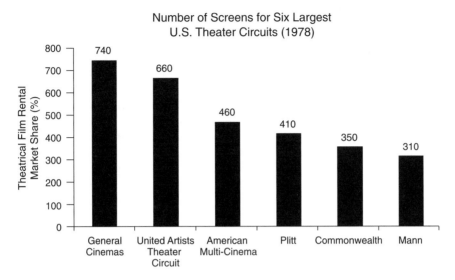

Number of Screens for Six Largest
U.S. Theater Circuits (1978)

SOURCE: *International Motion Picture Almanac,* 1979.

aters in key or sub-key status from 23 to 25 percent of the total in the late 1960s to 45 percent in the late 1970s; and 55 to 60 percent by 1981.[65] Undertaken mainly to defray soaring production and marketing costs, especially those of advertising on national television, saturation booking kept major films at a higher level of release for longer periods of time, during which higher admission prices could be charged. This resulted in a steady 7.7 percent annual growth in revenues throughout the decade, culminating in the record-breaking $2.8-billion box-office gross of 1979, although admissions grew only 2.1 percent. Meanwhile, the majors' increasing involvement with megabudget "event" pictures led them to impose blind-bidding on exhibitors in order to raise production capital and lay off risk, creating a shakeout in which the four chains listed above were left to dominate the American exhibition market with 2,719 screens—16 percent of the domestic total, nearly the percentage controlled by the majors before the Paramount decrees.[66]

Before the post-JAWS blockbuster era, there was a certain amount of give-and-take in distributor-exhibitor relationships, especially in the area of booking contracts. For example, if the exhibitor booked a flop at exorbitant rates, the distributor's sales department would traditionally offer "relief" by renegotiating the contract or giving the exhibitor a favorable deal on an upcoming release.[67] Such latitude was possible when there were seven major studios annually releasing twenty to twenty-five films each; but by 1977 there were six majors releasing twelve to fifteen films a year, and distributors had begun to enforce contracts calling for large advances and guaranteed runs of up to ten weeks. In this way, distributors could extract income from films like MIDWAY (Universal; Jack Smight, 1975) and LUCKY LADY (Fox; Stanley Donen, 1975) that exhibitors didn't want to rent and the public wouldn't pay to see. By limiting supply, the studios increased demand in classical Keynesian fashion (thus the terms "product shortage" and "film famine" so prevalent in mid-1970s trade publications).[68] Yet the 100–125 films per year produced by the majors during this period did not even come *close* to satisfying market demand, and, as distributors, they came to depend more and more on privately financed independent producers to supply exhibitors with a full year's supply of product.[69]

DISTRIBUTORS AND "INDIES"

To attract the independents, or "indies," the majors began to lower their distribution fees—typically, from the range of 30–35 percent of gross rentals down to 25 percent or lower. (The fee is charged for handling the film, exclusive of print and advertising costs, although these are negotiable as part of the deal—for example, the deal made by United Artists to distribute MGM films domestically called for a 22.5-percent fee, with United Artists advancing the cost of prints and advertising.[70] Another kind of distribution deal used in the 1970s, most commonly for negative pickups—that is, films acquired for distribution on the basis of a completed negative—involved a straight split of the gross rentals between producer and distributor without any deductions for costs, usually 40/60 percent—a division corresponding to the multiple of two-and-a-half used to calculate the break-even point.)[71] According to A. D. Murphy, by 1976 independent film production in the United States represented an investment of nearly $100 million, and "outside indie" production had reached a level of 300 pictures per year, or about two-thirds of the American total.[72] Furthermore, despite the elimination of tax-shelter financing in September 1976, there was an unprecedented boom in independently produced features in the first six months of 1977 as filmmaking's potential for short-term high yields continued to attract private investors away from stocks and real estate.[73] Yet *Variety* calculated that between 1970 and 1979 an independently produced English-language film without a major distributor stood only a 50-percent chance of getting a domestic theatrical release.[74]

Thus, as negative costs continued to rise toward the decade's end, the major risks of production were increasingly borne by the exhibitor and independent producer, not the distribution company (for whom by 1979 it typically cost $4 million to open a film nationally with a minimum of 500 prints).[75] For example, distributor outlays for the $55-million SUPERMAN (1978) were largely amortized by advance minimum

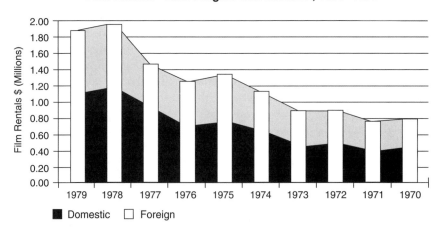

Film Rentals - Nine Largest U.S. Studios*, 1970–1979

SOURCE: *Warner Communications,* 1979 (Werthein & Co.).

* Allied Artists, Columbia, Disney, MGM, Paramount, 20th Century–Fox,
United Artists, Universal, and Warner Bros.

	1970	1971	1972	1973	1974	1975	1976	1977	1978	1979
American International	na	na	na	na	3.8	3.4	3.8	3.4	1.4	2.8
Buena Vista (Disney)	9.1	8.0	5.0	6.5	7.0	6.0	6.7	5.6	4.8	6.2
Columbia	14.1	10.2	9.1	7.0	7.0	13.1	8.3	11.5	11.6	14.0
MGM	3.4	9.3	6.0	4.6	---	---	---	---	---	---
Paramount	11.8	17.0	21.6	8.6	10.0	11.3	9.6	10.0	23.8	16.0
20th Century–Fox	19.4	11.5	9.1	18.8	10.9	14.0	13.4	19.5	13.4	16.0
United Artists	8.7	7.4	15.0	10.7	8.5	10.7	16.2	17.8	10.3	7.0
Universal	13.1	5.2	5.0	10.0	18.6	25.1	13.0	11.5	16.8	20.0
Warner Bros.	5.3	9.3	17.6	16.4	23.2	9.1	18.0	13.7	13.2	14.0
All others	15.3	22.1	11.6	17.4	11.0	7.3	11.0	7.0	4.7	4.0
Total	100.2	100.0	100.0	100.0	100.0	100.0	100.0	100.0	100.0	100.0

SOURCE: *Variety* reports.

Major American Distributors' Domestic Market Shares (1970–79).

guarantees, and the $36-million APOCALYPSE NOW (1979) was secured by the producer (Francis Ford Coppola) pledging his personal assets.[76] Despite the fact that advertising and promotion costs were soaring and that star talent was exerting leverage against the studios as never before, box-office dollars were rising far ahead of costs, and the industry had stabilized around a new product—the blockbuster, or "event" movie, prepackaged by agencies, pre-sold by marketing departments, and franchised through remakes, sequels, and series, so that its shelf-life might extend for decades. Hollywood's new focus on "special attractions" affected release schedules as well as booking practices. Instead of distributing their films at regular intervals throughout the year (as they had done when committed to supplying exhibitors with a full twelve months of their own product), the majors concentrated their most important releases in peak seasons—summer, Thanksgiving, Christmas-New Year's, Easter—which accounted for 20–25 weeks per year, to which another ten weeks might be added for good-to-average business.[77] With one-third of the year not covered by "Establishment" production, independent producers and exhibitor-producer combines like EXPRODICO were left to fill in during the "low seasons" of autumn and spring, with the majors as their distributors. But because the majors dominated the U.S. box office so completely, independents were left to scramble for 10–15 percent of the rental market—barely enough to recoup costs—and sometimes much less. (In 1977, for example, the majors accounted for 93 percent of American distributors' gross in the United States and Canada, and in the same year distributed all but one of the films that earned over $10 million in rentals.)[78] On the other hand, the distributor's share of box-office admissions rose steadily from 31 percent in 1970 to 45 percent in 1979 because film rentals grew much faster than grosses.[79] Combined with the revenue streams flowing from such ancillary markets as foreign distribution, network and syndicated television, and emerging pay cable and home video, surging theatrical rentals left the majors in an unchallengeable position of strength at the decade's end, in complete recovery from the deficits, buyouts, and near bankruptcies of the 1969–1971 recession.

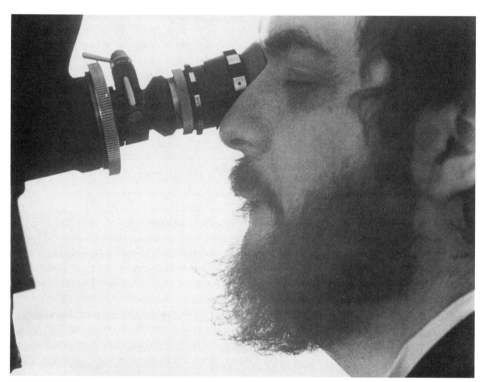

*Stanley Kubrick checking a shot for A Clockwork Orange (Warners, 1971). In the
three films that he made between 1971 and 1980, Kubrick appropriated and refined
new technologies of representation like no other director of his time.*

9

Technological Innovation and Aesthetic Response

I like to compare this revolution [in cinematography] of fast lenses plus pushed development to painting. . . . Impressionism also came out of a technological discovery, which was the tube of oil paint, as opposed to being limited to paint you had to prepare and mix yourself. The tubes were now ready-made, so you just took them in a box, went any place. You could paint Notre Dame at different hours of the day as Monet did. . . . So, in the case of cinematography as well: if we are doing things now that have not been done before, it is not only because of a revolution out of our genius, but also because nowadays you can do things you could not do before.

NESTOR ALMENDROS, ASC, C. 1980

While the 1970s didn't experience a technological-economic revolution on the order of the conversion to sound in the late 1920s, or to widescreen in the early 1950s, the decade witnessed a series of innovations and refinements that changed the way films were made for the rest of the century. These innovations came in three main areas: cinematography (lens and camera technology, stabilization systems and camera mounts); special effects (traveling matte photography, video and motion-control systems); and sound recording and playback (Dolby stereo optical sound, Dolby surround). Many were based on computers' increasing capacity to precisely regulate certain mechanical operations essential to production and on video's developing capability to monitor those operations and facilitate their remote control. These circumstances worked together to make the technology of filmmaking lighter, more flexible, and therefore more responsive to the wide variety of location contexts in which production now took place. Concurrent innovations in projection technology made exhibition more cost-effective and contributed to the spread of multiplex theaters.

Cinematography

Cinematography in the 1970s acquired a distinctive look that was characterized by the use of heavy lens diffusion, the introduction of fast lenses that could register images at very low levels of light, and the practice of "pushing" the film in the lab—overdeveloping it to increase its speed, thus accommodating enhanced lighting effects. The increased use of diffusion was an aesthetic phenomenon, seemingly a reaction to the high image definition made possible by recent refinements in film stock. Glass diffusion filters, or "fog filters," were long used to simulate fog or soften images in close-up, but cinematographers in the 1970s employed them for the first time throughout entire films to reduce image sharpness and stylize their work.[1] The introduction of fast lenses and overdevelopment, on the other hand, produced a technological revolution in cinematography that Nestor Almendros—one of the great cinematographers of the 1970s — compared to the revolution that occurred in painting in the late nineteenth century when premixed tubes of oil paint became widely available.[2]

The invocation of painting is instructive because a new aesthetic consciousness entered American cinematography during the 1970s, and the cameraman became an auteurist cult figure second only to the director. (As for direction, with *The Director's Event* [1969] and *The Film Director as Superstar* [1970], the titles of two popular books published early in the decade—*Hollywood Cameramen: Sources of Light* [1970] and *Behind the Camera: The Cinematographer's Art* [1971]—were indicative of this newly heightened status.)[3] The change was partly driven by an influx of European cameramen (Almendros, for example, had worked extensively with Rohmer and Truffaut), who found themselves able to work, with notable restrictions, in the American industry for the first time since its unionization in the 1920s. But it was cemented by young American cameramen, many from the East Coast, who ultimately took control of the closed-shop Hollywood cinematographers' union Local 659, International Photographers of the International Alliance of Theatrical Stage Employees (IATSE), ending its monopolistic control of high-paying jobs and lowering the rigid barriers to entry into the profession.[4] (Cinematographers had unionized and affiliated with IATSE, an AFL union, in 1928.)

LOCAL 659 AND OTHER BARRIERS TO ENTRY

Until the 1970s, Local 659 was the most conservative of all Hollywood unions, restricting the number of persons who could serve as directors of photography (DPs) to 200 of its senior members. Since only approved union members could be hired by unionized major studios, these 200 cameramen (who were by the mid-1960s all age sixty and over) dominated the profession.[5] When Conrad Hall (b. 1926), Haskell Wexler (b. 1926), Laszlo Kovacs (b. 1932), and Vilmos Zsigmond (b. 1930)—the four leading cinematographers of the early 1970s—began working in the 1960s, each had to overcome this archaic set of union rules before they could become DPs. (Kovacs and Zsigmond had emigrated together from Hungary after the 1956 revolution, which they documented in some 30,000 feet of film that was ultimately sold to CBS. They were both trained at the Budapest film academy, 1952–1956, but spent their entire professional careers in the American industry.) Most worked first as non-union cameramen for television or low-budget exploitation films, such as those produced by AIP, before breaking into the union, then struggled up its stepladder structure to become Group One cinematographers (who could plan camera set-ups and lighting but were not allowed to operate their own cameras) and full-fledged DPs. (Because of their early status as outsiders, Hall, Wexler, Kovacs, Zsigmond, and Owen Roizman [see below] made a pact never to take over a picture from another cameraman without that individual's approval.)[6]

The barriers to entry into the profession were considerable. As late as 1975, ten young cameramen, including Tak Fujimoto and Andrew Davis, filed a class action suit against Local 659 charging that they had been illegally denied entrance to the union, and therefore to jobs. (The suit was later settled out of court.) Moreover, if a production company wished to hire a foreign-born cameraman (as, for example, when BBS wanted to hire Almendros for a film to be entitled "Gone Beaver" in 1972), union regulations required that the film also employ a "standby" cameraman from its membership ranks, adding significantly—often prohibitively—to its costs.[7] Furthermore, the Immigration and Naturalization Service required union support before granting a temporary work permit to the foreign cameraman, and such support was rarely forthcoming within the West Coast jurisdiction of Local 659.[8] (Outside California, productions fared somewhat better—the great Belgian cinematographer Ghislain Cloquet was given permission to shoot Arthur Penn's MICKEY ONE in Chicago in 1965, and Czech cameraman Miroslav Ondricek shot TAKING OFF for Milos Forman in Manhattan in 1968, with the tacit support of the New York local. However, Local 659 even made it difficult for American cinematographers from out-of-state to work in Hollywood—as when it refused to let New York-based Gordon Willis work on Hal Ashby's HAROLD AND MAUDE in 1971.)

Some directors were able to employ foreign cinematographers when they shot on location in Southern right-to-work states—Monte Hellman used Almendros on COCKFIGHTER (1974), which was shot in Georgia; and Robert Altman hired French cameraman Jean Boffety to shoot THIEVES LIKE US (1974) on location in Mississippi.[9] The turning point arrived in 1978, when producer Dino De Laurentiis threatened to move KING OF THE GYPSIES (Frank Pierson, 1978) out of New York City if Swedish cinematographer Sven Nykvist, a frequent collaborator of Bergman, was not allowed to work on it.[10] The dispute was resolved by the New York local in De Laurentiis's favor, and an important precedent was established for flexing union rules. Yet when the Italian cinematographer Vittorio Storaro (Bernardo Bertolucci's cameraman, 1970–1978, and the DP on APOCALYPSE NOW [Francis Ford Coppola, 1979]) arrived in Hollywood to shoot the last five days of Warren Beatty's REDS (1981), having already shot the rest of it on international locations, Local 659 objected to his working in their jurisdiction and demanded that the film be finished by a union man—who was credited as "Director of Photography" while Storaro was given only a "Photographed By" credit. (In a letter to the American Society of Cinematographers, Storaro described this as "an act against the cinematographers of all nations as authors of their own work; an act against the very membership of the union in question; and act against the magic of the 'literature of light'—photography.")[11] Nevertheless, the Academy voted Storaro its award for Best Cinematography for his work on REDS (as it had done for APOCALYPSE NOW), and although they were still prevented from working on union films produced in Hollywood, between 1978 and 1984 foreign cameramen took that award exclusively, so great had their stylistic influence become.[12]

NEW CINEMATOGRAPHERS ENTER THE INDUSTRY MAINSTREAM
(AND HELP TO CHANGE ITS COURSE)

Yet during the 1970s the union began responding to an influx of younger men who would ultimately change the practice of cinematography in the American cinema— Hall, Wexler, Kovacs, Zsigmond, and a handful of dynamic others. Some were film school graduates like William Fraker (b. 1923) who had chosen to become cameramen precisely to bridge the generation gap created by the new producers and directors who came to dominate the youth-conscious Hollywood of the late 1960s (many of whom found it uncomfortable to work with older cinematographers and their preconceived notions about style dating from the studio era). In films such as ROSEMARY'S BABY (Roman Polanski, 1968) and BULLITT (Peter Yates, 1968), Fraker was among the first to use heavily diffused light, making it an available fashion for colleagues like Conrad Hall, whose use of it for BUTCH CASSIDY AND THE SUNDANCE KID (George Roy Hill, 1969) helped to win him an Academy Award. (TELL THEM WILLIE BOY IS HERE [Abraham Polonsky, 1969] is actually a better example of the technique.) Hall shot five features during the 1970s, and was particularly admired for his 1930s-style "period" photography on THE DAY OF THE LOCUST (John Schlesinger, 1975). Fraker, who had been Hall's camera operator on THE PROFESSIONALS (Richard Brooks, 1966), shot several distinctively stylized films in the next decade, including RANCHO DELUXE (Frank Perry, 1975), EXORCIST II: THE HERETIC (John Boorman, 1977), LOOKING FOR MR. GOODBAR (Richard Brooks, 1977), HEAVEN CAN WAIT (Warren Beatty, 1978), and 1941 (Steven Spielberg, 1979), and also provided additional photography for CLOSE ENCOUNTERS OF THE THIRD KIND (Steven Spielberg, 1977), most of which was shot by Zsigmond. Haskell Wexler won an Oscar for his black-and-white cinematography in WHO'S AFRAID OF VIRGINIA WOOLF? (Mike Nichols, 1966), and he experimented with desaturated color as early as 1967 on IN THE HEAT OF THE NIGHT (Norman Jewison), anticipating a major 1970s trend. Wexler directed the landmark *cinema verité*-style feature MEDIUM COOL in 1969, and in the 1970s he shot such important films as AMERICAN GRAFFITI (George Lucas, 1973), BOUND FOR GLORY (Hal Ashby, 1976)—for which he won a second Academy Award—and COMING HOME (Hal Ashby, 1978); Wexler also did the initial photography for Francis Ford Coppola's THE CONVERSATION (1974), collaborated with William Fraker and Bill Butler on the photography for Milos Forman's ONE FLEW OVER THE CUCKOO'S NEST (1975), and completed Nestor Almendros's work on DAYS OF HEAVEN (Terrence Malick, 1978) when Almendros had to leave to work with Truffaut.

As for the Hungarians, Laszlo Kovacs became associated with long-lens, rack-focus photography in the exploitation films he shot for Richard Rush (HELL'S ANGELS ON WHEELS [1967]; PSYCH-OUT [1968]) and Peter Bogdanovich (TARGETS [1968]), before becoming the house cinematographer for BBS (EASY RIDER [Dennis Hopper, 1969]; FIVE EASY PIECES [Bob Rafelson, 1970]; THE KING OF MARVIN GARDENS [Bob Rafelson, 1972], etc.). Kovacs had perfected long-take, deep-space staging as a economic necessity during his low-budget days, and used it to great effect in some of the decade's most notable period pieces—Peter Bogdanovich's PAPER MOON (1973), AT LONG LAST LOVE (1975), and NICKELODEON (1976); Scorsese's NEW YORK NEW YORK (1977); Norman Jewison's F.I.S.T. (1978); and Richard Lester's BUTCH AND SUNDANCE: THE EARLY DAYS (1979). In contrast to contemporary trends, Kovacs generally avoided lens diffusion and used bright, direct light whenever possible; the best example of this sharper, more naturalistic look is probably SHAMPOO (Hal Ashby, 1975).

Vilmos Zsigmond, easily the most distinctive stylist of the decade, cultivated a darker, more "textural" style based on soft light, long lenses, elaborate diffusion, and manipulated exposure.[13] His innovative use of filters and lab processes dramatically extended the boundaries of creative cinematography.[14] As a veteran of multiple 1960s exploitation films (many of which he and Kovacs worked on together, uncredited), Zsigmond was first widely praised for the impressionistic, sepia-toned photography of McCABE &

MRS. MILLER (Robert Altman, 1971), and for the constantly moving pan-and-zoom lens choreography of Altman's THE LONG GOODBYE (1973). He soon became the most sought-after of the New Hollywood cinematographers, creating an uncharacteristically stark and desaturated look for the natural locations of John Boorman's DELIVERANCE (1972), and lending Steadicam-like fluidity to the Panaflex camerawork of Steven Spielberg's debut feature THE SUGARLAND EXPRESS (1974) and radiant luminosity to his CLOSE ENCOUNTERS OF THE THIRD KIND (1977; additional photography by Fraker, but Academy Award for Best Cinematography to Zsigmond). He extemporized on VERTIGO's diaphanous lens diffusion for Brian De Palma's OBSESSION (1976), re-created the smoky haze of a steel mill town for Michael Cimino's THE DEER HUNTER (1978; for which he won the Academy Award for Best Cinematography), and used real smoke and dust to diffuse the natural light as it would have appeared in the late nineteenth-century Wyoming of HEAVEN'S GATE (Michael Cimino, 1980). From his earliest exploitation days, the majority of Zsigmond's work was in the widescreen format (the low-budget horror films he shot for Al Adamson were all in Technoscope)[15]—in the 1970s, he worked most often in Panavision anamorphic (the contemporary version of Cinema-Scope) and his genius for composing in the 2.35:1 aspect ratio was well known.

Several of the new breed of cameramen came from the New York teleproduction industry, where they began as assistants and operators on commercials. Among the most notable are Gordon Willis (b. 1931) and Owen Roizman (b. 1936). After he began to make features in 1970 (LOVING [Irvin Kershner]; THE LANDLORD [Hal Ashby]), Willis quickly became known as a "cinematographer's cinematographer" among his peers, but was so consistently ignored by the Academy for the rest of the decade that he was rumored to have been unofficially blackballed. (In 1983, he was finally nominated, and won, for his work on Woody Allen's ZELIG.) As Todd McCarthy has remarked, however, if there was a conspiracy against Willis it was one of artistic conservatism rather than industry politics, because Willis's dark and brooding style violated the rules of classical Hollywood cinematography more than that of any of the other new DPs.[16] At its most richly evocative in Francis Ford Coppola's THE GODFATHER (1972) and THE GODFATHER, PART II (1974), Alan J. Pakula's ALL THE PRESIDENT'S MEN (1976), and Woody Allen's ANNIE HALL (1977), his work influenced a whole generation of younger cameramen for whom he became, in the words of John Bailey (who filmed BOULEVARD NIGHTS [Michael Pressman, 1979]; AMERICAN GIGOLO [Paul Schrader, 1980]; and ORDINARY PEOPLE [Robert Redford, 1980]), the "preeminent American cinematographer."[17] Willis was particularly admired for his collaboration with production designers (e.g., Dean Tavoularis on the GODFATHER films) to achieve a film's overall look, and his perfectionism made him the most respected cinematographer of his generation.

Owen Roizman acquired a reputation for gritty realism in urban crime thrillers like THE FRENCH CONNECTION (William Friedkin, 1971) and THE TAKING OF PELHAM ONE TWO THREE (Joseph Sargent, 1974); but he was extremely versatile during the 1970s, shooting bright comedies (PLAY IT AGAIN, SAM [Herbert Ross]; THE HEARTBREAK KID [Elaine May], both 1972), open-air Westerns (THE RETURN OF A MAN CALLED HORSE [Irvin Kershner, 1975]), and expressive horror films (THE EXORCIST [William Friedkin, 1973]; THE STEPFORD WIVES [Bryan Forbes, 1975]).[18] Roizman collaborated most closely during this period with the director Sydney Pollack (THREE DAYS OF THE CONDOR [1975]; THE ELECTRIC HORSEMAN [1979]; ABSENCE OF MALICE [1981]; TOOTSIE [1982]), but he also did splendid work for Sidney Lumet (NETWORK [1976]) and Ulu Grosbard (TRUE CONFESSIONS [1981]).

John A. Alonzo (b. 1934) is another imaginative cinematographer who helped to give the cinema of the 1970s its unique look. Working first as an actor, then as a non-union camera operator, he won recognition assisting the legendary cinematographer James Wong Howe (1899–1976) on SECONDS (John Frankenheimer, 1966), one of the most visually innovative films of its day.[19] In the early 1970s, Alonzo was DP on several low-budget independent films (for example, Roger Corman's BLOODY MAMA [1970]) before shooting his first mainstream feature, HAROLD AND MAUDE (Hal Ashby, 1971), for which he was chosen when Local 659 refused the director permission to hire Gordon Willis (see above). After that, Alonzo worked extensively with Martin Ritt (SOUNDER [1972]; PETE 'N' TILLIE [1972]; CONRACK [1974]; NORMA RAE [1979]), as well as with Mike Nichols (THE FORTUNE [1975]), Dick Richards (FAREWELL, MY LOVELY [1975]), Michael Ritchie (THE BAD NEWS BEARS [1976]), and John Frankenheimer (BLACK SUNDAY [1977]). His most remarkable work of the decade was as cinematographer for Roman Polanski's period *film noir* CHINATOWN (1974), for which he won an Academy Award. Shot in the Panavision anamorphic ratio of 2.35:1, mainly with a 40mm lens, the film was an intense collaboration among Alonzo, Polanski, and art director Richard Sylbert, and is the most successful of numerous mid-1970s films (e.g., THE DAY OF THE LOCUST [1975]; GABLE AND LOMBARD [Sidney J. Furie, 1976]) that attempted to evoke in color what Todd McCarthy has called "the dreamy, nostalgic look of Hollywood in the early Panchromatic Age."[20] By and large, the film succeds because Alonzo strove to give CHINATOWN what he called a "classic" look that studiously avoided gimmicks."[21]

Toward the decade's end, several younger cinematographers achieved recognition—Michael Chapman (b. 1946) for his work with Philip Kaufman (THE WHITE DAWN [1974]; INVASION OF THE BODY SNATCHERS [1978]) and Martin Scorsese (TAXI DRIVER [1976], RAGING BULL [1980]); Caleb Deschanel (b. 1944) for THE BLACK STALLION (Carroll Ballard, 1979) and BEING THERE (Hal Ashby, 1979); and Dean Cundey for his collaborations with John Carpenter (HALLOWEEN [1978]; THE FOG [1980]; ESCAPE FROM NEW YORK [1981]; THE THING [1982]), which set new standards for roaming Steadicam/Panaglide photography. Other cinematographers contributing materially to the visual style of specific films during the decade were Bill Butler (b. 1921), who shot THE CONVERSATION (1974), JAWS (Steven Spielberg, 1975), ONE FLEW OVER THE CUCKOO'S NEST (1975; shared credit with Fraker and Wexler), and GREASE (Randal Kleiser, 1978); Richard H. Kline (b. 1926), DP on KING KONG (John Guillermin, 1976), WHO'LL STOP THE RAIN (Karel Reisz, 1978), and THE FURY (Brian De Palma, 1978); Mario Tosi, cameraman for HEARTS OF THE WEST (Howard Zieff, 1975), CARRIE (Brian De Palma, 1976), and THE STUNT MAN (Richard Rush, 1978; released 1980); and Bruce Surtees (b. 1936), who worked throughout the decade with both Don Siegel (THE BEGUILED [1971]; DIRTY HARRY [1972]) and Clint Eastwood (HIGH PLAINS DRIFTER [1973]; THE OUTLAW—JOSEY WALES [1976]), as well as with Philip Kaufman (THE GREAT NORTHFIELD, MINNESOTA RAID [1972]), Paul Mazursky (BLUME IN LOVE [1973]), Bob Fosse (LENNY [1974]), Arthur Penn (NIGHT MOVES [1975]), Herbert Ross (THE TURNING POINT [1977]), and John Milius (BIG WEDNESDAY [1978]).

As they became acknowledged masters of their craft, the new cinematographers were in constant demand by producers who valued both their discipline and their creativity in the new system of freelance packaging that replaced studio-originated production during the 1970s. Those in the top echelon found themselves positioned to pick and choose their projects based on their preferences for scripts, collaborators, and the relative artistic challenge of the production—very much like star performers, except that their salaries were regulated by union scale and rarely rose above $4,000 a week (Conrad Hall's $3,500 on Fox's BUTCH CASSIDY AND THE SUNDANCE KID, in fact, was the record through 1972).[22] Haskell Wexler, for example, usually signed on to projects that reflected his liberal politics (BOUND FOR GLORY [1976]; COMING HOME [1978]). Gordon Willis was known to favor scripts that promised particularly tricky lighting and focus situations (such as ALL THE PRESIDENT'S MEN [1976], with its all-fluorescent, deep-focus newsroom scenes). Many cinematographers found regular collaboration with certain directors the most rewarding way to practice their art (Zsigmond worked with Altman and Cimino; Willis with Pakula and Allen; Roizman with Pollack; and Alonzo with Ritt).

Whatever their aesthetic or cultural motives, however, all were heir to innovations in lens and camera technology that represented a quantum leap over the past—and they recognized this change and gloried in it. As John A. Alonzo said of the era in 1984: "We're in a marvelous period to be cinematographers, because of the new technology that keeps coming out. We look a thousand percent better to a producer than someone like Jimmy Wong Howe did. Yet they didn't know what he went through. I mean, that man was running around with a 165-pound camera and here we run around with a 45-pound camera [the Panaflex] that you can manipulate and move around [via the Steadicam or Panaglide system].... You can put the Panaflex in a bathroom without taking the walls out and shoot scenes in there. . . . [I]n the last ten years there have been radical changes."[23]

Lens Technology and Aesthetics

ZOOM LENSES: FORM AND FUNCTION

The use (and abuse) of the zoom lens is an unmistakeable hallmark of late 1960s' and early 1970s' film style in the United States and Europe. Most historians attribute this to the influence of television, whose cameras had been equipped with permanently mounted zoom lenses since the 1940s.[24] During the 1950s and 1960s, as more and more films came to be shot on location, television production techniques were adapted to feature filmmaking for their flexibility and economy. As early as 1960, for example, Hitchcock employed a television crew to shoot an entire theatrical feature (PSYCHO), and soon after that directors like John Frankenheimer (THE MANCHURIAN CANDIDATE [1962]; SEVEN DAYS IN MAY [1964]) were using television news-gathering styles to lend their films a *cinema-verité*-like immediacy. The zoom lens proved especially valuable in location shooting because of its capability for variable focus, since it could function as a telephoto lens at one extreme and a wide-angle lens at the other, traversing all of the stops in between. In 1963, the French Angenieux company introduced a zoom lens designed exclusively for film production with a zoom range of 10 to 1 (25mm to 250mm for 35mm cameras; 12mm to 120mm for 16mm cameras).[25] But American directors tended to avoid conspicuous zooms until the late 1960s, when the influence of various European "New Waves" began to be assimilated via such popular films as DARLING (John Schlesinger, 1965) and UN HOMME ET UNE FEMME (Claude Lelouch, 1966). (Similarly influential were the snap-zooms in Richard Lester's two Beatles films A HARD DAYS NIGHT [1964] and HELP! [1965], which borrowed the device from *cinema verité* styles.) Since the zoom lens distorts optical space by either collapsing it (telephoto position) or expanding it (wide-angle position), its use in narrative features tends to be self-reflexive; in teleproduction it was largely functional—providing optical enhancement for the coverage of live events (sports and news), and in dramatic programs it was a cheap substitute for tracking.

The European new-wave cinemas employed the lens expressively to create pictorial abstraction (Michelangelo Antonioni's RED DESERT [1964]) or to structure scenic space by hovering and focusing selectively within it (Miklos Jancso's THE ROUND UP [1965]; THE RED AND THE WHITE [1967]), but when American directors embraced the zoom in the late 1960s they initially used it to isolate detail within the frame, following the practice of television. In fact, many of them were veterans of television—Arthur Penn, Sam Peckinpah, John Frankenheimer, Robert Altman, Robert Mulligan, Sidney Lumet, Sydney Pollack, and Stuart Rosenberg—and some indulged in orgies of self-conscious zooming in otherwise worthy films (e.g., in Lumet's THE DEADLY AFFAIR [1967]; Rosenberg's COOL HAND LUKE [1967]; Pollack's THEY SHOOT HORSES, DON'T THEY? [1969]). Soon, however, zooming to create dramatic emphasis was blended with expressive stylization—Arthur Penn (BONNIE AND CLYDE [1967]; LITTLE BIG MAN [1970]) and Sam Peckinpah (THE WILD BUNCH [1969]; STRAW DOGS [1971]), for example, used zooms to heighten the optical violence of montage; and there was a mercifully brief fetish for using zooms to evoke the experience of tripping on LSD (THE TRIP [Roger Corman, 1967]; EASY RIDER [Dennis Hopper, 1969]). Slow, deliberate, but dramatically ambiguous zooms punctuated several landmark films of the era (notable among them are the poignant track-out zoom-in on Alice that concludes Penn's ALICE'S RESTAURANT [1969], the crane-and-zoom through the woods that begins Robert Mulligan's THE OTHER [1972], and the strangely unmotivated zoom that opens Francis Ford Coppola's THE CONVERSATION [1974]), but no American directors of the 1970s were more closely associated with the aesthetics of the zoom than Robert Altman and Stanley Kubrick.

COMPOSING FOR THE ZOOM: ALTMAN AND KUBRICK

Altman probably used the zoom more systematically during the 1970s than any film-maker before or since. His most salient films in this regard are M°A°S°H (1970), McCABE & MRS. MILLER (1971), THE LONG GOODBYE (1973), NASHVILLE (1975), and 3 WOMEN (1977), but virtually all of his 1970s work is composed of long takes structured by panning and zooming. Robin Wood wrote of Altman during this period, "the zoom is at once his means of guiding the audience's consciousness and of asserting his own presence in the film; but he has also grasped its potential for dissolving space and undermining our sense of physical reality."[26] Altman's cultivation of a fast, flexible pan-and-zoom style went hand-in-hand with his use of actor improvisation and ensemble playing, which in turn placed considerable creative responsibility on his cinematographers. According to Vilmos Zsigmond, Altman's director of photography on McCABE & MRS. MILLER, IMAGES (1972), and THE LONG GOODBYE, DPs had to operate their own cameras in such improvised situations in order to "grab" significant action.[27] By the early part of the decade, new camera viewfinders working on the principle of the single reflex lens made it possible for cinematographers to frame action more precisely than ever before, permitting the measured combination of zooming and tracking or rack

focus that became the hallmark of Altman's work. Furthermore, two new high-resolution, high-speed zoom lenses had become available early in the decade—the Taylor-
Hobson Cooke Varotal 5-to-1 (20mm to 100mm), and the Canon 5-to-1 (25mm to
125mm)—increasing the flexibility and precision of pan-and-zoom stylistics.[28]

Altman's use of the zoom was essentially nondemonstrative, sometimes even subliminal, approximating the mental processes of the viewer as he or she focused, panned,
and refocused on significant details within a seemingly arbitrary visual field, and it was
ideally suited to his sense of American social reality as both ambiguous and random.
Stanley Kubrick's resort to the zoom was more restrained and magisterial but no less
decisive in terms of aesthetic design. As early as DR. STRANGELOVE in 1964, Kubrick
had used a series of snap-zooms into the SAC bomber's control panels to bring the arm-
ing of its nuclear payload into tight close-up; and in 2001: A SPACE ODYSSEY (1968),
which was shot in a 65mm anamorphic process with a Super-Panavision lens for release
in 70mm Cinerama, he used several zooms as part of the elaborate special effects. But
for A CLOCKWORK ORANGE (1971) Kubrick envisioned the use of a 20-to-1 (24mm to
480mm) zoom lens, then manufactured by Angenieux only for 16mm filming. He
rented a similar lens (25mm to 500mm) from Samuelson Film Service in London, and
commissioned Ed DiGuilio of Cinema Products Corporation in Los Angeles to fit a
16mm Angenieux with a 1.6 extender so that it could be used for 35mm filming on a
modified, nonreflexed Mitchell BNC camera. (Kubrick liked to own his production
equipment and even built a customized location van for A CLOCKWORK ORANGE.)[29]
Renamed the Cine-Pro T9, the lens came equipped with a joystick control designed by
DiGuilio to insure its fluid automatic operation, since the motorized zoom controls of
the era often caused a slight vibration at the end of a movement; and it was delivered
in time for use on BARRY LYNDON (1975). Meanwhile, working closely with cinematographer John Alcott (DP Geoffrey Unsworth's assistant on 2001), Kubrick used
the rented Samuelson lens to accomplish the slow zoom-outs that open key scenes in
A CLOCKWORK ORANGE (for example, those in the Korova Milkbar, and the scenes of
Alex walking along the Thames), and he used multiple shorter zooms in montage
sequences of violent action (the gang rape by Billyboy and his droogs; Alex's murder of
the Cat Lady).

Kubrick's most elaborate use of the 20-to-1 zoom was reserved for the Cine-Pro T9
in his epic BARRY LYNDON (1975). The entire film was structured around a series of
slow backward zooms from telephoto close-up to panoramic wide-angle, evoking the
two major eighteenth-century painting genres (portraiture and landscape) and suggesting the rigidly ordered sociopolitical regime that will doom its title character. John
Alcott, who remained Kubrick's DP through THE SHINING in 1980, told *Millimeter*
magazine that the zoom in BARRY LYNDON "was used throughout the picture integrally
and not simply as a device to speed up production,"[30] and he later remarked of the practice to Michel Ciment: "Each time, it became an image in itself and not, as is usually the
case, a means of moving from one point in space to another. . . . [so] each shot was a
composition, like the zoom which moved out from the pistol during the duel at the
river's edge."[31] Alcott also used the telephoto end of the Cine-Pro to shoot close-ups during the film's large battle sequence, which was photographed by three cameras with
lenses of various focal length moving on an 800-foot track.[32] Here he anticipated the
now-standard use of the zoom as if it were a straight lens; this practice, as cinematographer Mario Tosi (HEARTS OF THE WEST [1975]; CARRIE [1976]; THE STUNT MAN

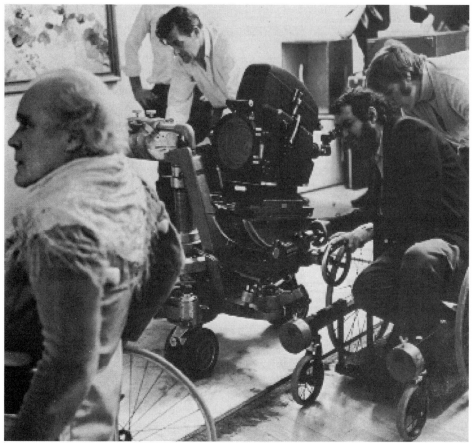

Kubrick and camera grips setting up a pre-Stedicam dolly shot for A CLOCKWORK ORANGE (1971). The camera is a nonreflexed Mitchell BNC modified by Cinema Products Corporation to accomodate a 20-to-1 (25mm to 500mm) zoom lens, shown here in its extreme wide-angle position. Patrick Magee, as the prominent writer, "Mr. Alexander," in the left foreground.

[1978]) has pointed out, can give a "continuity of look" to all shots in a sequence since the lens has the same optical properties (e.g., color values) at all focal lengths.[33] (Tosi further noted that, as opposed to a fixed lens, the zoom provides "much more freedom to find the frame size that fits perfectly" and can be used to make "small framing adjustments on motion during a pan to control the composition.")[34]

By the time of the THE SHINING (1980), Kubrick and Alcott were composing their shots for the Steadicam rather than the zoom, although few viewers will forget the slow zoom into the model of the Overlook's hedge maze that takes us outside, via a special effect, into the real thing. That same year Angenieux began to market a 25:1 ratio zoom (25mm to 625mm) for 35mm photography, signaling that the variable focal length lens had passed through its experimental stage to become an industry standard.

Although Altman and Kubrick set the standard for the expressive use of the zoom lens during the 1970s, it is difficult to imagine most American films of the decade without it.

Wide-angle shot of British troops marching into battle with the French during the
Seven Years' War in Stanley Kubrick's BARRY LYNDON (Warners, 1975), emphasizing
depth of field. According to director of photography John Alcott, this sequence was
photographed by three cameras with lenses of various focal lengths moving on an 800-
foot track. One of those lenses was the 20-to-1 (24-to-480mm) Cine-Pro T9 zoom that
Kubrick had commissioned from Ed DiGuilio's Cinema Products Corporation especially for this production. 35mm 1.66:1.

BARRY LYNDON: a shot of marching Prussian troops taken from the Cine-Pro T9 zoom's
extreme telephoto position (c. 480mm), collapsing depth of field and suggesting the
agglomeration of individual wills into a unified mass that characterizes all armies, but
especially Germanic ones. Throughout BARRY LYNDON, Kubrick and Alcott used the
zoom thematically, both to suggest the rigid sociopolitical order of the period and to
evoke eighteenth-century pictorial styles.

The lens appears ubiquitously across genres, and many works would be lesser achievements for its absence. In Sydney Pollack's 1972 Western JEREMIAH JOHNSON, photographed by Duke Callaghan, for example, long slow zoom-outs are essential to establishing the connection between the title character and the land. These rhythmic optical movements contribute to the saga-like quality of the narrative, and lend the film a majesty that straight lenses couldn't then afford. JAWS (1975), which was shot in anamorphic Panavision by Bill Butler, is largely staged in wide-angle depth, but at the crucial moment of the second shark attack on a young boy, Roy Scheider (the local sheriff), watching in horrified close-up from the beach, becomes the object of a VERTIGO-style track-out zoom-in that transfers his moment of psychological dislocation directly to the audience. Much of Alan J. Pakula's work of the 1970s depended on elaborate zoom effects, especially ALL THE PRESIDENT'S MEN (1976), shot by Gordon Willis, where slow aerial pull-backs are used to show Woodward and Bernstein trapped in maze-like configurations whose shapes are perceptible only from a bird's-eye view—for example, the famous Library of Congress shot where the camera pulls up from a close shot of the two men at the card catalogue to an aerial perspective from the ceiling in what appears to be a single continuous shot (but is actually a combination of tracking, zooming, and two dissolves).[35] According to Willis, the most optically difficult zoom in the film was a shot of Robert Redford (Woodward) on the telephone that pulls slowly back over several minutes to reveal the entire *Washington Post* newsroom, with action occurring on several different focal planes during the shot. (Willis had to use a split diopter to achieve this and other such shots in the film—that is, a partial lens element that splits the visual field so that the cameraman can focus on close and distant planes of action simultaneously.)[36]

Of course, for every calculated aesthetic use of the zoom during the decade, there were many more abuses of it to create specious interest where none inhered in character or plot, or to cut corners on camera movement, lighting, editing, and, at worst, actors' rehearsals. Furthermore, when it was still a novelty, even so masterful a director as Vittorio de Sica could allow the zoom to become obtrusive, as he does in THE GARDEN OF THE FINZI-CONTINIS (1971), where it seems to account for every third shot. (This was an unfortunate but understandable consequence of the fact that the Italian cinema embraced the zoom even more passionately in the early 1970s than the American—the list of major Italian films of the era whose form depends upon the zoom includes Bernardo Bertolucci's THE CONFORMIST [1971]; Luchino Visconti's DEATH IN VENICE [1971] and LUDWIG [1972]; Lina Wertmuller's THE SEDUCTION OF MIMI [1972], ALL SCREWED UP [1974], and SWEPT AWAY [1975]; Liliana Cavani's THE NIGHT PORTER [1974]; Federico Fellini's AMARCORD [1974]; Pier Paolo Pasolini's SALO [1975]; and Michelangelo Antonioni's THE PASSENGER [1975].)

LENSES OF FIXED FOCAL LENGTH

Besides the refinement of the zoom, there were several other significant innovations in lens technology during the 1970s. Canon, the Japanese company known worldwide for its still-camera lenses, entered the field of professional cinematography in 1971 with normal and anamorphic zoom lenses that possessed a new "Macrophotgraphy" feature, allowing for extremely close focus through the front element via a simple ring adjustment. This Macro facility made it possible for cinematographers to shoot very small objects with great magnification and no loss of definition. In 1974, Canon introduced a new series of fixed-focal-length "aspheric" lenses whose curvature was produced via computer technology rather than spherical reduction.[37] These high-resolution, high-speed lenses were widely adopted for long and intermediate range photography because they were less subject to optical distortion than spherical lenses. The German Zeiss Company also used computer technology to develop its SuperSpeed aspheric lens series in 1974—lenses of fixed focal length that had floating internal elements to vary focus. Moreover, Zeiss had produced the super-fast 50mm still-photography lens for NASA that Ed DiGuilio adapted for Kubrick to shoot the candle-lit interiors of BARRY LYNDON (1975);[38] and a whole range of Zeiss lenses, from 18mm to 85mm, were used for THE SHINING (1980).[39] Finally, Barry Salt notes a minor trend in 1970s cinematography toward the use of extremely wide-angle lenses (c. 10mm to 15mm) in normal dramatic scenes; he cites RANCHO DELUXE (Frank Perry, 1975), CHARLEY VARRICK (Don Siegel, 1973), DEATH WISH (Michael Winner, 1974), and—in 70mm—PATTON (Franklin Schaffner, 1970) as examples of this trend, linking it not to functional depth staging but contemporary fashions in still photography.[40]

"PUSHING" AND "FLASHING" FOR WIDE-ANGLE PHOTOGRAPHY

Most wide-angle lenses are "slow," because they employ large apertures to admit all available light. And because of the large aperture required for its wide-angle stops, the zoom is also a relatively slow lens, requiring either high illumination or "pushing" the film at the laboratory to increase its speed. This latter process, technically known as "forced development," enabled film stocks to be exposed with less light than was correct for their normal ASA rating. Underexposure, followed by overdevelopment to compensate, had been used for shooting night exteriors on location since the introduction of Kodak Ektachrome E.F. in 1965, and it was widely practiced during the 1970s to achieve aesthetic effects as well as functional ones. Gordon Willis, DP on THE GODFATHER (1972) and THE GODFATHER, PART II (1974), had his stock forced one stop in development to give the films a look that he described as "brown and black in feeling."[41] DP Michael Chapman pushed night-rated film an extra stop for TAXI DRIVER (1976) and INVASION OF THE BODY SNATCHERS (1978) to achieve dense blacks illuminated only by neon signs.[42] Nestor Almendros did the same for DAYS OF HEAVEN (1978), many of whose scenes were shot out-of-doors in what director Terrence Malick called "the magic hour"—the twenty to twenty-five minutes of light left after the sun had set.[43] To lend a documentary texture to the urban street-life dramas THE FRENCH CONNECTION (1971) and THE TAKING OF PELHAM ONE TWO THREE (1974), New York-based cinematographer Owen Roizman force-developed the entire footage of both films, and Vilmos Zsigmond pushed the film for THE LONG GOODBYE (1973) to accommodate both its low lighting levels and Altman's improvisational pan-and-zoom style.[44]

A similar laboratory procedure known as "flashing" or "fogging" was used by a number of innovative cinematographers during the 1970s. This was the process of exposing the negative briefly to white light in a printer before or after exposure in the camera to achieve certain visual effects. Like pushing, flashing produced a speed increase, but it also desaturated the color, and was first used for expressive effect in the late 1960s, most notably by DP Conrad Hall in HELL IN THE PACIFIC (John Boorman, 1968) and BUTCH CASSIDY AND THE SUNDANCE KID (1969).[45] The cinematographer most closely associated with flashing in the 1970s was Vilmos Zsigmond, who used it to lend an old-fashioned, faded quality (modeled on the paintings of Andrew Wyeth) to the images of MCCABE & MRS. MILLER (1971) and HEAVEN'S GATE (1980), for which he flashed both

Director of photography Vilmos Zsigmond achieved an old-fashioned, faded quality reminiscent of late-nineteenth-century sepia tones for Robert Altman's MCCABE & MRS. MILLER (1971) by flashing both the negative and the print. Zsigmond said that he modeled the look of the film (and of HEAVEN'S GATE, which he shot nine years later) on the paintings of Andrew Wyeth. 35mm Panavision anamorphic.

the negative and the print.[46] To achieve a similar softening of shadows and pasteling of colors, Haskell Wexler flashed nearly all of the Woody Guthrie biopic BOUND FOR GLORY (1976).[47] Lightflex, a system for flashing a predetermined amount of light on the film stock via a mechanical unit attached to the camera matte box, was introduced commercially in 1977 for Oswald Morris's shooting of THE WIZ (Sidney Lumet, 1978), and it took much of the guesswork out of the process, which during the early 1970s required extra handling of the negative in the lab.[48] Originated as "Colorflex" by the British cinematographer Gerald Turpin as a way of adding tints to YOUNG WINSTON (Richard Attenborough, 1972), Lightflex allowed cinematographers to introduce color and contrast variations in the film stock by selectively controlling the exposure during shooting.[49]

Lighting and Film Stock

The nearly complete transition from studio to location shooting during the 1970s led to improvements in lighting equipment and color film stock that opened new creative vistas for cinematographers, who, as noted earlier, had become increasingly sensitive to aesthetic issues as a by-product of auteur criticism. As Barry Salt points out, all-location production demanded smaller, lighter, and more powerful lighting units, and two new kinds of light source were introduced to meet this challenge.[50] The first was the xenon arc, which produced illumination of daylight intensity (a color temperature of 6,000 degrees Kelvin) by enclosing an electric arc within a quartz bulb filled with pressurized xenon gas. Originally marketed in 1970 as the "Sunbrute," xenons were first used as daylight fill for exterior locations and could be powered from a 30-volt D.C. source. (One of the earliest creative uses of xenons was to shine them through windows covered with translucent plastic sheets to light the daytime interior locations for Kubrick's BARRY LYNDON.) The other new light was the metal halide arc, developed for European television and adapted to film as the Osram HMI in 1974. In this unit, light was emitted from current arcing between two electrodes powered by an ordinary 120-volt A.C. source. Like the xenon, it produced two to three times more light (at 5,500 degrees Kelvin) than ordinary lamps, but consumed less power than xenons did.[51] HMI metal halide units were manufactured by Mole-Richardson in the United States after 1975.

As far as film stock is concerned, Eastman introduced new color negative type 5247 (7247 for 16mm) in 1973, with improved sharpness and finer grain, as well as simplified processing that benefited the laboratories.[52] But American cinematographers did not warm to this stock because of its increased color saturation and relatively low ASA rating (100). DP John Alonzo seemed to speak for the entire American Society of Cinematographers (ASC) when he said, "I think that 5247 is a very fine piece of mater-

By 1976, when Nestor Almendros was shooting Terrence Malick's DAYS OF HEAVEN (released 1978), film stocks had become "fast" enough to record at very low light levels, although not yet sensitive enough to shoot at night by flame-light alone. For this night sequence, just before the great crop fire, Almendros rigged kerosene lanterns with electric bulbs, so that the light was artificial but actually came from the lanterns. (He also used some fill light to make the background smoke distinctly visible.) 35mm Panavision spherical (1.85:1), blown up to 70mm for road-showing.

ial but why start out using it on a film and then find you can't shoot with it because you run into some dark sequences?"[53] In response, Kodak modified the emulsion to widen its exposure latitude and re-released the stock as "5247 Series 600" to great acclaim. It was adopted almost immediately for prestige productions like CLOSE ENCOUNTERS OF THE THIRD KIND (1977) because of its fine grain, and its versatility made it the preferred stock of such innovative cinematographers as Vilmos Zsigmond.[54] At about the same time that Kodak started marketing 5247, the Japanese photographic manufacturer Fuji introduced a motion picture negative stock that had the same ASA rating as the Eastman material but was significantly cheaper.[55] In the United States, Fuji was rarely used for features during the 1970s because it had less color fidelity than Kodak stock, but it was widely used in American teleproduction and in low-budget European features. One mainstream production shot on Fuji was the period *film noir* FAREWELL, MY LOVELY (1975); DP John Alonzo chose the stock because he wanted to give the film a different look than his work in CHINATOWN.[56] Near the end of 1980, Fuji introduced A250, a new fast negative stock (ASA 250), and the company became a leader in high-speed film for the next two decades. [57]

Camera Technology

According to Barry Salt, the 1970s was one of the most active periods in film history for the development of new cameras. In 1971, the French Eclair company introduced its lightweight ACL 16mm camera that could run off of one-lb. nickel-cadmium batteries.

Before the introduction of the lightweight 35mm Panaflex, cranes and tripod mounts were essential in stabilizing moving camera shots. In this production still from LITTLE FAUSS AND BIG HALSY *(Sidney J. Furie, 1970), the director and camera operator shoot a motorcycle race from a crane, while two operators at its base pan their cameras on tripods to follow the action. 35mm Panavision anamorphic.*

In 1972, in Germany, the Arnold and Richter company introduced the self-blimped (acoustically insulated) 35mm Arriflex 35 BL, which could be fully balanced on the cameraman's shoulder and weighed 15 lbs. unloaded. The Arriflex 35BL debuted in America in 1972, when it was used by DP Jack Priestley for location photography in Harlem for the United Artists production ACROSS 110TH STREET (Barry Shear, 1972).[58] But in Hollywood, Panavision became the industry leader with the appearance of the new Panaflex camera in 1973.

PANAVISION, INC., AND THE PANAFLEX 35MM CAMERA

Panavision, Incorporated, founded by Robert E. Gottschalk in 1953, had risen to prominence during the 1950s and 1960s by manufacturing the lenses that came to dominate widescreen filmmaking—the prismatic anamorphic lenses, which replaced the cylindrical CinemaScope lenses made by Bausch & Lomb, and the spherical lenses for 1:85 photography and 70mm Super Panavision (originally Ultra-Panavision 70). Initially, Panavision had designed its lenses to fit the studio workhorse Mitchell BNC, but in the early 1960s the company introduced its own camera, the Panavision Silent Reflex (PSR),

Weighing only 25 pounds when loaded with a 250-foot magazine, the Panavision Panaflex 35mm synch-sound reflex camera extended cinematography's flexibility and range by making it possible to shoot scenes in formerly inaccessible spaces. It was first used professionally by Vilmos Zsigmond on Steven Spielberg's THE SUGARLAND EXPRESS (1974) to shoot handheld dialogue sequences like this one inside a moving police car: Goldie Hawn, Michael Sacks.

which went on to become one of the world's most popular, not least because its reflex viewfinder was ideal for use with the newly popular zoom lens. The PSR, however, was relatively heavy, and Gottschalk committed Panavision to produce a new generation of cameras that would be light enough to be carried by hand but studio-durable.[59]

The result, after four years of development, was the Panaflex—a 35mm synch-sound reflex camera weighing just 25 lbs. when loaded with a 250-ft. magazine (34 lbs. with a 500-ft. magazine) and equipped with a variable speed motor (6–32 fps). It was first used by Vilmos Zsigmond on Steven Spielberg's THE SUGARLAND EXPRESS (1974) to shoot extensive handheld dialogue sequences among three people inside of a moving police car.[60] Another early use of the Panaflex was by Sven Nykvist, the regular DP for Ingmar Bergman, to shoot THE DOVE (Charles Jarrott, 1974), which took place mainly aboard a twenty-three-foot sailboat during a five-year trip around the world.[61] DP John Alonzo reported that the new camera proved invaluable in shooting Roman Polanski's CHINATOWN (1974), because "[y]ou can put a Panaflex in a bathroom without taking the walls out and shoot scenes in there."[62] The Panaflex underwent constant modification throughout the 1970s—for example, the viewfinder was redesigned to increase its brilliance, a thermostatically-controlled heating system was built in so that the camera could be used in sub-zero temperatures, and a one-hour 16mm conversion kit was introduced; as were several new lenses, including a series of super-fast wide-angle lenses (the "Ultra-Speed" series) and two new 10-to-1 zooms—a 25/250mm spherical and a 50/500mm anamorphic.[63] By the end of the decade, the Panaflex had become the industry standard in the United States and many other parts of the world, including the People's Republic of China, where it was adopted by the Beijing Film Studio in 1981.[64]

Director Alan J. Pakula and director of photography Gordon Willis setting up a shot on the Washington Post *newsroom set of* ALL THE PRESIDENT'S MEN *(Warners, 1976). The Panaflex camera, mounted on a pan-head tripod, is loaded with a 500-foot magazine, for a total weight of 34 pounds. 35mm 1.85:1.*

By 1980, the Panaflex camera—fitted with a series of super-fast wide-angle lenses (the "Ultra-Speed" series) and two new 10-to-1 zooms (a 25-to-250mm spherical and 50-to-500mm anamorphic)—had become the industry standard. Director Randal Kleiser is shown here on location for THE BLUE LAGOON *(1980) with a Panaflex equipped with 25-to-250 spherical zoom, mounted on a pan-head tripod and loaded with a 500-foot magazine. Director of photography: Nestor Almendros. 35mm Panavision spherical (1.85:1), blown up to 70mm for roadshowing.*

MITCHELL CAMERA AND OTHERS

In the United States and elsewhere, Panavision did not sell its equipment outright but rented it to production companies and cinematographers; the company also required a footage royalty on released prints struck from any negative made with Panavision cameras. Thus, despite the clear superiority of Panavision technology, many producers sought alternative equipment, creating a market for older companies like the Mitchell Camera Corporation and newer ones like Cinema Products, founded by former Mitchell engineer Edmund (Ed) DiGuilio in 1968. Mitchell made a number of efforts to compete in the new lightweight camera category, most notably with its Mark III 35mm, but met with little success. Cinema Products, on the other hand, made a small fortune by converting Mitchell BNCs into reflex cameras, and in 1973 introduced it own camera with the X35R. This was basically an improved BNC with an integral reflex shutter, which weighed 93 lbs. unloaded. Equipped with an Italian Technovision anamorphic lens, the Cinema Products X35R was used by Vittorio Storaro in shooting APOCALYPSE NOW (1979).[65]

Stabilization Systems and Camera Mounts

New cameras, lenses, and film stock notwithstanding, the most important innovation in cinematography during the 1970s was in the area of "floating" camera mounts.[66] Once professional hand-held 35mm cameras had been integrated into mainstream Hollywood production, there was a need for systems to stabilize them during movement. Early in the decade there was a variety of devices introduced to facilitate stability for one purpose or another. These included the "gyrocamera," a gyro-stabilized pan head developed for the Arriflex; the "Dynalens," a gyro-controlled liquid lens system designed to eliminate image wobbling in moving shots; the "Super-Grip," designed for mounting a hand-held camera on any smooth surface; the FERCO Dolly, a monorail system for tracking over rough terrain; and the "Fleximount," a large harness-braced camera support worn by the operator.[67] This latter was probably the model for Garrett Brown's revolutionary Steadicam system, which was first marketed by Cinema Products Corporation in 1976 and brought an extraordinary new mobility to American production practice. (Brown and Cinema Products, in fact, shared a 1978 Academy Award for its invention.)

THE STEADICAM REVOLUTION

Years in development, the Steadicam was a gimbal-jointed camera mount that attached to the operator's chest and waist by means of a harness; a small video camera attached

Once lightweight 35mm cameras like the Panaflex had been integrated into professional filmmaking, various systems were devised to stabilize them during movement. The most efficient was Garrett Brown's Steadicam, a gimbal-jointed camera mount that attached to the operator's chest and waist via a harness. First used commercially by director of photography Haskell Wexler in United Artists' BOUND FOR GLORY (Hal Ashby, 1976), the Steadicam (or proprietary versions of it like the Panaglide system) became the industry standard: David Carradine as Woody Guthrie. 35mm 1.85:1.

*Depicted here is a Steadicam Video SK, with video monitor
and Sony Hi-8 video camera, but its operating principle is
the same as the Steadicams used for 35mm filming during
the 1970s and after. (Steadicam is a registered trademark of
Cinema Products Corp., Los Angeles, California.)*

near the lens fed a high-intensity monitor that acted as a viewfinder, enabling the operator to frame his shots while in motion. (The video framing monitor was borrowed from the design of two anti-vibration helicopter mounts introduced in the late 1960s—the Tyler Camera Systems mount [1966] and Albert Lamorisse's "Helivision" [1967].)[68] The Steadicam was first used commercially by Haskell Wexler in BOUND FOR GLORY (1976), who deployed it to achieve a variety of "combination shots," where the camera begins on a moving crane or dolly then "steps off" with the operator to execute an elaborate maneuver that could not be done on the crane or dolly itself (such as going through a doorway, then twisting and turning down a hall). One famous example in BOUND FOR GLORY starts with a high-angle shot from a crane as it moves slowly over the set of a huge migrant labor camp and then booms down to pick up David Carradine (Woody Guthrie) sitting on a car; here the operator steps smoothly off the crane and follows Carradine as he makes his way through a crowd until he reaches another actor, after which the two of them walk together through more crowds of people and finally under

Francis Ford Coppola is shown directing a street scene in Santa Domingo for THE GODFATHER, PART II in 1974 (the Dominican Republic was used for the film's Cuban settings, since the U.S. trade embargo prevented shooting locations in Cuba itself). Just a few years later, instead of rigging a car to function as dolly, he would almost certainly have used a vibration-free Steadicam to stabilize the shot.

the flap of a tent. The vibration-free quality of the Steadicam in such shots was a function of both its shock-absorbing harness and its video viewfinder, as Wexler immediately understood: " . . . [T]he basic principle of Brown's device is that, since the viewing system on the camera is video, your eye does not have to be to the camera. Since your head is not attached to the camera, it's possible to actually run up and down stairs, to run through narrow passageways, or to hold the camera extended weightless in your hand and make shots which, when you see them on the screen, look like they were made from a miniature helicopter."[69]

It was clear to Wexler and other cinematographers who first used it that the Steadicam would significantly increase the fluidity of the camera by allowing it to go where it was either impossible or economically infeasible to lay dolly tracks—in short, virtually anywhere that the operator could physically carry it. As Ed DiGuilio of Cinema Products pointed out in *American Cinematographer*, the system made possible moving shots "of a totally different nature than have been possible heretofore." At the same time, it cut production costs by making it possible to shoot in tight interior locations, simulate crane shots from improvised ramps or stairs, and turn *any* vehicle—from a helicopter to a galloping horse—into a perfect camera platform since the Steadicam stabilizing devices had a shock-absorbing capacity of two to three feet, as opposed to only a few inches for previous stabilizers.[70] (Not all cameramen welcomed this stability—Bill Butler and his then-operator Michael Chapman preferred their choppy hand-held Panaflex shots on the water in JAWS to the fluidity that the Steadicam could have lent the situation.)[71] Another value of the Steadicam was discovered by Conrad Hall when he was shooting chase scenes for THE MARATHON MAN (John Schlesinger, 1976) with Dustin Hoffman in the streets of New York City. With only the operator present (in this case Garrett Brown himself), the actor could run down the street with the Steadicam either ahead of him or behind him and attract minimal attention—because the operator was not looking through a camera viewfinder as he followed the action, bystanders didn't realize that a film was being shot, enhancing the sequence's verisimilitude.[72] DP James Crabe created a similar Steadicam sequence for ROCKY (John G. Avildsen, 1976) when he followed the boxer on his famous run through the streets of Philadelphia and up the steps of the art museum. Another landmark use of the Steadicam (actually "Panaglide," which was Panavision's proprietary version of the system) was in the ur-slasher HALLOWEEN (1978), where cinematographer Dean Cundey's subjective hand-held tracking shots replicated the point of view of a psychotic killer as he stalked his victims—an innovative conceit imitated in hundreds of slasher and horror films to follow (whether

Because JAWS *(1975) was made one year before the introduction of the Steadicam, scenes on the water like this one were shot by director of photography Bill Butler and his operator Michael Chapman with a hand-held Panaflex. Both men have later said that, given the choice, they would have declined to use the Steadicam system anyway because the situation called for the shaky effect that hand-holding creates (Spielberg was fond of saying later that* JAWS *was "the most expensive hand-held movie ever made."): Roy Scheider, Robert Shaw, and Richard Dreyfuss bonded together in search of the Great White shark. 35mm Panavision anamorphic.*

Even after the Steadicam became widely available, some directors and cinematographers continued to use dollies for tracking shots on smooth surfaces, as here, where director George Roy Hill and director of photography Victor Kemper are shown setting up a shot on the ice for Universal's SLAP SHOT (1977). 35mm 1.85:1.

as crudely as in FRIDAY THE 13TH [Sean S. Cunningham, 1980], or as creatively as in WOLFEN [Michael Wadleigh, 1981], whose surrealistic stalking shots were provided by Garrett Brown.)

The film that most clearly demonstrated the full dynamic range of the Steadicam, however, was Stanley Kubrick's THE SHINING (1980), which had been conceived with the new system in mind. The interior sets of the hotel were designed by Roy Walker as a series of interconnecting rooms without flyaway walls or dolly-smooth floors; the exterior set of the hedge maze was designed so that *only* the Steadicam could be used to shoot it.[73] (Kubrick's affinity for this kind of movement was seen as early as the tracking shots along the trenches in PATHS OF GLORY [1957] and more recently in the hand-held orgy sequence in A CLOCKWORK ORANGE [1971].)[74] Kubrick had been impressed with demonstration footage from a prototype of the system in 1974 and arranged to meet Ed DiGuilio and Garrett Brown at FILM 77, a film equipment exhibition, in London in the summer of 1977. He subsequently hired Brown to shoot much of THE SHINING with the latest model of the Steadicam, which included a new 3-channel wireless servo lens control that allowed focus- and iris-pulling by radio remote. (Technically, Brown was the camera operator; John Alcott was DP, responsible for the film's complex lighting schema.) There was also a new video remote unit that transmitted the images that the

Steadicam was filming to a monitor so that the director could observe camera movement, image composition, and actors' performances in process.[75] The most memorable Steadicam shots in THE SHINING are those that follow Danny hurtling through corridor after corridor of the Overlook on his Big Wheel, with the camera riding just a few inches above the floor, and those that follow Jack and Danny running through the maze; but most of the film was shot with the Steadicam, including many of the stationary shots within constricted sets like the Torrances' apartment. (There *are* moving shots in the film that were taken from a conventional dolly, but Kubrick correctly assumed that the Steadicam would be given credit for these too.) For both moving and motionless shots, Brown employed an extreme wide-angle lens, the Cooke 18mm, that allowed him to pass close to walls and doors without optical distortion, further enhancing the Steadicam's mobility.[76] Brown would later refer to his assignment on THE SHINING as "the Steadicam Oympics," because Kubrick pushed the system to its limits in that film, fulfilling the prediction he had made in 1974 that the system would "revolutionize the way films are shot."[77] Aesthetics aside, however, the Steadicam was widely embraced as an economic boon to the industry—which, in a time of rapidly rising production costs, would no longer have to invest in expensive dollies and tracking setups.

WESSCAM AND THE LOUMA CRANE

Another stabilization system deployed during the 1970s was Wesscam, conceived by the Istec Corporation of Canada in 1972 and subsequently manufactured by Westinghouse. Wesscam was a remote-controlled gyro-stabilized camera system enclosed in a sphere that could be suspended from a helicopter or mounted on a crane with equal equanimity, and it was used extensively to film the 1976 Montreal Olympic Games.[78] Appearing among many impressive feature credits during the 1970s, the system was responsible for the elaborate maze shots in SLEUTH (Joseph L. Mankiewicz, 1972) and the remarkable penultimate shot of Michelangelo Antonioni's THE PASSENGER (1975), in which the system was transferred from an overhead track to a crane, with the camera running, in a single unbroken eight-minute trajectory.[79] Ultimately, Wesscam lacked the simplicity of the Steadicam, but another remote system was more successful.

The Louma crane, developed in France and manufactured by Samuelson Film Services in London, was a remote-controlled camera crane similar in design to a microphone boom.[80] Whereas formerly the operator, focus puller, and director all rode the crane together, the Louma crane was fitted with a gyroscopic pan-and-tilt mount that was controlled by servo-motors and was observable through a remote video viewing system.[81] The director and camera crew were relocated to a more convenient place from which they could aim the camera and control the lens aperture, focus, and zoom, without having to ride the crane itself. Because it was small and flexible, with a boom arm that could extend up to seven meters, the Louma could go where other cranes could not, and it was used in late 1970s Hollywood to shoot scenes for SUPERMAN (Richard Donner, 1978), MOONRAKER (Lewis Gilbert, 1979), and 1941 (1979), among others. A much simpler version of this idea was the "Little Big Crane" (so designated by key grip Richard Deats), a lightweight portable crane that could be totally disassembled and carried into a building. It had the obvious advantage of being able to go where conventional cranes could not because of their size and weight, and was used extensively in the production of HEAVEN'S GATE (1980).[82]

*From the penultimate shot in Michelangelo Antonioni's THE PASSENGER (1975), the
conclusion of an eight-minute circular track-and-crane shot executed by DP Luciano
Tovali using the remote-controlled, gyro-stabilized Wesscam camera system. Wesscam
competed briefly during the 1970s with the Steadicam, but was ultimately supplanted
by the simpler system: Maria Schneider, Jenny Runacre, Angel Del Pozo, Jose Maria
Cafarel, Jack Nicholson's feet. 35mm Dyaliscope anamorphic (a French proprietary
version of CinemaScope, widely used in Europe and the U.K.).*

CONCLUSION

The Steadicam and the Louma crane are prominent examples of the movement
throughout the 1970s toward smaller, lighter, and more flexible equipment in response
both to aesthetic demands and financial pressure to cut production costs. Both systems
relied on new technologies of remote video viewing and computer-assisted motion control that would find other applications within the industry as the decade drew to a close.
The former lead to the widespread use of video-assist technology as a production tool,
and the latter to a revolution in special effects that tilted the mainstream industry
toward the once marginal genres of science fiction, fantasy, and horror for much of the
1980s and beyond.

Video-Assist Technology

In the American cinema, video was first used to monitor production quality by Jerry
Lewis in two 1960s films (THE NUTTY PROFESSOR [Jerry Lewis, 1963] and WHO'S
MINDING THE STORE? [Frank Tashlin, 1963]). Lewis set up a video camera to run
beside the film camera so that he could evaluate his performance on playback.[83] This

Producer/director Bob Rafelson, Jessica Lange, Jack Nicholson, and DP Sven Nyskvist examine "video rushes" on the set of THE POSTMAN ALWAYS RINGS TWICE *(1981), a remake of the 1945 original directed by Tay Garnett. Half-inch video recording, introduced to consumers in 1976, made it possible for filmmakers to see their shots on videotape as soon as the camera operator had made them, rather than waiting for hours to develop and print the 35mm negative.*

idea of using video "rushes" caught on with several other directors. Carol Reed, for example, used video playback to check the lip synchronization and choreography of the seventeen musical numbers of OLIVER! (1968), and by 1970 an engineer named Bruce Hill had modified a Mitchell BNCR to accommodate an Ampex one-inch videotape recording and playback unit.[84] A version of the Hill system was used by John Guillermin to monitor the helicopter shots in THE TOWERING INFERNO (1974)—the first use of video assist to coordinate the shooting of a major Hollywood production, as opposed to checking performances after the fact. With the advent of the Steadicam and its video viewfinder in 1976, the possibilities for monitoring increased enormously. As Haskell Wexler was among the first to point out, the system represented a "marriage of the film and video media," and soon, he predicted (accurately), a small transmitter would be added to the Steadicam package that would send the video image to a Sony VCR "so that it will be possible for the director, or anyone else, . . . to see the shot on video tape immediately after the camera operator has made it."[85]

One interesting application of this principle appeared during the shooting of THE MUPPET MOVIE in 1979, where the film cameras were modified to incorporate compact, high-resolution video cameras whose images were carried by cable to both a VCR and as many as fifteen monitors, most of which were used by the individual puppeteers

Steven Spielberg, on the set of CLOSE ENCOUNTERS *(1977), was able to check shot composition on the video monitor to his camera's left; the monitor was fed with a signal from a video camera positioned just outside the frame on the camera's right. 35mm Panavision anamorphic, blown up to 70mm for road-showing.*

concealed beneath the set to position their Muppets for the cameras; larger monitors were used by the production staff to troubleshoot each take.[86] By the time of THE SHINING (1980), Kubrick was able to order two or three perfect takes on each scene for editing in post-production, monitoring all of them by video remote. As Garrett Brown wrote of the filming of the maze sequence, the director "mostly remained seated at the video screen, and we sent a wireless image from my camera out to an antenna on a ladder and thence to the recorder [for playback]."[87] (Kubrick had used video as early as 1967 to monitor the filming of the centrifuge sequence in 2001, and more recently to coordinate the camera work of BARRY LYNDON.)[88] Francis Ford Coppola employed videotape to pre-edit parts of APOCALYPSE NOW (1979) on location, and in the early 1980s, he valorized video-assist technology as never before by making it the basis for his "electronic cinema" method.[89] Used initially in the production of ONE FROM THE HEART (Francis Ford Coppola, 1982), this was basically a way to "pre-visualize" a film on video, creating an "electronic storyboard," so that it could actually be edited before it was shot (see below). According to Thomas Brown, director of Electronic Cinema at Zoetrope Studios, this meant that "the whole movie could be seen at any time" by the production crew and cast, before any film footage had been shot.[90] Used in this way, video assist enabled Coppola "at the beginning of each production day, to view an edited version of the previous day's shooting, complete with music and sound effects."[91] Although the electronic cinema method proved far less cost-effective than Coppola had envisioned (he used it only twice more himself—in THE OUTSIDERS and RUMBLE FISH [both 1983]), elements of it took root in the production community, and video-assist technology was adopted by most American directors over the next decade, with or without playback.[92]

Special Effects and Motion Control

In the same way that video assist technology changed the parameters of producing live-action sequences, so did automated motion control transform the production of special effects. Despite the well-deserved praise and the Academy Award accorded the special effects in 2001: A SPACE ODYSSEY in 1968, the technology of special effects had changed very little from the 1920s to the 1970s. The key to their achievement was traveling matte or "blue-screen" photography, in which models and miniatures are manipulated for the camera frame-by-frame in front a blue screen that leaves the background of the shot unexposed. The background is then superimposed—or "matted in"—during the printing process through double exposure. Any number of images can be layered on to the same piece of film in this way, but the matching of elements must be absolutely precise for the illusion to be seamless. The extraordinary verisimilitude of 2001's effects was accomplished through the painstaking efforts of Kubrick, and special photographic effects supervisor Douglas Trumbull and his crew, who spent 18 months and $6.5 million—or 60 percent of the film's total budget—to produce them. But except for its use of front projection on a vast scale in the "Dawn of Man" prologue and Trumbull's "slit-scan" photography in the "Stargate Corridor" sequence, there was nothing technically innovative about the film's special effects. The real secret of their success was the director's obsessive perfectionism.

By the mid-1970s there was a clear sense among production artists that the practice of special effects had not kept pace with the general technological acceleration of the industry. This can be observed, for example, in the ambivalent discourse surrounding the use of lasers and holograms in the science-fiction epic LOGAN'S RUN (Michael Anderson, 1976), whose special effects were touted to surpass those of 2001. In an article in *American Cinematographer*, L. B. Abbott, who would win a Special Achievement Award from the Academy for the film's visual effects (and had shared another with A. D. Flowers for THE POSEIDON ADVENTURE in 1972), lamented the decline of matte painting at the same time that he enthused over the use of laser holography to create futuristic effects.[93] Ironically, the matte paintings in LOGAN'S RUN were much more credible than the holograms, which didn't photograph very well, and most of its effects were rendered by conventional means. In fact, Abbott created much of the film's twenty-third-century environment through miniature, model, and matte-work techniques that had been available since he entered the cinema in 1926, the same ones used by virtually all special effects artists until STAR WARS (George Lucas) appeared in 1977 and revolutionized the practice of special effects for another twenty years—after which it came to be dominated by computer-generated imagery (CGI).

THE INNOVATIONS OF STAR WARS

Like those of 2001 (and parts of LOGAN'S RUN), the special effects in STAR WARS were accomplished through traveling matte photography. The crucial difference was that Lucas and his team at Industrial Light and Magic used a computerized motion-control system designed by John Dykstra (patented as "Dykstraflex") to make traveling matte work cost-effective for the first time. At its heart was a motorized camera mount governed by multi-track magnetic tape, which permitted the camera to pan, tilt, roll, and track eight vertical feet or forty-two horizontal feet in precisely repeatable movements. Operators could program their cameras to execute complicated maneuvers one frame at a time, and the sequences could then be infinitely repeated through numeric control.

The automation of traveling matte photography enabled the creation of special effects that were at once more complex and less expensive to achieve than ever before. Whereas Kubrick, for example, had spent $6.5 million to create thirty traveling mattes for 2001, Lucas spent only $2.5 million to create 365 traveling mattes for STAR WARS, and those of STAR WARS were arguably more dynamic.[94] (Another reason for the cost differential was that Kubrick shot his special effects sequences as complete takes and then edited them as if they were live-action footage; whereas Lucas followed the more conventional practice of pre-editing his effects sequences to the frame, so as not to shoot any footage that might wind up on the cutting room floor.)[95]

The epoch-making commercial success of STAR WARS created a late-1970s boom in state-of-the-art special effects and genres that supported them (most obviously, science fiction), reducing the high unemployment among film workers caused by the artificial "product shortage" at mid-decade. In a front-page article headlined "Film Effects Men Turn Trick at B. O.," Variety reported in July 1977 that a new breed of technicians was being attracted to Hollywood, one whose original training was not in the motion picture arts but in electronics and micro-circuitry.[96] These newly arrived electronics engineers and software programmers worked on the proprietary motion-control systems that appeared overnight to compete with "Dykstraflex"—Paramount, for example, overhauled its Magicam system, originated in 1975, though the studio switched to Dykstraflex for STAR TREK—THE MOTION PICTURE (Robert Wise, 1979).[97] Dykstraflex, which earned John Dykstra a 1977 Academy Award for "Scientific and Technical Achievement," was adopted by the producers of television's Battlestar Galactica series, but was replaced at ILM by Richard Edlund's even more sophisticated "Empireflex" system, used to film THE EMPIRE STRIKES BACK (Irvin Kershner, 1980); and Disney unveiled its $1-million ACES ("Automatic Camera Effects System") in 1979.[98] This latter used computer automation to control both camera and model in combination with Matte-Scan, another Disney system, that permitted the integration of matte paintings with live-action scenes while the camera was in motion on several axes; both were engaged to create the elaborate special effects for the studio's $17.5-million space epic THE BLACK HOLE (Gary Nelson, 1979).[99]

After STAR WARS, motion control became the industry standard for most traveling matte and miniature work, although it worked best with inanimate objects. It could not, for example, be used for the flying sequences of SUPERMAN (1978) because the movements of a human actor could not be precisely repeated for automated multiple exposure; after much costly trial and error, that film and its sequels adopted a system called "Zoptic," designed by Zoran Perisic, which basically combined front projection with zooms, pans, and tilts in continuous sequence.[100] Computer animation and computer graphics, which came to dominate special effects at the close of the century, were in their infancy for much of the 1970s, but at the end of the decade several groups were exploring their possible applications to film. There was interest among professional animators at several studios in automating some of their work, computer graphics research was in progress at Lucasfilm/ILM, and at Disney a project was in development that became TRON (Steven Lisberger, 1982), a landmark in early digital effects that featured

Disney used its new "Automatic Camera Effects System" (ACES) and Matte-Scan system to create breathtaking special effects for its space epic THE BLACK HOLE *(Gary Nelson, 1979), which failed at the box office nonetheless. ACES was a computer-automated motion-control system for traveling matte photography based on Industrial Light and Magic's "Dykstraflex," which had produced the special effects for* STAR WARS; *Matte-Scan integrated matte paintings with live-action sequences while the camera was in motion on several axes.* THE BLACK HOLE *was part of a late-1970s science-fiction boom driven by* STAR WARS; *it cost about $20 million to produce, thanks largely to its elaborate visual effects and returned just a little over $25 million in rentals. 35mm Technovision, blown up to 70mm for road-showing.*

sixteen minutes of computer-animated shots and twenty-five minutes of computer animation blended with live action.[101]

Dolby Stereo Optical Sound

That standards for sound recording and playback during the 1970s had not kept pace
with advances in cinematography was well understood by filmmakers at mid-decade. As
late as 1976, Arthur Penn could remark of his experiments with sound in THE MISSOURI
BREAKS: "[T]he question of sound is still very thorny. It doesn't match the visual sophistication. . . . We're all working still with radio [quality] mikes, trying to deal with it. I
don't know what the solution is going to be, but it's clearly the next major avenue of technology in films to be resolved."[102] Commenting at about the same time on the quality of
theatrical reproduction, Robert Altman said: "Sound in theaters—the overwhelming
majority of theaters—is just terrible. The acoustics, the speakers, everything."[103] Both
directors were dead right, but a major innovation in the technology of sound lay just
ahead with the introduction of Dolby-encoded stereo optical recording and playback. As
with so much else, the watershed for Dolby was STAR WARS, the first wide-release
Dolby stereo optical film, whose epoch-making success was understood to depend at
least partially on its high-powered, high-quality sound track. Early research by 20th
Century–Fox indicated that Dolby-equipped theaters significantly outgrossed non-
Dolby ones on the film's initial release, and *Variety* proclaimed "'Star Wars' Booms
Optical Tracks For Sound."[104] By Christmas 1977, five of the season's biggest releases
carried Dolby tracks, and the number of Dolby-equipped theaters had nearly doubled
to 200; it would increase to 800 by the end of 1978.[105] What followed has been accurately
called "the Second Coming of Sound," with STAR WARS as Dolby's THE JAZZ SINGER
(Alan Crosland, 1927), because within eight years of that film's release only a handful of
American films would be released in any other format.[106]

In 1977 most of the nation's 15,000 theaters were equipped to play optical prints only,
which until that point meant monaural sound. Stereophonic sound was the province of
magnetic recording and playback, and there were two magnetic systems available to
American theaters before Dolby—four-track CinemaScope stereo for 35mm anamorphic, introduced by Fox in THE ROBE (Henry Koster, 1953), and six-track Todd-AO
stereo for 70mm, introduced in AROUND THE WORLD IN EIGHTY DAYS (Michael
Anderson, 1956). Both of these systems placed their separate magnetic tracks directly
on the theatrical print of the film, outside the picture frame. Although magnetic prints
offered a very high quality of sound reproduction, magnetic striping and recording could
add as much as 50 percent to their cost over optical prints, and they degraded faster
because of excessive playback-head wear in the projector.[107] In the mid-1970s magnetic
prints cost about $1,200 to produce, while optical prints cost $800; and optical sound
tracks could be counted on to last for the life of the print, whereas magnetic sound tracks
usually wore out well before their images.[108] Moreover, exhibitors had to make expensive adjustments to projection equipment in order to play magnetic prints at their
proper frequency response (flat to 12kHz), and, because only about one-fourth of
America's theaters ever installed stereo magnetic equipment, distributors had to supply
both optical and magnetic versions of every stereo release. (An expensive compromise
adopted by Fox in the late 1950s was to produce "mag-optical" sound tracks, which had
both formats running side-by-side on the same print.)[109] For these reasons, most pro-

ducers chose not to invest in stereo recording and mixing, and before 1977 the American industry was geared to the production of monaural optical sound tracks, with stereo magnetic sound reserved for 70mm road shows and other special presentations. (There were a few exceptions—Nicolas Roeg's THE MAN WHO FELL TO EARTH [1976] was released in 35mm non-Dolbyized stereo magnetic—but these were rare.) Many 1970s films notable for their sound tracks—CABARET (Bob Fosse, 1972), THE EXORCIST (1973), and JAWS (1975), for example, all of which won Academy Awards for Best Sound—were recorded on film and played in theaters exclusively in monaural.

Since monaural films were the norm, stereo could have a defamiliarizing effect on movie audiences during the 1950s and early 1960s. As John Belton has pointed out, audiences were sometimes distracted by the practice of "voice-panning" whereby dialogue would travel from one speaker to another behind the screen to represent the movement of action across the frame.[110] The best stereo mixes of the era used voice-panning to create a spatial sound field that was directional and rich for both dialogue-music performance (as in THE KING AND I [Walter Lang, 1956]; and MY FAIR LADY [George Cukor, 1964]) and mass action scenes (SPARTACUS [Stanley Kubrick, 1960]; TARAS BULBA [Lee Thompson, 1962]), but stereo was associated exclusively with spectacle until it entered the mainstream home entertainment environment in the mid-1960s.[111] There it established itself somewhat arbitrarily as a two-channel, two-speaker format, although the earliest experiments with the technology at Bell Labs had been conducted with three distinct channels and at the time stereo magnetic movie sound tracks used at least four. (The term *stereo* derives from the Greek root for "solid," and the technique of stereophonic sound requires that multiple sources of sound be placed around the listener to re-create a three-dimensional sonic experience.)[112] Although Quadrophonic systems, which employed four speakers, were marketed briefly during the 1970s, binaural stereo imaging became the home entertainment standard through the era of the compact disc (CD). Most 35mm movie theaters, on the other hand, deployed three speakers—left, right, and center—behind the screen, and for films with monophonic optical sound tracks they were all fed by a single channel. Theaters capable of stereo playback normally had four speakers (six for 70mm)—left, center, right, and rear—one for each stereo magnetic track (the extra two speakers for 70mm were for tracks carrying base enhancers, or "baby boom" channels). Dolby stereo optical was a two-track, four-channel 35mm format that could maximize the dynamic range and frequency response of either theater system.

Dolby stereo optical grew out of the Dolby noise reduction (Dolby NR) system, which electronically reduces background noise and increases frequency response. Dolby NR was developed by Ray Dolby at Dolby Laboratories during the late 1960s for use in the recording industry (where, among other things, it helped to innovate stereo cassette recording by removing its inevitable hiss), and it entered the film industry in 1971 when Stanley Kubrick used it during the mixing stages of A CLOCKWORK ORANGE (1971), although the film itself was released with a standard monaural sound track. Dolby NR was subsequently applied to several musicals, where it was used for both monaural optical (STEPPENWOLF [Fred Haines, 1974]; STARDUST [Michael Apted, 1975]) and four-track stereo magnetic sound tracks (THE LITTLE PRINCE [Stanley Donen, 1974]; NASHVILLE [1975]) in both recording and theater playback.

Beginning in 1973, however, Eastman Kodak, RCA, and Dolby worked together to develop a simple two-channel stereo optical system that would have its left and right tracks running side-by-side in the area normally occupied by the monaural optical track.[113] (Monaural tracks were already bilateral, carrying two identical variable area channels to compensate for sound-head misalignment in the projector.)[114] This meant that an unconverted projector could run a stereo optical track and still generate a mono-compatible signal.[115] In the theater, Dolby stereo optical (Dolby SR) reproduced its two stereo tracks through the left and right speaker, and a third channel—synthesized by a logic circuit in the "Dolby Cinema Processor" from different phase relationships between the left and right track signals—was sent to the center speaker. The sound thus produced was indistinguishable from multi-track stereo magnetic, making high-fidelity stereo possible for the relatively modest conversion cost of about $5,000 per theater.[116] (Houses with outdated monaural equipment, however, could cost as much as $20,000 to convert, and there were plenty of these at the time.)[117] On the production side, it cost about $25,000 more to dub a film in Dolby stereo than in monaural and the conversion of an existing film-mixing studio to Dolby cost around $40,000, but these were relatively

Three-position mixing console used to mix dialogue, sound effects, and music in post-production; most of the levers are for equalizing volume and frequency response.

modest sums at a time when average negative costs had risen to $5 million per picture. Furthermore, the print cost of a Dolby stereo release was about the same as for a monaural production, and Dolby SR was so manifestly superior to its competition (for example, the short-lived Fox "Sound 360" system)[118] that the company's business quadrupled in the year following the release of STAR WARS.[119]

Before that occurred, however, Dolby developed a way of adding surround information to the optical track at the mixing stage via "stereo matrix" circuitry that encoded the information onto the two-track signal; the matrix was then decoded by the Dolby Cinema Processor in the theater to create a fourth channel.[120] The resulting surround signal was either sent to the rear speaker in existing four-speaker theaters, or could be distributed among new speakers positioned around the auditorium's side and back walls, so that the audience was literally "surrounded" by dimensional sound appropriate to a film's action—for example, helicopters flying overhead or source music (like a band playing) temporarily moving off-screen. There were several precedents for surround sound. Four-track CinemaScope magnetic had employed an "effects channel" which, like voice-panning, was designed to put the audience into the action.[121] And although it was technically more sophisticated, Dolby surround also had similarities with "Sensurround," the low-frequency sound system developed by MCA/Universal to simulate the seismic tremors in EARTHQUAKE (Mark Robson, 1974) and used for similar effects in MIDWAY (Jack Smight, 1976) and ROLLERCOASTER (James Goldstone, 1977). Essentially a monophonic amplification process combined with enormous speakers sta-

Ken Russell's TOMMY *(1975), the film that introduced Dolby stereo optical sound. This version of* The Who's *rock opera, adapted by Russell himself, represented the first time since the era of CinemaScope that four-channel stereo had accompanied a 35mm film.*

tioned at each corner of the auditorium, Sensurround filled the theater with a very low base and was capable of creating sound pressure waves comparable to those of an actual earthquake (8–14 Hz at 110–120 dB).[122] By selectively raising the volume of high frequency sounds in the mix, sound could be steered around the theater to create a quadrophonic effect not unlike that of Dolby surround. However, the obvious gimmickry and technical clumsiness of Sensurround doomed it after the arrival of Dolby stereo, and the system was last used in 1979 when added to BATTLESTAR: GALACTICA (Richard A. Colla) in post-production.[123]

Dolby stereo optical, then, was a two-track, four-channel 35mm format; it was first used in the musicals TOMMY (Ken Russell, 1975), LISZTOMANIA (Ken Russell, 1975), and A STAR IS BORN (Frank Pierson, 1976); also in 1975, Warners released BARRY LYNDON in partial Dolby, and LOGAN'S RUN (1976) became the first non-musical to be recorded entirely in the process (the film was also released in 70mm six-track stereo magnetic).[124] George Lucas and his producer Gary Kurtz approached Dolby Laboratories in 1975 to help them design a superior sound track for STAR WARS (1977), and Dolby saw the film as the perfect opportunity to demonstrate the range of its new system. Dolby engineers were involved at every stage of the film's planning, production, and mixing, with the goal that the sound heard in the theaters should be identical to that heard by the director during the mix.[125] The general release prints were Dolby-encoded stereo optical with a surround track and the 70mm six-track magnetic prints were also Dolbyized. As the first film to be both recorded and released in four-channel Dolby stereo (and the first to use Dolby NR throughout production), STAR WARS produced a revolution in theater sound that very soon caused a large-scale conversion to the system. (In production, however, audio still took a back seat to visual effects—only twenty workers handled the audio for STAR WARS, while 150 were employed on visual effects.)[126] It was followed almost immediately by several other blockbusters that exploited Dolby effects and confirmed its market potential, especially with young audiences (CLOSE ENCOUNTERS OF THE THIRD KIND [1977]; SATURDAY NIGHT FEVER [John Badham, 1977]; GREASE [1978]; and SUPERMAN [1978]), as well as by other films that had the lifelike reproduction of sound at their conceptual core (THE LAST WALTZ [Martin Scorsese, 1978]; THE SHOUT [Jerzy Skolimowski, 1978]; and DAYS OF HEAVEN [Terrence Malick, 1978]), which later (like GREASE) were shown in 70mm Dolby-encoded stereo magnetic because of the improved sound quality made possible by the wide-gauge format. (Early Dolby also had its share of flops—including THE WIZ [Sydney Lumet, 1978], FM [John A. Alonzo, 1978], AMERICAN HOT WAX [Floyd Mutrux, 1978], SGT. PEPPER'S LONELY HEARTS CLUB BAND [Michael Schultz, 1978], and HAIR [Milos Forman, 1979].) By the end of the decade, there were 1,200 Dolby-equipped American theaters, and by the mid-1980s Dolby counted over 6,000 installations worldwide, and almost 90 percent of all Hollywood films were being released in four-channel Dolby stereo.[127] For motion picture and theater sound, then, as for so much else, the 1970s were a formative decade, beginning as generally monaural and ending on the road to full stereo optical surround.

Sound Design and Post-Production

Michael Cimino, using Dolby SR for the first time during the production of THE DEER HUNTER (1978), said that it gives a director "the ability to create a *density of detail* of sound—a richness so you can demolish the wall separating the viewer from the film."[128]

Yet as subtle as Dolby stereo optical would prove to be at registering such sounds as insect chirps, bird calls, and human breathing, voices and lip movements were occasionally out of synchronization and directional stereo separation was often problematic. It soon became clear that to achieve an effective Dolby mix, the sound track had to be planned and even scripted as part of a film's overall production design—an imperative most brilliantly realized in Walter Murch's sound design for APOCALYPSE NOW (1979) and one that has become a central component of mainstream filmmaking ever since.

SOUND DESIGN

Murch was the conceptual and practical architect of what has become known as "sound design." Although the term didn't come into common usage until the mid-1970s, sound designers would have been called supervising sound editors in the pre-Dolby era. To paraphrase Marc Mancini, they are to modern multi-track sound systems what cinematographers are to lighting and visual composition or production designers to set construction and scenic display: they sculpt the sound of a motion picture from storyboarding through post-production, coordinating the work of a large number of performers, artists, and technical engineers, including the production sound mixer, the sound editor, the composer, the music editor and mixer, the ADR (automatic dialogue replacement) editor and mixer, the Foley artists, and the re-recording mixers.[129] It has been estimated that some 400 to 600 individual sound and source tracks are typically used to create a full feature-length sound track, and assembling one is an enormously complicated business.[130] The innovation of Dolby technology increased both the complexity and artistic range of the task, so that film school-trained specialists like Murch and Ben Burtt—the sound designer for STAR WARS and its sequels, as well as for the INDIANA JONES films and E.T.: THE EXTRA-TERRESTRIAL (Steven Spielberg, 1982)— were attracted to sound design as a major creative component of the filmmaking process.[131] As Murch put it in 1978 while working on APOCALYPSE NOW: "The challenges of putting together a sound track are not totally on the technical level. That's a very important part, but eighty percent is in finding the right and appropriate combination of sounds—and putting them in the right place."[132]

Murch's example is paradigmatic and exceptional at the same time. While still a student at the USC film school, he created the futuristic sound track for George Lucas's first features THX-1138 (1971; which he also co-wrote) and AMERICAN GRAFFITI (1973), and went on to design the sound for two of 1974's most critically esteemed films—Francis Ford Coppola's THE GODFATHER, PART II and THE CONVERSATION. For the latter, which was self-reflexively about electronic surveillance, Murch was nominated for an Academy Award, and he began using the credit "Sound Montage" for his sonic fabrications. Much of Murch's work at this stage involved the use of synthesizers to create experimental wave forms to suggest computers and other electronic noise for which there was no empirical analogue. What is now called Foley recording (see below) was available but not well developed at mid-decade, and Murch chose to record each of his effects separately and synchronize them by hand.[133] By the time of APOCALYPSE NOW (1979), which is considered to be a landmark in sound design, Murch was using ADR (automatic dialogue replacement, or "looping") sessions to supplement the detailed mapping of a 360-degree, spatially dimensional sound field for playback in Dolby 70mm six-track magnetic stereo—a full-frequency quadrophonic system that employed "split-surround," or "stereo surround," permitting the illusion of sound moving through all four quadrants of the theater, as when the helicopter in the film's credit sequence begins in the right rear, travels to the left rear, then moves to the left front and then to the right front.[134] (Although similar effects have been achieved since the early 1990s through Dolby Digital Stereo, DTS [Digital Theater Systems], SDDS [Sony Dynamic Digital Sound], or competing digital technologies; all movie sound before that time, both mono and stereo, was analog.)[135] Though APOCALYPSE NOW has not been re-released theatrically since 1979, Murch took advantage of the optical laserdisc format to remix its sound track twice: first in Digital Stereo in 1991, and then in 5.1-channel AC-3 in 1997, attempting to reproduce the original 70mm experience. Murch won an Academy Award for Best Achievement in Sound in APOCALYPSE NOW and inaugurated the "Sound Design" credit used in major films ever since. Over the next few decades, the sound designer became an integral member of the production team, often hired as early as the production designer and the DP, and as sound recording moved into the digital age, the role became increasingly complex. (Digital signal processing was first used in the post-production of a major Hollywood film to mix acoustical re-recorded sound with synthesized sounds for STAR TREK—THE MOTION PICTURE [1979].)[136]

FOLEY RECORDING

Like sound design, Foley recording came of age in the late 1970s. Named for Jack Foley, the Universal sound engineer who first conceived the idea during the late 1940s, Foley is the art of performing sound effects in post-production dubbing sessions rather than recording them while shooting (or, as in the studio era, cutting them into the sound track from a library of pre-recorded sounds). Foley is thus the sound-effects equivalent of ADR, in which actors watch their filmed performances on a screen and re-record some of their lines for remixing in a studio. A "Foley stage" is a dedicated recording studio that contains a variety of surfaces (for example, pits filled with concrete, sand, gravel, and leaves) and a large number of props (car doors, furniture, guns), as well as a movie screen or video monitor where Foley artists can study a film's action for synchronous, real-time recording of effects. Common Foley effects include footsteps, floors creaking, chairs scraping, clothes rustling, keys jingling, water splashing, etc. (Jack Foley once simulated the sound of Niagara Falls by spraying water from a garden hose onto a billboard.)[137] Foley artists can also remove incidental sounds that have been accidentally recorded in shooting and redub the sound track with more appropriate ones.

In 1971 there were only six to eight Foley artists in Hollywood, according to former sound editor Ross Taylor, who (with his partner Kitty Malone) performed the Foley on some of the 1970s' most important films, including CABARET (1972), THE GODFATHER (1972), THE EXORCIST (1973) (with its repulsive pea soup vomiting sequence), CHINATOWN (1974), STAR WARS (1977), THE DEEP (Peter Yates, 1977), and APOCALYPSE NOW (1979).[138] Taylor and Ross provided Foley dance steps for CABARET (all of the sound in the "Money-Money" number is Foley except the voice performances), machine-gun fire for THE GODFATHER, and the notorious vomiting sequence for THE EXORCIST. For THE DEEP, they collaborated with Hal Landker to develop a portable Foley system that included a twelve-by-three-foot swimming tank in which to produce the underwater effects.[139] The laser blasts in STAR WARS were created by hitting a tension wire that supported an antenna with a hammer and processing the sound in a synthesizer.[140] Yet the practice of Foley was so rare that until the mid-1970s there

A contemporary Foley artist walking in high heels on a Foley stage; he is synchronizing his footsteps with an image projected on a screen in front of him. Foley effects came of age during the 1970s, through their crucial appearance in such films as THE EXORCIST *(1973),* STAR WARS *(1977), and* APOCALYPSE NOW *(1979), whose visceral impact was heightened by a specialized use of sound. (Brian Vancho, Foley artist; Sound One Corp., New York.)*

was no established pay scale for it. By the 1980s, however, there were thirty or more full-time Foley artists, including a whole sub-group of "Foley walkers" who specialized in all sounds created by human feet, and ADR and Foley mixing had become a regular component of post-production sound engineering.[141] Foley became increasingly important with the advent of digital sound playback in theaters, whose precision demanded the vividness of studio-produced effects, and in 1990s it was a rare film that did not feature several Foley credits.

EXPERIMENTS IN ELECTRONIC EDITING

In addition to its innovations in electronic sound, the 1970s also witnessed the beginnings of electronic film editing. In 1967 the American broadcasting industry had adopted a time code to facilitate the electronic editing of NTSC videotape. This is essentially a system that encodes synchronized signals for each frame of video for the length of the tape so that it is "frame addressable" by computer, and therefore subject to precise (and speedy) electronic manipulation. In 1971, CMX, Inc., a partnership between CBS and the Memorex Corporation, introduced an electronic computerized editing system under the acronym of RAVE (Random Access Video Editing). This system, described as "a sophisticated fusion of tape recorders, computer memory banks and magnetic disks," was designed to read video time code, but CMX also touted its potential to reference motion picture edge numbering in the same way: "For a feature film, the computer could read out on paper the prescribed order of frame numbers for an entire production . . . [and a] technician then could cut the film according to instructions without recourse to the present method of winding and rewinding."[142] As it turned out, computer storage and access was still too limited to handle the amount of footage generated by a feature film, but visionary filmmakers like Coppola and Murch thought they could see the future in CMX technology. Together, they prepared a proposal to edit THE GODFATHER using the CMX system, which was rejected by Paramount, but six years later Coppola employed a linear video editing system to experiment with different story structures for APOCALYPSE NOW. Murch actually used it to compose the series of four-element overlapping dissolves in the first reel of the film, but the rest of it was put together on conventional editing machines (two flatbed Moviolas and two KEM eight-plates).[143] Coppola's unique perspective notwithstanding, there was considerable industry interest throughout the decade in the possibility of adapting time code and video editing techniques to film production, but a major stumbling block was the fact that film runs at 24 frames per second and video at 30. By mid-decade, it was possible to transfer film to video via a telecine conversion chain using the so-called "3-2 pulldown," which worked as follows. Because each video frame is composed of two interlaced fields of scan lines, the frame can be split in half and remain legible from top to bottom. In 3-2 pulldown technology, the film-video frame rate differential is addressed by allocating three fields of video to every second frame of film and two fields to the others. With the film thus transferred to video, it was then possible to edit the tape electronically, but converting the tape back into film was problematic because, as an article in *American Cinematographer* noted, "If one attempted to correlate video time code to film counts, the video frame on which a cut occurs may correspond to two different film frames."[144] This meant that until someone either a) devised a coding system that could distinguish between fields rather than frames, or b) developed a method for recording time code on the film stock itself, video could only be used to "pre-edit" films in the manner of Coppola's ONE FROM THE HEART (1982; see above), or Hal Ashby's SECOND-HAND HEARTS (1981), where cameras were run through a video editor and onto videotape so that the director could both evaluate shots and pre-assemble them.[145]

In 1982, Kodak would introduce a way to record an eight-digit SMPTE (Society of Motion Picture and Television Engineers) time code for each frame via a transparent magnetic coating on its film stock, creating the prospect of random-access electronic editing, research for which was ongoing at Lucasfilm Ltd., Zoetrope Studios, Lion's Gate, and other innovative production companies.[146] At the same time, CMX introduced a semi-computerized flatbed system called FLM-1, which correlated frame counts from film-to-tape transfers with conventional SMPTE time codes by running the film in constant synchronization with a 3/4-inch videotape recorder, obviating the 3-2 pulldown of a normal telecine chain.[147]

Projection

Before the 1970s, projection technology had changed little since the early days of the industry. In that decade, however, two significant innovations took place that greatly reduced the labor involved in projecting a 35mm or 70mm film on a screen, as well as cutting investment in projection hardware nearly in half. First, the high-intensity carbon arc lamps in projectors were replaced by more efficient xenon bulbs. Carbon arcs—in which electrical current arced across the gap between two carbon nodes—provided a brighter, whiter light than xenons (which nevertheless yielded a daylight-type light of a color temperature 6,000 degrees Kelvin), but they required constant vigilance for safety.[148] Xenons, originally developed by Xenotech, Inc. as searchlights for U.S. Army tanks, also contained an electrical arc, but one that was enclosed inside a quartz sleeve under high-pressure xenon gas, so that they could be left to operate unattended.

The other labor-saving device introduced during the 1970s was the horizontal platter system, in which the entire film was spliced together reel-by-reel and mounted on a four-foot-diameter platter for feeding into the projector; as the film wound its way through the machine, it was taken up by a lower platter. While this system required that the film be assembled into a single reel for presentation and disassembled for shipping after its run, it meant that there were no reel changes during projection, so that the projectionist could shuttle among several auditoria at once—a practice crucial to the operation of multiplexes. Once plattered, the film could be shown again and again over the length of its run by a relatively unskilled operator, eliminating the necessity for a unionized professional projectionist. (The membership of the Motion Picture and Video Projectionists Union was decimated as a result of this automation, declining in some parts of the country by as much as 90 percent.)[149] Finally, since there was no need to alternate reels, the platter system cut the number of projectors necessary to run a film in half, another big plus for the owners of multiplexes, enabling them to subdivide their equipment as cost-effectively as they had subdivided their auditoria. It was due in part to savings like these that exhibitors were able to continue to expand their holdings and prosper during an era of maximum "product shortage."

Coda: Technology and Narrative Form

Despite the many "revolutionary" innovations discussed above, between 1970 and 1979 the narrative form of American films changed very little as far as audiences were concerned. The trend toward rapid cutting that began in the 1960s under the influence of the French New Wave reached its zenith in 1976, when the average shot length approached six seconds; but jump cutting itself was largely abandoned as a means of scenic transition, and the long take remained the province of the European art film.[150] Lighter cameras contributed to a steady increase in location shooting (although the primary force was soaring studio overhead)—Vilmos Zsigmond, for example, used the new 25-lb. Panaflex camera to shoot extensive dialogue sequences inside a moving car for THE SUGARLAND EXPRESS (1974), but they don't appear to be much more realistic than the similarly staged process shots of BONNIE AND CLYDE (1967). In the same way, there was an increase in complicated moving-camera shots after 1976 thanks to the introduction of Steadicam/Panaglide technology, but the hand-held traveling shots of JAWS (1975) don't look much different from the Panaglide stalking sequences of HALLOWEEN (1978)— there are just more of them. Audiences that had gasped at the opening moments of THE SANDPIPER (Vincente Minnelli) in 1965, in which the camera seems to float above the crests of the waves off the Monterey coast via an extended helicopter shot,[151] had gotten used to cameras that roamed apparently free of physical limitations by the year of JAWS, NASHVILLE, and BARRY LYNDON. The ability to see beyond the pale of the natural universe delivered by the motion-control systems of Lucasfilm Ltd. in STAR WARS (1977) looked at the time like 2001: A SPACE ODYSSEY in overdrive (which, in a purely technical sense, it was); it would take another five years for the genres sustained by special effects—science fiction, fantasy, and horror—to consume the industry's production schedule and, in the terms of Peter Biskind, "infantilize" the American audience "by overwhelming it with sound and spectacle."[152] It was, in fact, in the domain of sound alone that a major formal change was apparent during the 1970s: audiences attending Dolby-equipped theaters showing Dolby-encoded films in the latter part of the decade would have detected a perceptible shift from undistinguished monaural to precision-honed stereo surround. Yet, as noted earlier, some of the 1970s films most notable for their sound tracks—THE GODFATHER, CABARET, AMERICAN GRAFFITI, THE EXORCIST, and JAWS, for example—were recorded and played in monaural.

The most striking change in American films during the 1970s came not at the level of form but of content, and two phenomena that bracketed the decade insured this. At its outset, the malfunctioning of the new MPAA ratings system gave the imprimatur of mainstream entertainment to the pornography of hardcore sex and graphic violence. Once that had occurred, both became irresistible box-office attractions, and everyone in the industry, from auteurist directors to studio financiers, had to acknowledge it—and then, of course, to compete with it. Thus, exploitation films like THE EXORCIST (1973) and JAWS (1975) were engineered by their producer-distributors to become international blockbusters, and serious filmmakers were forced to limn a fine line between art and decadence to sell their product at all. The fact that fallout from the twin calamities of Watergate and Vietnam was simultaneously poisoning the culture helped the process along, so that one of the decade's most distinguished films is about a deranged veteran of that war who goes on an ultraviolent killing spree to "rescue" a twelve-year-old prostitute from her pimp, having earlier tried and failed to assassinate a popular political candidate—Lee Harvey Oswald as John Wayne. Martin Scorsese's TAXI DRIVER (1976), which trades heavily in the depiction of paranoia, racial bigotry, perverse sexuality, and graphic gore, could not have been made in the United States before the MPPA began the segregation of audiences by age in late 1968. Yet by the end of the decade, Scorsese's film had been licensed for sale on home video—a medium that hadn't existed five years before, and one that would siphon off hardcore sexual materials from the nation's theaters into its homes. Together with much else.

In fact, what home video did for hardcore films it did for all movies—reduce them (literally) in stature and turn watching them, with or without masturbation, into a private act. How perfect, then, that what Tom Wolfe had branded as "the Me Decade" should end by making one of twentieth-century America's great public rituals a form of narcissistic gratification. (Although, if psychoanalytic film theorists are right, the movies may have never been anything else.) The crowning irony of the American Film Institute's 1998 ranking of great American films ("AFI's 100 Years . . . 100 Movies") was that by 1998 most Americans had never seen them on a movie screen. And whatever one may think of the AFI's list, it is noteworthy that twenty of the one hundred were made between 1969 and 1979 (including JAWS [1975], as number 47; and TAXI DRIVER [1976], as number 48), more by far than for any other decade, signaling the astonishing richness of the period. It was the last time in American film history that so much talent, so much art, and so much money have converged on the site of the motion picture screen. The results were often extreme, even explosive, because the films themselves mirrored our society at a time when it seemed to be coming apart, but the industry has never produced better ones, not even during the studio system's golden age. Yet for all of their innovativeness and energy, the films of the 1970s were in some sense autumn fruit, ripened through seven decades of economic, technological, and aesthetic development whose dynamics would change dramatically as the movies were shrunk and then digitized for electronic distribution in the decade to come.

10

Motion Picture Exhibition in 1970s America

Douglas Gomery [1]

O n the surface, the exhibition side of the movie industry seemed stable during the 1970s. While the major Hollywood studios struggled to redefine themselves within the TV age, the movie show seemed vanilla plain, as far from the golden days of the movie palace as one could imagine. The only change appeared to come at the popcorn stand, where the number of treats available at inflated prices seemed to increase daily. Indeed, during the 1970s the average theater saw its revenue share from concession sales rise from one-eighth to one-fifth of the total. But this seeming stasis masked considerable transformation. There was steady growth in the number of available indoor screens in commercial use, as multiplexing slowly pushed the figure from 10,000 towards 15,000.[2]

The 1970s surely was the decade when the theatrical moviegoing experience hit its nadir in the United States. Cluster after cluster of unadorned screening rooms typically offered only previews of Hollywood's latest features, maybe an ad or two, and then the blockbuster of the week. It was as if, realizing that they had lost the battle with TV, the exhibitors gave up almost all pretense of the competition that had long defined this sector of the industry. Gone were the architectural fantasies—screen number two offered even fewer amenities than were available at home. The movie house architecture seemed to become the international style at its soulless worst. Its function, in the age of television, seemed clear: collect the money, sell the popcorn, show the blockbuster, and then repeat the cycle all over again.

But simply focusing on this sad state of affairs loses sight of the real and significant changes in the presentation and viewing of movies that were taking place. Historically, not only was there increased interest in movie culture during the 1970s, there was continued growth in attendance as maturing baby boomers sought out their cinematic favorites. These boomers lived by and large in the suburbs surrounding America's cities, so new chains of exhibitors constructed new viewing sites in suburban shopping centers and malls. And demographics was not the only historical force pushing change.

Technology redefined the movie show during the 1970s. In theaters this came through new sound systems that were far superior to any available at home; but it was technical change in the home—from new forms of television—that revolutionized movie presentation, particularly as cable TV provided seemingly endless screenings of both new and old Hollywood favorites.

FUNDAMENTAL AUDIENCE CHANGES

To understand the basic causes transforming movie exhibition and presentation, we must began with the emergence of the new audience demographics. The baby boomers, folks born after 1945, came of age during the 1970s and generated more loyal movie fans than in any time in history. Living in the growing and expanding suburbs surrounding American cities, their interest caused more and newer venues of exhibition to appear. Their attendance kept theatrical exhibition alive and well despite many pundits' predictions that TV would kill going out to the movies. Baby boomers were altering all forms of American life, and none more so than moviegoing.[3]

The settling of the suburbs was one of the great postwar historical phenomena. Nearly all the new population growth in the United States after the war took place in the suburban rings around America's cities. American suburbs grew fifteen times faster than any other segment of the country. And once the movement to the suburbs began, more than one million acres of farmland were plowed under each year. In order to keep the move within the family budget, to purchase the biggest possible house, on the biggest possible lot, American families sought places where land prices were low and relatively spacious homes were affordable. Supported by Veterans Administration and Farmers Home Administration mortgages, home ownership in the United States increased by nearly 50 percent from 1945 to 1950, and went up another 50 percent in the decade after that. By 1960, for the first time in the history of the United States, more Americans owned houses than rented.[4]

After the Second World War, Americans accelerated a trek that they had begun at the turn of the century—the movement toward single family dwellings in the suburbs of America's cities. To appreciate the scope of this internal migration, compare it to the more famous transatlantic movement from Europe to the United States around the turn of the century. In 1907, when European emigration was at its peak, more than one million Europeans landed in the United States, precisely the magnitude of the suburban migration of the late 1940s and early 1950s. Coupled with this massive move to the suburbs was an equally historical increase in family size—the baby boom. The two-child family common since the turn of the century was joined in great numbers by families of three children or more. Somewhat cynically, economists fit children into their models as durable goods "consumed" by the parents. (Durable, versus nondurable, goods provide a stream of long-term, versus short-term, benefits. A child generates costs in terms of doctor's care, clothes, food, education, and so on. The benefits are traditionally explained in terms of increased labor value from children as workers around the house or in a family business, and in terms of increased psychic benefits to the parents, what some might call the "make-us-proud-of-you" effect.)

The baby boom of the 1940s and 1950s would constitute the core of the movie audience of the 1970s. The baby boom in the United States proved remarkable because it included all segments of the society. Bachelors and spinsters, childless couples, and couples with only one child all but vanished, and the odds of a mother with four children

having a fifth or sixth also actually declined. What developed was an unprecedented concentration of families with two or three children. That is, like other consumer durable
goods families went out and acquired children as fast as they could, though not in numbers larger than they could afford. With the pent-up demand, which had been put off
during the Great Depression and the Second World War, nearly everyone of family-
creating age acquired children.

Another stunningly reversed historical trend lay in the characteristics of the families
who were having more children. Demographers have tended to conclude that modernization leads to fewer children. The baby boom should have seen the lowest participation among the urban, educated, and rich, so it was unexpected when these groups
actually led the population explosion. Families with high school- and college-educated
parents, upper middle class in terms of income, had larger and larger families. Lawyers,
doctors, and executives contributed more proportionally to the baby boom than did the
factory workers and farmers usually thought to produce the biggest families. Likewise,
and equally unexpected, families in urban and suburban areas contributed more children than did rural Americans.[5]

EXHIBITORS REACT

The executives of the film industry were not oblivious to the economic consequences of
the vast social and demographic factors reconfiguring their potential audiences. Yet the
chief operating officers of the major Hollywood studios could not react because, according to the *United States v. Paramount Pictures et al.*, the antitrust case that had been
decided by the United States Supreme Court in May 1948, they had been given five
years (1945–1953) to divest themselves of the movie theater side of the film business.
After the Paramount case the movie industry—until the middle 1980s—divided into two
parts: Hollywood firms controlled production and distribution of films, while different
companies, for the first time since the days of the nickelodeon, dominated the exhibition marketplace.[6]

The five successor corporations that acquired the theater chains of the five major
Paramount defendants—Loew's, Inc.; Paramount; RKO; 20th Century–Fox; and
Warner Bros.—dealt with the changing face of the moviegoing audience as best they
could. They could acquire theaters, but only after having convinced a United States
District Court that such acquisitions would not unduly restrain trade. Each petition
required a formal hearing, often facing stiff opposition by attorneys representing the
Department of Justice. Significantly, time and again the closing of a downtown movie
palace and the purchase of one in the suburbs was *not* considered equivalent. It was not
until 1974 that the supervising judge in the United States District Court of New York
agreed to let one of the surviving former Big Five theater chains go into the suburbs of
a city where they had formerly held sway.

Indeed, by 1979 only Loew's, Inc. was still operated by its original successor corporation. In 1959, once Loew's had fully complied with the Court's decrees, the new corporation, which was no longer affiliated with MGM at all, operated fewer than one hundred
theaters. By 1978, Loew's had sold most of its original picture palaces and had transformed
itself into a small chain of multiplexes—sixty theaters with 125 screens. The Loew's corporation's principal business had become hotels, insurance, and cigarette manufacturing.[7]

In 1953, the former Paramount theaters were purchased by American Broadcasting
Companies, Inc., ABC television and radio. In 1948, the year of the Paramount consent

decrees, Paramount itself had been the largest of the Hollywood-owned circuits with nearly 1,500 theaters. But by 1957, after the specific divestitures ordered by the Court, ABC's Paramount division had just over 500. Thirteen years later the circuit numbered slightly more than 400, though the Paramount chain still generated millions of dollars in revenues and should be credited with providing the monies that kept ABC television going during the hard times of the 1950s and 1960s.[8] By the 1970s ABC was going great guns as a television network, and sold its theaters to one of its former employees, Henry Plitt, in two stages. In 1974, the northern division of 123 theaters was sold to Plitt for $25 million. Four years later ABC exited the theater business entirely, selling the remainder of the theaters (its southern division) to Plitt for approximately $50 million. By then theater revenues of more than $8 million per year constituted only one-twentieth of ABC's total business.[9]

The successor to 20th Century–Fox's theaters, the National General Corporation, controlled nearly 550 theaters at the time of the Fox divorcement and divestiture in 1951. Six years later, by court direction, the number had nearly been halved. The company struggled along, trying to deal with the new world of film exhibition, but grew little. Thus it surprised no one that in 1973 National General, still controlling some 240 theaters, was sold to a former employee, Ted Mann, who concentrated his activities in the Los Angeles area. Ironically, in 1985 Mann sold his chain to Paramount, and two years later Paramount merged them into the Cineamerica chain it owned and operated with Warner Communication. Thus the former Fox theaters became the core of a nationwide chain that is now controlled by Paramount and Warner Bros., which had long been two of Fox's chief rivals. And ownership of exhibition venues has once again returned to major Hollywood moviemaking powers.

The fates of the final two of the successor companies—RKO and Warner Bros.— would also become intertwined. RKO Theatres had only 124 theaters at the time of its divorcement in 1948. The chain was sold twice, and when the Glen Alden Corporation surfaced as owner in 1967 only thirty-two theaters were left. Meanwhile, the former Warner Bros. theaters had become the core of the Stanley Warner Theatre chain, beginning with more than 400 theaters at the time of the 1951 consent decree. But under court directives that forced sales, the number of theaters that Stanley Warner controlled fell to 300 by 1957, about 200 by 1960, and approximately 150 by 1967. In 1967, the Glen Alden Corporation merged what remained of the two chains into RKO-Stanley Warner, but the chain did not thrive, and yet another company, Cinerama, purchased it in the 1970s.[10]

The break-up of the Big Five movie theater circuits provided the openings in the theater business that keyed the changes of the 1970s, with new entrepreneurs responding to suburbanization and the baby boom. The first response involved the construction of more "auto-theaters" at the edges of all U.S. cities. Though drive-in theaters had, in fact, been around in small numbers since the mid-1930s, when the necessary building materials became available after the Second World War thousands of drive-ins opened in paved-over farm fields. The development of the drive-in was a peculiarly American phenomenon generated by the huge demand for auto-convenient movie exhibition by the millions of new suburbanites from coast to coast.[11] Sitting in parked cars, movie fans watched double and triple features on massive outdoor screens.

By 1952 the average attendance at drive-ins had grown to nearly four million patrons per week. One estimate had the public spending more at drive-ins that had not existed a mere decade before, than at live theater, opera, and professional and college football combined. By the early 1960s, drive-ins accounted for one out of every five movie viewers. For the first time, during one week in June of 1956, more people attended drive-ins than went to traditional "hard-top" theaters, thus sealing a pact initiated by early screenings in amusement parks and by traveling exhibitors, and stimulated by the air-conditioned movie palaces of the 1920s. Moviegoing attendance peaked when the weather was at its most pleasant, during the summer, a trend that has continued to the present day.

But the drive-in, even with CinemaScope or Panavision, did not provide a permanent solution to serving suburban America; or even, in the long run, a viable alternative to the basic comfort of the suburban television room. If the movie palace had been the grand-est of arenas in which to enjoy watching films, the family car was not. What fantasies it held, both for teens desperate to get a little unsupervised privacy, and for mom, dad, and the kids getting out of the house for a cheap night of fun, had little to do with the movie viewing experience. The lone attraction of the drive-in seemed to be that it was so inexpensive—two dollars a car for whomever could squeeze in. Pacific Theatres' slogan for its southern California customers became: "Come as you are in the family car." But price, convenience, and informality could not clear a foggy windshield or improve the sounds from the tinny loudspeaker hooked to the car window, which frequently fell off as someone climbed out to run to the restroom or buy more popcorn.

By the 1970s the drive-in had passed its heyday. The land that in the early 1950s had lain at the edge of town was becoming too valuable. Suburbanization had continued unabated and the acres required for a drive-in could be more profitably employed as space for a score of new homes. Furthermore, even drive-ins offering inexpensive triple features like NASHVILLE GIRL, BLAZING STEWARDESSES, and DIRTY MARY, CRAZY LARRY failed to make money, and as the receipts ebbed exhibitors sought longer term and more permanent responses to the suburbanization of America, and to the television in every household. Ironically, the sites they chose lay near the very drive-in theaters they were abandoning.

The 1970s suburban theater emerged from a radical transformation in American retailing. As the modern shopping center of the 1960s became its enclosed successor, the shopping mall, during the 1970s, the motion picture industry followed, and there-after came the familiar multiplex theaters and the mall cinemas ubiquitous in the latter quarter of the twentieth century. By 1980, to most Americans going to the movies meant going to the mall. To the exhibition industry the movement to the mall completed the transition from the downtown-oriented, run-zone-clearance system that had divided the nation into 30 zones whose theaters were classified (and admissions accordingly scaled) as first-run, second-run, or subsequent-run, with "clearance" periods mandated between each run in order to squeeze the maximum profit out of every release.

When the first movie houses were opened and before the 1960s, downtown had dom-inated the retailing scene in the United States. Outlying centers grew at the intersec-tions of transportation lines, and were accessed by public transportation and surrounded by apartment buildings, but postwar suburbia was based on the automobile and the single-family dwelling. There were very few shopping centers built in the 1920s or 1930s: Upper Darby in Philadelphia (1927), Highland Park in Dallas (1931), and River Oaks in Houston (1937) offer rare examples. The most famous shopping center of all was J. C. Nichols' Country Club Plaza, located in suburban Kansas City, Missouri, and opened in 1925. This is usually taken as the archetype for the modern, pre-planned shopping center since Country Club Plaza was auto-oriented, had extensive homoge-neous landscaping, and offered acres of free parking. But the Great Depression and

World War II called a halt to cloning, and as of 1945 there were only eight shopping centers in the United States.

However, the suburbanization of the late 1940s gave rise to increasing numbers of the shopping center as we know it today. The number of shopping centers grew from a few hundred in 1950 to near 3,000 in 1958 to more than 7,000 in 1963, with further extraordinary growth taking place in the late 1960s and 1970s. By 1980 the United States had 22,000 shopping centers. Even in major centers like New York City, Chicago, and San Francisco, the bulk of retail trade had moved to the edge of the city. And new regional centers emerged at the intersection of the major new highways built with funds from the 1956 Federal Highway Act. All shopping centers had acres of parking; increasingly they were enclosed from the elements; and their special services included soothing piped-in music, nurseries, band concerts, fashion shows, and, of course, movie theaters.[12]

The concept of the enclosed, climate-controlled shopping center or mall was first introduced at Minneapolis's Southland Shopping Center in 1956. Malls required large tracts of land and multi-million dollar financing, so it took time and planning before many more were built. The mall-building movement truly commenced in the late 1960s, and soon the Paramus Mall in Northern New Jersey; Tyson's Corner Shopping Center outside Washington, D.C.; Northridge near Milwaukee; Sun Valley in Concord, California; and Woodfield Mall in Shaumburg, Illinois, near Chicago's O'Hare airport provided the shopping hubs for their respective communities. Eventually, "superregional" malls were developed to draw shoppers from several states, not simply the nearby metropolitan areas. These malls contained hundreds of stores, at least four department store hubs, restaurants, hotels, ice skating rinks, and, of course, multiple movie "screens."[13]

The idea of an enclosed place in which to shop and play became one of the defining icons of the 1970s. Whether it be the theme-park Olde Mistick Village in Mystic, Connecticut (a whole shopping center representing a New England village); plain-vanilla Towne East in Wichita, Kansas; or the self-proclaimed world's largest mall in Edmonton, Alberta, Canada, the mall is defined by its similarity, not its differences. Everywhere a Sears, J.C. Penney, or Gimbels stood alongside a Dalton or Walden Bookstore and a Limited clothing store. Malls are among the most meticulously planned structures of the late twentieth century, brightly lit to promote a safe image, enclosed to keep out the elements, convenient to the highway to make a car trip seemingly effortless. Here was one-stop shopping superior to what any aging downtown could offer. Thus, by the late 1970s Americans were reported to be spending more time in shopping malls than anywhere outside their jobs or homes.[14]

The look of the shopping center was a knock-off of the international style: function dictated everything; stylistic considerations were set aside. For the movie theater this meant stripping all the art deco decoration that had made theaters of the 1930s and 1940s so attractive. Little of the earlier architecture survived. Though there was a necessary marquee to announce the films, the lobby became simply a place to wait, with a multipurpose concession stand, and a men's and women's room. The auditorium was a minimalist box with a screen at one end and seats in front, and it was as if one had come into a picture palace stripped of all possible decoration. Gone were the lobby cards, posters, and stills of an earlier generation.

The *Paramount* case had opened up the exhibition market for new shopping mall theaters; and the shopping center offered the locus for new power and profits. From these initial openings came the new theater chains, those that dominate the final decade of the twentieth century. Consider the case of General Cinema, a company that grew to become one of the largest national chains of the 1970s. When Philip Smith, the founder of General Cinema, built his first drive-in outside Detroit in 1935, the downtown movie palace was still king. Indeed, in Detroit his competition was the most powerful of the theater chains, the Paramount Publix circuit. A drive-in was the only way he could enter the market because Paramount did not absolutely control that market niche. But after the end of the Second World War Paramount signed a consent decree in 1949, and suddenly Detroit was an open market for the movies. Smith, the pioneer drive-in exhibitor, had a step on the competition, and prospered by building drive-in after drive-in. By 1949 the chain had more than twenty sites. Smith and his associates booked first-run films, admitting children free as long as their parents paid full fare. Smith sought to attract the suburban family by emphasizing vast concession stands enclosed within self-service cafeteria-style cinder block buildings, which often also included the projection booth and the manager's office. General Cinema likes to take credit for the introduction of the folding tray for cars, the extra-large sized (and more profitable) drinking cups, the barbecue hamburger, the pizza pie craze, and the wooden stirrer for coffee. Whether they were first or not does not matter. General Cinema concentrated on the concessions and the enormous profitability of this area of the business.[15]

Philip Smith died in 1961, just as the drive-in industry was reaching its zenith. His son, Richard Smith, a thirty-six-year-old Harvard-educated assistant to the president, went one step farther than his father and moved General Cinema into the new suburban shopping centers that were being built across the United States. By the late 1960s, General Cinema, as the company was then named, owned nearly one hundred shopping-center theaters, the largest such collection in the United States at the time. In 1967, General Cinema, with shopping-center theaters providing more than half its revenues, earned more than $2 million in profits on more than $40 million in revenues. And little of General Cinema's growth was due to the purchase of existing downtown theaters. In 1967 it had some 150 theaters in twenty-six states. By 1970 the number of theaters topped 200, with more than 250 screens. By mid-decade the numbers had doubled, with the number of General Cinema drive-ins declining from thirty-eight in 1966 to ten in 1978.[16]

As its profits rose, General Cinema diversified in 1968 into the allied soft-drink business—the company had recognized the importance of this aspect of the business as it developed its concession stands, first in the drive-ins and then in the suburban shopping center theaters. General Cinema first bought a Pepsi-Cola bottler with four plants in Florida and Ohio. Smith stated at the time that the young people of the country were the best movie customers as well as the best soft-drink customers. Moreover, he noted that the two businesses operated in similar fashion; both were decentralized. By the 1980s General Cinema would be one of the largest soft drink bottlers in the United States, far better known for this segment of its operation than its theaters.[17]

By the 1960s many exhibitors besides Richard Smith had come to realize that the shopping center cinema was beginning to define moviegoing. During the 1960s, with pre-planned malls opening in record numbers around the United States, innovative theater chains worked with shopping center developers to jam half a dozen multiplexes of prefab, indistinguishable design into malls across the nation. With acres of free parking, and easy access by super-highway, the movies in the shopping center grew to accommodate the majority of the nation's indoor screens, and became the locus of Hollywood's attentions. No company symbolizes the growth of the multiplex more than the Kansas

City-based American Multi-Cinema. As the shopping center world expanded to take over retailing in the United States, American Multi-Cinema made it a goal to offer each one a half dozen average indoor screens with a few hundred seats and one concession counter; staffed by two high-school students, one projectionist, and one manager who doubled as a ticket taker. Like the fast food operations across the nation, labor in the movie theater was reduced to low-cost, untrained servers and button pushers. With costs so low, it only required a few "boffo" box-office films a year to guarantee a profitable venture.[18]

Although the multi-cinema concept was not invented by American Multi-Cinema, that company took the concept to its logical extension, opening hundreds of similar operations from coast to coast. In July 1963, the predecessor company to American Multi-Cinema had opened the Parkway Twin, reputedly the nation's first twin-screen theater in a shopping center. Significantly, the Parkway—which was the first theater constructed in the Kansas City area since the late 1930s—presented first-run films. Parkway One had four hundred seats; Parkway Two had three hundred seats, but they had a common ticket booth and a single concession stand. The Parkway cost around $400,000 to build, and was watched closely from the beginning by the movie trade as a test case. It succeeded beyond all expectations.[19] The Metro Plaza complex, which American Multi-Cinema opened in December 1966 in Kansas City, was acclaimed as the world's first planned four-plex. The "first" six-plex came in January 1969 in Omaha, Nebraska. The "first" eight-plex came in 1974 in the Omni International Complex in Atlanta, with a total of 1,175 seats, in sum nearly the size of the downtown picture palace—the Omni International Complex contained auditoria ranging from 100 to 200 seats; with a shared concession stand, a single box-office, and common rest rooms.[20] While it is not clear that these actually were the first multiplexes of their size in the United States, they were certainly among the first.

American Multi-Cinema had emerged from Durwood Enterprises, which had been in business since 1920 (and as late as 1959 had but a dozen theaters, including a handful of drive-ins) and had found a way to prosper in the movie theater business. When company patriarch Edward Durwood died in 1960, his son, Stanley, expanded the company. In 1969 it was renamed American Multi-Cinema, a name more descriptive of its operation. As shopping centers were being built, this company in the heart of the United States took advantage of the opening. It was not a franchise system; rather it owned and operated all its screens.[21] Throughout the 1960s Stanley Durwood worked with architect Stanley Staas to design and build the Empire-4, the Midland-3, and the Brywood-6, in the Kansas City area. American Multi-Cinema duplicated this experience throughout the nation and by 1972 it owned more than 160 screens in nearly thirty cities in some thirteen states. As Stanley Durwood noted: "Four theaters [later six or more] enable us to provide a variety of entertainment in one location. We can present films for children, general audience, and adults, all at the same time." American Multi-Cinema would extend the concept so that new complexes in the late 1970s handled a dozen or more screens.[22]

A NEW THEATRICAL WORLD

The corporate triumphs of General Cinema and American Multi-Cinema led them and two other companies to develop national chains of hundreds of theaters each. These were the successors to the chains of the Big Five. The difference lay not only in the size of the auditoria (about 200 seats), and the number in any location (multiplexes of up to twenty screens), but also the fact that these chains did not concentrate in single regions of the country, but were spread the length and breadth of the United States. By the early 1980s, according to *Variety*, four chains dominated the United States.[23]

First in line was General Cinema, with 1,000 screens in some 350 locations in nearly all forty-eight continental states. Few of the original drive-ins were left by 1980; this was a multiplex operation pure and simple.

Second place was occupied by United Artists Communications, with slightly less than 1,000 screens in nearly 350 locations, with one in twenty being drive-ins. United Artists Theatre Circuit, Inc. grew to become one of the largest theater circuits in the nation, ironically more powerful than the more famous Hollywood producer of the similar name. It was a leader though the 1960s and 1970s in building multi-screen theater complexes in suburban shopping centers. United Artists had begun as an adjunct of Joseph M. Schenck's interest when he was the head of the United Artists' moviemaking company in the late 1920s and into the early 1930s. Although the two companies operated closely when Schenck was on top, he owned the theater chain outright and kept it separate from the moviemaking company. Thus when Schenck parted with United Artists to form 20th Century–Fox, he and his partners retained their hold on the theater chain; and United Artists Theatres represented the top movie palaces in such cities as Detroit, Chicago, and Los Angeles—and in partnership with others (including Sid Grauman) in Pittsburgh, Baltimore, Louisville, New York City, and Los Angeles with the famous Grauman's Chinese and Egyptian.

Third in size was American Multi-Cinema, with over 700 screens in 130 locations across the United States. None were drive-ins. And fourth place was held by Plitt Theatres, then based in Los Angeles, having moved from the former headquarters in Chicago, with 600 screens in nearly 300 locations. Again, none were drive-ins.

No other chain had more than 350 screens. The smaller circuits, with a couple of hundred theater screens, included the midwestern-based Commonwealth chain, the southern-based Martin Theatres, the Boston-based National Amusements, the Southern Cobb circuit, Kerasotes of Illinois, and Pacific of Southern California.

New Style of Moviegoing

What movie patrons received for their entertainment dollar with movies in the mall, save locational centrality, proved as far from the golden days of the movie palace as one could imagine. The clusters of unadorned screening rooms offered only feature films and concession stands. Space was at a premium, and screens were often sandwiched in the basement of a mall. It was as if, having realized they had lost the battle with television and the living room, the movie theaters gave up almost all pretense of the struggle at the level of architectural fantasy and the viewing experience, and actually produced interiors with *less* to offer than at home. Taking their cues from the dominant, Bauhaus-inspired trend in architecture, the new movie chains seemed to push the slogan of the international style to new lows of literalness: only function should dictate building form. The function in the age of television was clear: show blockbuster feature films and nothing else. Gone was the architectural ambience of the movie palace; any decoration on the side walls or around the screen seemed irrelevant. The movies became self-service: ushers were rarely sighted. The idea of live entertainment plus movies was something that grandmother and grandfather talked about. Only air conditioning continued to add a measure of pleasure. The mall theaters offered minimalist moviegoing.

Viewing conditions had reached an all-time low. To shoe-horn as many auditoria (rarely with more than 250 seats each) into a corner of a shopping center, projection booths rarely lined up with the screen. That is, one booth served two or more spaces, so the image invariably came out with one half of the movie larger than the other (a phenomenon called "keystoning"). To further skimp on costs, theater owners inadequately padded walls between auditoria. Thus, for example, as one tried to catch a quiet moment of ANNIE HALL (Woody Allen, 1977), more often than not the rousing battle sounds of STAR WARS (George Lucas, 1977) poured through the wall, drowning out dialogue and distracting attention.

Ironically, part of the sound problems resulted from one of the few improvements in the viewing experience. Dolby sound systems managed to outdo the television set by eliminating all extraneous noises and placing six-foot speakers in every corner of the auditorium, and behind the screen. The sound in 200-seat auditoria became so good that it could only have been properly accommodated in the 3,000-seat movie palaces of the 1920s.[24] Such systems, for a generation trained on home stereo and the portable cassette players, made sound at the movies far superior to all but the best home stereo systems. Four-inch television speakers were simply no match. Now, finally, the images of Panavision were coupled with new, clear sound, ratcheted to levels that offered the audiences of the 1980s a new, totally enveloping technological experience.

Unfortunately all this sound seemed largely to encourage television-trained viewers to talk during the screening. Television had trained movie fans at home to accept constant conversation as part of the standard viewing experience. By the 1980s, talking and constant commotion had become the norm at the movies in the mall.

Other interior amenities, once taken for granted by film fans, disappeared in the age of the multiplex. Waiting in the lobby of a movie palace that was designed to hold as many folks as could sit in the auditorium was a wonder-filled experience. In the multiplex, lines often spilled out into the mall, tangling with shoppers. What space there was in the lobby per se was invariably taken up by the popcorn stand, which in some cases also hawked T-shirts and posters, while attendants made change for the video games tucked into any corner adaptable as a "profit center." In many ways going to the movies had been reduced to the equivalent of standing in line at the K-Mart to buy a tire or pick out lawn furniture. The physical viewing conditions of the multiplex, save its advantage of superior sound, seemed a throwback to the nickelodeon era. Indeed, rarely was a live projectionist back there in the booth to deal with a film that tore apart. The social experience of vast crowds in a thousand-seat auditorium had been fragmented into screening rooms typically holding no more than 200 noisy patrons.

The suburbs and television had changed the nature of film in a number of ways, none more important than this fragmentation of viewing conditions. Indeed, drawing folks away from their television sets and living rooms required a diverse set of attractions, all designed to create *the* blockbuster. That is, so much money could be made on a single film, such as a STAR WARS (1977) or E. T.: THE EXTRA-TERRESTRIAL (Steven Spielberg, 1982), that fashioning blockbusters became the single purpose of the contemporary film industry. But no one could predict which film would become a blockbuster and which not. So theater owners tended to construct one large auditorium (with about 500 seats) surrounded by a half dozen auditoria with 100 seats each. Films were tested in the smaller auditoria and only the true blockbusters moved into the more spacious venue.

The multiplex put an end to folks over thirty-five regularly going out to the movies. By the late 1970s there were too many sticky floors, too many noisy patrons, too many films that seemed alike. Yet there was a reaction. Despite all sorts of predictions of the demise of the cinema experience, during the 1980s theaters would get better. They would also grow in number, making more screens available than had existed in the United States during the peak period of the late 1940s. As a new theater circuit that was not simply taking advantage of openings provided by suburbanization, or the *Paramount* case, Cineplex Odeon was set to offer a better moviegoing experience.

The changes began with sound. In the 1970s, into a nearly completely optical sound-track world of theatrical exhibition, came Sensurround. For EARTHQUAKE (Mark Robson, 1974) Universal added an eight-minute sequence in which Los Angeles is destroyed, with imagery that was enhanced by adding low-frequency sound waves to the sound track during the dubbing process to produce a rumbling effect. Theater owners were offered (for five hundred dollars per week) special speakers and an amplifier to produce the effect in their theaters. Sixty units were built, and the gimmick helped the film become one of the top box-office attractions of that year. The Sensurround system won a special Academy Award and was employed again for such films as MIDWAY (Jack Smight, 1976), ROLLERCOASTER (James Goldstone, 1977), and BATTLESTAR: GALACTICA (Richard A. Colla, 1979).

In 1977, Universal president Sidney J. Sheinberg declared: "Sensurround is as big a star as there is in the movie business today." He was wrong. The problem was that Sensurround worked best in a stand-alone theater. In multiplex situations the rumble poured through the walls into the other auditoria. Moreover the latter three films were not major box-office attractions. Thus the added expense and trouble seemed wasted, and the system was abandoned—although as of 1989 Universal still held the patents.[25] Despite Sensurround's failure, however, the industry had recognized that sound was one way theater owners could compete with television, since most TV sets at that time had only tinny, four-inch speakers. Eventually, the quest for new sound quality coalesced around Dolby sound, a high-fidelity stereo sound that provided clear, lifelike reproduction of the entire musical range, and accurate reproduction of the volume range.

Dolby, which was first introduced in 1975, is a process that uses 35mm release prints containing stereo optical tracks in which the sound is recorded as variable patterns of light and shade on the film strip itself. The optical system was maintained because Dolby prints cost no more to produce, they last the needed time under the wear and tear of constant use, and the theater equipment requires little in the way of special upkeep. Dolby noise reduction is a means of electronically reducing the background noise inherent in all recording media while not disturbing the sounds one is intended to hear, and it is at the heart of the Dolby stereo process because it paved the way for improvements in the full range of sound.[26]

Dolby Laboratories was founded in 1965 by physicist Ray M. Dolby to develop noise reduction techniques for the music industry. Through the late 1960s, Dolby's innovations made their way into improved home tape recorders, cassette decks, and FM receivers. Indeed Dolby helped bring about high-fidelity cassettes that had been hampered by problems inherent in slow recording speeds. In the 1970s, Dolby turned to the film industry. Although Stanley Kubrick did all the pre-mixes and masters for A CLOCKWORK ORANGE (1971) with Dolby noise reduction, the film was released with conventional optical mono sound. With CALLAN (Don Sharpe, 1974) came the first Dolby encoded mono sound track for general release. The first true Dolby stereo came with the release of the rock opera TOMMY (Ken Russell) in 1975. The sound track in that multi-sensuous experience impressed the young audience, but Ken Russell was hardly

Sound engineers at the Dolby Laboratories mixing the four-channel stereo sound track for APOCALYPSE NOW *(1979); 35mm Technovision anamorphic prints were released with four-channel stereo optical tracks; 70mm blow-ups had a six-track magnetic stereo.*

the household name to impress moguls in Hollywood. Indeed, in the first years, the films with Dolby seemed relegated to musicals: Ken Russell's LISZTOMANIA (1975), Robert Altman's NASHVILLE (1976), John Badham's SATURDAY NIGHT FEVER (1977). But it was with George Lucas's megahit, STAR WARS (1977) and Steven Spielberg's CLOSE ENCOUNTERS OF THE THIRD KIND (1977) that filmmakers took full advantage of the new recording techniques, and those films scored at the box office in part because of the improved sound. In a survey reported in July, 1977, the month after STAR WARS opened, 90 percent of those surveyed claimed that Dolby sound made a difference. By 1979 there were 1,200 Dolby-equipped theaters in the United States.[27]

The cost to convert a theater in the late 1970s, depending on how sophisticated the owner wanted the house to be, was under ten thousand dollars. By late in 1984, Dolby could claim some 6,000 installations in forty-five countries around the world, with the bulk in the United States. About one quarter of theaters in the United States in the mid-1980s had this special advantage, principally all first-run, suburban theaters, most often in the center and biggest auditorium of a six-plex or eight-plex. In the mid-1980s nearly 90 percent of all Hollywood films were being released in Dolby, with the common four channels of left front, center, right front, and surround.[28]

TV AS THE SUBSEQUENT-RUN CINEMA

The 1970s were also the age when Hollywood feature films regularly ended their exhibition life on television, and so Americans saw more and more movies on TV. No film established this more as a basic principle than THE WIZARD OF OZ (Victor Fleming,

1939) which had become a viewing staple by the 1970s. A 1950s deal between MGM and CBS made this tale of Kansas and Oz an classic. After NBC premiered *Saturday Night at the Movies* in September 1961 with HOW TO MARRY A MILLIONAIRE (Jean Negulesco, 1953), the neighborhood movie house was essentially dead, and the subsequent viewing of Hollywood feature films would be ever after on some form of television. By the mid-1950s it had become clear that Hollywood would not directly own and operate television stations (or networks), but would, rather, supply programing. With the coming of *The Late Show* in the mid-1950s and *Saturday Night at the Movies,* feature film showings became one of television's dominant programming forms.

Actually the movie show on television began in a minor way. In the late 1940s British film companies that had never been able to significantly break into the American theatrical market (in particular the Ealing, Rank, and Korda studios) willingly rented films to television. Monogram and Republic, long able to take only what the major Hollywood corporate powers left them, also jumped on board the television bandwagon with a vengeance. This multitude of small producers, all eager for the extra money, delivered some 4,000 titles to television before the end of 1950. Typical fare included B-class Westerns (Gene Autry and Roy Rogers from Republic, e.g.), and thrill-a-minute serials (Flash Gordon, also from Republic). But the repeated showings of this fare only served to remind longtime movie fans of the extraordinary number of treasures still resting comfortably in the vaults of MGM, Paramount, 20th Century–Fox, and Warner Bros.

To understand how and why the dominant Hollywood studios finally agreed to rent (or sell) their vast libraries of film titles to television, one must go back to May 1948, when eccentric millionaire Howard Hughes purchased control of the ailing RKO. In five years Hughes ran RKO into the ground. Debts soared past $20 million, and few new productions were approved to generate needed new revenues. By late 1953, it was clear that Hughes had to do something, and few industry observers were surprised in 1954 when he agreed to sell RKO to the General Tire and Rubber Company for $25 million. General Tire wanted the RKO back titles to present on its independent New York television station, WOR (today WWOR), along with other films it had acquired. In 1955, WOR regularly programmed a *Million Dollar Movie,* rerunning the same title throughout the week. Any number of later movie makers cited *Million Dollar Movie*'s repetitive screenings as inspiration for commencing their moviemaking career. George Romero, famous for making NIGHT OF THE LIVING DEAD (1968), for example, told an interviewer that seeing a screening of THE TALES OF HOFFMAN (Michael Powell, 1951) on *Million Dollar Movie* made him take up a career in film.

Profit figures from movie rentals to television impressed even the most recalcitrant Hollywood movie mogul. Within the space of the following twenty-four months all the remaining major companies released their pre-1948 titles to television. (Pre-1948 titles were free from the requirement of paying residuals to performer and craft unions; post-1948 titles were not.) For the first time in the sixty-year history of film a national audience was able to watch, at their leisure, a broad cross section of the best and worst of Hollywood talkies. (Silent films were only occasionally presented, usually in the form of compilations of the comedies of Charlie Chaplin and Buster Keaton.)

From the sale or lease to television of these libraries of films, Hollywood was able to tap a significant source of pure profit. This infusion of cash came precisely at a time when Hollywood needed money to support the innovation of widescreen spectacles, and television deals followed one after the other. Columbia Pictures, which had early on entered television production, quickly aped RKO's financial bonanza. In January 1956

Columbia announced that Screen Gems would rent packages of feature films to television stations. One hundred and four films constituted the initial package, from which Columbia realized an instant profit of $5 million.

From the middle 1950s on, the pre-1948 largely black-and-white films functioned as the mainstay of innumerable "Early Shows," "Late Shows," and "Late, Late Shows." Regular screenings of re-issues were rare in theaters in the early 1950s, and a decade later found more than one hundred different films aired each week on New York City television stations, with smaller numbers in less populous cities. In particular, the owned and operated stations of CBS invested in choice titles (including many from MGM). Each film was rotated, rested for three to six months, and then repeated again. Before 1961, the three television networks only booked feature films as occasional specials, as was the case for the CBS' ratings hit THE WIZARD OF OZ, not as regular programming.

But with color television a coming reality, the three television networks wanted to show *post*-1948 Hollywood features, principally those in color, in lucrative, attractive prime-time slots. This required agreements from the Hollywood craft unions, including the American Federation of Musicians, the Screen Actors Guild, the Screen Directors Guild, and the Writers Guild of America. In a precedent-setting action, the Screen Actors Guild, led by its then president, Ronald Reagan, went on strike and won guaranteed residuals for televised airings of post-1948 films. This set the stage for movie showings to become staples of prime-time television.[29]

The NBC network premiered the first prime-time series of recent films with *Saturday Night at the Movies,* in September 1961, showing HOW TO MARRY A MILLIONAIRE (1953), starring Marilyn Monroe, Betty Grable, and Lauren Bacall. Ratings were high and of the thirty-one titles shown during this initial season, fifteen were in color, and all were big-budget, post-1948 releases from 20th Century–Fox. All had their television "premiere" on *Saturday Night at the Movies.* NBC especially liked the color titles. RCA, pioneer in television color, owned NBC and used the network to spur sales of color television sets. CBS and ABC, seeing how their shows (CBS's *Have Gun, Will Travel* and *Gunsmoke,* and ABC's *Lawrence Welk*) fared against *Saturday Night at the Movies,* quickly moved to negotiate their own "Nights at the Movies." ABC, generally a distant third in the ratings during the 1960s, moved first, with a mid-season replacement, *Sunday Night at the Movies,* commencing in April 1962. CBS, the long-time ratings leader in network television, remained aloof and did not set in place its own "Night at the Movies," until September 1965.[30]

But with CBS joining the fray at the beginning of the 1965–1966 television season, the race was on. Television screenings of recent Hollywood movies became standard practice. In 1968 nearly 40 percent of all television sets in use at the time tuned in to Alfred Hitchcock's THE BIRDS (the theatrical release date was 1963). THE BRIDGE ON THE RIVER KWAI (David Lean, 1957), which was shown in 1966, and CAT ON A HOT TIN ROOF (Richard Brooks, 1958), shown in 1967, achieved ratings nearly as high. Clearly, recent feature films could be shown on television to blockbuster ratings: when GONE WITH THE WIND (Victor Fleming, 1939) was shown in two parts in early November of 1976, half the nation's television sets were tuned in to that one particular offering. By the fall of 1968, ABC, NBC, and CBS "Nights at the Movies" covered every night of the week. By the early 1970s, overlapping permitted ten separate "movie nights" each week. Throughout this period NBC remained the most committed network, in part because it wanted to use recent Hollywood features to help stimulate demand for RCA's color television sets.[31]

The success of the movie showings on the networks significantly affected affiliated stations. The number of "Late" and "Early" shows fell by 25 percent. Independent stations not affiliated with one of the three television networks continued to rely on pre-1948 features. Indeed, films on independent channels accounted for one-quarter of their schedules. With rediscovered hits like Warner Bros.' CASABLANCA (Michael Curtiz, 1943) and RKO's KING KONG (Merian C. Cooper, 1933) spaced judiciously throughout the viewing year, regular screenings of movies on television drew large audiences, but routine B-class thrillers and wacky low-budget war musicals spent their drawing power after one or two screenings. This unprecedented wave of movie programming quickly depleted the stock of attractive features that had not played on television. On the network level, the rule was to run a post-1948 feature twice ("premiere" and "rerun"), and then release it into syndication so that it then could be used by local stations for their "Late" or "Early" shows. Network executives searched for ways to maximize the audiences for repeated showings of blockbuster films.[32] It soon became clear to all who paid close attention that there were "too many" scheduled movie showings on television, and that there was "too little" new product coming into the pipeline to fill future slots with new theatrical films. Hollywood knew this, and the studios began to charge higher and higher prices for television screenings. Million-dollar price tags became commonplace, first for films that had done well at the box office, and then for those that might have not done so well but had won some sort of an award, in particular an Academy Award. For the widely heralded September 1966 telecast of THE BRIDGE ON THE RIVER KWAI, the Ford Motor Company put up nearly $2 million as the sponsor. When the film attracted some sixty million viewers against formidable competition, Hollywood insiders speculated that $10-million price tags would appear shortly.

TV network executives found a solution: make movies aimed for a television premiere. The networks could monitor production costs and guarantee fixed future rentals in the $300,000 to $500,000 range. Moreover, the networks could use these made-for-television movies to test new shows which might then be "downsized" to appear as regular series. The networks were used to paying the complete cost of pilot programs, so it was not a huge step to fashion them into stand-alone made-for-television films. Experiments began as early as 1964 when, in October, NBC aired SEE HOW THEY RUN (David Lowell Rich, 1964), starring John Forsythe, Senta Berger, Jane Wyatt, Franchot Tone, Leslie Nielson, and George Kennedy. Labeled "Project 120," in honor of its length in minutes, the experiment proved a modest success. The next entry, THE HANGED MAN (1964) came six weeks later. The idea was to do an anthology series to help NBC overtake CBS in the ratings war.[33]

Early in 1966, NBC contracted with Universal studios to create a regular series of "World Premiere" made-for-television movies. NBC specified that all films had to be in color, again to reinforce its leadership in that area. The agreement with Universal dictated that once the TV movie was shown twice on the network, rights reverted back to Universal which could release it to theaters in the United States (a rare occurrence), then to foreign theaters (more common), and finally to American television stations for their "Early" and "Late" shows (also common).[34] The initial entry for this continuing effort was FAME IS THE NAME OF THE GAME (Stuart Rosenberg, 1966), starring minor luminaries Jill St. John and Tony Franciosa, which was presented on a Saturday night in November 1966.

Made-for-television motion pictures took only five years to become a mainstay genre of American network television programming. By early in the 1970s, movies made for television outnumbered films that had been made for theatrical release on network "Nights at the Movies." After NBC led the way, ABC, seeing a successful trend, followed close behind. CBS, again smug with years of constantly leading the ratings with traditional series, eventually joined in. Profits proved substantial. A typical movie made for television cost three-quarters of a million dollars, far less than what Hollywood was demanding for rental of its recent blockbusters. And the ratings were phenomenal. Few expected that millions upon millions would tune in for THE WALTONS' THANKSGIVING STORY (1973), The NIGHT STALKER (John Llewellyn Moxey, 1971), A CASE OF RAPE (Boris Sagal, 1974), and WOMEN IN CHAINS (Bernard Kowalski, 1972). Such fare regularly outdrew what were considered the biggest films of the era, including THE GRADUATE (Mike Nichols, 1967; 1973 premiere on network television), WEST SIDE STORY (Robert Wise, 1961; 1972 premiere on network television), and GOLDFINGER (Guy Hamilton, 1964; 1972 premiere on network television). With the help of the made-for-television movie, network executives moved their "Nights at the Movies" to a full quarter share of all prime-time programming.[35]

One film in particular signaled that the made-for-television movie had come of age. *The ABC Movie of the Week* had premiered in the fall of 1969, sponsored by Barry Diller, then head of prime-time programming at ABC, later CEO of Paramount (1974–1984) and Fox (1984–1992), where he founded the Fox network. During the 1971–1972 television season, ABC's *Movie of the Week* series, which programmed only movies made for television, finished as the fifth-highest series of the year. On November 30, 1971, ABC presented a little-publicized made-for-TV movie entitled BRIAN'S SONG (Buzz Kulik, 1971), about a football player who dies of cancer. One-third of the households in the county watched, and half the people watching television that Tuesday night selected that movie over the fare offered on CBS and NBC. In its first five years, the ABC series accounted for four of the top twenty-five made-for-television movies for the period 1965 through 1980.[36]

BRIAN'S SONG vaulted to tenth place in all-time movie screenings on television. With THE WIZARD OF OZ accounting for five of the top nine ratings up to that November night, BRIAN'S SONG joined THE BIRDS (1963), THE BRIDGE ON THE RIVER KWAI (1957), and BEN-HUR (William Wyler, 1959) in that elite grouping. It demonstrated that movies made for television could win Emmys (five), the prestigious George Foster Peabody award, and citations from the NAACP and the American Cancer Society. When then President Richard M. Nixon declared BRIAN'S SONG one of his all-time favorite films, ABC reaped an unexpected publicity bonanza.

The movie manifested nothing particularly special from other typical early ABC movies made for television. Producer Paul Junger Witt had worked with ABC before with his *Partridge Family* series; and Buzz Kulik was a seasoned director of television series fare. But BRIAN'S SONG proved that success on the small screen could even be translated to theatrical features. Billy Dee Williams, who played football star Gale Sayers, had been kicking around Hollywood for years with little success. BRIAN'S SONG projected him into major roles in LADY SINGS THE BLUES (Sidney J. Furie, 1972), and MAHOGANY (Berry Gordy, 1975). James Caan, as the other leading figure in BRIAN'S SONG, moved on to stardom in THE GODFATHER (Francis Ford Coppola, 1972).[37] BRIAN'S SONG cost less than a half million dollars to make because stock footage from National Football League games kept production expenses at a minimum and shooting lasted only two weeks. But the impact of the first run of BRIAN'S SONG nearly equaled the publicity bonanza associated with a successful feature film. Books about the film's hero became best-sellers. The TV movie's music moved onto *Billboard*'s charts. The success of BRIAN'S SONG signaled that the networks should plan to react to unexpected hits, preparing publicity campaigns to take advantage of twists and turns in public opinion, even to shape it as only theatrical films had done in the past.[38]

By the late 1970s, the made-for-television motion picture had become a staple. One study found that for the three networks during the 1979–1980 television season, there were some 430 runs of movies of which 40 percent were telecasts of theatrical fare and 60 percent were made-for-television films. The three television networks booked just about the same number of theatrical features to show (about sixty), but CBS and NBC scheduled 50 percent more made-for-television films than rival ABC.[39] Furthermore, made-for-television movies made it possible to deal with topical or controversial material not deemed appropriate for regularly scheduled network series, particularly ones that could go into syndication, and as "evergreens" should not be dated in any way. And serious and celebrated actors and actresses who did not wish to work in series television could be featured in TV movies.

Another major change in movie-type programming came in the mid-1970s with the rise of the miniseries. Running over different nights, ROOTS (David Greene, et al., 1977), which is still considered the progenitor of the form, attracted nearly two-thirds of Americans when it was shown. Indeed, it was ROOTS that in a single week in January, 1977 drew an estimated 130 million households to tune in to at least one episode during the eight consecutive nights. Eighty million watched the final episode of this docudrama, breaking the audience record held by GONE WITH THE WIND (1939). From a variety of follow-up studies it seems that black viewing was higher than that of whites. ROOTS was a controversial show that provoked discussion, even rare interracial discussion, as some studies found. Television had discovered an event of its own, one that was the equal of a blockbuster theatrical film.[40]

The origins of the miniseries went back to 1971 when NBC invested more than $2 million in VANISHED (Buzz Kulik), a four-hour made-for-television movie planned for broadcast on two nights in March 1971. The ratings breakthrough came with NBC's THE BLUE KNIGHT (Robert Butler), which was broadcast in four one-hour segments between November 13 and 16, 1973. Starring William Holden, this tale of an aging policeman earned high ratings and critical acclaim, proving that miniseries could make a difference in crucial rating sweeps months. Miniseries typically commence on the night of the highest viewing, Sunday. If the series goes more than three nights, it invariably skips certain evenings, those with the top regular shows of that network.

TELEVISION REDEFINES U.S. MOVIE WATCHING

The coming of the movies to television has meant more than simply telecasting the best and worst of (sound) motion pictures from Hollywood's past and repeated presentations of TV movies. Television has changed the way Americans consume films. For example, in the 1970s a duo of reviewers from Chicago proved that TV would thereafter be the site of a new type of reviewing—TV style. Contrasting like Laurel and Hardy, Gene Siskel and Roger Ebert pioneered short, pithy weekly critiques of the latest in cinematic fare, reaching more potential movie viewers than any of the writers who plied their trade at a newspaper or magazine.

In terms of the number of screenings, the movie fan of the latter third of the twentieth century had never had it so good. Indeed movie showings in the 1970s on television seemed an endless stream, but increased viewing hardly represented the lone transformation that television imposed on the movies. The reliance on television for the presentation of motion pictures has extracted a high price in terms of viewing conditions. The television image is proportioned four by three while the standard motion picture image is much wider. To accommodate the changed proportions, the widescreen film is cut off at the sides to fit it onto the smaller video screen. Panning and scanning re-edit the widescreen film so the "action" shifts to the center of the frame, and the changes can be profound. For example, John Boorman's POINT BLANK (1967) employs cramped compositions with characters on the screen one moment and then off the next. On television POINT BLANK becomes a jumbled, confusing mess, because the widescreen compositions are fractured to place the action at the center of the screen.

Of course, films do not need to be panned and scanned. One can reduce the image for television until all of it fits on-screen; and in practice this technique of "letterboxing" fills the empty space above and below with a black matte. In the 1980s, there has been a great deal of lip service paid to letterboxing, but movie watchers en masse do not seem to care for it. Indeed, back in the 1960s as Hollywood studios tested their film to video transfers, letterbox prints were made to check the total quality of a widescreen movie's negative or master positive *before* it was transferred to video. These were element tests and the home viewer never saw them. Instead the studio filled the television frame with the center of the film and then panned and scanned to capture "all" the action. Today technicians can hide the panning and scanning, making them look "natural" in the course of the film, but these "additions" were never part of the original viewing experience.[41]

The biggest complaint from the average television viewer of motion pictures has long been against the interruption of the movie by advertisements. To fit the formula of commercial television a station allocates 25 percent of its prime-time slots to commercials. This means that in a ninety-minute slot the movie had to be trimmed to seventy-eight minutes; for a two-hour slot the film could not run more than ninety minutes. Cutting to fit the allotted time has been commonplace since the early 1950s. Stories of how television stations accomplished this heinous task are legendary. It is said that Fred Silverman, when he was a lowly film editor at WGN in Chicago, fit the ninety-six minute JAILHOUSE ROCK (Richard Thorpe, 1957) into a seventy-eight minute afternoon movie block by cutting all of Elvis's musical numbers![42]

Since over-the-air television could not rid itself of advertisements and time slots, a market arose for uninterrupted screenings of features on television. Enter cable television. Over-the-air television served as the principal second-run showcase for Hollywood films into the 1970s, but the number of TV stations in any one market was limited. Most of the nation had but three channels, which served up only network fare. The bigger cities did have independent stations that could counter-program, often with movies, but nowhere could the movie fan see his or her favorites as they had seen them in theaters. The emergence of cable television, principally through pay channels, took advantage of the frustrations of millions of Americans who watched most of their movies on television. But it took Time, Inc.'s subsidiary, Home Box Office (HBO), to innovate a profitable strategy during the 1970s. In retrospect HBO's success is not surprising. In one survey taken twenty years ago in the days before cable television became widespread, sample respondents were asked what they most disliked about film showings on TV networks. There were only two significant answers: constant advertisement interruptions and the long wait for blockbusters to appear. HBO solved both these problems—and more.[43]

HBO began as a microwave service in 1972 but it was not until 1975, when HBO went to satellite distribution, that it sparked the interest in cable television. In one of the most productive investments in television history, even before the satellite had been launched, Time gambled $7.5 million on a five-year lease to put HBO on RCA's satellite, Satcom I. HBO commenced national satellite distribution on September 30, 1975, and from a base of three hundred thousand subscribers moved, within five years, to six million. By giving its subscribers uncut, uninterrupted movies a few months after they had disappeared from theaters, growth during the late 1970s and into the early 1980s proved nothing less than spectacular. By 1983 the company could claim twelve million subscribers. Indeed, Time, Inc. proved so successful with its cable operations (read: HBO) that the video arm of the company surpassed the publishing activities in terms of profits generated.[44]

In 1976, Viacom International, a major television program supplier and owner of cable systems, created a rival to HBO with Showtime, which went to satellite distribution in 1979. In 1979, Warner Cable joined with its then partner American Express to create The Movie Channel. In 1980, Time created Cinemax as an all-movie complement to HBO, to appeal to younger audiences, in particular Yuppies. To further differentiate its product, during the 1980s Cinemax regularly scheduled more films than the competition, an average of eighty-five per month. The Movie Channel followed with an average of seventy-eight per month; Showtime had fifty-five, and HBO only fifty. But this was understandable since HBO and Showtime had contracted more of the blockbuster, star-laden titles, which the two repeated regularly.[45]

The Hollywood studios tried to establish their own pay-cable movie channel, Premiere. The major Hollywood studios argued that as HBO prospered through the 1970s it did so from Hollywood movies. The studios claimed that they received insufficient income from the showings on HBO and Showtime because those two, and those two alone, controlled the marketplace. To gain the upper hand, in April 1980 Columbia Pictures, MCA/Universal, Paramount, and 20th Century–Fox announced a joint deal with the Getty Oil Company to create Premiere as their own pay-television movie channel. They planned to withhold their films and only after they had played on Premiere would they be released for screening on HBO.[46] In response, HBO and Showtime asserted that this constituted a violation of antitrust law and the United States Department of Justice, near the end of the administration of President Jimmy Carter, agreed and filed suit. There was screaming and shouting, but in the end the four Hollywood companies backed off and Premiere never went into business. Ironically, had they tried a few years later, the administration of Ronald Reagan probably would have given the go ahead.[47]

In the format used by HBO and Showtime, during the course of a month, movies are scheduled from four to six times on different days and at different times during the daily schedule. The idea is to give the viewer several opportunities to watch each film, but not to quickly exhaust the movies that the pay service has to offer. Thus, the success of a pay-cable movie channel has been determined not by ratings for a single program, but by the general appeal and satisfaction level for the month as a whole. This was not tested by a rating system, but by whether the customers kept on writing their monthly checks.[48]

With all the changes and programming variations in the pay-per-view marketplace, the big winners were the Hollywood studios. Precise figures varied from deal to deal, but reliable estimates suggested that the major studios in the late 1970s gained from $5 to $7 million dollars per film from a deal with HBO/Cinemax, or Showtime/The Movie Channel. For a single year, this meant each of the six major studios stood to gain on average an extra $100 million. But movie viewers gained as well. For twenty years over-the-

air television had brought the best and worst of Hollywood into the home, but with significant disadvantages: constant interruptions for advertisements, sanitization of the
movie stories to please television's moralist critics, and waits of several years for hits to
appear. Pay-cable movie channels jettisoned the advertisements, and ran the films intact
only months after they had disappeared from movie theaters. (For theatrical failures, the
"clearance time" could be a matter of weeks.)[49]

HBO and its pay-cable competition were not the only significant additions to the
second-run cinema at home. Cable TV's superstations enabled rural and small-town
cable viewers to gain access to nationally distributed independent stations with dozens
of movies shown each week. Led by Ted Turner's WTBS, channel 17 from Atlanta,
superstations offered movies for approximately one-half of their broadcast day. WTBS
became so successful that by the middle 1980s Turner purchased MGM just to gain
access to its considerable movie library, feeding the superstation's forty movie screenings
per week.

Remarkably, despite all the new venues of home movie viewing, revenues at movie
houses increased steadily throughout the 1970s. Indeed, as the decade ended
Hollywood earned a record gross from the domestic box office. The baby boomers were
not only attending blockbusters in their full theatrical glory, but were also watching
more and more films at home. Thus, in totality, movie presentation was never more
active or healthy. And from this base—led by Cineplex Odeon—a revived theatrical
experience would commence in the 1980s, and with the innovation of home video even
more film viewing would take place at home. Surely, in historical perspective, the 1970s
were a pre-staging for a renewal of movie exhibition that would make the "Golden Age"
of Hollywood pale in comparison.

11

Looking Back and Turning Inward: American Documentary Films of the Seventies

WILLIAM ROTHMAN

In the revised and expanded version of his invaluable history of nonfiction film, Richard Barsam sees the sixties as a high-water mark for the American documentary cinema. It was a decade in which the politically committed social documentary flourished even as a new and experimental form of documentary, *cinema verité* or direct cinema, emerged. Barsam sums up the seventies, by contrast, as a decade in which few filmmakers were interested "either in the identification of social abuses or in the cinematic experimentation that, a decade earlier, had created direct cinema. Thus, much of their output, mired in tradition, seemed bland."[1]

In the seventies, filmmakers like Richard Leacock, D. A. Pennebaker, Albert and David Maysles, and Frederick Wiseman adhered to the strict *cinema verité* discipline they had mastered in the sixties, which calls upon filmmakers to wait silently for their human subjects to reveal themselves and to edit out signs of people's self-consciousness in the presence of the camera. A number of younger filmmakers, such as Alan and Susan Raymond, came to master that discipline, too. Nonetheless, Barsam is correct in suggesting that there was a general tendency in the seventies for documentary filmmakers to turn away from *cinema verité* as the "old masters" had practiced it (and continued to practice it).

Concurring with this suggestion, Michael Renov characterizes the seventies as the beginning of the "post-verité" period.[2] Rather than taking documentary film's turning away from *cinema verité* as signaling a retreat to blander and more traditional forms, however, Renov sees it as liberating. He praises a number of works of the seventies, which broke with the strict *cinema verité* discipline, for anticipating the profusion of films of the eighties and nineties that affirm their subjects' subjectivity, and especially the diaries, journals, and autobiographies that affirm the filmmaker's own subjectivity.[3]

In asserting that the seventies marked the beginning of the "post-verité" age, Renov consigns *cinema verité* to the past. He assumes that *cinema verité* was not flexible or resourceful enough to accommodate the affirmations of subjectivity that began to emerge in the seventies. He assumes that such films were repudiating *cinema verité*, although it is more fruitful as well as more accurate to view them as extending *cinema verité*, as, indeed, transforming it from within. Although Renov understands *cinema verité* (as exemplified by the Drew Associates productions and the early films of Leacock, Pennebaker, and the Maysles) to be fundamentally opposed to subjectivity, in fact, those films affirmed subjectivity no less than the films he champions. (How could one possibly view Leacock's A HAPPY MOTHER'S DAY [Richard Leacock and Joyce Chopra, 1963] or Pennebaker's DON'T LOOK BACK [1967], for example, as opposed to subjectivity?) The impulse to scrutinize people "scientifically," as if they were insects under a microscope, was characteristic of ethnographic film in the sixties and seventies, not *cinema verité*. From the outset, *cinema verité* in America, like the "classical" Hollywood cinema it took itself to be rebelling against, allied itself with the Emersonian view that the range of the human cannot be fixed in advance, that the human subject is always in the process of becoming.[4] To suppose that subjectivity first enters the documentary picture in a few forward-looking films of the seventies, and to view those films as repudiating *cinema verité*, is to deny the continuities between pre-seventies and post-seventies documentaries, hence to miss the importance of the seventies, both as a period of transition within the American documentary cinema and as a period of great vitality and achievement in its own right.

Economics

The task of assessing the American documentary cinema of the seventies is complicated both by the sheer number of documentaries made during the decade and by the sheer obscurity of so many of them.

For an all too brief period, coinciding with the Kennedy presidency, the earliest American *cinema verité* films, the Drew Associates productions (PRIMARY [1960]; ON THE POLE [1960]; the four films the Drew team made in 1960 and 1961 for the ABC-TV *Close-Up* series; the eleven films it made for the *Living Camera* series, including THE CHAIR [1962] and CRISIS: BEHIND A PRESIDENTIAL COMMITMENT [1963]), were broadcast in prime-time on network television. That was an event of national importance. But no less important was *cinema verité*'s expulsion from network television. A HAPPY MOTHER'S DAY (1963) marks this moment.[5] When a South Dakota woman gave birth to quintuplets, ABC commissioned Richard Leacock to film the hoopla. The network edited his footage but never broadcast it, so Leacock made his own version. No longer assured a national audience of millions for his work, but no longer obligated to mask his point of view behind a facade of journalistic objectivity, he was free to think of what he was creating simply as a film, *his* film. At that moment, *cinema verité* in America was reborn, disempowered but free, as a movement of independent film. The Drew team broke up, and Leacock, Pennebaker, and the Maysles brothers struck out on their own, their ranks soon joined by the likes of Frederick Wiseman, Edward Pincus, Les Blank, Alan and Susan Raymond, and, by the end of the seventies, literally thousands of documentary filmmakers who were incorporating into their work the adventure of filming "real people" going about their lives in the world.

In the seventies, a handful of documentaries enjoyed relatively significant theatrical runs, and a larger handful reached audiences nationwide through public television. On rare occasions, even commercial television still showed serious documentaries (for example, the 1976 Westinghouse-Group W series *Six American Families,* for which such distinguished documentary filmmakers as the Maysles brothers, Bill Jersey, Susan Fanshel, Arthur Barron, and Marc Obenhaus filmed the everyday life of six very different American families). But audiences for documentary films were usually small, and sometimes quite specialized. Except on the occasions in which they were screened at the venues in major cities and college campuses around the country that were open to the work of contemporary independent filmmakers, most documentaries received little or no public notice.

No individual or organization put money into documentaries in the hope of reaping profits. A crucial factor that made it possible for so many documentaries nonetheless to be made was the relatively ready availability of funds from public and private grant-giving entities. The National Endowment for the Arts, the American Film Institute, and the National Endowment for the Humanities provided funding for numerous documentary projects. State arts councils provided support, as did private foundations, ranging from the giant Rockefeller, Ford, and Guggenheim Foundations to small foundations such as The Film Fund created by Barbara Kopple, Obie Benz, and David Crocker, among others. To finance films meant to stimulate social change. A filmmaker like Amalie Rothschild, for example, was able to receive production grants from the American Film Institute Independent Filmmaker Program (1973), the National Endowment for the Arts (1977, 1978), the New York State Council on the Arts (1978), the Pinewood Foundation (1978), and the John Hay Whitney Foundation (1978) to help support her work in the seventies.[6] (In the late sixties and early seventies, the Corporation for Public Broadcasting, funded by the federal government, gave more grants to filmmakers than any other organization.[7] However, after Richard Nixon vetoed the 1972 CPB budget, public television stations were generally forced to turn to corporate funding to underwrite individual programs. Although in the late seventies an Independent Documentary Fund was established for public television, the imperative of not offending potential corporate underwriters led public television stations to gravitate increasingly to relatively conventional styles and noncontroversial subject matter.)

A glance at the final credits of any major documentary of the seventies suggests the ingenuity and persistence required for independent filmmakers to gather the resources to get their films in the can. HARLAN COUNTY, USA (Barbara Kopple, 1977), for example, thanks "individuals and organizations who have provided valuable support and assistance." The long list of individuals cited, added to the extensive list of people who are credited for technical work they did for the production, comprises a virtual Who's Who of New York's independent film community in the seventies. The almost equally long list of organizations includes, among others, the National Endowment for the Arts, the New York State Council on the Arts, the American Film Institute, the Abelard Foundation, the Menil Foundation, the Southern Regional Council, the United Methodist Church, and Duart Film Laboratories. (A disproportionate number of independently produced films in the seventies carry a "Color by Duart" because Irwin Young, brother of director Robert Young and owner of Duart Film Laboratories, was so committed to independent film, especially documentary, that he often made special deals with independent filmmakers that allowed them to defer post-production expenses.)

In addition to unsung heroes like Young, a diversity of other factors helped make it possible for so many documentary filmmakers to prevail in their struggles to finance their films. For example, the nonprofit Media Equipment Resource Center in New York pioneered in making equipment available to independent filmmakers, providing a model for similar organizations in other cities. Last, but unfortunately not least, explosive growth in the credit card industry made it possible, if undesirable (by the late seventies, after all, interest rates had risen to all-time highs), for filmmakers to go into debt to make their films.

In most cases, getting a completed documentary seen by its potential audience took even more ingenuity and persistence than getting it made in the first place. Numerous commercial distributors specialized in the 16mm nontheatrical market, ranging from relative giants, such as Films Incorporated, to the more filmmaker-friendly Serious Business Company (run by artist/filmmaker Freude Bartlett) and Direct Cinema, Ltd. (run by filmmaker/distributor/gadfly Mitchell Block).[8] Whether by choice or by necessity, many filmmakers distributed their films themselves. Their efforts at self-distribution were facilitated by distribution cooperatives, such as the Film-Makers' Cooperative, Canyon Cinema Cooperative, the Philadelphia Filmmakers' Co-op, and New Day Films.[9] (New Day was founded in 1971 by Amalie Rothschild, Julia Reichert, James Klein, and Liane Brandon to facilitate the distribution of films by and about women at an historical moment when a thriving feminist movement was engendering a proliferation of women's groups interested in screening and discussing such films.) There also were university distributors (for example, the University of California Extension Media Center; the NYU Film Library; Iowa Films, run by the University of Iowa; and the Audio-Visual Library Service of the University of Minnesota) and other nonprofit distributors, such as the Museum of Modern Art and the Donnell Library in New York.[10] Under the stewardship of Kitty Morgan, Independent Artists and Producers (ICAP), subsidized by grants from the National Endowment for the Arts, the New York State Council on the Arts, and the private Markle Foundation and thus able to return most of the rental revenues to the filmmakers, distributed independently produced films and videos to the then fledgling HBO and Showtime, to other cable systems, and to television stations abroad.[11] (German television, in particular, acquired numerous American documentaries, gravitating to those which exposed the dark underbelly of American life.)

Even for documentary filmmakers who were relatively successful in marketing their films, however, it remained a dream to be able to earn enough profits in rentals and sales to make a decent living, to pay off the debts they incurred making the films, and to finance their next films without having to depend on the whims of grant-giving agencies. Few documentary filmmakers in the seventies were able to support their expensive filmmaking habits solely by sales and rentals. (One exception was Pennebaker, whose sixties film DON'T LOOK BACK continued to reap dividends. Another was Wiseman, whose films were virtually guaranteed of being bought by almost every public television station in the country, and who distributed his films through his own production company, Zipporah Films, and supplemented his income by personal appearances.)

One reason so many documentary filmmakers gravitated to New York in the seventies was the opportunities the city provided to supplement their incomes—that is, pay off their debts—by working in various capacities within a film and television industry that, given New York's liberal tradition, was less rigid and more open to scruffy independent filmmakers, many of them women who were not about to let themselves be pushed around, than that of Los Angeles. Another was the generosity of the New York

State Council on the Arts. Yet another was New York's plethora of educational institutions where documentary filmmakers could teach, as adjuncts or as regular faculty members, in environments conducive to filmmaking.

New York was not the only major hub for documentary filmmakers in the seventies. The Boston area, for example, home to Harvard and MIT, was also home to the Harvard-based anthropological filmmaker Robert Gardner (whose major film of the seventies was RIVERS OF SAND [1974] and who also hosted a local television show dedicated to the work of independent filmmakers, especially documentarians); Alfred Guzzetti, also based at Harvard, whose major seventies film was FAMILY PORTRAIT SITTINGS (1976); Richard Leacock, who jointly presided over the faculty of the Graduate Film Section at MIT with his younger colleague Edward Pincus, an important if relatively little-known figure in documentary film of the seventies; Frederick Wiseman, whose work in the seventies was more widely seen than that of any other American documentary filmmaker; and John Marshall, who collaborated with Gardner on THE HUNTERS (1958), shot Wiseman's first film, TITICUT FOLLIES (1967), and in the seventies made a series of films about the !Kung Bushmen of the Kalahari as well as *cinema vérité* films closer to home. WGBH, one of the flagship PBS stations that was especially active in producing and acquiring documentaries, was also located in the Boston area.

In the seventies, filmmaking and film study programs sprang up in thousands of colleges and universities. More and more documentary filmmakers found themselves with university affiliations that freed them from the need to make a living by selling their services as hired hands to commercial production companies. It also gave them access to expensive camera, sound, and editing equipment they would otherwise have had to rent or purchase; it facilitated their efforts to secure grants; and the imperative of earning tenure in a "publish or perish" era provided a strong incentive to remain productive. Most university-based documentary filmmakers wanted their work to reach as wide an audience as possible, of course, but they were free to push the exigencies of the marketplace aside, if they wished, to pursue difficult subjects and challenging formal experiments without being unduly constrained by commercial considerations. (The academy may equal the marketplace in imposing its own conformities, but that is another story.)

The presence on so many college campuses of documentary filmmakers passionately committed to their work meant that the torch was passed to students all over the country. Increasingly, when documentaries were screened on or off college campuses, a sizable part of the audience was made up of film students, film teachers, and independent filmmakers, many of them documentary filmmakers, and many of them women. The establishment in the early seventies of the Association of Independent Video and Filmmakers (AIVF), New York-based but with a national membership, was indicative of the fact that a community of independent filmmakers had emerged, and had become conscious of itself as a community. As its name (and the name of its newsletter/journal, *The Independent*) suggests, the organization's goal was to help filmmakers secure their independence, financially as well as creatively. For the AIVF, furthering its members' independence was itself a political crusade. For most AIVF members, "independence" primarily meant independence from Hollywood studios, the networks, and the corporate world in general. The nonprofit AIVF, itself subsidized by grants, did not strive to wean filmmakers from dependence on grants. In the seventies, the major grant-awarding entities allowed decisions to be determined primarily by peer review panels—an NEA grant program for independent filmmakers was administered through the American Film Institute, for example—and were quite catholic in their choices. But

American society has always been ambivalent about public support for the arts, and the more restrictive Reagan era was just around the corner.

Television

By the end of the sixties, the hard-hitting network investigative documentary of the kind CBS pioneered in the fifties had already become an endangered species, with one of the last being THE SELLING OF THE PENTAGON (Peter Davis, 1971), made for CBS, an exposé of the ways the Defense Department was manipulating public opinion to bolster support for the Vietnam War. And by the end of the sixties, the networks had already for some years closed their doors to prime-time *cinema verité* documentaries of the kind Drew Associates had produced early in the decade. Although there were occasional exceptions, such as *Six American Families,* and although *Sixty Minutes* occasionally bought documentary footage from independent filmmakers (as did such syndicated shows as *That's Incredible!* and *Ripley's Believe It or Not),* network television in the seventies remained all but completely closed to documentaries.[12] Most of the documentaries broadcast nationwide were aired on public television.

In the mid-seventies, there were about 270 public television stations in the country. Approximately a third were licensed to colleges and universities, a third to public school systems, and a third to nonprofit organizations that mingled the social, cultural, religious, and educational interests of urban areas. Some stations were part of state networks—licensed, in fact, to the states themselves.[13] A number of individual PBS stations produced, and distributed to other stations, ongoing documentary series, such as *Nova*; multi-part series, such as the six-part 1977 series on female artists, *The Originals: Women in Art*; and individual documentaries, such as the *National Geographic* specials. Individual stations also acquired as many as fifteen hour-long documentaries a year, paying independent filmmakers, in the mid-seventies, up to $1,000 per hour for multiple screenings.[14] However, local stations were so far-flung and diverse that it was difficult, especially before videocassette recorders became universally available late in the decade, to establish relationships with more than a few of them. Filmmakers were also able to negotiate with consortia of stations, such as the Eastern Educational Network, which had about fifty member stations and bought perhaps ten or twelve single documentaries each year for about $100 per minute.[15] It was also possible for filmmakers to sell directly to PBS itself. (After the early seventies, CPB did not fund individual programs, but it did have funds for film acquisition. Decisions concerning which films to buy were made jointly by CPB and PBS.[16])

It must be said, however, that public television, which after the early seventies was heavily dependent on corporate underwriting to fund its programming, failed to furnish a national audience to more than a few documentary filmmakers. For the vast majority of documentary filmmakers in the seventies (or the eighties and nineties, for that matter), PBS was of little or no use in helping their films to reach audiences. For virtually none did it solve the problem of how to make documentary filmmaking self-supporting.

Theatrical and Nontheatrical Distribution

As detailed elsewhere in this volume, a general crisis in the film industry in the early seventies created a product shortage for exhibitors and thus a window of opportunity for independent producers, including documentary producers. In the seventies, several independently produced documentaries enjoyed considerable theatrical releases. Among them were WOODSTOCK (Michael Wadleigh, 1970), GIMME SHELTER (Albert and David Maysles and Charlotte Zwerin, 1970), MARJOE (Howard Smith and Sarah Kernochan, 1972), MILHOUSE (Emile De Antonio, 1973), HEARTS AND MINDS (Peter Davis, 1974), I. F. STONE'S WEEKLY (Jerry Bruck, Jr., 1973), ANTONIA: A PORTRAIT OF THE WOMAN (Jill Godmilow and Judy Collins, 1974), GENERAL IDI AMIN DADA (Barbet Schroeder, 1975), HARLAN COUNTY, USA, (1977), PUMPING IRON (Robert Fiore and George Butler, 1977), and BEST BOY (Ira Wohl, 1979).

The usual pattern, pioneered by Jerry Bruck, Jr. with I. F. STONE'S WEEKLY, was to open the film at a "showcase," preferably in New York. Frequently, the filmmakers appeared at these showcase screenings to introduce their works and answer questions. New York venues suitable for showcasing feature-length documentaries included the Whitney Museum's New American Filmmakers series, the Museum of Modern Art's Cineprobe series, Karen Cooper's Film Forum, or the Donnell Library, whose screenings were programmed by William Sloan (who also edited *Film Library Quarterly*, a journal that featured reviews and other coverage of contemporary documentaries). Outside New York, suitable venues included the Pacific Film Archive in Berkeley, run by Tom Luddy, which offered minimal press coverage but meant an important connection to other screenings and to distributors and festivals on the West Coast; the Vanguard Theater in Los Angeles, which ran a weekly "Contemporary Film" series; the

ANTONIA: A PORTRAIT OF THE WOMAN (Jill Godmilow and Judy Collins, 1974), which co-director Godmilow successfully distributed herself, was one of the most popular and best-loved documentaries of the seventies. (Photograph courtesy of Jill Godmilow.)

Northwest Film Study Center at Portland; the Rocky Mountain Film Center at Boulder; the Walker Art Center in Minneapolis; the American Film Institute theater in Washington, programmed by Michael Webb, which offered good press coverage and solid connections to other outlets and festivals; the Film Center at the School of the Art Institute of Chicago; the Walnut Street Film Theater in Philadelphia; and Center Screen in Cambridge.[17] Technically "nontheatrical," these all operated under nonprofit umbrellas and thus were eligible to receive grants from government agencies and private foundations. An alternative strategy was to open the film at a major film festival. For providing exposure to a documentary film that had a chance for a theatrical run, the top American film festivals included the New York Film Festival, FILMEX (Los Angeles International Film Exposition), and the fledgling Telluride Film Festival.

Favorable reviews attending the showcase opening increased a film's chance of securing first runs in commercial art theaters in major urban centers. Art-theater runs were followed by bookings on college campuses for quasi-theatrical one-night screenings, then by educational classroom rentals and sales of prints to schools and public libraries.

Jill Godmilow released ANTONIA: A PORTRAIT OF THE WOMAN (1974) in accordance with this pattern. First was a screening in the Whitney Museum "New American Filmmakers" series. The Whitney, which had an advertising budget, ran two major press screenings and individual screenings for critics who couldn't make the scheduled ones. As Godmilow describes it, "We provoked, and we prodded, and we pushed our materials to every radio, TV, newspaper, and magazine film critic in the city—from *Time* Magazine and *The Today Show* all the way down to the forty or fifty college newspapers and radio stations in the New York area."[18] Thanks to the reviews and media appearances (and, it must be added, thanks to the celebrity of the singer Judy Collins, then riding a crest of popularity), the Whitney sold out three and four shows a day for two weeks. With only a week's interruption in the run, ANTONIA: A PORTRAIT OF THE WOMAN and I. F. STONE'S WEEKLY (1973) opened as a double bill at the Quad Theater in Greenwich Village. "We did six pretty decent weeks at the Quad, trailed off badly through two more terrible ones, but managed to convince Larry Jackson at the Orson Welles Theater in Cambridge, Massachusetts, to give us a try, where ANTONIA eventually ran fifteen weeks."[19] In the ensuing twelve months, ANTONIA played in theaters in about twenty cities, mostly on the East and West Coasts. The length of the run and the degree of financial success varied, but the film did not lose money in any city.[20]

Even for documentary films, like ANTONIA, which enjoyed the luxury of theatrical openings, it was the nontheatrical market that provided the bulk of the revenues. For the vast majority of documentaries, the sole financial returns came from nontheatrical sales and rentals to schools, colleges, libraries, museums government agencies, hospitals, churches, and, for films by or about women, the women's groups that were springing up all over the country. In 1974, public school systems spent a total of $276 million on nonprint media, with the largest share ($62.3 million) going to 16mm films (64 percent of this was spent at the grade school level, 28 percent at the high school level).[21] The totality of nontheatrical rentals and sales of 16mm prints in the mid-seventies was about $140 million per year—not a trivial figure by any means, but obviously a drop in the bucket within the film industry as a whole.[22] The most important film festival in the seventies, for the nontheatrical market, was the American Film Festival, put on annually in New York by the Educational Film Library Association (EFLA).

Commenting in the mid-seventies on the nontheatrical market in an EFLA volume on 16mm distribution, Mitchell Block, whose distribution company, Direct Cinema,

Ltd., continues to distribute many classic and contemporary documentary films, wrote, rather disconsolately:

> [T]his business is underwritten by the government at all levels, including distribution. The buyers are public institutions, for the most part—libraries, schools, etc.; the markets are funded by grants and contracts; the only ones who don't really get a subsidy break are the for-profit distributors who must compete with state university film libraries. If the government provides a major share of the venture capital for filmmaking in a free market situation, then this distorts the entire market. Filmmakers find it difficult to raise money in the private sector because the selling price does not reflect the films' costs. This situation could be improved if the government simply funded the buyers at a level where the school systems and libraries could pay filmmakers and distributors a price that would reflect production costs. I believe that this would require that budgets be increased across the board 250 percent—just to maintain the present buying level. Unfortunately, this prospect seems unlikely in the near future and, in the meantime, filmmakers must cope with the present system.[23]

Colleges and Universities

In college and university film programs in the seventies it was quite typical for there to be a wall of mutual hostility, or at least mutual indifference, between those who taught production and those who taught history, criticism, and theory. But the documentary filmmaker's situation within the academy was especially anomalous. The original impulse to establish film on college campuses came largely from a post-Bazinian vision of film as a great art uniquely rooted in reality. Those who embraced such a vision were inclined to accord special importance to the great works of the documentary tradition. The new field of film study increasingly based its claim to legitimacy, though, on its embrace of the radical new theoretical frameworks and methodologies (poststructuralism, deconstruction, Althusserian Marxism, Lacanian psychoanalysis) that were revolutionizing the study of literature. The theories that came to dominate academic film study viewed films as discursive constructs, not as windows onto reality. Prior to the eighties, few if any critiques of documentary were published within film study. But the new theories made documentary films, or at least the claim sometimes made on their behalf that they were capable of revealing reality directly, seem philosophically naive, or worse, unfashionable. Even as the presence of documentary filmmakers was becoming a fact of life within the academy, documentaries were becoming more and more marginalized within academic film study. Shamefully, this was the case even though feminist theory was making ever greater inroads on film study in the late seventies, and so many contemporary documentaries were made by women and explicitly addressed feminist issues and themes.

Although many were increasingly isolated within their own film programs, campus-based documentary filmmakers began to have a major impact on documentary filmmaking itself. In the seventies, the foremost training ground for *cinema verité* filmmakers was the MIT Film Section. This graduate program, which awarded MFA degrees, was founded in 1969 by Edward Pincus, and quickly added the already legendary Richard Leacock to its faculty. The Film Section numbers among its alumni Ross McElwee, Joel DeMott, Jeff Kreines, Ann Schaetzel, Robb Moss, Steven Ascher, Michel Negroponte, and other filmmakers who went on to make major contributions to the American documentary in the eighties and nineties.

Documentary film's vexed relationship with academic film study was further complicated by the claims made by ethnographic filmmakers and their supporters that they were founding an academic discipline that was not a branch of film study (whose intellectual roots were in criticism and the humanities), but rather a visual branch of anthropology (whose roots were in the social sciences). In the early seventies, before its funding was cut, UCLA's Ethnographic Film Program, which was founded in the late sixties by Colin Young and Walter Goldschmidt and whose alumni included such filmmakers as David and Judith MacDougall, David Hancock, and Herb DiGioia, was the main university program in the United States for training ethnographic filmmakers.

Politics

In his 1968 campaign, Nixon had appealed to a "silent majority" who wished to put the turbulence of the sixties behind them. After Watergate, conservatives did not assume power until Reagan's election in 1980. But in the seventies a conservative mood was beginning to settle in. In this climate, Richard Barsam argues, "many American nonfiction filmmakers were more inclined to observe society than to confront it. However, some of them made social documentaries that were committed to principles of social justice."[24]

The exceptions Barsam cites include THE SELLING OF THE PENTAGON (1971), ON THE BATTLEFIELD (Peter Biskind, 1972), ATTICA (Cinda Firestone, 1973), HURRY TOMORROW (Richard Cohen, 1974), HEARTS AND MINDS (Peter Davis, 1974), HARLAN COUNTY, U.S.A. (Barbara Kopple, 1977), UNION MAIDS (Julia Reichert, James Klein, and Miles Mogulescu, 1976), and YOUTH TERROR (Helen Whitney, 1978). Many others could be added to this list. To name just a few: INTERVIEWS WITH MY LAI VETERANS (Joseph Strick, 1971), THE MURDER OF FRED HAMPTON (Michael Gray and Howard Alk, 1971), CHICAGO MATERNITY CENTER (Kartemquin Films, 1976), and THE WAR AT HOME (Glenn Silber and Barry Brown, 1979).

It should also be observed in this context that in the seventies numerous organizations as well as individual filmmakers were committed to using film and video as instruments of social change. The oldest of these was Newsreel, established in 1967 as a network of activist collectives centered in New York and San Francisco, with Norman Fruchter and Robert Kramer among its prime movers. In the early seventies, Newsreel produced and distributed such films as LINCOLN HOSPITAL (Newsreel, 1970), about a strike at a city-run health clinic in the South Bronx; WILMINGTON (Newsreel, 1970), which portrays Wilmington, Delaware, as a company town run by the Dupont family as if it were a private kingdom; ONLY THE BEGINNING (Newsreel, 1971), which documents the arrival of thousands of G.I.s in Washington to protest the Vietnam War; and THE WOMEN'S FILM (Newsreel USA, 1971), a militant feminist manifesto. In the course of the seventies Newsreel underwent structural changes, splitting into New York Newsreel and San Francisco Newsreel, and, in the mid-seventies, transforming itself from Newsreel, the militant collective, into Third World Newsreel, a nonprofit alternative media arts organization subsidized by public funds from government agencies as well as foundations and individual contributors. In its new incarnation, the organization specifically dedicated itself to fostering the creation, appreciation, and dissemination of independent film and video by and about people of color. In the seventies, Third World Newsreel produced and distributed such films as IN THE EVENT ANYONE DISAPPEARS (Third World Newsreel; Alan Siege, 1974), an examination of conditions faced by prisoners inside men's maximum security prisons in New Jersey; INSIDE WOMEN INSIDE (Third World Newsreel; Christine Choy and Canthi Maoris, 1978), containing firsthand accounts of inmates at North Carolina correctional centers; and PERCUSSION, IMPRESSIONS AND REALITY (Third World Newsreel; Alan Siege, 1978), about the social and political origins of traditional Puerto Rican music.

In the seventies there was also a proliferation of organizations and collectives, of varying degrees of militancy, committed to using film as an instrument for furthering specifically feminist causes and/or gay rights. These included the Twin Cities Women's Film Collective, the Berkeley Lesbian Feminist Film Collective, and the International Woman's Film Project.

Still other organizations attempted to utilize public access cable channels, which the cable industry was required by a 1972 law to provide to citizens in its hundred biggest markets, and to utilize other strategies as well, to develop community-oriented alternatives to conventional television. A key figure in this development was the filmmaker George Stoney, whose reputation had been established with such classic documentaries as ALL MY BABIES (1953). Stoney had directed the National Film Board of Canada's "Challenge for Change" project, which pioneered the idea of providing citizens access to the media to create a dialogue with agencies of government involved in social programs, before returning to the United States in 1970 to head the undergraduate film production program at NYU. (Through no fault of his own, Stoney did not last long in that position; NYU, whose Cinema Studies Department gravitated to the avant-garde and downplayed documentaries, was an exemplary instance of a university film program with little rapport between the filmmakers and the academics on its faculty. Nonetheless, Stoney has remained one of NYU's most distinguished professors. Over the years, he has become the "grand old man" of documentary at NYU and a towering figure within New York's independent film community. His films of the seventies include IN CHINA FAMILY PLANNING IS NO PRIVATE MATTER [1978] and ACUPUNCTURE AND HERBAL MEDICINE [1978].)

One of Stoney's first actions at NYU was to set up, with colleague Red Burns, an Alternate Media Center to promote and support the use of public access cable.[25] The Alternate Media Center, with funding from the Markle Foundation and the National Endowment for the Arts, trained organizers to work with interested community groups, cable companies, and city governments to develop public access to cable TV around the country. It was soon joined by such New York City organizations as Downtown Community Television, Global Village, and WNET-13's TV Lab; by Urban Planning Aid in Boston, and Communication for Change in Chicago; and by community video organizations in such places as Port Washington and Woodstock, New York. Two acclaimed productions to come out of this movement were the POLICE TAPES (Alan and Susan Raymond, 1976), a *cinema verité* slice of life shot at a South Bronx police station, which was funded by the TV Lab and grants from the National Endowment for the Arts and the Ford Foundation, and GIVING BIRTH (Julie Gustafson and John Reilly, 1976), produced by Global Village in association with the TV Lab, which advocated the techniques of natural childbirth.[26]

Despite all of this political activity, however, Barsam is not wrong in suggesting that documentary filmmakers in the seventies tended to pull back from protesting social or political injustices in the manner of so many documentaries of the sixties. However, his implication—that most documentaries of the seventies opted for observing rather than confronting society and hence were *not* committed to principles of social justice, that they were on Nixon's side, as it were—is highly misleading. Most documentary film-makers in the seventies kept faith with their (generally leftist) political principles, but they were responding to a changed political situation. The assassinations of Robert Kennedy and Martin Luther King, Jr., the election of Richard Nixon, the deaths of rock icons Janis Joplin and Jimi Hendrix, the withdrawal of Bob Dylan from the public stage (or, at least, from the role of prophet), and the killing at Altamont (simultaneous with the much-hyped Woodstock festival, touted in Michael Wadleigh's WOODSTOCK as the beginning of the revolution whose ending it really marked) all meant that the sixties were over. The political protests of the sixties were history, and by the mid-seventies the Vietnam War and the Nixon presidency had become history, too.

By exposing the gulf between the sanctimonious public Nixon and the coarse and mendacious private Nixon, the events history calls "Watergate," largely played out on television, brought down the Nixon presidency. Watergate was inextricably intertwined with Nixon's efforts to stop or discredit the ongoing public disclosures of the official lies, deceptions, and betrayals that were inseparable from the history of America's calamitous involvement in Vietnam. And Watergate coincided, as well, with the emergence of a new awareness, spearheaded by the women's movement, that America's "official" histories, as well as its media of mass entertainment, systematically suppress the roles played by women and minorities, and underwrite America's continuing unwillingness or inability to acknowledge painful truths about itself. Jimmy Carter was elected with the pledge that he would never lie to the American people. The 1976 election, coinciding with the Bicentennial of the American republic, promised to inaugurate a new era of honesty and freedom. At such a moment, many documentary filmmakers felt vindicated in their belief—were they wrong?—that there was no better way to express their commitment to principles of social justice than by making films that observed Americans living their private lives and reflected on who Americans have been, who they are, and who they are capable of becoming.

Folkloric Films

Organizations like the Kentucky-based Appalshop and the Memphis-based Center for Southern Folklore, whose agenda or mission was (and is) to document and affirm regional folk cultures, took quite seriously the principle, which the women's movement never tired of repeating, that the personal is the political.

Appalshop began in 1969 as a War on Poverty program to offer training in media pro-duction to young men and women of the Southern Appalachian mountains. They soon created their own nonprofit community-based media company and began making films about the culture and lives of the region's people, who "are shown pursuing that which is important to all of us—the chance to work, to live in health and peace, to share our lives with those we love, and to create and sustain that which is beautiful."[27] The goal was "to bring the voices of those who still work with their hands, those who see taking care of the land and water as something more than a passing trend, those who still believe in the power of people to take care of each other, into the discussion of what is important in the world."[28] Appalshop films of the seventies include JUDGE WOOTEN AND COON-ON-A-LOG (Herb E. Smith, 1971), a portrait of a local judge whose comments on recreation, retirement, and the mountaineer's relationship with the land are mixed with scenes of spectators on the banks of the Kentucky River applauding as someone's favorite coon dog plunges into the water and hustles a raccoon off a log; COAL MINER: FRANK JACKSON (Ben Zickafoose, 1971), which juxtaposes a miner's personal recollections of union organizing and mining with scenes of him in the mines; IN THE GOOD, OLD-FASHIONED WAY (Herb E. Smith, 1973), about the Old Regular Baptist Church, a unique product of Appalachian culture; STRIP MINING IN APPALACHIA (Gene DuBey, 1973), an examination of the desecration of land and communities brought about by surface mining of coal; TRADITION (Bill Hatton and Anthony Slone, 1973), a dual portrait of a moonshiner and a federal revenue agent; NATURE'S WAY (John Long and Elizabeth Barret, 1974), which profiles people who cure their own ailments using herbs, Native American folklore, and home remedies; CHAIRMAKER (Rick DiClemente, 1975), in which a rough-hewn rocking chair takes form under the experienced hands and well-worn knife of eighty-year-old Dewey Thompson from Sugarloaf Hollow, Kentucky; QUILTING WOMEN (Elizabeth Barret, 1976), which traces the process of traditional Appalachian quilting, from cutting out and piecing together the patterns to the quilting bee; and OAKSIE (Anthony Slone, 1979), a portrait of basket maker, fiddler, and harp player Oaksie Caudill.

IT AIN'T CITY MUSIC *(Tom Davenport, 1973) is representative of the movement, which grew explosively in the seventies, to document on film aspects of American folklore.*

The Center for Southern Folklore was founded in 1972 by Bill Ferris and Judy Peiser, who collaborated as filmmakers on a series of films such as GRAVEL SPRINGS FIFE AND DRUM (Bill Ferris, David Evans, and Judy Peiser, 1971), RAY LUM: MULE TRADER (Bill Ferris, Bobby Taylor, and Judy Peiser, 1973), and FANNIE BELL CHAPMAN: GOSPEL SINGER (Bill Ferris and Judy Peiser, 1975). Peiser's other films of the seventies include the charming HUSH HOGGIES HUSH (1978), in which a minister-farmer calls his pigs to dinner, says "Hush, hoggies, hush" to the squealing pigs, whereupon they fall silent as he reads from the Bible before they plunge with all four hooves into the feeding trough. Other films that the prolific Ferris directed or co-directed in the seventies under the auspices of the Center for Southern Folklore include DELTA BLUES SINGER: JAMES 'SONNY FORD' THOMAS (1970), BLACK DELTA RELIGION (Bill and Josette Ferris, 1973), MISSISSIPPI DELTA BLUES (Bill and Josette Ferris, 1974), GIVE MY POOR HEART EASE: MISSISSIPPI BLUESMEN (1975), and TWO BLACK CHURCHES (1975). He also made two films for the Yale University Media Design Studio in conjunction with the Center for Southern Folklore (I AIN'T LYING: FOLKTALES FROM MISSISSIPPI [1975], and MADE IN MISSISSIPPI: BLACK FOLK ART AND CRAFTS [1975]). In 1979, Ferris moved to Mississippi, where he established the Center for the Study of Southern Culture at the University of Mississippi. Peiser took over the reins of the Center for Southern Folklore.

Ferris and Peiser were key figures in the explosive growth in the seventies of films about American folklore and the ways individual Americans, and groups of Americans, maintain their ethnic and cultural identities within the multicultural American milieu. Among the many filmmakers associated with this movement are Jorge Preloran (whose films of the seventies include VALLE FERTIL [1972], COCHENGO MIRANDA [1975], THE WARAO [1975], ZERDA'S CHILDREN [1978], and LUTHER METKE AT 94 [Jorge Preloran and Steve Raymen, 1979]); Tom Davenport (whose films include THE UPPERVILLE SHOW [1970], THE SHAKERS [Tom Davenport and Dan Patterson, 1970], IT AIN'T CITY MUSIC [1973], HANSEL AND GRETEL [1975], BORN FOR HARD LUCK: SAM PEG LEG JACKSON [Tom Davenport and Dan Patterson, 1976], and RAPUNZEL, RAPUNZEL [1978]); and David Hancock and Herb DiGioia (whose films include NAIM AND JABAR [1973], AFGHAN NOMADS [1974], and AN AFGHAN VILLAGE [1974]).

Among the best of the folkloric films of the seventies was THE POPOVICH BROTHERS OF SOUTH CHICAGO (Jill Godmilow, 1978), about the importance of traditional Serbian music and musicians to the Serbian-American community in Chicago. The film was made by Jill Godmilow, widely known for the popular ANTONIA: A PORTRAIT OF THE WOMAN (1974). But the most celebrated creator of such films, and justly so, was Les Blank, who for over thirty years has been filming colorful individuals who represent ethnic and other American subcultures.

THE BLUES ACCORDIN' TO LIGHTNIN' HOPKINS (Les Blank, 1969), a portrait of the great Texas bluesman that features a generous helping of classic blues (including performances at an outdoor barbecue and a black rodeo) and a visit to Hopkins's boyhood town, set the tone for Blank's films of the seventies. These include SPEND IT ALL (1971), a rich portrayal of the lives and music of the Louisiana Cajuns; A WELL SPENT LIFE (1971), a glowing portrait of the legendary musicians (also lifelong husbands and sharecroppers) whom tough times made sweet, rather than bitter; HOT PEPPER (1973), a musical portrait of Zydeco King Clifton Chenier, "who combines the pulsating rhythms of Cajun dance music and black R&B with African overtones, belting out his irresistible music in the sweaty juke joints of South Louisiana"; DRY WOOD (1973), a look at black

Creole life in French Louisiana; CHULAS FRONTERAS (1976), a complex, insightful look at the Chicano experience as mirrored in the lives and music of the most acclaimed Norteño musicians of the Texas-Mexican border; ALWAYS FOR PLEASURE (1978), an "intense insider's portrait of New Orleans' street celebrations and unique cultural gumbo: Second-line parades, Mardi Gras, Jazz Fest," featuring live music from Professor Longhair, the Wild Tchoupitoulas, the Neville Brothers and more; and WERNER HERZOG EATS HIS SHOE (1979), in which German film director Werner Herzog really does eat his shoe to fulfill a vow to fellow filmmaker Errol Morris, "boldly exemplifying his belief that people must have the guts to attempt what they dream of."[29]

The overarching point is that many documentary filmmakers in the seventies who opted for observing society were actually confronting society. They were not turning their backs on social justice, they were experimenting with new ways of achieving social change. In any case, as more and more documentary filmmakers were coming to recognize, the medium of film itself overcomes or transcends the opposition between observing and confronting.

All of the major histories of documentary film accept the proposition that a fundamental distinction is to be drawn between American direct cinema (as films like those of Leacock, Pennebaker, or the Maysles brothers have been dubbed), in which the camera observes but does not participate in the events being filmed, and the more sophisticated filmmaking practice that Jean Rouch had in mind when he coined the term *"cinema verité"* to characterize his approach in making CHRONICLE OF A SUMMER (Jean Rouch and Edgar Morin, 1960) in France simultaneously with the Drew productions in America. In *cinema verité*, so the claim goes, the camera actively

ALWAYS FOR PLEASURE *(Les Blank, 1978), an "intense insider's portrait of New Orleans's street celebrations and unique cultural gumbo," is one of the most remarkable of the folkloric films of the seventies.*

provokes the revelations it records. To be sure, Rouch understood that the camera sometimes has to provoke reality into revealing its deepest truths. And yet Rouch also understood that observation is the camera's deepest way of provoking its subjects to reveal themselves. This means that *cinema verité* and "direct cinema" are *not* really in opposition. In Rouch's films no less than those of his American colleagues, it is the very presence of the camera when it is doing its mysterious work that provokes the revelations to which *cinema verité* aspires. And in their films as well as his, it is not reality as it is but reality as it is provoked by the act of filming that the camera documents. The world on film is capable of revealing its own reality, a reality that would not exist apart from the act of filming. Hence the world on film is capable of revealing its own truth: *Cinema* truth. *Cinema verité*.[30]

Ethnographic Films

The goal of the filmmakers who made folkloric films in the seventies, such as those made under the auspices of Appalshop or the Center for Southern Folklore, was to help America to acknowledge traditions internal to its own culture. Ethnographic films, by contrast, turned to other cultures, typically ones anthropologists consider primitive. The camera was used as an instrument of scientific observation, not revelation. Scientific truth, not cinema truth, was the goal. As the late Timothy Asch, perhaps the most respected American ethnographic filmmaker, put it, "The camera can be to the anthropologist what the telescope is to the astronomer or what the microscope is to the biologist."[31]

Asch is best known for the twenty-one films on the Yanomamo people of the Venezuelan rain forest, generally considered exemplary ethnographic films, which he made in collaboration with the anthropologist Napoleon Chagnon. Previous to that project, Asch had collaborated with John Marshall to re-edit footage of the !Kung Bushmen of the Kalahari that Marshall had shot as far back as the late fifties. Hand-synching the footage with wild sound, they released several films on Bushman life, such as N/UM TCHAI: THE CEREMONIAL DANCE OF THE !KUNG BUSHMEN (John Marshall and Timothy Asch, 1968), a film about a trance curing ceremony.

Prior to his partnership with Asch, Marshall had collaborated with Robert Gardner on THE HUNTERS (1958), made before synch-sound had become available to documentary filmmakers. Then he had served as Frederick Wiseman's cinematographer on TITICUT FOLLIES (1967), his first experience shooting synch sound. In a series of films he made about the Pittsburgh police department, of which THREE DOMESTICS (1972) is the best known, Marshall followed Wiseman's technique of using synch sound without narration, and perfected a long take style of shooting in which the camera follows the drama as it evolves. "Emphasizing the complexities of human interaction as opposed to the earlier stress on plot coherence evidenced in THE HUNTERS, Marshall developed the concept of 'sequence filming,'" Sharon R. Sherman writes. "Abandoning the artificial constraint of constructing a plot made up of events that may not have occurred in the proper time perspective, Marshall cut his footage into naturally occurring interactions between people that could be analyzed to indicate the importance of their behavior within their own culture or society."[32]

In his series of Yanomamo films, Asch adhered to Marshall's emphasis on "sequence filming" of complex social interactions. THE AX FIGHT (Timothy Asch and Napoleon

Changnon, 1973) is typical. The film is in five parts. Part 1 is the unedited footage of a fight that suddenly erupts in a Yanomamo village. In part 2, the screen is black as the filmmakers speculate on what happened. In part 3, written titles inform us what the fight was really about. Part 4 replays the original footage with a narrator explaining what we are seeing. Part 5 re-presents the original footage, sans narration but edited for narrative continuity like a Hollywood movie.

Eliot Weinberger observes, in the context of a devastating critique of ethnographic film's claims to scientific authority, "One of the curiosities of ethnographic film, evident to any outsider, is that the strictly scientific films often provide far less information than their reviled 'artistic' cousins. . . . Or, more damningly, they provide the same information."[33] In 1978, the Musée de L'Homme in Paris ran a festival of films about the Yanomamo, including several of the Asch-Chagnon films; a French television documentary; two films from a Yugoslavian TV series on the rain forest; a Canadian film from the television series *Full Speed to Adventure*, focusing on two Canadian missionaries living with the community; a Japanese television film; three videos by New York avant-gardist Juan Downey; and unedited footage shot in the early 1960s by a woman who was in Venezuela prospecting for gold. In a review of the festival written at the time for *Film Library Quarterly*, Jen Sloan points out that both the images and the information presented in these films were surprisingly similar.[34] As Weinberger puts it, "The moment one erases the stylistic differences, the ethnographic differences between a research film and an episode of *Full Speed to Adventure* are less than meets the eye.[35]

Indeed, as Weinberger adds, the "amateurs" often turned out ethnographically richer films than those who claimed scientific authority for their work. He considers the case of THE NUER (Hilary Harris, George Breidenbach, and Robert Gardner, 1970). Karl Heider, in his influential *Ethnographic Film*, which attempted to set methodological standards for the scientific discipline of visual anthropology, acknowledged that THE NUER was a visually beautiful film, but treated it as the classic example of how not to make an ethnographic film.[36] And yet, as Weinberger argues, THE NUER contains far more ethnographic information than THE AX FIGHT.

> We see what the Nuer look like, what they make, what they eat, what their music sounds like, their leisure activities, body art, architecture, fishing and cattle-herding, local fauna, diseases, rites of exorcism, spiritual possession, and so on. Most of all, as a study of a community based on cattle, it is a startling revelation of the cow. Even an untrained urban eye finds itself immediately differentiating the cows as individuals—much as the Nuer know the personal history of each; a history which, through bride-prices and ritual exchange, is inextricably tangled with their own histories. Moreover, it becomes evident in the course of the film how an entire aesthetic could be derived form the close observation of cattle—how the shapes and textures of the herds are recapitulated in so much of what the Nuer made.[37]

David and Judith MacDougall, alumni of the UCLA Ethnographic Film Program, argued for the need for ethnographic filmmakers to move beyond the strict *cinema verité* discipline by acknowledging their own presence in their films. Films such as TO LIVE WITH HERDS (David and Judith MacDougall, 1972) and their "Turkana Conversations" trilogy (THE WEDDING CAMELS [1977], LORANG'S WAY [1979], and A WIFE AMONG WIVES [1982]) revolve around conversations—exchanges among the subjects being filmed, but also between the subjects and the filmmakers, who sometimes appear on the screen. They also employ titles written in the first person ("We put the following to Lorang . . ."). And when the filmmakers speak in voice-over narrations, they speak not as "Voices of God" but in their own voices ("I was sure Lorang's wives were happy together"; "It doesn't feel like we're making progress"). Although the MacDougalls had found solutions to some of the political and moral dilemmas of ethnographic filmmaking, however, it is not clear what scientific value, if any, their films can claim. Again, Weinberger's criticisms have the ring of truth:

> The films focus on the family of a wealthy man. . . . The film rarely leaves the family compound, and for nearly six hours we watch and listen to people largely talking about money and complaining. . . . Lorang is an Arthur Miller character: the self-made man disgusted by his good-for-nothing sons. But, in the absence of any dramatic catalyst—this being life and not theater—he's a character who goes nowhere. After the first half-hour or so, we only get more of the same. (The wives mainly repeat everything their husbands say.) And the film gives us no way to evaluate whether Lorang is more representative of the Turkana or of the universal *nouveau riche*. In many ways, the trilogy is like an excruciating evening with one's least favorite relatives. There's no doubt it is a precise representation of this particular family, but can it be considered ethnographic, a representation of a people?[38]

The films of Timothy Asch stand or fall on their scientific value. But the films of the MacDougalls do not seem in the same way to be in earnest pursuit of scientific knowledge. They envision their subjects as playing out a familiar human comedy unaltered by being set in exotic landscapes and acted by so-called primitives. They present Lorang and his family, for example, as types we already know all too well. (What should we know that we do not already know about rich people like this who talk about money and kvetch about their relatives?) Films such as these must stand or fall on their value as films, their revelations of *cinema* truth.

Among the American filmmakers usually discussed in the context of visual anthropology in the seventies, Robert Gardner and John Marshall were exceptional for creating works that transcend the limitations of visual anthropology, works that call for being viewed as films, not as science. Both Gardner and Marshall view human existence in poetic, yet tragic, terms. For both, the tragedy is the failure of all human society to fulfil the human longing for acknowledgment and love; society is the mask by which we veil from ourselves the truth that we live inhuman lives.

For Gardner, culture is the system of masks and lies humans create to deny the truth of our condition, a truth that nonetheless can be recognized by anyone with eyes to see. It is the system by which we hide our cruelty and our tenderness from each other and from ourselves. Like his first film, DEAD BIRDS (1963), and his later films, such as DEEP HEARTS (1981) and FOREST OF BLISS (1985), Gardner's most ambitious film of the seventies, RIVERS OF SAND (1974), is a sublime and beautiful poem. Its subject is the Hamar people near the border of Ethiopia and the Sudan. A Hamar woman is the film's central figure. "In DEAD BIRDS, warfare was central and birds became a symbol for men," Sharon Sherman writes. "In RIVERS OF SAND, Gardner examines the role of pain in the relationships between men and women, and the metaphor is a set of grinding stones."[39] Each society Gardner films becomes a metaphor for the tenderness and cruelty of all human existence, the tenderness and cruelty we all are capable of recognizing when we look deep into our own hearts. Gardner's films are about people he does not claim especially to love, but the human need for love, the other face of the human resistance to loving and being loved, is his great subject.

Marshall's subject is the powerlessness of love in the face of forces that are transforming the world into a place unfit for human habitation. Except as a scientist, Timothy Asch had no attachment to the Yamomamo people, or at least none that any of his twenty-one films about them acknowledged. But Marshall's films about the !Kung Bushmen of the Kalahari Desert are no more films about "ethnographic others" than Gardner's films are. They are about people who are important to Marshall, personally. And his culminating film about the Bushmen, N!AI: STORY OF A KUNG WOMAN (1978), revolves around a woman he first filmed when he was a young man and she an eight-year-old. (The young N!ai is a central figure in A JOKING RELATIONSHIP [1971], which Marshall released in 1971 but shot a decade earlier.) To Marshall, N!ai is no anthropological informant, she is a woman he knows, cares about, yet feels powerless to save. Marshall's own story (son of the anthropologist Lorna Marshall, he lived among the Bushmen from his childhood) is inseparable from the story of this people and this person. And the story is a tragedy: This nomadic people is being herded into camps, dying out *as* a people, and what he loves about N!ai is dying out, too.

The words "dying out" suggest that this is occurring naturally, that no one is responsible, that what is happening is not murder or genocide. Marshall's films point no accusing finger, but their premise and conclusion is that this is a tragedy for which no one is completely exempt from guilt—including Marshall himself. His films inscribe his knowledge that his fate is to tell this tragic story, hence that he plays a role within this tragedy, that he, too, is a figure of tragedy, a tragic figure. His powerlessness to avert this people's fate cannot be separated from the tragedy that is their fate, and his.

Gardner's and Marshall's films bear an intimate relationship to one another. Gardner turns to a particular people to make a film that speaks an unspeakable truth about humanity, then moves on. (That humans are nomads is one of these unspeakable truths.) Gardner films others to formulate statements that are really about himself; his films unburden his own heart by creating cruel and tender poetry. But Marshall's films, too, are implicated in the cruelty, as well as the tenderness, that is an alienable part of being human.

Cinema verité's *"Old Masters"*

In the seventies, the "old masters" of American *cinema verité*—Richard Leacock, Donn Alan Pennebaker, Albert and David Maysles, Frederick Wiseman—kept faith with their belief in "cinema truth" by continuing to adhere to the strict *cinema verité* discipline they had practiced in the sixties.

Leacock directed QUEEN OF THE APOLLO (1970), a unique glimpse of a New Orleans debutante at a Mardi Gras ball, and ISABELLA STEWART GARDNER (1977). He was co-cinematographer (with D. A. Pennebaker) on Norman Mailer's MAIDSTONE (1971), and also helped shoot several other relatively major productions. He did most of his filming, however, with the experimental Super-8mm synch-sound rigs he helped to develop, and for his own pleasure and the pleasure of his friends, rather than for public consumption. Leacock's main impact on the world at large, in the seventies, was as a mentor and role model for younger filmmakers.

Pennebaker made several major films during the seventies, although none that rank among his best-known works. They include ONE PM (1971), a collaboration with Jean-Luc Godard about the making of Godard's ONE AM (an aborted film on American radicalism, in which Godard, visible only through a perpetual haze of smoke from his Gauloises, seems more like Peter Sellers *playing* Godard than the real thing); TOWN BLOODY HALL (1972, released in 1979), a record of a tumultuous "Dialogue on Women's Liberation" at New York's Town Hall featuring Germaine Greer, Diana Trilling, and Norman Mailer; THE CHILDREN'S THEATER OF JOHN DONAHUE (1971); KEEP ON ROCKING (1972); ZIGGY STARDUST AND THE SPIDERS FROM MARS (1973); ORIGINAL CAST ALBUM: COMPANY (1978); and THE ENERGY WAR (1979).

In the seventies, Albert and David Maysles were at the top of their form. Their initial film of the decade was GIMME SHELTER (1970), about the Rolling Stones' ill-fated Altamont concert, at which an audience member was killed. CHIRSTO'S VALLEY CURTAIN (Albert and David Maysles and Ellen Giffard, 1974) was the first of their several films about Christo, the visionary artist who wraps buildings and monuments, hangs curtains across landscapes, and so on. GREY GARDENS (Albert and David Maysles, Ellen Hovde, Muffie Meyer, and Susan Froemke, 1975), is a complex film about the relationship of a mother and daughter, relatives of Jacqueline Kennedy Onassis so reclusive they had not left their house in twenty years. THE BURKS OF GEORGIA (1976), made for the Westinghouse-Group W *Six American Families* series, documents the daily life of a poverty-stricken family with thirteen children living in rural Georgia, depicting the family's pride and love for one another and their overriding concern with keeping the family together. And RUNNING FENCE (David Maysles and Albert Maysles and Charlotte

GIMME SHELTER (David and Albert Maysles and Charlotte Zwerin, 1970), the Maysles brothers' film about the Rolling Stones' ill-fated Altamont concert. Dave and Al Maysles, among the earliest masters of cinema verité filmmaking, were at the peak of their form in the seventies.

Zwerin, 1978), follows the Maysles brothers' favorite subject, Christo, as he conceptualizes, builds, and presents a twenty-four-and-a-half-mile long, eighteen-foot-high fence of white fabric across Sonoma and Marin counties.

Of *cinema verité*'s "old masters," however, it was Frederick Wiseman whose work in the seventies was the most widely seen and received the most critical attention. Of all documentary filmmakers, Wiseman has over the years created the body of work most widely recognized as constituting a coherent authorship. Unlike Leacock, Pennebaker, and the Maysles brothers, Wiseman was not a Drew Associates alumnus. After completing law studies at Yale and Harvard, he worked as a lawyer in Paris and taught law at Boston University. His first film, TITICUT FOLLIES (1967), was an unbearably powerful indictment of the inhumanity of the Bridgewater prison. His two other films of the sixties, HIGH SCHOOL (1968) and LAW AND ORDER (1969), achieve the more distanced tone characteristic of his later works, which allows them to be enjoyable even as they retain a sharply critical edge as they study the American institutions that are their subjects, institutions that are in theory committed to freedom yet which operate by imposing strict discipline.

Producing and distributing his films through his own production company, Zipporah Films, Wiseman has enjoyed a regular outlet on public television since the early seventies. During the seventies, he continued to add a film a year to the institutional series that has been his life's work. HOSPITAL (1970) won an Emmy for "Outstanding Achievement in News Documentary Programming." BASIC TRAINING (1971), ESSENE (1972), JUVENILE COURT (1973), PRIMATE (1974), WELFARE (1975), and MEAT (1976)

PRIMATE *(Frederick Wiseman, 1974), like Wiseman's other films of the seventies, is among his most eloquent and devastating critique of American institutions. (Photograph courtesy of Zipporah FIlms.)*

received less public recognition, but are also among his most eloquent and powerful critiques of an American society whose institutions reveal it to be hypocritical and resistant to change.

Although Wiseman's idiosyncratic filmmaking method—he takes sound but does not shoot his own films, for example, and never uses a narrator—serves to an unusual degree to efface his presence from his films; at every moment the viewer is aware of his authorial point-of-view, which is established primarily in the editing, not in the shooting. In their forgoing of a linear narrative, Wiseman's films are often compared to mosaics. However, mosaics are meant to be viewed from a position that allows their pieces to blend seamlessly. Wiseman treats each sequence as a self-contained scene. For each such scene, he prepares a transcript that primarily focuses not on the ways the camera's subjects reveal themselves (or mask themselves) visually, but on what they say, on the ideas that underlie their words, on the tensions or conflicts among these ideas. In putting together successions of scenes, Wiseman edits them in such a way that the transitions bring out the inner logic of each scene, the conflicts of ideas at play within it, and the logical connection between the scenes, the dialectical relationships between their conflicts. For every shot of every sequence, his editing by this means fixes a specific set of logical relationships that define its place and meaning within the work as a whole.

Wiseman has said that as an editor he takes it to be his task to give the viewer enough information to think the film through. And yet thinking the film through means following the film's thinking. Wiseman's filmmaking method respects the viewer's freedom, as it respects the freedom of the people being filmed. But it also locks us and them into rigid structures. Wiseman's films, like the American institutions they study, impose strict discipline even as they affirm freedom. His early films were powerful protests against American institutions, and by the late seventies his authorship had *become* an American institution. This threw it into a state of crisis. Every year saw a new Wiseman film, but works like CANAL ZONE (1977), SINAI FIELD MISSION (1978), and MANOEUVRE (1979) seemed to have a less sharply critical edge than his earlier films. After MODEL (1980), a study of a modeling agency, Wiseman made SERAPHITA'S DIARY (1982), his only fiction film, which sank without a trace. There was a hiatus of three years before he returned to the institutional series that has continued to occupy him. Without denying the gaps that remained between American ideals and American social realities, his films of the eighties and nineties emphasize the remarkable fact that, for all their resistance to change, American institutions do change; indeed, they are instruments of change. Even Wiseman's films have changed. They now acknowledge that the perspective from which they view America, their way of thinking about America, is not outside or above the society they study. (Have they then forfeited their right to protest? Not if America is a free country.)

AN AMERICAN FAMILY

Like Wiseman's films, the controversial AN AMERICAN FAMILY (Craig Gilbert, 1973), whose ten million viewers per episode made it public television's highest-rated program of the seventies, was motivated by its producer's intention to confront American society with truths about itself. Believing that vast changes were occurring in American society, Craig Gilbert proposed to NET a documentary series about a representative American family that would put a truthful view of family life on prime-time television, as opposed to the unrealistic images usually shown. From May 30 to December 31, 1971, Alan and Susan Raymond, devoted followers of the strict *cinema verité* discipline, filmed three hundred hours of 16mm color film—about an hour and a half a day—of the lives of the members of the Loud family of Santa Barbara, California: Pat and William and their children Lance, Kevin, Grant, Delilah, and Michele.[40]

AN AMERICAN FAMILY is a product of a singular moment in the history of public television; it could not have been made earlier, or later. When the new Public Broadcasting System was created in 1969, NET (National Educational Television) merged with New York City's educational station, WNDT-13, to become WNET-13, one of the flagship PBS stations. AN AMERICAN FAMILY was produced by NET and WNET-13 during the brief period, 1970–1973, in which funds for individual PBS programs were available from the Corporation for Public Broadcasting. CPB provided half of the series' $1.2-million budget. The Ford Foundation provided the other half.[41]

The proposal Gilbert submitted to NET and the Ford Foundation envisioned combining *cinema verité* passages with other types of documentary material so as to analyze this family's place in a broad historical context. As it turned out, however, AN AMERICAN FAMILY dispenses with such an analytical apparatus. Although the episodes occasionally use third-person and first person voice-over narration, non-diegetic music, interviews, and home movies, they primarily focus *cinema verité* style on the everyday lives of its family members, which take on the qualities of a television soap opera. In the course of the series, son Lance declares his homosexuality, and parents Bill and Pat separate and decide to divorce. As Jeffrey Ruoff argues, these events, unanticipated by the filmmakers when they chose the Louds, enabled the series as a whole to seem to show life as it is for this particular family, while bringing home the point that the American family itself was in a state of crisis.[42] In illustrating this theme, the series allowed for very different responses, however. Many viewers identified strongly with one or more of the family members. As Ruoff writes, "Pat Loud took up the mantel of the liberated housewife. Her son Lance became a symbol for an entire generation of openly gay men."[43] For viewers who identified with the family, the series showed that the "traditional" American family no longer existed, except on television. For viewers who were harshly critical of the Louds, however, the series demonstrated the urgent need to restore traditional family values. In any case, it is no exaggeration to suggest, as Ruoff does, that in tandem with its contemporary, Norman Lear's iconoclastic network situation comedy *All in the Family*, AN AMERICAN FAMILY did as much as any single television show to change the ways family life is represented in American television, with unfathomable effects on the ways family life in America is actually lived.[44]

Looking Back and Turning Inward

Forgoing the confrontational politics of the sixties and yet keeping faith with their political principles, many documentary filmmakers in the seventies turned to retrospective reflections on history. Examples include I AM SOMEBODY (Madeline Anderson, 1970), a pioneering film by one of the first African-American women to write, produce, and direct major nonfiction films, which chronicles the efforts of a group of South Carolina nurses in the struggle for civil rights in the late sixties; UNION MAIDS (1976), which employs still photographs, found footage, and interviews, in a manner characteristic of innumerable documentaries of the seventies, to portray the role of women within the labor movement in Chicago in the thirties; WITH BABIES AND BANNERS: STORY OF THE WOMEN'S EMERGENCY BRIGADE (Anne Bohlen, Lyn Goldfarb, and Lorraine Gray, 1978), about the role of women in the General Motors Sit-Down Strike of 1936–1937, including interviews with several Brigade members as they met on the fortieth anniversary of the strike and archival footage of the events discussed; THE WOBBLIES (Deborah Shaffer and Stewart Bird, 1979), which sketches the history of the Industrial Workers of the World from its founding in 1905; and THE LIFE AND TIMES OF ROSIE THE RIVETER (Connie Field, 1980), in which several women who worked in the shipyards during World War II recount their experiences at work and offer comments on society's expectations of them during and after the war, their narratives interspersed—in the manner characteristic of seventies documentaries—with War Department films, newsreels, and Hollywood movies made during the period that concerned women working outside the home.

Even hard-hitting political documentaries of the seventies tended to have a retrospective dimension. HEARTS AND MINDS (1974) and THE WAR AT HOME (1979), for example, looked back on the Vietnam War, which had already come to an end. Perhaps more typical of the seventies, though, are films that looked at history from a personal perspective, as did so many of the folkloric films discussed above. The makers of such films combined explorations of history with explorations in the realm of the personal or private, revealing their subjects' often masked feelings, capturing intimate moments in their private lives, and in some cases meditating on the filmmakers' feelings as well, and their relationships to their subjects. (In AN AMERICAN FAMILY, we might note in this context, the first episode announced the parents' breakup. All the episodes that followed showed how the family arrived at their present situation, giving the entire series a retrospective dimension.)

The general tendency for documentary films of the seventies, at once to look back and turn inward, can be appreciated by comparing DON'T LOOK BACK (1967), Pennebaker's classic *cinema verité* chronicle of Bob Dylan's 1965 London tour, with two films about rock performers that book-ended the seventies. As edited by Charlotte Zwerin, GIMME SHELTER, the Maysles brothers' 1970 film about the Rolling Stones' Altamont concert, frames its concert footage with shots of Mick Jagger and other Stones viewing, on a moviola, footage of the killing that took place only a few yards from the stage, footage that the film has just presented to us. Jagger is reflecting, as we are, on the implications of this violent event, which has already happened and which symbolizes for us now, as it already symbolized for him then, the end of the innocent optimism of the sixties. THE LAST WALTZ (1979), Martin Scorsese's elegiac film about the Band's final tour before calling it quits after years on the road, combines diverse kinds of documentary material (live concert footage, *cinema verité*-style observations of the Band members offstage, interviews, archival footage) in the characteristic manner of so many documentaries of the seventies in order to engender a nostalgic meditation on the end of the era we call "the sixties," an era that kept living on, the film suggests, as long as the Band kept on touring.

HARLAN COUNTY, U.S.A.

HARLAN COUNTY, U.S.A. (1976), which won the Academy Award for best documentary feature of 1976, likewise has both a retrospective dimension and an inward-looking aspect. The film documents the strike against the Brookside Mine of the Eastover Mining Company in Harlan County, Kentucky, in the early 1970s. The company's refusal to recognize the miners' decision to allow the United Mine Workers of America to represent them led to the strike, which lasted more than a year and included violent battles between company "gun thugs" and the picketing miners and their "women-folk." Like a number of documentaries of the seventies, HARLAN COUNTY, U.S.A. straddles the gap between two documentary traditions, *cinema verité* and the politically committed protest film, and thereby revises and extends the conventions of both.

HARLAN COUNTY, U.S.A. employs *cinema verité* technique to allow events to speak for themselves scene by scene. However, although there is no narrator, the film alters the strict *cinema verité* discipline by employing written titles, whose authority is not to be questioned, both to inform us of events not captured on film but crucial to the story and to place the film's events in the context of larger struggles by, and within, the mineworkers union. In placing its events in historical context the film unabashedly sides with the miners, who emerge as true heroes and heroines of the working class.

HARLAN COUNTY, U.S.A. (Barbara Kopple, 1976), which won the Academy Award for Best Documentary Feature in 1976, straddles the gap between two documentary traditions, cinema verité *and the politically committed protest film, and thereby revises both traditions.*

In two other ways, as well, the film diverges from strict *cinema verité* discipline. First, folk songs or union songs, such as "Which Side Are You On?" sometimes sung on camera and sometimes not, provide a Greek Chorus-like commentary on the action. The songs are sung by Hazel Dickens, a singer of authority whose weathered face and equally weathered voice mark her as representative of the miners and their families whose faith, endurance, and courage her songs celebrate. The songs thus provide a medium through which the miners are able to speak for themselves within the film; or, rather, a medium through which the miners' wives, mothers, and daughters are able to speak for them, to express their feelings directly to us as it is not ordinarily possible for people to do within a *cinema verité* film. Second, although none of the filmmaking crew ever appears on screen, Barbara Kopple, the director, emerges as an important character. We never see her, but there are several crucial occasions during which others address her and we hear her responses. Among all these earthy Appalachian voices, Kopple's decidedly non-Southern voice stands out. Viewers cannot but be aware that everything on view had to have been filmed, and that in the filming the filmmakers stood shoulder-to-shoulder with the miners and their families, at times putting themselves in harm's way.

Kopple's courage and resourcefulness, manifest within the film, give credence to the credit at the end that acknowledges, before going on to name some of them, "the people of the coal fields who let us become part of their lives and participate in their struggles." These people allowed the filmmakers to participate in their struggles, and the filmmakers' work allows us, too, to participate, at least vicariously. Viewing HARLAN COUNTY, USA, we know which side we are on, and we ponder whether we would be as brave as these miners, or these filmmakers, had we been in their place.

Although HARLAN COUNTY, U.S.A. is in the tradition of the political protest documentary, it modifies that tradition's conventions too. The film's *cinema verité* mode, which enables us to become absorbed in the world of the film as we become absorbed in the worlds of fiction films, transforms Harlan County, making it as much a mythical world as an out-of-the-way corner of the "real" world. The world of HARLAN COUNTY, U.S.A. is and is not our world, the "real" world. In our world conflicts are complex and we cannot easily know which side is right or where we stand. These miners and their families inhabit a world that brutally victimizes those who do not stand up for their rights, but it is also a world where heroism is possible. We would not trade places with these people, but we cannot but envy them their opportunities to prove their courage and their faith. Should they ultimately prevail in their struggles they would join our world, a world in which heroism like theirs is all but impossible, and we would no longer wish to live vicariously through them. HARLAN COUNTY, U.S.A. reveals a place in America but apart from America, real but mythical, where the good fight is still being fought. The pleasure we take in the film reveals that we wish for there to exist such a place. This wish sets us apart from the miners and their families within the film. Insofar as we harbor this wish, we cannot simply be on their side. Nor can Barbara Kopple.

Kopple was in her mid-twenties when she made HARLAN COUNTY, U.S.A. Her youthful sincerity shines through every frame. In allowing her to make this film, the miners and their families allowed her to participate in their heroic struggles. Making the film took courage, as the film attests, but hers was not a heroic struggle in the same sense. Harlan County emerges in the film as a vestige of a simpler world, more brutal but also more romantic than our world, where it is still possible for ordinary men and women to be heroes and heroines, and where filmmaking too can be an heroic enterprise. HARLAN COUNTY, U.S.A. is itself a vestige of the tradition of the political protest documentary. But in its nostalgia for the working-class heroes and heroines that tradition innocently celebrated, and its all but explicit acknowledgment that the world of clear-cut heroes and villains (if it ever really existed) is all but completely past, HARLAN COUNTY, U.S.A. brings the tradition of political protest documentary into the seventies.

Formal Innovations

In looking back and turning inward, documentary filmmakers in the seventies were no more retreating from the formal experimentation of the sixties than they were retreating from their commitment to the principles of social justice. As surely as the pioneering *cinema verité* filmmakers of the sixties, they were experimenting with new techniques, formally as well as thematically charting new territory.

One such formal innovation, to which we have already alluded more than once, was the creation of hybrid forms that bridged the gap between the two dominant documentary forms of the sixties: the "conventional" documentary, whose visuals illustrate assertions made by a "Voice of God" narrator; and the *cinema verité* documentary, which aspires to be as purely observational as possible and whose mode is revelation, as it is in dramatic fiction films, rather than assertion. As has been noted, innumerable documentary films of the seventies juxtaposed *cinema verité* sequences with interviews and sequences composed of other kinds of documentary material (archival footage, home movies, etc.). Often, in such films, filmmakers spoke their own voice-over narrations or allowed people within the films to narrate, so that the narrators speak not as authority figures but as their human selves. Their words and voices at once reveal and mask who they are, as is the case when human beings speak in the "real" world. In interview passages the people speaking (whether to an on-screen or off-screen interviewer or directly to the camera) are often presented not as authoritative experts but as human beings who have their own private motives (which they may have motives for masking) for saying what they say the way they say it in the camera's presence. And when archival footage, home movies, or photographs are employed in such films, this "found footage" tends to take on the revelatory quality of *cinema verité* footage. Emile De Antonio, one of the great originals of the American documentary cinema who did not shoot his films *cinema verité*-style but compiled them out of archival film and television clips and interviews, sometimes spoke contemptuously of *cinema verité*. ("*Cinema verité* is first of all a lie, secondly a childish assumption about the nature of film. . . . Only people without feelings or convictions could even think of making *cinema verité*.")[45] Yet in De Antonio's masterful films (POINT OF ORDER [1963]; RUSH TO JUDGMENT [1967]; IN THE YEAR OF THE PIG [1969]; AMERICA IS HARD TO SEE [1970]; MILHOUSE: A WHITE COMEDY [1972]; PAINTERS PAINTING [1972]; UNDERGROUND [1976]; and IN THE KING OF PRUSSIA [1983]), the mode is revelation, as it is in *cinema verité* films. Clips of Senator Joseph McCarthy or Richard Nixon, originally taken by anonymous television cameramen, placed in the context in which De Antonio places them, engender revelations of character as vivid and compelling as those in any *cinema verité* film (or any Hollywood film, for that matter).

Films of the seventies that combined *cinema verité* passages with interviews and other kinds of documentary material were extending, not repudiating, *cinema verité*. In the best of such films the people interviewed or filmed *cinema verité*-style or addressing us directly in voice-over narrations reveal themselves vividly as characters. What

these people say (and what they leave unsaid) matters within the film because their saying of these words here and now reveals something about who they have been, who they
are, and who they are capable of becoming. They are creatures of history, as we are. If
they have been written out of history, history needs to be rewritten so as to acknowledge
them. That is what such films undertook to do.

Film Portraits

If a single documentary genre epitomized the seventies, it was the film portrait.
Countless documentaries of the period were portraits of individuals, or incorporated
portraits or elements of portraits into their overall form.

The subjects of many film portraits of the seventies were public figures, often artists,
whether contemporaneous or historical personages. Such films include GERTRUDE
STEIN: WHEN THIS YOU SEE, REMEMBER ME (Perry Miller Adato, 1971) and other
films about artists that filmmakers like Perry Miller Adato also made for public televi-
sion, such as GEORGIA O'KEEFFE (Perry Miller Adato, 1977), made for the PBS *The
Originals: Six Woman Artists* series; ANGELA DAVIS: PORTRAIT OF A REVOLUTIONARY
(Yolande du Luart, 1971); THE ITINERARY OF ELIE WIESEL (Charles D. Jones, 1972);
I. F. STONE'S WEEKLY (1973); ANAIS NIN OBSERVED (Robert Snyder, 1974); JANIS
(Howard Alk and Seaton Findlay, 1974); GENERAL IDI AMIN DADA (1975); NEVER
GIVE UP: IMOGEN CUNNINGHAM (Ann Hershey, 1975); THE LIFE AND DEATH OF
FRIDA KAHLO (Karen and David Crommie, 1976); and ELIZABETH SWADOS: THE
GIRL WITH THE INCREDIBLE FEELING (Linda Feferman, 1977).

The subjects of a number of other portrait films of the seventies were people who
walked the thin edge between fame and anonymity. A prominent example was MARJOE
(1972), a portrait of teenage evangelist Marjoe Gortner, which gave its subject a notoriety that he was able to parlay into a moderately successful show business career. Another
popular favorite was ANTONIA: A PORTRAIT OF THE WOMAN (1974). The film is a
touching portrait of Antonia Brico, Judy Collins's music teacher, who had once enjoyed
her fifteen minutes of fame as that novelty of novelties, a world-class female conductor,
but whose career had foundered in an America not yet ready to accept a woman in that
role. ANTONIA was one of the most widely seen documentaries of the seventies. Its popularity led to a revival of Brico's conducting career in the years before her death. Less
widely seen was CHARLEEN (Ross McElwee, 1978), an early film by Ross McElwee,
then a student at the MIT Film Section, about his outspoken friend, Charleen, a poet
who had been a protege of Ezra Pound (and who would steal the show in McElwee's
breakthrough film of the eighties, SHERMAN'S MARCH [1986]). Several film portraits in
the seventies by and about African-American women touch on the relative lack of public recognition accorded to minority and women artists, such as VALERIE: A WOMAN, AN
ARTIST, A PHILOSOPHY OF LIFE! (Monica Freeman, 1975), a portrait of Valerie
Maynard, a New York-based printmaker and sculptor who was at one time Artist-in-
Residence at the Studio Museum in Harlem; CLEMENTINE HUNTER, ARTIST
(Madeline Anderson, 1976); SYVILLA: THEY DANCE TO HER DRUM (Ayoka Chenzira,
1979); and VARNETTE'S WORLD: A STUDY OF A YOUNG ARTIST (Carroll Blue, 1979), a
tribute to visual artist Varnette Honeywood.

In numerous other portrait films, the subjects were anything but public figures. Most
of the films produced under the auspices of Appalshop and the Center for Southern

Folklore can be placed in this category. Other examples include JANIE'S JANIE (Geri Ashur, 1971), which follows a young welfare mother as she struggles to assert her own identity; YUDIE (Mirra Bank, 1974), a portrait of a woman who tells of her life and of growing up on New York's Lower East Side; GREY GARDENS, the 1975 Maysles brothers film about a pair of eccentric recluses, mother and daughter; LITTLE BOY (Danny Lyon, 1977), one of a series of films Danny Lyon made in the seventies about Chicanos and Native Americans; and CHICANA (Sylvia Morales, 1979).

Still other documentaries of the seventies include portraits or elements of portraits of a number of individuals, not just one. I AM SOMEBODY (1970), IT HAPPENS TO US (Amalie Rothschild, 1971), THE WOMAN'S FILM (Louise Alamo, Judy Smith, Ellen Sorin, 1971), ANYTHING YOU WANT TO BE (Liane Brandon, 1971), CHRIS AND BERNIE (Deborah Schaffer and Bonnie Friedman, 1974), MEN'S LIVES (Will Roberts and Josh Hanig, 1975), WE ARE OURSELVES (Ann Hershey, 1976), UNION MAIDS (1976), WITH BABIES AND BANNERS: STORY OF THE WOMEN'S EMERGENCY BRIGADE (1978), TO OURSELVES, OUR SONS, OUR FATHERS: A COLLECTION OF PERSONAL STATEMENTS BY MEN (Michael Chaire and Len Grossman, 1978), GAY WOMEN SPEAK (Laird Sutton, 1979), THE OTHER SIDE (Danny Lyons, 1979), and ROSIE THE RIVETER (1980) are examples of such films, which generally had strong feminist or gay rights messages.

Family Portrait Films

An important group of portrait films of the seventies comprises a genre or subgenre that can be called the "family portrait films." Examples include the films of the *Six American Families* television series. More typical of the period, however, are the numerous documentaries which focus on one or more members of the filmmaker's own family. The Academy Award-winning BEST BOY (1979), which follows the director's retarded, middle-aged cousin Philly over a span of three years, is a prominent member of this latter category. Others include ITALIANAMERICAN (Martin Scorsese, 1974), in which the director's parents talk over dinner at their New York apartment, interweaving their own experiences as Italian Americans with the history of New York itself; AN OLD-FASHIONED WOMAN (Martha Coolidge, 1974), which examines the relationship between the filmmaker and her grandmother; NANA, MOM AND ME (Amalie Rothschild, 1974), which revolves around interactions among the filmmaker, her artist mother, and her grandmother, and reflects on the differing motivations, philosophies, and rivalries that went into shaping their relationships with each other; and JOE AND MAXI (Maxi Cohen and Joel Gold, 1977), about the filmmaker's troubled relationship with her dying father.

Family portrait films such as these, which focus on members of the filmmaker's own family, exemplify a second important formal innovation characteristic of documentaries of the seventies. When the first *cinema verité* filmmakers ventured with their cameras into the world to film human beings going about their lives, they thought of themselves as effecting a liberating break with traditional documentary practices, and with the practices of Hollywood studio filmmaking, too, which they took to be dehumanizing. In turn, many younger documentary filmmakers in the seventies came to feel that the strict *cinema verité* discipline practiced by *cinema verité*'s "old masters" was itself dehumanizing. To wait silently for the camera's subjects to reveal themselves requires filmmakers to efface themselves in ways no child of the sixties was likely to find acceptable. At the same time, it gave filmmakers the power to intrude into the private lives of their sub-

jects without allowing their own privacy to be intruded upon. Many of these younger
cinema verité filmmakers, uncomfortable filming strangers from a position of invisibil-
ity, thus began making films about family members, subjects they knew so intimately
that they found it natural to put themselves and their relationship to their subjects
explicitly into their films. Even as they were filming they would go about their own
everyday lives, conversing with others from their place behind the camera and on occasion allowing others to film them. Who the filmmaker is, what role filming plays within
his or her form of life, how the act of filming affects the filmmaker's own life and the
lives of the people he or she is filming, are questions *internal* to family portrait films like
BEST BOY; ITALIANAMERICAN; NANA, MOM AND ME; and JOE AND MAXI.

When filmmakers film members of their own families, they find themselves with
opportunities (whether wished for or not) to settle old scores. Family portrait films thus
pose especially acutely some of the moral issues that are unavoidable in documentary
filmmaking. Increasingly, documentary filmmakers in the seventies understood it to be
a moral imperative to find ways of acknowledging *within their films* the reality of the act
of filming for both filmmaker and subjects. The challenge is to resolve the conflicts
between the filmmaker's assumption of authorship of the film and the subjects' right to
authorize public revelations about them. Of all the family portrait films of the seventies,
Alfred Guzzetti's FAMILY PORTRAIT SITTINGS (1976) is perhaps the most forthright in
confronting this challenge.[46]

The sound track of FAMILY PORTRAIT SITTINGS incorporates the voices of members of the filmmaker's family reminiscing and reflecting about their lives. This taped

*NANA, MOM AND ME (Amalie Rothschild, 1974), which revolves around interactions
among the filmmaker, her artist mother, and her grandmother, is representative of the
numerous documentaries of the seventies that focus on one or more members of the
filmmaker's own family. (Photograph courtesy of Amalie Rothschild.)*

material is sometimes employed in synch-sound sequences in which the speaker is shown addressing the camera. At other times, the taped voices are accompanied by other kinds of imagery—shots taken through the windshield of a car driving down a dreary Philadelphia street; shots of Abruzzo, Italy; shots of still photographs; home movies; *cinema verité* footage, shot in the present, of family members at work or at family gatherings. Functioning as narrations, the voices together tell the story of the two of the filmmaker's family in America from before the emigration from Italy to the time the film was being made. World historical events such as the large-scale migration of Southern Europeans to America around the turn of the century, the Depression, and World War II figure crucially. The spoken material is also organized thematically. The first part of the film concerns emigration and marriage; the second, childbirth and death; the third, work and politics. This organization by themes, in turn, helps the film chart the concepts through which the family members understand themselves, their relationships, and their world. The film presents this family's place in history from the outside, considering its family as a "case." But the film also posits its own making as a moment *within* the family's history. The author implied by the film is an analytical investigator, but he is also a family member—Alfred, son of Susan and Felix, husband of Deborah, and father of Benjamin. Alfred has the power to decide what will be filmed and where each shot will be placed, but as a character he is subject to the camera's revelations, and as a member of this family his perspective is limited. What then gives this film the authority to speak about, and in the name of, family and film-making? How can Alfred Guzzetti, from his place within his family, create a film that speaks with authority on issues such as what it means to be a family member, an American, a human being, a filmmaker? How can he honor his family without allowing it to dictate to him? How can his family authorize his film without denying his authorship of it? Part of the authority of FAMILY PORTRAIT SITTINGS derives from its form, which enables its author's perspective to emerge from within the family, and to be authorized by the family, even as he claims the work as his own.

Film Diaries

From family portrait films like BEST BOY, ITALIANAMERICAN, AN OLD-FASHIONED WOMAN, NANA, MOM AND ME, JOE AND MAXI or FAMILY PORTRAIT SITTINGS, it is only a short step to the autobiographical or diary film.

One of the most notable of the diary films of the seventies is JOYCE AT 34 (Joyce Chopra and Claudia Weill, 1972), a woman filmmaker's account of her pregnancy and labor and her thoughts about negotiating the unavoidable conflicts between work and mothering. (Taking seriously the film's double authorship, the fact that it is Claudia Weill—a woman, a filmmaker, and a close friend of Joyce Chopra—who shot the film, Helene Keyssar argues persuasively that the film can also be viewed a dialogue between two women about being a woman in the society in which they live.)[47] Another is the avant-garde filmmaker Jonas Mekas's REMINISCENCES OF A JOURNEY TO LITHUANIA (1974). However, the most famous and influential of all diary films remains to this day DAVID HOLZMAN'S DIARY (Jim McBride, 1967), which envisions the filming of one's own life as an act of such folly or hubris that no good can possibly come of it. Ironically, this archetypal diary film is not a documentary at all, but a fiction film posing as a documentary. Undeterred by his friend Jim McBride's cautionary tale, Edward Pincus began the most ambitious of the period's experiments in autobiographical filmmaking. The project resulted in Pincus's monumental DIARIES: 1971–1976 (1981), whose editing was completed ten years after the commencement of shooting, and the brilliant and eloquent LIFE AND OTHER ANXIETIES (Edward Pincus and Steven Ascher, 1977), DIARIES's sequel (although its editing was completed several years earlier).

Far less well-known than Robert Leacock, D. A. Pennebaker, the Maysles brothers, or Frederick Wiseman, Pincus is nonetheless a seminal figure by virtue of his influence as the founder of the MIT Film Section in 1969, over which he and Leacock presided in the seventies; his two books on 16mm filmmaking; his development, with engineer Stuart Cody, of a 16mm documentary rig that made it possible for the first time for the person shooting to take sound as well, dispensing with the need for a sound recordist; and, last but not least, his own films.

As a philosophy graduate student at Harvard in the early sixties, Pincus was struck by the affinity between *cinema verité* and the emphasis, within certain schools of contemporary philosophy, on the ordinary or the everyday. At the height of the civil rights movement, he interrupted his graduate studies and put the ordinary or everyday on hold to travel to Mississippi with his friend David Newman, who took sound, to document the activities of civil rights workers. The resulting film, BLACK NATCHEZ (Edward Pincus and David Newman, 1967), was at once a committed political documentary and a classic instance of a film made in accordance with the strict *cinema verité* discipline.

While Pincus was filming BLACK NATCHEZ, he encountered an African-American man named Panola, the town drunk, who kept hectoring the filmmaker to let him star in a film. Perhaps because he believed he could fit Panola into his larger documentary, perhaps because he thought Panola was such a poignant victim of racial injustice that he could make a separate little film about him, perhaps because liberal guilt made him unable to say no, or perhaps because it was the only way to shut Panola up, Pincus began filming this man who kept insisting that he was a movie star. Panola proved quite uncontainable within the framework of BLACK NATCHEZ, however. He was too self-destructive to be cast as society's victim and too rambunctious to behave like a proper *cinema verité* subject. He kept mugging for the camera, addressing Pincus directly, and finally took control over the filming, telling the filmmaker what to shoot and when to stop shooting. Pincus found his experience filming Panola so disturbing that it was half a decade before he could bring himself to look back on it, to acknowledge what the resulting footage revealed about his subject and about himself. Even then, he gave it to others to edit under his general supervision. As much as any single work, the resulting film, PANOLA (Edward Pincus and David Newman, 1970), shot in the sixties but edited at the threshold of the new decade, at once looks back and turns inward, and can be thought of as inaugurating the American documentary cinema of the seventies. In a similar fashion, DIARIES, which Pincus began shooting in 1971 and did not finish editing until 1981, when the changed filmmaker could look back on a decade of change, can be thought of as summing up the period.

In the devastating long take that culminates PANOLA, the protagonist-subject, obviously drunk, greets the filmmaker and invites or commands him to enter his crumbling shack. Saying "Look! Look!" he directs Pincus to train his camera on the pathetic trappings of his life of poverty, a life that, at least on the outside, could not be more different from the filmmaker's own. In exposing his despair and rage to the camera, Panola is giving a self-conscious performance. Yet he seems so driven by emotions he cannot control that we cannot help but feel that it is indecent to be viewing him like this. Surely,

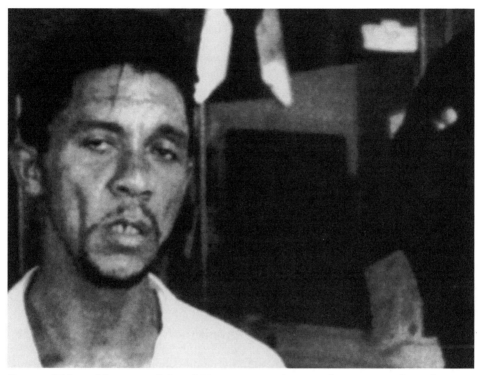

PANOLA (Edward Pincus and David Newman, 1970), as much as any single work, at once looks back and turns inward, and can be thought of as inaugurating the American documentary cinema of the seventies.

Pincus had no right to keep filming Panola in such a state. No less surely, though, Pincus had no right to stop filming in the middle of Panola's performance. When Panola's despair and rage are spent, his performance is complete, and he is satisfied that the camera has captured everything, he says, "Now I have shown you. Go." Covering his eyes, he adds, with great sadness, "You do not know what I am talking about." The scene fades out, and the final credits are accompanied only by the sounds of children playing, reminding us that the world is still out there, that there is still hope.

In his detailed account of this passage, James Lane suggests that Panola's volatile, self-conscious performance "unsuccessfully attempted to draw out the filmmakers from behind the gaze of their direct-cinema camera."[48] Panola's repeated commands to look, Lane writes, provoke "no reaction from the filmmakers other than their continued shooting, indicating their lasting reliance on the noninterventionist principles of direct cinema. The documentarists' refusal to interact is problematized by Panola's persistent enjoining."[49] And yet what Panola persistently enjoins Pincus to do *is* to look, that is, to *film* everything Panola is presenting to the camera.

Panola is calling upon this middle-class white man who has never known privation, who assumes a privileged place behind the camera as if it were his birthright, to acknowledge that he does not know who this black man he is filming really is. America's racist social system must be changed. The *cinema verité* filmmaker's relationship to his subjects, separate and inherently unequal, mirrors that unjust system, so Panola has taken it into his own hands to change it. What gives this passage its Shakespearean depth, however, is the sense that Panola is also talking about, and from, a metaphysical isolation that no merely political change can alter. Panola is calling upon the filmmaker to acknowledge that no one—no one black or white, rich or poor, male or female, adult or child—knows him as he is "on the inside." Every human being is unknown to every other. For Pincus to acknowledge what Panola is talking about, he must acknowledge not only how different they are, but also how they are alike. The filmmaker behind the camera is no less unknown than the camera's subject. When Panola takes off his mask to make his unknownness known, he is not only speaking to Pincus, he is speaking for him, declaring their bond. The filmmaker must find a way within his completed work to acknowledge that bond, or else he will be denying his subject's humanity, and his own.

What Pincus learned from his encounter with Panola was a new understanding of the depth of his own responsibility, as a filmmaker, to his subjects and to himself. His aspiration, when he turned from filming strangers to filming his own life in DIARIES and LIFE AND OTHER ANXIETIES, was to overcome or transcend the inhumanity of the *cinema verité* filmmaker's role by filming the world without withdrawing from the world. His goal was to transform filming itself into an everyday activity. He undertook to film what he was capable of knowing if he was capable of knowing anything, namely, his own everyday experience. To make his form of life knowable, he had to be willing to reveal himself as completely as Panola had, even if this meant speaking and being spoken to when he was behind the camera filming. On occasion he had to let himself be filmed by others, let himself appear on film as the mortal creature of flesh and blood he is.

In DIARIES, as in DAVID HOLZMAN'S DIARY, conflicts emerge between Pincus's project and the demands of his wife, children, parents, lovers, and friends who call upon him to acknowledge them as human beings who are separate from him—and from his project. Nonetheless, by the end of the film it seems that filming his life has helped the filmmaker to become the kind of person on whom no experience is lost. Pincus's filming of his own life seems, at least provisionally, to have come to a good end.

Pincus's gifted MIT students (they were also Robert Leacock's students), such as Steven Ascher, Michel Negroponte, Mark Rance, Ann Schaetzel, Joel DeMott, Robb Moss, and Ross McElwee, went on in the eighties and nineties to make films that sustained Pincus's revisions or extensions of the strict *cinema verité* discipline as exemplified by the filmmaking practice of his colleague, Leacock. In their films, the problematic relationship between filming and living one's life in a fully human way is central, as it is in DIARIES. In their films, too, filmmaking is a romantic quest, and there is, as in Pincus's work, the suggestion that there may be an inhuman aspect to filming one's life *even if* the filmmaker speaks and emerges as a character among others; *even if* people directly address the filmmaker behind the camera; and *even if* the filmmaker becomes a visible, embodied presence in the film. Nonetheless, in these students' work, too, filming comes, at least provisionally, to a good end.

Although DIARIES (1081) and LIFE AND OTHER ANXIETIES (1977) broke with the conventions of the strict *cinema verité* discipline, insofar as their mode was revelation, not assertion, they were transgressing its letter, not its spirit. By making filming a natural part of a human way of life, their aspiration was to make film a bridge, not a barrier, between filmmaker and subject. Yet this was a central aspiration for Leacock as well, and, indeed, for all the "old masters" of *cinema verité*. Leacock's A HAPPY MOTHER'S DAY (1963), after all, culminates emotionally when the stoical Mrs. Fischer, the mother of the film's title, gives a sly grin to the filmmaker's camera, acknowledging their secret bond, and the camera begins to pan from one to another of the good people of Aberdeen, South Dakota, who are gathered together to honor this woman they do not really know; the filmmaker and his subject authorize this silent summation of her world. And Pennebaker's DON'T LOOK BACK (1967) culminates in a gesture of the camera that likewise declares the bond between filmmaker and subject—between Pennebaker, who has embraced a filmmaking practice that makes filming itself an adventure, and the quixotic Bob Dylan, who in his life and art affirms the principle "Don't look back."[50]

In the seventies, documentary filmmakers no longer felt bound by the injunction to not look back. But filming remained an adventure for them. In the eighties and the nineties, that adventure continued.

Conclusion

In the seventies, when the women's movement was in the ascendancy, a community of documentary filmmakers, within a larger community of independent filmmakers, many of them women and many based on college campuses, emerged and became conscious of itself *as* a community. Within the history of documentary film in America, this was a momentous event. The works of these documentary filmmakers, in the seventies, were marked by a general tendency to take on a retrospective dimension, to take the form of reflections on history. They were also marked by a general tendency to further the explorations of the realm of the personal or private, which made *cinema verité* in the sixties such a dramatic departure from the mainstream documentary tradition. Often, documentary films of the seventies combined these two tendencies: reflecting on history from a personal perspective, or reflecting on history's impact on the private lives of individuals. In at once looking back and turning inward, documentaries of the seventies experimented with two key formal innovations. One was the creation of hybrid forms that juxtaposed *cinema verité* sequences with interviews and/or sequences composed of other kinds of documentary material (archival footage, home movies, etc.). The other was a new willingness for filmmakers to converse with others even as they were filming them, breaking the silence that strict *cinema verité* discipline demands and forgoing the pretense that filmmakers are "flies on the wall" whose presence has no effect on the people they are filming.

12

Avant-Garde Cinema
of the Seventies

ROBIN BLAETZ

The writing of any history of the avant-garde in the arts is an undertaking fraught with difficulties due to the esoteric nature of much experimental work. When the art under consideration is the cinema, the problem is magnified. Since the entrance of film studies into the university in the 1960s, mainstream cinema has received increasing critical attention, which has led to the establishment of a canon of films deserving of and receiving ongoing consideration. But avant-garde film has rarely found its way into either film scholarship or undergraduate syllabi. While the following chapter attempts to account for experimental filmmaking practices in the 1970s in the United States, it inevitably omits films of value that have failed to receive either notice or adequate distribution. Furthermore, due partially to growing interest in film by the National Endowment for the Arts and by universities, which occasionally hired and taught the work of avant-garde filmmakers, the 1970s was a decade of tremendous diversity in experimental filmmaking. While filmmakers who had been active for decades—such as Stan Brakhage, James Broughton, or Bruce Conner—continued to work, a new generation of artists influenced by Minimalism, film theory, and feminism exploded the parameters of the avant-garde with a multitude of experimental films.

On December 1, 1970, Anthology Film Archives in New York City opened its doors as the first institution solely dedicated to the preservation, exhibition, and study of avant-garde cinema. Avant-garde film—also identified as underground, experimental, or New American cinema—is generally a 16mm filmmaking practice that occurs outside of the Hollywood-based industry, which it often opposes (purposefully or not) by exploring aspects of cinematic space, time, and perception ignored by mainstream narrative feature film. P. Adams Sitney wrote a manifesto for the Anthology Film Archives that expressed its desire to preserve the great artistic monuments of the cinema just as a museum conserves and presents the other visual arts.[1] With roots going back almost thirty years, to the first films of Maya Deren in the early 1940s, there was plenty of material to organize. The critical enterprise of selecting those films to be saved and maintaining a program of continual reevaluation was assumed by Sitney and filmmakers

James Broughton, Ken Kelman, Peter Kubelka, and Jonas Mekas. The group chose the best print of each film, which was then shown cyclically in the archive's Invisible Cinema, designed by Kubelka with blinders around each of its ninety seats to facilitate the viewer's total concentration in complete darkness and isolation. Neither dubbing nor subtitles were acceptable, and no one was admitted into the screening space once a film had begun. Other public venues for screening the avant-garde in the 1970s came to include the Museum of Modern Art, Film Forum, the Collective for Living Cinema, the Millennium Film Workshop, and the Whitney Museum in New York, as well as several museums and theaters in San Francisco, Chicago, and Minneapolis.

Throughout the 1970s Anthology Film Archives published several books that addressed the films in its collection, including *The Essential Cinema* (1975) and *The Avant-Garde Film Reader* (1978). At the same time, many of the people involved in the archive, as well as graduate students from recently founded cinema studies programs and other interested scholars, contributed critical essays about the avant-garde cinema to journals such as *Film Culture* (edited by Mekas), *Millennium Film Journal*, and *The Cinema News*. Writing on experimental cinema also appeared in *Wide Angle, Camera Obscura, Field of Vision, October, Quarterly Review of Film Studies, Screen, Afterimage*, and *Artforum*. In sum, the 1970s was the first decade to witness the broad acceptance of cinema as a serious art form.

In addition, experimental films that veered from the expectations created by Hollywood narrative cinema were no longer dismissed as incoherent but seen as worthy of attention. The earliest and most influential model for the study of avant-garde cinema was provided by P. Adams Sitney's formalist, descriptive essays and by his indispensable history of experimental cinema in the United States, *Visionary Film* (published 1974; revised and expanded 1978). Other approaches have included the investigation of the relation of the avant-garde to dominant cinema, which is typified by Scott MacDonald's critical essays in the 1970s and his later collections of interviews with filmmakers, and the consideration of this marginal cinema in relation to the larger culture. This latter concern, which came to the fore in the 1980s, is typified by David James's *Allegories of Cinema: American Film in the Sixties* (Bloomington: Indiana University Press, 1989).

Using the work of the writers noted above and diverse essays and reviews about the experimental films of the 1970s, this chapter is organized in a loose chronology. In order not to suggest too narrow an evolution, I address the entire career of a given filmmaker at her or his first introduction. Since the avant-garde tends to be prolific, I examine or note representative films in the text and provide a fuller filmography at the end of the chapter. I begin with a consideration of the 1970s films of filmmakers who started working before 1970, then turn to the work of newer artists who engage film traditions from earlier years, including first-person cinema, the diary film, films that refer to Hollywood, and graphic cinema.[2] Next, I deal with the influential art movements of the 1960s, particularly Minimalism, as they affected the coming decade, and the resulting body of films that have been described as *Structural*. From this point I trace the dominant films and concepts as they appear chronologically, including feminist cinema, work influenced by film theory, and punk film. While I try to be as inclusive as possible, the vagaries of film distribution and reception and the brevity of this chapter will invariably lead to omissions and misrepresentations. The following chronicle is but an introduction to a vast array of films that deserve a much fuller account.

Unlike narrative film, avant-garde cinema cannot be organized or understood as thematically linked to the social or political movements of its day in any direct way. The films of the 1970s in particular are often not *about* anything except cinema itself. David James has described these films as visual events that cannot be recoded into another discursive mode, like criticism.[3] Although any film that challenges the habitual ways of seeing engendered by Hollywood cinema ultimately has a political function, few films have this as their original intention. Sitney describes the trajectory of the American avant-garde since the 1940s as a continual condensation of cinematic form, in which the shape and material of the film become its sole content. While Sitney believes this process leads to what he calls a "mythic encounter" involving the viewer, the film, and the world,[4] others, like James, believe that the cinema of the 1970s fully engages a critique of representation, in which relations between film language and any extra-textual reality are rigorously analyzed and reduced.[5]

Stan Brakhage, who started making films in the 1950s and is the best known and most prolific filmmaker of the American avant-garde, continued his influential work throughout the 1970s. His signature first-person use of the camera, in which the movement of the apparatus defines consciousness itself, was expanded from documenting immediate perception to recording the filmmaker's encounter with memory and the world at large. Brakhage himself best described his lifelong project in the opening lines of his often-reprinted manifesto of 1963, entitled *Metaphors on Vision*: "Imagine an eye unruled by man-made laws of perspective, an eye unprejudiced by compositional logic, an eye which does not respond to the name of everything but which must know each object encountered in life through an adventure of perception. . . . Imagine a world before the 'beginning was the word.'" This union of body and camera that records the very process of experiencing the world regardless of all established codes of visual language is inherently documentary. Brakhage's work as an editor was to join and layer what he had discovered in the world, to suggest in a single work of art the endless correspondences in and the richness of perceptual experience. Since Brakhage's films, which range in length from minutes to many hours, manifest neither thematic unity nor recognizable technique, they are virtually indescribable. However, they reflect the concerns of the seventies to the degree that they use the world as raw material, yet eliminate all recognizable imagery through abstraction.

Sitney describes Brakhage's project, along with those of several of the younger filmmakers of the 1970s including Diana Barrie, Warren Sonbert, Dore O., and even Kenneth Anger, in naming autobiography as the key genre of the avant-garde. Sitney writes in *The Avant-Garde Film Reader* that "the very quest for a cinematic strategy which relates the moments of shooting and editing to the diachronic continuity of the film-maker's life is the true theme of our contemporary avant-garde film."[6] Brakhage's strategy is the assemblage of filmed images of the past—such as home movies, photographs, or albums of photographs—to suggest all that was *not* recorded of any given experience. The juxtaposition between the images that remain of the past and the indescribable depths of individual memory trigger an examination of cinematic representation and its limitations. Several multi-part films made or completed by Brakhage in the early 1970s examine the nature of childhood vision and experience as a universal phenomenon. Both parts of the proposed "The Book of the Film," the four-part SCENES FROM UNDER CHILDHOOD (1967–1970) and the three-part THE WEIR-FALCON SAGA (1970), counter the rigidity of adult vision with the freedom of the child's perception. Much like his earlier work, these films are marked by dazzling speed and fluidity and a trove of visual and thematic correspondences, created by his freely roaming camera, superimposition, dissolves, and rapid editing. The films provide a glimpse into the lost vision of the past, to which the conventional imagery of photographs and home movies can only refer.

The more than fifty films that Brakhage made in the 1970s have been described by Sitney as marked by the "horrors of solipsism."[7] Among these films is a trilogy comprising EYES (1971), DEUS EX (1971), and the best-known THE ACT OF SEEING WITH ONE'S OWN EYES (1971)—for which Brakhage took his first-person camera into a police station, hospital, and morgue, respectively. Influenced by Frederick Wiseman's films about similar institutions, Brakhage attempted to interact in the broader social realm rather than in his preferred domestic sphere—which he had created with his wife, Jane Brakhage, and his children in rural Colorado. Dana Polan has described these films as Brakhage's failed attempt to confront the urban dangers that he had abandoned.[8] The poetic abstraction carried out by distorting lenses, slow motion recording, rapid cutting, and various masking devices could not eliminate the hard facts of violence and death.

The most successful of Brakhage's films of the 1970s are generally thought to be THE RIDDLE OF LUMEN (1972) and especially THE TEXT OF LIGHT (1974). Both films take light as their sole subject and allow any symbolic or referential content to dissolve in color, movement, and shape. THE TEXT OF LIGHT came to be shot through an ashtray extending from the camera lens after Brakhage apparently placed his malfunctioning camera next to an ashtray on a friend's desk and happened to see the novel image that was created.[9] Shooting frame by frame over several months and editing, or composing, in the camera as a way to preserve the actual trail of perception, the film loses all reference to the things of the world except by way of the light and color infusing them. The

THE RIDDLE OF LUMEN by Stan Brakhage (1972) is a study of light in which all referential content dissolves in color, movement, and shape.

viewer senses multiple phenomena—including people, animals, city lights, and land-scapes—but sees them anew. As in all of Brakhage's best work, the world is not tran-scended but instead allowed to reveal all that most viewers have been taught to ignore.

The four films made by Warren Sonbert in the 1970s exhibit a similar concern with exploring the full range of the language of cinema as a means of documenting the film-maker's perceptions of public behavior. CARRIAGE TRADE (1968–1972) consists of hand-held shots of ten to fifteen seconds in length on various stocks of film with myriad light conditions, distances, angles, and focus, which show the world in a montage that reflects Sonbert's perceptual activity. While the spectacular series of images, which are linked according to graphic matches, visual motifs, and thematic connections, refer to recog-nizable things, there is no narrative line. NOBLESSE OBLIGE (1978–1981) continues the use of rapid, elliptical editing and superimposition, yet with a focus on symbols of American democracy that are countered by images of angry people in varied situations and scenes of destruction and disaster. While the film was a response to actual events (the killings of Harvey Milk and George Moscone in San Francisco), it seeks only to sug-gest the wealth of possible related images and perceptions, which are then left to the viewer to connect. Like Brakhage, Sonbert stretches the viewer's sense of the possibili-ties of perceptual activity available in the world.

The Scandinavian filmmaker Gunvor Nelson and the German filmmaker Dore O. both worked in the United States during the 1970s. Nelson's films are largely recognized for their dreamlike lyricism, which in MOON'S POOL (1972) is created through under-water photography of moving bodies that are juxtaposed with shots of landscapes. However, Nelson also made a straightforwardly poetic film about birth, KIRSA NICHOLINA (1970), and the funny and pointed TAKE-OFF (1972), in which the conven-tions of striptease are mocked. However, while Dore O.'s films are also known for their delicate beauty, she worked more closely in the tradition of Brakhage where the world is meaningful to the degree that it engages perceptual activity that can be cinematically conveyed. KASKARA (1974) poetically suggests the nature of summer by dissolving and superimposing images of a landscape through a door and window, thus merging inside and outside with people coming and going.

The degree to which the cinema, as the art of light, is perceived as a way to see the world more deeply is evident in the films released by Kenneth Anger in the 1970s. RABBIT'S MOON, which was made in 1950 but not released until 1971, uses a Pierrot figure who reaches for the moon, and a Columbine, who is revealed by a magic lantern, to suggest literally and metaphorically the desire for and benefits of an ever more focused and brighter light. Yet Anger's larger project, LUCIFER RISING, which he started in the middle of his career in 1966 and finished in 1980, suggests the complex-ity of his relation to both the cinema and the occult. With his simultaneous adoration of and repulsion by Hollywood's excess and star culture, Anger created his demonic Lucifer, as God of Light, to embody this contradiction. David James describes the fig-ure as inhabiting "Anger's cinema as both the figure of its mythology and its basis as for-mal practice and material event. As an agent of Lucifer, Anger documents magic, and his practice is itself magic; his lifework is MAGICK, the cinematograph is his Magical Weapon, and his films are a Magick Lantern Cycle." In other words, Anger celebrates the Lucifer who is both the attractive light and spectacle inherent in film as a material form, and the means through which Hollywood perpetuates its normalizing and repres-sive social vision. The interruption of the sheer beauty of Anger's images—often with disturbing sounds, characters, actions, and editing patterns—forces a continual reappraisal of the institutions of cinema and the ambiguous relations between film, the world, and the unconscious.

While not involved in the occult to the same degree as Anger, Storm de Hirsch was a poet and filmmaker who considered her work to be part of visionary, mystical experience. De Hirsch was active in the 1960s, exploring ritual and dream through the manipulation of the film itself through scratching, painting, and split screen. MY EXPERIMENT IN MEDITATION (1971) continues this tradition with fluid colors and alternating zooms. De Hirsch's later films, some of which are part of her "Hudson River Diary," and others that are made in Super-8 as opposed to the more usual 16mm, are impressionistic documentations of her travels and observations that she calls *cine-sonnets*.

One filmmaker who attempted to remain unknown, thus exemplifying the dilemma of a history of the avant-garde, is Diana Barrie, who made twenty-six films in the 1970s. Scott MacDonald's interview with her in *A Critical Cinema*[10] introduces an artist whose own interests span the concerns of the decade. Her early work not only reflects Anger's interest in dream and occult imagery, but is involved with first-person cinema, in which the camera and the light are intimately tied to the actions of the filmmaker. For example, THE ANNUNCIATION (1973–1974) is a Super-8 film in which the female filmmaker gives light to the Mary figure, who, as a filmic phenomenon, is herself made of light. This film presages several of the key concerns of the decade, including investigations of cinematic form, the use of found footage, and the examination of the cinematic construction of gender and the origins of filmmaking. The visually stunning MY VERSION OF THE FALL (1978) turns to another primal female, Eve, and to the hand-tinting of the early days of the cinema. In the film Barrie reverses the story of the Fall by ending her version in the middle of the actual film and then running it in reverse as both a literal undoing of the text and a metaphoric erasure of one of the basic narratives of Western culture.

A second major form that was explored by filmmakers who started their work in earlier decades and continued into the 1970s is the diary or chronicle film, as distinct from the first-person, more lyrical film described above. Unlike documentary films, in which events in the world are recorded as straightforwardly as possible and edited rhetorically, these films employ a full range of formal devices to document private lives and experiences, political issues in relation to private lives, and the filmmaker's interpretation of broader cultural phenomena. Unlike the documenting of a filmmaker's perceptual experiences in the world, as found in Brakhage's autobiographical films, the diary or chronicle film allows the referential world a more recognizable and conventional presence. Yet James Broughton's observation that "Looking is a grasping act. Seeing is a receiving act," indicates that continuities exist between the two modes of filmmaking.[11]

Broughton, who started working in avant-garde film in San Francisco in the 1940s, is the best known of the poetic autobiographical filmmakers. As a poet and the author of a book of film theory called *Seeing the Light* (1977), Broughton made films that are light-hearted but searching combinations of spoken poetry, images from nature, and theatrical enactment of mythic concepts. At the same time, the camera itself and the cinema's ability to remake the world poetically are ever-present concerns. In HIGH KUKUS (1973), a single image of water that is disturbed by wind, debris, and insects is shown while Broughton's voice-over describes all that cannot be seen in the image, such as the sky, the tree, or the mud below. As Sitney quotes from the film, "Anywhere you look at it,/Said the Camera,/this is the way it is./ . . . /I have no meaning./Said the film,/I just unreel myself."[12] This childlike openness is present in Broughton's best-known film, TESTAMENT (1974), in which the filmmaker tells his life story in reverse to explain his artistic avoca-

This luminous figure from Dreamwood *by James Broughton (1972), embodies the filmmaker's lifelong celebration of the male body.*

tion. Accompanied by the reading of one of his poems, the film includes documentary footage of Broughton's hometown as it celebrates him and sections from several of his older films featuring images that have become iconic in his work, particularly a metallic nude Pan figure who leaps through a meadow. The most powerful sequence in the film is a series of still portraits of Broughton shown in reverse order from old age to infancy that speak movingly of the fragility of life and the power of cinema as an art form.

Broughton began working with the Canadian filmmaker Joel Singer in the late 1970s on a series of films, such as Song of the Godbody (1977), that celebrate the male body, Walt Whitman, and the pleasures derived from cinematically manipulating images of the human body. Singer also made films on his own that were more formal in their concerns. For example, Sliced Light (1976) is a black-and-white film of a landscape that is subordinated as subject matter by the camera's activity. Much like the films of Ernie Gehr discussed below, the pans, swish pans, telephoto shots, zooms, and superimpositions are the real subject of the film.

Two of the pioneers of avant-garde filmmaking who continued working into the 1970s were Sara Kathryn Arledge and Rudy Burkhardt. Arledge made the first experimental dance films in the early 1940s, then returned to make Tender Images (1978) and Interior Gardens, I (1978). Burkhardt, who made the first of his lyrical, often humorous films in 1938 and collaborated with Joseph Cornell in the 1950s, worked on brief, poetic documentaries in the 1970s. Whether the subject observed is a lakefront in Maine in SUMMER (1970), the streets of New York in DOLDRUMS (1972), or the painter Alex Katz in ALEX KATZ PAINTING (1978), Burkhardt's later films are best described as impressionistic collages of recognizable images. With his casual, musing sensibility, Burkhardt believed that if he framed the everyday world in the right way it would speak for itself.

Two lesser known filmmakers working in the 1970s, Tom Chomont and Robert Huot, engaged the personal diary film most rigorously. Chomont, who rarely distributes his films due to their personal nature, used the sparest equipment to make small, meticulous films about, as Scott MacDonald says, "what it is like to *be* Tom Chomont."[13] In the twenty-two artisanal films he made during the decade, Chomont used formal devices such as mirror printing to make emotional experience concrete. As was common to avant-garde artists of this period, Chomont felt that the filming of the banal material world could release what he believed to be a mystical essence. Huot came to cinema from painting, where he started as an Abstract Expressionist and moved to Minimalism. Although he was part of a circle that included Hollis Frampton (who is discussed below), Huot was a diarist who recorded the smallest details of his life with straightforward sincerity. Using the formal limitation of the single roll of film, his serial presentation of the events of his life, which for a time included his relationship with the dancer and choreographer Twyla Tharp, who was then his wife, was free of all narrative drive. The fourteen films that he made in the 1970s convey a sense that the unwinding of time is experienced as both progressive and cyclical.[14]

Freude (Freude Bartlett) was also involved in autobiographical diary filmmaking in the 1970s, as well as in the exhibition and distribution of avant-garde films made in San Francisco. Rejecting the usual system of distributing experimental films through cooperatives, such as Filmmaker's Co-op in New York or Canyon Cinema on the West Coast, her Serious Business Company advocated aggressive marketing of avant-garde film. Printing brochures, assembling film packages, and traveling with the films, Freude attempted to educate the public and earn more money for the filmmakers she represented. As a filmmaker in the 1970s, Freude made five poetic explorations of her daily life that suggest the connections between humans and animals and between life in the home and the natural world. Like others in the autobiographical genre, her films differ from documentary to the extent that they use formal devices such as superimposition, dissolves, and alternations between sound and silence, to express more about the experience of life than is conventionally conveyed through either narrative or *cinema verité* recording of the world.

Perhaps the most personal of the autobiographical filmmakers of the 1970s was the performance artist Carolee Schneemann. Her 1967 film FUSES was the first in a series of works documenting her relationship with another filmmaker, James Tenney (both of whom are featured in several of Brakhage's early films). In this first film and in PLUMB LINE, which was made between 1968 and 1972, Schneemann manipulated the actual film itself in every possible way: painting it, reversing it, splitting and quartering the screen, and superimposing multiple layers of film. In addition, not only is the film the product of a collage of images made in the camera, but it was edited just after it was filmed in order to capture most fully the intensity of the experience. FUSES in particular has had a difficult history, partially due to its explicit erotic content. While most of the small number of avant-garde films made by women have been incorporated into feminist study, Schneemann's work frequently has been dismissed for its unquestioning use of the conventionally beautiful, naked female body and its concentration on a heterosexual love relationship.

Counter to Schneemann's work is that of Anne Severson (now known as Alice Anne Parker) who made NEAR THE BIG CHAKRA in 1972. While Severson's film is at least as sexually explicit as Schneemann's, in showing close-ups of the vulvas of thirty-seven women of all ages over seventeen minutes, its serial presentation and de-eroticizing of the female body made it an icon of early feminist cinema.

Jonas Mekas, one of the founders of Anthology Film Archives and *Film Culture*, made two films that pushed the personal diary film into a broader social realm. In 1971 Mekas made REMINISCENCES OF A JOURNEY TO LITHUANIA, documenting his return to his homeland after living for many years in New York City as a displaced person. While the images in the film are recognizably Lithuanian landscapes and other locations, the film actually documents the very moment of Mekas perceptions of these spaces, as well as his conscious search for significant images. Shots are as short as one frame in length and are made with an incessantly mobile, handheld camera that zooms, cuts, reframes, and pulls focus in tandem with Mekas's shifting attention. Influenced by the filmmaker's commitment to the spontaneity and sincerity of the Beat movement, the camera and in-camera editing mediate Mekas's encounter with his past. LOST, LOST, LOST (1976) continues his autobiographical search for a meaningful life in his adopted country. Using the same techniques to explore both his expatriate and film communities, Mekas suggested the ties between experimental cinema and fully living life, as well as the power of art and the community of artists to facilitate personal renewal. David James quotes a line from the film spoken by Mekas in his distinct, plaintive accent as he wanders through a field: "It was very quiet, like in a church and we were the monks of the order of cinema."[15] Mekas's films document a profound faith in avant-garde cinema as a positive personal, social, and artistic phenomenon.

Located professionally and aesthetically between the work and careers of Mekas and Brakhage is the West Coast filmmaker Bruce Baillie, who also founded the Canyon Film Society, *The Canyon Cinema News*, and the distribution agency Canyon Cinema Cooperative. As an artist documenting the world around him, Baille was most active in the 1960s but completed QUICK BILLY in 1971, and ROSLYN ROMANCE (IS IT REALLY TRUE?) in 1978. The former film is the most extreme example of Baillie's dense layering of images, in which the world is almost totally abstracted into what P. Adams Sitney calls a "pulsating matrix," where beings and things seem to mutate together in a suggestion of birth and death.[16] Baillie's earlier work addressed the tensions between the natural, organic world and the mechanical, urban one by documenting both with the same poetic, fluid style, characterized by graphic matches. His later, more expressive work suggests that the two worlds must be merged cinematically as a means of retraining the viewer's perceptual faculties. ROSLYN ROMANCE extends Baillie's concerns past diary film to suggest a tapestry of time as well as space, in its blending of photographs from the past with the filmic present and its depictions of seasons in transition. In this personal work, the filmmaker, who appears in the film, tries to find a balance between nature and technology (represented here by the cinema itself), ritual and everyday life, and memories of the past versus the lived, fully perceived present.

Among the many filmmakers working in the 1970s who moved from the diary film to experiment with new ways of chronicling the culture at large, as opposed to the self in some relation to the world, is Chick Strand. Strand had been an ethnographic filmmaker before beginning a body of work that uses the full range of cinema's formal devices to analyze the social forces that determine women's lives. Films such as ELASTICITY (1976) and MUJER DE MILFUEGOS (1976) are marked by a ritualistic tone created through repetition, associative editing, slow motion produced through step printing, superimposition, and freeze frames. Where the former film uses found footage to present and parody stereotypical female conduct as a way of suggesting how contemporary female identity is formed, the latter conveys the sense that deeper structures determine behavior. In an isolated, ruined villa, the black-garbed woman in MUJER DE MILFUEGOS is depicted enacting domestic chores such as sweeping as if they are timeless rituals. The mythic quality created by the film's pacing and editing, which is further suggested by red-tinted sequences evoking sex, birth, and death, prevents a simplistically, feminist reading of the film.

After the first-person poetic film and the diary film, the third strain of filmmaking to move into the 1970s from earlier decades comments on Hollywood and popular culture. After making some of the best known films of the early avant-garde, beginning in 1958 with A MOVIE, Bruce Conner continued assembling his stunning compilation films through the 1960s. Conner's short films are made entirely of found footage—which includes entertainment, industrial, and archival films as well as film leader, title sequences, and trailers. Conner's filmmaking consists of editing together unrelated pieces of film according to visual and thematic associations, then creating an equally complex aural track from sound effects and popular music. Unlike the majority of avant-garde filmmakers who mask footage of the modern, industrial world through layering, quick cutting, or the introduction of visual metaphor, Conner works with both the referent depicted in the footage and the status of the footage as a pop culture product. MARILYN TIMES FIVE (1974) loop prints a sequence of a woman, who may be Marilyn Monroe, stripping and singing, "I'm through with love," five times. The repetition deflates the erotic charge of the image, which in turn reveals that the actual subject of the film is not the profilmic event but the formal device. The autobiographical VALSE TRISTE (1978) diverges from all of Conner's other work with its use of fades to suggest causality, the passing of time, and dream. MONGOLOID (1978) captures the world as seen by someone with Down's syndrome, using the device of Conner's COSMIC RAY (1962), in which a popular song provides the structure for the film. (In the early 1970s, Standish Lawder continued the found footage tradition in a number of short compilation films such as DANGLING PARTICIPLE [1970], which uses instructional films, and RAINDANCE [1972], which is composed of footage from an old cartoon showing falling rain.)

A less analytical and more camp attitude toward Hollywood and its products was taken by George Kuchar, who started making films with his brother Mike in the 1950s. The brothers worked in 8mm, with George moving to 16mm in 1966. The nineteen films that Kuchar made in the 1970s were often collaborations with friends who shared an attraction to and repulsion by the glamour of Hollywood in the 1930s and 1940s. The titles of the films suggest their tone, from DEVIL'S CLEAVAGE (1973) to I, AN ACTRESS (1977) to SYMPHONY FOR A SINNER (1979). Scott MacDonald describes Kuchar's devoted audience as loving "to guffaw at the ludicrous costumes and sets, at the outrageous over- and under-acting, at the zaftig leading ladies and the geeky leading men, at the absurd plots and the cheap, raucous mise-en-scène, at the overly melodramatic music."[17] This description could just as easily be applied to the followers of John Waters, who was strongly influenced by George Kuchar. While both filmmakers were interested in the gap between the banality of everyday life and the illusions and desires created by

Hollywood, Waters's approach was more distanced and cynical. Working exclusively in Baltimore with a stable group of actors and technicians and higher budgets, Waters pushed Kuchar's aesthetic into popular culture in six features made in the 1970s. Films such as PINK FLAMINGOES (1972) are full-length narratives that combine intelligent observation, unpretentious humor, and outrageous plots. Waters and his main actor, Divine, were able to shock and offend the audience, while at the same time provoking laughter at their perspicacious audacity.

The fourth and final category of films that began in earlier decades and continued through the 1970s is graphic cinema, which ranges from hand-drawn animation to sophisticated experimentation with computers. James and John Whitney started working in the 1940s with the assumption that both traditional animation and the use of pre-existing music were uncinematic. They were concerned with the formal properties of the medium, including the illusion of movement and depth, light, frame, screen, and editing patterns. James Whitney was particularly interested in the serial presentation of abstract form in patterns of theme and variation. As the titles of his three films from the 1970s indicate, he became increasingly intrigued by Eastern philosophy and practices. He believed that films such as DWIJA (1976), with its loops, superimposition, solarization, and rephotography that dissolve mandala-like form into pure light, manifested the effects of meditation and served as an aid to the practice. John Whitney was a composer of music who applied the mathematical principles of twelve-tone music to the construction of films in computers that he designed. In his five films of the 1970s, ranging from OSAKA (1970) to ARABESQUE (1975), John Whitney transformed complex sound tracks, geometric form, and color into stunning films that seem to defy the two dimensionality of screen space. (Another filmmaker from the early years of animation was Jules Engel, who made three films in the 1970s after beginning his career with Walt Disney in the 1930s.)

Both Stan Vanderbeek and Ed Emshwiller continued the tradition of experimentation with computer-generated cinema in the 1970s. Echoing Maya Deren's original avant-garde films (e.g., RITUAL OF TRANSFIGURED TIME, 1946), both filmmakers turned to dancers to provide the human form that is then manipulated by video and computer techniques through fragmentation and speed adjustment. The attempt to create a dialogue between conventionally conceived and executed art and technology is evident in Van Der Beek's FILM FORM #1 (1970) and Emshwiller's SCAPEMATES (1972). Both films use video to transform the dancer's body and the journey through space by way of color and abstraction. Many of the films of the West Coast filmmaker Scott Bartlett also used computer and electronic manipulation of the image. Taking advantage of earlier work done in the mixing of media, Bartlett's films explore the experimental technique as vocabulary in his varied films. While MEDINA (1972) and GREENFIELD (1977) document the filmmaker's experience of Morocco and a ritual celebration of the summer solstice, respectively, other films take on mythic subjects and/or the nature of perception.

Robert Breer came to graphic cinema in the 1950s as an abstract painter in search of greater dynamism. Using hard-edged abstract animation and brilliant color, Breer's seven quickly-paced films of the 1970s generally explore the perception of depth and scale in film through the interplay of geometric form. FUJI (1973) breaks the pattern to a degree by integrating live-action footage of a man on a train passing by Mt. Fuji, with loose, lyrical drawings of the same imagery. Breer often shows his films in loop format, since he sees them as objects through which to explore the difference between normal and cinematic perception. A second animator to begin work in the 1950s was Larry Jordan, who started his career by finishing six films that had been initiated by Joseph Cornell, and later completing a film about the artist, CORNELL, 1965 (1978). Like his mentor, Jordan was a collage artist who applied the editing techniques of dissolves and superimpositions to brilliantly colored, cut-out imagery, often taken from old steel engravings, to create magical juxtapositions. Jordan's THE RIME OF THE ANCIENT MARINER (1977), which is narrated by Orson Welles, uses engravings by Gustave Doré combined with rich color and inserted imagery of various animals. With its characteristic use of quirky synthesizer sound, the film serves as a good example of Jordan's meticulous and haunting work.

The final filmmaker in this brief analysis of graphic cinema is Jordan Belson, who began with single-frame animation in the 1960s before moving toward Brakhage-like meditations on perception in the 1970s. As David James writes, the geometrical shapes of Belson's films are "kinesthetic optical effects [which] are both produced in response to the visual and visionary experience of altered states of consciousness and used to achieve them."[18] Belson was interested in awakening perceptual activity so that the external world could be understood to lead into an inner realm. MEDITATION (1971) tries to approach the mind's eye by layering circular imagery made of radiating light and water. CHAKRA (1972) uses cosmic imagery that suggests rain, clouds, and planets, while LIGHT (1974) invokes light in motion to suggest that the material phenomena of the world can be united with the consciousness of the perceiver through the agency of cinema.

Working at the same time as the filmmakers who continued their careers into the 1970s from earlier decades, were those artists who were influenced by the broadly-based movement in the arts known as Minimalism. Within the visual arts, Minimalism emerged in the early 1960s as a reaction to the emotive excess of second-generation Abstract Expressionism. Rather than being an articulation of the artist's psyche, the Minimalist art work was a material object, sometimes made of industrial matter, that tended to neither refer to, represent, nor comment on anything outside of itself. Contrary to most notions of artistic creation and skill, the majority of the artist's work involved the determination of the formal system of the piece. What remained was an object with a specific material presence that confronted the viewer at first encounter, with no suggestion that any more could be read from or into the work. In the earliest days of Minimalism, the Austrian filmmaker Peter Kubelka made a series of short formalist films that shared many of these same concerns. Films such as ADEBAR (1956–1957), SCHWECHATER (1957–1958), ARNULF RAINER (1958–1960), and UNSERE AFRIKAREISE (1961–1966) are the medium's most meticulously constructed works of art. While Kubelka's work lacked the requisite absence of content and separation from the artist's hand, its formal concerns presaged the powerful influence that Minimalism was to have on film by the 1970s.

Where painters, sculptors, and dancers had to make an effort to keep the imprint of the artist's hand or body from the work by employing manufacturing processes, commonplace objects, or task-related movements, filmmakers worked with an industrial product from the start. However, film as generally understood was a photographic medium with an assumed reference to things outside itself. The artists who came to be known as *Structural* or *Material* filmmakers found their greatest challenge in foregrounding the chosen form of the film so as to prevent the viewer from inferring reference to a world outside the film, thus preventing a story from being seen as encoded or, worse, recorded. Ernie Gehr, who is discussed below, expressed this new rigorous concept of film in stating: "Film is a real thing and as a real thing is not imitation."[19]

Like Minimalism, Structural filmmaking produced unprecedented amounts of theory and criticism by artists and scholars to explain its purported simplicity. The most important member of the group, Hollis Frampton, took great pains in his work and in his writing to redefine film according to Structural precepts. In a presentation called "Lecture," given on October 30, 1968, Frampton foregrounded form as the topic of the lecture itself and through the material that was presented and performed.[20] A pre-recorded text was played while Frampton, the speaker, operated a projector from the back of the room. The piece was intended to illustrate that self-expression in art was a short-lived phenomenon; that artists are only interested in "reconstructing the fundamental conditions and limits" of their art; and most crucially, that the film being projected during the talk (that is, the light emitted by the empty projector) "is only a rectangle of white light. . . . But it is all films. We can never see *more* within our rectangle, only *less*." Thus, the project of Structural film was the formal delineation of all the possibilities for defining the rectangle of white light through its methodical reduction.

A second major influence on Structural film in the 1970s was Andy Warhol, who made films between 1963 and 1974. Warhol's first films, which the artist conceived himself but had executed by assistants, SLEEP and EAT (1963), are Minimalist works of art in which the titles precisely state what is seen in the film. SLEEP is a six-hour film of a man sleeping, in a fixed-frame film of unedited one-hundred foot rolls that flare every two and three-quarter minutes as they end. EAT, which is forty-five minutes long, uses the same technique to record a man eating a mushroom. These films and the eight-hour EMPIRE (1964), in which a camera records the Empire State Building overnight, overtly challenge the audience to consider the nature of the cinema. Since the films show neither a narrative event nor the perceptual adventures of a filmmaker, the viewer is left to contemplate the form itself. In these films, the formal properties include the effect of light on emulsion, the limitations of the frame, the presence of off-screen space, the brevity of the roll of film, the arbitrariness of film length, and the effect of the camera on the subject. P. Adams Sitney interprets Warhol's films as a direct commentary on American avant-garde cinema. Through parody and reduction, Warhol explodes "the myth of compression and the myth of the filmmaker" embodied by the style, concerns, and persona of a filmmaker like Brakhage. Sitney describes Warhol's legacy to Structural film as the challenge to orchestrate duration by directing "the wandering attention that [triggers] ontological awareness" toward a goal.[21]

Warhol's films became less influential in the avant-garde during the 1970s. His films of the mid-1960s were closer to those of George Kuchar in their fascination with the influence of Hollywood and the performance of the self. Using scripts, sound, zooms, pans, and in-camera editing, films such as THE CHELSEA GIRLS (1966) or BIKE BOY (1967) are more involved with ironic parody of star culture than with the form of the film. By the time the Structural filmmakers had started working, Warhol had very little to do with his films outside of providing the milieu in which they were created. Paul Morrissey wrote, photographed, or directed most of Warhol's work of the 1970s, which were chiefly fragmentary, rough-hewn narratives about Hollywood notions of female glamour and exhibitionism, often performed by transvestites. Finally, with films like ANDY WARHOL'S FRANKENSTEIN (Paul Morrissey, 1974), Warhol simply "presented" a film that had been made by Carlo Ponti's production company as the ultimate fulfillment of his authorial distancing.

The work of artists who were not primarily filmmakers but who used film to document conceptual, body, or earth art were more influential than Warhol by 1970. Yoko Ono, Vito Acconci, and John Baldessari were known for films that recorded or were part of performance pieces, while Robert Smithson recorded his earth work "Spiral Jetty" in a film of the same name in 1970, and Bruce Naumann made ART MAKE-UP: GREEN, BLACK, WHITE, PINK in 1971. In addition, installation artists such as Nam June Paik and Taka Iimura in New York and Pat O'Neill in Los Angeles explored film projection and other aspects of the medium in gallery settings. Through the use of loop prints, the pieces called attention to aspects of duration, the screen, and the light emitted from the projector.

Two of the films of the late 1960s that most influenced the next decade were Tony Conrad's THE FLICKER (1966) and Michael Snow's WAVELENGTH (1967). The former film is clearly about the optical effects of quickly alternating frames of film. With its absence of referentiality or implied significance, it is a purely structural analysis of a single cinematic phenomenon. While Kubelka's ARNULF RAINER (1958–1960), for example, is also a mathematically calculated alternation of black and white frames with a

ONE SECOND IN MONTREAL by Michael Snow (1969) is an early structural film in which over thirty photographs are shown for increasingly long periods of time for half of the film, then in decreasing intervals until the film ends. The viewer's attention wanders between the banal content of the images and the subtle temporal variations between shot lengths.

corresponding sound track, the formal system is hidden from the observer by its complexity. Moreover, Kubelka believed that the film evoked natural images in the viewer's mind.[22] Although Snow's WAVELENGTH displays a similar rigor, its complexity suggests the reasons that Minimalist concepts had to be transformed as they made their way into the cinema.

While films can be made that foreground the material nature of the medium in a rationally constructed, immediately perceivable way, few films can be totally abstract because the cinema is largely a photographic art form. The referential world can have a minimal presence, as does the corridor in Gehr's SERENE VELOCITY (1970), or an arbitrary one, like the barn in Larry Gottheim's BARN RUSHES (1971), but the thing recorded is almost always in some way pertinent to the action of the dominant formal device. In addition, as Paul Arthur and others have indicated, rarely is the complete organizational system of a film immediately graspable by the viewer.[23]

Indeed, very few films can be defined as purely Structural, although the influence of the technique explored in these films has been considerable. In the best of the Structural films and those that follow, Minimalist simplification permits awareness of the often elegant workings of the cinema, which are often so skillfully hidden in narrative film, in relation to content evoked by the imagery.[24] The short films made by the Canadian filmmaker Joyce Weiland in 1967, 1933 and SAILBOAT, epitomize this deceptive simplicity. The sailboat on the ocean depicted in the latter film becomes the ideal device with which to explore the film's topic, the illusion of screen depth.

WAVELENGTH, made by another Canadian filmmaker who strongly influenced experimental film in the United States, was celebrated at its first appearance as a revolutionary artwork. Michael Snow's film is a forty-five minute forward zoom through a loft space that ends on a black-and-white photograph of waves in an ocean, accompanied by an electronic sine wave that becomes increasingly more compressed and shrill. The zoom pauses occasionally so that day turns into night, and things happen in the room, such as the moving of furniture, the collapse of a man, and the making of a telephone call by a distraught woman. But, as P. Adams Sitney suggests, more important than the things that happen in the room are the things that happen *to* the room cinematically through the use of the zoom, superimposition, negatives, and colored gels.[25] This observation strikes the viewer forcefully as less and less of the room remains to be explored. In one of many analyses of the Structural films of the 1970s, Annette Michelson's 1971 essay in *Artforum*, "Toward Snow," elucidates the power of WAVELENGTH and indicates the crucial role that film came to play in the aesthetic discourse of the time. Michelson writes of the experience of Snow's film, "we are proceeding from uncertainty to certainty, as our camera narrows its field, arousing and then resolving our tension of puzzlement as to its ultimate destination, describing in the splendid purity of its one, slow movement, the notion of 'horizon' characteristic of every subjective process and fundamental as a trait of intentionality."[26]

Snow's next two films also explored the workings of a camera set in a single space. BACK AND FORTH (1969) features a camera that swings from side to side and up and down, across an area in which various banal happenings occur, such as a janitor sweeping and a girl reading. As the speed of the camera accelerates, the space is flattened and the events blur until the credits appear and the actions shown in the film return in a series of superimpositions. The film is less a perceptual experience than an illustration of the ways in which the camera can dissolve time. THE CENTRAL REGION (1971) is a three-hour film in which a camera on a tripod designed and programmed by Snow to

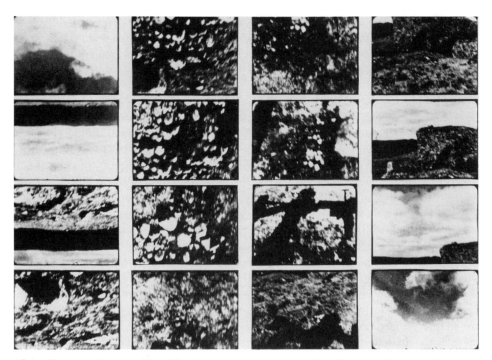

The collection of images filmed by the moving camera in THE CENTRAL REGION *(LA RÉGION CENTRALE) by Michael Snow (1971) has been seen both as a metaphor for the working of consciousness and as a thorough investigation of the mechanics of the cinema.*

move in 360-degree arcs simply records the barren plateau on which it is placed. The viewer is aware of the camera's movement, the tripod, and focus, until the camera's pace increases to make the world, rather than the camera, seem to be in motion. Snow's last major film of the seventies is RAMEAU'S NEPHEW BY DIDEROT (THANX TO DENNIS YOUNG) BY WILMA SCHOEN (1974). Almost five hours long, the film is a comprehensive, serial construct with twenty-four loosely connected episodes that explore every conceivable approach to the combination of sound and image that might be used as a means of representing the world on film.

The most straightforward of all the Structural filmmakers is Ernie Gehr, for whom film is simply light, time, and the illusion of movement, without reference to events in the world or subjectivity. HISTORY (1970) is his purest film. Shot without a lens, the film was exposed to a black cloth then reprinted to reveal the grain of the film, before being shown at sixteen frames per second to emphasize the flicker of the projector. Gehr's best known work is SERENE VELOCITY (1970), in which an empty corridor is shot through the night with a zoom that is altered every four frames, with an ever-increasing ratio and cyclical alterations of exposure, so that the continual optical jolts become ever more extreme. Even though the illusion of distance between the ends of each zoom grows, the eye compensates due to the phenomenon of persistence of vision in order to create the sense of a coherent space. In 1979 Gehr released EUREKA (also known as GEOGRAPHY), which was one of several influential works to use an early film as its raw material. EUREKA is composed of a four-minute film that was made in San Francisco between 1903–1905 of a Hale's Tour trolley car as it makes its way through the city. Each frame of the film is reprinted eight times to extend the event, which makes a pulse of light occur every eight frames. This tactic not only allows the viewer more time to study the chaotic activity of people and traffic in the street, but it emphasizes every sign of deterioration on the film to reveal the emulsion itself. The viewer is made acutely aware of the passage of time and its effects.

Ken Jacobs also worked with an artifact from cinema's earliest years. In addition to his use of three-dimensional film in performance pieces in the 1970s, Jacobs made TOM, TOM, THE PIPER'S SON (1971). The film uses a ten-minute film of the same title shot by Billy Bitzer in 1905, which it re-presents in multiple ways. By running the original film backwards, at different speeds, with shifting focus, and from various distances, countless heretofore unseen elements are revealed. Not only does the viewer see new things in the *mise-en-scène* and performance, but the film itself—as an abstract pattern of light and shadow—is really *seen* for the first time.

One of the more rigorous of the Structural filmmakers was Bill Brand, who also returned to early cinema in an attempt to analyze the materiality of film. Brand's films are often simple explorations of the filmic material itself. RATE OF CHANGE (1972)

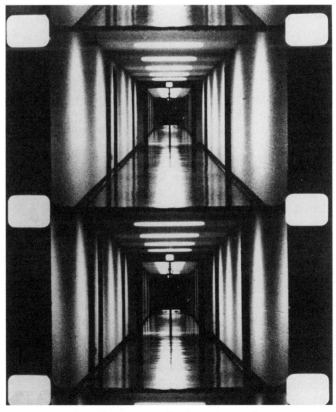

SERENE VELOCITY *by Ernie Gehr (1970) uses the zoom to create a purely cinematic space and time, to explore the way in which persistence of vision creates the illusion of motion in the cinema.*

shows a tinted, frameless strip of celluloid, while TOUCH TONE PHONE FILM (1973) features the motion of a strip of film slipping in the projector. DEMOLITION OF A WALL (1974) is Brand's most complex work. Using six frames from a Lumière film in which a group of men knock over a wall with sledgehammers, Brand explores the place of the frame in the single shot. Each of the six frames is step-printed four times, then every permutation of the six images and the six musical tones accompanying them is played out, which results in 720 changes over a thirty-minute period. Brand's later films used computers to continue his analysis of the basic units of visual language in film and the role of memory in deciphering cinematic structures. (Similar to Brand in his rigor is the American filmmaker Peter Gidal, who worked in the European avant-garde. Gidal's theoretical writing and his strenuously Structural-Material films examined the nature of film, particularly the mobile frame and off-screen space, and the processes of cinematic signification.)

Two influential films of the 1970s made by filmmakers active through the decade were PRODUCTION STILLS (1970) by Morgan Fisher and PRINT GENERATION (1973–1974) by J. J. Murphy. The structure of Fisher's film is determined by the fixing of eight Polaroid images to a white wall, which becomes the white screen when it is projected. The length of the film is determined by the time it takes for a four-hundred foot roll of 16mm film to go through the camera. As one hears the crew talking and sees the white wall/screen, images that are taken from the filming of this very wall during PRODUCTION STILLS appear on the screen. Thus, the film is the documentary of its own production through still and motion photography. J. J. Murphy made quintessentially Minimalist films, in which he formulated an elementary concept and set it in motion. HIGHWAY LANDSCAPE (1971–1972) simply shows a section of highway, with sounds that make one speculate about directionality. PRINT GENERATION is a series of sixty commonplace images in a one-minute loop accompanied by ocean sound, which is reprinted repeatedly. The result of this process of reprinting is that each print contains less and less of the original matter, and consequently of the imagery and sound, of the original film.

Perhaps the most important figure in the avant-garde of the 1970s was Hollis Frampton, who made numerous films and wrote a series of theoretical essays during the decade (published in 1983 as *Circles of Confusion* by the Visual Studies Workshop Press in Rochester, New York). Frampton had been a photographer in New York in the 1960s, where he was part of a circle of serious Minimalist artists that included the sculptor Carl Andre. In addition, he had spent time with Ezra Pound in Washington, D.C., in the late 1950s, where he formulated the notion that visual images could refer to the world without being subservient to narrative. As a theorist and poet of the cinema, Frampton made films that analyze every element of the structure of cinema as well as the nature of photographic representation. More than most Structural filmmakers, Frampton made films that investigated properties as basic as the frame or the illusion of depth, for example, which were also evocative and moving.

In the essay "A Pentagram for Conjuring the Narrative," Frampton asks, "what are the irreducible axioms of that part of thought we call the art of film?" He likens film to the waterfall and the gas jet, which are not things but "stable patterns of energy" that have a characteristic shape in space and time.[27] The boundaries that define film as such are the frame and the photographic illusion, with the latter due to the assumption that every photograph implies the existence of some actual phenomenon.

ZORN'S LEMMA by Hollis Frampton (1970) systematically examines the processes of signification used in the visual and aural tracks of the cinema and reveals the degree to which any filmic image exceeds the attempt to translate it into language.

Frampton makes the important distinction that the photographic illusion is not a representation, since any photograph is an abstraction of its original matter. Finally, since it occurs in time, every film contains at least the narrative of its own making. Another essay in *Circles of Confusion*, entitled "For a Metahistory of Film: Commonplace Notes and Hypotheses," suggests that all cinema contains references to the medium's history and that Frampton's project is the making of all the films that need to be made to complete this history.

In the late 1960s, Frampton made a series of films with titles such as Surface Tension (1968) and Palindrome (1969) that refer to academic disciplines that interested him, physics and linguistics respectively. Zorn's Lemma (1970), which takes its title from mathematical set theory, is one of Frampton's best known works. Over an hour's time, each of the film's three sections explores possibilities for the creation of both cinematic language and meaning. The first part is a dark screen with voices rhythmically reading the *Bay State Primer*, an old-fashioned text that was designed to simultaneously teach the alphabet, grammar, and Christian dogma. The central section is longest and is a silent serial presentation in which the twenty-four letters of the Latin alphabet (with I/J and U/V combined) appear for a second at a time, photographed for the most part from existing signs in New York City. In arbitrary order and at irregular intervals, each letter is replaced by an image, which then takes the letter's spot in the alphabet. For example, a shot of a fire burning replaces each regular occurrence of the letter X, while the painting of a room and the peeling of a tangerine appear in place of other letters. This rhythmic, preordained process, which is also a game of guessing and remembering, teaches that although one can read the manifold properties of the shot and the sequence, cinema cannot be reduced to language. The final segment shows a couple walking into deep space in a snowstorm while women's voices metronomically read one word at a time from a medieval text called *On Light, or the Ingression of Forms*. The words are made meaningless by the reading style, with the film ending as the people finally disappear into the snow-filled distance and the screen becomes the pure white rectangle that is, for Frampton, the most complete film.

Between 1971 and 1972, Frampton made a series of seven films entitled "Hapex Legomena," which is a term from philology referring to those words of which only a single instance survives in all the ancient textual sources, so that the meaning must be inferred through its specific context. Each film investigates one aspect of the material of cinema, with (Nostalgia) [sic] (1971), the first part, considering the nature of the photographic illusion, the relation of still and motion photography, and the relation of sound and image. In the film, an autobiographical text describing a series of photographs taken by Frampton is spoken by Michael Snow. After appearing for several seconds, each photograph is seen to be lying on a hot-plate that proceeds to imprint its coiled form before gradually burning the photograph to a crisp. Thus the property of motion, which defines the cinema, does not occur in connection with any narrative but only in relation to the actual photographic paper. This procedure also makes the concrete photograph doubly ephemeral by turning it into cinema, which only exists in the instance of projection, and by burning it. Moreover, one soon realizes that the aural text describes not what is seen, but the next photograph in the series. The viewer then must both accumulate and remember visual imagery in preparation for the next reading, while recalling the visuals of the previous image in accordance with what is being heard. Filled as it is with irony, unintentional associations, and parodies of the art world, the film typifies Frampton's investigations of film.

The other sections of "Hapex Legomena" include POETIC JUSTICE (1972), which considers the generic film script through having an actual script read as it lies on a table; CRITICAL MASS (1973), about editing between sound and image; TRAVELLING MATTE (1971), about framing; ORDINARY MATTER (1972), about the projector and stop motion; REMOTE CONTROL (1972), about the relation between video and film; and SPECIAL EFFECTS (1972), which ponders the powerful desire to find significance in the most minimal image. Between 1972 and his death in 1984, Frampton worked on another body of work that he called "The Magellan Cycle." The unfinished piece consists of over twenty-five films of various lengths that were to be shown over a year and a day, in segments ranging from very short films to several longer films intended for the solstices and equinoxes. The thirty-six hours of film in the completed film cycle explore epic themes conceptually and expressively, without recourse to narrative, in sections with titles such as: STRAITS OF MAGELLAN: DRAFTS & FRAGMENTS (1974), and THE BIRTH OF MAGELLAN: DREAMS OF MAGELLAN (DREAM 1: MATRIX) (1979), and LAMENTATIONS. In an extensive essay and an interview with Frampton concerning the films, William Simon suggests that the films teach its viewers how to interpret in the act of viewing, and calls "The Magellan Cycle" a utopian, "grammatically complete synopsis of the [infinite cinema]."[28]

While Frampton, Snow, Gehr, and others mentioned above were concerned with the material and structure of film and the relation of film to language, another group of filmmakers was interested in the relation of film structure to perception. Paul Sharits made the first color flicker films in the late 1960s, such as N:O:T:H:I:N:G (1968) and T,O,U,C,H,I,N,G, (1968) with the sole intention of affecting the consciousness of the viewer by working with cinema as light. The alternating colors in the films soften the cuts and frequently produce, in the viewer's mind, pulsations of colors that are not actually present. Sharits also uses recognizable imagery in his films, which he empties of meaning through the flicker effect, superimposition, and rephotography from the screen that distorts and blurs. In 1970, Sharits made S:TREAM:S:S:ECTION:S:ECTION:S:S:ECTIONED, which features female voices repeating the word "exochorion" in counterpoint, along with scratched color footage of moving water. As the words begin to metamorphose into other words and phrases, and as the eye shifts from seeing only depth in flowing water to seeing only the surface of the film in the scratched emulsion, the film produces extraordinary perceptual experiences. In over fifteen films, with titles like ANALYTICAL STUDIES I: THE FILM FRAME (1971–1976), and several installations, Sharits spent the 1970s analyzing the perceptual effects of the most basic aspects of cinema.

In the same years, George Landow (also known as Owen Land) made films that questioned not only the formal means through which film induces psychological states, but also the ways that film manipulates the audience's logical responses. As the title of his 1971 film REMEDIAL READING COMPREHENSION suggests, Landow believes that part of the project of the avant-garde is to undo commonplace assumptions about film in relation to concrete reality and authority. With characteristic irony, this film combines found color test footage; a faked commercial about rice containing the phrase: "suppose your name is Madge and you have just cooked some rice"; flashes of text in a speed-reading manual; a sleeping woman whose dream appears as a comic book word balloon; and a rephotographed image of the filmmaker running, with the superimposed words: "This Is A Film About You . . . . Not About Its Maker." The issue of address is central to the film. The viewer must consider whether or not to assume the position of the "you" of the film, which in turn determines whether the film is understood to represent the world in a conventional way or to challenge film's relation to reality. (A slightly anomalous film in the larger career of the San Francisco filmmaker Robert Nelson, called BLEU SHUT [1970], shows similar concerns. Through the use of grids, buzzer sounds, mock commercials, and a timing clock in the corner of the frame, Nelson parodies television game shows and their relation to consumerism.)

Landow's 1976 film NEW IMPROVED INSTITUTIONAL QUALITY: IN THE ENVIRONMENT OF LIQUIDS AND NASALS A PARASITIC VOWEL SOMETIMES DEVELOPS most directly addresses the ways in which film reflects and participates in authoritarian modes of learning, as well as the tendency to condense real experience and memory into film-like stories. Unlike the first version of this film (1969), in which the viewer took an absurd I.Q. test, in this version an older man responds to a voice tonally addressed to a young child by obeying its orders. The audience observes and shares the man's confusion and paralysis in reaction to ambiguous directions like: "answer the telephone, put a number four on what you would touch," when a telephone is heard ringing on the film's sound track. Landow forces the viewer to participate in the film through his mode of address, which provides a visceral sense of the degree to which the representational strategies of narrative film are equated with reality.

Although the best known experimental films of the 1970s are those made by the Structural filmmakers who dealt methodically either with pure form or with the capabilities of cinema's formal properties to evoke perceptual experience, many other filmmakers experimented with the medium during the decade. One tendency of the period is exemplified by Larry Gottheim, who made a series of short, meticulously planned formal films about the experience of perception. For example, FOG LINE (1970) is a single fixed shot of a meadow in which mist slowly rises and alters the graininess of the image, the color, and the focus of the visible world. BARN RUSHES (1971) uses a series of camera movements, particularly a leftward track with a rightward pan, to film the side of a barn. The cinematic processes change the viewer's perception of the world; the barn jumps in the frame as it shimmers and blurs in the changing light. Barry Gerson worked in a similar mode, in which aspects of the everyday world are delicately considered through cinematic properties such as the play of light or the adjustment of focus. INVERSION (1973), like many of Gerson's brief films, is composed around a window to suggest the layering and merging of different kinds of space. Gerson pays careful attention to the phenomenal world, and the illusions it produces, as a way of suggesting a more spiritual realm beneath it.

Other filmmakers of the decade who received critical attention include James Benning and Ken Kobland. Benning made a series of films that formally document the midwestern industrial landscape through the exploration of depth, scale, color, and motion. ONE WAY BOOGIE-WOOGIE (1977) lives up to its Mondrian-inspired title in its use of objects like cars or signs as flat blocks of color in a series of sixty, one-minute shots accompanied by a sound track of radio and industrial noise. Ken Kobland made a number of films in the late 1970s that use more unusual cinematic techniques to explore space, often with a sense of humor. FRAME (1976) plays with flat versus deep space and off-screen space through the blue-screen process, while NEAR AND FAR/NOW AND THEN (1979) layers swish pans of fall scenery with postcards held in front of the camera by the filmmaker's hands, accompanied by magisterial music and a combination of cartoon and ambient sound.

Indicative of the diversity of filmmaking in the 1970s is the fact that Hollis Frampton programmed the 29th of February, in the year-long "Magellan Cycle," to show any one of the films of Yvonne Rainer. Although Rainer and Frampton both have deep roots in Minimalism and are considered to be involved in the Structural project, Frampton felt that Rainer's work was the direct opposite of his, due to her concern with narrative.[29] Rainer was a choreographer who brought Minimalism to dance, particularly through a series of performances in the Judson Church in New York in the early 1960s. In place of the theatricality and display of skill characteristic of traditional dance, Rainer worked with a series of movement tasks that involved improvisation and ordinary actions, as well as spoken texts and film. As concerns with narrative, emotion, and the forms of classical Hollywood cinema began to dominate her work, Rainer turned to filmmaking. However, it was not until the end of the decade that she stopped using the stylized performing body as the principal tool in her films.

After making a series of short dance films in the late 1960s, Rainer made her first longer, narrative work in 1972, entitled LIVES OF PERFORMERS. The film is a collage of dances, photographs of performances, improvisations, commentary, and a performance based on stills from the 1928 film by the German director G. W. Pabst, PANDORA'S BOX. Rainer intended this episodic juxtaposition of material from her own life, particularly her romantic relationships, and conventional representations of similar material to highlight the ways in which the subject is created in language. Because of her interest in melodrama, female experience, and sexist representation, as well as the new complex images of women that she had created, feminists immediately laid claim to Rainer's

JOURNEYS FROM BERLIN/1971 *by Yvonne Rainer (1979) challenges filmic narration through the use of episodic structure, indeterminate spaces, and the juxtaposition of fiction and documentary to reconcile personal involvement with radical politics, feminism, and psychoanalysis. (Photograph courtesy of Zeitgeist Films.)*

films. However, Rainer asserted in these early years that her work was about the possibilities for structuring content, not about the content itself. The well-known sequence in FILM ABOUT A WOMAN WHO . . . (1974), called "An Emotional Accretion in 48 Steps," supports Rainer's argument. With a love affair as its subject matter, two characters woodenly perform forty-eight possible ways of relating to one another in discrete, preordained segments. Multiple formal possibilities for behavior are explored in relation to sound, address, performance style, and composition in the frame.

By the end of the 1970s, the importance of Rainer's work in feminist film studies, the influence of her deadpan style in relation to melodrama, her complex use of written and spoken text, and her commitment to emotional and experiential concerns were widely recognized. Unlike her male counterparts in Minimalist-inspired film, Rainer (as well as her director of photography, filmmaker Babette Mangolte) used film self-reflexively, in order to question representation, and politically, to examine the repercussions of Hollywood's dominance. JOURNEYS FROM BERLIN/1971 (1979) is a three-hour film that challenges conventional means of filmic narration through episodic construction, destabilized space, the interplay of fiction and documentary, and the use of several performers per character. The film includes long psychoanalytic sections with several therapists, diary readings, a long tracking shot across a crowded mantelpiece, and documentary shots of the Berlin Wall, Stonehenge, New York, and Europe seen from a moving train. However, it is chiefly committed to exploring the relationships among feminism, psychoanalysis, politics, personal needs and memories, and morality. The film is purposefully difficult and irreconcilable, which makes the spectator attentive and suggests the insolubility of the dilemmas it presents. In particular, the question remains as to how one lives morally in an era of political violence, when the courage of others provides models of behavior that are both extraordinary and ambiguous.

Rainer's films helped to end the Structural era of avant-garde filmmaking in the 1970s by exhibiting a concern with content. Other influential filmmakers in the transition include the Belgian Chantal Ackerman, who made NEWS FROM HOME in New York in 1976. This film catalogs the sights of the city in straightforward long takes, which are modified by the reading of letters from the filmmaker to her mother in Belgium. Outside of Rainer's work, most experimental films of the early to mid-1970s were divorced from social and political life in the United States. The careful exploration of the medium seemed to preclude concern with the era's multiple political assassinations, the Vietnam War, Watergate, and increasing activity in the Civil Rights and Feminist movements. The avant-garde's concern with perceptual experience, mystical states of consciousness, and logical puzzles investigating cinematic form waned as the decade ended.[30] In the late-1970s, the avant-garde turned to documentary, autobiography, and punk filmmaking in an effort to comment on the larger social and political sphere, in addition to continuing its investigation of the language of cinema.

Marjorie Keller made a number of films throughout the decade that follow this trajectory. Keller's films explore the nature of the medium through sound/image interplay, shifts in focus, and rapid editing of thematically and visually associated imagery. The films range in tone and appearance from Brakhage-like flurries of indistinct images to echoes of Landow's humorous reconstructions to Rainer-like documentary footage. What is different and consistent in Keller's films is a concern with autobiography and social situations. MISCONCEPTION (1973–1977) is a formally complex combination of imagery and sound associated with the pregnancy and childbirth experienced by Keller's sister. While the film is a personal tribute to her sister and a pointed commentary on

Brakhage's lyrical childbirth films of the early 1960s, it is also about misguided and confusing cultural conceptions about birth. Also working throughout the decade was Barbara Hammer, who produced a body of visually compelling films about lesbian experiences and goddess imagery that has continued to grow. Finally, Su Friedrich made COOL HANDS, WARM HEART in 1979, a film that documents women performing personal hygiene rituals in public spaces, which was the first in a series of rigorous, formally challenging films about women's contradictory relation to political and social history.

The increased attention paid to women filmmakers of the past and the growing number of women making films was closely connected with the rise in feminist film theory that was precipitated by Laura Mulvey's 1975 *Screen* article, "Visual Pleasure and Narrative Cinema." The psychoanalytically inclined essay called attention to the fact that, despite decades of formal experimentation in the cinema, women in avant-garde as well as Hollywood films continued to play the role of non-acting object of the male gaze. David James believes that the writing of feminist theory was itself a "subcultural practice of cinema," which in turn led to a search in the next decade for a new kind of film language.[31] Mulvey had called for a counter-cinema, in the tradition of the "feminine writing" of French feminists such as Luce Irigaray and Hélène Cixous. This alternative and thus difficult filmmaking practice was intended to subvert the binary structures of patriarchy. While Friedrich, as well as Jackie Raynal and Leslie Thornton, responded to this call in various ways at the end of the decade, the avant-garde of the 1980s actually saw the rise of feminist filmmaking on a large scale. (The only film made by the collective of film theorists that included Anthony McCall, Claire Pajaczkowska, Andrew Tyndall, and Jane Weinstock, was SIGMUND FREUD'S DORA [1979], which encapsulates the concerns of the time. Investigating one of Freud's key cases and the facts surrounding it, the film also explores the silent and passive place of women in Hollywood representation, the mechanics of the gaze in narrative film, and women's social roles. This rigorous and poetic film provided a model for both filmmakers and theorists during the next decade.)

Other filmmakers were inspired by elements of film theory that were not necessarily feminist. After his work in New York University's cinema studies department, Manuel De Landa made THE ITCH SCRATCH ITCH CYCLE in 1976, which explores the way in which filmic space is created through shot/counter shot, in a story about a confrontation between a man and a woman. DeLanda was also interested in documenting and commenting on the dirtier aspects of urban New York in films such as ISMISM (1979). This concern with the life of the street characterized the filmmaking trend of the mid-to-late 1970s known variously as No Wave, Punk, or Super-8, which can be understood to be avant-garde to the extent that it rejects commercial cinema. Filmmakers such as Beth B. and Scott B., Vivienne Dick, Amos Poe, and many others rejected the poetic, personal, and art world affiliations of the traditional avant-garde. They used cheap equipment—which they learned to use in the act of filming—to make gritty, primitive, socially-aware narratives about life on the streets, which they then screened in bars and clubs. The influences they claimed were B-level *film noir* of the 1940s, as well as Warhol, the Kuchars, Anger, and Jack Smith's outrageous orgy film FLAMING CREATURES (1963).

Beth B. and Scott B. collaborated on a number of anti-commercial and purportedly anti-avant-garde films. BLACK BOX (1978) is about a man who is obsessed with the television show *Mission Impossible* and is subsequently captured by thugs who torture him in a black box. Before the film ends, the viewers are subjected to the sounds and lights experienced in the black box. Other experiments in form included a weekly punk melodrama of 1979 called THE OFFENDERS, which was screened between musical sets at the New York club, Max's Kansas City. The Irish filmmaker Vivienne Dick was known in the 1970s for spontaneous, collaborative films in which the camera participates to invoke confession and to combine urban sites through in-camera editing. Single rolls of unedited Super-8 sound film structure the 1978 GUÉRILLÈRE TALKS, while SHE HAD HER GUN ALL READY (1978) uses a handheld camera to create the tension in a drama about two women.

Eric Mitchell's KIDNAPPED (1978) seems the most appropriate example of the raw personal films created with the Super-8 sound cameras that became widely available to consumers in 1974. Mitchell's hour-long film of unedited, aimless pans of his punk friends hanging around his slum apartment pretending to be terrorists has been described as a "1960s underground movie happening today."[32] Mitchell's self-reflexive film marks an ironic reverse trajectory by returning to a classic Warhol situation, but with a complete rejection of the ambiguous glamour of Hollywood that inspired Warhol. Due to the social and political context of its introduction in the 1970s, Super-8 film-making tended to document the grittier aspects of urban life in films by Becky Johnston, Paula Gladstone, or Dave Lee. Other filmmakers, such as Ericka Beckman or Greg Sharits, used the freedom given by the small camera to create special effects in and out of the camera. While Beckman created dreamscapes through superimposing fragments of images, Sharits made more formal films by superimposing lights and buildings.

Avant-garde filmmaking in the United States in the 1970s is part of the coming of age of cinema itself as a fully developed, malleable art form. The Structural filmmakers, the graphic artists, and filmmakers influenced by feminist film theory fully and brilliantly articulated the formal parameters of cinema as well as the ideological implications of conventional practices. The lyrical and autobiographical filmmakers who had started their work in earlier decades, as well as the iconoclastic No Wave filmmakers of the late 1970s, reinforced the notion that film can be a personal as well as an institutional prac-tice. The results of the experimentation of the 1970s have been the acceptance of film as a field of study, the recognition of the cultural influence of the cinema, and the cata-loguing of the vocabulary of cinema for the study of film and for the next generation of filmmakers.

Avant-Garde Cinema Filmography

Acconci, Vito
SEE THROUGH, 1970

Ackerman, Chantal
NEWS FROM HOME, 1976

Anger, Kenneth
RABBIT'S MOON, 1972
LUCIFER RISING, 1966–80

Arledge, Sara Kathryn
INTROSPECTION, 1941–1946
TENDER IMAGES, 1978
INTERIOR GARDENS, I, 1978

B., Beth and Scott B.
G-MAN, 1978
BLACK BOX, 1978
LETTERS TO DAD, 1979
THE OFFENDERS, 1979

Baillie, Bruce
QUICK BILLY, 1967–1970
ROSLYN ROMANCE (IS IT REALLY
    TRUE?), 1978

Baldessari, John
SCRIPT, 1973

Ball, Gordon
FATHER MOVIE, 1977
SITTING, 1977
ENTHUSIASM, 1979

Barrie, Diana
THE ANNUNCIATION, 1973–1974
MY VERSION OF THE FALL, 1978

Bartlett, Scott
LOVEMAKING, 1970
SERPENT, 1971
1970, 1972
MEDINA, 1972
SOUND OF ONE, 1976
GREENFIELD, 1977
HEAVY METAL, 1979

Beckman, Ericka
WHITE MAN HAS CLEAN HANDS,
    1977
WE IMITATE; WE BREAK-UP, 1978
THE BROKEN RULE, 1979
OUT OF HAND, 1980

Belson, Jordan
WORLD, 1970
COSMOS, 1971
MEDITATION, 1971
CHAKRA, 1972
LIGHT, 1974
CYCLES, 1975
MUSIC OF THE SPHERES, 1977

Benning, James
11×14, 1976
ONE WAY BOOGIE-WOOGIE, 1977
GRAND OPERA, 1978

Brakhage, Stan
SCENES FROM UNDER CHILDHOOD,
    1967–1970
THE ANIMALS OF EDEN AND
    AFTER, 1970
THE MACHINE OF EDEN, 1970
THE WEIR-FALCON SAGA, 1970
WESTERN HISTORY, 1971
Pittsburgh Trilogy:
    THE ACT OF SEEING WITH ONE'S
        OWN EYES, 1971
    EYES, 1971
    DEUS EX, 1971
ANGELS, 1971
DOOR, 1971
FOX FIRE CHILD WATCH, 1971
THE PEACEABLE KINGDOM, 1971
SEXUAL MEDITATION: ROOM WITH
    VIEW, 1972
SEXUAL MEDITATION: FAUN'S
    ROOM, YALE, 1972
SEXUAL MEDITATION: OFFICE
    SUITE, 1972
SEXUAL MEDITATION: HOTEL,
    1972
SEXUAL MEDITATION: OPEN FIELD,
    1972
THE PRESENCE, 1972
THE PROCESS, 1972
THE RIDDLE OF LUMEN, 1972
THE SHORES OF PHOS: A FABLE,
    1972
THE WOLD SHADOW, 1972
SINCERITY I, 1973
AQUARIEN, 1974
CLANCY, 1974
DOMINION, 1974
FLIGHT, 1974
"HE WAS BORN HE SUFFERED, HE
    DIED," 1974
HYMN TO HER, 1974
SKEIN, 1974
SOL, 1974
STAR GARDEN, 1974
THE STARS ARE BEAUTIFUL, 1974
THE TEXT OF LIGHT, 1974
SHORT FILMS, 1–10, 1975
SINCERITY II, 1975
SHORT FILMS, 1–4 1976

SUPER 8 FILMS (10), 1976
TRAGOEDIA, 1976
THE DOMAIN OF THE MOMENT,
    1977
THE GOVERNOR, 1977
BIRD, 1978
BURIAL PATH, 1978
CENTRE, 1978
PURITY, AND AFTER, 1978
SINCERITY III, 1978
SLUICE, 1978
DUPLICITY I & II, 1978
NIGHTMARE SERIES, 1978
THOT-FAL'N, 1978
CREATION, 1979

Brand, Bill
TREE, 1970
ALWAYS OPEN/NEVER CLOSED,
    1971
PONG PING PONG, 1971
RATE OF CHANGE, 1972
ZIP TONE CAT TUNE, 1972
MOMENT, 1972
TOUCH TONE PHONE FILM, 1973
"Acts of Light":
    RATE OF CHANGE, 1972
    ANGULAR MOMENTUM, 1973
    CIRCLES OF CONFUSION, 1974
DEMOLITION OF A WALL, 1974
THE TRAIL TO KOSKINO, HIS FIRST
    HUNT, 1976
WORKS IN THE FIELD, 1978

Breer, Robert
GULLS AND BUOYS, 1972
FUJI, 1973
RUBBER CEMENT, 1975
77, 1977
LMNO, 1978
T.Z., 1979

Broughton, James
THE GOLDEN POSITIONS, 1970
THIS IS IT, 1971
DREAMWOOD, 1972
HIGH KUKUS, 1973
TESTAMENT, 1974
THE WATER CIRCLE, 1975

EROGENY, 1976
TOGETHER, 1976
WINDOWMOBILE, 1977
SONG OF THE GODBODY, 1977 (with
  Joel Singer)
HERMES BIRD, 1979

Burkhardt, Rudy
MADE IN MAINE, 1970
SUMMER, 1970
INSIDE DOPE, 1971
DOLDRUMS, 1972
CATERPILLAR, 1973
DEFAULT AVERTED, 1975
SAROCHE, 1975
DWELLINGS, 1975
CITY PASTURE, 1975
SODOM AND GOMORRHA, NEW
  YORK 10036, 1976
GOOD EVENING EVERYBODY, 1977
ALEX KATZ PAINTING, 1978
MOBILE HOMES, 1979

Child, Abigail
SOME EXTERIOR PRESENCE, 1977
PERIPETEIA 1, 1977
DAYLIGHT TEST SECTION, 1978
PERIPETEIA 2, 1978
ORNAMENTALS, 1979
PACIFIC FAR EAST LINES, 1979

Chomont, Tom
PORTRET, 1971
ARIA, 1971
LOVE OBJECTS, 1971
ONDERSOEK/RESEARCH, 1972
LJIN, II, 1972
RE:INCARNATION, 1972 (with Peter
  Erdmann)
BILD, 1974
., 1974
ABDA, 1974
REBIRTH, 1974
LYNNE, 1975
UNTITLED, 1975
CROSSCURRENTS, 1977
MODERN ART, 1977
THE HEAVENS, 1977
SPACE TIME STUDIES, 1977

EARTH, 1978
ASTRAL LOGIC, 1978
LIFE STYLE, 1978
MOUSE IN YOUR FACE, 1978
MINOR REVISIONS, 1979

Conner, Bruce
MARILYN TIMES FIVE, 1974
CROSSROADS, 1976
TAKE THE 5:10 TO DREAMLAND,
  1977
MONGOLOID, 1978
VALSE TRISTE, 1978

Conrad, Tony
FILM FEEDBACK, 1974

de Hirsch, Storm
MY EXPERIMENT IN MEDITATION,
  1971
HUDSON RIVER DIARIES, 1973
LACE OF SUMMER, 1973
SEPTEMBER EXPRESS, 1973
GEOMETRICS OF THE KABBALAH,
  1975

De Landa, Manuel
SHIT, 1975
SONG OF A BITCH, 1976
SALIVA DILDO—PREMATURE
  EJACULATOR, 1976
THE ITCH SCRATCH ITCH CYCLE,
  1976
INCONTINENCE, 1978
ISMISM, 1979

Dick, Vivienne
SHE HAD HER GUN ALL READY,
  1978
GUÉRILLÈRE TALKS, 1978
BEAUTY BECOMES THE BEAST, 1979

Emshwiller, Ed
CAROL, 1970
FILM WITH THREE DANCERS, 1970
BRANCHES, 1970
CHOICE CHANCE WOMAN DANCE,
  1971
SCAPEMATES, 1972

Thermogenesis, 1972
Chrysalis, 1973
Sunstone, 1979

Engel, Jules
Train Landscape, 1975
Shapes and Gestures, 1976
Rumble, 1977

Fisher, Morgan
Production Stills, 1970
Production Footage, 1971
Picture and Sound Rushes, 1973
The Wilkinson Household Fire Alarm, 1973
Cue Rolls, 1974
240x, 1974
Projection Instructions, 1976

Frampton, Hollis
Zorn's Lemma, 1970
"Hapex Legomena":
(Nostalgia), 1971
Poetic Justice, 1972
Critical Mass, 1973
Travelling Matte, 1971
Ordinary Matter, 1972
Remote Control, 1972
Special Effects, 1972
"The Magellan Cycle," 1972–1984
Apparatus Sum (Studies for Magellan: #1), 1972
Tiger Balm (Memoranda Magelani: #1), 1972
Yellow Springs (Vanishing Point: #1), 1972
Public Domain, 1972
Less, 1973
Autumnal Equinox, 1974
Noctiluca (Magellan's Toys: #1), 1974
Winter Solstice, 1974
Straits of Magellan: Drafts & Fragments, 1974
Summer Solstice, 1974

Solariumagelani, 1974
Banner, 1974
Ingenivm Nobis Ipsa Pvella Fecit, 1975
Drum, 1975
Pas de Trois, 1975
Magellan: At The Gates of Death. Part I; The Red Gate, 1976; Part II: The Green Gate, 1976
Otherwise Unexplained Fires, 1976
Not the First Time, 1976
For Georgia O'Keeffe, 1976
Quaternion, 1976
Tuba, 1976
Procession, 1976
More Than Meets the Eye, 1979
Gloria!, 1979
The Birth of Magellan: Dreams of Magellan (Dream I: Matrix), 1979

Freude
Shooting Star, 1970
Sweet Dreams, 1971
Folly, 1972
One and the Same, 1973
Women and Children at Large, 1973

Friedrich, Su
Cool Hands, Warm Heart, 1979
Scar Tissue, 1979

Gehr, Ernie
History, 1970
Field, 1970 (long, short versions)
Serene Velocity, 1970
Three, 1970
Still, 1969–1971
Shift, 1972–1974
Behind the Scenes, 1975
Table, 1976
Untitled, 1977

EUREKA, 1979 (also known as
GEOGRAPHY)
HOTEL, 1979

Gerson, Barry
SUNLIGHT/FLOATING/AFTERNOON,
1970
BEADED LIGHT/DISSOLVING/
BEYOND, 1970
ENDURANCE, 1979/REMEMBRANCE/
METAMORPHOSIS, 1970
MOVEMENTS, 1971
CONVERGING LINES/ASSIMILATION,
1971
PORTRAIT OF DIANA/PORTRAIT OF
ANDREW NOREN, 1970–1972
SHADOW SPACE, 1973
INVERSION, 1973
LUMINOUS ZONE, 1973
TRANSLUCENT APPEARANCES, 1975
CELLULOID ILLUMINATIONS, 1975
THE SECRET ABYSS, 1979

Gibbons, Joe
SPYING, 1978–1979
WELTSCHMERZ, 1979
CONFIDENTIAL, 1979

Gidal, Peter
ROOM FILM, 1973
FILM PRINT, 1974
CONDITION OF ILLUSION, 1975
KOPENHAGEN/1930, 1977
SILENT PARTNER, 1977
4TH WALL, 1978

Gladstone, Paula
THE DANCING SOULS OF THE
WALKING PEOPLE, 1974–1978

Gottheim, Larry
CORN, 1970
FOG LINE, 1970
THOUGHT (SWING), 1970
DOORWAY, 1971
BARN RUSHES, 1971
HARMONICA, 1971

"Elective Affinities":
HORIZONS, 1973
MOUCHES VOLANTES, 1976
FOUR SHADOWS, 1978
TREE OF KNOWLEDGE, 1980

Hammer, Barbara
A GAY DAY, 1973
SISTERS, 1973
DYKETACTICS, 1974
JANE BRAKHAGE, 1974
WOMEN'S RITES OF TRUTH IS THE
DAUGHTER OF TIME, 1974
X, 1974
PSYCHOSYNTHESIS, 1975
SUPERDYKE, 1975
MOON GODDESS, 1976
WOMEN I LOVE, 1976
THE GREAT GODDESS, 1977
MULTIPLE ORGASM, 1977
DOUBLE STRENGTH, 1978

Huot, Robert
NUDE DESCENDING THE STAIRS,
1970
ONE YEAR, 1971
TURNING TORSO DRAWDOWN, 1971
THE SEX LIFE OF THE ARTIST AS A
YOUNG MAN, 1971
ROLLS: 1971, 1972
STRIP, 1972
THIRD ONE-YEAR MOVIE—1972,
1973
ACCENTUATE THE POSITIVE, 1973
FACE OF FACES, 1973
DIARY FILM #4, 1973
BEAUTIFUL MOVIE, 1975
DIARY 1974–1975, 1975
CHINA 1978, 1978
FADES AND CLOSE-UPS, 1978

Jacobs, Ken
TOM, TOM, THE PIPER'S SON, 1971
THE DOCTOR'S DREAM, 1978

Johnston, Becky
SLEEPLESS NIGHTS

Jordan, Larry
THE SACRED ART OF TIBET, 1972
ORB, 1973
ONCE UPON A TIME, 1974
THE RIME OF THE ANCIENT
    MARINER, 1977
ANCESTORS, 1978
CORNELL, 1965, 1978
MOONLIGHT SONATA, 1979

Keller, Marjorie
SHE/VA, 1971
THE OUTER CIRCLE, 1973
OBJECTION, 1974
SUPERIMPOSITION, 1975
BY 2'S AND 3'S: WOMEN, 1976
MISCONCEPTION, 1973–1977
THE WEB, 1977
ON THE VERGE OF AN IMAGE OF
    CHRISTMAS, 1978
ANCIENT PARTS AND FOREIGN
    PARTS, 1979
SIX WINDOWS, 1979

Kobland, Ken
FRAME, 1976
FRANCE, 1976
LOBBY, 1977
VESTIBULE (IN 3 EPISODES),
    1977–1978
PICKING UP THE PIECES, 1978
NEAR AND FAR/NOW AND THEN,
    1979

Kuchar, George
PAGAN RHAPSODY, 1970
PORTRAIT OF RAMONA, 1971
THE SUNSHINE SISTERS, 1972
DEVIL'S CLEAVAGE, 1973
I MARRIED A HEATHEN, 1974
THE DESPERATE AND THE DEEP,
    1975
BACK TO NATURE, 1976
A REASON TO LIVE, 1976
THE ASPHALT RIBBON, 1977
KY KAPERS, 1977
WILD NIGHT IN EL RENO, 1977

I, AN ACTRESS, 1977
FOREVER AND ALWAYS, 1978
MONGOLOID, 1978
ONE NIGHT A WEEK, 1978
PRESCRIPTION IN BLUE, 1978
BLIPS, 1979
THE POWER OF THE PRESS,
    1979
SYMPHONY FOR A SINNER, 1979

Landow, George (Owen Land)
REMEDIAL READING
    COMPREHENSION, 1971
WHAT'S WRONG WITH THIS
    PICTURE, 1972
THANK YOU JESUS FOR THE
    ETERNAL PRESENT, 1973
NO SIR, ORISON, 1975
WIDE ANGLE SAXON, 1975
NEW IMPROVED INSTITUTIONAL
    QUALITY: IN THE ENVIRONMENT
    OF LIQUIDS AND NASALS A
    PARASITIC VOWEL SOMETIMES
    DEVELOPS, 1976
ON THE MARRIAGE BROKER JOKE,
    1977–1979

Lawder, Standish
DANGLING PARTICIPLE, 1970
NECROLOGY, 1970
ROADFILM, 1970
COLORFILM, 1972
RAINDANCE, 1972

Lee, Dave
TO A WORLD NOT LISTENING,
    1980

Levine, Saul
NOTES OF AN EARLY FALL, 1976

Lipton, Lenny
CHILDREN OF THE GOLDEN WEST,
    1975

McCall, Anthony
LINE DESCRIBING A CONE, 1973

McCall, Anthony, Claire
Pajaczkowska, Andrew Tyndall,
Jane Weinstock
SIGMUND FREUD'S DORA, 1979

Mekas, Jonas
REMINISCENCES OF A JOURNEY TO
LITHUANIA, 1971
LOST, LOST, LOST, 1976
IN BETWEEN: 1964–68, 1978
NOTES FOR JEROME, 1978
PARADISE NOT YET LOST, 1979

Mitchell, Eric
KIDNAPPED, 1978

Murphy, J. J.
HIGHWAY LANDSCAPE, 1971–1972
IN PROGRESS, 1971–1972
ICE, 1972
SKY BLUE WATER LIGHT SIGN, 1972
PRINT GENERATION, 1973–1974
SUMMER DIARY, 1976
MOVIE STILLS, 1977
SCIENCE FICTION, 1979

Nares, James
ROME '78, 1978

Naumann, Bruce
ART MAKE-UP: GREEN, BLACK,
WHITE, PINK, 1971

Nelson, Gunvor
KIRSA NICHOLINA, 1970
TAKE-OFF, 1972
MOON'S POOL, 1972
TROLLSTENEN, 1973–1976
BEFORE NEED, 1979

Nelson, Robert
BLEU SHUT, 1970
R.I.P., 1970
KING DAVID, 1970 (with Mike
Henderson)
NO MORE, 1971
WORLDLY WOMAN, 1973 (with Mike
Henderson)

REST IN PIECES, 1974
DEEPWESTURN, 1974 (with Mike
Henderson)
SUITE CALIFORNIA: STOPS AND
PASSES, PART I, 1976
SUITE CALIFORNIA: STOPS AND
PASSES, PART II, 1978

O., Dore
KALDALON, 1970–1971
BLONDE BARBAREI, 1972
KASKARA, 1974

Ono, Yoko
FLY, 1970
ERECTION, 1970
APOTHEOSIS, 1971

Poe, Amos
NIGHT LUNCH, 1975
THE BLANK GENERATION, 1975
UNMADE BEDS, 1975
THE FOREIGNER, 1977

Rainer, Yvonne
LIVES OF PERFORMERS, 1972
FILM ABOUT A WOMAN WHO . . . ,
1974
KRISTINA TALKING PICTURES, 1976
JOURNEYS FROM BERLIN/1971, 1979

Raynal, Jackie
DEUX FOIS, 1970

Schneemann, Carolee
FUSES, 1967
PLUMB LINE, 1968–1972
KITCH'S LAST MEAL, 1973–1978

Serra, Richard and Joan Jonas
PAUL REVERE, 1971

Severson, Ann (Alice Anne Parker)
RIVERBODY, 1970
INTRODUCTION TO HUMANITIES,
1972
NEAR THE BIG CHAKRA, 1972

ANIMALS RUNNING, 1974
THE STRUGGLE OF THE MEAT, 1974

Sharits, Paul
S:TREAM:S:S:ECTION:S:ECTION:
S:S:ECTIONED, 1970
INFERENTIAL CURRENT, 1971
AXIOMATIC GRANULARITY 1972–1973
ANALYTICAL STUDIES I: THE FILM
FRAME, 1971–1976
ANALYTICAL STUDIES II:
UNFRAMED LINES, 1971–1976
ANALYTICAL STUDIES III: COLOR
FRAME PASSAGES, 1973–1974
SYNCHRONOUSOUNDTRACKS,
1973–1974
COLOR SOUND FRAMES, 1974
SHUTTER INTERFACE, 1975
APPARENT MOTION, 1975
ANALYTICAL STUDIES IV: BLANK
COLOR FRAMES, 1975–1976
EPILEPTIC SEIZURE COMPARISON,
1976
DREAM DISPLACEMENT, 1976
TAILS, 1976
DECLARATIVE MODE, 1976
EPISODIC GENERATION, 1977–1978

**Singer, Joel (see also James
Broughton)**
BREAKDOWN, 1974
JUDY, 1974
ADIEU BEAUSEJOUR, 1975
PERISPHERE, 1975
SLICED LIGHT, 1976
BEHEMOTH, 1977

Smithson, Robert
SPIRAL JETTY, 1970

Snow, Michael
THE CENTRAL REGION (LA RÉGION
CENTRALE), 1971
RAMEAU'S NEPHEW BY DIDEROT
(THANX TO DENNIS YOUNG) BY
WILMA SCHOEN, 1974
TWO SIDES TO EVERY STORY, 1974

BREAKFAST (TABLE TOP DOLLY),
1972–1976

Sonbert, Warren
CARRIAGE TRADE, 1968–1972
RUDE AWAKENING, 1972–1976
DIVIDED LOYALTIES, 1975–1978
NOBLESSE OBLIGE, 1978–1981

Strand, Chick
MASORI MONIKA, 1970
ELASTICITY, 1976
GUACAMOLE, 1976
MUJER DE MILFUEGOS, 1976
CARTOON LE MOUSSE, 1979
FEVER DREAM, 1979
KRISTALLNACHT, 1979
LOOSE ENDS, 1979
SOFT FICTION, 1979

Van Der Beek, Stan
COLLISDEOSCOPE, 1970
FILM FORM #1, 1970
VIDEOSPACE, 1972
WHO HO RAY #1, 1972
SYMMETRICKS, 1972

Warhol, Andy
TRASH, 1970
WOMEN IN REVOLT (SEX), 1971
ANDY WARHOL'S BAD, 1971
HEAT, 1972
HAIRCUT, 1972
L'AMOUR, 1973 (Directed by Paul
Morrissey)
ANDY WARHOL'S FRANKENSTEIN,
1974 (Directed by Paul Morrissey)
ANDY WARHOL'S DRACULA, 1974
(Directed by Paul Morrissey)

Waters, John
MONDO TRASHO, 1970
MULTIPLE MANIACS, 1970
PINK FLAMINGOES, 1972
FEMALE TROUBLE 1975
DESPERATE LIVING, 1977

Weiland, Joyce
    Pierre Vallières, 1972
    Solidarity, 1973
    The Far Shore, 1976

Whitney, James
    Dwija, 1976

Wu Ming, 1977
Kang Jing Xiang, 1978

Whitney, John
    Osaka, 1970
    Matrix, 1971–1972 (3 films)
    Arabesque, 1975

Appendixes

ANNUAL U.S. BOX OFFICE RECEIPTS, 1970–1979 ($ MILLIONS)

YEAR	U.S. BOX OFFICE RECEIPTS	% OF U.S. PERSONAL SPENDING	% OF U.S. RECREATIONAL SPENDING	% OF SPECTATOR RECREATIONAL SPENDING
1970	1,162	0.19	2.86	48.00
1971	117	0.18	2.74	47.74
1972	1,644	0.22	3.03	47.01
1973	1,524	0.20	3.50	50.77
1974	1,909	0.28	4.10	53.99
1975	2,115	0.26	3.84	51.81
1976	2,036	0.27	4.12	53.36
1977	2,372	°	°	°
1978	2,653	0.28	°	°
1979	2,806	0.29	°	°

° Figures not available.

SOURCE: U.S. Department of Commerce, Social and Economic Statistics Administration.

APPENDIX 2

AVERAGE WEEKLY ATTENDANCE, 1970–1980

YEAR	AVERAGE WEEKLY ATTENDANCE	YEAR	AVERAGE WEEKLY ATTENDANCE
1970	17,700,000	1976	18,400,000
1971	15,800,000	1977	20,400,000
1972	18,000,000	1978	21,800,000
1973	16,600,000	1979	21,600,000
1974	19,400,000	1980	19,600,000
1975	19,900,000		

SOURCE: Motion Picture Association of America.

APPENDIX 3

INFLATION 1970–1980, ACCORDING TO "CONSUMER PRICE INDEX" FIGURES COMPILED BY THE U.S. DEPARTMENT OF COMMERCE

YEAR	RISE IN INFLATION OVER PREVIOUS YEAR	YEAR	RISE IN INFLATION OVER PREVIOUS YEAR
1970	5.7%	1976	5.8%
1971	4.4%	1977	6.5%
1972	3.2%	1978	7.6%
1973	6.2%	1979	11.3%
1974	11.0%	1980	11.1%
1975	9.1%		

Note: What this table shows is that from 1970 through 1980 the domestic value of the U.S. dollar dropped by almost 80 percent, with 30 percent of the decline occurring in the three-year period 1978–1980.

SOURCE: *Statistical Abstract of the United States* (Washington, D.C.: Department of Commerce, 1997).

APPENDIX 4

AVERAGE TICKET PRICE IN THE
U.S. EACH YEAR, 1970–1980

YEAR	ADMISSION PRICE	YEAR	ADMISSION PRICE
1970	$1.552	1976	$2.128
1971	$1.645	1977	$2.230
1972	$1.695	1978	$2.340
1973	$1.768	1979	$2.510
1974	$1.874	1980	$2.69
1975	$2.048		

SOURCE: Motion Picture Association of America.

APPENDIX 5

NUMBER OF MOVIE THEATERS
IN THE U.S., 1970–1980

YEAR	FOUR-WALLED THEATERS		DRIVE-INS		TOTAL	
1970	10,000		3,750		13,750	
1971	10,335		3,770		14,105	
1972	10,580		3,790		14,370	
1973	10,850		3,800		14,650	
1974	9,645	(11,612)	3,519	(3,772)	13,164	(15,384)
1975	9,857	(12,168)	3,535	(3,801)	13,392	(15,969)
1976	10,044	(12,692)	3,536	(3,802)	13,580	(16,494)
1977	(information unavailable)					
1978	9,047	(12,671)	3,233	(3,580)	12,280	(16,251)
1979	9,021	(13,331)	3,197	(3,570)	12,218	(16,901)
1980	8,895	(14,029)	3,102	(3,561)	11,997	(17,590)

Figures in parentheses indicate number of *screens* as opposed to number of theaters, representing the growth of multiplexes.

SOURCE: Motion Picture Association of America.

APPENDIX 6

MAJOR COMPANY SHARE OF NEW RELEASES HANDLED BY NATIONAL DISTRIBUTORS, 1970–1980

COMPANY	1970	1971	1972	1973	1974	1975	1976	1977	1978	1979	1980	TOTAL, 1970–1980 NUMBER	PERCENT
TOTAL NEW RELEASES	267	282	279	237	238	195	191	167	171	189	192	2408	100%
MPAA COMPANIES:													
ALLIED ARTISTS	7	8	8	1	3	7	6	4	2	—	—	46	1.9
AVCO EMBASSY	11	6	13	11	10	15	8	5	10	11	10	110	4.6
COLUMBIA	28	37	27	16	21	15	15	10	14	20	15	218	9.1
METRO-GOLDWYN-MAYER	21	20	22	16	°	°	°	°	°	°	°	79	3.3
PARAMOUNT	16	21	14	26	23	11	18	15	14	16	17	191	7.9
20TH CENTURY–FOX	14	16	25	14	18	19	18	14	7	14	16	175	7.3
UNITED ARTISTS	40	26	20	18	21	21	22	14	19	23	22	246	10.2
UNIVERSAL	17	16	16	19	11	10	13	17	21	15	18	173	7.2
WARNER	15	17	18	22	15	19	11	14	18	19	24	192	8.0
TOTAL	169	167	163	143	122	117	111	93	105	118	122	1430	
MPAA COMPANIES AS % OF TOTAL NEW RELEASES	63.3%	59.20%	58.4%	60.3%	51.3%	60.0%	58.1%	55.7%	61.4%	62.4%	63.5%		59.4%
BUENA VISTA (DISNEY)	4	5	4	4	5	6	5	5	5	5	3	51	2.1
AMERICAN INTERNATIONAL	25	24	28	19	18	17	17	18	13	11	9	199	8.3
MPAA COMPANIES, BUENA VISTA AND AMER. INTERNAT'L AS % OF TOTAL NEW RELEASES	74.2%	69.5%	69.9%	70.0%	60.9%	69.6%	69.6%	69.5%	71.9%	70.9%	69.8%		69.8%

° Distributed by United Artists.

SOURCE: Motion Picture Association of America.

APPENDIX 7

MARKET DOMINATION BY SIX LEADING DISTRIBUTORS* OF THEATRICAL FILMS, 1977 AND 1980 (RENTALS IN $ MILLIONS)

	1977	1980
Top 10 grossing films in North America		
Number handled	9	10
Rentals	$344.8	$460.7
Films with $10 million or more in North American rentals		
Number handled	23 of 28	29 of 33
Rentals	$622.6	$775.0
Films with $2 million or more in North American rentals	53 of 78	69 of 96

* Columbia, Paramount, Twentieth Century–Fox, United Artists (distributing for Metro-Goldwyn-Mayer), Universal, and Warner. MPAA member companies in 1980, which included the above plus Avco Embassy, Buena Vista (Disney), and Filmways, distributed 32 of the 33 films earning rentals of $10 million or more, and 79 of the 96 films earning rentals of $2 million or more in the United States-Canadian market.

SOURCE: *Variety*, January 4, 1978; January 14, 1981. (Reissues are excluded.)

APPENDIX 8

MARKETING EXPENSES* FOR MAJOR RELEASES, 1970–1980 ($ MILLIONS)

	RELEASES				ADVERTISING				
YEAR	TOTAL	NEW	RE-ISSUES	TOTAL	NET. TV	LOCAL TV	NEWS-PAPER	SPOT RADIO	AVERAGE AD SPENDING PER PICTURE
1980	235	193	42	703.8	103.3	102.4	486.1	12.0	2.99
1979	214	188	26	600.1	64.1	94.2	433.6	8.2	2.80
1978	191	171	20	513.4	44.9	72.2	389.5	6.8	2.69
1977	199	167	32	410.0	30.7	55.1	321.1	3.1	2.06
1976	220	190	30	372.5	14.8	64.1	291.8	1.8	1.69
1975	233	193	40	341.4	13.4	59.3	267.7	1.0	1.47
1974	278	233	45	295.4	10.4	55.9	229.1	1.0	1.07
1973	286	248	38	253.3	6.0	30.8	216.5	1.0	0.89
1972	317	278	39	236.6	4.0	23.6	208.0	1.0	0.75
1971	314	282	32	223.7	3.9	21.6	197.7	0.5	0.71
1970	306	267	39	207.7	3.9	15.5	187.8	0.5	0.68

COMPOUND ANNUAL GROWTH RATE: 12.54 PERCENT

* This table shows that throughout the 1970s motion picture marketing expenses rose at an average annual rate of more than 12.5 percent.

SOURCES: Television Bureau of Advertising, Radio Advertising Bureau, MaGavern Guild Radio, Newspaper Advertising Bureau.

APPENDIX 9

MAJOR STUDIO REVENUES AND AFTER-TAX PROFITS, 1970–1980* ($ MILLIONS)

YEAR	COLUMBIA				20TH CENTURY–FOX			
	FILM REVENUES	TOTAL REVENUES	PROFITS	OPERATING INCOME	FILM REVENUES	TOTAL REVENUES	PROFITS	OPERATING INCOME
1970	137.9	242.1	6.2		160.0	252.4	[76.4]	[77.2]
1971	113.0	233.3	[28.8]		143.2	226.8	9.7	12.4
1972	110.0	233.5	[3.4]	7.3	118.8	201.4	7.8	8.1
1973	101.5	205.4	[50.0]	[61.5]	152.6	253.5	10.7	12.1
1974	111.3	250.1	[2.3]	24.9	159.7	280.1	11.0	12.9
1975	170.3	325.5	10.5	33.2	210.8	342.7	22.7	28.9
1976	152.2	332.1	11.5	28.3	217.2	355.0	10.7	17.1
1977	153.5	390.5	34.6	30.8	321.5	501.5	50.8	69.7
1978	269.0	574.6	68.8	80.1	346.6	610.9	58.4	91.1
1979	263.1	613.3	39.0	59.0	316.4	658.0	57.3	63.8
1980	341.6	691.8	44.9	59.5	581.9	847.3	54.6	55.2

YEAR	MGM				UNITED ARTISTS		
	FILM REVENUES	TOTAL REVENUES	PROFITS	OPERATING INCOME	FILM REVENUES	TOTAL REVENUES	PROFITS
1970	98.5	169.6	[8.2]			211.0	[45.0]
1971	111.1	169.3	7.8		97.2	204.3	1.0
1972	134.5	155.6	9.2		152.7	315.0	10.8
1973	138.8	159.6	2.1		164.0	322.6	14.0
1974	125.1			26.8	141.9	288.6	9.9
1975	100.7			31.9	187.4	319.7	11.5
1976	96.1			32.0	229.5	377.7	16.0
1977	110.7			26.6	318.5	474.1	26.6
1978	138.8	182.9	19.6	39.2	294.2	416.8	28.8
1979	159.2	193.3	29.4	60.1	381.0	468.9	26.6
1980	141.6	181.9	16.5	36.4		424.8	20.1

* The profit figures in this chart are "net profits," and the operating income figures correspond to "gross profits." Since the taxes of studios owned by conglomerates were paid by the parent company, there were no after-tax profits reported for Paramount (Gulf & Western), Universal (MCA), or Warner Bros. (WCI), during this period.

APPENDIX 9 (CONT.)

	PARAMOUNT				UNIVERSAL				
YEAR	FILM & TV REVENUES	FILM REVENUES	TOTAL REVENUES	PROFITS	OPERATING INCOME	FILM REVENUES	TOTAL REVENUES	PROFITS	FILM ENTERTAINMENT PROFITS	OPERATING INCOME
1970		101.0	240.9		2.0	96.9	220.0		13.3	32.4
1971		139.0	278.7		20.1	56.7	194.6		16.7	15.0
1972		142.0	291.0		31.2	61.9	204.6		20.9	19.9
1973		120.0	277.5		38.7	87.5	227.7		27.1	20.2
1974		103.0	298.1		18.7	205.0	387.5		59.2	68.0
1975		175.0	360.3		29.9	289.1	509.9		95.5	124.0
1976		152.0	451.4		49.6	213.4	506.9		90.2	100.6
1977	232.0	150.0	469.6		36.2	222.8	561.4		95.1	107.4
1978	384.0	287.0	802.0		84.1	318.7	724.4		128.4	159.8
1979	551.0	427.0	966.7		116.4	305.0	781.5		139.0	174.3
1980	603.0	392.0	1041.6		100.1	397.7	767.7			133.9

	WARNER BROS.				TOTAL U.S. CORPORATE PROFITS ($ BILLION)
YEAR	WARNER BROS. FILM REVENUES	WARNER BROS. TOTAL REVENUES	WARNER BROS. TOTAL PROFITS	OPERATING INCOME	
1970	64.2	114.9		7.0	37.0
1971	86.3	124.3		14.8	44.3
1972	144.3	193.4		23.1	54.6
1973	152.7	209.5		31.1	67.1
1974	275.3	319.0		57.7	74.5
1975	202.3	255.9		41.7	70.6
1976	221.7	285.2		42.2	92.2
1977	253.6	353.2		58.0	104.5
1978	261.3	393.0		79.9	121.5
1979	433.7	609.7		117.6	
1980	369.6	668.9		60.8	

SOURCE: Joel Finler, *The Hollywood Story* (New York: Crown, 1988), pp. 286–87. Finler's figures derive from the annual financial reports of the film companies, the *Film Daily Year Book*, *Moody's Manual of Investments, Motion Picture Almanac,* and the *U.S. Department of Commerce Survey of Current Business.*

APPENDIX 10

LATE SIXTIES FLOPS
(PRODUCTIONS THAT EXPERIENCED COST OVERRUNS
AND LOWER-THAN-ANTICIPATED RENTALS)

TITLE	YEAR	STUDIO	COST (MILLIONS)	DOMESTIC RENTALS (MILLIONS)
DOCTOR DOLITTLE	1967	20th Century–Fox	17.0	6.2
CAMELOT	1967	Warner Bros.	17.0	14.0
CHITTY CHITTY BANG BANG	1968	United Artists	16.0	7.0
THE BATTLE OF BRITAIN	1968	United Artists	12.0	2.5
STAR	1968	20th Century–Fox	14.5	4.2
CHARGE OF THE LIGHT BRIGADE	1968	United Artists	12.0	1.0
GAILY GAILY	1969	United Artists	9.0	1.0
PAINT YOUR WAGON	1969	Paramount	18.0	14.5
THE PARTY	1969	United Artists	6.0	1.0
THE GREAT WHITE HOPE	1970	20th Century–Fox	9.9	2.8
RYAN'S DAUGHTER	1970	20th Century–Fox	15.0	14.6
LITTLE BIG MAN	1970	Cinema Center	15.0	15.0
THE ADVENTURERS	1970	Paramount	17.0	7.7
CATCH-22	1970	Paramount	18.0	12.2
DARLING LILI	1970	Paramount	22.0	3.5
THE ONLY GAME IN TOWN	1970	20th Century–Fox	10.0	1.5
THE LAST VALLEY	1970	Cinerama	6.0	1.0
THE MOLLY MAGUIRES	1970	Paramount	11.0	1.0
ON A CLEAR DAY YOU CAN SEE FOREVER	1970	Paramount	10.0	5.3

SOURCE: Aubrey Solomon. *Twentieth Century Fox: A Corporate and Financial History* (Metuchen, N.J.: Scarecrow Press, 1988), p. 162.

APPENDIX 11

HIT MOVIES OF THE 1968–1969 SEASON

TITLE	YEAR	STUDIO	COST (MILLIONS)	DOMESTIC RENTALS (MILLIONS)
THE GRADUATE	1967	Avco Embassy	3.0	49.0°
BONNIE AND CLYDE	1967	Warner Bros.	3.0	24.1
PLANET OF THE APES	1968	20th Century–Fox	5.8	15.0
BULLITT	1968	Warner Bros.	5.5	19.0
2001: A SPACE ODYSSEY	1968	MGM	11.0	24.1
FUNNY GIRL	1968	Columbia	14.1	26.3
BOB, CAROL, TED AND ALICE	1968	Columbia	2.0	14.6
OLIVER!	1969	Columbia	10.0	16.8
EASY RIDER	1969	Columbia	0.6	19.1
GOODBYE, COLUMBUS	1969	Paramount	1.5	10.5
MIDNIGHT COWBOY	1969	United Artists	3.2	20.3
THE LOVE BUG	1969	Disney	5.0†	23.1

°Denotes most revenue from 1968.

† Denotes approximation—Disney never released cost figures.

SOURCE: Aubrey Solomon, *Twentieth Century Fox: A Corporate and Financial History* (Metuchen, N.J.: Scarecrow Press, 1988), p. 162.

APPENDIX 12

TOP TWENTY RENTAL FILMS, 1970–1980

TITLE	STUDIO	RENTALS IN MILLIONS OF DOLLARS
1970		
LOVE STORY‡	Paramount	48.7
AIRPORT	Universal	45.2
M°A°S°H‡	20th Century–Fox	36.7
PATTON‡	20th Century–Fox	28.1
IN SEARCH OF NOAH'S ARK	Sunn	23.8
WOODSTOCK	Warner Bros.	16.4
RYAN'S DAUGHTER‡	MGM	14.6
TORA! TORA! TORA! ‡	20th Century–Fox	14.5
THE ARISTOCATS°	Disney	11.5
JOE	Can/MGM	9.5
CATCH-22	Paramount	9.3
THE BOATNIKS	Disney	9.2

APPENDIX 12 (CONT.)

TITLE	STUDIO	RENTALS IN MILLIONS OF DOLLARS
FIVE EASY PIECES	Columbia	8.9
THE ADVENTURERS	Paramount	7.8
THE OUT OF TOWNERS	Paramount	7.4
BENEATH THE PLANET OF THE APES	20th Century–Fox	7.3
CHISUM	Warner Bros.	6.0
A MAN CALLED HORSE	Cinerama	6.0
DIARY OF A MAD HOUSEWIFE	Universal	5.9
ON A CLEAR DAY	Paramount	5.7
1971		
FIDDLER ON THE ROOF‡	United Artists	38.2
BILLY JACK	Warner Bros.	32.5
THE FRENCH CONNECTION‡	20th Century–Fox	26.3
SUMMER OF '42	Warner Bros.	20.5
DEEP THROAT	Damiano	20.0
DIAMONDS ARE FOREVER	United Artists	19.8
DIRTY HARRY	Warner Bros.	18.1
A CLOCKWORK ORANGE‡	Warner Bros.	17.5
LITTLE BIG MAN	NG	17.0
THE LAST PICTURE SHOW‡	Columbia	14.1
THE OWL AND THE PUSSYCAT	Columbia	12.2
CARNAL KNOWLEDGE	Emb	12.1
THE HOSPITAL‡	United Artists	9.5
WILLARD	AIP	9.3
THE ANDROMEDA STRAIN	Universal	8.0
BIG JAKE	Cin Center	7.5
THE STEWARDESSES	Coons	7.0
KLUTE‡	Warner Bros.	7.0
NICHOLAS AND ALEXANDRA‡	Columbia	6.9
SHAFT‡	MGM	6.1
1972		
THE GODFATHER‡	Paramount	86.3
THE POSEIDON ADVENTURE‡	20th Century–Fox	42.1
WHAT'S UP, DOC?	Warner Bros.	28.5
DELIVERANCE‡	Warner Bros.	22.6
JEREMIAH JOHNSON°	Warner Bros.	21.9
CABARET‡	AA/ABC	20.2
THE GETAWAY	NG/Warner Bros.	18.4
LADY SINGS THE BLUES	Paramount	11.0
SOUNDER‡	20th Century–Fox	9.5
PETE 'N TILLIE	Universal	8.7
EVERYTHING YOU ALWAYS . . . SEX	United Artists	8.5
BEDKNOBS AND BROOMSTICKS ‡	Disney	8.3
THE COWBOYS	Warner Bros.	7.0

APPENDIX 12 (CONT.)

TITLE	STUDIO	RENTALS IN MILLIONS OF DOLLARS
FRENZY	Universal	6.3
SKYJACKED	MGM	6.1
SONG OF THE SOUTH (reissue)	Disney	5.9
ESCAPE FROM THE PLANET OF THE APES	20th Century–Fox	5.5
BUTTERFLIES ARE FREE‡	Columbia	5.5
THE NEW CENTURIONS	Columbia	5.5
2001: A SPACE ODYSSEY (reissue)	MGM	5.4

1973

TITLE	STUDIO	RENTALS IN MILLIONS OF DOLLARS
THE EXORCIST‡	Warner Bros.	89.3
THE STING‡	Universal	78.2
AMERICAN GRAFFITI‡°	Universal	55.3
THE WAY WE WERE‡	Columbia	25.8
PAPILLON	AA	22.5
MAGNUM FORCE	Warner Bros.	20.1
ROBIN HOOD°	Disney	17.2
LAST TANGO IN PARIS	United Artists	16.7
PAPER MOON	Paramount	16.6
LIVE AND LET DIE	United Artists	16.0
SERPICO	Paramount	14.6
JESUS CHRIST SUPERSTAR	Universal	13.1
CHARIOTS OF THE GODS	Sunn	12.4
ENTER THE DRAGON	Warner Bros.	11.5
THE WORLD'S GREATEST ATHLETE	Disney	10.5
MARY POPPINS (reissue)	Disney	9.0
THE DAY OF THE JACKAL	Universal	8.7
WALKING TALL	Ind	8.5
BILLY JACK (reissue)	Warner Bros./Ind	8.3
HIGH PLAINS DRIFTER	Warner Bros.	7.3

1974

TITLE	STUDIO	RENTALS IN MILLIONS OF DOLLARS
THE TOWERING INFERNO‡	20th-Warner Bros.	48.8
BLAZING SADDLES	Warner Bros.	47.8
EARTHQUAKE‡	Universal	35.9
THE TRIAL OF BILLY JACK	Warner Bros.	31.1
BENJI	Mulberry	30.8
THE GODFATHER, PART II‡	Paramount	30.7
YOUNG FRANKENSTEIN	20th Century–Fox	30.1
AIRPORT 1975	Universal	25.3
THE LONGEST YARD	Paramount	23.0
THAT'S ENTERTAINMENT!	MGM	19.1
MURDER ON THE ORIENT EXPRESS	Paramount	19.1
HERBIE RIDES AGAIN	Disney	17.1

APPENDIX 12 (CONT.)

TITLE	STUDIO	RENTALS IN MILLIONS OF DOLLARS
THE THREE MUSKETEERS	20th Century–Fox	15.4
DIRTY MARY, CRAZY LARRY	20th Century–Fox	15.2
FOR PETE'S SAKE	Columbia	14.5
THE TEXAS CHAINSAW MASSACRE	New Line	14.4
THE GREAT GATSBY‡	Paramount	14.2
LENNY‡	United Artists	11.5
FREEBIE AND THE BEAN	Warner Bros.	12.5
THUNDERBOLT AND LIGHTFOOT	United Artists	9.3

1975

JAWS‡	Universal	129.5
ONE FLEW OVER THE CUCKOO'S NEST‡	United Artists	60.0
ROCKY HORROR PICTURE SHOW°	20th Century–Fox	3.5 (40.0, 1976–79)
SHAMPOO‡	Columbia	24.5
DOG DAY AFTERNOON‡	Warner Bros.	22.5
RETURN OF THE PINK PANTHER	United Artists	22.1
GRIZZLY ADAMS	Sunn	21.9
THREE DAYS OF THE CONDOR	Paramount	21.5
FUNNY LADY	Columbia	19.3
THE OTHER SIDE OF THE MOUNTAIN	Universal	18.0
TOMMY	Columbia	17.8
APPLE DUMPLING GANG	Disney	16.6
THE HINDENBURG‡	Universal	14.5
LUCKY LADY	Universal	12.1
LET'S DO IT AGAIN	Warner Bros.	11.8
ISLAND AT THE TOP OF THE WORLD	Disney	10.5
NO DEPOSIT, NO RETURN	Disney	10.5
HUSTLE	Paramount	10.4
THE MAN WITH THE GOLDEN GUN	United Artists	10.0
BARRY LYNDON‡	Warner Bros.	9.9
WALKING TALL	FW/CRC	9.4

1976

ROCKY‡	United Artists	56.5
A STAR IS BORN‡	Warner Bros.	37.1
KING KONG‡	Paramount	36.9
ALL THE PRESIDENT'S MEN‡	Warner Bros.	31.0
SILVER STREAK	20th Century–Fox	30.0
THE OMEN‡	20th Century–Fox	28.5
THE BAD NEWS BEARS	Paramount	24.3
THE ENFORCER	Warner Bros.	24.1
MIDWAY	Universal	21.6
SILENT MOVIE	20th Century–Fox	21.2

APPENDIX 12 (CONT.)

TITLE	STUDIO	RENTALS IN MILLIONS OF DOLLARS
TO FLY	IMAX	20.3
THE PINK PANTHER STRIKES AGAIN	United Artists	19.9
MURDER BY DEATH	Columbia	19.1
NETWORK‡	MGM	15.1
MARATHON MAN	Paramount	16.6
CARRIE	United Artists	15.2
TAXI DRIVER	Columbia	11.7
FREAKY FRIDAY	Disney	11.7
ODE TO BILLY JOE	Warner Bros.	11.6
THE OUTLAW JOSEY WALES	Warner Bros.	10.6

1977

STAR WARS‡°	20th Century–Fox	193.8
CLOSE ENCOUNTERS OF THE THIRD KIND‡	Columbia	82.8
SATURDAY NIGHT FEVER	Paramount	74.1
SMOKEY AND THE BANDIT	Universal	59.0
THE GOODBYE GIRL‡	MGM-Warner Bros.	41.9
OH, GOD!	Warner Bros.	31.5
THE DEEP	Columbia	31.2
THE RESCUERS°	Disney	30.1
THE SPY WHO LOVED ME	United Artists	24.3
SEMI-TOUGH	United Artists	22.9
A BRIDGE TOO FAR	United Artists	20.4
HIGH ANXIETY	20th Century–Fox	19.2
ANNIE HALL‡	United Artists	19.0
THE OTHER SIDE OF MIDNIGHT	20th Century–Fox	18.4
PETE'S DRAGON	Disney	18.4
THE GAMBLER	Warner Bros.	17.7
THE TURNING POINT	20th Century–Fox	17.1
LOOKING FOR MR. GOODBAR	Paramount	16.9
AIRPORT '77	Col-Universal	15.1
THE BAD NEWS BEARS II	Paramount	15.1

1978

GREASE	Paramount	96.3
SUPERMAN‡	Warner Bros.	82.8
NATIONAL LAMPOON'S ANIMAL HOUSE	Universal	70.9
EVERY WHICH WAY BUT LOOSE	Warner Bros.	51.9
JAWS 2	Universal	50.4
HEAVEN CAN WAIT	Paramount	49.4
HOOPER	Warner Bros.	34.9
CALIFORNIA SUITE‡	Columbia	29.2
THE DEER HUNTER‡	EMI-Universal	28.0
FOUL PLAY	Paramount	27.5

APPENDIX 12 (CONT.)

TITLE	STUDIO	RENTALS IN MILLIONS OF DOLLARS
UP IN SMOKE	Paramount	26.3
REVENGE OF THE PINK PANTHER	United Artists	25.4
THE END	United Artists	20.7
THE CHEAP DETECTIVE	Columbia	19.2
HALLOWEEN	Compass	18.6
MIDNIGHT EXPRESS‡	Columbia	15.0
HOUSE CALLS	Universal	15.0
COMA	MGM	14.8
COMING HOME‡	United Artists	13.5
THE OMEN II	20th Century–Fox	12.1

1979

KRAMER VS. KRAMER‡	Columbia	59.9
STAR TREK	Paramount	56.0
THE JERK	Universal	43.0
ROCKY II	United Artists	42.1
ALIEN‡	20th Century–Fox	40.3
APOCALYPSE NOW‡	United Artists	37.9
10	Orion/Warner Bros.	37.4
THE AMITYVILLE HORROR	AIP	35.4
MOONRAKER	United Artists	34.0
THE MUPPET MOVIE	ITC/AFD	32.8
THE ELECTRIC HORSEMAN	Columbia	30.2
THE MAIN EVENT	Warner Bros.	26.4
THE CHINA SYNDROME	Columbia	25.8
THE BLACK HOLE	Disney	25.4
1941	Universal	23.2
ESCAPE FROM ALCATRAZ	Paramount	21.5
MEATBALLS	Paramount	21.2
ALL THAT JAZZ‡	20th-Columbia	20.0
STARTING OVER	Paramount	19.1
THE ROSE	20th Century–Fox	19.1

1980

THE EMPIRE STRIKES BACK‡	20th Century–Fox	141.7
NINE TO FIVE	20th Century–Fox	59.1
STIR CRAZY	Columbia	58.3
AIRPLANE!	Paramount	40.6
ANY WHICH WAY YOU CAN	Warner Bros.	40.5
SMOKEY AND THE BANDIT II	Universal	39.0
COAL MINER'S DAUGHTER‡	Universal	35.5
PRIVATE BENJAMIN	Warner Bros.	34.4
THE BLUES BROTHERS	Universal	32.1

APPENDIX 12 (CONT.)

TITLE	STUDIO	RENTALS IN MILLIONS OF DOLLARS
THE SHINING	Warner Bros.	30.9
THE BLUE LAGOON	Columbia	28.8
POPEYE	Paramount	24.5
URBAN COWBOY	Paramount	23.8
ORDINARY PEOPLE‡	Paramount	23.1
SEEMS LIKE OLD TIMES	Columbia	21.6
CHEECH & CHONG'S NEXT MOVIE	Universal	21.5
CADDYSHACK	Orion	20.0
BRUBAKER	20th Century–Fox	19.0
FRIDAY THE 13TH	Paramount	17.1
DRESSED TO KILL	AIP/Orion	15.9

Note: A slash between studio names indicates a producer/distributor relationship; a hyphen indicates co-production.

° denotes multiple releases; the dollar amount given in parentheses after a year is the average price of all tickets sold, including half-price children's.

‡ denotes a major Oscar.

SOURCES: *Variety, The Hollywood Reporter.*

APPENDIX 13

NORTH AMERICAN RENTALS IN EXCESS OF $22.25 MILLION, 1970–1980

TITLE	YEAR	STUDIO	$ MILLIONS
STAR WARS	1977	20th Century–Fox	193.8
THE EMPIRE STRIKES BACK	1980	Lucas/20th Century–Fox	141.7
JAWS	1975	Universal	129.5
GREASE	1978	Paramount	96.3
THE EXORCIST	1973	Warner Bros.	88.5
THE GODFATHER	1972	Paramount	86.3
SUPERMAN	1978	co-prod. Salkind/Warner Bros.	82.8
CLOSE ENCOUNTERS OF THE THIRD KIND	1977	Columbia	82.8
THE STING	1973	Universal	78.2
SATURDAY NIGHT FEVER	1977	Paramount	74.1
NATIONAL LAMPOON'S ANIMAL HOUSE	1978	Universal	70.9
ONE FLEW OVER THE CUCKOO'S NEST	1975	Fantasy/United Artists	60.0
KRAMER VS. KRAMER	1979	Columbia	59.9
NINE TO FIVE	1980	20th Century–Fox	59.1

APPENDIX 13 (CONT.)

TITLE	YEAR	STUDIO	$ MILLIONS
SMOKEY AND THE BANDIT	1977	Universal	59.0
STIR CRAZY	1980	Columbia	58.3
ROCKY	1976	Chartoff-Winkler/United Artists	56.5
STAR TREK—THE MOTION PICTURE	1979	Paramount	56.0
AMERICAN GRAFFITI	1973	Universal	55.2
EVERY WHICH WAY BUT LOOSE	1978	Warner Bros.	51.9
JAWS 2	1978	Universal	50.4
HEAVEN CAN WAIT	1978	Paramount	49.4
TOWERING INFERNO	1974	co-prod. 20th/Warner Bros.	48.8
LOVE STORY	1970	Paramount	48.7
BLAZING SADDLES	1974	Warner Bros.	47.8
AIRPORT	1970	Universal	45.2
THE JERK	1979	Universal	43.0
ROCKY II	1979	Chartoff-Winkler/United Artists	42.1
THE POSEIDON ADVENTURE	1972	20th Century–Fox	42.1
THE GOODBYE GIRL	1977	co-prod. WB/MGM	41.9
AIRPLANE!	1980	Paramount	40.6
ANY WHICH WAY YOU CAN	1980	Warner Bros.	40.5
ALIEN	1979	20th Century–Fox	40.3
SMOKEY AND THE BANDIT II	1980	Universal	39.0
FIDDLER ON THE ROOF	1971	Mirisch/United Artists	38.2
APOCALYPSE NOW	1979	Omni-Zoetrope/United Artists	37.9
'10'	1979	Orion/Warner Bros.	37.4
A STAR IS BORN	1976	Warner Bros.	37.1
KING KONG	1976	DeLaurentiis/Paramount	36.9
M*A*S*H	1970	20th Century–Fox	36.7
EARTHQUAKE	1974	Universal	35.9
COAL MINER'S DAUGHTER	1980	Universal	35.5
THE AMITYVILLE HORROR	1979	AIP	35.4
HOOPER	1978	Warner Bros.	34.9
PRIVATE BENJAMIN	1980	Warner Bros.	34.4
MOONRAKER	1979	Eon/United Artists	34.0
THE MUPPET MOVIE	1979	ITC/AFD	32.8
BILLY JACK	1971	Warner Bros.	32.5
THE BLUES BROTHERS	1980	Universal	32.1
OH, GOD!	1977	Warner Bros.	31.5
THE DEEP	1977	Columbia	31.2
THE TRIAL OF BILLY JACK	1974	Warner Bros.	31.1
ALL THE PRESIDENT'S MEN	1976	Warner Bros.	31.0
THE SHINING	1980	Warner Bros.	30.9
THE GODFATHER, PART II	1974	Paramount	30.7
THE ELECTRIC HORSEMAN	1979	Columbia	30.2
YOUNG FRANKENSTEIN	1974	20th Century–Fox	30.1
SILVER STREAK	1976	20th Century–Fox	30.0
CALIFORNIA SUITE	1978	Columbia	29.2

APPENDIX 13 (CONT.)

TITLE	YEAR	STUDIO	$ MILLIONS
THE OMEN	1976	20th Century–Fox	28.5
WHAT'S UP, DOC?	1972	Warner Bros.	28.5
THE BLUE LAGOON	1980	Columbia	28.5
PATTON	1970	20th Century–Fox	28.1
THE DEER HUNTER	1978	co-prod. EMI/U	28.0
FOUL PLAY	1978	Paramount	27.5
UP IN SMOKE	1978	Paramount	26.3
THE FRENCH CONNECTION	1971	20th Century–Fox	26.3
THE MAIN EVENT	1979	Warner Bros.	26.3
THE CHINA SYNDROME	1979	Columbia	25.8
AIRPORT 1975	1974	Universal	25.4
THE BLACK HOLE	1979	Buena Vista	25.4
THE WAY WE WERE	1973	Columbia	25.0
THE REVENGE OF THE PINK PANTHER	1978	Jewel/United Artists	25.0
THE BAD NEWS BEARS	1976	Paramount	24.3
POPEYE	1980	co-prod. Par/Disney	24.5
THE SPY WHO LOVED ME	1977	Eon/United Artists	24.3
THE ENFORCER	1976	Warner Bros.	24.1
IN SEARCH OF NOAH'S ARK	1970	Sunn	23.8
URBAN COWBOY	1980	Paramount	23.8
1941	1979	co-prod. Col/Universal	23.2
ORDINARY PEOPLE	1980	Paramount	23.1
THE LONGEST YARD	1974	Paramount	23.0
SEMI-TOUGH	1977	Merrick/United Artists	22.9
DELIVERANCE	1972	Warner Bros.	22.6
PAPILLON	1973	Allied Artists	22.5
DOG DAY AFTERNOON	1975	Warner Bros.	22.5

SOURCES: Joel Finler, *The Hollywood Story* (New York: Crown: 1988), pp. 277–78; *Variety*; *The Hollywood Reporter*.

APPENDIX 14
MAJOR ACADEMY AWARDS, 1970–1980

1970

Picture: PATTON (20th Century–Fox)
Director: Franklin J. Schaffner, PATTON
Actor: George C. Scott, PATTON (declined award)
Actress: Glenda Jackson, WOMEN IN LOVE
Supporting Actor: John Mills, RYAN'S DAUGHTER
Supporting Actress: Helen Hayes, AIRPORT
Writing:
  (Adapted screenplay) M•A•S•H—Ring Lardner, Jr
  (Original story and screenplay) PATTON—Francis Ford Coppola and Edmund H. North
Cinematography: RYAN'S DAUGHTER—Freddie Young
Art Direction–Set Decoration: PATTON—Urie McCleary, Gil Parrondo; Antonio Mateos,
Pierre-Louis Thevenet
Film Editing: PATTON—Hugh S. Fowler
Sound: PATTON—Douglas Williams and Don Bassman
Music:
  (Song) "For All We Know" (LOVERS AND OTHER STRANGERS)—music by Fred Karlin;
lyrics by Robb Royer and James Griffin (a.k.a. Robb Wilson and Arthur James)
  (Original Score) LOVE STORY—Francis Lai
  (Original Song Score) LET IT BE—The Beatles
Costume Design: CROMWELL—Nina Novarese
Special Visual Effects: TORA! TORA! TORA!—A.D. Flowers and L.B. Abbott
Documentary:
  (Short) THE GIFTS (The Water Quality Office of the Environmental Protection Agency)
  (Feature) CHARIOTS OF THE GODS (Terra-Filmkunst GmbH.)
Foreign Language Film: INVESTIGATION OF A CITIZEN ABOVE SUSPICION, Italy
Irving G. Thalberg Award: Ingmar Bergman
Jean Hersholt Humanitarian Award: Frank Sinatra
Honorary Awards:
  Lillian Gish
  Orson Welles

1971

Picture: THE FRENCH CONNECTION (20th Century–Fox)
Director: William Friedkin, THE FRENCH CONNECTION
Actor: Gene Hackman, THE FRENCH CONNECTION
Actress: Jane Fonda, KLUTE
Supporting Actor: Ben Johnson, THE LAST PICTURE SHOW
Supporting Actress: Cloris Leachman, THE LAST PICTURE SHOW
Writing:
  (Adapted screenplay) THE FRENCH CONNECTION—Ernest Tidyman
  (Original story and screenplay) THE HOSPITAL—Paddy Chayefsky

APPENDIX 14 (CONT.)

Cinematography: FIDDLER ON THE ROOF—Oswald Morris
Art Direction–Set Decoration: NICHOLAS AND ALEXANDRA—John Box, Ernest Archer, Jack Maxsted, Gil Parrondo; Vernon Dixon
Film Editing: THE FRENCH CONNECTION—Jerry Greenberg
Sound: FIDDLER ON THE ROOF—Gordon K. McCallum and David Hildyard
Music:
    (Song) "Theme from SHAFT" (SHAFT)—music and lyrics by Isaac Hayes
    (Original Score) MARY, QUEEN OF SCOTS—John Barry
    (Adaptation Score) FIDDLER ON THE ROOF—John Williams
Costume Design: NICHOLAS AND ALEXANDRA—Yvonne Blake and Antonia Castillo
Special Visual Effects: BEDKNOBS AND BROOMSTICKS—Alan Maley, Eustace Lycett, and Danny Lee
Documentary:
    (Short) ADVENTURES IN PERCEPTION (Han van Gelder Filmproduktie for Netherlands Information Service)
    (Feature) ALASKA WILDERNESS LAKE (Alan Landsburg Prods.)
Foreign Language Film: THE GARDEN OF THE FINZI-CONTINIS, Italy
Honorary Awards:
    Charlie Chaplin

1972

Picture: THE GODFATHER (Paramount)
Director: Bob Fosse, CABARET
Actor: Marlon Brando, THE GODFATHER
Actress: Liza Minnelli, CABARET
Supporting Actor: Joel Grey, CABARET
Supporting Actress: Eileen Heckart, BUTTERFLIES ARE FREE
Writing:
    (Adapted screenplay) THE GODFATHER—Mario Puzo and Francis Ford Coppola
    (Original story and screenplay) THE CANDIDATE—Jeremy Larner
Cinematography: CABARET—Geoffrey Unsworth
Art Direction–Set Decoration: CABARET—Rolf Zehetbauer, Jurgen Kiebach; Herbert Strabel
Film Editing: CABARET—David Bretherton
Sound: CABARET—Robert Knudson and David Hildyard
Music:
    (Song) "The Morning After" (THE POSEIDON ADVENTURE)—music and lyrics by Al Kasha and Joel Hirschhorn
    (Original Score) LIMELIGHT—Charles Chaplin, Raymond Rasch, and Larry Russell
    (Adaptation Score) CABARET—Ralph Burns
Costume Design: TRAVELS WITH MY AUNT—Anthony Powell
Documentary:
    (Short) HUNDERTWASSER'S RAINY DAY (Argos Films-Schamoni Film Prod./K-Z Nexus Films)
    (Feature) APE AND SUPER-APE (Netherlands Ministry of Culture, Recreation, and Social Welfare)

APPENDIX 14 (CONT.)

Foreign Language Film: THE DISCREET CHARM OF THE BOURGEOISIE, France
Jean Hersholt Humanitarian Award: Rosalind Russell
Honorary Awards:
    Charles S. Boren, leader for 38 years of the industry's enlightened labor relations and architect of its policy of non-discrimination
    Edward G. Robinson

1973

Picture: THE STING (Universal)
Director: George Roy Hill, THE STING
Actor: Jack Lemmon, SAVE THE TIGER
Actress: Glenda Jackson, A TOUCH OF CLASS
Supporting Actor: John Houseman, THE PAPER CHASE
Supporting Actress: Tatum O'Neal, PAPER MOON
Writing:
    (Adapted screenplay) THE EXORCIST—William Peter Blatty
    (Original story and screenplay) THE STING—David S. Ward
Cinematography: CRIES AND WHISPERS—Sven Nykvist
Art Direction–Set Decoration: THE STING—Henry Bumstead; James Payne
Film Editing: THE STING—William Reynolds
Sound: THE EXORCIST—Robert Knudson and Chris Newman
Music:
    (Song) "The Way We Were" (THE WAY WE WERE)—music by Marvin Hamlisch; lyrics by Alan Bergman and Marilyn Bergman
    (Original Score) THE WAY WE WERE—Marvin Hamlisch
    (Adaptation Score) THE STING—Marvin Hamlisch
Costume Design: THE STING—Edith Head
Documentary:
    (Short) BACKGROUND (D'Avino and Fucci-Stone Prods.)
    (Feature) ALWAYS A NEW BEGINNING (Goodell Motion Pictures)
Foreign Language Film: DAY FOR NIGHT, France
Irving G. Thalberg Award: Laurence Weingarten
Jean Hersholt Humanitarian Award: Lew Wasserman
Honorary Awards:
    Henri Langlois, for his devotion to the art of film
    Groucho Marx

1974

Picture: THE GODFATHER, PART II (Paramount)
Director: Francis Ford Coppola, THE GODFATHER, PART II
Actor: Art Carney, HARRY AND TONTO
Actress: Ellen Burstyn, ALICE DOESN'T LIVE HERE ANYMORE
Supporting Actor: Robert De Niro, THE GODFATHER, PART II
Supporting Actress: Ingrid Bergman, MURDER ON THE ORIENT EXPRESS

Appendix 14 (cont.)

Writing:

(Adapted screenplay) THE GODFATHER, PART II—Francis Ford Coppola and Mario Puzo

(Original story and screenplay) CHINATOWN—Robert Towne

Cinematography: THE TOWERING INFERNO—Fred Koenekamp and Joseph Biroc

Art Direction–Set Decoration: THE GODFATHER, PART II—Dean Tavoularis, Angelo Graham; George R. Nelson

Film Editing: THE TOWERING INFERNO—Harold F. Kress and Carl Kress

Sound: EARTHQUAKE—Ronald Pierce and Melvin Metcalfe, Sr.

Music:

(Song) "We May Never Love Like This Again" (THE TOWERING INFERNO)—music and lyrics by Al Kasha and Joel Hirschhorn

(Original Score) THE GODFATHER, PART II—Nino Rota and Carmine Coppola

(Adaptation Score) THE GREAT GATSBY—Nelson Riddle

Costume Design: THE GREAT GATSBY—Theoni V. Aldredge

Documentary:

(Short) CITY OUT OF WILDERNESS (Francis Thompson, Inc.)

(Feature) ANTONIA: A PORTRAIT OF THE WOMAN (Rocky Mountain Prods.)

Foreign Language Film: AMARCORD, Italy

Irving G. Thalberg Award: Arthur B. Krim

Honorary Awards:

Howard Hawks, a master American filmmaker

Jean Renoir, a genius who, with grace, responsibility, and enviable devotion through silent film, sound film, feature, documentary, and television, has won the world's admiration

Special Achievement Award:

Visual Effects: Frank Brendel, Glen Robinson, and Albert Whitlock for EARTHQUAKE

1975

Picture: ONE FLEW OVER THE CUCKOO'S NEST (United Artists)

Director: Milos Forman, ONE FLEW OVER THE CUCKOO'S NEST

Actor: Jack Nicholson, ONE FLEW OVER THE CUCKOO'S NEST

Actress: Louise Fletcher, ONE FLEW OVER THE CUCKOO'S NEST

Supporting Actor: George Burns, THE SUNSHINE BOYS

Supporting Actress: Lee Grant, SHAMPOO

Writing:

(Adapted screenplay) ONE FLEW OVER THE CUCKOO'S NEST—Laurence Hauben and Bo Goldman

(Original story and screenplay) DOG DAY AFTERNOON—Frank Pierson

Cinematography: BARRY LYNDON—John Alcott

Art Direction–Set Decoration: BARRY LYNDON—Ken Adam and Roy Walker; Vernon Dixon

Film Editing: JAWS—Verna Fields

Sound: JAWS—Robert L. Hoyt, Roger Heman, Earl Madery, and John Carter

Music:

(Original Song) "I'm Easy" (NASHVILLE)—music and lyrics by Keith Carradine

(Original Score) JAWS—John Williams

(Adaptation Score) BARRY LYNDON—Leonard Rosenman

APPENDIX 14 (CONT.)

Costume Design: BARRY LYNDON—Ulla-Britt Soderlund and Milena Canonero
Documentary:
    (Short) ARTHUR AND LILLIE (Department of Communication, Stanford University)
    (Feature) THE CALIFORNIA REICH (Yasny Talking Pictures)
Foreign Language Film: DERSU UZALA, USSR
Irving G. Thalberg Award: Mervyn LeRoy
Jean Hersholt Humanitarian Award: Jules C. Stein
Honorary Awards:
    Mary Pickford
Special Achievement Awards:
    Sound Effects: Peter Berkos for THE HINDENBURG
    Visual Effects: Albert Whitlock and Glen Robinson for THE HINDENBURG

1976

Picture: ROCKY (United Artists)
Director: John G. Avildsen, ROCKY
Actor: Peter Finch, NETWORK
Actress: Faye Dunaway, NETWORK
Supporting Actor: Jason Robards, ALL THE PRESIDENT'S MEN
Supporting Actress: Beatrice Straight, NETWORK
Writing:
    (Adapted screenplay) ALL THE PRESIDENT'S MEN—William Goldman
    (Original story and screenplay) NETWORK—Paddy Chayefsky
Cinematography: BOUND FOR GLORY—Haskell Wexler
Art Direction–Set Decoration: ALL THE PRESIDENT'S MEN—George Jenkins;
George Gaines
Film Editing: ROCKY—Richard Halsey and Scott Conrad
Sound: ALL THE PRESIDENT'S MEN—Arthur Piantadosi, Les Fresholtz, Dick Alexander, and
Jim Webb
Music:
    (Original Song) "Evergreen" (Love Theme From A STAR IS BORN)—music by Barbra
Streisand; lyrics by Paul Williams
    (Original Score) THE OMEN—Jerry Goldsmith
    (Adaptation Score) BOUND FOR GLORY—Leonard Rosenman
Costume Design: FELLINI'S CASANOVA—Danilo Donati
Documentary:
    (Short) AMERICAN SHOESHINE (Titan Films)
    (Feature) HARLAN COUNTY, U.S.A. (Cabin Creek Films)
Foreign Language Film: BLACK AND WHITE IN COLOR, Ivory Coast
Irving G. Thalberg Award: Pandro S. Berman
Special Achievement Awards:
    Visual Effects: Carlo Rambaldi, Glen Robinson, and Frank Van der Veer for KING KONG
    Visual Effects: L. B. Abbott, Glen Robinson, and Matthew Yuricich for LOGAN'S RUN

APPENDIX 14 (CONT.)

1977

Picture: ANNIE HALL (United Artists)
Director: Woody Allen, ANNIE HALL
Actor: Richard Dreyfuss, THE GOODBYE GIRL
Actress: Diane Keaton, ANNIE HALL
Supporting Actor: Jason Robards, JULIA
Supporting Actress: Vanessa Redgrave, JULIA
Writing:
   (Adapted screenplay) JULIA—Alvin Sargent
   (Original story and screenplay) ANNIE HALL—Woody Allen and Marshall Brickman
Cinematography: CLOSE ENCOUNTERS OF THE THIRD KIND—Vilmos Zsigmond
Art Direction–Set Decoration: STAR WARS—John Barry, Norman Reynolds, and Leslie Dilley; Rober Christian
Film Editing: STAR WARS—Paul Hirsch, Marcia Lucas, and Richard Chew
Sound: STAR WARS—Don MacDougall, Ray West, Bob Minkler, and Derek Ball
Music:
   (Original Song) "You Light Up My Life" (YOU LIGHT UP MY LIFE)—music and lyrics by Joseph Brooks
   (Original Score) STAR WARS—John Williams
   (Adaptation Score) A LITTLE NIGHT MUSIC—Jonathan Tunick
Costume Design: STAR WARS—John Mollo
Visual Effects: STAR WARS—John Stears, John Dykstra, Richard Edlund, Grant McCune, and Robert Black
Documentary:
   (Short) AGUEDA MARTINEZ: OUR PEOPLE, OUR COUNTRY (Esparza Production)
   (Feature) THE CHILDREN OF THEATRE STREET (Mack-Vaganova Company)
Foreign Language Film: MADAME ROSA, France
Irving G. Thalberg Award: Walter Mirisch
Jean Hersholt Humanitarian Award: Charlton Heston
Honorary Awards:
   Margaret Booth, for her exceptional contribution to the art of film editing in the motion picture industry
   Gordon E. Sawyer and Sidney P. Solow, in appreciation for outstanding service and dedication in upholding the high standards of the Academy of Motion Picture Arts and Sciences
Special Achievement Awards:
   Sound Effects Editing: Frank E. Warner for CLOSE ENCOUNTERS OF THE THIRD KIND
   Benjamin Burtt, Jr., for the creation of the alien, creature, and robot voices in STAR WARS

1978

Picture: THE DEER HUNTER (EMI Films-Universal)
Director: Michael Cimino, THE DEER HUNTER
Actor: Jon Voight, COMING HOME
Actress: Jane Fonda, COMING HOME

APPENDIX 14 (CONT.)

Supporting Actor: Christopher Walken, THE DEER HUNTER
Supporting Actress: Maggie Smith, CALIFORNIA SUITE
Writing:
    (Adapted screenplay) MIDNIGHT EXPRESS—Oliver Stone
    (Original story and screenplay) COMING HOME—Nancy Dowd, story; Waldo Salt and
Robert C. Jones, screenplay
Cinematography: DAYS OF HEAVEN—Nestor Almendros
Art Direction–Set Decoration: HEAVEN CAN WAIT—Paul Sylbert and Edwin O'Donovan;
George Gaines
Film Editing: THE DEER HUNTER—Peter Zinner
Sound: THE DEER HUNTER—Richard Portman, William McCaughey, Aaron Rochin, and
Darin Knight
Music:
    (Original Song) "Last Dance" (THANK GOD IT'S FRIDAY)—music and lyrics by Paul Jabara
    (Original Score) MIDNIGHT EXPRESS—Giorgio Moroder
    (Adaptation Score) THE BUDDY HOLLY STORY—Joe Renzetti
Costume Design: DEATH ON THE NILE—Anthony Powell
Documentary:
    (Short) THE DIVIDED TRAIL: A NATIVE AMERICAN ODYSSEY (A Jerry Aronson
Production)
    (Feature) THE LOVERS' WIND (Ministry of Culture and Arts of Iran)
Foreign Language Film: GET OUT YOUR HANDKERCHIEFS, France
Jean Hersholt Humanitarian Award: Leo Jaffe
Honorary Awards:
    Walter Lantz, for bringing joy and laughter to every part of the world through his
unique animated motion pictures
    Laurence Olivier
    King Vidor
    The Museum of Modern Art Department of Film for the contribution it has made to
the public's perception of movies as an art form
    Linwood G. Dunn, Loren L. Ryder, and Waldon O. Watson, in appreciation for out-
standing service and dedication in upholding the high standards of the Academy of Motion
Picture Arts and Sciences
Special Achievement Awards:
    Visual Effects: Les Bowie, Colin Chilvers, Denys Coop, Roy Field, Derek Meddings,
and Zoran Perisic for SUPERMAN

1979

Picture: KRAMER VS. KRAMER (Columbia)
Director: Robert Benton, KRAMER VS. KRAMER
Actor: Dustin Hoffman, KRAMER VS. KRAMER
Actress: Sally Field, NORMA RAE
Supporting Actor: Melvyn Douglas, BEING THERE
Supporting Actress: Meryl Streep, KRAMER VS. KRAMER

APPENDIX 14 (CONT.)

Writing:
  (Adapted screenplay) KRAMER VS. KRAMER—Robert Benton
  (Original story and screenplay) BREAKING AWAY—Steve Tesich
Cinematography: APOCALYPSE NOW—Vittorio Storaro
Art Direction–Set Decoration: ALL THAT JAZZ—Philip Rosenberg and Tony Walton;
Edward Stewart and Gary Brink
Film Editing: ALL THAT JAZZ—Alan Heim
Sound: APOCALYPSE NOW—Walter Murch, Mark Berger, Richard Beggs, and Nat Boxer
Music:
  (Original Song) "It Goes Like It Goes" (NORMA RAE)—music by David Shire; lyrics by
Norman Gimbel
  (Original Score) A LITTLE ROMANCE—Georges Delerue
  (Adaptation Score) ALL THAT JAZZ—Ralph Burns
Costume Design: ALL THAT JAZZ—Albert Wolsky
Visual Effects: ALIEN—H. R. Giger, Carlo Rambaldi, Brian Johnson, Nick Allder, and
Denys Ayling
Documentary:
  (Short) DAE (Vardar Film/Skopje)
  (Feature) BEST BOY (Only Child Motion Pictures, Inc.)
Foreign Language Film: THE TIN DRUM, Federal Republic of Germany
Irving G. Thalberg Award: Ray Stark
Jean Hersholt Humanitarian Award: Robert Benjamin
Honorary Awards:
  Hal Elias, for his dedication and distinguished service to the Academy of Motion
Picture Arts and Sciences
  Alec Guinness
  John O. Aalberg, Charles G. Clarke, and John G. Frayne, in appreciation for outstand-
ing service and dedication in upholding the high standards of the Academy of Motion
Picture Arts and Sciences
Special Achievement Awards:
  Sound Editing: Alan Spelt for THE BLACK STALLION

1980

Picture: ORDINARY PEOPLE (Paramount)
Director: Robert Redford, ORDINARY PEOPLE
Actor: Robert De Niro, RAGING BULL
Actress: Sissy Spacek, COAL MINER'S DAUGHTER
Supporting Actor: Timothy Hutton, ORDINARY PEOPLE
Supporting Actress: Mary Steenburgen, MELVIN AND HOWARD
Writing:
  (Adapted screenplay) ORDINARY PEOPLE—Alvin Sargent
  (Original story and screenplay) MELVIN AND HOWARD—Bo Goldman
Cinematography: TESS—Geoffrey Unsworth (posthumous) and Ghislain Cloquet
Art Direction–Set Decoration: TESS—Pierre Guffroy; Jack Stephens

APPENDIX 14 (CONT.)

Film Editing: RAGING BULL—Thelma Schoonmaker
Sound: THE EMPIRE STRIKES BACK—Bill Varney, Steve Maslow, Gregg Landaker, and
Peter Sutton
Music:
    (Original Song) "Fame" (FAME)—music by Michael Gore; lyrics by Dean Pitchford
    (Original Score) FAME—Michael Gore
Costume Design: TESS—Anthony Powell
Documentary:
(Short) DON'T MESS WITH BILL (Insight Productions Inc.)
(Feature) AGEE (James Agee Film Project)
Foreign Language Film: MOSCOW DOES NOT BELIEVE IN TEARS, USSR
Special Achievement Award:
    Visual Effects: Brian Johnson, Richard Edlund, Dennis Muren and Bruce Nicholson for
THE EMPIRE STRIKES BACK
Honorary Awards:
    Henry Fonda
    Fred Hynes, in appreciation of outstanding service and dedication in upholding the high
standards of the Academy of Motion Picture Arts and Sciences

SOURCE: Academy of Motion Picture Arts and Sciences.

Notes

CHAPTER 1 (INTRODUCTION: A DECADE OF CHANGE)

1. From 1969 to 1978, the networks spent nearly $1.5 billion on television rights to theatrical features, enough to subsidize production at several major studios. See William Lafferty, "Feature Films on Prime-Time Television," in *Hollywood in the Age of Television*, Tino Balio, ed. (Boston: Unwin Hyman, 1990), pp. 247–248.

2. James Lardner, *Fast Forward: Hollywood, the Japanese, and the Onslaught of the VCR* (New York: W. W. Norton, 1987), pp. 171–175.

3. Tom Bierbaum, "Study Puts '85 Homevid Retail Biz at $4.55 Bil," *Daily Variety*, January 7, 1986, p. 1.

4. Quoted in Mark Litwak, *Reel Power: The Struggle for Influence and Success in the New Hollywood* (New York: William Morrow, 1986), p. 91. Murphy comments: "Agents see the big money raised [from outside investors] and then demand ever greater amounts for their clients. They know you have fifty million in outside money. The outer bounds of financial limits are broken."

5. Suzanne Mary Donahue, *American Film Distribution: The Changing Marketplace* (Ann Arbor: UMI Research Press, 1987), p. 31.

6. Myron Meisel, "Industry: The Sixth Annual Grosses Gloss," *Film Comment* 17, no. 2 (March–April 1981), p. 64.

7. Jim Hillier, *The New Hollywood* (London: Studio Vista, 1992), p. 10.

8. Litwak, *Reel Power*, pp. 93–94.

9. "Hollywood S.O.S. on Subsidy: Rally Steams Up Alien Exclusion," *Variety*, December 2, 1970, p. 3. In many unions (e.g., International Alliance of Laborers Craft Services, International Alliance of Lamp Operators 728, and Story Analysts 854) unemployment ran about 50 percent, and in some others (International Alliance of Set Designers 847, Illustrators and Matte Artists 750) 65 percent and higher; see "H'wood's Production Slump Sparks Record Drop in Craft Employment," *Variety*, January 21, 1970, pp. 5, 71.

10. Andew Laskos, "The Hollywood Majors," in *Anatomy of the Movies*, David Pirie, ed., New York: Macmillan, 1981), p. 13.

11. Tino Balio, "Introduction to Part II," *Hollywood in the Age of Television*, pp. 260–261.

12. Joseph R. Dominick, "Film Economics and Film Content: 1964–1983," in *Current Research in Film: Audience, Economics, and Law*, Vol. 3, Bruce A. Austin, ed. (Norwood, NJ: Ablex Publishing, 1987), p. 146.

13. Stuart Byron, "The Industry," *Film Comment* 16, no. 1 (January–February 1980), p. 39.

14. Douglas Gomery, *Shared Pleasures: A History of Movie Presentation in the United States* (Madison: University of Wisconsin Press, 1992), p. 67; Tino Balio, *Grand Design: Hollywood as a Modern Business Enterprise, 1930–1939* (*History of the American Cinema*, Vol. 5 [New York: Charles Scribner's Sons, 1993]), p. 20.

15. A. D. Murphy, "Ten Years of Film Change," *Variety*, August 9, 1978, p. 1.

16. Balio, "Introduction to Part I," *Hollywood in the Age of Television*, p. 29.

17. "55–60 percent Firstrun, Where's Subrun Biz?: This Jan.–Feb. Is Unusual 'Shakeout,'" *Variety*, January 21, 1981, p. 3.

18. Thomas Guback, "The Evolution of the Motion Picture Theater Business in the 1980s," *Journal of Communication* 37, no. 2 (Spring 1987), pp. 67–69.

19. Peter Guber, "The Cartridge Revolution," *Cinema*, May 2, 1970; reprint in *The Movie Business: American Film Industry Practice*, A. William Bluem and Jason E. Squire, eds. (New York: Hastings House Publishers, 1972), pp. 258–291.

20. Quoted in Leonard J. Leff and Jerold L. Simmons, *The Dame in the Kimono: Hollywood, Censorship, and the Production Code from the 1920s to the 1960s* (New York: Grove Weidenfield, 1990), p. 270.

21. "Pix Say Sony's Betamax Infringes on Copyrights," *Variety*, November 17, 1976, pp. 1, 75.

22. Blay paid Fox an advance of $300,000 against a $500,000 per year minimum; a year later Fox, bought Magnetic Video from Blay for $7.2 million. See "20th–Fox First Major Studio to Enter Home Vidtape Market with Pix; License 50 Pre-'72s," *Variety*, August 8, 1977, pp. 3, 24; and Stephen Klain, "H-wood Pix on Home Tape at $50 Per; 20th–Fox Catalogue First to Hit New Market," *Variety*, December 7, 1977, pp. 1, 90.

23. Other notable collaborations among the majors during the 1970s include Universal-Paramount's SORCERER (William Friedkin, 1977); Fox-Columbia's ALL THAT JAZZ (Bob Fosse, 1979); Universal-Columbia's 1941 (Steven Spielberg, 1979) and THE ELECTRIC HORSEMAN (Sidney Pollack, 1979); and Paramount-Disney's POPEYE (Robert Altman, 1980).

24. See, for example, Robert Lindsey, "The New Tycoons of Hollywood," *The New York Times Magazine*, August 7, 1977, pp. 12–23; and Mike Bigrave, "The New Moguls" in David Pirie, ed., *Anatomy of the Movies* (New York: Macmillan, 1981), pp. 62–79.

25. Peter N. Carroll, *It Seemed Like Nothing Happened: The Tragedy and Promise of America in the 1970s* (New York: Holt, Rinehart and Winston, 1982).

26. Michael Pye and Lynda Myles, *The Hollywood Brats: How the Film Generation Took Over Hollywood* (New York: Holt, Rinehart and Winston, 1979).

27. Litwak, *Reel Power*, p. 155.

CHAPTER 2 (FORMATIVE INDUSTRY TRENDS, 1970–1979)

1. In 1969, United Artists lost $89 million, MGM lost $72 million, Fox lost $65 million—losing another $77.4 million in 1970, and Warners took a $25 million write-off of 1969 pictures in development.

2. "Columbia, Warners Alone of Majors 'Started' More Pix in 1969 Than 1968," *Variety*, December 3, 1969, p. 1.

3. *Los Angeles Times*, March 17, 1971, p. 1: "If the country as a whole is in a recession, the motion picture business is in an out and out depression. More than half of the 30,000 local film union members are out of work. In some crafts joblessness is said to be running 85–90 percent."

4. Stuart Byron, "'Instant Majors': A Short Cut," *Variety*, October 25, 1967, pp. 5, 21; and "American International Expected Inheritor of Cinerama Releasing, One of 'Instant Majors' of 1967," *Variety*, July 31, 1974, p. 3.

4a. Anthony Slide, *The New Historical Dictionary of the American Film Industry* (Lanham, MD and London: The Scarecrow Press, 1998), p. 44

5. Tino Balio, "Introduction to Part II," *Hollywood in the Age of Television* (Boston: Unwin Hyman, 1990), pp. 259–260.

6. Suzanne Mary Donahue, *American Film Distribution: The Changing Marketplace* (Ann Arbor: UMI Research Press, 1987), p 105.

7. David V. Picker, "The Film Company as Financier-Distributor," in *The Movie Business Book*, Jason E. Squire, ed. (Englewood Cliffs, NJ: Prentice Hall, 1983), p. 153.

8. Abel Green, "Topheavy Film Studio Fade: Film Biz Ducks Overhead Load," *Variety*, October 29, 1969, pp. 1, 24.

9. A. D. Murphy, "Film Trade Sanity Asserts Itself," *Variety*, April 12, 1972, pp. 3, 20.

10. A. D. Murphy, "Tax Break to Ease Pix Crisis: 'Schrieber Plan' to Cut Charges," *Variety*, September 15, 1971, p. 3. Another way Nixon helped the film industry—though inadvertently—was through his historic 8.75 percent devaluation of the U.S. dollar in August 1971, which automatically made foreign currency more valuable. Gene Arnell estimated that this produced a paper gain for the industry of about $34 million a year in overseas film and television sales ("Devaluation: Film Biz Boon," *Variety*, December 22, 1971, p. 1). See also Paul Harris, "Film Biz in 1971 Nixon 'Milk Deal'?: McCloskey Sees Tax Hanky-Panky," *Variety*, August 21, 1974, p. 1.

11. J. Hoberman, "Ten Films That Shook the World," *American Film* 10, no. 8 (June 1985), p. 36.

12. Andrew Laskos, "The Hollywood Majors," in *Anatomy of the Movies*, David Pirie, ed. (New York: Macmillan, 1981), pp. 13–14.

13. Quoted in "Alan Hirschfield at Columbia: Some 40–50 percent of Our $38–42 Million Production Has Been Co-Financed," *Variety*, August 14, 1974, p. 5.

14. In addition to Columbia, only United Artists depended significantly on tax shelter investments, having raised about 20 percent of its $52 million production budget for 1975 from this source. Smaller sums contributed to production capital at Warners, Paramount, American International, and Allied Artists, and no outside money was used at 20th Century–Fox, Walt Disney Productions, or MCA, whose Universal Studios was buoyed by a $95.5 million post-JAWS profit. See Robert Lindsey, "Film Investments Earn Tax Breaks—and Criticism," The *New York Times*, March 28, 1976, sec. E, p. 1.

15. "Tax Lures Revive Berlin as Production Center," *Variety*, September 8, 1976, pp. 5, 34; "German Tax Shelters Luring Yanks," *Variety*, December 8, 1976; "U.S. Tax Shelter Deals Migrate to Australia," *Variety*, May 5, 1979, p. 27.

16. "Possible Tax Ruling Bonanza: Judge Upsets Old Guideline," *Variety*, June 23, 1971, p. 3.

17. "Disney Tax Credit Retroactive to 1962," *Variety*, June 6, 1973, pp. 3, 6.

18. Martin Dale, *The Movie Game: The Film Business in Britain, Europe and America* (London: Cassell, 1997), p. 157.

19. From a record high of one billion in the postwar euphoria of 1946, average weekly attendance declined by 50 percent over the next decade (1947–1957) and another 60 percent between 1957 and 1965. After bottoming out in 1971, attendance rose slowly but steadily throughout the seventies until it plateaued at twenty-three million in the mid-eighties with little change since. The prevailing industry consensus is that such a market can support the production of fewer than 200 features per year. See Cobbett Steinberg, *Reel Facts: The Movie Book of Records*, rev. ed. (New York: Vintage Books, 1981), pp. 45–46.

20. Lee Beaupre, "Hits Few: Beasts of Burden: Analysis of 1971 Boom-Bust Biz," *Variety*, November 29, 1972, p. 6.

21. Thomas Schatz, "The New Hollywood," in *Film Theory Goes to the Movies*, Jim Collins, Hilary Radner, and Ava Preacher Collins, eds. (New York: Routledge, 1993), p. 16.

22. "Making the Movies into a Business," *Business Week*, June 23, 1973, pp. 123–124.

23. John Izod, *Hollywood and the Box Office, 1895–1986* (New York: Columbia University Press, 1988), p. 183.

24. See Mark Litwak, *Reel Power: The Struggle for Influence and Success in the New Hollywood* (New York: William Morrow, 1986), pp. 233–234; and David Lees and Stan Berkowitz, *The Movie Business* (New York: Vintage Books, 1981), pp. 144–147. The major studios have developed their own market research departments (in 1969 Paramount was the first to do so; see "Paramount Puts Science Into Sell," *Variety*, February 5, 1969, p. 5). Test screenings are conducted by independent firms like Lieberman Research Worldwide and National Research Group (NRG). See Frank Rose, "This Is Only a Test," *Premiere* 9, no. 12 (August 1996), pp. 27–30.

25. Justin Wyatt, *High Concept: Movies and Marketing in Hollywood* (Austin: University of Texas Press, 1994), p. 157.

26. See James Monaco, *American Film Now* (New York: Oxford University Press, 1979), pp. 26–26; John Izod, *Hollywood and the Box Office*, pp. 184–185; and Nancy Griffin and Kim Masters, *Hit and Run: How Jon Peters and Peter Guber Took Sony for a Ride in Hollywood* (New York: Simon & Schuster, 1996), pp. 82–86.

27. Myron Meisel, "Industry: The Sixth Annual Grosses Gloss," *Film Comment* 17, no. 2 (March–April 1981), p. 64. According to a study by Theodore E, James, Jr., a general partner of Montgomery Securities in San Francisco, the *average* advertising budget on a 1979 film was $2.5 million, with total ad expenditure ($514 million, including newspapers) equaling 23 percent of domestic rentals (*Marketing and Media Decisions*, March 1981, p. 150). Five years earlier, in 1973, the industry's media expenditures were a little more than half that sum ($273 million), the main difference being the rise of saturation booking with its heavy reliance on TV advertising. See Jeffrey Kaye, "Epic Price Tags for Epic Films," *Washington Post*, November 18, 1979, sec. G, pp. 1, 14, 16; and Stephen Farber, "Shelf Life," *Film Comment* 19, no. 3 (May–June 1983), pp. 39–43.

28. Lees and Berkowitz, *The Movie Business*, p. 158.

29. Stanford Blum, "Merchandising," in Jason E. Squire, ed., *The Movie Business Book*, 2nd ed. (New York: Simon & Schuster, 1992), pp. 408–409.

30. Lees and Berkowitz, p. 155.
31. Litwak, *Reel Power*, p. 242.
32. Robert Lindsey, "Product Pluggers Find Gold in Silver Screen," The *New York Times*, February 25, 1977, sec E, p. 3.
33. Richard Albarino, "'Billy Jack' Hits Reissue Jackpot: Unique Game Plan Produces a $60-Mil Bonanza," *Variety*, November 7, 1973, pp. 1, 63.
34. William Bates, "Hollywood in the Era of the 'Super-Grosser'," The *New York Times*, December 24, 1978, sec. E, p. 1.
35. Izod, *Hollywood and the Box Office*, p. 185.
36. A. D. Murphy, "Pick Picture Playoff Patterns," *Variety*, March 17, 1976, p. 1.
37. As a subsidiary of Mann Theaters, Ted Mann Productions financed such films as BUSTER AND BILLIE (Daniel Petrie, 1974), LIFEGUARD (Daniel Petrie, 1976), and BRUBAKER (Stuart Rosenberg, 1980). General Cinema Corporation, the nation's largest, financed a number of unsuccessful films during the decade and in 1979 attempted to acquire a 20-percent share of Columbia Pictures. On EXPRODICO, see "Film Famine Could Revive EXPRODICO," *Variety*, February 14, 1979, p. 7.
38. Donahue, *American Film Distribution* (1987), pp. 32, 179.
39. The earning figures given for films in this book, unless otherwise noted, are for domestic (U.S. and Canada) film rentals. See Christopher Reynolds, *1995 Hollywood Power Stats* (Valley Village, CA: Cineview Publishing, 1995), p. 89.
40. A. D. Murphy, "Distribution and Exhibition: An Overview," in *The Movie Business Book*, Jason E. Squire, ed. (Englewood Cliffs, NJ: Prentice Hall, 1983), pp. 256–257.
41. David V. Picker, "The Film Company as Financier-Distributor," in *The Movie Business Book*, Jason E. Squire, ed. (Englewood Cliffs, NJ: Prentice Hall, 1983), p. 153.
42. Ibid.
43. Harlan Jacobson, "'Product Shortage' Has Been Cry of Exhibitors Since Consent Decrees," *Variety*, September 8, 1976, p. 3.
44. "300 Indie Films Pace Production," *Variety*, June 9, 1976, p. l.
45. "10-Year Diary of Fast-Fade 'Indie' Pix," *Variety*, October 8, 1980, p. 10.
46. Lees and Berkowitz, *The Movie Business*, p. 74.
47. Leo Janos, "The Hollywood Game Grows Rich—and Desperate," The *New York Times*, February 12, 1978, sec. E, p. 15.
48. "Agent Power Now Rules Hollywood," *Variety*, January 9, 1974, p. 9.
49. David Pirie, "The Deal," in *Anatomy of the Movies*, David Pirie, ed. (New York: Macmillan, 1981), p. 45.
50. Litwak, *Reel Power*, p. 49.
51. Michael Conant, "The Paramount Decrees Reconsidered," in *The American Film Industry* (rev. ed.), Tino Balio, ed. (Madison: University of Wisconsin Press, 1985), p.552.
52. "Japan New No. 1 Market for U.S. Films; 60 percent of $1.9-Bil World Rentals from Domestic B.O.," *Variety*, July 11, 1979, p. 1.
53. John Lipman, "'Star Wars' Distribution Deal Leaves 20th Century–Fox with Power of Force," The *Wall Street Journal*, April 3, 1998, sec. A, p. 9; Neal Gabler, "The End of the Middle," The *New York Times Magazine*, November 16. 1997, p. 78.
54. These figures are for 1980, quoted from *Border Crossing: Film in Ireland, Britain and Europe*, John Hill et al., eds. (Belfast: Institute of Irish Studies, 1994), p. 75. See also "Special Report: Hollywood Abroad—Market and Image," *American Film* 7, no. 2 (November 1981), pp. 44–50; and Steven S. Wildman and Stephen E. Siwek, *International Trade in Films and Television Programs* (Cambridge, MA.: Ballinger Publishing, 1988), pp. 17–18.
55. Andreas Fuchs, "United International Marketing," *Film Journal International* 101, no. 6 (June 1998), p. 18.
56. "TV's 'Season of the Feature Films,'" *Variety*, October 2, 1967, p. 1; and "TV's New 'Untouchables'—Pictures," *Variety*, December 13, 1967, p. 1.
57. William Lafferty, "Feature Films on Prime-Time Television," in Tino Balio, ed. *Hollywood in the Age of Television*, p. 247.
58. Schatz, "The New Hollywood," in *Film Theory Goes to the Movies*, Jim Collins, Hilary Radner, and Ava Preacher Collins, eds. (New York: Routledge, 1993), pp. 15–16.
59. Michele Hilmes, *Hollywood and Broadcasting: From Radio to Cable* (Urbana and Chicago:

University of Illinois Press, 1990), pp. 186–187.

60. Martin S. Quigley and Associates, *First Century of Film* (New York: Quigley Publishing Company, Inc., 1995), p. xxi.

61. Richard Maltby and Ian Craven, *Hollwood Cinema* (Oxford: Blackwell, 1995), p. 478.

62. By way of comparison, the domestic box-office gross for 1995 was $5.43 billion. See Anne Thompson, "The 21st Annual 'Grosses Gloss'," *Film Comment* 32, no. 2 (March–April 1996), p. 60.

63. The figure of $640 million represents the pre-tax profits of the film and television divisions of the six majors for 1979; they fell to $477 million in 1980, and $301 million in 1981. See Stephen J. Sansweet, "Wall Street Goes to the Movies," *American Film* 8, no. 1 (October 1982), p. 46.

64. John F. Berry and Jack Egan, "After the Moguls: A New Breed Rules Hollywood," *Washington Post*, February 5, 1978, sec. M, p. 6.

65. *The Hollywood Reporte*r, November 22, 1980, "Wall Street Embracing Film Co.s Now That Rick Is Virtually Gone," p. 1.

66. Stephen Farber, "The Return of the Grown-Up Movie," *American Film* 7, no. 3 (December 1981), p. 51.

67. A term coined by J. Hoberman in "Ten Films That Shook the World" (*American Film* 10, no. 8 [June 1985], p. 45) that came into wide industry use.

68. "Loss of Control Over Film Costs Stressed by 'Heaven's Gate' Fiasco," *Variety*, January 14, 1981, p. 33.

CHAPTER 3 (MANUFACTURING THE BLOCKBUSTER: THE "NEWEST ART FORM OF THE TWENTIETH CENTURY")

1. Quoted in Michael Pye and Lynda Myles, *The Movie Brats: How the Film Generation Took Over Hollywood* (New York: Holt, Rinehart and Winston, 1979), p. 89.

2. David Gordon, "The Movie Majors," in *Sight and Sound* 48, no. 3 (Summer 1979), p. 152.

3. Quoted in Earl C. Gottschalk, Jr., "The Spectaculars," The *Wall Street Journal*, August 10, 1974, p. 1.

4. Lee Beaupre, "Hits Few: Beasts of Burden: Analysis of 1971 Boom-Bust Biz," *Variety*, November 30, 1972, pp. 5–6.

5. Ibid.

6. Andrew Laskos, "The Money and the Power," in *Anatomy of the Movies,* David Pirie, ed., (New York: Macmillan, 1981), pp. 12–13.

7. The *average* advertising budget on a 1979 film was $2.5 million, with total advertising expenditures ($514 million including newspapers) equaling 23 percent of domestic rentals ("Brand Report 63: Movies," *Marketing and Media Decisions*, March 1981, p. 150).

8. For example, the ten most bankable stars in 1980, according to Ian Jessel, marketing director of Lord Grade's ITC, were Robert Redford (box-office value estimated at $5 million per film), Clint Eastwood ($4 million), Robert De Niro ($3 million), Warren Beatty ($2 million), Steve McQueen ($2 million), Al Pacino ($2 million), Woody Allen ($2 million), Dustin Hoffman ($2 million), Barbra Streisand ($1.5 million; $3 million with songs), and Paul Newman ($1.5 million). (See Paul Kerr, "Stars and Stardom," in *Anatomy of the Movies,* David Pirie, ed., [New York: Macmillan, 1981], p. 104.) Of course, bankability was all relative to a star's latest hit. In 1979, following critical acclaim for her role in the sleeper THE CHINA SYNDROME (James Bridges, 1979), Columbia paid Jane Fonda $2 million to appear in a film entitled "Her Brother's Keeper," which hadn't been written yet and was never produced. (Aljean Harmetz, "Columbia Pays $2 Million to Jane Fonda for Film," The *New York Times*, September 28, 1979.)

9. Lee Beaupre, "How to Distribute a Film," *Film Comment* 13, no. 4 (July–August 1977), p. 46.

10. Tony Schwartz, "U.A. Pays $2.5 Million for Book by Gay Talese," The *New York Times*, October 7, 1979.

11. Charles Schreger, "Who's Afraid of the Pix Sequel Jinx?; H'Wood Riding Remake Cycle," *Variety*, November 23, 1977, p. 5. See also Omar Hendrix, "What Will 'Jaws' and 'Exorcist' Do for an Encore?," *New York Times*, June 27, 1976; Judy Klemesrud, "Can He Make the 'Jaws' of Outer Space?," *New York Times*, May 15, 1977; and David Lewin, "Can the Makers of 'Star Wars' Do It Again?," *New York Times*, December 2, 1979. On remakes and sequels as defensive production and marketing strategies, see Stephen M. Silverman, "Hollywood Cloning: Sequels, Prequels, Remakes, and Spin-Offs," *American Film* 3, no. 9 (July-August 1978), pp. 24–30; and Constantine

Verevis, "Re-Viewing Remakes, *Film Criticism* 21, no. 3 (Spring 1997), pp. 1–19.

12. Joseph R. Dominick, "Film Economics and Film Content, 1964–1983," in *Current Research in Film: Audience, Economics, and Law,* Vol. 3, Bruce A. Austin, ed. (Norwood, NJ: Ablex, 1987), p. 146. In a related study, however, Thomas Simonet found that although the 1970s did see an increase in the number of "recycled-script films" (i.e., remakes, sequels, or series films) over the 1960s, the figure remained far below that of the high studio era as represented by the 1940s. (Thomas Simonet, "Conglomerates and Content: Remakes, Sequels, and Series in the New Hollywood," in *Current Research in Film: Audiences, Economics, and Law,* Vol. 3, Bruce A. Austin, ed. (Norwood, NJ: Ablex, 1987), pp. 162.

13. Quoted in J. Hoberman, "Ten Films That Shook the World," *American Film* 10, no. 8 (June 1985), p. 35.

14. Evans had come to Paramount as a vice president in charge of production in 1966 from 20th Century–Fox, where he had worked as an independent producer since 1960.

15. "'Love Story' Boffo: Turns Around Par," *Variety,* January 6, 1971, p. 5; and "$100-M of 'Love': Big Grosses for 'Love Story' May Approach $100-M," *Variety,* April 7, 1971, p. 3.

16. Peter Bart, then vice-president of production at Paramount, says that studio head Stanley Jaffe and distribution chief Frank Yablans discussed the GODFATHER project with about "30 completely inappropriate directors, all of whom turned them down." He also reports that Sam Peckinpah was seriously considered and wanted the film, but the nod of course went to Coppola. See Peter Biskind, "Making Crime Pay," *Premiere,* August 1977, pp. 80–86, 107–108.

17. *Variety,* April 5, 1972, p. 3.

18. Thomas Schatz, "The New Hollywood," in *Film Theory Goes to the Movies,* Jim Collins, Hilary Radner, and Ava Preacher Collins, eds. (New York: Routledge, 1993), p. 16.

19. "Airport," *Variety Movie Guide* '97, Derek Elley, ed. (London: Hamlyn, 1996), p. 12.

20. Douglas Gomery, *Shared Pleasures: A History of Movie Presentation in the United States* (Madison: University of Wisconsin Press, 1992), p. 227; "Universal Encourages Theaters to Four-Wall 'Rollercoaster,'" *Variety,* February 9, 1977, p. 4.

21. Gary Arnold, "Chalking 'Graffiti' Up to Experience," The *Washington Post,* May 26, 1974, sec. E, p. 3.

22. Stephen Farber, "Hollywood's New Sensationalism: The Power and the Gory," The *New York Times,* July 7, 1974, sec. E, p. 1.

23. Richard Albarino, "'Billy Jack' Hits Reissue Jackpot: Unique Game Plan Produces a $60-Mil Bonanza," *Variety,* November 7, 1974, pp. 1, 63.

24. Syd Silverman, "U.S. Four-Walling: Boon or Threat?," *Variety,* November 7, 1974, p. 64; and "Hollywood Up Against the Wall-to-Wall: Feds Eye Distrib Reentry Into Exhibition," *Variety,* April 3, 1974, pp. 1, 36. See also Richard Moses, "The Rise, Fall, and Second Coming of Four-Walling," *Variety,* January 8, 1975; Wayne Kabak, "On Four-Walling," *Film Comment* 11, no. 6 (November–December 1975), pp. 30–31.

25. Frederick Wasser, "Four-Walling Exhibition: Regional Resistance to the Hollywood Film Industry," *Cinema Journal* 34, no. 2 (Winter 1995), p. 57. See also Frank Segers, "N.Y. Exhibs Fear the 'Exorcist' Devil: If WB Designs Four-Wall Plan," *Variety,* February 27, 1974, p. 5; "Fear 'Wall' Deals Local Ad Crypt: Big 15 percent Shops Seen a Chocker," *Variety,* April 17, 1974, p. 7.

26. Farber, "Hollywood's New Sensationalism: The Power and the Gory," p. 1.

27. Ibid.

28. See Justin Wyatt, *High Concept: Movies and Marketing in Hollywood* (Austin: University of Texas Press, 1994), pp. 8–13.

29. J. Hoberman, "Ten Films That Shook the World," p. 35.

30. Schatz, "The New Hollywood," p. 17.

31. Then, as now, publishers regularly vetted prepublication galley proofs to Hollywood producers in hopes of a movie rights sale, with the important difference that many publishers and movie studios are now owned by the same conglomerates.

32. Carl Gottlieb, *The Jaws Log* (New York: Dell, 1975), pp. 15–19. This copiously illustrated paperback provides an informative account of the production of the film by one of the collaborators on the screenplay. It was rushed into print in 1975 as part of the promotion campaign.

33. JAWS was actually photographed by Bill Butler, as DP, and his operator Michael Chapman. Since the Steadicam was not yet available, all of the shots at sea, including those that comprise the film's last thirty minutes, were hand-held, making JAWS (as Spielberg and Chapman were both fond of pointing out) "the most expensive hand-held movie ever made." (See "Michael Chapman" in

Masters of Light: Conversations with Contemporary Cinematographers, Dennis Schaefer and Larry Salvato, eds., [Berkeley: University of California Press, 1985], p. 102.)

34. Harlan Jacobson, "U Introducing Nat'l Co-op Ads on 'Jaws': Assess Exhibs Share of TV Buys," *Variety,* April 16, 1975, p. 3.

35. Pye and Myles, *The Movie Brats,* p. 236.

36. Stuart Byron, "First Annual Grosses Gloss," *Film Comment* 12, no. 2. (March–April 1976), p. 30.

37. Ibid.

38. Spielberg told *The Hollywood Reporter* a week after JAWS opened that Universal had originally planned "a mass-saturation blitzkrieg campaign in 1,000 theaters" but got cold feet after a March preview in Long Beach indicated that the film needed some re-editing. (Quoted in Joseph McBride, *Steven Spielberg: A Biography* [New York: Simon & Schuster, 1997], p. 258.)

39. See A. D. Murphy, "1975 Record Film B.O. Nears $1.9-Bil: 'Variety' Key City Grosses Up More Than 90 percent," *Variety,* January 14, 1976, pp. 1, 86; A. D. Murphy, "Universal Pics Make Film History: 1975 World Rentals at Alltime High of $289-Mil," *Variety,* January 21, 1976, p. 1; and A. D. Murphy, "Universal's Whale of Pix Biz Share: 'Jaws' Makes U No. 1 with 25 percent of Domestic Gross," *Variety,* February 11, 1976, p. 1.

40. Pye and Myles, *The Movie Brats,* p. 237.

41. Justin Wyatt, *High Concept: Movies and Marketing in Hollywood* (Austin: University of Texas Press, 1994), p. 117.

42. Quoted in J. Hoberman, "Ten Films That Shook the World," p. 36.

43. Addison Verrill, "'Kong' Wants 'Jaws' Boxoffice Crown," *Variety,* December 22, 1976, p. 1.

44. Farber, "Hollywood's New Sensationalism: The Power and the Gory," p. 1.

45. Michael Pye, *Moguls: Inside the Business of Show Business* (New York: Holt, Rinehart and Winston, 1980), pp. 192–194.

46. Nancy Griffin and Ken Masters, *Hit and Run: How Jon Peters and Peter Guber Took Sony for a Ride in Hollywood* (New York: Simon & Schuster, 1996), p. 84.

47. Ibid., p. 85.

48. Wyatt, *High Concept,* p. 146.

49. James Monaco, *American Film Now: The People, the Power, the Money, the Movies* (New York: Oxford University Press, 1979), p. 25.

50. Quoted in Griffin and Masters, p. 85.

51. Monaco, p. 25.

52. "Alan Hirschfield at Columbia: Some 40–50 percent of Our $38–42 Million Production Program Has Been Co-Financed," *Variety,* August 14, 1974, p. 5. In fact, there was German tax-shelter money in CLOSE ENCOUNTERS, which the producers had qualified to receive by beginning the shoot on the last two days of 1975 (the formation of tax shelters for production finance became illegal on January 1, 1976), then shutting down until the following May. (See Jim McBride, *Steven Spielberg: A Biography* [New York: Simon & Schuster, 1997], pp. 270–271.)

53. Pye and Myles, *The Movie Brats,* p. 240; Thomas Guback, "Theatrical Film," in Benjamin M. Compaine, *Who Owns the Media?: Concentration of Ownership in the Mass Communications Industry,* 2nd ed. (White Plains, N.Y.: Knowledge Industry Publications, Inc., 1982), p. 230.

54. Monaco, *American Film Now,* pp. 24–25; Vincent Canby, "'Somebody Must Put a Lid on Budgets'," *The New York Times,* November 27, 1977, sec. E, p. 14; John Baxter, *Steven Spielberg: The Unauthorized Biography* (New York: HarperCollins, 1996), p. 169.

55. Olen J. Earnest, "STAR WARS: A Case Study of Motion Picture Marketing," in *Current Research in Film: Audiences, Economics, and Law,* Vol. 1, Bruce A. Austin, ed. (Norwood, NJ: Ablex, 1985), p. 6. For all his research, however, Lucas did not fully understand the cultural dimensions he was tapping into: when the STAR WARS was in production, for example, he told a *New York Times* reporter—with apparent seriousness—that the film was basically "an effort to interest young people in space exploration." (See Donald Goddard, "From 'American Graffiti' to Outer Space," *New York Times,* September 9, 1976.)

56. David Pirie, "The Deal," in *Anatomy of the Movies,* David Pirie, ed. (New York: Macmillan, 1981), p. 54.

57. Dale Pollock, *Skywalking: The Life and Films and George Lucas* (Hollywood: Samuel French, 1990), pp. 136–137.

58. Pye and Myles, *The Movie Brats,* p. 131. STAR WARS action figures proved so popular that in the Christmas following the film's release demand far exceeded supply. The licensed manufacturer,

Kenner, was forced to ship empty boxes to retailers with IOU certificates for later redemption so that parents could at least have something to put under the tree. (See Tiuu Lunk, *Movie Marketing* [Los Angeles: Silman-James Press, 1997], pp. 253–257.)

59. Quoted in Pollock, p. 158.
60. Earnest, p. 14.
61. Ibid., p. 12.
62. Quoted in John Seabrook, "Letter from Skywalker Ranch: Why Is the Force Still with Us?," *The New Yorker*, January 6, 1997, p. 44.
63. Ibid., p. 40.
64. James Sterngold, "The Return of the Merchandiser," The *New York Times*, January 30, 1997, sec. C, p. 1.
65. Ibid., sec. C, p. 6.
66. Ibid., sec. C, p. 1.
67. Tiiu Lunk, *Movie Marketing: Opening the Picture and Giving It Legs* (Los Angeles: Silman-James Press, 1997), pp. 254–255.
68. A. D. Murphy, "Twenty Years of Weekly Film Ticket Sales in U.S. Theaters," *Variety*, March 15–21, 1989, p. 26.
69. William Bates, "Hollywood in the Era of the 'Super-Grosser'," The *New York Times*, December 24, 1978, sec. E, p. 1.
70. Stephen J. Sansweet, "Wall Street Goes to the Movies," *American Film* 8, no. 1 (October 1982), p. 46.
71. Quoted in Bates, "Hollywood in the Era of the 'Super-Grosser'," sec. E, p. 1.
72. Leo Janos, "The Hollywood Game Grows Rich—and Desperate," The *New York Times*, February 12, 1978, sec. E, pp. 4, 15.
73. Bates, "Hollywood in the Era of the 'Super-Grosser'," sec. E, p. 1.
74. Ibid.
75. Janos, p. E15.
76. Joseph McBride, "Newly Cordial to Low Budget Features: Part of Flight from $-Mad Stars," *Variety*, December 15, 1976, pp. 5, 23.
77. See "Pix Look For Cut of Music Biz Action: Disk Boom Cues H'wood Themes," *Variety*, November 16, 1977, p. 5.
78. Alexander Doty, "Music Sells Movies: (Re)New(ed) Conservatism in Film Marketing," *Wide Angle* 10, no. 2, p. 76.
79. Peter Guralnick, *Careless Love: The Unmaking of Elvis Presley* (Boston: Little, Brown & Company), pp. 366–367. The exact quote is, "Nothing could be simpler or more logical [in Parker's thinking]: the soundtrack album promoted the movie release, the movie release guaranteed a certain level of sales and publicity for the album."
80. *Film Journal*, August 1980, p. 45.
81. Quoted in Thomas Maromaa, "The Sound of Movie Music," *New York Times*, March 28, 1976, sec. E, p. 15.
82. "A Hit Is Born and Made," *Variety*, February 9, 1977, p. 124.
83. Michael Pye, *Moguls: Inside the Business of Show Business* (New York: Holt, Rinehart and Winston, 1980), p. 273.
84. Post-release telephone surveys for STAR WARS showed that 40 percent of its audience had seen the film three or four times by the end of August 1977; most of these were teenagers and some of them had seen the film between thirty and thirty-five times. (See Earnest, "Case Study," p. 16.)
85. Quoted in Stuart Byron, "Fourth Annual Grosses Gloss," *Film Comment* 15, no. 2 (March–April 1970), p. 72.
86. J. Hoberman, "Ten Films That Shook the World," p. 42.
87. A. D. Murphy, "Audience Demographics, Film Future: Loss of Youth Adjustment Due," *Variety*, August 20, 1975, pp. 3, 74. In this article Murphy predicted a "diminishing dichotomy between films made strictly for the young and those made for general audiences," resulting in a "truly mass audience" but also "the later ultimate sterilization of content." In other words, the Hollywood of Steven Spielberg.
88. Stephen Farber, "The Return of the Grown-Up Movie," *American Film* 7, no. 12 (December 1981), p. 51. This second-wave youth market had grown even larger by the decade's end: a survey conducted for the MPAA in the summer of 1979 indicated that 49 percent of all movegoers were between the ages of twelve and twenty, and another 27 percent between twenty-one and

twenty-nine. By this accounting, then, 76 percent of the national audience was under thirty as the 1980s began.

89. R. Serge Denisoff and William D. Romanowski, *Risky Business: Rock in Film* (New Brunswick, NJ: Transaction Publishers, 1991), p. 235.

90. Quoted in Susan Sackett, *The Hollywood Reporter Book of Box Office Hits*, rev. ed. (New York: Billboard Books, 1996), p. 261.

91. Quoted in Bates, "Hollywood in the Era of the 'Super-Grosser'," sec. E, p. 1.

92. Ibid.

93. "'Superman,' Pair, in $50-M. Super Budget," *Variety*, March 22, 1978, pp. 3, 26.

94. Quoted in Walter Powell, "The Blockbuster Decades," in *American Media and Mass Culture: Left Perspectives*, Donald Lazere, ed. (Berkeley: University of California Press, 1987), p. 61.

95. "Brand Report 47: Motion Pictures," in *Marketing and Media Decisions* 14, no. 11 (November 1979), p. 152.

96. Quoted in "Million-and-More Per Pic Sell on TV," *Variety*, March 26, 1980, pp. 5, 42.

97. "Brand Report 63: Movies," in *Marketing and Media Decisions* 16, no. 3 (March 1981), p. 150.

98. Jon Lewis, *Whom God Wishes to Destroy: Francis Ford Coppola and the New Hollywood* (Durham: Duke University Press, 1995), p. 45; and "Brand Report 47: Motion Pictures," in *Marketing and Media Decisions* 14, no. 11 (November 1979), p. 158.

99. Alan Stanbrook, "Hollywood's Crashing Epics," *Sight and Sound* 50, no. 2 (Spring 1981), p. 82; and Michael Dempsey, "After the Fall: Post-Cimino Hollywood," *American Film* 6, no. 10 (September 1981), p. 53. See also Jordan R. Young, "Studio Heads Forecast for 1981: The Year of Cost-Effective Filmmaking," *Millimeter*, January 1981, pp. 169–181.

100. Lee Beaupre, "Hits Few: Beasts of Burden: Analysis of 1971 Boom-Bust Biz," *Variety*, November 29, 1972, pp. 5–6.

101. Andrew Fogelson, quoted in Bates, "Hollywood in the Era of the 'Super-Grosser'," sec. E, p. 1.

102. A. D. Murphy, "Winter, Spring, Summer or Fall, B.O.'s Now a Year-Round Ball," *Variety*, March 15–21, 1989, pp. 1, 26.

103. Quoted in Bates, "Hollywood in the Era of the 'Super-Grosser'," sec. E, p. 1.

104. Schatz, "The New Hollywood," p. 25.

105. David Lees and Stan Berkowitz, *The Movie Business* (New York: Vintage Books, 1981), p. 183.

106. A. D. Murphy, p. 26.

CHAPTER 4 (THE AUTEUR CINEMA: DIRECTORS AND DIRECTIONS IN THE "HOLLYWOOD RENAISSANCE")

1. "Pix Must Broaden Market: 18 percent of Public; 76 percent of Audience," *Variety*, March 20, 1968, pp. 1, 78.

2. Another European pickup of 1966, Allied Artist's A MAN AND A WOMAN (Claude Lelouch) was similarly rewarded by American audiences for its stylistic éclat, earning $6.3 million to become #15 on *Variety*'s annual grosses chart (BLOWUP was #13).

3. The youth market was deemed so critically important that the majors actually hired full-time scholastic liaison officers to build public relations within the student community. See Eric Spilker, "Majors Staff Up For Youth: Assign Contacts to Cover Field," *Variety*, June 24, 1970, pp. 3, 60.

4. "Modern Films for the Masses," *Variety*, April 17, 1968, p. 23.

5. Ibid.

6. See, for example, Abel Green, "Era of Young Film Presidents: Stan Jaffe, 30, Latest of Breed," *Variety*, July 29, 1970, pp. 3, 22.

7. "Evans' Par Credo: Stress Story, Encourage Youth, Mix in Experience," *Variety*, February 21, 1967, p. 9.

8. Andrew Sarris, "Notes on the Auteur Theory in 1962," *Film Culture*, No. 27 (Winter 1962–1963).

9. Andrew Sarris, *The American Cinema: Directors and Directions, 1929–1968* (New York: E. P. Dutton & Company, 1968).

10. Anthologized in Kael, *I Lost It At the Movies* (Boston: Little, Brown, 1965), pp. 264–288.

11. Kael, "Raising Kane," *The New Yorker*, February 20, 1971, pp. 43–89; and February 27, 1971, pp. 44–81; reprint. in *The 'Citizen Kane' Book* (Boston: Little, Brown, 1971), pp. 1–84.

12. Eric Sherman and Martin Rubin, eds., *The Director's Event: Interviews with Five American Film-makers* (New York: New American Library, 1969); and Joseph Gelmis, ed., *The Film*

Director as Superstar: Kubrick, Lester, Mailer, Nichols, Penn, Polanski, and Others (New York: Doubleday, 1970). The directors interviewed by Sherman and Rubin are Peter Bogdanovich, Samuel Fuller, Abraham Polonsky, Budd Boetticher, and Arthur Penn. Gelmis interviewed sixteen directors representing New Hollywood cinema, as well as the American underground and the European art cinema.

13. Thomas M. Pryor, "Youth with 'em, Exhibs Grin," *Variety*, November 13, 1968, p. 1.

14. "'Visual' Mod & 'Verbal' Crix: Kubrick's Sure '2001' to Click," *Variety*, April 10, 1968, p. 3.

15. Ibid.

16. Jon Lewis, *Whom God Wishes to Destroy: Francis Ford Coppola and the New Hollywood* (Durham: Duke University Press, 1995), p. 19.

17. Gary Crowdus and Richard Porton, "The Importance of a Singular, Guiding Vision: An Interview with Arthur Penn," *Cineaste* 20, no. 2 (Spring 1993), p. 12.

18. "'Brutal Films Pale Before Televised Vietnam'—Valenti," *Variety*, February 21, 1968, p. 2. See also Abel Green, "Year of Violence & Mergers: Diversify Biz, Defy Morality," *Variety*, January 3, 1968, pp. 1, 41, 43, 45.

19. Two 1969 Supreme Court decisions were also involved in the creation of the ratings system. In *Ginsberg v. New York*, the Court ruled that the government could protect minors from sexually explicit materials; in *Interstate Circuit v. Dallas*, the Court affirmed the basic constitutionality of local censorship ordinances. Together, the two decisions suggested that communities could establish their own censorship guidelines for minors, so the MPAA set out to beat them to it.

20. "Mom-Pop Film Code: G-M-R-X: Trade Education Vs. Legislation," *Variety*, October 6, 1968, pp. 3, 9; and "MPAA's New Code & Rating Rules," op. cit., pp. 8–9.

21. Quoted in Stephen Farber, *The Movie Rating Game* (Washington, DC: Public Affairs Press, 1972), p. 46.

22. Stephen Prince, *Savage Cinema: Sam Peckinpah and the Rise of Ultraviolent Movies* (Austin: University of Texas Press, 1998), p. 26.

23. According to CARA's 1969 annual report, nearly a third of the 325 films rated that year (102) were re-edited to secure a rating change, including ALICE'S RESTAURANT, BOB & TED & CAROL & ALICE, BUTCH CASSIDY AND THE SUNDANCE KID, DARLING LILI, GOODBYE COLUMBUS, IF. . . . , LAST SUMMER, THE LEARNING TREE, A MAN CALLED HORSE, and THE REIVERS. See Stephen Farber, *The Movie Rating Game* (Washington, DC: Public Affairs Press, 1972), pp. 55–72.

24. The credited producers of EASY RIDER are Raybert Productions and the Pando Company, and the distributor was Columbia Pictures. Raybert was founded in 1965 by Bob Rafelson and Bert Schneider; it became BBS during the film's production with the addition of Steve Blauner to the partnership. Pando Productions was a company formed by Peter Fonda in 1968 specifically to raise finance capital for EASY RIDER.

25. Quoted in Michael Pye and Lynda Myles, *The Movie Brats: How the Film Generation Took Over Hollywood* (New York: Holt, Rinehart, and Winston, 1979), p. 191.

26. Seth Cagin and Philip Dray, *Born to Be Wild: Hollywood and the Sixties Generation* (Boca Raton, FL: Coyote, 1994), p. 71.

27. *The Hollywood Reporter*, December 17, 1970, p. 28.

28. Quoted in Tag Gallagher, "Night Moves," *Sight and Sound* 44, no. 2 (Spring 1975), p. 87.

29. See, for example, Lee Beaupre, "Few 'Superstar' Directors: 'Unreliable' As Most Players," *Variety*, August 9, 1972, pp. 3, 26.

30. "Rackmil: Spartacus's Take Nears $12-Mil," *Variety*, February 14, 1962, p. 7.

31. Vincent LoBrutto, *Stanley Kubrick: A Biography* (New York: Donald I. Fine Books, 1997), p. 202.

32. Robert Sklar, "Stanley Kubrick and the American Film Industry," in *Current Research in Film: Audience, Economics, Law*, Vol. 4, Bruce A. Austin, ed. (Norwood, NJ: Ablex Publishing, 1988), p. 114.

33. The score for A CLOCKWORK ORANGE is a mixture of prerecorded classical performances (as with 2001) and electronic music composed and performed by Walter Carlos on a Moog synthesizer. It was the first feature film to use Dolby noise reduction for its re-recording mix, although Kubrick didn't use the Dolby system in production until the 1980s.

34. Vincent Canby, quoted in Vincent LoBrutto, *Stanley Kubrick: A Biography* (New York: Donald I. Fine Books, 1997), p. 361.

35. Vincent LoBrutto, *Stanley Kubrick: A Biography*, p. 359.

36. J. Hofsess, "The Shining: Stanley Kubrick is Hoping His Film of Stephen King's Horror Story Will Be a Monster Hit," *The Washington Post*, June 1, 1980, sec. H, p. 1.

37. According to his diary, Arthur Bremmer was inspired by A CLOCKWORK ORANGE during his stalking of presidential candidate George Wallace, which culminated in his shooting Wallace in Laurel, Maryland, on May 15, 1972. Three years later, screenwriter Paul Schrader used Bremmer's diary as background for the character of Travis Bickle in TAXI DRIVER (Martin Scorsese, 1976). And five years after that, John Hinckley, Jr., attempted to assassinate President Ronald Reagan on March 30, 1981 in an apparent effort to act out Bickle's role in the film, stemming from his obsession with Jodie Foster, who had played a 12-year-old prostitute in it. (See Franklin L. Ford, *Political Murder: From Tyrannicide to Terrorism* [Cambridge: Harvard University Press, 1985].)

38. A. Verrill, "Give Sales Exec Hard Time: Kubrick-Katz Monitor Menace," *Variety*, March 8, 1972, p. 3.

39. "Kubrick Keeping Next Pic a Secret, Even from Warner," *Variety*, October 4, 1972, p. 3

40. Norman Kagan, *The Cinema of Stanley Kubrick*, new ed. (New York: Continuum, 1989), pp. 189–190.

41. David McGillivray, "Flops," in *Anatomy of the Movies*, David Pirie, ed., (New York: Macmillan, 1981), p. 306.

42. This is Thomas Allen Nelson's term from *Kubrick: Inside a Film Artist's Maze* (Bloomington: Indiana University Press, 1982), pp. 165–196.

43. Sklar ("Stanley Kubrick and the American Film Industry") says $12 million; John Baxter says $13 million (*Stanley Kubrick: A Biography* [New York: Carroll & Graf, 1997; p. 307]; Harlan Kennedy says $18 million ("Kubrick Goes Gothic: The Shining—an $18 Million Scare," *American Film* 5, no. 8 [June 1980], pp. 49–52).

44. Vincent LoBrutto, *Stanley Kubrick: A Biography*, p. 449.

45. Kubrick's involvement with production administration led him to experiment with various state-of-the-art information processing systems at different points in time—in the early 1970s he employed the new German Definitiv display filing system, allowing for an infinite cross-referencing of materials, to help him strategize location shoots for A CLOCKWORK ORANGE and BARRY LYNDON; more recently he has used computer modeling for budget allocation, and computerized editing systems for pre-assemblage of his films on video.

46. Produced in England for $17 million, FULL METAL JACKET earned $22.7 in the North American market.

47. "Details, Details," *Entertainment Weekly*, no. 372 (March 28, 1997), p. 9.

48. Garner Simmons, *Peckinpah: A Portrait in Montage* (Austin: University of Texas Press, 1982), p. 71.

49. David Weddie, *"If They Move . . . Kill 'em!": The Life and Times of Sam Peckinpah* (New York: Grove Press, 1994). pp. 369–370.

50. See, for example, Michael Bliss, ed., *Doing It Right: The Best Criticism on Sam Peckinpah's The Wild Bunch* (Carbondale: Southern Illinois University Press, 1994).

51. These were restored to theatrical prints for Warner's 1995 re-release of THE WILD BUNCH.

52. Weddie, p. 387.

53. Simmons, p. 137.

54. See, for example, Lee Beaupre, "Debate Over Brutality: 'Violence' as Substitute for 'Stars'; Explicit Horrors of '72 Pix—and Why; Recall Torture Shows of Ancient Rome," *Variety*, January 3, 1973, p. 16.

55. Pauline Kael, quoted in Marshall Fine, *Bloody Sam: The Life and Films of Sam Peckinpah* (New York: Donald I. Fine, 1991), p. 210.

56. Quoted in Marshall Fine, *Bloody Sam: The Life and Films of Sam Peckinpah*, p. 208.

57. Weddie, p. 428.

58. The term comes from a book by Western writer Max Evans, who played the shotgun guard in *Cable Hogue* and wrote an account of the production entitled *Sam Peckinpah: Master of Violence*. Peckinpah had optioned Evans's novel *The Hi-Lo Country* in 1963, with the intention of filming it, and the two became lifelong friends. (The novel was finally filmed in 1999, directed by Stephen Frears from a screenplay by WILD BUNCH co-writer Walon Green, with Martin Scorsese as executive producer.)

59. Robert Evans, *The Kid Stays in the Picture* (Beverly Hills, CA: Dove Books, 1994), pp. 248–250.

60. Weddie, p. 441.

61. Aubrey basically dumped PAT GARRETT & BILLY THE KID in order to take a write-off. During his brief stewardship of MGM production, Aubrey concentrated mainly on exploitation films with

budgets under $2 million, reasoning that, if they failed, the economic impact would be minimal. PAT GARRETT was budgeted at $3 million and went over budget during principal photography in Mexico. (See Peter Bart, *Fade Out: The Calamitous Final Days of MGM* [New York: William Morrow, 1990], pp. 40, 43–44.)

62. Simmons, *Peckinpah: A Portrait in Montage*, p. 223.

63. Weddle, p. 504.

64. Fine, *Bloody Sam: The Life and Films of Sam Peckinpah*, pp. 306–307.

65. Weddle, p. 519.

66. Peckinpah also worked with some of the biggest stars of the decade, including Dustin Hoffman, Steve McQueen, Ali McGraw, James Caan, Robert Duvall, and Kris Kristofferson.

67. "'Cold Day' Made Less Seductive; Thereby Excapes X of R Tag," *Variety*, July 2, 1969, p. 3.

68. Quoted in Alan Karp, *The Films of Robert Altman* (Metuchen, NJ: Scarecrow Press, 1981), p. 8.

69. Patrick McGilligan, *Robert Altman: Jumping Off the Cliff* (New York: St. Martin's Press, 1988), p. 328.

70. Lion's Gate was named after the suspension bridge that spans Burrard Inlet to link downtown Vancouver with the city's North Shore, first encountered by Altman while on location for THAT COLD DAY IN THE PARK.

71. C. Kirk McClelland, *On Making a Movie: Brewster McCloud* (New York: New American Library, 1971), p. 7.

72. As part of its contract for use of the Astrodome, MGM was obligated to premiere BREWSTER MCCLOUD there. Projected on a 150-by-70–foot screen for a crowd of approximately 24,000, the film was inaudible and created a bad first impression for the press, the public, and MGM, which apparently decided to dump it on the exploitation circuit on the basis of the experience.

73. Virginia Wright Wexman and Gretchen Bisplinghof, *Robert Altman: A Guide to References and Resources* (Boston: G. K. Hall, 1984), p. 43.

74. Ibid., p. 365.

75. Quoted in Judith M. Kass, *Robert Altman: American Innovator* (New York: Popular Library, 1978), p. 176.

76. McGilligan, *Robert Altman: Jumping Off the Cliff*, p. 381.

77. See Lear Levin, "Robert Altman's Innovative Sound Techniques," *American Cinematographer* 61, no. 6 (April 1980), pp. 336–339, 368, 384–385.

78. McGilligan, p. 447.

79. "De Laurentiis Dismisses Altman from *Ragtime*," The *New York Times*, June 22, 1976, sec. H, p. 31.

80. Wexman and Bipslinghoff, p. 61.

81. Vincent Canby, "The New Movie—Cool and Disorienting," The *New York Times*, May 22, 1977, sec. H, p. 1.

82. Spacek won Best Supporting Actress for her role in THREE WOMEN from the New York Film Critics, and Duvall shared the Best Actress award at Cannes for her part.

83. Charles Schreger, "Altman, Dolby, and the Second Sound Revolution," in *Film Sound: Theory and Practice*, ed. Elizabeth Weis and John Belton (New York: Columbia University Press, 1985), p. 350.

84. "Robert Altman Co. Sets Up Plant For Self and Tenants," *Variety*, February 7, 1979, pp. 3, 49; and Justin Wyatt, "Economic Constraints/Economic Opportunities: Robert Altman as Auteur," *The Velvet Light Trap*, 38 (Fall 1996), p. 57.

85. Even when he resumed filmmaking in the 1990s, Altman worked not for the majors but for the independent, art-house distributors Fine Line Features (a subsidiary of New Line Cinema—THE PLAYER [1992]; SHORT CUTS [1993]), Miramax (READY TO WEAR [1994]; KANSAS CITY [1996]), and Island (a subsidiary of Polygram—THE GINGERBREAD MAN [1998]).

86. See. for example, ch. 11, "Who's Afraid Virginia Woolf?" in Leonard J. Leff and Jerold L. Simmons, *The Dame in the Kimono: Hollywood, Censhorship, and the Production Code from the 1920s to the 1960s* (New York: Grove Weidenfeld, 1990), pp. 241–266.

87. "High Court's 'Carnal' Ruling Seen As Crucial For Cinema Freedom," *Variety*, June 26, 1974, pp. 1, 79.

88. The Directors Company produced only three films—Bogdanovich's PAPER MOON (1973) and DAISY MILLER (1974) and Coppola's THE CONVERSATION (1974)—before Yablans withdrew Paramount from the agreement.

89. At LONG LAST LOVE, budgeted at $6 million, was rushed into release by Fox, and after a disastrous opening, the director recut the film several times, so that it now exists in both a 115-minute (video) and 121-minute version. (See Thomas J. Harris, *Bodganovich's Picture Shows* [Metuchen, NJ: Scarecrow Press, 1990], pp. 183–198.)

90. Collected now in Peter Bogdanovich's 850-page compilation *Who the Devil Made It?* (New York: Alfred A. Knopf, 1997).

91. When its producer, 20th Century–Fox, shelved THEY ALL LAUGHED as unreleasable, Bogdanovich bought it from the studio for $5 million and tried to distribute it himself through his own company, Moon Pictures. Its commercial failure contributed materially to his bankruptcy in 1985.

92. Bogadanovich began an affair with Dorothy Stratten, a former *Playboy* playmate turned actress, in London during the filming of THEY ALL LAUGHED. This was discovered by her former husband, Paul Snyder, who had hired a private detective to have her trailed, and Snyder shot her to death two weeks after the picture's completion. Amid considerable controversy, Bogdanovich wrote a memoir about Dorothy entitled *The Killing of the Unicorn: Dorothy Stratten 1960–1980* (New York: Alfred A. Knopf, 1984), and later married her half-sister Louise B. Stratten (in 1988). Bob Fosse's grim biopic STAR 80 (1983) is about Stratten's life and murder.

93. Bogdanovich filed suit against MASK's distributor Universal/MCA and producer Martin Starger for having made unauthorized cuts in the film and tampering with its sound track (a matter of eliminating about ten minutes of Bruce Springsteen music that the studio had failed to acquire the rights for). Bogdanovich publicly disowned the Universal version, although it garnered some of the best reviews of his career; his position was strongly supported by the Director's Guild of America, but some observers felt he had lost his reason over the Stratten affair. (See Andrew Yule, *Picture Shows: The Life and Films of Peter Bogdanovich* (New York: Limelight Editions, 1992), pp. 207–212.)

94. Thomson notes that "many Americans began to take directors more seriously because of what he [Bogdanovich] wrote." (See *A Biographical Dictionary of Film*, 3rd ed. [New York: Alfred A. Knopf, 1994], p. 74.)

95. William Peter Blatty, *William Peter Blatty on "The Exorcist" from Novel to Film* (New York: Bantam, 1974), p. 41.

96. The rating itself was controversial, and Jack Valenti was called on to publicly defend it by pointing out that THE EXORCIST contained no "overt sex" or "excessive violence." Nonetheless, many cities restricted the film to those under eighteen.

97. Stephen Farber, "A Unique Freak Show: *The Exorcist*," *Film Comment* 10, no. 3 (May–June 1974), p. 34.

98. *Variety,* February 9, 1973, p. 44

99. CIC would become UIP (United International Pictures) in 1981, when MGM/UA joined the distributorship.

100. William Friedkin, SORCERER Symposium, Director's Guild of America, June 6, 1978. The title was Friedkin's, as he explained at the symposium: "The title SORCERER occurred to me to represent several things. Each character was a kind of evil wizard, a specialist. One with explosives, another a wheel man, another is a manipulator of people, and the fourth is a trigger man. Then the sorcerer, really, was fate." The logistics of SORCERER were complicated enough to require two directors of photography (John M. Stephens and Dick Bush, BSC) and four sound designers led by Jean-Louis Ducarme, and all four were nominated for an Academy Award); its musical score was composed and performed by Tangerine Dream.

101. Dale Pollack, "*Cruising*: Protests on the Picket Lines," *Los Angeles Times*, Calendar, February 18, 1980, p. 1; and "*Cruising* Tails Off," *Los Angeles Times*, Calendar, March 16, 1980, p. 3.

102. *Variety,* February 12, 1980, p. 14.

103. Larry Gross, "What Ever Happened to William Friedkin?," *Sight and Sound* 5, no. 12 (December 1995), pp. 14–15.

104. In 1990, Rafelson and Schneider sued Columbia for return of the negatives, prints, and outtakes from this process. See *Variety*, November 12, 1990, p. 4.

105. On the imaginative, cost-effective lighting style of THE KING OF MARVIN GARDENS, see Laszlo Kovacs, "Dialogue on Film," *American Cinematographer* 55, 10 (October 1974), pp. 2–13.

106. Patrick McGilligan, *Jack's Life: A Biography of Jack Nicholson* (New York: W. W. Norton, 1994), p. 267.

107. Harold Schneider would later produce BLACK WIDOW (1987). Rafelson's professional association with former BBS colleagues continued throughout his career—for example, Jack Nicholson starred in two of his post-1970s films (THE POSTMAN ALWAYS RINGS TWICE [1981] and MAN TROUBLE [1992]), and Carole Eastlake wrote the screenplay for one of them (MAN TROUBLE).

108. Stephen Farber, "Hearts and Bodies," *New West,* May 10, 1976, p. 82.

109. *Variety,* December 12, 1971.

110. "Producer's Appeals Make Mockery of MPAA's 'R' for Vulgar Words Often Loaded as 'Shock Value'," *Variety,* February 7, 1979, pp. 4, 49.

111. Joseph McBride, "Song for Woody: Joseph McBride on the Set of *Bound for Glory,*" *Film Comment* 12, no. 6 (November–December 1976), p. 26.

112. In 1962 Pakula formed a production company with Robert Mulligan and produced six films over the next seven years with Mulligan as director, including the Oscar-nominated hit TO KILL A MOCKINGBIRD (1962), LOVE WITH THE PROPER STRANGER (1963), BABY, THE RAIN MUST FALL (1965), INSIDE DAISY CLOVER (1965), UP THE DOWN STAIRCASE (1967), and THE STALKING MOON (1969).

113. Paramount was nervous about the controversial nature of THE PARALLAX VIEW and held up its release by several months, presumably to see which way the political wind was blowing. The film was finally released in June 1974, two months before Nixon was forced to resign the presidency on August 9, 1974. On the analogical relationship between the events of the film and the JFK assassination, see Art Simon, *Dangerous Knowledge: The JFK Assassination in Art and Film* (Philadelphia: Temple University Press, 1996).

114. Richard T. Jameson, "The Pakula Parallax," *Film Comment* 12, no. 5 (September–October 1976), p. 8.

115. Allen's first venture into film was to produce and co-write the script of WHAT'S UP, TIGER LILY? (1966), a redubbed, parodic version of a Japanese spy movie called KAGI NO KAGI (KEY OF KEYS [Senkichi Taniguchi, 1964]).

116. According to its editor, Ralph Rosenberg, ANNIE HALL was anything but a mainstream romantic comedy in its first cut, which was originally entitled "Anhedonia"(meaning the inability to experience pleasure). In his memoir, *When the Shooting Stops . . . the Cutting Begins* (New York: Viking, 1979), Rosenberg describes this version as "the surrealistic and abstract adventures of a neurotic Jewish comedian" in which Alvy Singer's relationship with Annie Hall is just another thread (p. 275). But Allen and Rosenberg "began cutting in the direction of that relationship" when they realized its potential (p. 281). In the course of five test screenings, the title was changed from "Anhedonia" to "Anxiety," to "Alvy and Annie," and finally to "Annie Hall" (p. 289).

117. Allen's last United Artists film was STARDUST MEMORIES (1980); his association with Orion began with A MIDSUMMER NIGHT'S SEX COMEDY (1982) and lasted through SHADOWS AND FOG (1992); Columbia-TriStar distributed HUSBANDS AND WIVES (1992) and A MANHATTAN MURDER MYSTERY (1993); with BULLETS OVER BROADWAY (1994), Allen's distributor became Miramax.

118. Although most of Allen's art films, or "chamber films," as he calls them (after Bergman), failed commercially during the seventies and eighties, by the mid-nineties, his films were averaging a domestic gross of $10–15 million regardless of content, and he had developed a large following in Europe, where pre-sold distribution rights helped to subsidize his independence in the United States. (See Peter Cowie, "Introduction" to *Annie Hall* [BFI Modern Classics Series; London: BFI, 1996].)

119. *Variety,* March 22, 1974, p. 11.

120. Peter Biskind, *Easy Riders, Raging Bulls* (New York: Simon & Schuster, 1998), p. 249.

121. Biskind, pp. 297–298.

122. Schatz, *Old Hollywood/New Hollywood: Ritual, Art, and Industry* (Ann Arbor: UMI Research Press, 1983), p. 203.

123. The new aspect ratio had the unfortunate effect of cropping off the dancers' feet.

124. Lewis, *Whom God Wishes to Destroy: Francis Ford Coppola and the New Hollywood* (Durham: Duke University Press, 1995), p. 13.

125. George Lucas has said: "Francis saw Zoetrope as a sort of alternative EASY RIDER studio where he could do the same thing: get a lot of young talent for nothing, make movies, hope that one of them would be a hit, and eventually build a studio that way." (Quoted in Dale Pollack, *Skywalking: The Life and Films of George Lucas* [Hollywood: Samuel French, 1990], p. 88.)

126. Richard Albarino, "Coppola: Creative Over Company Man: Ownership, Final Cut, Playoff Are Seen As Vital," *Variety*, August 21, 1974, pp. 3, 6.
127. Pye and Myles, *The Movie Brats*, p. 86.
128. Ibid., p. 111.
129. The provisional figure cited in the development deal was $12 million. When UA executives saw a rough cut of APOCALYPSE NOW, they decided to reduce the studio's principal investment in the film to $7.5 million and loan Coppola the remaining $25 million. This loan, secured by the director's profit interest in the GODFATHER films (6 points in the original; 10–15 points on the sequel) and the assets of American Zoetrope, forced Coppola to carry the burden of investment risk, but, as Jon Lewis argues, it gave him "a degree of control over his own destiny that neither he nor any other director of his generation had ever enjoyed" (Lewis, p. 42).
130. "General Studios Finally Coppola's; but He Stays with Frisco Base," *Variety*, March 12, 1980, pp. 3, 40.
131. Lane Maloney, "Coppola: Inflation Propelling Film to Electronics, Satellites," *Variety*, March 26, 1980, p. 40.
132. Lewis, p. 59.
133. Before that happened, however, Coppola shot the two last Zoetrope films on location in Tulsa, Oklahoma, both adapted from the youth novels of S. E. Hinton. THE OUTSIDERS (1983) was a film of teenage rebellion thematically and formally indebted to Nicholas Ray's REBEL WITHOUT A CAUSE (1955), whereas RUMBLE FISH (1983) was a highly allusive family melodrama shot in a black-and-white style deliberately evocative of German Expressionism. The former was a box-office hit and propelled Coppola into a deal to direct THE COTTON CLUB (1984), a Robert Evans production, for release through Orion. A big-budget gangster film (projected at $20 million; final cost $47 million) set in Harlem during the 1920s and featuring the music of Duke Ellington, THE COTTON CLUB received mixed reviews and broke even at the box office. Faced with enormous debt, Coppola directed two films in rapid succession for Tri-Star, PEGGY SUE GOT MARRIED (1986), a thoughtful treatment of the previous year's BACK TO THE FUTURE (Robert Zemeckis, 1985) formula which became his highest-grossing film of the decade, and GARDENS OF STONE (1987), a melancholy account of a Vietnam-era military burial unit at Arlington National Cemetery, which was, almost inevitably, a commercial failure. TUCKER: THE MAN AND HIS DREAM (1988), produced with George Lucas's backing for Paramount, fared little better at the box office, but was perceived by critics as a major comeback for Coppola as auteur. Based on the true story of Preston Thomas Tucker, the visionary entrepreneur who successfully fought post-war Detroit to manufacture what he called "the first completely new car in 50 years" but was ruined by monopolistic collusion before he could market it, Coppola's film was crafted as both a roman à clef and homage to Orson Welles's CITIZEN KANE (1941). It was followed by the successful sequel THE GODFATHER, PART III (1990), which Coppola wrote with Puzo for Paramount to continue the Corleone saga into the present. Produced for $57 million and earning $70 million, the film received Academy Award nominations for best picture, best director, and best actor. But Coppola's true redemption as far as Hollywood was concerned came with BRAM STOKER'S DRACULA (1992), which was produced on time and just slightly under budget for $50 million for Columbia. The film grossed $200 million worldwide in its first four months. For all its contemporary music-video patina, DRACULA is a knowing compendium of silent film special effects; and this unlikely triumph of cinematic style over exhausted genre and jaded audience signaled that Coppola's auteurist impulse had not only survived the industry upheaval of the previous three decades but, in some sense, prevailed.
134. Ted Ashley, the executive in charge at Warners, turned the negative of THX-1138 over to in-house editor Rudi Fehr, who cut a little over four minutes from the film. The footage was restored for re-release of the film after the success of STAR WARS in 1977.
135. Pye and Myles, *The Movie Brats*, p. 237.
136. The huge profits from E.T. (1982) and POLTERGEIST (Tobe Hooper, 1982), for which he was executive producer, enabled Spielberg to form Amblin Entertainment in 1984. There he was co-executive producer for some of the eighties' most successful entertainment—GREMLINS (Joe Dante, 1984), BACK TO THE FUTURE (Robert Zemeckis, 1985), AN AMERICAN TAIL (Don Bluth, 1986; animated), and their various sequels, as well as the live-action/animated WHO FRAMED ROGER RABBIT? (Robert Zemeckis, 1988), with Disney's Touchstone Pictures. Spielberg also co-produced his own work through Amblin in partnership with other studios—for example, with

Warner Bros., he collaborated on THE COLOR PURPLE (1985), an adaptation of Alice Walker's Pulitzer Prize-winning account of growing up black and female in the Depression-era South, and EMPIRE OF THE SUN (1987), a version of J. G. Ballard's novel about life in a Japanese prison camp in China during World War II; and with Universal he produced a remake of Victor Fleming's romantic fantasy A GUY NAMED JOE (1943) entitled ALWAYS (1989). These "adult" films met with varying degrees of critical and financial disappointment, inducing Spielberg to return to the world of childhood with HOOK (1991; produced with Sony Pictures/TriStar), an inflated, star-studded version of *Peter Pan* that was considered a financial failure even though it earned $65 million in domestic rentals. The epochal success of JURASSIC PARK (1993) briefly confirmed the impression that Spielberg worked best with juvenile material—at least until the release of deeply serious SCHINDLER'S LIST (1993), a somber film about the Holocaust that was hailed as a masterpiece and won Academy Awards for Best Picture, Best Director, Best Screenplay, Art Direction, Cinematography, Editing, and Score.

137. "Taxi Dancer: Martin Scorsese Interviewed by Jonathan Kaplan," *Film Comment* 13, no. 4 (July–August 1977), pp. 41–43.
138. For a contemporary reaction to TAXI DRIVER's exploitation component—its "playing both sides of the box-office dollar"—see Patricia Patterson and Manny Farber, "The Power and the Gory," *Film Comment* 12, no. 3 (May-June 1976), pp. 26–30.
139. Quoted in Les Keyser, *Martin Scorsese* (Boston: Twayne Publishers, 1992), p. 112.
140. Anthony DeCurtis, "Martin Scorsese," *Rolling Stone*, November 1, 1990, p. 106.
141. Gelmis, *The Film Director as Superstar*, "Brian De Palma," p. 29.
142. Laurent Bouzereau, *The De Palma Cut* (New York: Dembner Books, 1988), p. 37.
143. Pauline Kael, Review of PHANTOM OF THE PARADISE, *The New Yorker*, November 11, 1974, p. 44.
144. Herrmann received posthumous nominations for both OBSESSION and TAXI DRIVER (Martin Scorsese, 1976) but lost to Jerry Goldsmith for his score for THE OMEN (Richard Donner, 1976). Herrmann's importance to "film generation" directors lay not only in the fact that he was himself a great (and somewhat neglected) composer, but also that his scores were closely associated with the premiere auteurs of the American cinema—Hitchcock and Welles.
145. Robert E. Kapsis, *Hitchcock: The Making of a Reputation* (Chicago: University of Chicago Press, 1992), pp. 196–198.
146. Cohen would later write the screenplay for GHOST STORY (John Irvin, 1981) from Peter Straub's best-selling novel and adapt CARRIE as a Broadway musical, which closed after three weeks in 1988.
147. Roger Greenspun, "Carrie, and Sally and Leatherface Among the Film Buffs," *Film Comment* 13, no. 1 (January-February 1977), p. 17.
148. Kapsis, pp. 204–205.
149. Pye and Myles, *The Movie Brats*, pp. 167–168.
150. Kapsis, pp. 214–215. On the hue and cry over DRESSED TO KILL, see Charles Lyons, "Murder of Women Is Not Erotic: Feminists against DRESS TO KILL (1980)," in *The New Censors: Movies and the Culture Wars* (Philadelphia: Temple University Press, 1997), pp. 53–80.
151. The class of 1965–1970 also included writer-directors Matthew Robbins (DRAGONSLAYER) and Willard Huyck (FRENCH POSTCARDS), cinematographer Caleb Deschanel (THE BLACK STALLION), editor Walter Murch (APOCALYPSE NOW), composer Basil Poledouris (BLUE LAGOON, CONAN THE BARBARIAN), writer Dan O'Bannon (ALIEN), and writer-director Robert Zemeckis (USED CARS, the BACK TO THE FUTURE series, WHO FRAMED ROGER RABBIT?, and FORREST GUMP). Dale Pollock has described this group and its UCLA/NYU counterparts as "the cinematic equivalent of the Paris writer's groups in the 1920s" (*Skywalking*, pp. 47–48). Less ethereally, in a 1983 press release USC claimed that "41 of the 42 all-time highest grossing films have USC alumni affiliated with them."
152. Garth Jowett, *Film: The Democratic Art* (Boston: Little, Brown and Company, 1976), p. 437.
153. Garth Jowett and James M. Linton, *Movies as Mass Communication*, 2nd ed. (Newbury Park, CA: SAGE Publications, 1989), p. 59.
154. Auteurism as a marketing tool was not completely new to the industry—Hitchcock's cameos in his films from THE LODGER (1926) through FAMILY PLOT (1976) were both "signatures" *and* marketing hooks. Several other directors or director-producers enjoyed a similar celebrity during the studio era,

including C. B. DeMille, Walt Disney, and Frank Capra (as suggested by the title of the latter's auto-biography, *The Name Above the Title* [New York: Macmillan, 1971; reprint. Da Capo Press, 1997])

155. Pye and Myles, *The Movie Brats*, p. 81.

CHAPTER 5 (GENRES I: REVISION, TRANSFORMATION, AND REVIVAL)

1. See, for example, Morris Dickstein, "Summing Up the Seventies: Issues," *American Film*, December 1979, pp. 28, 55–57; Stephen Schiff, et al., "Midsection: Dueling Genres," *Film Comment* 18, no. 2 (March-April 1982), pp. 33–48; Robert Sklar, *Movie-Made America: A Cultural History of American Movies*, rev. ed. (New York: Vintage Books/Random House, 1994), pp. 327–329; Douglas Gomery, "The New Hollywood," in Geoffrey Nowell-Smith, ed., *The Oxford History of World Cinema* (New York: Oxford University Press, 1996), pp. 475–482.

2. See Peter Lloyd, "The American Cinema 3: An Outlook," *Monogram*, no. 1 (April 1971), pp. 11–13; Thomas Elsaesser, "The Pathos of Failure: American Films in the 70s," *Monogram*, no. 6 (1975), pp. 13–19; Sybil De Gaudio, "Columbia and the Counterculture: Trilogy of Defeat," in Bernard F. Dick, ed., *Columbia Pictures: Portrait of a Studio* (Lexington: University of Kentucky Press, 1992), pp. 182–190.

3. Distributed by United Artists, A HARD DAY'S NIGHT and HELP! earned $4.5 and $4.2 million respectively in rentals to become the sixteenth highest grossing films of 1964 and 1965. A French (Les Films 13) production, A MAN AND WOMAN was picked up by Allied Artists and returned $6.3 million in rentals, making it the fifteenth highest earning film of 1966; it also won Academy Awards for Best Story/Screenplay and Best Foreign Language Film. Another film that exposed the American mass audience to New Wave form was Tony Richardson's TOM JONES (1963), the highest-earning film of the year ($17.1 million in rentals) and winner of Oscars for Best Film, Best Screenplay, and Best Original Score. Made for Woodfall Productions, UK, and distributed by United Artists, this adaptation of an 18th-century picaresque novel offered French New Wave technique by way of British social realism.

4. Among much other invective about BONNIE AND CLYDE, Crowther wrote in his *New York Times* review of 1967 that it was "a cheap piece of bald-faced slapstick comedy that treats the hideous depredations of that sleazy, moronic pair as though they were as full of fun and frolic as the jazz-age cutups in THOROUGHLY MODERN MILLIE. . . . It has Beatty clowning broadly as the killer who fondles various types of guns with as much nonchalance and dispassion as he airily twirls a big cigar, and it has Dunaway squirming grossly as his thrill-seeking, sex-starved moll."

5. Robert B. Ray, *A Certain Tendency of the Hollywood Cinema, 1930–1980* (New Jersey: Princeton University Press, 1985), p. 287.

6. See Robert Self, "The Art Cinema of Robert Altman," *The Velvet Light Trap* 19, pp. 30–34; and Justin Wyatt, "Economic Constraints/Economic Opportunities: Robert Altman as Auteur," *The Velvet Light Trap*, 38 (Fall 1996), pp. 52–67.

7. Quoted in Seth Cagin and Philip Dray, *Born to Be Wild: Hollywood and the Sixties Generation* (Boca Raton: Coyote Press, 1994), p. 101. Aubrey said this in Rome, where he had flown to see Antonioni's new cut of the film after its censorious re-editing by his MGM predecessor Louis F. Polk, Jr.

8. Stephen Schiff, "The Repeatable Experience," *Film Comment* 18, no. 2 (March–April 1982): 35–36.

9. These figures are cited in the U.S. Supreme Court's opinion in the *United States v. Paramount Pictures* case of 1947, quoted in Gerald Mast, ed., *The Movies in Our Midst: Documents in the Cultural History of Film in America* (Chicago: University of Chicago Press, 1982), p. 601.

10. Thomas Schatz, *Old Hollywood/New Hollywood: Ritual, Art, and Industry* (Ann Arbor, MI: UMI Research Press, 1983), p. 223.

11. An additional $180,000 was spent on EASY RIDER's postproduction, making its total costs about $550,000. The film's $19.2 million in rentals would therefore represent an approximate investment return of 37:1. On the stampede to reproduce the film's success, see Hank Werba, "'Rider's' $50,000 Gross?': Fonda Parlays 325G into Hit," *Variety*, November 5, 1969, pp. 29–30; and Aubrey Tarbox, "Dreamy Cheapness of 'Rider'." *Variety*, December 10, 1969, pp. 5, 32.

12. Stanley Kauffman, "Celebrating the Film Generation," in Louis M. Savary and J. Paul Carrico, eds., *Contemporary Film and the New Generation* (New York: Association Press, 1971), p. 51.

13. The Maysle Brothers had tried but failed to raise the $400,000 Woodstock Ventures was asking for the festival's film rights. Warners came in to the deal by guaranteeing the promoters 50-percent profit participation in the film, and a sound-track album to be released on the Warner Reprise label.

14. Abel Green, "B. O. Dictatorship By Youth: Kids As Talent and Consumers," *Variety*, January 7, 1970, pp. 3, 36. See also Stanley Penn, "Movie Makers See Box Office This Year In Low-Cost, Timely Films Liked by Young," The *Wall Street Journal*, Friday, March 27, 1970, p. 20.

15. "Variety B.O. Charts' 1969 Results," *Variety*, April 29, 1970, p. 26.

16. The AIP biker pic was a standard 1960s exploitation form (THE WILD ANGELS [Roger Corman, 1966]; THE BORN LOSERS ["T. C. Frank," i.e., Tom Laughlin, 1967]) and one of the models for EASY RIDER. After EASY RIDER, bikers were imbued with a kind of existential angst that had a number of bad consequences, including the Hell's Angels being hired to provide security at Altamont. Another was an hour-long NBC-TV series called *Then Came Bronson,* produced by Robert H. Justman and directed by William A. Graham, that ran from September 1969 to September 1970, and featured Michael Parks as a middle-class dropout on an EASY RIDER-like quest for identity and meaning.

17. Barry Salt, *Film Style & Technology: History & Analysis*, 2nd ed. (London: Starword, 1992), pp. 279–280.

18. R. Serge Denisoff and William D. Romanowski, *Risky Business: Rock in Film* (New Brunswick, NJ: Transaction Publishers, 1991), p. 169.

19. Ibid., pp. 175–176.

20. Stephen Farber, *The Movie Rating Game* (Washington, D. C.: Public Affairs Press, 1972), pp. 40–41.

21. See Rick Setlow, "'Alienated' Themes Blah B.O.: Drug 'Culture' Turns Off Folks." *Variety*, February 17, 1971, pp. 5, 22.

22. Roger Corman's AIP biker film THE WILD ANGELS (1966), starring Peter Fonda, and his LSD paean THE TRIP (1967), scripted by Jack Nicholson and starring both Fonda and Dennis Hopper, were the prototypes for EASY RIDER.

23. On the failure of youth-cult see "When 'Youth' Pix Bore Young: Metro's Rule Is 'Forget It Fast,'" *Variety*, August 26, 1970, pp. 1, 48; Joe Cohen, "'Teen Power' Fading at B. O.: Elder Backlash Cues Nostalgia," *Variety*, February 24, 1971, pp. 1, 61; Addison Verrill, "Youth Angles Can Drop Dead: Second Thoughts About 4 at WB," *Variety*, July 21, 1971, p. 5; and "Youth Shuns Youth-Lure Films: 74 percent of Patrons But They Stray," *Variety*, November 3, 1971, pp. 1, 48.

24. Timothy Leary, *The Politics of Ecstasy* (London: Paladin, 1972), p. 291.

25. Schiff, "The Repeatable Experience," p. 35.

26. Eric Barnouw, *Tube of Plenty: The Evolution of American Television*, 2nd rev. ed. (New York: Oxford University Press, 1990), pp. 197–198.

27. Robert B. Ray, *A Certain Tendency of the Hollywood Cinema, 1930–1980,* p. 264.

28. Christopher Anderson, *Hollywood TV: The Studio System in the Fifties* (Austin: University of Texas Press, 1994). p. 291.

29. Peter N. Carroll, *It Seemed Like Nothing Happened: The Tragedy and Promise of America in the 1970s* (New York: Holt, Rinehart and Winston, 1982), p.17.

30. Thomas Schatz, "The Western," in Wes D. Gehring, ed., *Handbook of American Film Genres* (New York: Greenwood Press, 1988), p. 33.

31. Stephen Farber, *The Movie Rating Game*, pp. 67–69.

32. Vilmos Zsigmond (b. 1930) and Laszlo Kovacs (b. 1932) were both trained at the Budapest Academy of Dramatic and Cinematographic Art and came together to the United States in the wake of the Hungarian revolution of 1956. Both made a living by working on exploitation films before becoming prominent mainstream cinematographers in the 1970s. See chapter 9.

33. In a chart of "The Most Profitable Stars Since 1932," compiled by Paul Kerr from information given in *Variety* and *Motion Picture Almanac*, John Wayne was first in bankability among all Hollywood stars in 1951–1955, and second from 1956 to 1970; in 1971, he was first again, fell to fourth in 1972, ninth in 1973, tenth in 1974, and then fell out of the top ten altogether for the rest of the decade. Nevertheless, from 1932–1980, Wayne was on average the most profitable star in the industry. See Paul Kerr, "Stars and Stardom," in David Pirie, ed., *Anatomy of the Movies* (New York: Macmillan, 1981), pp. 110–111.

34. John Wayne's Batjac Productions was formed in 1950 and named for the shipping company in THE WAKE OF THE RED WITCH (Edward Ludwig, 1949), in which he starred.

35. The author wishes to thank Dana Polan for this valuable suggestion (and many others).

36. Christopher Frayling, *Spaghetti Westerns* (London: Routledge & Kegan Paul, 1981), pp. 284–285.

37. Ray, *A Certain Tendency of the Hollywood Cinema*, p. 257.

38. Phil Hardy, *The Western* (New York: William Morrow, 1983), p. 340.

39. This *Variety* review is quoted from Derek Elly, ed., *Variety Movie Guide '97* (London: Hamlyn, 1996). p. 98. For example, in "The Repeatable Experience" Stephen Schiff says "In BLAZING SADDLES, Mel Brooks dealt a punishing blow to the Western" (p. 35).

40. Edward Buscomb, ed., *The BFI Companion to the Western*, new ed. (London: Andre Deutsch/BFI, 1983), p. 251.

41. Noted in Garry Wills, *John Wayne's America: The Politics of Celebrity* (New York: Simon & Schuster, 1997), p. 312.

42. Lee Clark Mitchell, *Westerns: Making the Man in Fiction and Film* (Chicago: University of Chicago Press, 1996), p. 259.

43. Jeff Gerth, "Nixon and the Mafia," *Sundance* 1, no. 3, p. 30.

44. David A. Cook, *A History of Narrative Film*, 3rd ed. (New York: W. W. Norton, 1996), pp. 450–451.

45. Geoffrey O'Brien, "The Return of Film Noir," *New York Review of Books* 38, no. 14 (August 15, 1991), p. 45.

46. Michael Ryan and Douglas Kellner, *Camera Politica: The Politics and Ideology of Contemporary Hollywood Film* (Bloomington: Indiana University Press, 1988), p. 82.

47. Roman Polanski, *Roman on Polanski* (London: Heinemann, 1984), pp. 306–307.

48. Liner notes, Laserdisc edition of *Night Moves* (Burbank, CA: Warner Home Video, 1992).

49. Quoted in Seth Cagin and Philip Dray, *Born to Be Wild: Hollywood and the Sixties Generation* (Boca Raton, FL: Coyote Press, 1994), p. 173.

50. Ryan and Kellner, p. 83.

51. Kael quoted in Greil Marcus, "The Style of the 70's: Pop Culture," The *New York Times*, June 5, 1977, p. 1E.

52. Virginia Campbell and Edward Marguiles, "Twenty Movies to Kill For," *Movieline* 4, no. 11 (August 1993), p. 53.

53. Cagin and Dray, p. 173.

54. Quoted in Douglas Brode, *Money, Women, and Guns: Crime Movies from Bonnie and Clyde to the Present* (New York: Citadel Press, 1995), p. 54. Brode points out that WALKING TALL (1973) was both an homage to director Phil Karlson's earlier rural crime film THE PHENIX CITY STORY (1955) and a modernization of HIGH NOON (Fred Zinnemann, 1952).

55. Richard Thompson, "What's Your 10–20?," *Film Comment* 16, no. 4 (July–August 1980), pp. 35–37. I am indebted to Dana Polan for calling my attention to this unique article on how the "redneck movie . . . took over the action film in the Seventies like unchecked Kudzu" (p. 34) and to the phenomenon of the new South in general.

56. Fox Butterfield, "Southern Curse: Why America's Murder Rate Is So High," The *New York Times*, July 26, 1998, op-ed, p. 1.

57. Roger Watkins, "'Demented Revenge' Hits World Screen: Many at Mifed Express Disgust," *Variety*, October 29, 1980, p. 33.

58. Richard Hofstader, *The Paranoid Style in American Politics and Other Essays* (New York: Vintage Books, 1967), p. 14.

59. Robert J. Landry, "Pix Fascination with Assassination: Themes Echoing News Headlines," *Variety*, September 5, 1973, pp. 1, 41.

60. Cagin and Dray, *Born to Be Wild*, p. 160.

61. It was Robert Redford who convinced Woodward and Berstein to focus their book on their Watergate investigation; their original project had been to write a biography of former attorney general John Mitchell. Redford had wanted only to produce the movie, but Warners insisted that he also co-star as part of the deal.

62. Jonathan Schell, *The Time of Illusion* (New York: Alfred A. Knopf, 1976), p. 363.

63. Seymour Martin Lipset and William Schneider, *The Confidence Gap: Business, Labor and Government in the Public Mind* (New York: The Free Press, 1983), pp. 36–37.

64. Abel Green, "Pix in 'Major' Retrenchment," *Variety*, October 8, 1969, p. 3.

65. Kenneth Von Gunden, "The RH Factor," *Film Comment* 15, no. 5 (September–October 1979), p. 55.

66. Clive Hirschhorn, *The Hollywood Musical* (New York: Crown, 1981), p. 405.

67. Stephen Grover, "Hard Act to Follow: Making Broadway Hit Into a Movie Involves Much Work, Big Risks," The *Wall Street Journal*, December 23, 1976, pp. 1, 17.

68. "The Yellow Brick Road to Profit," *Time*, January 23, 1978, p. 46.

69. Charles Schreger, "The Second Coming of Sound," *Film Comment* 14, no. 5 (September–October 1978), p. 36.

70. Dave Marsh, "Schlock Around the Rock," *Film Comment* 14, no. 4 (July–August 1978), p. 8; and R. Serge Denisoff and William D. Romanowski, *Risky Business: Rock in Film* (New Brunswick, NJ: Transaction Publishers, 1991), pp. 224–225.

71. See Rebee Garifalo, *Rockin' Out: Popular Music in the USA* (Boston: Allyn and Bacon, 1997). pp. 240–241; and Paul Friedlander, *Rock and Roll: A Social History* (Boulder, CO: Westview Press, 1996), p. 233.

72. Douglas Gomery, *Shared Pleasures: A History of Movie Presentation in the United States* (Madison: University of Wisconsin Press, 1992), p. 226.

73. Charles Schreger, "The Second Coming of Sound," *Film Comment* 14, no. 5 (September–October 1978), p. 37.

74. Douglas Pratt, *Laserdisc Newsletter*, April 1993, p. 2.

75. Barry Salt, *Film Style & Technology: History & Analysis*, Second Edition (London: Starword, 1992), p. 282.

76. Bruce F. Kawin, *How Movies Work* (Berkeley: University of California Press, 1992), p. 470.

77. "'Star Wars' Heralds Advent of New Sound Era Via Dolby Rigs," *Variety*, May 17, 1978, p. 132.

78. *Box Office*, August 21, 1978, p. 19; *Variety*, September 5, 1979, p. 6; *Variety*, October 1984, pp. 7, 44.

79. "Pix Look for Cut of Music Biz Action: Disk Boom Cues H'Wood Themes," *Variety*, November 16, 1977, p. 5.

80. Schreger, "The Second Coming of Sound," p. 36.

81. Mitch Tuchman, "Industry," *Film Comment* 14, no. 6 (November–December 1978), p. 70.

82. Robin Wood, *Hollywood from Vietnam to Reagan* (New York: Columbia University Press, 1986), p. 84.

83. See Robert Phillip Kolker, *A Cinema of Loneliness: Penn, Kubrick, Scorsese, Spielberg, Altman*, 2nd ed. (New York: Oxford University Press, 1988), pp. 17–18; and Thomas Schatz, *Old Hollywood/New Hollywood: Ritual, Art, and Industry* (Ann Arbor: UMI Research Press, 1983), pp. 261–262.

84. According to Stephen Rebello in *Alfred Hitchcock and the Making of Psycho* (New York: Dembner, 1990), the director wanted to imitate the success of AIP. Screenwriter Joseph Stefano told him: "When I asked him why he [Hitchcock] had bought the book [Robert Bloch's 1959 novel *Psycho*], he said he noticed that American-International was making movie after movie for under a million dollars, yet all made ten to thirteen million" (p. 40).

85. Robert E. Kapsis, *Hitchcock: The Making of a Reputation* (University of Chicago Press, 1992), pp. 58–62. "For the younger moviegoer, in particular, attending PSYCHO came to be perceived as a major social event not to be missed" (p. 62).

86. Ibid., p. 60.

87. Gregory Waller, "Introduction," *American Horrors: Essays on the Modern American Horror Film* (Urbana: University of Illinois Press, 1987), p. 5.

88. Estimate of Douglas Pratt, *The Laser Disc Newsletter*, April 1993, no. 103, p. 3.

89. Addison Verrill, "New Tide of Film Gore Rises: Other Shore of Sexplicit Wave," *Variety*, June 2, 1971, p. 1.

90. Harry Ringel, "THE EXORCIST," *Cinefantastique* 3, no. 2 (Summer 1974), p. 24.

91. Stephen Farber, "Hollywood's New Sensationalism: The Power and the Gory," The *New York Times*, July 7, 1974, p. 1, 63.

92. In 1998, Nick Freand Jones produced a 25th anniversary documentary on the production and cultural positioning of THE EXORCIST for the BBC. Entitled THE FEAR OF GOD, it contains outtakes and the film's original, more positive ending. See "Lucifer Rising," *Sight and Sound* 8, no. 7 (July 1998), pp. 6–11. See also, David E. Williams, "Demonic Convergence," *American Cinematographer* 79, no. 8 (August 1998), pp. 88–97, on Owen Roizman's expressive cinematography for the film.

93. Other films inspired by the Gein killings include DERANGED (Alan Ormsby/Jeff Gillen, 1974), a fictionalized account of the actual case; SILENCE OF THE LAMBS (Jonathan Demme, 1991), whose serial killer "Buffalo Bill" is based on Gein by way of the Thomas Harris source novel (Gein made masks of human flesh and was known to have worn the flayed skin of his victims); and the parodic ED AND HIS DEAD MOTHER (Jonathan Wacks, 1993).

94. Quoted in "Once Upon a Time in Texas: THE TEXAS CHAINSAW MASSACRE as Inverted Fairytale," *Necromonicon, Book One*, Andy Black, ed. (London: Creation Books, 1996), p. 7.

95. On the TEXAS CHAINSAW MASSACRE controversy, see Roger Greenspun, "Carrie, and Sally and Leatherface Among the Film Buffs." *Film Comment* 13, no. 1 (January–February 1977), pp. 14–17.

96. "Majors Borrow Horror Success From Indies, Often 'Outsiders,'" *Variety*, November 5, 1980, p. 30.

97. Dick Atkins, *Method to the Madness: Hollywood Explained* (Livingston, NJ: Prince Publishers, 1975), pp. 107–108.

98. Tony Williams, *Larry Cohen: The Radical Allegories of an Independent Filmmaker* (Jefferson, NC: McFarland, 1997), p. 129; and Robin Wood, *Hollywood from Vietnam to Reagan*, p. 106.

99. Ibid., p. 106.

100. An analysis of variants of subjective tracking or "unclaimed point-of-view" shots in the horror film is provided in Isabel Cristina Pinedo, *Recreational Terror: Women and the Pleasures of Horror Film Viewing* (Albany: SUNY Press, 1997), pp. 51–55.

101. Richard Meyers, *For One Week Only: The World of Exploitation Films* (Piscataway, NJ: New Century Publishers, 1983), p. 140.

102. Peter Birge and Janet Maslin, "Getting Snuffed in Boston," *Film Comment* 12, no. 3 (May–June 1976), pp. 35, 63.

103. Linda Williams, *Hardcore: Power, Pleasure, and the "Frenzy of the Visible"* (Berkeley: University of California Press, 1989), pp. 193–194.

104. Laura Lederer, ed., *Take Back the Night: Women on Pornography* (New York: Morrow, 1980), p. 274.

105. Regarding this idea of a "generic confusion between horror and hardcore," it is worth noting that in the first edition of *The X-Rated Videotape Guide* (New York: Arlington House, 1984), author Robert H. Rimmer chose to include three horror films in his filmography "to show how filmmakers are using the R category to get away with material that would get them arrested if they simply added a penis or vagina to their films" (p. 39). The three films were THE TEXAS CHAINSAW MASSACRE, HALLOWEEN, and FRIDAY THE 13TH.

106. Not to be confused with Lucio Fulci's ZOMBIE (aka ZOMBIE FLESH EATERS, 1979), an Italian gore fest originally entitled ZOMBIE 2 to make it appear to be a sequel to Dargento's version of the Romero film.

107. Robert E. Kapsis, "Hollywood Genres and the Production of Culture Perspective," *Current Research in Film: Audiences, Economics, and Law*, vol. 5, Bruce A. Austin, ed. (Norwood, NJ: Ablex Publishing, 1991), p. 73.

108. Lawrence Cohn, "Gore Perpetual Fave of Young Film Fans," *Variety*, August 20, 1981, pp. 7, 42.

109. Roger Ebert, "Why the Movies Aren't Safe Anymore," *American Film*, March 1981, p. 56.

110. Ibid.

111. *Film Comment* 15, no. 5 (September-October 1979), p. 1 (content logo for Tom Figenshu, "Screams of a Summer Night," pp. 49–53; and Kenneth Von Gunden, "The RH Factor, " pp. 54–57).

112. See, for example, Janet Maslin, "Bloodbaths Debase Movies and Audiences," The *New York Times*, November 11, 1982, sec. D, pp. 1, 15; and "'Horrorpix More Obscene Than Porn' To Des Ryan, Philly Critic," *Variety*, February 3, 1982.

113. Robert E. Kapsis, *Hitchcock: The Making of a Reputation*, pp. 269–270.

114. "Horrid Year for Horror," *Variety*, January 25, 1984, pp. 3, 36; and Janet Maslin, "Tired Blood Claims the Horror Film as a Fresh Victim," The *New York Times*, November 1, 1981, sec. D, pp. 15, 23.

115. See "'Violent' or 'Horror' Tag Fits One-Third of Top-Money Films," *Variety*, May 26, 1981; and Kapsis, *Hitchcock*, p. 268.

116. Roger Watkins, "'Demented Revenge' Hits World Screen,: Many at Mifed Express Disgust," *Variety*, October 29, 1980, p. 3.

117. Vera Dika, *Games of Terror: Halloween, Friday the 13th, and the Films of the Stalker Cycle* (Rutherford, NJ: Associated University Press, 1990), pp. 132–133.

118. Cohn, "Gore," p. 7; and "Majors Borrow Horror Success From Indies," p. 30.

119. Quoted in Robert E. Kapsis, "Hollywood Genres," p. 81.

120. Lawrence Cohn, "Horror, Sci-Fi Pix Earn 37 percent of Rentals," *Variety*, November 19, 1980, p. 5.

121. *Variety*, January 25, 1984, p. 36.

122. Liner notes, *Colossus: The Forbin Project/Silent Running*, a Widescreen Encore Edition Double Feature laserdisc (Universal City, CA: Universal Home Video, 1997).

123. The insect sequences of THE HELLSTROM CHRONICLES and PHASE IV were shot by Ken Middleton, who also photographed the cockroaches for the revenge-of nature feature BUG (1975).

124. Charles Matthews, *Oscar: A to Z* (New York: Doubleday, 1995), p. 504.

125. Dale Pollack, *Skywalking: The Life and Films of George Lucas* (Hollywood: Samuel French, 1990), p. 158.

126. Frederic Jameson, "Postmodernism and Consumer Society," in *Movies and Mass Culture*, John Belton, ed. (New Brunswick, NJ: Rutgers University Press, 1996), p. 190.

127. J. Hoberman, "1975-1985: Ten Years That Shook the World," *American Film* 10, no. 8 (June 1985), p. 42.

128. Quoted in Hoberman, p. 41.

129. See Christopher Lasch, "The Narcissist Society," The *New York Review of Books*, September 30, 1976, pp. 8, 28; and *The Culture of Narcissism* (New York: Norton, 1978); Peter Marin, "The New Narcissism," *Harper's*, October 1975, pp. 45–48; Tom Wolfe, "The 'Me' Decade and the Third Great Awakening," *New York*, August 23, 1976.

130. Peter N. Carroll, *It Seemed Like Nothing Happened: The Tragedy and Promise of America in the 1970s* (New York: Holt, Rinehart and Winston, 1982), p. 280.

131. The linkage between INVASION OF THE BODY SNATCHERS, released December 22, 1978, the discovery of the mass suicides at Jonestown, Guyana, on November 21, 1978, and the shooting of George Moscone and Harvey Milk by Dan White at San Francisco's City Hall three days later, is noted by Robert Eberwein in "Remakes and Cultural Studies," in *Play It Again, Sam: Retakes on Remakes*, Andrew Horton and Stuart Y. McDougal, eds. (Berkeley: University of California Press, 1998), pp. 25–27. Eberwein also notes the coincidence between the film's alien conspiracy and the report of the House Select Committee on Assassinations at the end of 1978 that President John F. Kennedy and Dr. Martin Luther King, Jr. were "probably assassinated as a result of conspiracy."

132. Quoted in Charles Freund, "Pods over San Francisco," *Film Comment* 15, no. 1 (January-February 1979), p. 23.

133. In a 1977 *New York Times* op-ed piece, Ben Boya listed fear of the future as one of three main reasons for science fiction's newfound success among American audiences; the others were the genre's sense of basic morality and its novelty "[i]n an era when almost every new film is a remake of an earlier film." ("Why Hollywood Finds Profits Out of This World," The *New York Times*, November 13, 1977, op-ed.)

134. In 1996, INDEPENDENCE DAY and TWISTER; in 1997, ANACONDA, ASTEROID, DANTE'S PEAK, FIRE ON THE MOUNTAIN (ABC-TVM), THE LOST WORLD: JURASSIC PARK, SPEED 2: CRUISE CONTROL, TURBULENCE, TITANIC, VOLCANO; in 1998, ARMAGEDDON, DEEP IMPACT, FIRESTORM, GALILEO'S WAKE, HARD RAIN, VIRUS, and TSUNAMI.

135. Quoted in Nick Roddick, "Only the Stars Survive: Disaster Movies in the Seventies," in *Performance and Politics in Popular Drama*, David Brady et al., eds. (London: Cambridge University Press, 1981), pp. 243, 262. In his definition of the form, Roddick includes science fiction movies set in future worlds where catastrophes have already occurred (for example, SOYLENT GREEN, THE OMEGA MAN, ZARDOZ, and LOGAN'S RUN) or will occur during the course of the film, which broadens the category considerably.

136. Andrew C. Revkin, "Motherly? Not Her! Nature Is Trying to Kill You," The *New York Times*, April 20, 1997, sec. H, p. 19.

137. For example, Michael Ryan and Douglas Kellner argue that plurivalent disaster films like 1974's EARTHQUAKE and THE TOWERING INFERNO pose a populist critique of corporate capitalism, expressing a deep-seated mistrust of the liaison between politics and business. (*Camera Politica: The Politics and Ideology of Contemporary Hollywood Film* [Bloomington: Indiana University Press, 1988], pp. 52–57.)

138. The *Wall Street Journal*, January 7, 1975, p. 22.

139. John Brosnan, *Movie Magic: The Story of Special Effects in Cinema* (New York: New American Library, 1976). p. 252.

140. Liner notes, Widescreen Special Edition of THE POSEIDON ADVENTURE (New York: CBS Fox, 1991). Regarding the film's realism, Maurice Yacowar links it with Fox's TITANTIC (Jean Negulesco, 1953) and Rank's A NIGHT TO REMEMBER (Roy "Ward" Baker, 1958), both of which, like THE HINDENBURG (Robert Wise, 1975) are based on a real event (Maurice Yacowar, "The Bug in the Rug: Notes on the Disaster Genre," in *Film Genre Reader II*, Barry Keith Grant, ed. [Austin: University of Texas Press, 1995], p. 263). A better analogy might be with MGM's THE LAST VOYAGE (Andrew L. Stone, 1960), for which a real ship was sunk.

141. See, for example, Lawrence Shaffer, "The Good Dumb Film: THE POSEIDON ADVENTURE," *Film Comment* 9, no. 5 (September–October, 1973), pp. 52–55.

142. Brosnan, p. 259.

143. Quoted in *Variety Movie Guide '97*, ed. Derek Elley (London: Hamlyn, 1996), p. 270.

144. Liner notes, Widescreen Laserdisc Edition of THE TOWER INFERNO (Beverly Hills, CA: Twentieth Century–Fox Home Entertainment, Inc., 1995).

145. John Culhane, *Special Effects in the Movies: How They Do It* (New York: Ballantine Books, 1981), p. 146.

146. Quoted from *Variety Movie Guide '97*, p. 419.

147. Thomas Schatz, "The New Hollywood," in *Film Theory Goes to the Movies*, Jim Collins, Hilary Radner, and Ava Preacher Collins, eds. (New York: Routledge, 1993), pp. 18–19.

148. J. Hoberman, "1975–1985: Ten Films That Shook the World," *American Film* 10, no. 8 (June 1985), p. 35.

149. Joseph McBride, *Steven Spielberg: A Biography* (New York: Simon & Schuster, 1997), p. 234–235.

150. Marc Sigoloff, *The Films of the Seventies: A Filmography of American, British, and Canadian Films, 1970–1979* (Jefferson, NC: MacFarland, 1984), p. 289.

151. John Fleming, "Special Effects," in David Pirie, *Anatomy of the Movies*, p. 180.

CHAPTER 6 (GENRES II: EXPLOITATION AND ALLUSION)

1. Donald Bogle, *Toms, Coons, Mulattos, Mammies, and Bucks: An Interpretive History of Blacks in American Films*, 3rd ed. (New York: Continuum, 1996), p. 223.

2. "'Black Is Beautiful' at B.O.," *Variety*, June 17, 1970, p. 1.

3. George Gent, "Black Films Are In, So Are Profits," The *New York Times*, July 18, 1972, p. 14E. See also Mel Gussow, "The Baadasss Success of Melvin Van Peebles," The *New York Times*, August 20, 1972. pp. 8–9E.

4. Quoted in Bogle, pp. 235–236. For more on the SWEETBACK controversy, see Jon Hartman, "The Trope of Blaxploitation in Critical Responses to SWEETBACK," *Film History* 6, no. 3 (Autumn 1994), pp. 382–404; Michel Euvard, "SWEET SWEETBACK'S BAADASSSSS SONG: Melvin Van Peebles," *CinemAction: Le cinema noir americain* (Paris: Le Cerf, 1987), pp. 144–150; and Manthia Diawara, "Black American Cinema: The New Realism," in *Black American Cinema*, Manthia Diawara, ed. (New York: Routledge, 1993), pp. 10–25.

5. "Black Movie Boom," *Newsweek*, September 6, 1971, p. 66.

6. James Robert Parish and George H. Hill, *Black Action Films* (Jefferson, NC: McFarland, 1989), p. 254.

7. Lee Beaupre, "One-Third Film Public: Negro; Columbia and UA Pitch for Biz," *Variety*, November 29, 1967, p. 3.

8. Addison Verrill, "WB's on 'n' Off Black Capers: 'Superspade' of Zanuck Not One," *Variety*, July 19, 1972, p. 7.

9. Addison Verrill, "'Super Fly' a Blackbuster [sic] Phenom; Gross Already Tops $5,000,000 In Limited Dates; How About an Oscar?," *Variety*, October 4, 1972, pp. 3, 26.

10. Robert J. Landry, "Black Pix: 'Menial' to 'Mean': Crime Reaction Like Italians," *Variety*, August 23, 1972, pp. 5, 22.

11. Addison Verrill, "Black Pix and White Market: True Trend or Just Novelty?," *Variety*, September 8, 1971, pp. 3, 25.

12. "Domestic B.O. Bounces Back: MPAA Notes 20 Percent Gain Over 1971," *Variety*, October 4, 1972, p. 3. See also, Lee Beaupre, "U.S. 'Downtown' Pix Snapback: Not Only N.Y.C.; Boom in 'Action'," *Variety*, August 30, 1972, pp. 1, 24.

13. Quoted in Bogle, *Toms, Coons, Mulattos, Mammies, and Bucks*, p. 241.

14. Addison Verrill, "Black Film Explosion," *Variety*, January 9, 1974, p. 30.

15. "U.S. Black Audience-Slated Films: 25 New 1974 Titles," *Variety*, January 8, 1975, p. 18.

16. Landry, "Black Pix: 'Menial' to 'Mean,'" p. 5.

17. Quoted in Bogle, p. 242.

18. Darius James, *That's Blaxploitation: Roots of the Baadasssss 'Tude* (New York: St. Martin's Press, 1995), p. 38.

19. Ibid., p. 166.

20. Quoted in James Robert Parish and George H. Hill, *Black Action Films*, p. 298.

21. Ed Guerrero, *Framing Blackness: The African American Image in Film* (Philadelphia: Temple University Press, 1993), p. 105.

22. Ibid., p. 77.

23. Steven J. Kendall, *New Jack Cinema: Hollywood's African American Filmmakers* (Silver Spring, MD: J. L. Denser, 1994), pp. v–vii.

24. Ibid., p. 169.

25. Lawrence Cohn, "The Box Office: Poetic Justice," *Premiere*, July 1994, p. 41.

26. Darius James, p. 31.

27. Parish and Hill, p. 219.

28. I. C. Jarvie, *Window on Hong Kong: A Sociological Study of the Hong Kong Film Industry and Its Audience* (Hong Kong: Centre of Asian Studies, University of Hong Kong, 1977), pp. 48–51, 87–89. Most of these films were produced in the Mandarin dialect, the official dialect of mainland China, which had replaced Cantonese, the chief dialect of southern China and Hong Kong, as the predominant language of Chinese cinema in the late 1960s; in the 1980s and 1990s Cantonese displaced Mandarin once more. In practice, most contemporary Hong Kong action films are shot "wild" for postdubbing into Cantonese, Mandarin, and/or English.

29. Craig A. Reid, "Fighting without Fighting: Film Action Fight Choreography," *Film Quarterly* 47, no. 2 (Winter 1993–94), p. 30.

30. "Kung Fu Choppy Big B.O.," *Variety*, April 25, 1973, p. 5. THE BIG BOSS (1971) was distributed in the U.S. by Warner Bros. as FISTS OF FURY; the original Hong Kong title for THE CHINESE CONNECTION (1972) was FIST OF FURY but was changed by Warners to avoid redundancy and to cash in on the popularity of Fox's THE FRENCH CONNECTION, which had just won the 1971 Oscar for Best Picture and Best Director (William Friedkin).

31. See Lou Gaul, *The Fist That Shook the World, The Cinema of Bruce Lee* (Baltimore: Midnight Marquee Press, 1997).

32. Gene Moskowitz, "Kung-Fu: Fixture on Global Screen: Demand Still Brisk, Sez Shaw," *Variety*, December 19, 1973, p. 17.

33. "Swish! Thwack! Kung Fu Films Make It," The *New York Times*, June 16, 1973. p. 1, 13 E.

34. "U.S. Rage of Chop-Socky Films: Karate Breaks Out of Chinatown," *Variety*, January 9, 1974, p. 72.

35. Randall Clark, *At a Theater or Drive-In Near You: The History, Culture, and Politics of the American Exploitation Film* (New York: Garland, 1995), p. 131. On their first U.S. appearance in the early 1970s, Hong Kong kung fu movies played almost exclusively at inner city theaters and did not attract white audiences. During the 1980s, however, white teenagers comprised a significant share of the television and video markets for these films.

36. Quoted in "Swish! Thwack!," p. 13 E.

37. Stuart M. Kaminsky, *American Film Genres*, 2nd ed. (Chicago: Nelson-Hall, 1985), p.73; Reid, "Fighting without Fighting," p. 35.

38. Verna Glaessner, *Kung Fu: Cinema of Vengeance* (New York: Crown, 1974), pp. 24–26.

39. Benjamin Svetkey, "Why Movie Ratings Don't Work," *Entertainment*, November 26, 1994, p. 30.

40. Alex McNeil, *Total Television: A Comprehensive Guide to Programming from 1948 to 1980* (New York: Penguin, 1980), p. 392.

41. Richard Meyers, Amy Harlib, Bill and Karen Palmer, *Martial Arts Movies* (Secaucus, NJ: Citadel Press, 1985), p. 36.

42. Logan Bey, *Hong Kong Action Cinema* (Woodstock, NY: The Overlook Press, 1995), p. 24.

43. Thomas Weisser, "Pretenders to the Throne: Bruce Le, Bruce Li, Dragon Lee, and Bruce Liang," in *Asian Cult Cinema* (New York: Boulevard Books, 1997), pp. 221–222.

44. Bill Palmer, Karen Palmer, and Richard Meyers, *The Encyclopedia of Martial Arts Movies* (Metuchen, NJ: Scarecrow, 1995), pp. 43–47.

45. Frank Miller, *Censored Hollywood: Sex, Sin, and Violence on Screen* (Atlanta: Turner Publishing, 1994), pp. 222–223.

46. Stephen Farber, *The Movie Ratings Game* (Washington, DC: Public Affairs Press, 1972), p. 57.

47. This softcore-hardcore distinction is synthesized from several sources, among them Robert H. Rimmer, *The X-Rated Videotape Guide* (New York: Arlington House, 1984); Linda Williams, *Hard Core: Power, Pleasure, and the "Frenzy of the Visible"* (Berkeley: University of California Press, 1989); Joseph W. Slade, "Pornography in the Late Nineties," *Wide Angle* 19, no. 3 (July 1997), pp. 1–12; and Gail Dines, Robert Jensen, and Ann Russo, *Pornography: The Production of and Consumption of Inequality* (New York: Routledge, 1998). The fact that this list of sources is longer than the distinction itself says something about the difficulty of defining almost any terms dealing with pornography, which the U.S. Supreme Court has rendered virtually indefinable as a whole.

48. Joseph W. Slade, "The Porn Market and Porn Formulas: The Feature Film of the Seventies," *Journal of Popular Film and Television* 6, no. 2 (1977), p. 175.

49. Edward De Grazia and Roger K. Newman, *Banned Films: Movies, Censorship, and the First Amendment* (New York: Bowker, 1982), pp. 297–303.

50. Addison Verrill, "Broader, Less Sexy, Sherpix: Expands, Funds, & Censor-Wary," *Variety*, July 7, 1971, p. 5.

51. Linda Williams, *Hard Core: Power, Pleasure, and the "Frenzy of the Visible,"* p. 98.

52. "Welcome to the Doll House: The Influence of Russ Meyer," *Gadfly* 1, no. 7 (September 1997), p. 21.

53. Addison Verrill, "Nary a Loan trip to Bank: Audubon, at 10, Is Only a Depositor," *Variety*, October 14, 1970, p. 3.

54. Ibid.

55. Eddie Muller and Daniel Faris, *Grindhouse: The Forbidden World of "Adults Only" Cinema* (New York: St. Martin's Press, 1996), p. 139.

56. Roger B. Rollin, "Triple-X: Erotic Movies and Their Audiences," *Journal of Popular Film and Television* 10, no. 1 (1982), p. 18.

57. Verrill, op-cit., p. 3.

58. William Rostler, *Contemporary Erotic Cinema* (New York: Penthouse/Ballantine, 1973), p. 39.

59. See also Bruce Williamson, "Porno Chic," in *Flesh and Blood: The National Society of Film Critics on Sex, Violence, and Censorship*, Peter Keough, ed. (San Francisco: Mercury House, 1995), pp. 10–28. (Originally published in *Playboy*, August 1973.)

60. Ralph Blumenthal, "Porno Chic," *The New York Times Magazine*, January 21, 1973, p. 28.

61. Jon Lewis, "Money Matters: Hollywood in the Corporate Era," in *The New American Cinema*, Jon Lewis, ed. (Durham: Duke University Press, 1998), p. 91.

62. Leonard J. Leff and Jerold L. Simmons, *The Dame in the Kimono: Hollywood Censorship, and the Production Code from the 1920s to the 1960s* (New York: Grove Weidenfeld, 1990), p. 276.

63. See, for example, Adele Olivia Gladwell, "LAST TANGO IN PARIS: Circles of Sex and Death," *Necronomicon, Book One*, ed. Andy Black (London: Creation Books International, 1996), pp. 131–140; and John Whitehead, "Carcasses of THE LAST TANGO IN PARIS," *Gadfly* 1, no. 5 (July 1997), pp. 12–13.

64. De Grazia and Newman, *Banned Films*, pp. 363–366.

65. Personal experience of the author, retained as expert witness by attorneys for the festival pending prosecution.

66. Quoted in Tino Balio, *United Artists: The Company That Changed the Film Industry* (Madison: University of Wisconsin Press, 1987), p. 298.

67. Champlin quoted in Leff and Simmons, *The Dame in the Kimono*, p. 276.

68. David Shipman, *Caught in the Act: Sex and Eroticism in the Movies* (London: Elm Tree Books, 1985), p. 144.

69. Quoted in Muller and Faris, *Grindhouse*, p. 146.

70. Harlan Jacobson, "If 'Snuff' Killings Are Real, Film Violence Faces New Test," *Variety*, December 12, 1975, p. 4.

71. Quoted in Charles Lyons, *The New Censors: Movies and the Culture Wars* (Philadelphia: Temple University Press, 1997), p. 65.

72. Ibid.

73. Leaflet, "Snuff, c. 1976"; clipping file, Billy Rose Theater Collection, Library of Performing Arts, New York City Public Library.

74. Cited in Roger Greenspun, "Carrie, Sally and Leatherface Among the Film Buffs," *Film Comment* 13, no. 1 (January-February 1977), p. 14. (Koch's original article appeared in *Harper's* for November 1976.)

75. A. D. Murphy, "Over 50 percent 'Restricted' Ratings in U.S.: Untabulated X's as Self-Imposed," *Variety*, November 5, 1975, p. 7. In fact, this ratio held true until the formulation of the NC-17 rating in 1990. According to the MPAA, CARA rated 8,460 features from 1968–1988, of which 4.3 percent were given an X and 47.8 percent an R. (Laura Landro, "After 20 Years, Movies' Ratings System Is Still Assailed by Special-Interest Groups," *Wall Street Journal*, November 1, 1988, sec. B, p. 1.)

76. Joseph McBride, "Childhood's Innocence Getting Lost? Teen Harlots, Perverts in Scripts," *Variety*, February 9, 1977, p. 7.

77. Ibid.

78. *Paris Adult Theatre I v. Slaton*, decided by the Supreme Court on the same day as *Miller v. California*, also figured in the "community standards" definition of obscenity. On the immediate confusion occasioned by the rulings, see Earl C. Gottschalk, "A Dirty Deal? Pornography Ruling Causing Confusion and Chaos, Many Traditional Publishers and Filmmakers Say," The *Wall Street Journal*, July 16, 1973, p. 28.

79. Quoted in "High Court's 'Carnal' Ruling Seen As Crucial For Cinema Freedom," *Variety*, June 26, 1974, p. 1, 79.

80. De Grazia and Newman, *Banned Films*, pp. 350–357, 362–366.

81. Quoted in Larry Michie, "Justice Dept.'s Porno Stance: 'Impossible Burden' Removed; Case Load Eased," *Variety*, July 4, 1973. p. 1.

82. Muller and Faris, *Grindhouse*, p. 135.

83. Robert H. Rimmer, *The X-Rated Video Guide* (New York: Arlington House, 1984), p. 5. Although adult males still dominate the market, the heterosexual couples audience for pornography seems to have carried over from theatrical features to video, according to both scholarship (see, for example, Stephen Prince, "The Pornographic Image and the Practice of Film Theory," *Cinema Journal* 27, no. 2 [Winter 1988], pp. 27–39) and industry statistics. According to the Adult Film Association of America's figures for 1991, 40 percent of those renting X-rated tapes were single men, 29 percent were men with women, 15 percent were single women, 13 percent were men with men, and 3 percent were women with women (cited in John Johnson, "Into the Valley of Sleaze," *The Los Angeles Times Magazine*, February 17, 1991, p. 16).

84. The sex industry, calculated to have annual revenues of $9 billion in 1996 as against film industry box-office receipts of $5.9 billion, has always been a critical factor in media revolutions, as is the case with the Internet today. See, for example, Frank Rose, "Sex Sells," *Wired* 5, 12 (December 1997), pp. 219–224, 276–280.

85. Samuel Z. Arkoff, "Famous Myths of the Film Industry," *Journal of the Producers Guild of America* 11, no. 3 (September 1969), p. 6.

86. Quoted in Earl C. Gottschalk, Jr., "The Spectaculars," The *Wall Street Journal*, August 10, 1974, p. 1.

87. Noel Carroll, "The Future of Allusion: Hollywood in the Seventies (and Beyond)," *October* 20 (1982), pp. 51–81; J. Hoberman, "Facing the Nineties," *Vulgar Modernism: Writing on Movies and Other Media* (Philadelphia: Temple University Press, 1991), pp. 1–10.

88. See Wes D. Gehrig, "Parody," in *Handbook of American Film Genres*, Wes. D. Gehrig, ed. (Westport, CT: Greenwood Press, 1988), p. 145; and Steve Neale and Frank Krutnik, "Definitions, Genres, and Forms," in *Popular Film and Television Comedy* (New York: Routledge, 1990), ed. Steve Neale and Frank Kuntuik, p. 19.

89. Peter Biskind, "The Last Crusade," *Seeing Through Movies*, Mark Crispin Miller, ed. (New York: Pantheon, 1990), p. 117.

90. Carroll, "The Future of Allusion," pp. 56, 62.

91. Uncredited American remakes of foreign films during the 1970s include THE CONVERSATION (Francis Ford Coppola, 1974), a version of Antonioni's BLOWUP (1966); SORCERER (William

Friedkin, 1977), which remakes Clouzot's THE WAGES OF FEAR (1952); WHICH WAY IS UP? (Michael Schulz, 1977), a remake of Lina Wertmuller's THE SEDUCTION OF MIMI (1972); and WILLIE AND PHIL (Paul Mazursky, 1980), a remake of Truffaut's JULES AND JIM (1961).

92. The series was continued into subsequent decades with MGM/United Artists' THAT'S DANCING! (Jack Haley, Jr., 1985) and THAT'S ENTERTAINMENT III (Bud Friedgen, 1994).

93. Joseph McBride, "Sports No Longer Poison; 30 Game-Related Pics," *Variety*, January 5, 1977, p. 22.

94. Stephen Farber, "The Return of the Grown-Up Movie," *American Film* 7, no. 12 (December 1981), p. 51.

95. "Industry Economic Review," *The Movie Business Book,* Jason E. Squire, ed. (Englewood Cliffs, NJ: Prentice Hall, 1983), p. 354.

96. Stanley Calvell, *Pursuits of Happiness: The Hollywood Comedy of Remarriage* (Cambridge: Harvard University Press, 1981), pp. 3–4.

97. Thomas Deegan, "No-Fault Divorce Films: Hollywood's Changing Morality," *Cineaste* 15, no. 2 (1986), p. 24.

98. James Harwood, "Films Gotta Cater to 'Aging' Audience: 'Youth Appeal' Now Booby Trap," *Variety*, February 23, 1977, pp. 7, 34.

99. Op. cit.

100. Liner notes, Special Widescreen Laserdisc Edition of BODY HEAT (Burbank: Warner Home Video, 1996).

101. "Lawrence Kasdan interviewed by Dan Yakir," *Film Comment* 17, no. 5 (September–October 1981), p. 53.

102. J. Hoberman, "Introduction," *Vulgar Modernism: Writing on Movies and Other Media* (Philadelphia: Temple University Press, 1991), p. 7.

CHAPTER 7 (ORDERS OF MAGNITUDE I: MAJORS, MINI-MAJORS, "INSTANT MAJORS," AND INDEPENDENTS)

1. Justin Wyatt, *High Concept: Movies and Marketing in Hollywood* (Austin: University of Texas Press, 1994), pp. 71, 85.

2. Oliver E. Williamson, "The Modern Corporation: Origins, Evolution, Attributes," in *Industrial Organization*, Anindya Sen, ed. (New Delhi: Oxford University Press, 1996), pp. 73–74.

3. Financial information derived from John Douglas Eames, *The MGM Story: The Complete History of Fifty-Seven Roaring Years*, 2nd ed. (New York: Crown Publishers, 1982), pp. 278, 284, 290, 296, 304, 310, 322–325; and Christopher Reynolds, *1995 Hollywood Power Stats* (Laurel Canyon, CA: Cineview Publishing, 1995), pp. 55–88.

4. Eames, *The MGM Story*, p. 346.

5. Domenico Meccoli, "Conglomerates Gobble Up Movies," *Successo* 12 (March 1970), p. 90.

6. Robert H. Stanley, *The Celluloid Empire: A History of the American Movie Industry* (New York: Hastings House, 1978), p. 257.

7. Meccoli, p. 90.

8. Jerzy Toeplitz, *Hollywood and After: The Changing Face of Movies In America*, Boleslaw Sulik, trans. (Chicago: Henry Regnery Company, 1974), pp. 26–27.

9. Addison Verrill, "Aubrey Vows a Turnaround: Unflappable at MGM Stock Pow," *Variety*, January 21, 1970, p. 5.

10. Axel Madsen, *The New Hollywood: American Movies in the 70s* (New York: Thomas Y. Crowell, 1975), pp. 11–12.

11. Quoted in Madsen, p. 13.

12. John Izod, *Hollywood and the Box Office, 1895–1986* (New York: Columbia University Press, 1988). p. 175.

13. Madsen, p. 12.

14. The *New York Times*, October 30, 1973, sec. E, p. 1.

15. "MGM Scrams Theatre Distribution: Fewer Features, More TV, Overseas Selloff," *Variety*, September 19, 1973, p. 1.

16. Frank Segers, "Krim Bullish About MGM Features: Bottom Not Out of Theatre Pix," *Variety*, November 14, 1973, pp. 5, 20.

17. Peter Bart, *Fade Out: The Calamitous Final Days of MGM* (New York: William Morrow and Company, 1990), p. 58.

18. Quoted in Eames, *The MGM Story,* p. 368.

19. Bart, *Fade Out,* p. 25; Joel W. Finler, *The Hollywood Story* (New York: Crown, 1988), p. 126.

20. Quoted in "Making the Movies into a Business," *Business Week,* June 23, 1973, p. 117.

21. A. D. Murphy, "Banks New Collateral Idea: MGM Example on Pic-by-Pic Rule," *Variety,* February 10, 1971, pp. 5, 20.

22. Bart, *Fade Out,* p. 55.

23. Madsen, *The New Hollywood,* p. 12. In addition to being a ruthless network/studio chief, Aubrey was also a heavy drinker and legendary womanizer who earned character roles in contemporary *roman à clef* novels by Jacqueline Susan (*The Love Machine*), Harold Robbins (*The Inheritors*), and Keefe Brasselle (*The Cannibals*); see Bart, *Fade Out,* pp. 33–34.

24. Joel W. Finler, *The Hollywood Story* (New York: Crown, 1988) p. 154,

25. John Douglas Eames, *The Paramount Story* (New York: Crown, 1985), p. 224.

26. Tino Balio, "Adjusting to the New Global Economy: Hollywood in the 1990s," in Albert Moran, ed., *Film Policy: International, National and Regional Perspectives* (London: Routledge, 1996), p. 28.

27. See Robert Evans, *The Kid Stays in the Picture* (Beverly Hills, CA: Dove Books, 1994).

28. Jim Hillier, *The New Hollywood* (London: Studio Vista, 1993), p. 15.

29. Eames, *The Paramount Story,* p. 225.

30. A, D, Murphy, "Barry Diller, 32, New Par Chairman: Bluhdorn Move Surprises Film Trade," *Variety,* September 25, 1974, p. 2.

31. George Mair, *The Barry Diller Story: The Life and Times of America's Greatest Entertainment Mogul* (New York: John Wiley & Sons, 1997), pp. 65, 67.

32. Justin Wyatt, *High Concept,* p. 85.

33. Thomas Guback, "Theatrical Film," in Benjamin M. Compaine, ed., *Who Owns the Media? Concentration of Ownership in the Mass Communications Industry* (White Plains, NY: Knowledge Industry Publications, 1979). p. 202; and Seymour M. Hersh, "Gulf and Western Tax Practices Coming Under Wide Examination," The *New York Times,* July 26, 1977, p. 10.

34. Quoted in J. Hoberman, "1975–1985: Ten Years That Shook the World," *American Film* 10, no. 8 (June 1985), p. 35.

35. Quoted in Michael Pye and Lynda Myles, *The Movie Brats: How the Film Generation Took Over Hollywood* (New York: Holt, Rinehart and Winston, 1979), p. 89.

36. Jon Lewis, *Whom God Wishes to Destroy: Francis Ford Coppola and the New Hollywood* (Durham: Duke University Press, 1995), pp. 16–18.

37. "Big Warner Cash in Indie Films," *Variety,* June, 9, 1954, p, 5.

38. "Nearly All WB Net from 'Giant,'" *Variety,* December 11, 1957, p. 4.

39. "Revolving Production Fund for WB; Clarification From Kinney National," *Variety,* January 21, 1970.

40. Guback, "Theatrical Film," p. 202.

41. Robert Lindsey, "The New Tycoons of Hollywood," *The New York Times Magazine,* August 7, 1977, p. 18.

42. "Making the Movies into a Business," *Business Week,* June 23, 1973, p. 118.

43. Ibid.

44. Ibid.

45. A. D. Murphy, "WB Paces U.S. Majors With 20 percent of Market: UA, Par, U Tied at 15 percent Level," *Variety,* January 23, 1980, pp. 3, 100.

46. John Baxter, *Stanley Kubrick: A Biography* (New York: Carroll & Graf, 1997), pp. 245–246.

47. A. D. Murphy, "First Artists, NGP Library to WB; Boasberg Unit to Be Dissolved," *Variety,* November 28, 1973, p. 3.

48. Ibid.

49. Charles Schreger, "Orion-Style 'Independence' Within WB: Nature of Pact Becoming Clearer," *Variety,* August 2, 1978, p. 5; and Phillip H. Wiggins, "Warner to Back Ladd in Film Unit," The *New York Times,* July 5, 1979, p. 6.

50. A. D. Murphy, "WB Net: Two-Thirds Music: New SEC Rule Uncovers Facts," *Variety,* March 1, 1972, p. 3.

51. Stephen Klain, "WCI Sees Explosive Growth in Cable TV: Films & Disks Still Are Basic," *Variety,* April 30, 1980, pp. 3, 50.

52. Robert Gustafson, "'What's Happening to Our Pix Biz?' From Warner Bros. to Warner Communications Inc.," in Tino Balio, ed., *The American Film Industry,* rev. ed. (Madison: University of Wisconsin Press, 1985), p. 579.

53. Richard Gold, "Time's Move of the Year: Vaults to Media Pinnacle," *Variety*, July 5, 1989, p, 1; and Balio, *The American Film Industry,* p. 28.

54. According to George Custen, the Zanucks initially laid off 2,000 employees and shut the studio down, so that for part of 1962–1963 the only Fox income was from television series residuals and the $18 million gross from Darryl's independently produced World War II epic THE LONGEST DAY (Ken Annakin, 1962); yet by riding the boom-or-bust wave between 1963 and 1968 the Zanucks made Fox the second most profitable studio in Hollywood (after United Artists). See George F. Custen, *Twentieth Century's Fox: Darryl Zanuck and the Culture of Hollywood* (New York: Basic Books, 1997), pp. 367–368.

55. "Making the Movies into a Business," *Business Week*, June 23, 1973, p. 118.

56. Gene Arneel, "Radical Knife on Fox Costs: Study Domestic Sales Patterns," *Variety*, August 5, 1970, p. 3.

57. Leonard Mosley, *Zanuck: The Rise and Fall of Hollywood's Last Tycoon* (Boston: Little, Brown,, 1984), p. 371.

58. Steven M. Silverman, *The Fox That Got Away: The Last Days of the Zanuck Dynasty at Twentieth Century Fox* (Secaucus, NJ: Lyle Stuart, 1988), p. 172.

59. "Making the Movies into a Business," *Business Week*, June 23, 1973, p. 118.

60. Aubrey Solomon, *Twentieth Century-Fox: A Corporate and Financial History* (Metuchen, NJ: Scarecrow, 1988), p. 172.

61. Gene Arneel, "Name of the Fox Game: Sane; 11 Pix Incoming, None Over $2-Mil," *Variety*, January 27, 1971, p. 3.

62. "Nicholson Format at Fox; Own Finances & Own Exploiting," *Variety*, June 14, 1972, p. 5.

63. Robert H. Stanley, *The Celluloid Empire,* pp. 250–251.

64. Quoted in Madsen, *The New Hollywood,* p. 18.

65. "Fox Buys St. Paul Coke Bottler In $27.5 Diversification Move," *Variety*, July 7, 1977, pp. 3, 34.

66. Quoted in William Bates, "Hollywood in the Era of the Super-Grosser," The *New York Times*, December 24, 1978, sec. E, p. 1.

67. "20th–Fox First Major Studio to Enter Home Vidtape Market with Pix; License 50 Pre-'72s," *Variety*, August 10, 1977, pp. 3, 30; Stephen Klain, "H'Wood Pix on Home Tape at $50 Per: 20th–Fox Catalogue First to Hit New Market," *Variety*, December 7, 1977, pp. 1, 90.

68. Andrew J. Neff, "20th's Prod. Budget in '79 Tops $70-Mil: To Release 11 Pix This Year," *Variety*, February 14, 1979, pp. 3, 64.

69. Solomon, *Twentieth Century–Fox,* p. 186.

70. David Pirie, *Anatomy of the Movies,* (New York: Macmillan, 1981), p. 30.

71. Silverman, *The Fox That Got Away,* p. 288.

72. Ibid., p. 193.

73. Bernard F. Dick, *City of Dreams: the Making and Remaking of Universal Pictures* (Lexington: University of Kentucky Press, 1997), pp. 141–146.

74. Ibid., p. 165.

75. "Banks Biggest Film Loan?: MCA Gets $134-M in Re-Financing," *Variety*, March 3, 1971, p. 3.

76. A. D. Murphy, "MCA Pinpoints Film Side: 1972 Rise 32 percent; Tax Credit Vital," *Variety*, April 4, 1973, p. 3.

77. A. D. Murphy, "Universal Pics Make Film History: 1975 World Rentals at Alltime High of $289-Mil," *Variety*, January 21, 1976, p. 1.

78. Dick, p. 171.

79. Bart, *Fade Out,* p. 30.

80. Stanley, *The Celluloid Empire,* p. 267; and Guback, "Theatrical Film," p. 231.

81. *Hollywood Reporter*, February 27, 1979, p. 13.

82. Dan E. Moldea, *Dark Victory: Ronald Reagan, MCA, and the Mob* (New York: Viking, 1986), p. 56; David G. Wittles, "The Star-Spangled Octopus," The *Saturday Evening Post*, August 1946.

83. Finler, *The Hollywood Story,* p. 218.

84. Quoted in Moldea, p. 269.

85. Stephen Farber, "The Return of the Grown-up Movie," *American Film* 7, no. 3 (December 1981), p. 51.

86. Andrew Neff, "MCA Joins Congloms; Billionaire Elite: U Among Subsids Generating Lucre," *Variety*, February 28, 1979, pp. 3, 18.

87. Moldea, p. 264.

88. Ibid. p. 277.
89. Ronald Grover, "Lights, Camera, Auction," *Business Week*, December 10, 1990, pp. 27.
90. Gary Arlen, "A Premiere Approach," *American Film* 6, no. 1 (October 1980), pp. 25–27.
91. Dick, *City of Dreams*, p. 167.
92. Stanley, *The Celluloid Empire*, p. 238.
93. Bernard F. Dick, "From the Brothers Cohn to Sony Corp.," in Bernard F. Dick, ed., *Columbia Pictures: Portrait of a Studio* (Lexington: University of Kentucky Press, 1992), p. 20.
94. Bo Burlington, "Politics Under the Palms," *Esquire* 87, no. 2 (February 1977), p. 51.
95. Madsen, *The New Hollywood,* p. 16.
96. Lucian K. Truscott IV, "Hollywood's Wall Street Connection," The *New York Times*, February 26, 1978; see also Dick, *Columbia Pictures*, p. 28.
97. Richard Albarino, "Columbia Evades Kiss of Debt: Warrant Deal for Radio-TV Outlets," *Variety*, October 10, 1973, p. 2.
98. "Begelman As Columbia Pictures Chief Probable; Would Bring New Dispensation On Films, Also At CMA," *Variety*, August 14, 1973, p. 3.
99. Bad times for BBS began in December 1973 when David Begelman moved to eliminate all vestiges of the Schneider regime at Columbia. The new management seized BBS royalties on previous films, took back their 16mm rights, and tried to cancel the rest of the six-picture deal. But the studio was still prepared to release the BBS-produced anti-Vietnam war documentary HEARTS AND MINDS (Peter Davis, 1974) until Begelman saw it and refused to release it, demanding that Columbia's logo be removed from the film. Bert Schneider filed suit against Columbia, claiming suppression on political grounds (although, in fact, it was the film's dim commercial prospects that drove Begelman to shelve it). In court, BBS won the right to buy the film back from Columbia for $1,000,000, and, distributed by Henry Jaglom's independent Rainbow Pictures, HEARTS AND MINDS went on win the 1974 Academy Award for Best Documentary Feature. (See Bo Burlington, "Politics Under the Palms," pp. 52–53.) Schneider had one more film to distribute when he closed BBS in 1975, a documentary called THE GENTLEMAN TRAMP that focused on Charlie Chaplin's film career and his demonization by right-wing politicians and press. This had limited theatrical distribution and playoff on PBS, after which Schneider produced one last feature, Terrence Malick's extraordinary DAYS OF HEAVEN (1978). This film was the first American work of French cinematographer Nestor Almendros, whom Schneider had earlier attempted to bring to the U.S. to shoot the aborted BBS production GONE BEAVER against the vociferous (and successful) protest of powerful Local 659 of the International Photographers of the Motion Picture Industries. (See "BBS & Hollywood Unions: Camera Import Nix for 'Beaver'," *Variety*, November 8, 1972, p. 3.)
100. Quoted in Madsen, *The New Hollywood,* p. 16.
101. Ibid.
102. "Columbia Rental Decade Double-Plus: Recent Upturn Sharpens Data," *Variety*, January 21, 1976, p, 5.
103. Robert Lindsey, "Film Industry Fears an Inquiry By U.S., but None Is Seen Soon," The *New York Times*, May 9, 1978, p. 3A.
104. Quoted in Pirie, p. 29.
105. Dick, *Columbia Pictures*, p. 33.
106. Stanley, *The Celluloid Empire*, p. 241; A. D. Murphy, "Col Into Pinballs Via $50-Mil Deal: D. Gottlieb Deal Broadens Base," *Variety*, December 8, 1976, pp. 3, 87.
107. Richard Albarino, "Al Hirschfield: Call It Co-Financing: Risk in Shabby Tax Shelter," *Variety*, August 14, 1974, p. 5.
108. "Columbia Pic: 'Love That Tax Shelter': Would Hate It If It's Abated," *Variety*, August, 1975, p. 3.
109. James Monaco, *American Film Now: The People, the Power, the Money, the Movies* (New York: Oxford University Press, 1979), p. 25; and "'Close Encounters' Propels Columbia," The *New York Times*, May 12, 1978, p. 1B. The film's $8-million promotional budget brought total investment in CLOSE ENCOUNTERS to $25.5 million, less $6.75 million in outside money, so that its $21 million in advance guarantees from exhibitors put it $2 million over costs before it was even released.
110. Joseph McBride, "Kirk's CPI Salvo Sparks Legal Warfare: KK Spells Out 2 Takeover Bids," *Variety*, October 1, 1980, pp. 3, 36.
111. David McClintick, *Indecent Exposure: A True Story of Hollywood and Wall Street* (New York: William Morrow, 1982), p. 509.

112. "Time Is Money For Columbia Picts.: Pay-Cable Also Tied to Production Deal," *Variety*, June 23, 1976, pp. 1, 30.

113. *Fortune*, December 1, 1980, pp. 108–109.

114. John Huey and Stephen J. Sansweet, "Coca Cola to Pay over $820 Million for Movie Firm." The *Wall Street Journal*, January 20, 1982; Dick, *Columbia*, pp. 34–35.

115. Finler, *The Hollywood Story*, p. 200.

116. Tino Balio, *United Artists: The Company That Changed the Film Industry* (Madison: University of Wisconsin Press, 1987). p. 307.

117. Stanley, *The Celluloid Empire*, p. 254.

118. See, for example, Abel Green, "Era of Young Film Presidents: Stan Jaffe, 30, Latest of Breed," *Variety*, July 29, 1970, pp. 3, 22.

119. Balio, p. 315.

120. Ibid., p. 318.

121. Frank Segers, "Krim Bullish About MGM Features: Bottom Not Out of Theater Pix," *Variety*, November 14, 1973, p. 5.

122. A. D. Murphy, "United Artists 'Stabilized': Sheds Fat: Debt Offloaded 20 Percent; MGM Deal Boon; Avoids CATV," *Variety*, March 27, 1974, p. 7.

123. Robert Lindsey, "The Film Giant with No Studio," The *New York Times*, March 27, 1977, p. 15.

124. A. D. Murphy, "Boomy United Artists Contributes Fiscal Glow to Transamerica," *Variety*, July 20, 1977, p. 3.

125. Harlan Jacobson, "UA Reaps Record $275-Mil Rentals: See $120-Mil From Foreign," *Variety*, November 23, 1977, pp. 3, 28; and A. D. Murphy, "UA Global Rentals," *Variety*, January 11, 1978, p. 3.

126. Quoted in Peter J. Schuyten, "United Artists' Script Calls for Divorce," *Fortune* 97 (January 16, 1978), pp. 130–131.

127. Michael Deeley and Barry Spikings, co-directors of EMI's film division, quoted in Aljean Harmetz, "Orion's Star Rises in Hollywood," The *New York Times*, April 19, 1978, p. 2E.

128. A. D. Murphy, "'High Noon' in UA Executive Suite: Andy Albeck New Prez as Vet Showmen Exit," *Variety*, January 18, pp. 1, 3.

129. Patrick McGilligan, "Breaking Away, Mogul Style," *American Film*, 5, 8 (June 1980), p. 29. See also "Rise and Shine: Mike Medavoy Interviewed by Anne Thompson," *Film Comment* 23, no. 3 (May–June 1987), pp. 55–58.

130. Steven Bach, *Final Cut: Dreams and Disaster in the Making of 'Heaven's Gate'* (New York, William Morrow, 1985).

131. Geri Fabrikant, "UA Faces Economics of 210-Minute Film: 'Heaven's Gate' Is a Recoup Problem," *Variety*, October 1, 1980, pp. 7, 36.

132. "Transamerica Writes Off 'Gate' As Admitted Loss; No Specifics," *Variety*, November 26, 1980, p. 3.

133. Geri Fabrikant, "UA, Directors' Paradise, Under Loss Cloud: 'Heaven's Gate' Is Hellish Dilemma," *Variety*, November 26, 1978, p. 3.

134. Bach, *Final Cut*, p. 374.

135. Michael Dempsey, "After the Fall: Post-Cimino Hollywood," *American Film* 6, no. 10 (September 1981), p. 53.

136. Balio, *United Artists*, p. 343; Bruce Orwall and Lisa Bannon, "Kerkorian's Script for Restoring MGM Casts Him as Savior of the Faded Studio, The *Wall Street Journal*, July 18, 1996, sec. B, p. 1; Martin Peers and Chris Petrikin, "One More Roar in Ailing Lion: Bidders Invited to Take Stock in Cash-Starved MGM," *Variety*, August 10–16, 1998, p. 1.

137. Stanley, *The Celluloid Empire*, p. 261.

138. Douglas Gomery, "Disney's Business History: A Reinterpretation," *Disney Discourse: Producing the Magic Kingdom*, Eric Smoodin, ed. (New York: Routledge, 1994), p. 77.

139. Quoted in Alan Bryman, *Disney and His Worlds* (New York: Routledge, 1995), p. 36.

140. Jon Lewis, "Disney After Disney: Family Business and the Business of Family," in *Disney Discourse: Producing the Magic Kingdom*, Eric Smoodin, ed. (New York: Routledge, 1994), p. 97.

141. "Making the Movies into a Business," *Business Week*, p. 119.

142. Bryman, *Disney and His Worlds*, p. 38.

143. Lewis, "Disney After Disney," p. 99.

144. John Culhane, "The Old Disney Magic," *The New York Times Magazine*, August 1, 1976, pp. 32–36.
145. "Hardest Sell In Hollywood; 'G'," *Variety*, August 2, 1978, p. 6.
146. Aljean Harmetz, "Disney Studio to Release PG Film It Didn't Make," The *New York Times*, January 15, 1979, p. 2E.
147. Aljean Harmetz, "Disney Studio Risks $17.5 Million on 'Black Hole,'" The *New York Times*, March 4, 1979, p. 5E.
148. Pamela G. Hollie, "'Animators' Loss Shakes Disney," The *New York Times*, October 10, 1979, p. 16B.
149. Leonard Maltin, *The Disney Films* (New York: Hyperion, 1995), p. 286.
150. Balio, *United Artists,* p. 273.
151. Richard deCordova, "The Mickey in Macy's Window," in *Disney Discourse*, Eric Smoodin, ed., p. 205.
152. Marc Eliot, *Walt Disney: Hollywood's Dark Prince* (New York: Birch Lane Press, 1993), p. 272.
153. Joe Flower, *Prince of the Magic Kingdom: Michael Eisner and the Re-making of Disney* (New York: John Wiley & Sons, 1991), p. 103.
154. Mark Thomas McGee, *Faster and Furiouser: The Revised and Fattened Fable of American International Pictures* (Jefferson, NC: McFarland & Company, 1984), p. 25.
155. Ibid., p. 150.
156. Stanley, *The Celluloid Empire*, p. 243.
157. McGee, pp. 150; 42.
158. Stanley, p. 244.
159. David Gordon, "The Movie Majors," *Sight and Sound* 4E, 3 (Summer 1979); "Majors," p. 152; Guback, "Theatrical Films," p. 231.
160. McGee, p. 153.
161. Stanley, p. 258.
162. Derek Elley, *The Epic Film: Myth and History* (London: Routledge & Kegan Paul, 1984), p. 21.
163. "The Producer: Joseph E. Levine," in *Filmmakers on Filmmaking*, Vol. 2, Joseph McBride, ed. (Los Angeles: J.P. Tarcher, Inc., 1983), pp. 28–29.
164. Ibid.
165. Guback, "Theatrical Film," p. 231.
166. Douglas Gomery, "Joseph E. Levine," *International Dictionary of Films and Filmmakers — 4: Writers and Production Artists*, Second Edition, ed. Samantha Cook, et al. (Detroit: St. James Press, 1993), pp. 472–473.
167. Michael Conant, "The Paramount Decrees Reconsidered," in *The American Film Industry*, rev. ed., Tino Balio, ed. (Madison: University of Wisconsin Press, 1985), p. 555.
168. Suzanne Mary Donahue, *American Film Distribution: The Changing Marketplace* (Ann Arbor: UMI Research Press, 1985), p. 224; Dan Yakir, "Bob Rehme: New Power in Hollywood," *Film Comment* 17, no. 4 (July-August 1981), p. 74.
169. "Perenchio, Lear Form Embassy; Horn Chairman," *The Hollywood Reporter*, January 21, 1982, p. 4. See also Anthony Slide, *The American Film Industry: A Historical Dictionary* (New York: Greenwood Press, 1986), p. 110.
170. Slide, pp. 110–111.
171. Gene Fernett, *American Film Studios: An Historical Encyclopedia* (Jefferson, NC: McFarland, 1988), p. 146.
172. Erwin Kim, *Franklin J. Schaffner* (Metuchen, NJ: Scarecrow Press, 1985), p. 292.
173. Ibid., p. 447, n. 142.
174. John Huston, *An Open Book* (New York: Alfred A. Knopf, 1980), p. 353.
175. Stuart Kaminsky, *John Huston: Maker of Magic* (Boston: Houghton Mifflin, 1978). p. 202.
176. Guback, "Theatrical Film," p. 231.
177. Michael Conant, "The Paramount Decrees Reconsidered," pp. 556–557.
178. Lee Beaupre, "How to Distribute a Film," *Film Comment* 13, no. 4 (July-August 1977), p. 48.
179. James Lardner, *Fast Forward: Hollywood, the Japanese, and the Onslaught of the VCR* (New York: W. W. Norton, 1987), p. 178.
180. Quoted in Ed Naha, *The Films of Roger Corman: Brilliance on a Budget* (New York: Arco Publishing, 1982), p. 70.
181. Donahue, *American Film Distribution,* p. 227.
182. Pirie, p. 92.

183. Quoted in Naha, p. 72.
184. David Chute, "The New World of Roger Corman," *Film Comment* 18, no. 2 (March–April 1982), p. 30.
185. "The Making of a Modern-Day Movie Mogul," *Business Week*, May 16, 1977, p. 117.
186. Stuart Byron, "'Instant Majors': A Short-Cut: Whole U.S. Films Trade Shuffles," *Variety*, October 25, 1967, pp. 5, 21.
187. Robert B. Frederick, "Palmieri: Consent Decree Ban Stands: NGP Filmmaking as 'Experiment'," *Variety*, April 29, 1969, pp. 3, 78.
188. Stanley, *The Celluloid Empire*, p. 245.
189. Jack Gold, "C.B.S. Is Dropping Its Theater Films," The *New York Times*, January 10, 1972, p. 6. See also Gordon Stulberg, "Film Company Management," in *The Movie Business Book*, Jason E. Squire, ed. (Englewood Cliffs, NJ: Prentice Hall, 1983), pp. 143–150 (about Stulberg's experience as president of Cinema Center Films).
190. Ibid., p. 7.
191. Frederick, "Palmieri: Consent Decree Ban Stands," p. 78.
192. A. D. Murphy, "First Artists, NGP Library to WB: Boasberg Unit To Be Dissolved," *Variety*, November 28, 1973, p. 3.
193. The *New York Times*, quoted in "'Instant Majors': A Short Cut," *Variety*, October 25, 1967, p. 5.
194. Gary Edgerton, *American Film Exhibition and An Analysis of the Motion Picture Industry's Market Structure, 1963–1980* (New York: Garland Publishing, Inc, 1983), pp. 53–54.
195. John Belton, *Widescreen Cinema* (Cambridge: Harvard University Press, 1992), p. 110.
196. Lee Beaupre, "ABC Pix: Post-Mortem 'Audit': Flops, Successes in $35 Million Loss," *Variety*, May 30, 1973, pp. 5, 22.
197. Frank Segers, "CRC Goes On, No 'Merger'; Joe Sugar Remains President; AIP Takes Distribution Burden," *Variety*, August 7, 1974, pp. 3, 21.
198. Ibid., p. 3.
199. William Lafferty, "Feature Films on Prime-Time Television," in *Hollywood in the Age of Television*, Tino Balio, ed. (New York: Ungar, 1992), p. 249.
200. A. D. Murphy, "Film Distribs' '70-Mkt. Shares: Fox Tops at 19 percent; Indies' Cut Soars," *Variety*, January 13, 1971, p. 38.
201. David Gordon, "Why the Movie Majors are Major," in *The American Film Industry*, Tino Balio, ed. (Madison: University of Wisconsin Press, 1976), p. 460.
202. Barry R. Litman, *The Motion Picture Mega-Industry* (Boston: Allyn and Bacon, 1998), p. 15.
203. Tino Balio, "Introduction to Part II," *Hollywood in the Age of Television*, p. 260.
204. Gary Edgerton, *American Film Exhibition*, p. 51.
205. A. D. Murphy, "Distribs' B.O. Share Below 40 Percent: Talent Generation Shift, Screen Expansion, Price War Contributing Factors," *Variety*, August 21, 1984, p. 1.
206. David Lees and Stan Berkowitz, *The Movie Business* (New York: Vintage, 1981), p. 135.
207. A. D. Murphy, "Distribution and Exhibition: An Overview," in *The Movie Business Book*, Second Edition, Jason E. Squire, ed. (New York: Simon & Schuster, 1992), p. 278.
208. Edgerton, p. 72.
209. "Youngstein Angle Re EXPRODICO," *Variety*, January 31, 1979, p. 7; "Film Famine Could Revive EXPRODICO: Product Flow Cooled Exhibs," *Variety*, February 14, 1979, p. 7.
210. Suzanne Mary Donahue, *American Film Distribution*, p. 105.
211. Harlan Jacobson, "Mann, Loews, RKO File 'Consent' Pleas: Seek-Film-Making Okay of Palmieri," *Variety*, April 4, 1979, pp. 3, 22; Frank Segers, "Distribs: Don't Unglue Consent Pacts: Argue Chains Would Hog Firstrun Dates," *Variety*, May 30, 1979, p. 7; and Harlan Jacobson, "Justice Dept. Okays Loew's Prod. Bid: Govt. to Modify Consent Decree," *Variety*, December 5, 1979, pp. 3, 36.
212. Quoted in "Loew's Gets OK to Enter Pic Production: Some Taboos Still Remain," *Variety*, March 5, 1980, p. 44.
213. Ibid.
214. Harold L. Vogel, *Entertainment Industry Economics: A Guide for Financial Analysis* (New York: Cambridge University Press, 1986), p. 113.
215. "Film-making Gets Some Tightfisted Angels," *Business Week*, February 5, 1972, pp. 68–69; Robert J. Landry, "Short Take for a U.S. Film History: WWII to 1976," *Variety*, January 5, 1977, p. 12; "Parents Mag., Filmmaker: Talks on with Paramount, Fox," *Variety*, June 6, 1973, pp. 3, 22;

Stuart Byron, "Don Rugoff: Ballyhoo with a Harvard Education," *Film Comment* 11, no. 3 (May–June 1975), pp. 20–27.

216. Martin Dale, *The Movie Game: The Film Business in Britain, Europe, and America* (London: Cassell, 1997), p. 55.

217. David Gordon, "The Movie Majors," *Sight and Sound* 48, no. 3 (Summer 1979), p. 5.

218. Richard Maltby, *Harmless Entertainment: Hollywood and the Ideology of Consensus* (Metuchen, NJ, 1983), p. 322.

219. Douglas Gomery, "The American Film Industry in the 1970's: Stasis in the 'New Hollywood,'" *Wide Angle* 5, no. 4 (1983), p. 53.

220. A. D. Murphy, "Japan Now No. 1 Market for U.S. Films: 60 percent of $1.9-Bil. World Rentals From Domestic B.O.," *Variety*, July 11, 1979, pp. 1, 6.

221. Thomas Schatz, "Boss Men," *Film Comment* 26, no. 1 (January–February 1990), p. 28.

222. "The Agent: Sue Mengers" in *Filmmakers on Filmmaking*, Vol. 1, Joseph McBride, ed., p. 170.

223. Pirie, p. 30.

224. Bach, *Final Cut*, p. 417.

CHAPTER 8 (ORDERS OF MAGNITUDE II: COSTS, AGENTS, STARS)

1. "In 10 Years, Film Costs Tripled," *Variety,* January 7, 1970, p. 10.

2. Alan Stanbrook, "Hollywood's Crashing Epics," *Sight and Sound* (Spring 1981), p. 82.

3. Leonard Klady, "Budgets in the Hot Zone: The Sum Also Rises," *Variety*, March 16–22, 1998, p. 80.

4. Stuart Byron, "The Industry," *Film Comment* 16, no. 1 (January–February 1980), p. 38.

5. Jim Waters, "These 'Angels' Rush In Where Others Fear to Tread: His Money Talks in Hollywood," *The New York Times*, September 5, 1976, p. 8E.

6. Mitch Tuchman, "Helter Shelter: Now Do We Write Off Hollywood?," *Film Comment* 13, no. 1 (January-February 1977), p. 22.

7. Michael Pye, *Moguls: Inside the Business of Show Business* (New York: Holt, Rinehart and Winston, 1980), p. 187.

8. Tuchman, p. 24.

9. Quoted in Mark Litwak, *Reel Power: the Stuggle for Influence and Success in the New Hollywood* (New York: William Morrow and Company, Inc., 1986), p. 91.

10. Quoted in Pye, *Moguls*, p. 186.

11. Quoted in Paul Kerr, "Stars and Stardom," in David Pirie, ed. (New York: Macmillan, 1981), p. 107.

12. A. H. Howe, "A Banker Looks at the Picture Business—1971," *Journal of the Motion Picture Producers Guild of America* 13, no. 2 (June 1971), pp. 2–7.

13. Patrick McGilligan, "Bank Shots: Patrick McGilligan Interviews Two Film Financiers," *Film Comment* 12, no. 5 (September-October 1976), p. 25.

14. Stephen Holden, "At the Top By Way of the Bottom Line," *The New York Times*, February 22, 1998, Arts, p. 15.

15. Martin Dale, *The Movie Game* (London: Cassell, 1997), p. 42.

16. Robert Lindsey, "All Hollywood Loves a Blockbuster—and Chips Off the Old Blockbuster," *The New York Times*, May 1976, p. 1E.

17. Nancy Hass, "Now You See Them . . . and See Them Again," *The New York Times*, November 16, 1997, "Art and Leisure" section, p. 26.

18. Frank Rose, *The Agency: William Morris and the Hidden History of Show Business* (New York: HarperCollins, 1995), pp. 306, 319–320.

19. Ibid., p. 338.

20. Ibid., p. 339.

21. Johnnie L. Roberts, "Doc Hollywood: King of the Deal," *Newsweek*, June 12, 1995, p. 49.

22. Rose, p. 333.

23. Quoted in Dale, p. 44.

24. Robert Slater, *Ovitz: The Inside Story of Hollywood's Most Controversial Power Broker* (New York: McGraw-Hill, 1997), p. 73.

25. Charles Schreger, "CAA: Packaging of an Agency," *The Los Angeles Times*, April 23, 1979, part IV, p. 13.

26. Aljean Harmetz, "Film Costs: Scenario of Greed," The *New York Times*, February 15, 1978, p. 1E.

27. Mark Liwak, *Reel Power*, p. 42.

28. Stephen Farber, "Film Notes: Rising Stars and Falling Moguls," The *New York Times*, January 19, 1975, p. 14E. Screenwriter Jon Axelrod, who was hired by Peters to rewrite the script (and later fired), asked convincingly "How do you explain to stockholders that a hairdresser is going to direct a $5-million film?"

29. James Monaco, *American Film Now*, Second Edition (New York: New American Library, 1984), p. 47.

30. Joseph McBride, *Steven Spielberg: A Biography* (New York: Simon & Schuster, 1997), pp. 236–237.

31. "The Agent: Sue Mengers," in *Filmmakers on Filmmaking*, Vol. 1, Joseph McBride, ed. (Los Angeles: J. P. Tarcher, 1983), p. 165.

32. "The Casting Director: Joyce Selznick," in *Filmmakers on Filmmaking*, Vol. 2, Joseph McBride, ed. (Los Angeles: J. P. Tarcher, 1983), pp. 177–179.

33. Kirk Honeycutt, "Stalmaster, the Master Caster," *American Film* 5, no. 8 (June 1980), pp. 34–40; 61; 67.

34. Michael F. Mayer, *The Film Industries*, rev. ed. (New York: Hastings House, 1978), p. 18.

35. John W. Cones, *Film Finance & Distribution: A Dictionary of Terms* (Los Angeles: Silman-James Press, 1992), pp. 93–94.

36. Michael Angeli, "My Name Is Bond, Completion Bond," The *New York Times*, June 22, 1991, p. 12E.

37. Jeff Berg, quoted in Karen Stabiner, "Playing Hardball with a Hot Agent," *American Film* 6, no. 9 (July-August 1981), pp. 45–67.

38. Yablans quoted in Peter Biskind, *Easy Riders, Raging Bulls: How the Sex-Drugs-and-Rock 'n' Roll Generation Saved Hollywood* (New York: Simon & Schuster, 1998), p. 281.

39. David Puttnam, with Neil Watson, *The Undeclared War: The Struggle for Control of the World's Film Industry* (London: HarperCollins, 1997), p. 280.

40. Dennis McDougal, *The Last Mogul: Lew Wasserman, MCA, and the Hidden History of Hollywood* (New York: Crown, 1998), pp. 152–153.

41. At United Artists, producer-directors like Norman Jewison were not fined but forced to pay for cost overruns out their own pocket. Concerning the elimination of budget overrides on *F.I.S.T.* (1978) see "Jewison Must Pay His Over-Bill! Ouch!!: United Artists Enforces Rule," *Variety*, July 20, 1977, pp. 3, 26.

42. Andrew Laskos, "The Hollywood Majors," in David Pirie, ed., *Anatomy of the Movies*, p. 34.

43. Aljean Harmetz, "Film Figures Decry Profit-Sharing Evils," The *New York Times*, February 5, 1978, p. 8E.

43A. An analysis of the Academy Awards and nominations made between 1970 and 1980 (see Appendix 14) reveals that women nominated in the Best Actress category almost never appeared in films that were nominated for Best Picture or other major awards, confirming the long-held suspicion that the industry doesn't offer women key roles in its best (i.e., most cost-intensive) films.

44. Peter Bart quoted in Harmetz, "Film Costs," p. 1E. See also Molly Haskel, "What Makes Streisand Queen of the Box Office?" The *New York Times*, March 9, 1975, p. 7E.

45. Quoted in David Pirie, "The Deal," Pirie, ed., *Anatomy of the Movies*, p. 50.

46. Quoted in Leo Janos, "The Hollywood Game Grows Rich—and Desperate," The *New York Times*, February 12, 1978, p. 15E.

47. A. H. Weiler, "3 Stars Form Film Production Outfit," The *New York Times*, June 12, 1969, p. 4E.

48. David Thomson, *Beneath Mulholland: Thoughts on Hollywood and Its Ghosts* (New York: Alfred A. Knopf, 1997), p. 10.

49. "Won't Wait for Brando, Keitel Fired: Ufland Furious at F. F. Copppola," *Variety*, April 21, 1976, p. 3. Harvey Keitel took the McQueen role, which became Marlon Brando's "Kurtz," after Coppola fired Keitel.

50. Aljean Harmetz, "Columbia Pays $2 Million to Jane Fonda for Film," The *New York Times*, September 28, 1979, p. 5E.

51. Puttnam and Watson, *The Undeclared War*, p. 282.

52. Ben Stein, "Holy Bat-Debt!," *Entertainment Weekly* (April 26, 1991), p. 12.

53. See Joan Didion, "The White Album," *The White Album* (New York: Pocket Books, 1979); Andrew Sarris, Review of "Comes a Horseman," The *Village Voice*, 1978; Tom Wolfe, "The Me Decade and the Third Great Awakening." Arkoff told the MPAA in 1973: "For one or two years, everybody was

scaled down. But now major studios are letting themselves be sucked into the same goddam pattern. The $750,000-to-$1-million actor that no studio wanted to pay more than $250,000 for last year is getting $750,000 again, but now, in addition, he's getting a piece of the gross." (Quoted in Axel Madsen, *The New Hollywood* [New York: Thomas Y. Crowell, 1975], p. 15.)

54. Litwak, *Reel Power*, p. 156.
55. Coblenz quoted in Litwak, p. 159. See also Wayne E. Baker and Robert R. Faulkner, "Role as Resource in the Hollywood Film Industry," *American Journal of Sociology* 97, no. 2 (September 1991), pp. 287–292.
56. Gary Edgerton, *American Film Exhibition and An Analysis of the Motion Picture Industry's Market Structure, 1963–1980* (New York: Garland Publishing, Inc., 1983), p. 55.
57. David Londoner, "The Changing Economics of Entertainment," in Tino Balio, ed., *The American Film Industry*, rev. ed. (Madison: University of Wisconsin Press, 1985), p. 615.
58. "Book Pix That Stimulate Food, Drink; Argue Stands Are Sites' Salvation," *Variety*, January 28, 1979, p. 7.
59. Jim Hillier, *The New Hollywood* (London: Studio Vista, 1992), p. 16; Cobbett Steinberg, *Reel Facts: The Movie Book of Records*, updated ed. (New York: Random House, 1982), p. 84.
60. James Monaco, *American Film Now*, p. 393.
61. Tino Balio, "Introduction to Part I," *Hollywood in the Age of Television*, Tino Balio, ed. (Boston: Unwin Hyman, 1990), p. 29.
62. Douglas Gomery, "If You've Seen One, You've Seen the Mall," in Mark Crispin Miller, ed., *Seeing Through Movies* (New York: Pantheon, 1990). p. 68.
63. Edgerton, p. 44; Douglas Gomery, *Shared Pleasures: A History of Movie Presentation in the United States* (Madison: University of Wisconsin Press, 1992), pp. 98–99; Mary Suzanne Donahue, *American Film Distribution: The Changing Marketplace* (Ann Arbor: UMI Research Press, 1987), p. 107.
64. Thomas Guback, "The Evolution of the Motion Picture Theater Business in the 1980s," *Journal of Communication* 37, no. 2 (Spring 1987), pp. 68–69.
65. A. D. Murphy, "Distribution and Exhibition: An Overview," in *The Movie Business Book*, Jason E. Squire, ed. (Englewood Cliffs, NJ: Prentice Hall, 1983), p. 261; and "55–60 Percent Firstrun, Where's Subrun Biz?: This Jan.–Feb. Is Unusual 'Shakeout'," *Variety*, January 21, 1981, p. 3.
66. Edgerton, pp. 55–57.
67. Todd McCarthy, "The Exorcism of 'The Heretic': Why They Had to Destroy This Film in Order to Save It," *Film Comment* 13, no. 5 (September–October 1977), p. 48.
68. See, for example, "Theatre Crisis Over Film Famine: Exhibs Spotlight Problems at NATO Meeting," *Variety*, October 1, 1975, pp. 1, 119.
69. A. D. Murphy, "Pinch Picture Playoff Patterns: Majors Can't Supply Full Year's Product," *Variety*, March 17, 1976, p. 34.
70. Lee Beaupre, "Industry," *Film Comment* 14, no. 4 (July–August 1978), p. 68.
71. Ibid., p. 69.
72. A. D. Murphy, "300 Indie Films Pace Production: Invest $100-Mil Outside Majors," *Variety*, June 9, 1976, p. 32.
73. James McBride, "Independent Productions Rise Despite Tax Shelter Collapse; Films Better Risk Than Stocks," *Variety*, June 15, 1977, p. 2.
74. Lawrence Cohn, "10-Year Diary of Fast-Fade 'Indie' Pix: Risky for Thesps When Directing," *Variety*, October 15, 1980, p. 13.
75. "Marketing Still After-Thought? Kahn, Powell, Rosenfield and Goldberg Agree that Too Often There's Little Input," *Variety*, October 31, 1979, p. 28.
76. David J. Londoner, "The Changing Economics of Entertainment," p. 617.
77. Murphy, "Pinch Picture Playoff Patterns," p. 34.
78. David Gordon, "The Movie Majors," *Sight & Sound* 48, no. 3 (Summer 1979), p. 151; Douglas Gomery, "The American Film Industry in the 1970s: Stasis in the 'New Hollywood'," *Wide Angle* 5, no. 4 (1983), p. 53.
79. Londoner, pp. 615–616.

CHAPTER 9 (TECHNOLOGICAL INNOVATION AND AESTHETIC RESPONSE)

1. Barry Salt, *Film Style & Technology*, 2nd ed. (London: Starword Press, 1992), p. 272.
2. "Nestor Almendros," in Ellen Oumano, *Film Forum: Thirty-Five Top Filmmakers Discuss Their Craft* (New York: St. Martin's Press, 1985), pp. 85–84.
3. Charles Higham, *Hollywood Cameramen: Sources of Light* (Bloomington: Indiana University Press, 1970); Leonard Maltin, *Behind the Camera: the Cinematographer's Art* (New York: New American Library, 1971); reprinted and enlarged as *The Art of the Cinematographer: A Survey and Interviews with Five Masters* (New York: Dover Publications, 1978). While both collections deal primarily with classical cinematographers, they acknowledge the revolutionary practice of the emerging generation of William Fraker, Haskell Wexler, Conrad Hall, etc., and Maltin's book features an interview with Hall himself.
4. "Film Union Sued Over Job Policy," The *New York Times*, December 5, 1975.
5. Axel Madsen, *The New Hollywood: American Movies in '70s* (New York: Thomas Y. Crowell, 1975), p. 82.
6. "Vilmos Zsigmond," in Dennis Schaefer and Larry Salvato, *Masters of Light: Conversations with Contemporary Cinematographers* (Berkeley: University of California Press, 1984) p. 324.
7. Lee Beaupre, "BBS & Hollywood Unions: Camera Import Nix for 'Beaver'," *Variety*, November 8, 1972, p. 3.
8. Ibid.
9. Todd McCarthy, "That Euro-wood Look: Speed of Light," *Film Comment* 25, no. 5 (September-October, 1989), p. 32.
10. Ibid.
11. Quoted in "Vittorio Storaro," in Dennis Schaefer and Larry Salvato, *Masters of Light: Conversations with Contemporary Cinematographers* (Berkeley: University of California Press, 1984), p. 232.
12. Todd McCarthy, "Hollywood Style '84," *Film Comment* 20, no. 2 (March-April 1984), pp. 32–33.
13. Ibid., p. 37.
14. "Vilmos Zsigmond," in Schaefer and Salvato, p. 312.
15. David Konow, *Schlock-O-Rama: The Films of Al Adamson* (Los Angeles: Lone Eagle Publishing Co., 1998), p. 24.
16. McCarthy, p. 33.
17. Quoted in "Gordon Willis," Schaefer and Salvato, p. 284.
18. On Roizman's unusual cinematography for THE EXORCIST, see David E. Miller, "Demonic Convergence," *American Cinematographer* 79, no. 8 (1998), pp. 88–97.
19. "John Alonzo," Schaefer and Salvato, p. 23.
20. Ibid. p. 32; McCarthy, p. 34.
21. John A. Alonzo, "Shooting 'Chinatown,'" *American Cinematographer* 56, no. 5 (May 1975), p. 527.
22. Lee Beaupre, "BBS & Hollywood Unions," p. 30.
23. "John Alonzo," in Schaefer and Salvato, pp. 24, 40.
24. Bary Salt, *Film Style & Technology*, p. 279; Richard Zacks, "Veni, Vidi, Video . . . ," *Film Comment* 18, no. 3 (May-June 1982), p. 35; John Belton (and Lyle Tector), "The Bionic Eye: The Aesthetics of the Zoom," *Film Comment* 16, no. 5 (September-October, 1980), p. 15.
25. Salt, p. 253.
26. Quoted in Belton, p. 13.
27. "Vilmos Zsigmond," in Schaefer and Salvato, p. 317.
28. Salt, p. 279.
29. Ed DiGuilio, "Two Special Lenses for 'Barry Lyndon,'" *American Cinematographer* 57, no. 3 (March 1976), pp. 276, 336.
30. Quoted in Vincent LoBrutto, *Stanley Kubrick: A Biography* (New York: Donald I. Fine, 1997), p. 389.
31. Quoted in Michel Ciment, *Kubrick*, Gilbert Adair, trans. (New York: Holt, Rinehart and Winston, 1980), p. 216.
32. LoBrutto, p. 390.
33. "Mario Tosi," in Schaefer and Salvato, p. 241.
34. Ibid.
35. "Gordon Willis," in Schaefer and Salvato, p. 298.

36. Ibid., p. 296.
37. Salt, *Film Style & Technology,* p. 279.
38. Di Guilio, "Two Special Lenses," pp. 276–277, 318.
39. "John Alcott, Chief Cameraman," in Michel Ciment, *Kubrick,* p. 216.
40. Salt, p. 280.
41. Quoted in Salt, p. 272.
42. "Michael Chapman," in Schaefer and Salvato, pp. 111–112.
43. "Nestor Almendros," in Schaefer and Salvato, pp. 15–18.
44. "Owen Roizman" and "Vilmos Zsigmond," in Schaefer and Salvato, pp. 197–198, 322–323.
45. Salt, p. 252.
46. "Vilmor Zsigmond," in Schaefer and Salvato, pp. 326, 333.
47. "Haskell Wexler," in Schaefer and Salvato, pp. 264–265.
48. "John Bailey," in Schaefer and Salvato, p. 59.
49. Gerry Turpin, BSC, "The Turpin Colorflex System as Used for 'Young Winston'," *American Cinematographer* 1, no. 54 (January 1973), pp. 30–33, 70–71, 82–83; and "Lightflex: A Whole New World of Color on the Screen, " *American Cinematographer* 11, no. 59 (November 1978), pp. 1086–1087, 1119, 1125–1128.
50. Salt, *Film Style & Technology,* p. 271.
51. Ibid.
52. "Kodak Announces New Improved 5247/7247 Eastman Color Negative," *American Cinematographer* 54, no. 1 (January 1973), p. 46; Frederic Goodich, "Advantages of Shooting 7247 on 'How Does a Rainbow Feel?'" *American Cinematographer* 57, no. 3 (March 1976), pp. 328–331, 354; Herb A. Lightman, "ABC's Wide World of Sports Uses New Kodak 7247 16mm Color Negative for the First Time," *American Cinematographer* 55, no. 5 (May 1974), pp. 578–589.
53. "John Alonzo," Schaefer and Salvato, p. 42.
54. "Vilmos Zsigmond," in Schaefer and Salvato, pp. 314, 322.
55. Salt, p. 269.
56. "John Alonzo," in Schaefer and Salvato, p. 30.
57. Salt, p. 285.
58. Charles Loring, "Arriflex 35BL Makes Production Debut in 'Across 110th Street'," *American Cinematographer* 53, no. 8 (August 1972), pp. 876–877.
59. Scott Henderson, "The Panavision Story," *American Cinematographer* 58, no. 4 (April 1977), pp. 414–415.
60. Herb A. Lightman, "The New Panaflex Camera Makes Its Production Debut," *American Cinematographer* 54, no. 5 (May 1973), p. 567.
61. Milton Forman, "The Filming of 'The Dove'," *American Cinematographer* 55, no. 3 (March 1974), pp. 280–281.
62. "John Alonzo," in Schaefer and Salvato, p. 41.
63. Henderson, "The Panavision Story," pp. 423, 432.
64. "Panavision Goes to China," *American Cinematographer* 12, no. 62 (December 1981), pp. 1240–1241.
65. Salt, p. 276.
66. The term "floating camera mounts" derives from D. W. Samuelson, "A Survey of Current Film Production Techniques," *American Cinematographer* 58, no. 9 (September 1977), p. 922.
67. William Dykes, "Filming 'The Castle' with the Gyrocamera," *American Cinematographer* 50, no. 5 (May 1969), pp. 489–494; "Product Report: 'The Dynalens'," *American Cinematographer* 50, no. 5 (May 1969), pp. 476–478; 498; Ken Phelps, "Evolution of the 'Super-Grip'," *American Cinematographer* 53, no. 7 (July 1972), p. 788; Urs B. Furrer, "An Affair with a Dolly," *American Cinematographer* 53, no. 5 (May 1972), pp. 633–634; Salt, *Film Style & Technology,* p. 278.
68. Warren Maitland, "The Sky Is Not the Limit," *American Cinematographer* 47, no. 2 (February 1966), pp. 102–105; "The Tyler Vibrationless Mini-Mount," *American Cinematographer* 48, no. 12 (December 1967), pp. 878–881, 910; "Helivision II," *American Cinematographer* 52, no. 6 (June 1971), pp. 576–577, 810–811.
69. Quoted in "The First Feature Use of Steadicam-35 on 'Bound for Glory'," *American Cinematographer* 57, no. 7 (July 1976), p. 791.
70. Ed DiGuilio, "Steadicam-35—A Revolutionary New Concept in Camera Stabilization," *American Cinematographer* 57, no. 7 (July 1976), p. 802.

71. "Bill Butler," in Schaefer and Salvato, p. 91; "Michael Chapman," in Schaefer and Salvato, p. 102.

72. Ibid., DiGuilio, p. 779.

73. Garrett Brown, "The Steadicam and 'The Shining,'" *American Cinematographer* 61, no. 8 (August 1980), p. 786.

74. Ciment, *Kubrick*, p. 214.

75. Ibid., p. 216.

76. Brown, "The Steadicam and 'The Shining'," p. 826.

77. Quoted in Brown, p. 786.

78. Ernest McNabb, "The Wesscam Remote-Control Gyro-Stabilized Camera Mount," *American Cinematographer* 57, no. 10 (October 1976), pp. 1101, 1153.

79. William J. Schwartz, "Shooting 'The Schedule Master' with Wesscam," *American Cinematographer* 61, no. 4 (April 1980), pp. 391, 370.

80. Salt, p. 278.

81. David W. Samuelson, "Introducing the LOUMA Crane," *American Cinematographer* 60, no. 12 (December 1979), pp. 1126–1127.

82. Richard Deats, "Introducing the 'Little Big Crane'," *American Cinematographer* 61, no. 11 (November 1980), pp. 1128–1129, 1146, 1171.

83. Jean-Piere Geuens, "Through the Looking Glasses: From the Camera Obscura to Video Assist," *Film Quarterly* 49, no. 3 (Spring 1996), p. 19.

84. "Electronic Aids to Film Making," *American Cinematographer* 50, no. 8 (August 1969), p. 798.

85. "'Bound for Glory,'" *American Cinematographer* 57, no. 7 (July 1976), p. 779.

86. Bob Fisher and Don Kader, "Film-Video System Plays Key Role in Shooting 'The Muppet Movie'," *American Cinematographer* 60, no. 7 (July 1979), p. 702.

87. Brown, "The Steadicam and 'The Shining'," p. 852.

88. Ciment, *Kubrick*, p. 216.

89. Douglas M. Stewart, Jr., "Electronic Cinema: Zoeptrope Plans for the Future with Today's Technology," *On Location* 5, no. 8 (December 1981), p. 64.

90. Thomas Brown, "The Electronic Camera Experiment," *American Cinematographer* 63, no. 1 (January 1982), p. 76.

91. Ibid., p. 79.

92. Geuens, "Through the Looking Glasses," p. 20.

93. L. B. "Bill" Abbott, ASC, "Magic for the 23rd Century," *American Cinematographer* 57, no. 6 (June 1976), pp. 642–643, 676–677, 700–701; and Strawberry Gatts, "The Use of Holograms in 'Logan's Run'," *American Cinematographer* 57, no. 6 (June 1976), pp. 650–651, 668–669, 706.

94. Robert Blalack and Paul Roth, "Composite Optical and Photographic Effects for 'Star Wars'," *American Cinematographer* 7, no. 58 (July 1977), pp. 706–708, 772.

95. John Culhane, *Special Effects in the Movies: How They Do It* (New York: Ballantine Books, 1981), p. 159.

96. James Harwood, "Film Effects Men Turn Trick at B.O.: 'Star Wars' Spotlights New Breed of Wizards," *Variety*, July 27, 1977, p. 1.

97. Joe Matza, "Magicam," *American Cinematographer* 56, no. 1 (January 1975), pp. 34–37, 72–73, 112–113.

98. Bruce Nicholson, "Composite Optical Photography for 'The Empire Strikes Back'," *American Cinematographer* 61, no. 6 (June 1980), pp. 562–563, 571, 612–613.

99. "Disney's New Matte Scan System," *American Cinematographer* 61, no. 1 (January 1980), p. 36.

100. "'Superman,' Pair, in $50-M. Super Budget: Technology Was Big Grief," *Variety*, March 22, 1978, p. 3; "Zoran Perisic, Zoptics Effect Wiz, Due to Try Fortune in California," *Variety*, March 19, 1980, p. 36.

101. Edwin E. Catmull, Ph.D., "New Frontiers in Computer Animation," *American Cinematographer* 60, no. 2 (October 1979), pp. 1000–1003, 1049–1953; "Computer Research and Development at LUCASFILM," *American Cinematographer* 63, no. 8 (August 1982), pp. 773–775; "Computer Imagery for 'TRON'," *American Cinematographer* 63, no. 8 (August 1982), pp. 802–805, 820–823.

102. "What Is a Western?: Arthur Penn Interviewed by Stuart Byron and Terry Curtis Fox," *Film Comment* 12, no. 4 (July–August 1976), p. 39.

103. Quoted in Charles Schreger, "The Second Coming of Sound," *Film Comment* 14, no. 5 (September–October 1978), p. 37.

104. "'Star Wars' Booms Optical Tracks for Sound, Dolby Labs Cashing In," *Variety*, November 23, 1977, p. 22.

105. "Dolby Factor In Super-Grossers Increase Use of Stereo Gear," *Variety*, February 28, 1979, p. 40.

106. Schreger, pp. 34, 36.

107. Ioan Allen, "The Dolby Sound System for Recording 'Star Wars'," *American Cinematographer* 58, no. 7 (July 1977), p. 748. Schreger, p. 37.

108. John Belton (and Lyle Tector), "The Bionic Eye: The Aesthetics of the Zoom," *Film Comment* no. 16, no. 5 (September–October, 1980), p. 152.

109. John Belton, *Widescreen Cinema* (Cambridge: Harvard University Press, 1992), p. 208. See also Belton, "1950s Magnetic Sound: The Frozen Revolution," in *Sound Theory, Sound Practice*, Rick Altman, ed. (New York: Routledge, 1992), pp. 154–167.

110. Review of "MAN OF LA MANCHA and TARAS BULBA," *Widescreen Review* 2, no. 6 (November–December 1993), p. 87.

111. Anthony Chiarella, "The Surround of Music: 5.1-Channel Audio Can Bring the Musical Experience Home," *Home Theater* 5, no. 2 (February 1998), p. 50.

112. Bruce F. Kawin, *How Movies Work* (Berkeley: University of California Press, 1992), p. 470.

113. Allen, "The Dolby Sound System," p. 748.

114. Stephen Handzo, "Appendix: A Narrative Glossary of Film Sound Technology," *Film Sound: Theory and Practice*, Elisabeth Weis and John Belton, eds. (New York: Columbia University Press, 1985), p. 422.

115. Salt, *Film Style & Technology*, p. 282.

116. "'Star Wars Heralds Advent of New Sound Era Via Dolby Rigs," *Variety*, May 17, 1978, p. 132.

117. Ibid.

118. Leonard Kroll, "The 20th Century–Fox 'Sound 360' System," *American Cinematographer* 58, no. 12 (December 1977), pp. 1257, 1312–1313. Another surround format, Ambisonics, proposed the use of four signals rather than three, to create a spherical rather than a horizontal sound field; it was never deployed. (See Giovanni Abrate, "Ambisonics: The Forgotten Surround Sound System," *WideGauge Film and Video Monthly* 3, no. 5 [May 1998]), pp. 1, 14–15.)

119. "'Star Wars' Heralds Advent of New Sound Era," p. 132.

120. Allen, "The Dolby Sound System," p. 748; "Michael Di Cosimo and Robert Warren," in Vincent LoBrutto, *Sound-on-Film: Interviews with Creators of Film Sound* (Westport, CT: Praeger, 1991) p. 130.

121. "Tomlinson Holman," in Lobrutto, p. 206.

122. Scott Michael Bosco, "Sensurround in the Theater," *Home Theater* 2, no. 6 (June 1995), p. 27.

123. See also Lee Beaupre, "Screen Need: TV-Defying Gimmicks: Gropes For Theater Lures, *Variety*, March 20, 1974, p. 7; "Sensurround," *American Cinematographer* 55, no. 11 (November 1974), pp. 1312–1313, 1345–1351; Jerry Christian, "The Sound Effects [for EARTHQUAKE]," *American Cinematographer* 55, no. 11, p. 1314; Ronald Pierce, "The Sound Mixing [for EARTHQUAKE]," *American Cinematographer* 55, no. 11, pp. 1315, 1344; Robert Leonard, "Recording 'Rollercoaster' Sound in Sensurround," *American Cinematographer* 58, no. 6 (June 1977), pp. 596, 648–649; and Robert L. Hoyt, "Mixing 'Rollercoaster' in Sensurround," *American Cinematographer* 58, no. 6 (June 1977), pp. 597, 651.

124. "'Star Wars' Heralds Advent of New Sound Era Via Dolby Rigs," p. 9.

125. Allen, "The Dolby Sound System," p. 746.

126. Linda Trefz, "Audio Achievements in Feature Films," *Millimeter* 10, no. 11 (November 1982), p. 90.

127. *Box Office*, August 21, 1978, p. 19; *Variety*, September 5, 1979, p. 6, and October 1984, pp. 7, 44.

128. Quoted in Schreger, "The Second Coming of Sound," p. 36.

129. Marc Mancini, "The Sound Designer," in *Film Sound: Theory and Practice*, Elisabeth Weis and John Belton, eds., p. 361; Vincent LoBrutto, "Introduction," *Stanley Kubrick: A Biography*, p. xi.

130. David Weinberg, "The Motion Picture Soundtrack Jigsaw Puzzle, Part 2," *Widescreen Review* 6, no. 2, issue 24 (May 1997), p. 100.

131. See John Michael Weaver: Studying the Art of Soundtrack Design," *Audio + Music Education* (Emeryville, CA: Cardinal Business Media, Inc., 1995), pp. 38–43.

132. Quoted in Schreger, p. 37.

133. "Walter Murch" in Vincent LoBrutto, *Sound-on-Film: Interviews with Creators of Film Sound* (Westport, CT: Praeger, 1994), p. 87.

134. Ibid., p. 91.
135. Gary Reber, "Sound Wars at a Theatre Near You," *Widescreen Review* 4, no. 2, Issue 13 (March-April 1995), p. 85; Mark Elson, "The Sounds of Battle, Volume 1," *Home Theater* 2, no. 8 (August 1994), p. 18.
136. Frank Serafine, "The New Motion Picture Sound," *American Cinematographer* 61, no. 8 (August 1980), pp. 796–798.
137. *Cassell Companion to Cinema*, Jonathan Law, ed. (London: Market House Books, Ltd., 1997), p. 206.
138. "Ross Taylor and Kitty Malone," in LoBrutto, *Sound-on-Film*, pp. 61–63.
139. Hal Landaker, "A New Portable Foley (Sync Sound Effects) Recording Stage," *American Cinematographer* 58, no. 8 (August 1980), pp. 716–717, 758–759.
140. Scott Kim, "Sounds Like," *New Media* (September 1994), p. 116.
141. Michael Fremer, "The Making of a Soundtrack," *Stereophile Guide to Home Theater* 3, no. 3 (Fall 1997), p. 63.
142. Jack Gould, "Computer to Save Millions in Film Editing Due Soon," The *New York Times*, March 14, 1971, 5B. See also Gary Jones, "Welcome Aboard the Film/Tape Bandwagon," *American Cinematographer* 52, no. 6 (June 1971), pp. 566–567, 614, on electronic editing of 16mm film.
143. Walter Murch, *In the Blink of an Eye: A Perspective on Film Editing* (Los Angeles: Silman-James Press, 1995), pp. 78–79.
144. "Video Assisted Film Editing," *American Cinematographer* 63, no. 3 (March 1982), p. 297.
145. Ric Gentry, "First Class Cinematography for *Second Hand Hearts*," *Millimeter* 9, no. 11 (November 1981), p. 104.
146. "Time Code on Film: Kodak's Transparent Magnetic Coating for Film," *American Cinematographer* 63, no. 8 (August 1982), pp. 771–772; Mark Schubin, "Video Research," *Videography*, February 1982, pp. 57–59.
147. "Video Assisted Film Editing," pp. 305–306.
148. Salt, p. 271.
149. John Lippman, "Screened Out," The *Wall Street Journal*, p. R7.
150. Salt, *Film Style & Technology*, p. 283.
151. Warren Maitland, "The Sky Is Not the Limit," *American Cinematographer* 47, no. 2 (February 1966), p. 103.
152. Peter Biskind, "Blockbuster: The Last Crusade," in Mark Crispin Miller, *Seeing Through Movies* (New York: Pantheon Books, 1990), p. 124.

CHAPTER 10 (MOTION PICTURE EXHIBITION IN 1970S HOLLYWOOD)

1. Douglas Gomery teaches at the University of Maryland and is author of ten books including *Shared Pleasures: A History of Movie Presentation in the United States* (Madison: University of Wisconsin Press, 1992). He dedicates this chapter to T. P. Moon whose counsel and advise fashioned the best parts of this research and writing.
2. The number of drive-ins is not counted here: they declined in number and importance during the 1970s as is discussed below. Indeed the official figures from the Department of Commerce in 1982 revealed a shade under 15,000 screens as compared with about 10,700 a decade earlier. From 1972 to 1982 the number of drive-ins fell from 3700 to 3000.
3. See, in particular, *Variety*, January 28, 1979, p. 7.
4. Landon Y. Jones, *Great Expectations: America and the Baby Boom Generation* (New York: Random House, 1981), pp. 43–54; Louise Russell, *The Baby Boom Generation and the Economy* (Washington, DC: The Brookings Institution Press, 1982), pp. 8–20; Louis H. Masotti and Jeffrey K. Hadden, eds., *Suburbia in Transition* (New York: New Directions, 1974), pp. 46–70; Philip C. Dolce, ed., *Suburbia* (Garden City, NJ: Anchor, 1976), pp. 1–59.
5. The aforementioned history and analysis of the baby boom is based on Landon Y. Jones, *Great Expectations*, pp. 11–78; Paul C. Light, *Baby Boomers* (New York: W. W. Norton, 1988), pp. 19–44; Richard A. Easterlin, *Birth and Fortune: the Impact of Numbers on Personal Welfare*, 2nd ed. (Chicago: University of Chicago Press, 1987), pp. 3–33.
6. The specific case docket is *United States v. Paramount Pictures et al.*, 334 U. S. 131 (1948). For the reaction of the film industry during the 1970s see Michael Conant, "The Paramount Decrees Reconsidered," *Law and Contemporary Problems* 44, no. 4 (Autumn 1981), pp. 79–107.

7. For the historical background see Michael Conant, *Antitrust in the Motion Picture Industry*, (Berkeley: University of California Press, 1960), p. 108; *Variety*, September 7, 1960, pp. 5, 15; *Variety*, June 19, 1957, pp. 3, 7.

8. Hunt Williams, *Beyond Control: ABC and the Fate of the Networks* (New York: Antheneum, 1989), pp. 37–41; Sterling Quinlan, *Inside ABC: American Broadcasting Company's Rise to Power* (New York: Hastings House, 1979), pp. 23–45.

9. The *Wall Street Journal*, October 18, 1973, p. 14; see also American Broadcasting Companies, Inc., Annual Report, 1978.

10. Michael Conant, *Antitrust in the Film Industry*, pp. 108–109; The *Wall Street Journal*, April 22, 1959, p. 18; The *Wall Street Journal*, August 7, 1967, p. 24; The *Wall Street Journal*, August 21, 1967, p. 2; *Moody's Industrial Manual* (New York: Moody's, 1978), p. 1497.

11. Andrew Horton, "Turning On and Turning Out at the Drive-in: An American Phenomenon Survives and Thrives," *Journal of Popular Film* 5, nos. 3 and 4 (Fall 1976), pp. 233–244.

12. Peter O. Muller, *Contemporary Suburban America* (Englewood Cliffs, NJ: Prentice Hall, 1981), pp. 120–124; Edward T. Thompson, "The Shopping Center Macy's Built," *Fortune* 61, no. 2 (1960), pp. 195–200; The *New York Times*, January 16, 1957, p. 30; *Business Week*, October 11, 1952, pp. 124–128; John C. Van Nostrand, "The Queen Elizabeth Way: Public Utility Verses Public Space," *Urban History Review* 12, no. 4 (October 1983), pp. 1–23.

13. Thomas Harrison, "The Advent of the Super Regional Shopping Center," *The Appraisal Journal* 36 (January 1968), pp. 90–97; The *Wall Street Journal*, February 20, 1969, pp. 1, 21; The *Washington Post*, February 20, 1977, pp. 22–23; Kenneth T. Jackson, *Crabgrass Frontier: The Suburbanization of the United States* (New York: Oxford University Press, 1985), pp. 257–261.

14. William Severini Kowinski, "The Malling of America," *New Times*, May 1, 1978, pp. 33–34.

15. *Motion Picture Herald*, February 16, 1966, p. 23; *Motion Picture Herald*, November 9, 1966, p. 22.

16. *Motion Picture Herald*, September 27, 1967, p. 14; *Moody's Industrial Manual, 1971*, p. 421; *Barrons*, October 14, 1974, p. 39; *Barrons*, July 10, 1978, p. 32; *Business Week*, May 20, 1972, p. 31.

17. *Forbes*, April 15, 1968, p. 71; *Barrons*, July 18, 1966, p. 20.

18. *Business Week*, March 14, 1970, p. 29; *International Motion Picture Almanac–1979* (New York: Quigley Publications, 1979), p. 30A; *Barrons*, June 28, 1971, p. 11; The *Wall Street Journal*, February 8, 1977, p. 46.

19. *Variety*, May 29, 1963, p. 17; *Variety*, July 17, 1963, p. 15.

20. *Box Office*, August 6, 1973, p. SE-1; *Box Office*, August 27, 1973, p. 5.

21. *Box Office*, June 17, 1974, p. 6.

22. *Box Office*, August 28, 1972, p. C-1; *Box Office*, January 2, 1972, p. W-1; *Box Office*, July 20, 1970, p. 48; *Variety*, December 29, 1976, p. 20. The quotation is from *Box Office*, December 18, 1972, p. E-9.

23. *Variety*, November 10, 1982, p. 92.

24. Please remember that there had been earlier attempts during the 1950s to bring the stereo experience coupled with CinemaScope. But audio quality fell drastically during the 1960s, so Dolby seemed like a wholly new revolution in theatrical sound.

25. The *New York Times*, April 12, 1977, p. 23; *Premiere*, November 1987, p. 9.

26. *Motion Picture Herald*, "Modern Theatres," November 15, 1976, p. 28; *Box Office*, October 16, 1978, p. SE-1; *Film Journal*, September, 1980, pp. 23–24; *American Cinematographer* 56, no. 9 (September 1975), pp. 1032–1033, 1088–1091.

27. Rich Warren, "Ray Dolby: Quiet on the Set," *Video*, April, 1988, p. 61; *Box Office*, August 21, 1978, p. 19; *Film Journal*, April, 1980, p. 45.

28. *Box Office*, August 21, 1978, p. 19; *Variety*, September 5, 1979, p. 6; *Variety*, October 31, 1984, pp. 7, 44; *Video*, September, 1989, p. 31.

29. David F. Prindle, *The Politics of Glamour: Ideology and Democracy in the Screen Actors Guild* (Madison: University of Wisconsin Press, 1988), pp. 82–90.

30. *Radio-Television Daily*, July 30, 1962, p. 32; *Variety*, June 21, 1972, p. 34; *Variety*, September 20, 1978, pp. 48, 66; Cobbett Steinberg, *Reel Facts* (New York: Random House, 1978), pp. 355–357; Tim Brooks and Earle Marsh, *The Complete Directory to Prime Time Network TV Shows, 1946–Present* (New York: Ballantine, 1979), pp. 416–420.

31. *Motion Picture Herald*, January 18, 1967, p. 1; Neil Hickey, "The Day the Movies Ran Out," *TV Guide*, October 23, 1965, pp. 6–9; Cobbett Steinberg, *Reel Facts*, pp. 355–357

32. Ryland A. Taylor, "The Repeat Audience for Movies on TV," *Journal of Broadcasting* 17, no. 1 (Winter 1972–1973), pp. 95–100.

33. Jon Krampner, "In the Beginning..The Genesis of the Telefilm," *Emmy* 11, no. 6 (December 1989), pp. 30–35; Henry Harding, "First Attempts at Making Movies for TV," *TV Guide*, July 4, 1964, p. 14; Alvin H. Marill, *Movies Made for Television* (Westport, CT: Arlington House, 1980), pp. 1–12.

34. *Variety*, August 18, 1971, p. 30; *Variety*, June 14, 1972, p. 29; *Broadcasting*, January 15, 1973, p. 37; The *Washington Post*, October 6, 1974, pp. E1–E2; Douglas Stone, "TV Movies and How They Get That Way," *Journal of Popular Film and Television* 7, no. 2 (1979), pp. 147–149.

35. Dick Adler and Joseph Finnigan, "The Year America Stayed Home for the Movies," *TV Guide*, May 20, 1972, pp. 6–10; *Broadcasting*, September 25, 1972, p. 61; *Broadcasting*, January 15, 1973, p. 37; Caroline Meyer, "The Rating Power of Network Movies," *Television* 25, no. 3 (March 1968), pp. 56, 84; Joseph R. Dominick and Millard C. Pearce, "Trends in Network Prime-Time Programming, 1953–74," *Journal of Communication* 26, no. 1 (Winter 1976), pp. 74–75.

36. Patrick McGilligan, "Movies Are Better Than Ever—on Television," *American Film* 5, no. 5 (March 1980), pp. 52–53.

37. *Variety*, December 8, 1971, p. 34; John W. Ravage, *Television: The Director's Viewpoint* (Boulder, CO: Westview Press, 1978), pp. 103–112; Christopher Wicking and Tise Vahimagi, *The American Vein: Directors and Directions in Television* (New York: E. P. Dutton, 1979), pp. 27–28.

38. Martin Kasindorf, "Movies Made for Television," *Action*, January/February, 1974, pp. 13–15; Eileen Lois Becker, "The Network Television Decision Making Process: A Descriptive Examination of the Process within the Framework of Prime-Time Made-for-TV Movies," Unpublished MA Thesis, University of California at Los Angeles, pp. 19–56; *Variety*, 8 December 1971, p. 34; The *New York Times*, January 28, 1972, p. 91; *Variety*, December 15, 1971, p. 29.

39. Peter J. Dekom, ed., *The Selling of Motion Pictures in the '80s: New Producer/Distributor/Exhibitor Relationships* (Los Angeles: Privately published, 1980), pp. 302–312.

40. John Howard, George Rothbart, and Lee Sloan, "The Response to 'Roots': A National Survey," *Journal of Broadcasting* 22, no. 3 (Summer 1978), pp. 279–287; K. Kyoon Hur, "Impact of 'Roots' on Black and White Teenagers," *Journal of Broadcasting* 22, no. 3 (Summer 1978), pp. 289–307; Stuart H. Surlin, "'Roots' Research: A Summary of Findings," *Journal of Broadcasting* 22, no. 3 (Summer 1978), pp. 309–320; Leslie Fishbein, "*Roots*: Docudrama and the Interpretation of History," in John E. O'Connor, ed., *American History/American Film: Interpreting the Video Past* (New York: Frederick Ungar Publishing Company, 1983), pp. 279–305; David L. Wolper, *The Inside Story of TV's "Roots"* (New York: Warner Books, 1978).

41. Ty Burr, "The Letterbox Dilemma," *Video Review*, February, 1990, pp. 40–43.

42. John Belton, "The Pan & Scan Scandals," *The Perfect Vision* 1, no. 1 (Summer 1987), pp. 41–49; Michael Kerbel, "Edited for Television," *Film Comment* 13, no. 3 (May–June 1977), pp. 28–30; Michael Kerbel, "Edited for Television II," *Film Comment* 13, no. 4 (July–August 1977), pp. 38–40; The *Washington Post*, March 6, 1988, sec. G, pp. 1, 6, 7; Susan Tyler Eastman, Sydney W. Head, and Lewis Klein, eds., *Broadcast/Cable Programming: Strategies and Practices*, 3rd ed. (Belmont, CA: Wadsworth Publishing Company, 1989), pp. 214–215.

43. Diane Brown, Joseph M. Ripley II, and Lawrence W. Lichty, "Movies on Television: What the Audience Says," *Radio-Television-Film Audience Studies*, Department of Speech, University of Wisconsin, no. 1, March, 1966, pp. 1–3.

44. The history of the origins of HBO is vividly told in George Mair, *Inside HBO* (New York: Dodd, Mead, 1988), pp. 1–35, and Curtis Prendergast, *The World of Time Inc: The Intimate History of a Changing Enterprise, 1960–1980* (New York: Atheneum, 1986), pp. 489–512. See also The *New York Times*, March 7, 1983, Sec. D., pp. 1, 8; *Broadcasting*, November 15, 1982, p. 48; Robert Lindsey, "Home Box Office Moves in on Hollywood," *The New York Times Magazine*, June 12, 1983, pp. 31–33; *Electronic Media*, November 30, 1987, p. 22; *Broadcasting*, November 15, 1990, p. 48.

45. Eastman, Head, and Klein, *Broadcast/Cable Programming*, pp. 333–334.

46. Dale Pollock and Peter Warner, "Premiere: Studios Tell Why Hollywood Empire Struck Back," *Watch*, July, 1980, pp. 36–39.

47. H. Polskin, "Inside Pay-Cable's Most Savage War," *Panorama*, March, 1981, pp. 54–58; *Broadcasting*, January 5, 1981, p. 31; *Cablevision*, January 19, 1981, pp. 26–27.

48. Eastman, Head, and Klein, pp. 324–328; *Multichannel News*, July 31, 1989, pp. 1, 50.
49. The *Wall Street Journal*, May 12, 1988, p. 28.

CHAPTER 11 (LOOKING BACK AND TURNING INWARD: AMERICAN DOCUMENTARY FILMS OF THE SEVENTIES)

1. Richard Barsam, *Non-Fiction Film: A Critical History*, rev. ed. (Bloomington and Indianapolis: Indiana University Press, 1992), p. 329.
2. Michael Renov, "New Subjectivities: Documentary and Self-Representation in the Post-Vérité Age," Part Three of "Transformations in Film as Reality" series, in *Documentary Box* (http://www.cit.yamagata.yamagata.jp/yidff/ff/box/box7/en/b7enf2-1.html, 1998).
3. One such work of the seventies that Renov rightly celebrates in this context, a work not usually considered in discussions of documentaries, is video artist Wendy Clarke's ongoing "Love Tapes" project, begun late in the decade. (To make a "Love Tape," Clarke seats a subject in a booth with a monitor and a self-activated camera and gives the person three minutes to say what love means to him or her. To date, she has taped thousands of individuals in this way.) Another is LOST, LOST, LOST (1975) by avant-garde filmmaker Jonas Mekas, also not usually considered in discussions of documentaries, which revolves around Mekas's own history and experience but surrounds it in layers of historical documentation.
4. This theme is more fully developed in the chapters on A HAPPY MOTHER'S DAY and DON'T LOOK BACK in William Rothman, *Documentary Film Classics* (New York and Cambridge: Cambridge University Press, 1998), pp. 109–210; and in William Rothman, "Eternal Vérités," in Charles Warren, ed., *Beyond Document: Essays on Non-Fiction Film* (Hanover, NH: Wesleyan University Press, 1996), pp. 79–100.
5. For a discussion of the significance of A HAPPY MOTHER'S DAY within the history of American documentary film, see William Rothman, *Documentary Film Classics*, pp. 109–143.
6. See the biography of Amalie Rothschild at http://raven.ubalt.edu/staff/simon/WIF/RothschildFilm.htm.
7. David C. Stewart, "Getting It On—Public Television Market," in Judith Trojan and Nadine Covert, eds., *16mm Distribution* (New York: Educational Film Library Association, 1977), p. 116.
8. Esme J. Dick, "Commercial Distribution," in Trojan and Covert, pp. 41–52.
9. Judith Trojan, "Film Cooperatives," in Trojan and Covert, pp. 58–60.
10. Stephen C. Johnson, "University Film Distribution," in Trojan and Covert, pp. 53–57.
11. Kitty Morgan, "ICAP: Independent Cinema Artists and Producers," in Trojan and Covert, pp. 118–121.
12. Bernice Coe, "The Television Market," in Trojan and Covert, pp. 104–109.
13. Stewart, in Trojan and Covert, p. 111.
14. Ibid., p. 112.
15. Ibid., p. 113.
16. Ibid., p. 116.
17. Appendix 2, "Showcases for Independent Film and Video Work," in Trojan and Covert, p. 169.
18. Jill Godmilow, "Paying Dues: A Personal Experience with Theatrical Distribution," in Trojan and Covert, p. 94.
19. Ibid., p. 95.
20. Ibid.
21. Nadine Covert, "Non-Theatrical Distribution," in Trojan and Covert, p. 48.
22. Ibid., p. 50.
23. Mitchell Block, "Slicing the Pie: A Financial Analysis of 16mm Distribution," in Trojan and Covert, pp. 78–79.
24. Barsam, *Non-Fiction Film: A Critical History*, p. 350.
25. Jack C. Ellis, *The Documentary Idea* (Englewood Cliffs, NJ: Prentice Hall, 1989), p. 276.
26. Ibid., pp. 277–278.
27. This quote is taken from "About Appalshop," on Appalshop's WWW home page (http://www.uky.edu/Projects/Appal/), p. 1.
28. Ibid., p. 2.
29. All quotes are from "Les Blank's Flower Films," on the website for Flower Films, the distribution company Blank set up to distribute his films and other films that have an affinity with his work (http://www.picpal.com/lesnhar.html), pp. 2–5.

30. For a fuller development of this theme, see the chapter on CHRONICLE OF A SUMMER in William Rothman, *Documentary Film Classics*, pp. 66–108.
31. Quoted in Eliot Weinberger, "The Camera People," in Warren, *Beyond Document,* p. 149.
32. Sharon R. Sherman, *Documenting Ourselves: Film, Video and Culture* (Lexington, KY: The University Press of Kentucky, 1998), p. 38.
33. Weinberger, p. 154.
34. Quoted in Weinberger, p. 155.
35. Ibid., pp. 157–159.
36. Ibid., p. 156.
37. Ibid., pp. 156–157.
38. Ibid., pp. 158–159.
39. Sherman, pp. 44–45.
40. Jeffrey Ruoff, "Family Programming, Television, and American Culture" forthcoming from the University of Minnesota Press), unpaged, p. 49. Throughout the ensuing discussion of *An American Family*, I rely on Ruoff's illuminating and meticulously researched case study.
41. Ruoff, pp. 41–48.
42. Ibid., pp. 45–47.
43. Ibid., p. 102.
44. Ibid., pp. 199–209.
45. Quoted in Alan Rosenthal, *The Documentary Conscience: A Casebook in Film Making* (Berkeley: University of California Press, 1980), p. 211.
46. There is a detailed reading of this film in William Rothman, "Alfred Guzzetti's FAMILY PORTRAIT SITTINGS," in *Quarterly Review of Film Studies* 1 (Winter 1977), pp. 1–25. Reprinted in William Rothman, *The "I" of the Camera* (New York and Cambridge: Cambridge University Press, 1982), pp. 200–216.
47. Helene Keyssar, "The Toil of Thought: On Several Nonfiction Films by Women," in Warren, *Beyond Document,* pp. 124–127.
48. James Lane, "The Career and Influence of Ed Pincus," in *Journal of Film and Video* 49 (Winter 1997), p. 7.
49. Ibid., p. 7.
50. For an extended reading of DON'T LOOK BACK, see the chapter on the film in William Rothman, *Documentary Film Classics*, pp. 144–210.

CHAPTER 12 (AVANT-GARDE CINEMA OF THE SEVENTIES)

1. P. Adams Sitney, ed., *The Essential Cinema: Essays on the Films in the Collection of Anthology Film Archives* (New York: Anthology Film Archives and New York University Press, 1975), p. vi.
2. The loose criterion for inclusion was the appearance of at least three extended references to a film-maker in secondary material, which of course excludes many interesting films and filmmakers.
3. David James, *Allegories of Cinema: American Film in the Sixties* (Princeton: Princeton University Press, 1989), p. 43.
4. P. Adams Sitney, *Visionary Film: The American Avant-Garde* (New York: Oxford, 1979), p. 369.
5. James, p. 237.
6. P. Adams Sitney, *The Avant-Garde Film: A Reader of Theory and Criticism* (New York: New York University Press, 1978), p. 200.
7. Sitney, *Visionary Film*, p. 420.
8. Dana Polan, *The Political Language of Film and the Avant-Garde* (Ann Arbor, MI: University Micro-films, 1985), p. 63.
9. James, p. 55.
10. Scott MacDonald, *A Critical Cinema: Interviews with Independent Filmmakers* (Los Angeles: University of California Press, 1988), pp. 317–333.
11. William C. Wees, *Light Moving in Time: Studies in the Visual Aesthetics of Avant-Garde Film* (Berkeley: University of California Press, 1992), p. 126.
12. Sitney, *Visionary Film*, p. 431.
13. MacDonald, *A Critical Cinema*, p. 6.
14. Ibid., p. 9.
15. James, p. 112.
16. Sitney, *Visionary Film*, p. 225.

17. MacDonald, *A Critical Cinema*, p. 298.
18. James, p. 128.
19. Sitney, *Avant-Garde Film Reader*, p. 247.
20. Ibid., 275–280.
21. Sitney, *Visionary Film*, pp. 371, 374.
22. Ibid., 297.
23. Paul Arthur, "Structural Film: Revisions, New Versions, and the Artifact, Part Two," *Millennium Film Journal* 4, no. 5 (Spring 1979b), pp. 122–134.
24. James, p. 244.
25. Sitney, *Visionary Film*, p. 374.
26. Annette Michelson, "Toward Snow," *Artforum* 9, no. 10 (June 1971a), p. 31.
27. Sitney, *Avant-Garde Film Reader*, p. 284.
28. William Simon, "Talking About Magellan: An Interview with Hollis Frampton," *Millennium Film Journal* nos. 7, 8, 9 (Fall, Winter 1980–1981), p. 15.
29. Ibid., p. 26.
30. James, pp. 260–263.
31. Ibid., p. 309.
32. J. Hoberman, "The Avant-Garde Film Now," *Film Comment* 17, no. 3 (May–June 1981), p. 43.

Bibliography

The following selected bibliography lists publications that the authors found most useful in the preparation of their respective chapters.

Chapters 1 through 9

PRINCIPAL NEWSPAPERS, TRADE JOURNALS, AND PERIODICALS

The *Los Angeles Times*
The *New York Times*
The *Washington Post*
The *Wall Street Journal*
Box Office
Film Journal International
Variety
Action

American Cinematographer
Journal of the Motion Picture and Television Engineers
Millimeter
On Location
American Film
Film & Video
Film Comment

Film Quarterly
Sight and Sound
Newsweek
Time
Business Week
Fortune
Forbes

Newspaper and trade press articles are not listed individually in the Bibliography except where they have provided seminal information and analysis; for example, several of A. D. Murphy's *Variety* pieces on industry trends.

ARTICLES, PARTS OF BOOKS, UNPUBLISHED MANUSCRIPTS

Abbott, L. B. "Bill." "Magic for the 32rd Century." *American Cinematographer* 57, no. 6 (June 1976).

Abrate, Giovanni. "Ambisonics: The Forgotten Surround Sound System." *Wide Gauge Film and Video Monthly* 3, no. 5 (May 1998).

Adler, Dick, and Joseph Finnigan. "The Year America Stayed Home for the Movies." *TV Guide*, May 20, 1972.

Albarino, Richard. "'Billy Jack' Hits Reissue Jackpot: Unique Game Plan Produces a $60-Mil Bonanza." *Variety*, November 7, 1973.

Allan, Stuart. "New Tools, New Ideas: New Technologies and Techniques Provide Infinite Means of Expression for Feature Film and TV Cinematographers." *Film & Video* 11, no. 3 (March 1994).

———. "Masters of Light: The 1993 Oscar Nominees for Best Cinematography Bring Their Careers and Films into Focus." *Film & Video* 11, no. 5 (May 1994).

———. "Vilmos Zsigmond: Interview." *Film & Video* 11, no. 7 (July 1994).

Allen, Ioan. "The Dolby Sound System for Recording 'Star Wars'." *American Cinematographer* 58, no. 7 (July 1977).

Alonzo, John. "Shooting 'Chinatown'," *American Cinematographer* 56, no. 5 (May 1975).

American Cinematographer. "Kodak Announces New Improved 5247/7247 Eastman Color Negative." Vol. 54, no. 1 (January 1973).

American Cinematographer. "The First Feature Use of the Steadicam-35 on 'Bound for Glory'." Vol. 57, no. 7 (July 1976).

American Cinematographer. "Disney's Matte Scan System." Vol. 61, no. 1 (January 1980).

American Cinematographer. "Video Assisted Film Editing." Vol. 63, no. 3 (March 1982).

American Cinematographer. "Time Code on Film: Kodak's Transparent Magnetic Coating for Film." Vol. 63, no. 8 (August 1982).

Angeli, Michael. "My Name Is Bond, Completion Bond." The *New York Times*, April 2, 1991.

Ansen, David. "The Dark Side of a Hit." (On STAR WARS reissue.) *Newsweek*, January 20, 1997.

Arkoff, Samuel Z. "Famous Myths of the Film Industry." *Journal of the Producers Guild of America* 11, no. 3 (September 1969).

Arlen, Gary. "A Premiere Approach." *American Film* 6, no. 1 (October 1980).

Atkinson, Michael. "The Squalor of the 1970s." *Movieline* 4, no. 11 (August 1993).

Auster, Al, and Leonard Quart. "American Cinema of the Sixties." *Cineaste* 13, no. 2 (1984).

Baker, Robin. "Computer Technology and Special Effects in Contemporary Cinema." In Philip Haward and Tana Wollen, eds., *Future Visions: New Technologies of the Screen.* London: BFI, 1993.

Baker, Wayne E., and Robert R. Faulkner. "Role as Resource in the Hollywood Film Industry." *American Journal of Sociology* 97, no. 2 (September 1991).

Balack, Robert, and Paul Roth. "Composite Optical and Photographic Effects for 'Star Wars'." *American Cinematographer* 7, no. 58 (July 1977).

Balio, Tino. "Introduction" to Parts 1 and 2. In Tino Balio, ed., *Hollywood in the Age of Television.* Boston: Unwin Hyman, 1990.

———. "Adjusting to the New Global Economy: Hollywood in the 1990s." In Albert Moran, ed., *Film Policy: International, National and Regional Perspectives.* London: Routledge, 1996.

Bart, Peter. "What Hollywood Isn't Telling MCA's New Owners." *Variety*, December 3, 1990.

Bates, William. "Hollywood in the Era of the Super-Grosser." The *New York Times*, December 24, 1978.

Beaupre, Lee. "BBS & Hollywood Unions: Camera Import Nix for 'Beaver'." *Variety*, November 8, 1972.

———. "Hits Few: Beasts of Burden: Analysis of 1971 Boom-Bust Biz." *Variety*, November 30, 1972.

———. "Debate Over Brutality: 'Violence' as Substitute for 'Stars'; Explicit Horrors of '72 Pix— and Why; Recall Torture Shows of Ancient Rome." *Variety*, January 3, 1973.

———. "How to Distribute a Film." *Film Comment* 13, no. 4 (July–August 1977).

———. "Industry." (On distribution deals.) *Film Comment* 14, no. 4 (July–August 1978).

———. "Industry: Grosses Gloss: Breaking Away at the Box-Office." *Film Comment* 16, no. 2 (March–April 1980).

———, and Anne Thompson. "Industry: Eighth Annual Grosses Gloss." *Film Comment* 19, no. 2 (March–April 1983).

Belton, John. "The Bionic Eye: Zoom Aesthetics." *Cineaste* 9, no. 1 (Winter 1980–1981).

———. "The Pan & Scan Scandals." *The Perfect Vision* I, no. 1 (Summer 1987).

———. "1950s Magnetic Sound: The Frozen Revolution." In Rick Alman, ed., *Sound Theory, Sound Practice.* New York: Routledge, 1992.

———, and Lyle Tector. "The Bionic Eye: The Aesthetics of the Zoom." *Film Comment* 16, no. 5 (September–October 1980).

Berry, John F., and Jack Eagan. "After the Moguls: A New Breed Rules Hollywood." The *Washington Post*, February 5, 1978.

Bierbaum, Tom. "Study Puts '85 Homevid Retail Biz at $4.55 Bil." *Daily Variety*, January 7, 1986.

Bigrave, Mike. "The New Moguls." In David Pirie, ed., *Anatomy of the Movies.* New York: Macmillan, 1981.

Birge, Peter, and Janet Maslin. "Getting Snuffed in Boston." *Film Comment* 12, no. 3 (May–June 1976).

Biskind, Peter. "The Last Crusade." In Mark Crispin Miller, ed., *Seeing Through Movies.* New York: Pantheon, 1990.

Blair, Iain. "A Conversation with Director Robert Zemeckis About Pushing the Digital Envelope in *Forrest Gump*." *Film & Video* 11, no. 7 (July 1994).

Blum, Stanford. "Merchandising." In Jason E. Squire, ed., *The Movie Business Book*. 2nd ed. New York: Simon & Schuster, 1992.

Blumenthal, Ralph. "Porno Chic." The *New York Times Magazine*, January 21, 1973.

Bosco, Scott Michael. "Sensurround in the Theater." *Home Theater* 2, no. 6 (June 1995).

Boya, Ben. "Why Hollywood Finds Profits Out of This World." The *New York Times*, November 13, 1977.

Braudy, Leo. "The Sacraments of Genre: Coppola, De Palma, Scorsese." *Film Quarterly* 34, no. 3 (Spring 1986).

Brigman, William E. "Politics and the Pornography Wars." *Wide Angle* 19, no. 3 (July 1997). (Special Issue on pornography, guest editor Joseph W. Slade.)

Brown, Garrett. "The Steadicam and 'The Shining'." *American Cinematographer* 61, no. 8 (August 1980).

Brown, Peter H. "Hollywood Space Wars." The *Washington Post*, November 25, 1979.

Brown, Thomas. "The Electronic Camera Experiment." *American Cinematographer* 63, no. 1 (January 1982).

Burlington, Bo. "Politics Under the Palms." *Esquire* 87, no. 2 (February 1977).

Business Week. "Film-making Gets Some Tightfisted Angels" (February 5, 1972).

Business Week. "Making the Movies into a Business" (June 23, 1973).

Business Week. "Marvin Davis' New Scenario for Fox" (May 30, 1983).

Byron, Stuart. "'Instant Majors': A Short Cut; Whole U.S. Film Trade Shuffles." *Variety*, October 25, 1967.

———. "The Industry: First Annual 'Grosses Gloss'." *Film Comment* 12, no. 2 (March–April 1976).

———. "Industry: Second Annual Grosses Gloss." *Film Comment* 13, no. 2 (March–April 1977).

———. "Industry: Third Annual Grosses Gloss." *Film Comment* 14, no. 2 (March–April 1978).

———. "Industry: Fourth Annual Grosses Gloss." *Film Comment* 15, no. 2 (March–April 1979).

———. "The Industry." (In "The Seventies" Midsection.) *Film Comment* 16, no. 1 (January–February 1980).

———, and Terry Curtis Fox. "What Is a Western?: Arthur Penn Interviewed by Stuart Byron and Terry Curtis Fox." *Film Comment* 12, no. 4 (July–August 1976).

Canby, Vincent. "Explicit Violence Overwhelms Every Other Value on the Screen." The *New York Times*, October 17, 1976.

———. "The New Movie—Cool and Disorienting." The *New York Times*, May 22, 1977.

———. "Let's Call It 'The Accountant's Theory' of Filmmaking." The *New York Times*, July 10, 1977.

———. "Somebody Must Put a Lid on Budgets." The *New York Times*, November 27, 1977.

Carroll, Noel. "The Future of Allusion: Hollywood in the Seventies (and Beyond)." *October* 20 (1982).

———. "Back to Basics." In Philip S. Cook, et al., eds., *American Media: The Wilson Quarterly Reader*. Washington: The Wilson Center Press, 1989.

Castell, David. "Hollywood in the 1970s." In Jack Lodge, et al., eds., *Hollywood: Sixty Great Years*. New York: Barnes & Noble Books, 1994.

Catmull, Edwin E. "New Frontiers in Computer Animation." *American Cinematographer* 60, no. 2 (October 1979).

Christian, Larry. "The Sound Effects [for EARTHQUAKE]." *American Cinematographer* 55, no. 11 (November 1974).

Chute, David. "Tom Savini: Maniac." *Film Comment* 17, no. 4 (July–August 1981).

———. "The New World of Roger Corman." *Film Comment* 18, no. 2 (March–April 1982).

Cohen, M. "7 Intricate Pieces: The Corporate Style of BBS." *Take One* (November 1973).

Cohn, Lawrence. "Gore Perpetual Fave of Young Film Fans." *Variety*, August 20, 1981.

Conant, Michael. "The Paramount Decrees Reconsidered." In Tino Balio, ed., *The American Film Industry*. Madison: University of Wisconsin Press, 1985.

Cook, Bruce. "Summing Up the Seventies: Talents." *American Film* 5, no. 2 (December 1979).

Cook, David A. "American Horror: *The Shining*." *Literature/Film Quarterly* 12, no. 1 (Spring/Summer 1984).

———. "Auteur Cinema and the 'Film Generation' in 1970s Hollywood." In Jon Lewis, ed., *The New American Cinema*. Durham: Duke University Press, 1998.

———. "Ballistic Balletics: Styles of Violent Representation in *The Wild Bunch* and After." In Stephen Prince, ed., *Sam Peckinpah's "The Wild Bunch."* Cambridge: Cambridge University Press, 1998.

Corliss, Richard. "Happy Days Are Here Again." *Film Comment* 15, no. 4 (July–August 1979).

———. "The New Conservatism." (In "The Seventies" Midsection.) *Film Comment* 16, no. 1 (January–February 1980).

———. "Fellini Go Home!" *Time*, January 13, 1997.

Coupland, Douglas. "The Abiding Urge to Watch Things Go Ka-Boom!" The *New York Times*, February 9, 1997.

Cowie, Elizabeth. "*Film Noir* and Women." In Joan Copjec, ed., *Shades of Noir*. London: Verso, 1993.

Cowie, Peter. "Introduction." In *Annie Hall* (BFI Modern Classics Series). London: BFI, 1996.

Crowdus, Gary, and Richard Porton. "The Importance of a Singular, Guiding Vision: An Interview with Arthur Penn." *Cineaste* 20, no. 2 (Spring 1993).

Culhane, John. "The Old Disney Magic." The *New York Times Magazine*, August 1, 1976.

Dale, Martin. *The Movie Game: The Film Business in Britain, Europe, and America*. London: Cassell, 1997.

Deats, Richard. "Introducing the 'Little Big Crane'." *American Cinematographer* 61, no. 11 (November 1980).

DeCordova, Richard. "The Mickey in Macy's Window." In Eric Smoodin, ed., *Disney Discourse: Producing the Magic Kingdom*. New York: Routledge, 1994.

De Curtis, Anthony. "Martin Scorsese." *Rolling Stone*, November 1, 1990.

Deegan, Thomas. "No-Fault Divorce Films: Hollywood's Changing Morality." *Cineaste* 15, no. 2 (1986).

Delgaudio, Sybil. "Columbia and the Counterculture: Trilogy of Defeat." In Bernard F. Dick, ed., *Columbia Pictures: Portrait of a Studio*. Lexington: University of Kentucky Press, 1992.

Dempsey, Michael. "After the Fall: Post-Cimino Hollywood." *American Film* 6, no. 10 (September 1981).

Dick, Bernard R. "From the Brothers Cohn to Sony Corp." In Bernard F. Dick, ed., *Columbia Pictures: Portrait of a Studio*. Lexington: University of Kentucky Press, 1992.

Dickstein, Morris. "Summing Up the Seventies: Issues." *American Film* 5, no. 2 (December 1979).

DiGuilio, Ed. "Two Special Lenses for 'Barry Lyndon'." *American Cinematographer* 57, no. 3 (March 1976).

———. "Steadicam-35—A Revolutionary New Concept in Camera Stabilization." *American Cinematographer* 57, no. 7 (July 1976).

Dominick, Joseph R. "Film Economics and Film Content, 1964–1983." In Bruce A. Austin, ed., *Current Research in Film: Audience, Economics, and Law*. Vol. 3. Norwood, NJ: Ablex Publishing, 1987.

———, and Millard C. Pearce. "Trends in Network Prime-Time Programming, 1953–74." *Journal of Communication* 26, no. 1 (Winter 1976).

Doty, Alexander. "Music Sells Movies: (Re) New (ed) Conservatism in Film Marketing." *Wide Angle* 10, no. 2 (1988).

Earnest, Olen J. "*Star Wars*: A Case Study of Motion Picture Marketing." In Bruce A. Austin, ed., *Current Research in Film: Audiences, Economics, and Law*. Vol. 1. Norwood, NJ: Ablex Publishing, 1985.

Ebert, Roger. "Why the Movies Aren't Safe Anymore." *American Film* 6, 5 (March 1981).

Eberwein, Robert. "Remakes and Cultural Studies." In Andrew Horton and Stuart Y. McDougal, eds., *Play It Again, Sam: Retakes on Remakes*. Berkeley: University of California Press, 1998.

Ehrenstein, David. "The Aesthetics of Failure." ("The Hard Part, III: Getting It Right.") *Film Comment* 19, no. 3 (May–June 1983).

Eidsvik, Charles. "Machines of the Invisible: Changes in Film Technology in the Age of Video." *Film Quarterly* 47, no. 2 (Winter 1988–1989).

Elsaesser, Thomas. "The Pathos of Failure: American Films in the 70s." *Monogram*, no. 6 (1975).

Elson, Mark. "The Sound of Battle, Volume 1." *Home Theater* 2, no. 8 (August 1994).

Farber, Stephen. "A Unique Freak Show: *The Exorcist*." *Film Comment* 10, no. 3 (May–June 1974).
———. "Hollywood's New Sensationalism: The Power and the Gory." The *New York Times*, July 7, 1974.
———. "The Man Who Brought Us Greetings from the Vietcong." The *New York Times*, May 4, 1975.
———. "Why Do Critics Love Trashy Movies?" *American Film* 7, no. 4 (April 1981).
———. "The Return of the Grown-up Movie." *American Film* 7, no. 12 (December 1981).
———. "Shelf Life." ("The Hard Part, II: Getting It Shown.") *Film Comment* 19, no. 3 (May-June 1983).
Feldman, Hans. "Kubrick and His Discontents." *Film Quarterly* 30, no. 1 (Fall 1976).
Figenshu, Tom. "Screams of a Summer Night." *Film Comment* 15, no. 5 (September–October 1979).
Fisher, Bob, and Don Kader. "Film-Video System Plays Key Role in Shooting 'The Muppet Movie'." *American Cinematographer* 60, no. 7 (July 1979).
Fleming, John. "Special Effects." In David Pirie, ed., *Anatomy of the Movies*. New York: Macmillan, 1981.
Franklin, H. Bruce. "Visions of the Future in Science Fiction Films from 1970 to 1982." In Annette Kuhn, ed., *Alien Zone: Cultural Theory and Contemporary Science Fiction Cinema*. London: Verso, 1990.
Fremer, Michael. "The Making of a Soundtrack." *Stereophile Guide to Home Theater* 3, no. 3 (Fall 1997).
Freund, Charles. "Pods over San Francisco." *Film Comment* 15, no. 1 (January–February 1979).
Fuchs, Andreas. "United International Marketing." *Film Journal International* 101, no. 6 (June 1998).
Funt, Peter. "So They Robbed a Bank and Lived Happily Ever After." The *New York Times*, January 6, 1974.
Gabler, Neal. "The End of the Middle." The *New York Times Magazine*, November 16, 1997.
Gadfly. "Welcome to the Doll House: The Influence of Russ Meyer." Vol. 1, no. 7 (September 1997).
Garvin, David A. "Blockbusters: The Economics of Mass Entertainment." *Journal of Cultural Economics* (June 1981).
Gatts, Strawberry. "The Use of Holograms in 'Logan's Run'." *American Cinematographer* 57, no. 6 (June 1976).
Gehrig, Wes D. "Parody." In Wes D. Gehrig, ed., *Handbook of American Film Genres*. Westport, CT.: Greenwood Press, 1988.
Gent, George. "Black Films Are In, So Are Profits." The *New York Times*, July 18, 1972.
Gentry, Ric. "First Class Cinematography for *Second Hand Hearts*." *Millimeter* 9, no. 11 (November 1981).
———. "Rob Bottin: Exploring the Magic of Make-Up." *Millimeter* 10, no. 9 (September 1982).
Geuens, Jean-Pierre. "Through the Looking Glasses: From the Camera Obscura to Video Assist." *Film Quarterly* 49, no. 3 (Spring 1996).
Gomery, Douglas. "The American Film Industry in the 1970s: Stasis in the 'New Hollywood'." *Wide Angle* 5, no. 4 (1983).
———. "Corporate Ownership and Control in the Contemporary US Film Industry: A Report by Douglas Gomery." *Screen* 25, nos. 4-5 (July–October 1984).
———. "Movie Merger Mania." *On Film* 13 (Fall 1984).
———. "*Brian's Song*: Television, Hollywood, and the Evolution of the Movie Made for Television." In Horace Newcomb, ed., *Television: The Critical View*. 4th ed. New York: Oxford University Press, 1987.
———. "Hollywood's Business." In Philip S. Cook et al., eds., *American Media: The Wilson Quarterly Reader*. Washington: The Wilson Center Press, 1989.
———. "If You've Seen One, You've Seen the Mall." In Mark Crispin Miller, ed., *Seeing Through Movies*. New York: Pantheon, 1990.
———. "Who Killed Hollywood?" *Wilson Quarterly* (Summer 1991).
———. "Disney's Business History: A Reinterpretation." In Eric Smoodin, ed., *Disney Discourse: Producing the Magic Kingdom*. New York: Routledge, 1994.
———. "The New Hollywood." In Geoffrey Nowell-Smith, ed., *The Oxford History of World Cinema*. New York: Oxford University Press, 1996.

Gordon, David. "Why the Movie Majors Are Major." In Tino Balio, ed., *The American Film Industry*. Madison: University of Wisconsin Press, 1976.

———. "The Movie Majors." *Sight and Sound* 48, no. 3 (Summer 1979).

Gottschalk, Earl C., Jr. "A Dirty Deal? Pornography Ruling Causing Confusion and Chaos, Many Traditional Publishers and Filmmakers Say." The *Wall Street Journal*, July 16, 1973.

———. "The Spectaculars." The *Wall Street Journal*, August 10, 1974.

Grant, Steven. "Blood Brothers: Splatterateurs George Romero and Wes Craven Resurrect the Horror Film." *Video* (October 1986).

Green, Abel. "Pix in 'Major' Retrenchment." *Variety*, October 6, 1969.

———. "Topheavy Film Studio Fade: Film Biz Ducks Overhead Load." *Variety*, October 29, 1969.

———. "B.O. Dictatorship By Youth: Kids as Talent and Consumers." *Variety*, January 7, 1970.

Greenspun, Roger. "Carrie and Sally and Leatherface Among the Film Buffs." *Film Comment* 3, no. 1 (January–February 1977).

Grimes, T. "BBS: Auspicious Beginnings, Open Endings." *Movie* (Winter 1986).

Grobel, Lawrence. "Glory Days." (Two-part interview with Robert Evans.) *Movieline* 4, no. 11 (August 1993).

Gross, Larry. "What Ever Happened to William Friedkin?" *Sight and Sound* 5, no. 12 (December 1995).

Grover, J. "Lights, Camera, Auction." *Business Week*, December 10, 1990.

Guback, Thomas. "Theatrical Film." In Benjamin M. Compaine, ed. *Who Owns the Media? Concentration of Ownership in the Mass Communications Industry*. White Plains, NY: Knowledge Industry Publications, 1979.

———. "Film as International Business: The Role of American Multinationals." In Gorham Kindem, ed., *The American Movie Industry: The Business of Motion Pictures*. Carbondale: University of Southern Illinois Press, 1982.

———. "The Evolution of the Motion Picture Theater Business in the 1980s." *Journal of Communication* 37, no. 2 (Spring 1987).

Guber, Peter. "The Cartridge Revolution." *Cinema*, May 2, 1970.

Gustafson, Robert. "What's Happening to Our Pix Biz? From Warners Bros. to Warner Communications Inc." In Tino Balio, ed., *The American Film Industry*. Rev. ed. Madison: University of Wisconsin Press, 1985.

Hammer, Joshua. "The Fall of Frank Mancuso." *Newsweek*, May 6, 1991.

Handzo, Stephen. "Appendix: A Narrative Glossary of Film Sound Technology." In Elisabeth Weis and John Belton, eds., *Film Sound: Theory and Practice*. New York: Columbia University Press, 1985.

Harding, Henry. "First Attempts at Making Movies for TV." *TV Guide*, July 4, 1964.

Harmetz, Aljean. "Film Costs: Scenario of Greed." The *New York Times*, February 15, 1978.

———. "Disney Incubating New Artists." The *New York Times*, July 25, 1978.

———. "Orion's Star Rises in Hollywood." The *New York Times*, April 19, 1978.

———. "Disney Studio Risks $17.5 Million on 'Black Hole'." The *New York Times*, March 4, 1979.

Harrison, Thomas. "The Advent of the Super Regional Shopping Center." *The Appraisal Journal* 36, no. 1 (January 1968).

Harwood, James. "Films Gotta Cater to 'Aging' Audience: 'Youth Appeal' Now Booby Trap." *Variety*, February 23, 1977.

———. "Sony Defeats Majors on Copying; Private Use Stressed—Enforcement Impossible." *Variety*, October 3, 1979.

Hass, Nancy. "Now You See Them . . . and See Them Again." The *New York Times*, November 16, 1997.

Henderson, Scott. "The Panavision Story." *American Cinematographer* 58, no. 4 (April 1977).

Hoberman, J. "Veni, Vidi, Video . . . ." *Film Comment* 18, no. 3 (May–June 1982).

———. "1975–1985: Ten Years That Shook the World." *American Film* 10, no. 8 (June 1985).

———. "Facing the Nineties." In *Vulgar Modernism: Writing on Movies and Other Media*. Philadelphia: Temple University Press, 1991.

Hollie, Pamela G. "Animators' Loss Shakes Disney." The *New York Times*, October 10, 1979.

Honeycutt, Kirk. "Stalmaster, the Master Caster." *American Film* 5, no. 8 (June 1980).

Howe, A. H. "A Banker Looks at the Picture Business—1971." *Journal of the Motion Picture Producers Guild of America* 13, no. 2 (June 1971).

Hoyt, Robert L. "Mixing 'Rollercoaster' in Sensurround." *American Cinematographer* 58, no. 6 (June 1977).

Huey, John, and Stephen J. Sansweet. "Coca Cola to Pay Over $820 Million for Movie Firm." The *Wall Street Journal*, January 20, 1983.

Jacobson, Harlan. "If 'Snuff' Killings Are Real, Film Violence Faces New Test." *Variety*, December 12, 1975.

———. "'Product Shortage' Has Been Cry of Exhibitors Since Consent Decrees." *Variety*, September 8, 1976.

———. "Govt. To Modify Consent Decree." *Variety*, December 5, 1979.

———. "Film Exhibition." (In "The Seventies" Midsection.) *Film Comment* 16, no. 1 (January–February 1980).

———. "Hollywood Lays an Egg." *Film Comment* 18, no. 3 (May-June 1982).

Jameson, Frederic. "Postmodernism and Consumer Society." In John Belton, ed., *Movies and Mass Culture*. New Brunswick, NJ: Rutgers University Press, 1996.

Jameson, Richard T. "The Pakula Parallax." *Film Comment* 12, no. 5 (September–October 1976).

Janos, Leo. "The Hollywood Game Grows Rich—and Desperate." The *New York Times*, February 12, 1978.

Jenkins, Henry. "Historical Poetics." In Joanne Hollows and Mark Jancovich, eds., *Approaches to Popular Film*. Manchester: Manchester University Press, 1995.

Johnson, John. "Into the Valley of Sleaze." The *Los Angeles Times Magazine*, February 17, 1991.

Jones, Gary. "Welcome Aboard the Film/Tape Bandwagon." *American Cinematographer* 52, no. 6 (June 1971).

Jones, Nick Freand. "Lucifer Rising." (On THE EXORCIST.) *Sight and Sound* 8, no. 7 (July 1998).

Kabak, Wayne. "On Four-Walling." *Film Comment* 11, no. 6 (November–December 1975).

Kael, Pauline. "Raising Kane." Parts 1 and 2. *The New Yorker*, February 20, 1971; February 27, 1971.

Kaplan, Jonathan. "Taxi Dancer: Martin Scorsese Interviewed by Jonathan Kaplan." *Film Comment* 13, no. 4 (July–August 1977).

Kapsis, Robert E. "Hollywood Genres and the Production of Culture Perspective." In Bruce A. Austin, ed., *Current Research in Film: Audiences, Economics, and Law*. Vol. 5. Norwood, NJ: Ablex Publishing, 1991.

Kawin, Bruce. Review of *"The Funhouse* and *The Howling."* *Film Quarterly* 35, no. 1 (Fall 1981).

Kaye, Jeffrey. "Epic Price Tags for Epic Films." The *Washington Post*, November 18, 1979.

Kehr, David. "A Star Is Made." ("Star Making in the Seventies"). *Film Comment* 15, no. 1 (January–February 1979).

Kelly, Kevin, and Paula Parisi. "Beyond Star Wars: What's Next for George Lucas." *Wired*, February 1997.

Kennedy, Harlan. "Kubrick Goes Gothic: *The Shining*—an $18 Million Scare." *American Film* 5, no. 8 (June 1980).

———. "Things That Go Howl in the Id." *Film Comment* 18, no. 2 (March–April 1982).

Kerbel, Michael. "Edited for Television." Parts 1 and 2. *Film Comment* 13, no. 3 (May-June 1977); 13, no. 4 (July–August 1977).

Kerr, Paul. "Stars and Stardom." In David Pirie, ed., *Anatomy of the Movies*. New York: Macmillan, 1981.

Kilday, Gregg. "Industry: Ninth Annual Grosses Gloss." *Film Comment* 20, no. 2 (March–April 1984).

———. "Tenth Annual Grosses Gloss." *Film Comment* 21, no. 2 (March–April 1985).

Klain, Stephen. "H-Wood Pix on Home Tape at $50 Per; 20th–Fox Catalogue First to Hit New Market." *Variety*, December 7, 1977.

Klawens, Stuart. "Hollywood's Fabulous Follies." *Newsweek* (Special Issue: A Century of Movies) (Summer 1998).

Kowinski, William Severini. "The Malling of America." *New Times*, May 1, 1978.

Krampner, Jon. "In the Beginning . . . The Genesis of Telefilm." *Emmy* 11, no. 6 (December 1989).

Kroll, Leonard. "The 20th Century–Fox 'Sound 360' System." *American Cinematographer* 58, no. 12 (December 1977).

Lafferty, William. "Feature Films on Prime-Time Television." In Tino Balio, ed., *Hollywood in the Age of Television*. New York: Ungar, 1992.

Landaker, Hal. "A New Portable Foley-Synch Sound Effects Recording Stage." *American Cinematographer* 58, no. 8 (August 1980).

Landro, Laura. "Saga of a Sequel: 'Godfather III' Filming Begins after 15 Years and 3 Studio Regimes." The *Wall Street Journal*, February 9, 1990.

———. "Giants Talk Synergy But Few Make It Work." The *Wall Street Journal*, September 25, 1995.

Landry, Robert J. "Black Pix: 'Menial' to 'Mean'; Crime Reaction Like Italians." *Variety*, August 23, 1972.

Lasch, Christopher. "The Narcissist Society." The *New York Review of Books*, September 30, 1976.

Laskos, Andrew. "The Greatest Movies Never Made." *American Film* 4, no. 10 (September 1979).

———. "The Hollywood Majors." In David Pirie, ed., *Anatomy of the Movies*. New York: Macmillan, 1981.

———. "The Money and the Power." In David Pirie, ed., *Anatomy of the Movies*. New York: Macmillan, 1981.

Law, Johnathan, ed. *Cassell Companion to Cinema*. London: Market House Books, Ltd., 1997.

Leonard, Robert. "Recording 'Rollercoaster' in Sensurround" *American Cinematographer* 58, no. 6 (June 1977).

Levin, Lear. "Robert Altman's Innovative Sound Techniques." *American Cinematographer* 61, no. 4 (April 1980).

Lewis, Jon. "Disney After Disney: Family Business and the Business of Family." In Eric Smooden, ed., *Disney Discourse: Producing the Magic Kingdom*. New York: Routledge, 1994.

———. "Money Matters: Hollywood in the Corporate Era." In Jon Lewis, ed., *The New American Cinema*. Durham: Duke University Press, 1998.

Lightman, Herb A. "The New Panaflex Camera Makes Its Production Debut." *American Cinematographer* 54, no. 5 (May 1973).

Lindsey, Robert. "Film Union Sued Over Job Policy." The *New York Times*, December 7, 1975.

———. "All Hollywood Loves a Blockbuster—and Chips Off the Old Blockbuster." The *New York Times*, May 1976.

———. "Film Investments Earn Tax Breaks—and Criticism." The *New York Times*, March 28, 1976.

———. "Product Pluggers Find Gold in Silver Screen." The *New York Times*, February 15, 1977.

———. "The Film Giant with No Studio." *The New York Times*, March 27, 1977.

———. "Entertainment Industry Is Facing Broad Monopoly Inquiry by U.S." The *New York Times*, February 4, 1978.

———. "The New Tycoons of Hollywood." The *New York Times Magazine,* August 7, 1977.

———. "The New New Wave of Film Makers." The *New York Times*, May 28, 1978.

Lippman, John. "'Star Wars' Distribution Deal Leaves 20th Century Fox with Power of Force." The *Wall Street Journal*, April 3, 1998.

Lloyd, Peter. "The American Cinema 3: An Outlook." *Monogram*, no. 1 (April 1971).

Londoner, David. "The Changing Economics of Entertainment." In Tino Balio, ed., *The American Film Industry*. Rev. ed. Madison: University of Wisconsin Press, 1985.

Lovell, Glenn. "Movies and Manipulation: How Studios Punish Critics." *Columbia Journalism Review* (January–February, 1997).

Lyman, Rick. "The Intense Tussle to Dominate What Used to Be the Dog Days." The *New York Times*, July 20, 1997.

Magid, Ron. "An Expanded Universe: Digital and Analog Special Effects Collide in the Retooled Version of *Star Wars*." American Cinematographer 78, no. 2 (February 1997).

———. "George Lucas: Past, Present and Future." *American Cinematographer* 78, no. 2 (February 1997).

Mancini, Marc. "The Sound Designer." In Elisabeth Weis and John Belton, eds., *Film Sound: Theory and Practice*. New York: Columbia University Press, 1985.

Marcus, Greil. "The Style of the 70's: Pop Culture." The *New York Times*, June 5, 1977.

Maromaa, Thomas. "The Sound of Movie Music." The *New York Times*, March 28, 1976.

Marsh, Dave. "Schlock Around the Rock." *Film Comment* 14, no. 4 (July–August 1978).

Marshall, Scott. "CinemaScope: The 'Poor Man's' Cinerama." *Widescreen Review* 6, 4, issue no. 25 (December 1997).

Maslin, Janet. "Tired Blood Claims Horror Film as a Fresh Victim." The *New York Times*, November 1, 1981.

———. "Bloodbaths Debase Movies and Audiences." The *New York Times*, November 11, 1982.

Matza, Joe. "Magicam." *American Cinematographer* 56, no. 1 (January 1975).

McBride, Joseph. "Newly Cordial to Low Budget Feature: Part of Flight from $-Mad Stars." *Variety*, December 15, 1976.

———. "Childhood's Innocence Getting Lost? Teen Harlots, Perverts in Scripts." *Variety*, February 9, 1977.

———. "Song for Woody: Joseph McBride on the Set of *Bound for Glory*. " *Film Comment* 12, no. 6 (November–December 1976).

———. "Sports No Longer Poison; 30 Game-Related Pics." *Variety*, January 5, 1977.

McCarthy, Todd. "The Exorcism of 'The Heretic': Why They Had to Destroy This Film in Order to Save It." *Film Comment* 13, no. 5 (September–October 1977).

———. "Trick or Treat: John Carpenter Interviewed by Todd McCarthy." *Film Comment* 16, no. 1 (January–February 1980).

———. "Hollywood Style '84." *Film Comment* 2, no. 20 (March–April 1984).

———. "That Euro-wood Look: Speed of Light." *Film Comment* 25, no. 5 (September–October, 1989).

McDonough, Tom. "I Am a Camera: Gordon Willis Makes the Stars Go Dark—Without Extinguishing Them." *American Film* 12, no. 9 (May 1986).

———. "Traveling Light: A New Wave of Young, European-Trained Cinematographers Is Bringing a 'Slapdash Smart' Look to American Films." *American Film* 13, no. 3 (December 1987).

McGilligan, Patrick. "Bank Shots: Patrick McGilligan Interviews Two Film Financiers." *Film Comment* 12, no. 5 (September–October 1976).

———. "Transitions: Summing Up the Seventies." *American Film* 5, no. 2 (December 1979).

———. "Movies Are Better Than Ever—On Television." *American Film* 5, no. 5 (March 1980).

———. "Breaking Away, Mogul Style." *American Film* 5, no. 8 (June 1980).

McGillivray, David. "Flops." In David Pirie, ed., *Anatomy of the Movies*. New York: Macmillan, 1981.

McNabb, Earnest. "The Wesscam Remote-Control Gyro-Stabilized Camera Mount." *American Cinematographer* 57, no. 10 (October 1976).

Meccoli, Domenico. "Conglomerates Gobble Up Movies." *Successo* 12 (March 1970).

Meisel, Myron. "Industry: The Sixth Annual Grosses Gloss." *Film Comment* 17, no. 2 (March–April 1981).

———. "Industry: Seventh Annual Grosses Gloss." *Film Comment* 18, no. 2 (March–April 1982).

Meyer, Caroline. "The Rating Power of the Network Movies." *Television* 25, no. 3 (March 1968).

Mims, Sergio Alejandro. "Looking Ahead: The Eighties." *American Film* 5, no. 2 (December 1979).

———. "1970–1975: le phenomene de la "blaxploitation." *CinemAction: Le cinema noir ameri-cain*. Paris: Cerf, 1987.

Monaco, James. "Some Late Clues to the Lester Direction: A New Look at the Director." *Film Comment* 10, no. 3 (May-June 1974).

Moses, Richard. "The Rise, Fall, and Second Coming of Four-Walling." *Variety*, January 8, 1975.

Moskowitz, Gene. "Kung Fu: Fixture on Global Screen." *Variety*, December 19, 1973.

Moss, Robert F. "The Brutalists: Making Movies Mean and Ugly." *Saturday Review*, October 14, 1980.

Murphy, A. D. "Banks New Collateral Idea: MGM Example on Pic-by-Pic Rule." *Variety*, February 18, 1971.

———. "Tax Break to Ease Pix Crisis: 'Schreiber Plan' to Cut Charges." *Variety*, September 15, 1971.

———. "Pinch Picture Playoff Patterns: Majors Can't Supply Full Year's Product." *Variety*, March 17, 1975.

———. "Audience Demographics, Film Future: Loss of Youth Adjustment Due." *Variety*, August 20, 1975.

————. "Universal Pics Make Film History: 1975 World Rentals at Alltime High of $289-Mil." *Variety*, January 21, 1976.

————. "Universal's Whale of Pix Biz Share: 'Jaws' Makes U No. 1 With 25% of Domestic Gross." *Variety*, February 11, 1976.

————. "300 Indie Films Pace Production: Invest $100-Mil Outside Majors." *Variety*, June 15, 1977.

————. "Ten Years of Film Change." *Variety*, August 9, 1978.

————. "Japan Now No. 1 Market for U. S. Films: 60% of $1.9-Bil World Rentals From Domestic B. O." *Variety*, July 11, 1979.

————. "Distribution and Exhibition: An Overview." In Jason E. Squire, ed., *The Movie Business Book*. Englewood Cliffs, NJ: Prentice Hall, 1983.

————. "Twenty Years of Weekly Film Ticket Sales in U.S. Theaters." *Variety*, March 15–21, 1989.

Musico, Guiliana. "The Commerce of Classicism." (Essay Review of Tino Balio's *Grand Design*.) *Quarterly Review of Film & Video* 15, no. 3 (1994).

Newsweek. "Black Movie Boom" (September 6, 1971).

Newsweek. "Godfather of the Movies" (Coppola as producer.) (November 25, 1974).

Newsweek. "The Mouse That Roared: In the Midst of a Creative Crisis in Hollywood a New Disney Team Has a Bold Vision of the Future" (March 22, 1986).

Nicholson, Bruce. "Composite Optical Photography for 'The Empire Strikes Back'." *American Cinematographer* 61, no. 6 (June 1980).

O'Brien, Geofrey. "The Return of Film Noir." *The New York Review of Books*, August 15, 1991.

————. "Horror for Pleasure." *The New York Review of Books*, April 22, 1993.

Orwall, Bruce, and Lisa Bannon. "Kerkorian's Script for Restoring MGM Casts Him as Savior of the Faded Studio." The *Wall Street Journal*, July 18, 1996.

Patterson, Patricia, and Manny Farber. "The Power and the Gory." (On TAXI DRIVER.) *Film Comment* 12, no. 3 (May-June 1976).

Paul, William. "Hollywood Harakiri: Notes on the Decline of an Industry and an Art." *Film Comment* 13, no. 2 (March-April 1977).

Perkins, Tessa. "The Politics of 'Jane Fonda'." In Christine Gledhill, ed., *Stardom: Industry of Desire*. London: Routledge, 1991.

Phillips, Joseph D. "Film Conglomerate Blockbusters: International Appeal and Product Homogenization." *Journal of Communication* 25, no. 2 (Spring 1975).

Picker, David V. "The Film Company as Financier-Distributor." In Jason E. Squire, ed., *The Movie Business Book*. Englewood Cliffs, NJ: Prentice Hall, 1983.

Pierce, Ronald. "The Sound Mixing [for *Earthquake*]." *American Cinematographer* 55, no. 11 (November 1974).

Pietschmann, Ricard J. "The New Little Kings of Hollywood." *Los Angeles*, December 15, 1987.

Pirie, David. "The Deal." In David Pirie, ed., *Anatomy of the Movies*. New York: Macmillan, 1981.

Pollack, Dale, and Peter Warner. "Premiere: Studios Tell Why Hollywood Empire Struck Back." *Watch*, July 1980.

Polskin, H. "Inside Pay-Cable's Most Savage War." *Panorama*, March 1981.

Porter, John. "Blaxploitation: Beautiful, Baby," *White's Guide to Movies* 1, no. 2 (February 1999).

Powell, Walter. "The Blockbuster Decades." In Donald Lazere, ed., *American Media and Mass Culture: Left Perspectives*. Berkeley: University of California Press, 1987.

Rapping, Elayne. "Hollywood's Youth Cult Films." *Cineaste* 16, nos. 1-2 (1987–1988).

Reid, Craig A. "Fighting without Fighting: Film Action Fight Choreography." *Film Quarterly* 47, no. 2 (Winter 1993–1994).

Revkin, Andrew. "Motherly? Not Her! Nature Is Trying to Kill You." The *New York Times*, April 20, 1997.

Roddick, Nick. "Only the Stars Survive: Disaster Movies in the Seventies." In David Brady, et al., eds., *Performance and Politics in Popular Drama*. London: Cambridge University Press, 1981.

Rollin, Roger B. "Triple-X: Erotic Movies and Their Audiences." *Journal of Popular Film and Television* 10, no. 1 (1982).

Rutter, Carol. "Colorific: Vittorio Storaro Interviewed by Carol Rutter." *Film Comment* 25, no. 5 (September–October 1989).

Ryan, James. "Look, Ma, No Pixels: Plastic Triumphs on the Set." The *New York Times*, May 4, 1997.

Salemson, Harold J., and Maurice Zolotow. "It Didn't Begin with Begelman: A Concise History of Film Business Finagling." *Action*, July–August 1978.

Samuleson, D. W. "A Survey of Current Film Production Techniques." *American Cinematographer* 58, no. 9 (September 1977).

———. "Introducing the LOUMA Crane." *American Cinematographer* 61, no. 4 (April 1980).

Sansweet, Stephen J. "Wall Street Goes to the Movies." *American Film* 8, no. 1 (October 1982).

Sargeant, Jack. "Hallucinations and Homecomings: Notes on Conrad Rooks' 'Chappaqua'." In Jack Sargeant, *Naked Lens: Beat Cinema*. London: Creation Books, 1997.

Sarris, Andrew. "Notes on the Auteur Theory in 1962." *Film Culture*, no. 27 (Winter 1962–1963).

———. "Notes on the Auteur Theory in 1970." *Film Comment* 6, no. 1 (Spring 1970).

———. "Film Criticism in the Seventies." *Film Comment* 14, no. 1 (January-February 1978).

———. "After 'The Graduate'." *American Film* 3, 9 (July–August 1978).

———. "Sixties Cinema." In Andrew Sarris, ed., *Politics and Cinema*. New York: Columbia University Press, 1978.

Schatz, Thomas. "The Western." In Wes. D. Gehring, ed., *Handbook of American Film Genres*. New York: Greenwood Press, 1988.

———. "Boss Men." *Film Comment* 26, no. 1 (January–February 1990).

———. "The New Hollywood." In Jim Collins, et al., eds., *Film Theory Goes to the Movies*. New York: Routledge, 1993.

Schiff, Stephen. "The Repeatable Experience." *Film Comment* 18, no. 2 (March–April 1982).

———, et al. "Midsection: Dueling Genres." *Film Comment* 18, no. 2 (March–April 1982).

Schregar, Charles. "Who's Afraid of the Pix Sequel Jinx?; H-Wood Riding Remake Cycle," *Variety*, November 23, 1977.

———. "The Second Coming of Sound." *Film Comment* 14, no. 5 (September–October 1978).

———. "CAA: Packaging of an Agency." The *Los Angeles Times*, April 23, 1979.

Schuyten, Peter J. "United Artists' Script Calls for Divorce." *Fortune* 97 (January 16, 1978).

Schwartz, Tony. "Hollywood's Hottest Stars." *New York*, July 30, 1984.

Seabrook, John. "Letter from Skywalker Ranch: Why Is the Force Still With Us?" *The New Yorker*, January 6, 1977.

Seidman, Robert, and Nicholas Leiber. "Arthur Penn: Making Peace with the 60s." *American Film* 7, no. 3 (December 1981).

Self, Robert. "The Art Cinema of Robert Altman." *The Velvet Light Trap*, no. 19 (1986).

Serafine, Frank. "The New Motion Picture Sound," *American Cinematographer* 61, no. 8 (August 1980).

Seydor, Paul. "Sam Peckinpah." *Sight and Sound* 5, no. 10 (October 1994).

Shaffer, Lawrence. "The Good Dumb Film: *The Poseidon Adventure*." *Film Comment* 9, no. 5 (September–October 1973).

Shapiro, Eben, and Thomas R. King. "Lights! Camera! Checkbook!: Costs Menace Movie Makers." The *Wall Street Journal*, December 21, 1995.

Sherman, Stratford P. "Coming Soon: Hollywood's Epic Shakeout." *Fortune*, April 30, 1984.

Shumway, David R. "Rock 'n' Roll Sound Tracks and the Production of Nostalgia. *Cinema Journal* 38, 2 (Winter 1999).

Silverman, Stephen M. "Hollywood Cloning: Sequels, Prequels, Remakes, and Spin-Offs." *American Film* 3, no. 9 (July–August 1978).

Simonet, Thomas. "Industry: Beyond the Fanny of the Cohn." *Film Comment* 16, no. 1 (January–February 1980).

———. "Conglomerates and Content: Remakes, Sequels, and Series in the New Hollywood." In Bruce A. Austin, ed., *Current Research in Film: Audiences, Economics, and Law* Vol. 3. Norwood, NJ: Ablex Publishing, 1987.

Sklar, Robert. "When Looks Could Kill: American Cinema of the Sixties." *Cineaste* 16, nos. 1-2 (1987–1988).

———. "Stanley Kubrick and the American Film Industry." In Bruce A. Austin, ed., *Current Research in Film: Audience, Economics, Law*. Vol. 4. Norwood, NJ: Ablex Publishing, 1988.

Slade, Joseph W. "The Porn Market and Porn Formulas: The Feature Film of the Seventies." *Journal of Popular Film and Television* 6, no. 2 (1977).

————. "Pornography in the Late Nineties," *Wide Angle* 19, no. 3 (July 1997).

Stabiner, Karen. "Playing Hardball with a Hot Agent." *American Film* 6, no. 9 (July–August 1981).

Stanbrook, Alan. "Hollywood's Crashing Epics." *Sight and Sound* 50, 2 (Spring 1981).

Sterngold, James. "The Return of the Merchandiser: As the Millennium Approaches, Star Wars Is Back on Screen and in Stores." The *New York Times*, January 30, 1997.

Stewart, Douglass M., Jr. "Electronic Cinema: Zoetrope Plans for the Future with Today's Technology." *On Location* 5, no. 8 (December 1981).

Stone, Douglas. "TV Movies and How They Get That Way." *Journal of Popular Film and Television* 7, no. 2 (1979).

Stulberg, Gordon. "Film Company Management." In Jason E. Squire, ed., *The Movie Business Book*. Englewood Cliffs, NJ: Prentice Hall, 1983.

Suid, Lawrence. "Hollywood and Vietnam." *Film Comment* 15, no. 5 (September–October 1979).

Svetkey, Benjamin. "Why Movie Ratings Don't Work." *Entertainment Weekly*, November 25, 1994.

Swerdlow, Joel. "The Shark Attacks Tonight: Blockbuster Movies Feed TV's Voracious Appetite for Prime-Time Ratings." The *Washington Post*, November 4, 1979.

Tarbox, Aubrey. "Dreamy Cheapness of 'Rider'; Kadish: Everyone Now Raps 'Star'." *Variety*, December 10, 1969.

Taylor, Ryland A. "The Repeat Audience for Movies on TV." *Journal of Broadcasting* 17, no. 1 (Winter 1972–1972).

Thompson, Anne. "Industry: Tenth [*sic*] Annual Grosses Gloss." (Actually the Eleventh Annual Grosses Gloss.) *Film Comment* 22, no. 2 (March–April 1986).

————. "Industry: The 12th Annual Grosses Gloss." *Film Comment* 23, no. 2 (March–April 1987).

Thompson, David. "The Decade When Movies Mattered." *Movieline* 4, no. 11 (August 1993).

Thompson, Richard. "What's Your 10-20?" *Film Comment* 16, no. 4 (July–August 1980).

Time. "The Shock of Freedom in Films" (December 8, 1967).

Trachtenberg, Jeffrey A. "G&W After Bludorn," *Forbes*, December 3, 1984.

Trefz, Linda. "Audio Achievements in Feature Films: Using Sound for Its Full Effect." *Millimeter* 10, no. 11 (November 1982).

Truscott, Lucian K. IV. "Hollywood's Wall Street Connection." The *New York Times*, February 26, 1978.

Tuchman, Mitch. "Helter Shelter: Now Do We Write Off Hollywood?" *Film Comment* 13, no. 1 (January–February 1977).

————. "Industry: Post-Tax-Shelter Hollywood Has a New Mogul: Uncle Sam." *Film Comment* 14, no. 6 (November–December 1978).

Turpin, Gerry. "The Turpin Colorflex System as Used for 'Young Winston'." *American Cinematographer* 1, no. 54 (January 1973).

————. "Lightflex: A Whole New World of Color on the Screen." *American Cinematographer* 11, no. 59 (November 1978).

Variety. "'Brutal Films Pale Before Televised Vietnam'—Valenti" (February 21, 1968).

Variety. "Pix Must Broaden Market: 18% of Public; 76% of Audience" (March 20, 1968).

Variety. "MPPA's New Code & Rating Rules" (October 6, 1968).

Variety. "Columbia, Warners Alone of Majors 'Started' More Pix in 1969 Than 1968" (December 3, 1969).

Variety. "'Black Is Beautiful' at B.O." (June 17, 1970).

Variety. "Kung Fu Choppy Big B.O." (April 25, 1973).

Variety. "Agent Power Now Rules Hollywood" (January 9, 1974).

Variety. "High Court 'Carnal' Ruling Seen As Crucial For Cinema Freedom" (June 26, 1974).

Variety. "Alan Hirschfield at Columbia: Some 40–50% of Our $38–42 Million Production Program Has Been Co-Financed" (August 14, 1974).

Variety. "Pix Says Sony's Betamax Infringes on Copyrights" (November 17, 1976).

Variety. "Disney Tax Credit Retroactive to 1962" (December 8, 1976).

Variety. "20th–Fox First Major Studio to Enter Home Vidtape Market with Pix.; License 50 Pre-72s" (August 8, 1977).

Variety. "Film Famine Could Revive EXPRODICO" (February 14, 1979).

Variety. "German Tax Shelters Luring Yanks" (May 5, 1979).

Variety. "Loss of Control Over Film Costs Stressed by 'Heaven's Gate' Fiasco" (January 14, 1981).

Verevis, Constantine. "Re-Viewing Remakes." *Film Criticism* 21, no. 3 (Spring 1997).

Verrill, Addison. "Black Film Explosion." *Variety*, January 9, 1974.

———. "'Kong' Wants 'Jaws' Boxoffice Crown." *Variety*, December 22, 1976.

———. "'Violent' or 'Horror' Tag Fits One-Third of Top-Money Films." *Variety*, May 26, 1981.

Von Gunden, Kenneth. "The RH [*Rocky Horror*] Factor." *Film Comment* 15, no. 5 (September–October 1979).

Walker, Beverly. "Soon/Maybe Never to Be a Major Motion Picture." *Film Comment* 16, no. 4 (July–August 1980).

The *Wall Street Journal*. "A Taste for Disaster" (January 7, 1975).

Waller, Gregory. "Introduction." In Gregory Waller, ed., *American Horrors: Essays on the Modern American Horror Film*. Urbana: University of Illinois Press, 1987.

Warren, Rich. "Ray Dolby: Quiet on the Set," *Video*, April 1988.

Wasser, Frederick. "Four-Walling Exhibition: Regional Resistance to the Hollywood Film Industry." *Cinema Journal* 34, no. 2 (Winter 1995).

Waterman, David. "Prerecorded Home Video and the Distribution of Theatrical Feature Films." In Eli M. Noam, ed., *Video Media Competition: Regulation, Economics, and Technology*. New York: Columbia University Press, 1985.

Watkins, Roger. "'Demented Revenge' Hits World Screen: Many at Midfed Express Disgust." *Variety*, October 29, 1980.

Watson, Russell, and Corie Brown. "The 100 Best of 100 Years: A List of the Greatest U.S. Movies of the Century Puts the American Film Institute in the Spotlight." *Newsweek* (Special Issue: A Century of Movies) (Summer 1998).

Weaver, John Michael. "Studying the Art of Soundtrack Design." In *Audio & Music Education*. Emeryville, CA: Cardinal Business Publications, 1997.

———, and Pete Elia. "An Introduction to the Audio Post-Production Process. " In *Audio & Music Education*. Emeryville, CA: Cardinal Business Publications, 1997.

Weinberg, David. "The Motion Picture Soundtrack Jigsaw Puzzle, Part 2." *Widescreen Review* 6, 2, issue no. 24 (May 1997).

Weintraub, Bernard. "Who Drives the Box Office? Girls." The *New York Times*, February 23, 1998.

Werba, Hank. "'Rider's' $50,000,000 Gross? Fonda Parlays 325G into Hit." *Variety*, November 5, 1969.

White, Armond. "Illuminations [on American cinematography]." *Film Comment* 25, no. 5 (September–October 1989).

———. "Unbearable Lightness: Sven Nykvist Interviewed by Armond White." *Film Comment* 25, no. 5 (September–October 1989).

Williamson, Bruce. "Porno Chic." In Peter Keough, ed., *Flesh and Blood: The National Society of Film Critics on Sex, Violence, and Censorship*. San Francisco: Mercury House, 1995.

Wise, Ron. "'Black Is Beautiful' at B.O.; Chi Pattern as Industry Trend." *Variety*, June 17, 1970.

Wolfe, Tom. "The 'Me' Decade and the Third Great Awakening." *New York*, August 23, 1976.

Wood, Robin. "Beauty Bests the Beast." *American Film* 8, no. 10 (September 1983).

Wyatt, Justin. "High Concept, Product Differentiation, and the Contemporary U. S. Film Industry." In Bruce A. Austin, ed., *Current Research in Film: Audiences, Economics, and Law*. Vol. 5. Norwood, NJ: Ablex Publishing, 1991.

———. "Economic Constraints/Economic Opportunities: Robert Altman as Auteur." *The Velvet Light Trap*, 38 (Fall 1996).

Yacowar, Maurice. "The Bug in the Rug: Notes on the Disaster Genre." In Barry Keith Grant, ed., *Film Genre Reader II*. Austin: University of Texas Press, 1995.

Yakir, Dan. "Marketing a Movie Is More Than Selling Jell-o." The *New York Times*, January 6, 1980.

———. "Industry: Campaigns and Caveats." *Film Comment* 16, no. 3 (May–June 1980).

———. "Bob Rehme: New Power in Hollywood." *Film Comment* 17, no. 4 (July–August 1981).

———. "Lawrence Kasdan Interviewed by Dan Yakir." *Film Comment* 17, no. 5 (September–October 1981).

Young, Jordan R. "Studio Heads Forecast for 1981: The Year of Cost-Effective Filmmaking." *Millimeter* 9, no. 1 (January 1981).

————. "Studio Heads Forecast for 1982: Banking on Home Distribution." *Millimeter* 10, no. 1 (January 1982).

Zwick, Edward. "Film View: Why Hollywood Makes Movies By the Numbers." The *New York Times*, January 12, 1997.

BOOKS

Adair, Gilbert. *Vietnam on Film: From "The Green Berets" to "Apocalypse Now."* New York: Proteus, 1981.

Adelman, M. A. *The Genie Out of the Bottle: World Oil Since 1970.* Cambridge: MIT Press, 1995.

Adler, Renata. *A Year in the Dark: A Year in the Life of a Film Critic, 1968–1969.* New York: Random House, 1969.

Alloway, Lawrence. *Violent America: The Movies, 1946–1964.* New York: Museum of Modern Art, 1971.

Altman, Rick. *The American Film Musical.* Bloomington: Indiana University Press, 1987.

————, ed. *Sound Theory, Sound Practice.* New York: Routledge, 1992.

Anderegg, Michael, ed. *Inventing Vietnam: The War in Film and Television.* Philadelphia: Temple University Press, 1991.

Anderson, Christopher. *Hollywood TV: The Studio System in the Fifties.* Austin: University of Texas Press, 1994.

Arnold, Edwin T., and Eugene D. Miller, Jr. *The Films and Career of Robert Aldrich.* Knoxville: University of Tennessee Press, 1986.

Atkins, Dick. *Method to the Madness: Hollywood Explained.* Livingston, NJ: Prince Publishers, 1975.

Auster, Albert, and Leonard Quart. *How the War Was Remembered: Hollywood and Vietnam.* New York: Praeger, 1988.

Austin, Bruce A, ed. *Current Research in Film: Audiences, Economics, and Law.* Vol. 1. Norwood, NJ: Ablex Publishing, 1985.

————, ed. *Current Research in Film: Audiences, Economics, and Law.* Vol. 3. Norwood, NJ: Ablex Publishing, 1987.

————, ed. *Current Research in Film: Audiences, Economics, and Law.* Vol. 4. Norwood, NJ: Ablex Publishing, 1988.

————, ed. *Current Research in Film: Audiences, Economics, and Law.* Vol. 5. Norwood, NJ: Ablex Publishing, 1991.

Bach, Steven. *Final Cut: Dreams and Disaster in the Making of 'Heaven's Gate.'* New York: William Morrow and Company, 1985.

Balio, Tino. *United Artists: The Company Built by the Stars.* Madison: University of Wisconsin Press, 1976.

————, ed. *The American Film Industry.* Madison: University of Wisconsin Press, 1976.

————, ed. *The American Film Industry.* Rev. ed. Madison: University of Wisconsin Press, 1985.

————. *United Artists: The Company That Changed the Film Industry.* Madison: University of Wisconsin Press, 1987.

————, ed. *Hollywood in the Age of Television.* New York: Ungar, 1992.

————. *Grand Design: Hollywood as a Modern Business Enterprise, 1930–1939.* History of the American Cinema, vol. 5. New York: Charles Scribner's Sons, 1993.

Barnouw, Eric. *Tube of Plenty: The Evolution of American Television.* 2nd ed. New York: Oxford University Press, 1990.

Barsam, Richard. *Nonfiction Film: A Critical History.* Rev. and exp. Bloomington: Indiana University Press, 1992.

Bart, Peter. *Fade Out: The Calamitous Final Days of MGM.* New York: William Morrow and Company, 1990.

Base, Ron. *"If the Other Guy Isn't Jack Nicholson, I've Got the Part": Hollywood Tales of Big Breaks, Bad Luck, and Box-Office Magic.* Chicago: Contemporary Books, 1994.

Baughman, James L. *The Republic of Mass Culture: Journalism, Filmmaking, and Broadcasting in America since 1941.* Baltimore: Johns Hopkins University Press, 1992.

Baxter, John. *Stunt: The Story of the Great Movie Stunt Men.* Garden City, NY: Doubleday & Company, 1974.

————. *Steven Spielberg: The Unauthorized Biography*. New York: HarperCollins, 1996.

————. *Stanley Kubrick: A Biography*. New York: Carroll & Graf, 1997.

Belton, John. *Widescreen Cinema*. Cambridge: Harvard University Press, 1992.

————. *American Cinema/American Culture*. New York: McGraw-Hill, 1994.

Bernardoni, James. *The New Hollywood: What the Movies Did with the New Freedoms of the Seventies*. Jefferson, NC: McFarland, 1991.

Bey, Logan. *Hong Kong Action Cinema*. Woodstock, NY: The Overlook Press, 1995.

Biskind, Peter. *Easy Riders, Raging Bulls: How the Sex-Drugs-and-Rock 'n' Roll Generation Saved Hollywood*. New York: Simon & Schuster, 1998.

Bliss, Michael. *Brian De Palma*. Metuchen, NJ: Scarecrow, 1983.

————, ed. *Doing It Right: The Best Criticism on Sam Peckinpah's* The Wild Bunch. Carbondale: Southern Illinois University Press, 1994.

Bluem, A. William, and Jason E. Squire, eds. *The Movie Business: American Film Industry Practice*. New York: Hastings House, 1972.

Blum, Richard A. *American Film Acting: The Stanislavski Heritage*. Ann Arbor: UMI Research Press, 1984.

————, and Richard D. Lindheim. *Primetime: Network Television Programming*. Boston: Focal Press, 1987.

Bogdanovich, Peter. *Who the Devil Made It*. New York: Alfred A. Knopf, 1997.

Bogle, Donald. *Toms, Coons, Mulattos, Mammies, and Bucks: An Interpretive History of Blacks in American Films*. 3rd ed. New York: Continuum, 1996.

Bonadio, Felice A. *A. P. Giannini: Baker of America*. Berkeley: University of California Press, 1994.

Bookbinder, Robert. *The Films of the Seventies*. New York: Citadel Press, 1982.

Bordwell, David. *On the History of Film Style*. Cambridge: Harvard University Press, 1997.

Bordwell, David, Janet Staiger, and Kristin Thompson. *The Classical Hollywood Cinema: Film Style and Mode of Production to 1960*. New York: Columbia University Press, 1985.

Bouzereau, Laurent. *The De Palma Cut*. New York: Dembner Books, 1988.

————. *Ultraviolent Movies*. New York: Citadel Press, 1996.

Boyer, Jay. *Sidney Lumet*. New York: Twayne Publishers, 1993.

————. *Bob Rafelson: Hollywood Maverick*. New York: Twayne Publishers, 1996.

Brenner, Marie. *Going Hollywood: An Insider's Look at Power and Pretense in the Movie Business*. New York: Delacorte Press, 1978.

Breskin, David. *Inner Views: Filmmakers in Conversation*. Rev. ed. Da Capo Press, 1997.

Brode, Douglas. *Money, Women, and Guns: Crime Movies from 'Bonnie and Clyde' to the Present*. New York: Citadel Press, 1995.

Brosnan, John. *Movie Magic: The Story of Special Effects in Cinema*. New York: New American Library, 1976.

Brottman, Mitika. *Offensive Films: Toward an Anthropology of Cinema Vomitif*. Westport, CT: Greenwood Press, 1997.

Brown, Gene. *Movie Time: A Chronology of Hollywood and the Movie Industry from Its Beginnings to the Present*. New York: Macmillan, 1995.

Bryman, Alan. *Disney and His Worlds*. New York: Routledge, 1995.

Buscomb, Edward, ed. *The BFI Companion to the Western*. Rev. ed. London: Andre Deutsch/BFI, 1983.

Cagin, Seth, and Philip Dray. *Born to Be Wild: Hollywood and the Sixties Generation*. Boca Raton: Coyote Press, 1994. Originally published as *Hollywood Films of the Seventies: Sex, Drugs, Violence, Rock 'n' Roll & Politics* (New York: Harper & Row, 1984).

Carney, Raymond. *American Dreaming: The Films of John Cassavetes and the American Experience*. Berkeley: University of California Press, 1985.

Carr, Robert E., and R. M. Hayes. *Wide Screen Movies: A History and Filmography of Wide Gauge Filmmaking*. Jefferson, NC: McFarland, 1988.

Carroll, Peter N. *It Seemed Like Nothing Happened: The Tragedy and Promise of America in the 1970s*. New York: Holt, Rinehart and Winston, 1982.

Caute, David. *Joseph Losey: A Revenge on Life*. London: Faber and Faber, 1994.

Cavell, Stanley. *Pursuits of Happiness: The Hollywood Comedy of Remarriage*. Cambridge: Harvard University Press, 1981.

Champlin, Charles. *George Lucas: The Creative Impulse: Lucasfilm's First Twenty Years*. New York: Harry N. Abrams, Inc., 1992.

Chapple, Steve, and Reebee Garofalo. *Rock 'n' Roll Is Here to Pay: The History and Politics of the Music Industry*. Chicago: Nelson-Hall, 1978.

Chown, Jeffrey. *Hollywood Auteur: Francis Coppola*. New York: Praeger, 1988.

Ciment, Michel. *Kubrick*. Translated by Gilbert Adair. New York: Holt, Rinehart and Winston, 1980.

Clagett, Thomas D. *William Friedkin: Films of Aberration, Obsession and Reality*. Jefferson, NC: McFarland, 1990.

Clarens, Carlos. *Crime Movies: From Griffith to the Godfather and Beyond*. New York: W. W. Norton, 1980.

Clark, Randall. *At a Theater or Drive-In Near You: The History, Culture, and Politics of the American Exploitation Film*. New York: Garland, 1995.

Clover, Carol. *Men, Women, and Chainsaws: Gender in the Modern Horror Film*. New Jersey: Princeton University Press, 1992.

Collins, Jim, Hilary Radner, and Ava Preacher Collins. *Film Theory Goes to the Movies*. New York: Routledge, 1993.

Compaine, Benjamin M. *Who Owns the Media? Concentration of Ownership in the Mass Communications Industry*. Rev. ed. White Plains, NY: Knowledge Industry Publications, 1982.

Cones, John W. *Film Finance & Distibution: A Dictionary of Terms*. Los Angeles: Silman-James Press, 1992.

Cook, David A. *A History of Narrative Film*. 3rd ed. New York: W. W. Norton, 1996.

Copjec, Joan, ed. *Shades of Noir: A Reader*. London: Verso, 1993.

Cowie, Peter. *Coppola: A Biography*. Rev. ed. New York: Da Capo Press, 1994.

Coyne, Michael. *The Crowded Prairie: American National Identity in the Hollywood Western*. London: I. B. Tauris, 1997.

Creed, Barbara. *The Monstrous-Feminine: Film, Feminism, Psychoanalysis*. London: Routledge, 1993.

Crenshaw, Marshall. *Hollywood Rock: A Guide to Rock 'n' Roll in the Movies*. Edited by Ted Mico. New York: Agincourt Press/HarperCollins, 1994.

Crowdus, Gary, ed. *The Political Companion to American Film*. Lakeview Press, 1994.

Culhane, John. *Special Effects in Movies: How They Do It*. New York: Ballantine Books, 1981.

Cunningham, Frank A. *Sidney Lumet: Film and Literary Vision*. Lexington: University of Kentucky Press, 1991.

Curran, Daniel. *Guide to American Cinema, 1965–1995*. Westport, CT: Greenwood Press, 1998.

Custen, George F. *Twentieth Century's Fox: Darryl Zanuck and the Culture of Hollywood*. New York: Basic Books, 1997.

Daniels, Bill, David Leedy, and Steven D. Sills. *Movie Money: Understanding Hollywood's (Creative) Accounting Practices*. Los Angeles: Silman-James Press, 1998.

David, Saul. *The Industry: Life in the Hollywood Fast Lane*. New York: Times Books, 1981.

De Grazia, Edward and Roger K. Newman. *Banned Films: Movies, Censorship, and the First Amendment*. New York: Bowker, 1982.

Dekom, Peter J., ed. *The Selling of Motion Pictures in the 80's: New Producer/Distributor/Exhibitor Relationships*. Los Angeles: privately published, 1980.

Denby, David, ed. *Film 70/71: An Anthology by the National Society of Film Critics*. New York: Simon & Schuster, 1971.

———. *Film 72–73: An Anthology by the National Society of Film Critics*. Indianapolis: Bobb-Merrill, 1973.

Denisoff, Serge, and William D. Romanowski. *Risky Business: Rock in Film*. New Brunswick, NJ: Transaction Publishers, 1991.

Diawara, Manthia, ed. *Black American Cinema*. New York: Routledge, 1993.

Dick, Bernard, ed. *Columbia Pictures: Portrait of a Studio*. Lexington: University of Kentucky Press, 1992.

———. *The Merchant Prince of Poverty Row: Harry Cohn of Columbia Pictures*. Lexington: University of Kentucky Press, 1993.

―――. *City of Dreams: The Making and Remaking of Universal Pictures*. Lexington: University of Kentucky Press, 1997.

Dika, Vera. *Games of Terror: Halloween, Friday the 13th, and the Films of the Stalker Cycle*. Rutherford, NJ: Associated University Presses, 1990.

Dines, Gail, Robert Jensen, and Ann Russo. *Pornography: The Production and Consumption of Inequality*. New York: Routledge, 1998.

Dittmar, Linda, and Gene Michaud, eds. *From Hanoi to Hollywood: the Vietnam War in American Film*. New Brunswick, NJ: Rutgers University Press, 1990.

Doherty, Thomas. *Teenagers & Teenpics: The Juvenilization of American Movies in the 1950s*. Boston: Unwin Hyman, 1988.

Dolce, Philip C., ed. *Suburbia*. Garden City, NY: Anchor, 1976.

Donahue, Mary Suzanne. *American Film Distribution: The Changing Marketplace*. Ann Arbor: UMI Research Press, 1987.

Dunne, John Gregory. *The Studio*. New York: Farrar, Straus & Giroux, 1968.

―――. *Monster: Living Off the Big Screen*. New York: Random House, 1997.

Dworkin, Susan. *Double De Palma: A Film Study of Brian De Palma*. New York: Newmarket Press, 1984.

Dyer, Richard. *Heavenly Bodies: Film Stars and Society*. New York: St. Martin's Press, 1986.

Eames, John Douglas. *The MGM Story: The Complete History of Fifty-Seven Roaring Years*. 2nd rev. ed. New York: Crown Publishers, 1982.

―――. *The Paramount Story*. New York, Crown Publishers, 1985.

Easterlin, Richard A. *Birth and Fortune: The Impact of Numbers on Personal Welfare*. 2nd ed. Chicago: University of Chicago Press, 1987.

Eastman, Susan Tyler, Sydney W. Head, and Lewis Klein, eds. *Broadcast/Cable Programming: Strategies and Practices*. 3rd ed. Belmont, CA: Wadsworth Publishing Company, 1989.

Edgerton, Gary. *American Film Exhibition and An Analysis of the Motion Picture Industry's Market Structure, 1963–1980*. New York: Garland Publishing, Inc., 1983.

Eliot, Marc. *Walt Disney: Hollywood's Dark Prince*. New York: Birch Lane Press, 1993.

Elley, Derek. *The Epic Film: Myth and History*. London: Routledge & Kegan Paul, 1984.

―――, ed. *Variety Movie Guide '97*. London: Hamlyn, 1996.

Evans, Robert. *The Kid Stays in the Picture*. Beverly Hills, CA: Dove Books, 1994.

Eysenck, H. J., and D. K. B. Nias. *Sex, Violence, and the Media*. New York: St. Martin's Press, 1978.

Farber, Stephen. *The Movie Rating Game*. Washington, DC: Public Affairs Press, 1972.

―――. *Outrageous Conduct: Art, Ego, and the "Twilight Zone" Case*. New York: Arbor House, 1988.

―――, and Marc Green. *Hollywood Dynasties*. New York: Delilah Books, 1984.

Fernett, Gene. *American Film Studios: An Historical Encyclopedia*. Jefferson, NC: McFarland & Company, 1988.

Fine, Marshall. *Bloody Sam: The Life and Films of Sam Peckinpah*. New York: Donald I. Fine, 1991.

Finler, Joel W. *The Hollywood Story*. New York: Crown Publishers, 1988.

Flower, Joe. *Prince of the Magic Kingdom: Michael Eisner and the Remaking of Disney*. New York: John Wiley & Sons, 1991.

Frank, Sam. *Sex in the Movies*. Secaucus, NJ: Citadel Press, 1986.

Frayling, Christopher. *Spaghetti Westerns*. London: Routledge & Kegan Paul, 1981.

French, Michael. *US Economic History Since 1945*. Manchester: University of Manchester Press, 1997.

Friedlander, Paul. *Rock and Roll: A Social History*. Boulder, CO: Westview Press, 1996.

Garofalo, Reebee. *Rockin' Out: Popular Music in the USA*. Boston: Allyn and Bacon, 1997.

Gaul, Lou. *The Fist That Shook the World: The Cinema of Bruce Lee*. Baltimore: Midnight Marquee Press, 1997.

Gehring, Wes D. *Handbook of American Film Genres*. New York: Greenwood Press, 1988.

Gelmis, Joseph, ed. *The Film Director as Superstar: Kubrick, Lester, Mailer, Nichols, Penn, Polanski, and Others*. New York: Doubleday, 1970.

Glaessner, Verna. *Kung Fu: Cinema of Vengeance*. New York: Crown, 1974.

Goldman, William. *Adventures in the Screen Trade: A Personal View of Hollywood and Screenwriting.* New York: Warner Books, 1984.

Gomery, Douglas. *The Hollywood Studio System.* New York: St. Martin's Press, 1986.

———. *Shared Pleasures: A History of Movie Presentation in the United States.* Madison: University of Wisconsin Press, 1992.

Gottlieb, Carl. *The Jaws Log.* New York: Dell, 1975.

Grant, Barry Keith, ed. *Film Genre Reader II.* Austin: University of Texas Press, 1995.

Gray, Ian. *Sex, Stupidity, and Greed: Inside the American Movie Industry.* New York: Juno Books, 1997.

Griffin, Nancy, and Ken Masters. *Hit and Run: How Jon Peters and Peter Guber Took Sony for a Ride in Hollywood.* New York: Simon & Schuster, 1996.

Grover, Ron. *The Disney Touch: Disney, ABC & the Quest for the World's Greatest Media Empire.* Rev. ed. Chicago: Irwin Professional Publishing, 1997.

Guback, Thomas. *The International Film Industry: Western Europe and America Since 1946.* Bloomington: Indiana University Press, 1969.

Guerrero, Ed. *Framing Blackness: The African American Image in Film.* Philadelphia: Temple University Press, 1993.

Handling, Piers, ed. *The Shape of Rage: The Films of David Cronenberg.* New York: New York Zoetrope, 1983.

Hanke, Ken. *Ken Russell's Films.* Metuchen, NJ: Scarecrow, 1984.

———. *A Critical Guide to Horror Film Series.* New York: Garland Publishing, Inc., 1991.

Hardy, Phil. ed. *The Overlook Film Encyclopedia: Horror.* Woodstock, NY: The Overlook Press, 1995.

———, ed. *The Overlook Film Encyclopedia: Science Fiction.* Woodstock, NY: The Overlook Press, 1995.

———, ed. *The Overlook Film Encyclopedia: The Western.* Woodstock, NY: The Overlook Press, 1995.

Harris, Thomas J. *Bogdanovich's Picture Shows.* Metuchen, NJ: Scarecrow Press, 1990.

Haskell, Molly. *From Reverence to Rape: The Treatment of Women in the Movies.* New York: Penguin Books, 1974.

Hayes, R. M. *Trick Cinematography: The Oscar Special-Effects Movies.* Jefferson, NC: McFarland, 1986.

Hill, John, Martin McLoone, and Paul Hainsworth. *Border Crossing: Film in Ireland, Britain and Europe.* Belfast: Institute of Irish Studies, 1994.

Hill, Lee, ed. *Easy Rider.* London: BFI Modern Classics, 1996.

Hillier, Jim. *The New Hollywood.* London: Studio Vista, 1992.

Hilmes, Michele. *Hollywood and Broadcasting: From Radio to Cable.* Chicago: University of Illinois Press, 1990.

Hirsch, Foster. *Film Noir: The Dark Side of the Screen.* New York: Da Capo, 1983.

Hirschhorn, Clive. *The Hollywood Musical.* New York: Crown Publishers, 1981.

———. *The Warner Bros. Story.* New York: Crown Publishers, 1981.

———. *The Universal Story.* New York: Crown Publishers, 1983.

Hoberman, J. *Vulgar Modernism: Writing on Movies and Other Media.* Philadelphia: Temple University Press, 1991.

———, and Jonathan Rosenbaum. *Midnight Movies.* New York: Harper & Row, 1983.

Hodgson, Godfrey. *America in Our Time.* Garden City, NY: Doubleday, 1976.

Hoff, Joan. *Nixon Reconsidered.* New York: Basic Books, 1994.

Hofstader, Richard. *The Paranoid Style in American Politics and Other Essays.* New York: Vintage Books, 1967.

Horton, Andrew. *The Films of George Roy Hill.* New York: Columbia University Press, 1984.

———, and Stuart Y. McDougal, eds. *Play It Again, Sam: Retakes on Remakes.* Berkeley: University of California Press, 1998.

Huston, John. *An Open Book.* New York: Alfred A. Knopf, 1980.

Izod, John. *Hollywood and the Box Office, 1895–1986.* New York: Columbia University Press, 1988.

———. *The Films of Nicholas Roeg: Myth and Mind.* London: Macmillan, 1992.

Jackson, Kenneth T. *Crabgrass Frontier: The Suburbanization of the United States*. New York: Oxford University Press, 1985.

Jacobs, Diane. *Hollywood Renaissance*. South Brunswick, NJ: A. S. Barnes & Company, 1977.

James, Darius. *That's Blaxploitation: Roots of the Baadasssss 'Tude*. New York: St. Martin's Press, 1995.

James, David. *Allegories of Cinema: American Film in the Sixties*. New Jersey: Princeton University Press, 1989.

Jarvie, I. C. *Window on Hong Kong: A Sociological Study of the Hong Kong Film Industry and Its Audience*. Hong Kong: Centre for Asian Studies, University of Hong Kong, 1977.

Jewell, Richard B., with Vernon Harbin. *The RKO Story*. New York: Arlington House, 1982.

Johnson, Robert K. *Francis Ford Coppola*. New York: Twayne Publishers, 1977.

Jones, Landon Y. *Great Expectations: America and the Baby Boom Generation*. New York: Random House, 1981.

Jowett, Garth. *Film: The Democratic Art*. Boston: Little, Brown and Company, 1976.

———, and James M. Linton. *Movies as Mass Communication*. 2nd ed. Newbury Park, CA: SAGE Publications, 1989.

Kael, Pauline. *I Lost It at the Movies*. Boston: Little, Brown, 1965.

———. *Kiss Kiss Bang Bang*. Boston: Little, Brown, 1968.

———. *Going Steady*. Boston: Little, Brown, 1970.

———. *The "Citizen Kane" Book*. Boston: Little, Brown, 1971.

———. *Deeper into Movies*. Boston: Little, Brown, 1973.

———. *Reeling*. Boston: Little, Brown, 1976.

Kagan, Norman. *The Cinema of Stanley Kubrick*. Rev. ed. New York: Continuum, 1989.

Kaminsky, Stuart. *John Huston: Maker of Magic*. Boston: Houghton Mifflin, 1978.

———. *American Film Genres*. 2nd ed. Chicago: Nelson-Hall, 1985.

Kanfer, Stefan. *Serious Business: The Art and Commerce Animation in America from Betty Boop to "Toy Story."* New York: Scribners, 1997.

Kapsis, Robert E. *Hitchcock: The Making of a Reputation*. Chicago: University of Chicago Press, 1992.

Karp, Alan. *The Films of Robert Altman*. Metuchen, NJ: Scarecrow Press, 1981.

Karnow, Stanley. *Vietnam: A History*. New York: Penguin, 1984.

Kass, Judith M. *Robert Altman: American Innovator*. New York: Popular Library, 1978.

Kawin, Bruce F. *How Movies Work*. Berkeley: University of California Press, 1992.

Kelly, Mary Pat. *Martin Scorsese: A Journey*. New York: Thunder's Mouth Press, 1991.

Kendall, Steven J. *New Jack Cinema: Hollywood's African American Filmmakers*. Silver Spring, MD: J. L. Denser, 1994.

Keough, Peter, ed. *Flesh and Blood: The National Society of Film Critics on Sex, Violence, and Censorship*. San Francisco: Mercury House, 1995.

Keyser, Les. *Hollywood in the Seventies*. San Diego: A. S. Barnes, 1981.

———. *Martin Scorsese*. Boston: Twayne Publishers, 1992.

Kim, Erwin. *Franklin J. Schaffner*. Metuchen, NJ: Scarecrow Press, 1985.

Kindem, Gorham, ed. *The American Movie Industry: The Business of Motion Pictures*. Carbondale: University of Southern Illinois Press, 1982.

Kobal, John. *Gotta Sing, Gotta Dance: A History of Movie Musicals*. Rev. ed. New York: Exeter Books, 1983.

Kolker, Robert Phillip. *A Cinema of Loneliness: Penn, Kubrick, Scorsese, Spielberg, Altman*. 2nd ed. New York: Oxford University Press, 1988.

Konow, David. *Schlock-O-Rama: The Films of Al Adamson*. Los Angeles: Lone Eagle Publishing Co., 1998.

Kramer, Stanley, with Thomas M. Coffey. *A Mad, Mad, Mad, Mad World: A Life In Hollywood*. New York: Harcourt Brace, 1997.

Kuhn, Annette, ed. *Alien Zone: Cultural Theory and Contemporary Science Fiction Cinema*. London: Verso, 1990.

Lanning, Michael Lee. *Vietnam at the Movies*. New York: Fawcett Columbine, 1994.

Lanza, Joseph. *Fragile Geometry: The Films, Philosophy, and Misadventures of Nicolas Roeg*. New York: PAJ Publications, 1989.

La Polla, Franco. *Il Nuovo Cinema Americano (1967–1975)*. 2nd ed. Venice, Italy: Marsilio Editori, 1985.

Lardner, James. *Fast Forward: Hollywood, the Japanese, and the Onslaught of the VCR*. New York: W. W. Norton, 1987.

Lashner, Marilyn A. *The Chilling Effect in TV News: Intimidation by the Nixon White House*. New York: Praeger, 1984.

Law, Jonathan, ed. *Cassell Companion to Cinema*. London: Market House Books, Ltd., 1997.

Lazarus, Paul N., III. *The Film Producer: A Handbook for Producing*. St. Martin's Press, 1992.

Lederer, Laura, ed. *Take Back the Night: Women on Pornography*. New York: Morrow, 1980.

Lees, David, and Stan Berkowitz. *The Movie Business*. New York: Vintage, 1981.

Lehman, Peter, and William Luhr. *Blake Edwards*. Athens: Ohio University Press, 1981.

Leff, Leonard J., and Jerold L. Simmons. *The Dame in the Kimono: Hollywood Censorship and the Production Code from 1920s to the 1960s*. New York: Grove Weidenfeld, 1990.

Lev, Peter. *The Euro-American Cinema*. Austin: University of Texas Press, 1993.

Lewis, Jon. *Whom God Wishes to Destroy . . . Francis Ford Coppola and the New Hollywood*. Durham: Duke University Press, 1995.

———, ed. *The New American Cinema*. Durham: Duke University Press, 1998.

Light, Paul C. *Baby Boomers*. New York: W. W. Norton, 1988.

Lipset, Seymour Martin, and William Schneider. *The Confidence Gap: Business, Labor and Government in the Public Mind*. New York: The Free Press, 1983.

Litman, Barry R. *The Motion Picture Mega-Industry*. Boston: Allyn and Bacon, 1998.

Litwak, Mark. *Dealmaking in the Film & Television Industry: From Negotiations to Final Contracts*. Los Angeles: Silman-James, 1994.

———. *Reel Power: The Struggle for Influence and Success in the New Hollywood*. Beverly Hills, CA: Silman-James Press, 1986.

LoBrutto, Vincent. *Selected Takes: Film Editors on Editing*. Westport, CT: Praeger, 1991.

———. *By Design: Interviews with Film Production Designers*. Westport, CT: Praeger, 1992.

———. *Sound-on-Film: Interviews with Creators of Film Sound*. Westport, CT: Praeger, 1994.

———. *Stanley Kubrick: A Biography*. New York: Donald I. Fine, 1997.

Lourdeaux, Lee. *Italian and Irish Filmmakers in America: Ford, Capra, Coppola, and Scorsese*. Philadelphia: Temple University Press, 1990.

Luhr, William, and Peter Lehman. *Returning to the Scene: Blake Edwards*, vol. 2. Athens: Ohio University Press, 1989.

Lumet, Sidney. *Making Movies*. New York: Alfred A. Knopf, 1995.

Lunk, Tiuu. *Movie Marketing: Opening the Picture and Giving It Legs*. Los Angeles: Silman-James, 1997.

Lyons, Charles. *The New Censors: Movies and the Culture Wars*. Philadelphia: Temple University Press, 1997.

Madsen, Axel. *The New Hollywood: American Movies in the 1970s*. New York: Thomas Y. Crowell, 1975.

Mair, George. *Inside HBO: The Billion Dollar War between HBO, Hollywood, and the Home Video Revolution*. New York: Dodd, Mead & Company, 1988.

———. *The Barry Diller Story: The Life and Times of America's Greatest Entertainment Mogul*. New York: John Wiley & Sons, 1997.

Malkiewicz, Kris. *Cinematography: A Guide for Film Makers and Film Teachers*. 2nd ed. New York: Prentice Hall, 1989.

———, assisted by Barbara J. Gyboski. *Film Lighting: Talks with Hollywood's Cinematographers and Gaffers*. New York: Prentice Hall, 1986.

Maltby, Richard. *Harmless Entertainment: Hollywood and the Ideology of Consensus*. Metuchen, NJ: Scarecrow, 1983.

———, and Ian Craven. *Hollywood Cinema: An Introduction*. Oxford: Blackwell, 1995.

Maltin, Leonard. *The Art of the Cinematographer: A Survey and Interviews with Five Masters*. New York: Dover, 1978.

———. *The Disney Films*. 3rd Edition. New York: Hyperion, 1995.

Man, Glen. *Radical Visions: American Film Renaissance, 1967–1976*. Westport, CT: Greenwood Press, 1994.

Marmorstein, Gary. *Hollywood Rhapsody: Movie Music and Its Makers, 1900–1975*. New York: Schirmer Books, 1997.

Marshall, Garry, with Lori Marshall. *Wake Me When It's Funny: How to Break into Show Business and Stay There*. New York: Newmarket Press, 1995.

Martin, Michael T. *Cinemas of the Black Diaspora: Diversity, Dependence, and Oppositionality*. Detroit: Wayne State University Press, 1995.

Massotti, Louis H., and Jeffrey K. Haddon, eds. *Suburbia in Transition*. New York: New Directions, 1974.

Mast, Gerald, ed. *The Movies in Our Midst: Documents in the Cultural History of Film in America*. Chicago: University of Chicago Press, 1982.

Matthews, Charles. *Oscar: A to Z*. New York: Doubleday, 1995.

Maxford, Howard. *The A–Z of Horror Films*. Bloomington: Indiana University Press, 1997.

Mayer, Michael F. *The Film Industries*. Rev. ed. New York: Hastings House, 1978.

McBride, Joseph, ed. *Filmmakers on Filmmaking*. Vols. 1 and 2. Los Angeles: J. P. Tarcher, 1983.

———. *Steven Spielberg: A Biography*. New York: Simon & Schuster, 1997.

McCarthy, Todd, and Charles Flynn. *Kings of the Bs: Working Within the Hollywood System*. New York: E. P. Dutton, 1975.

McCarty, John. *Splatter Movies: Breaking the Last Taboo*. Albany, NY: FantaCo Enterprises, 1981.

———. *The Modern Horror Film: 50 Contemporary Classics*. New York: Citadel Press, 1990.

———. *Hollywood Gangland: The Movies' Love Affair with the Mob*. New York: St. Martin's Press, 1993.

———, ed. *The Fearmakers: The Screen's Directorial Masters of Suspense and Terror*. New York: St. Martin's Press, 1994.

———. *The Sleaze Merchants: Adventures in Exploitation Filmmaking*. New York: St. Martin's Press, 1995.

McClelland, C. Kirk. *On Making a Movie: Brewster McCloud*. New York: New American Library, 1971.

McClintick, David. *Indecent Exposure: A True Story of Hollywood and Wall Street*. New York: William Morrow and Company, 1982.

McDougal, Dennis. *The Last Mogul: Lew Wasserman, MCA, and the Hidden History of Hollywood*. New York: Crown Publishers, 1998.

McGee, Mark Thomas. *Faster and Furiouser: The Revised and Fattened Fable of American International Pictures*. Jefferson, NC: McFarland & Company, 1984.

McGilligan, Patrick. *Robert Altman: Jumping Off the Cliff*. New York: St. Martin's Press, 1988.

———. *Jack's Life: A Biography of Jack Nicholson*. New York: W. W. Norton, 1994.

———. *Backstory 3: Interviews with Screenwriters of the 1960s*. Berkeley: University of California Press, 1997.

McGinniss, Joe. *The Selling of the President 1968*. New York: Pocket Books, 1969.

McKinnon, Kenneth. *Misogyny in the Movies: The De Palma Question*. Cranbury, NJ: Associated University Presses, 1990.

McNeil, Alex. *Total Television: A Comprehensive Guide to Programming from 1948 to 1980*. New York: Penguin, 1980.

Mellen, Joan. *Women and Their Sexuality and the New Film*. New York: Dell, 1973.

Menville, Douglas, and R. Reginald. *Things to Come: An Illustrated History of the Science Fiction Film*. New York: Times Books, 1977.

———. *Future Visions: The New Golden Age of Science Fiction Film*. North Hollywood, CA: Newcastle Publishing Company, 1985.

Meyers, Richard. *For One Week Only: The World of Exploitation Films*. Piscataway, NJ: New Century Publishers, 1983.

———. *SF 2: A Pictorial History of Science Fiction Films From "Rollerball" to "Return of the Jedi."* Secaucus, NJ: Citadel Press, 1984.

Meyers, Richard, et al. *Martial Arts Movies: From Bruce Lee to the Ninjas*. Secaucus. NJ: Citadel Press, 1985.

Miller, Frank. *Censored Hollywood: Sex, Sin, and Violence on Screen*. Atlanta: Turner Publishing, 1994.

Miller, Mark Crispin. *Seeing Through Movies*. New York: Pantheon, 1990.

Mintz, Marilyn D. *The Martial Arts Film*. Cranbury, NJ: A.S. Barnes, 1978.

Mintz, Morton, and Jerry S. Cohen. *America, Inc. Who Owns and Operates the United States?* New York: Dell, 1971.

Mitchell, Lee Clark. *Westerns: Making the Man in Fiction and Film*. Chicago: University of Chicago Press, 1996.

Moldea, Dan E. *Dark Victory: Ronald Reagan, MCA, and the Mob*. New York: Viking, 1986.

Monaco, James. *Media Culture: Television, Radio, Records, Books, Magazines, Newspapers, Movies*. New York: Dell, 1978.

———. *How To Read a Film: The Art, Technology, Language, History, and Theory of Film and Media*. Rev. ed. New York: Oxford University Press, 1981.

———. *American Film Now: The People, the Power, the Money, the Movies*. 2nd ed. New York: New American Library, 1984.

Moran, Albert, ed. *Film Policy: International, National and Regional Perspectives*. London: Routledge, 1996.

Mordden, Ethan. *Medium Cool: The Movies of the 1960s*. New York: Alfred A. Knopf, 1990.

Morsiani, Alberto, ed. *Rosso Italiano (1977/1987)*. Verona: *Sequenze* (17), 1988.

Mosley, Leonard. *Zanuck: The Rise and Fall of Hollywood's Last Tycoon*. Boston: Little, Brown, 1984.

Mott, Donald R., and Cheryl McAllister Saunders. *Steven Spielberg*. Boston: Twayne Publishers, 1986.

Muller, Eddie, and Daniel Faris. *Grindhouse: The Forbidden World of "Adults Only" Cinema*. New York: St. Martin's Press, 1996.

Muller, Peter O. *Contemporary Suburban America*. Englewood Cliffs, NJ: Prentice Hall, 1981.

Murch, Walter. *In the Blink of an Eye: A Perspective on Film Editing*. Los Angeles: Silman-James Press, 1995.

Murray, James. *To Find an Image: Black Films from Uncle Tom to Superfly*. Indianapolis: Bobbs-Merrill, 1973.

Naha, Ed. *The Films of Roger Corman: Brilliance on a Budget*. New York: Arco Publishing, 1982.

Neale, Steve, and Frank Krutnik. *Popular Film and Television Genres*. New York: Routledge, 1990.

———, and Murray Smith. *Contemporary Hollywood Cinema*. New York: Routledge, 1998.

Nelson, Thomas Allen. *Kubrick: Inside a Film Artist's Maze*. Bloomington: Indiana University Press, 1982.

Ness, Richard. *Alan Rudolph: Romance and a Crazed World*. New York: Twayne Publishers, 1996.

The *New York Times* Staff. *The End of a Presidency*. New York: Holt, Rinehart and Winston, 1974.

Newman, Kim. *Nightmare Movies: A Critical Guide to Contemporary Horror Films*. New York: Harmony Books, 1988.

———, ed. *The BFI Companion to Horror*. London: Cassell, 1996.

Noam, Eli M., ed. *Video Media Competition: Regulation, Economics, and Technology*. New York: Columbia University Press, 1985.

Obst, Lynda. *Hello, He Lied—and Other Truths from the Hollywood Trenches*. New York: Broadway Books, 1996.

Oldham, Gabriella, ed. *First Cut: Conversations with Film Editors*. Berkeley: University of California Press, 1992.

Oumano, Ellen, ed. *Film Forum: Thirty-Five Top Filmmakers Discuss Their Craft*. New York: St. Martin's Press, 1985.

Palmer, Bill, Karen Palmer, and Ric Meyer. *The Encyclopedia of Martial Arts Movies*. Metuchen, NJ: Scarecrow, 1995.

Palmer, James, and Michael Riley. *The Films of Joseph Losey*. Cambridge: Cambridge University Press, 1993.

Palmer, R. Barton. *Hollywood's Dark Cinema: The American Film Noir*. New York: Twayne Publishers, 1994.

Palmer, William J. *The Films of the Seventies: A Social History*. Metuchen, NJ: Scarecrow, 1987.

Parish, James Robert, and George H. Hill. *Black Action Films*. Jefferson, NC: McFarland, 1989.

Park, James. *British Cinema: The Lights That Failed*. London: B. T. Batsford, 1990.

Pasquariello, Nicholas. *Sounds of Movies: Interviews with the Creators of Feature Sound Tracks*. San Francisco: Port Bridge Books, 1996.

Paul, William. *Laughing Screaming: Modern Hollywood Horror and Comedy*. New York: Columbia University Press, 1994.

Perry, Jeb H. *Screen Gems: A History of Columbia Pictures Television from Cohn to Coke, 1948–1983*. Metuchen, NJ: Scarecrow, 1991.

Phillips, Julia. *You'll Never Eat Lunch in This Town Again*. New York: Signet Books, 1992.

Pinedo, Isabel Cristina. *Recreational Terror: Women and the Pleasures of Horror Film Viewing*. Albany: SUNY Press, 1997.

Pirie, David, ed. *Anatomy of the Movies*. New York: Macmillan, 1981.

Polan, Dana. *Power and Paranoia: History, Narrative, and the American Cinema, 1940–1950*. New York: Columbia University Press, 1986.

Pollack, Dale. *Skywalking: the Life and Films of George Lucas*. Hollywood: Samuel French, 1990.

Porter, William E. *Assault on the Media: The Nixon Years*. Ann Arbor: University of Michigan Press, 1976.

Prince, Stephen. *Savage Cinema: Ultraviolence and the Films of Sam Peckinpah*. Austin: University of Texas Press, 1999.

Prindle, David F. *Risky Business: The Political Economy of Hollywood*. Boulder, CO: Westview Press, 1993.

Puttnam, David, with Neil Warson. *The Undeclared War: The Struggle for Control of the World's Film Industry*. London: HarperCollins, 1997.

Pye, Michael. *Moguls: Inside the Business of Show Business*. New York: Holt, Rinehart and Winston, 1980.

———, and Linda Myles. *The Hollywood Brats: How the Film Generation Took Over Hollywood*. New York: Holt, Rinehart and Winston, 1979.

Quart, Leonard, and Albert Auster. *American Film and Society since 1945*. 2nd ed. Revised and Expanded by Leonard Quart. New York: Praeger, 1991.

Quigley, Martin S., and Associates. *First Century of Film*. New York: Quigley Publishing Company, Inc., 1995.

Quinlan, Sterling. *Inside ABC: American Broadcasting Company's Rise to Power*. New York: Hastings House, 1979.

Ravage, John W. *Television: The Director's Viewpoint*. Boulder, CO: Westview Press, 1978.

Ray, Robert B. *A Certain Tendency of the Hollywood Cinema, 1930–1980*. New Jersey: Princeton University Press, 1985.

Rebello, Stephen. *Alfred Hitchcock and the Making of 'Psycho'*. New York: Dembner, 1990.

Reed, Joseph W. *American Scenarios: The Uses of Film Genre*. Middletown, CT: Wesleyan University Press, 1989.

Reid, Mark A. *Redefining Black Film*. Berkeley: University of California Press, 1993.

Reynolds, Christopher. *1995 Hollywood Power Stats*. Valley Village, CA: Cineview Publishing, 1995.

Rhines, Jesse Algernon. *Black Film/White Money*. New Brunswick, NJ: Rutgers University Press, 1996.

Rimmer, Robert H. *The X-Rated Video Guide*. New York: Arlington House, 1984.

Rose, Frank. *The Agency: William Morris and the Hidden History of Show Business*. New York: HarperCollins, 1995.

Rosenblum, Ralph, and Robert Karen. *When the Shooting Stops . . . the Cutting Begins: A Film Editor's Story*. New York: Viking Press, 1979.

Rosenfield, Paul. *The Club Rules: Power, Money, Sex, and Fear—How It Works in Hollywood*. New York: Warner Books, 1992.

Rosow, Eugene. *Born to Lose: The Gangster Film in America*. New York: Oxford University Press, 1978.

Rostler, William. *Contemporary Erotic Cinema*. New York: Penthouse/Ballantine, 1973.

Roven, Jeff. *A Pictorial History of Science Fiction Films*. Secaucus, NJ: Citadel Press, 1975.

Rowe, John Carlos, and Rick Berg, eds. *The Vietnam War and American Culture*. New York: Columbia University Press, 1991.

Russell, Diana E., ed. *Making Violence Sexy: Feminist Views on Pornography*. New York: Teacher's College Press, 1993.

Russell, Louise. *The Baby Boom Generation and the Economy*. Washington, DC: The Brookings Institution Press, 1982.

Ryan, Michael, and Douglas Kellner. *Camera Politica: The Politics and Ideology of Contemporary Hollywood Film*. Bloomington: Indiana University Press, 1988.

Sackett, Susan. *The Hollywood Reporter Book of Box Office Hits*. Rev. ed. New York: Billboard Books, 1996.

Salamon, Julie. *The Devil's Candy: 'The Bonfire of the Vanities' Goes to Hollywood*. Boston: Houghton Mifflin Company, 1991.

Salt, Barry. *Film Style & Technology*. 2nd ed. London: Starword, 1992.

Samuels, Stuart. *Midnight Movies*. New York: Collier Books, 1983.

Sanderson, Mark. *Don't Look Now*. London: BFI Modern Classics, 1996.

Sanjek, Russell. *American Popular Music and Its Business: The First Four Hundred Years*. Vol. 3, *From 1900 to 1984*. New York: Oxford University Press, 1988.

Sansweet, Stephen J. *Star Wars: From Concept to Screen to Collectible*. San Francisco: Chronicle Books, 1992.

Sarris, Andrew. *The American Cinema: Directors and Directions, 1929–1968*. New York: E. P. Dutton & Company, 1968.

———. *Politics and Cinema*. New York: Columbia University Press, 1978.

Savini, Tom. *Bizarro! The Art & Technique of Special Make-Up Effects*. New York: Harmony Books, 1983.

Schaefer, Dennis, and Larry Salvato. *Masters of Light: Conversations with Contemporary Cinematographers*. Berkeley: University of California Press, 1984.

Schatz, Thomas. *Hollywood Genres: Formulas, Filmmaking, and the Studio System*. Philadelphia: Temple University Press, 1981.

———. *Old Hollywood/New Hollywood: Ritual, Art, and Industry*. Ann Arbor: UMI Research Press, 1983.

———. *The Genius of the System: Hollywood Filmmaking in the Studio Era*. New York: Pantheon, 1988.

———. *Boom and Bust: Hollywood in the 1940s*. History of the American Cinema. Vol. 6. New York: Charles Scribner's Sons, 1997.

Schell, Jonathan. *The Time of Illusion*. New York: Alfred A. Knopf, 1976.

Schickel, Richard. *Clint Eastwood: A Biography*. New York: Vintage Books, 1997.

Sen, Anindya, ed. *Industrial Organization*. Delhi: Oxford University Press, 1996.

Sennett, Ted. *Hollywood Musicals*. New York: Harry N. Abrams, Inc., 1981.

Sheehan, Neil. *A Bright Shining Lie: John Paul Vann and America in Vietnam*. New York: Random House, 1988.

Sherman, Eric. *Selling Your Film: A Guide to the Contemporary Marketplace*. Los Angeles: Acrobat Books, 1990.

———, and Martin Rubin, eds. *The Director's Event: Interviews with Five American Film-makers*. New York: New American Library, 1969.

Shipman, David. *Caught in the Act: Sex and Eroticism in the Movies*. London: Elm Tree Books, 1985.

Sigoloff, Marc. *The Films of the Seventies: A Filmography of American. British, and Canadian Films, 1970–1979*. Jefferson, NC: MacFarland, 1984.

Silver, Alain, and Elizabeth Ward. *Film Noir: An Encyclopedic Reference to the American Style*. Rev. ed. Wooodstock, NY: The Overlook Press, 1992.

Silverman, Steven M. *Public Spectacles*. New York: E. P. Dutton, 1981.

———. *The Fox That Got Away: The Last Days of the Zanuck Dynasty at Twenitieth–Century Fox*. Secaucus, NJ: Lyle Stuart, 1988.

Simmons, Garner. *Peckinpah: A Portrait in Montage*. Austin: University of Texas Press, 1982.

Simon, Art. *Dangerous Knowledge: The JFK Assassination in Art and Film*. Philadelphia: Temple University Press, 1996.

Sinclair, Andrew. *Spiegel: The Man Behind the Pictures*. Boston: Little, Brown and Company, 1987.

Sklar, Robert. *Movie-Made America: A Cultural History of American Movies*. Rev. ed. New York: Vintage Books/Random House, 1994.

Slater, Robert. *Ovitz: The Inside Story of Hollywood's Most Controversial Power Broker*. New York: McGraw-Hill, 1997.

Slide, Anthony. *The American Film Industry: A Historical Dictionary*. New York: Greenwood Press, 1986.

———. *The International Film Industry: A Historical Dictionary*. New York: Greenwood Press, 1989.

————. *The New Historical Dictionary of the American Film Industry*. Lanham, MD: Scarecrow, 1998.

Smoodin, Eric, ed. *Disney Discourse: Producing the Magic Kingdom*. New York: Routledge, 1994.

Sobel, Robert. *The Age of Giant Corporations: A Microeconomic History of American Business, 1914–1970*. Westport, CT: Greenwood Press, 1972.

Solomon, Aubrey. *Twentieth Century–Fox: A Corporate and Financial History*. Metuchen, NJ: Scarecrow, 1988.

Spoto, Donald. *Stanley Kramer: Filmmaker*. Hollywood: Samuel French, 1990.

Squire, Jason E., ed. *The Movie Business Book*. Englewood Cliffs, NJ: Prentice Hall, 1983.

————. *The Movie Business Book*. 2nd ed. New York: Simon & Schuster, 1992.

Stanley, Robert H. *The Celluloid Empire: A History of the American Movie Industry*. New York: Hastings House, 1978.

Steinberg, Cobbett. *Reel Facts: The Movie Book of Records*. Rev. ed. New York: Random House, 1982.

Stempel, Tom. *Framework: A History of Screenwriting in the American Film*. New York: Continuum, 1988.

Stern, Lee Edward. *The Movie Musical*. New York: Pyramid Communications, 1974.

Stern, Leslie. *The Scorsese Connection*. Bloomington: Indiana University Press, 1995.

Taub, Eric. *Gaffers, Grips, and Best Boys*. New York: St. Martin's Press, 1994.

Taylor, John Russell. *Directors and Directions: Cinema for the Seventies*. New York: Hill and Wang, 1975.

Taylor, Philip M. *Steven Spielberg*. London: B.T. Batsford, Ltd., 1992.

Thomas, Tony. *Music for the Movies*. 2nd ed. Beverly Hills, CA: Silman-James Press, 1997.

————, and Aubrey Solomon. *The Films of 20th Century–Fox*. Rev. ed. Secaucus, NJ: Citadel Press, 1985.

Thompson, David. *A Biographical Dictionary of Film*. 3rd ed. New York: Alfred A. Knopf, 1994.

————. *Beneath Mulholland: Thoughts on Hollywood and Its Ghosts*. New York: Alfred A. Knopf, 1997.

Threadgill, Derek. *Shepperton Studios: An Independent View*. London: BFI, 1994.

Toeplitz, Jerzy. *Hollywood and After: The Changing Face of Movies in America*. Translated by Boleslaw Sulik. Chicago: Henry Regnery Company, 1974.

Travers, Peter, ed. *The "Rolling Stone" Film Reader: The Best Film Writing from "Rolling Stone" Magazine*. New York: Pocket Books, 1996.

Tudor, Andrew. *Monsters and Mad Scientists: A Cultural History of the Horror Movie*. Oxford: Basil Blackwell, 1989.

Turan, Kenneth, and Stephen E. Zito. *Sinema: American Pornographic Films and the People Who Make Them*. New York: Praeger, 1974.

Turner, Graeme. *Film As Social Practice*. London: Routledge, 1988.

Vogel, Harold L. *Entertainment Industry Economics: A Guide for Financial Analysis*. New York: Cambridge University Press, 1986.

Von Gunden, Kenneth. *Postmodern Auteurs: Coppola, Lucas, De Palma, Spielberg and Scorsese*. Jefferson, NC: McFarland, 1991.

Walker, Alexander. *Stardom: The Hollywood Phenomenon*. New York: Stein and Day, 1970.

Waller, Gregory, ed. *American Horrors: Essays on the Modern American Horror Film*. Urbana: University of Illinois Press, 1987.

Ward, Ed, Geoffrey Stokes, and Ken Tucker. *Rock of Ages: The "Rolling Stone" History of Rock & Roll*. Englewood Cliffs, NJ: Rolling Stone Press/Prentice Hall, Inc., 1986.

Wasko, Janet. *Movies and Money: Financing the American Film Industry*. Norwood, NJ: Ablex Publishing Company, 1982.

————. *Hollywood in the Information Age*. Austin: University of Texas Press, 1994.

Weaver, James B., III, and Ron Tamborini, eds. *Horror Films: Current Research on Audience Preferences and Reactions*. Mahwah, NJ: Lawrence Erlbaum, 1996.

Weddie, David. *"If They Move . . . Kill 'em!": The Life and Times of Sam Peckinpah*. New York: Grove Press, 1994.

Weis, Elizabeth, and John Belton. *Film Sound: Theory and Practice*. New York: Columbia University Press, 1985.

Weisser, Thomas. *Spaghetti Westerns—the Good, the Bad and the Violent: A Comprehensive, Illustrated Filmography of 558 Eurowesterns and Their Personnel, 1961–1977.* Jefferson, NC: McFarland, 1992.

———. *Asian Cult Cinema.* New York: Boulevard Books, 1997.

Wexman, Virginia Wright, and Gretchen Bisplinghof. *Robert Altman: A Guide to References and Resources.* Boston: G. K. Hall, 1984.

Wicking, Christopher, and Tise Vahimagi. *The American Vein: Directors and Directions in Television.* New York: E. P. Dutton, 1979.

Wildman, Steven S., and Stephen E. Siwek. *International Trade in Films and Television Programs.* Cambridge, MA: Ballinger Publishing, 1988.

Williams, Hunt. *Beyond Control: ABC and the Fate of the Networks.* New York: Athenaeum, 1989.

Williams, Linda. *Hard Core: Power, Pleasure, and the "Frenzy of the Visible."* Berkeley: University of California Press, 1989.

Williams, Tony. *Larry Cohen: The Radical Allegories of an Independent Filmmaker.* Jefferson, NC: McFarland, 1997.

Wills, Garry. *John Wayne's America: The Politics of Celebrity.* New York: Simon & Schuster, 1997.

Wingrove, David. *The Science Fiction Film Source Book.* Essex, England: Longman, 1985.

Witcover, Jules. *The Year the Dream Died: Revisiting 1968 in America.* New York: Warner Books, 1997.

Wood, Robin. *Hollywood from Vietnam to Reagan.* New York: Columbia University Press, 1986.

Wyatt, Justin. *High Concept: Movies and Marketing in Hollywood.* Austin: University of Texas Press, 1994.

Wyver, John. *The Moving Image: An International History of Film, Television, and Video.* London: Basil Blackwell/BFI, 1989.

Yule, Andrew. *Fast Fade: David Puttnam, Columbia Pictures, and the Battle for Hollywood.* New York: Delacorte, 1989.

———. *Picture Shows: The Life and Films of Peter Bogdanovich.* New York: Limelight Editions, 1992.

Zucker, Harvey Marc, and Lawrence J. Babich. *Sports Films: A Complete Reference.* Jefferson, NC: McFarland, 1987.

Zucker, Joel S. *Arthur Penn: A Guide to References and Resources.* Boston: G.K. Hall, 1980.

———. *Francis Ford Coppola: A Guide to References and Resources.* Boston: G. K. Hall, 1984.

Chapter 11

Barnouw, Erik. *Documentary: A History of the Nonfiction Film*, rev. ed. New York: Oxford University Press, 1983.

Barsam, Richard Meran. *Non-Fiction Film, A Critical History*, rev. and exp. Bloomington: Indiana University Press, 1992.

Benson, Thomas, and Carolyn Anderson. *Reality Fictions: The Films of Frederick Wiseman.* Carbondale: Southern Illinois University Press, 1989.

Bullert, B.J. *Public Television: Politics and the Battle over Documentary Film.* New Brunswick: Rutgers University Press, 1997.

Cholodenko, Alan. *The Films of Frederick Wiseman.* (Harvard University Ph.D. Thesis.) University Microfilms International, 1987.

Cooper, Thomas. *Natural Rhythms: The Indigenous World of Robert Gardner.* New York: Anthology Film Archives, 1995.

Crawford, Peter Ian, and David Turton. *Films as Ethnography.* Manchester: Manchester University Press, 1992.

De Brigard, Emilie. *Anthropological Cinema.* New York: Museum of Modern Art, 1974.

Devereaux, Leslie, and Roger Hillman, eds. *Essays in Film Studies, Visual Anthropology and Photography.* Berkeley: University of California Press, 1995.

Ellis, Jack. *The Documentary Idea: A Critical History of the English-Language Documentary Film and Video.* New York: Prentice Hall, 1989.

Erens, Patricia. "Women's Documentaries as Social History." *Film Library Quarterly* 14, 2 (1981): 4–9.

Grant, Barry Keith. *Voyages of Discovery: The Cinema of Frederick Wiseman*. Urbana-Champaign: University of Illinois Press, 1992.

————, and Jeannette Sloniowski, eds. *Documenting the Documentary: Close Readings of Documentary Film and Video*. Detroit: Wayne State University Press, 1998.

Guynn, William. *Cinema of Nonfiction*. Teaneck, NJ: Fairleigh Dickinson University Press, 1990.

Heider, Karl. *Ethnographic Film*. Austin: University of Texas Press, 1978.

Hockings, Paul, ed. *Principles of Visual Anthropology*. The Hague: Mouton, 1975.

Holmlund, Chris, and Cynthia Fuchs, eds. *Between the Sheets, in the Streets: Queer, Lesbian, and Gay Documentary*. Minneapolis: University of Minnesota Press, 1997.

Kaplan, E. Ann. *Women and Film: Both Sides of the Camera*. New York: Methuen, 1983.

Kreuger, Eric. "An American Family: An American Film," *Film Comment* 9 (November–December 1973): 16–19.

Lane, James. "The Political Aesthetics of the Feminist Documentary Film," *Quarterly Review of Film Studies* 3, 3 (1978): 507–523.

Lewin, Roy. *Documentary Experience: 15 Interviews with Film Makers*. Garden City, NY: Doubleday, 1971.

Loizos, Peter. *Innovation in Ethnographic Film: From Innocence to Self-Consciousness, 1955–85*. Chicago: University of Chicago Press, 1993.

Mamber, Stephen. *Cinema Verité in America: Studies in Uncontrolled Documentary*. Cambridge: MIT Press, 1974.

Marcorelles, Louis. "Leacock at MIT." *Sight and Sound* 18, 2 (1974): 104–107.

————. *Living Cinema: New Directions in Contemporary Film-Making*. New York: Praeger, 1973.

Naficy, Hamid. "'Truthfull Witness': An Interview with Albert Maysles," *Quarterly Review of Film Studies* 6, 2 (1981): 155–179.

Nichols, Bill. *Ideology and the Image: Social Representation in the Cinema and Other Media*. Bloomington: Indiana University Press, 1981.

————. *Representing Reality: Issues and Concepts in Documentary*. Bloomington: Indiana University Press, 1991.

————. *Blurred Boundaries: Questions of Meaning in Contemporary Culture*. Bloomington: Indiana University Press, 1994.

Pincus, Edward. "New Possibilities in Film and the University." *Quarterly Review of Film Studies* 2, 2 (1977): 159–178.

Platinga, Carl. *Ordered Images: Rhetoric and Representation in Nonfiction Film*. New York and Cambridge: Cambridge University Press, 1996.

Renov, Michael. "The Image of Analysis: Newsreel's Re-Search for a Radical Film Practice." *Wide Angle* 6, 3 (1984): 76–82.

————. "New Subjectivities: Documentary and Self-Representation in the Post-Vérité Age." *Documentary Box*, 1998. Available from: http://www.cit.yamagata.jp/yidff/ff/box/box7/en/b7enf2-1.html

————, ed. *Theorizing Documentary*. London: Routledge, 1993.

Rosenthal, Alan. *The Documentary Conscience: A Casebook in Filmmaking*. Berkeley: University of California Press, 1988.

Rothman, William. *Documentary Film Classics*. Cambridge: Cambridge University Press, 1997.

————. *The "I" of the Camera*. Cambridge: Cambridge University Press, 1988.

Ruby, Jay. "The Image Mirrored: Reflexivity and the Documentary Film." *Journal of the University Film Association* 29, 4 (1977): 3–12.

————, ed. *A Crack in the Mirror: Reflexive Perspectives on Anthropology*. Philadelphia: University of Pennsylvania Press, 1982.

Ruoff, Jeffrey. "Family Programming, Television, and American Culture (unpublished manuscript).

Sherman, Sharon R. *Documenting Ourselves: Film, Video and Culture*. Lexington, KY: The University Press of Kentucky, 1998.

Trojan, Judith, and Nadine Covert, eds. *16mm Distribution*. New York: Educational Film Library Association, 1977.

Warren Charles, ed. *Beyond Document: Essays on Non-Fiction Film*. Hanover, NH: Wesleyan University Press, 1996.

Waugh, Thomas. *Show Us Life: Toward a History and Aesthetics of the Committed Documentary.* Metuchen, NJ: Scarecrow Press, 1984.
———. "Beyond Verité: Emilie de Antonio and the New Documentary of the Seventies." in Bill Nichols, ed. *Movies and Methods II.* Berkeley: University of California Press, 1985, 233–258.

Chapter 12

ARTICLES, THESES, AND PARTS OF BOOKS

Alloway, Lawrence, "Network: The Art World Described as a System," *Artforum* 11,1 (September 1972).
Andrew, B. "On Yvonne Rainer." *Cinemanews* nos. 5/6 (Spring 1980).
Arthur, Paul. "The Calisthenics of Vision: Open Instructions on the Films of George Landow." *Artforum* 10,1 (September 1971b).
———. "Structural Film: Revisions, New Versions, and the Artifact." *Millennium Film Journal* nos. 1/2 (Spring/Summer 1978).
———. "'Quixote' and its Contexts." *Film Culture* nos. 67/68/69 (1979a).
———. "Structural Film: Revisions, New Versions, and the Artifact. Part Two." *Millennium Film Journal* nos. 4/5 (Spring 1979b).
———. "Last of the Machine: Avant-garde Film since 1965." *Millennium Film Journal* nos.16/17/18 (Fall/Winter 1986–1987).
———. "Beauty, Flesh, and The Empire of Absence: Resighting Warhol." *The Independent* (December 1988).
Baillie, Bruce. "Interview." *Film Comment* 7,1 (January–February 1971).
———. "Letter." *Cinemanews* 4,1 (July-August 1977).
———. "Miscellaneous Writings." *Film Culture* nos. 67/68/69 (1979a).
Bannon, Anthony. "Baillie's Use of Light: A Reading of His Notebooks." *Film Culture* nos.67/68/69 (1979a).
Barnett, G. "Interview/Jonas Mekas." *Literature/Film Quarterly* 1,2 (1973).
Bergstrom, Janet. "Rereading the Work of Claire Johnston." *Camera Obscura* 3–4 (1979).
Bershon, Wanda. "Zorn's Lemma." *Artforum* 10, 1 (September 1971b).
Bourdon, David. "Andy Warhol as Filmmaker." *Art in America* 59,3 (May 1971).
Brakhage, Stan. "Metaphors on Vision." *Film Culture* no. 30 (Autumn 1963).
———. "Brakhage Uncensored." *Cinemanews* no. 6 (1978).
———. "Stan Brakhage Speaks on '23rd Palm Branch' at Filmmakers Cinematheque, April 22, 1967." *Film Culture* nos. 67/68/69 (1979a).
———. "Stan Brakhage: The Text of Light." *Cantrill Filmnotes* nos. 21/22 (1977).
Brooks, Virginia. "Film, Perception, and Cognitive Psychology." *Millennium Film Journal* nos. 14/15 (1984–1985).
Broughton, James. "The Necessity of Living Poetically in an Electronic Age" and "Twelfth Independent Film Award." *Film Culture* no. 61 (1975).
Buchloh, Benjamin H. D. "The Andy Warhol Line." In Gary Garrels, ed., *The Work of Andy Warhol.* Seattle: Bay Press and the Dia Foundation, 1989.
Buchsbaum, Jonathan. "Composing for Film: The Work of Bill Brand." *Millennium Film Journal* no. 3 (Winter 1979).
———. "Narrative/Diegesis—Threshold, Limits." *Screen* 23,2 (1982).
Cage, John. "On Film." In Richard Kostelanetz, ed., *John Cage,* New York: Praeger, 1970.
Callenbach, Ernest. "*Quick Billy.*" *Film Quarterly* 24, 3 (1971).
Camper, Fred. "*Remedial Reading Comprehension* by George Landow." *Film Culture* no. 52 (Spring 1971).
———. "On L. Hock's Piece on *Remedial Reading Comprehension.*" *Film Culture* nos. 63/64 (1976).
Carroll, Noel. "Avant-Garde Film and Film Theory." *Millennium Film Journal* nos. 4/5 (Spring 1979b).
Cathcart, Linda. "An Interview with Paul Sharits." *Film Culture* nos. 65/66 (1978).

Chalfen, Richard. "Cinema Naivete: A Study of Home Moviemaking as Visual Communication." *Studies in the Anthropology of Visual Communication* 2 (1975).

Chin, Daryl. "Walking on Thin Ice: The Films of Yoko Ono." *The Independent* (April 1989).

Cornwall, Regina. "Works of Ernie Gehr from 1968 to 1972." *Film Culture* nos. 63/64 (1976).

———. "Hittin on *A lot of Near Mrs.*" *Film Reader* 3 (1978).

———. "Please Sound and Light Talk: *Hearing is Deceiving: Rameau's Nephew* by Michael Snow." *Afterimage* 7 (Summer 1978).

Cowan, B. "*Serene Velocity.*" *Take-One* 4,1 (1974).

Davidson, David. "Warren Sonbert's Noblesse Oblige." *Millennium Film Journal* nos. 4/5 (Spring 1979b).

Dawson, J. "A World Beyond Freud." *Sight and Sound* 49,3 (1980).

Delauretis, Teresa. "Snow on the Oedipal Stage." *Screen* 22,3 (1981).

Deren, Maya. "Cinematography: The Creative Uses of Reality." *Daedalus*, 89,1 (Winter 1960).

Eco, Umberto. "Articulations of the Cinematic Code." In Bill Nichols, ed., *Movies and Methods*. Berkeley: University of California Press, 1976.

Estevez, Sue Ann. "Bruce Baille's *Roslyn Romance (Is It Really True?)*. *Millennium Film Journal* nos. 4/5 (Spring 1979b).

Fisher, Lucy. "Frampton and the Magellan Metaphor." *American Film* 4,7 (May 1979).

Foreman, Richard. "On Ernie Gehr's Film *Still.*" *Film Culture* nos. 63/64 (1976).

Forney, Darrell. "A New Film by Robert Nelson: *Bleu Shut.*" *West Art* 8,13 (1971).

Frampton, Hollis. "For a Metahistory of Film: Commonplace Notes and Hypotheses." *Artforum* 10, 1 (September 1971).

———. "(nostalgia): voice-over narration for film of that name, dated 1/8/71" *Film Culture* nos. 53/55 (Spring 1972).

———. "A Pentagram for Conjuring the Narrative." In Dennis Wheeler, ed., *Form and Structure in Recent Film*. Vancouver: Vancouver Art Gallery, 1972.

———. "Digressions on the Photographic Agony." *Artforum* 9,3 (1972).

———. "Stan and Jane Brakhage, Talking." *Artforum* 11,5 (January 1973).

———. "The Withering Away of the State of Art." *Artforum* 13,4 (December 1974).

———. "Notes on Composing in Film." *October* 1 (Spring 1976).

———. "Mind Over Matter." *October* 6 (Fall 1978).

———. "Film in the House of the World." *October* 17 (Summer 1981).

Fredericksen, Don. "Modes of Reflexive Film." *Quarterly Review of Film Studies* 4,3 (Summer 1979).

Fried, Michael. "Art and Objecthood." In Gregory Battcock, ed. *Minimal Art: A Critical Anthology*. New York: E. P. Dutton, 1968.

Gartenberg, J. "The Avant-Garde." *Films in Review* no. 33 (June–July 1982).

Gehr, Ernie. "Program Notes for a Film Showing at the Museum of Modern Art, NYC, Feb. 2, 1971 at 5:30 P.M." *Film Culture* nos. 53/55 (Spring 1972).

———. "Interview by Jonas Mekas, March 24, 1971." *Film Culture* nos. 53/55 (Spring 1972).

———. "Discussions." *Film Culture* nos. 70/71 (1983).

Gidal, Peter. "Theory and Definition of Structural/Materialist Film." *Studio International* 190,978 (December 1975).

———. "The Anti-Narrative (1978)." *Screen* 20,2 (Summer 1979).

Glick, M. "*Eureka* by Ernie Gehr." *Film Culture* nos. 70/71 (1983).

Grindon, Leger. "Significance Reexamined: A Report on Bruce Conner." *Post Script* 4 (1985).

Gunning, Tom. "The Participatory Film." *American Film* 1 (October 1975).

———. "The Critique of Seeing with One's Own Eyes: Ernie Gehr's Untitled (1976)." *Millennium Film Journal* nos. 4/5 (Spring 1979b).

Hanlon, Lindley. "Lost Mekas Looks at His Past." *Thousand'Eyes* 2 (March 1977).

Heath, Stephen. "Repetition Time: Notes around 'Structural/Materialist Film'." *Wide Angle* 2,3 (1978).

Hill, Jerome. "Brakhage's *Eyes.*" *Film Culture* no. 52 (Spring 1971).

———. "Interview/Jonas Mekas." *Film Culture* nos. 56/57 (Spring 1973).

Hills, M. "Robert Nelson Interview." *Cinemanews* nos. 3/4 (1978).

———, and D. Gerstein. "St. Hollis (part 2)." *Cinemanews* nos. 3/4 (1978).

Hoberman, J. "The Avant-Garde Now." *Film Comment* 17,3 (May–June 1981).
———. "Ernie Gehr's Geography." *Millennium Film Journal* no. 3 (Winter 1979).
———. "A Context for Vivienne Dick." *October* 20 (Spring 1982).
Hock, L. "Reconsidered Analyses of *Remedial Reading Comprehension*." *Film Culture* nos. 63/64 (1976).
Huyssen, Andreas. "The Search for Tradition: Avant-Garde and Postmodernism in the 1970s." *New German Critique* 22 (Winter 1981).
Jacoby, Roger. "Willard Maas and Marie Menken: The Last Year." *Film Culture* nos. 63/64 (1976).
James, David. "Semiology and Independent Film: A Review of Research and Criticism." *Quarterly Review of Film Studies* 3,3 (Summer 1978).
Jenkins, Bruce. "Frampton Unstructured: Notes for a Metacritical History." *Wide Angle* 2,3 (1978).
———, and Noel Carroll. "*Text of Light*." *Film Culture* nos. 67/68/69 (1979a).
Johnston, Claire. "Women's Cinema as Counter Cinema." In Claire Johnston, ed., *Notes on Women's Cinema*. London: Society for Education in Film and Television, 1973.
Jordan, Larry. "Interview." *Canyon Cinemanews* no. 3 (May-June 1976).
———. "Survival in the independent-non-commerical-avant-garde-experimental-personal-expressionistic film market of 1974." *Cinema News* nos. 2/3/4 (1979).
Keller, Marjorie. "*Rabbit's Moon* by Kenneth Anger." *Film Culture* nos. 67/68/69 (1979a).
———. "Excerpts from Journal of *Daughters of Chaos*, 1980." *Cinematograph* 1 (1985).
Kelman, Ken. "Animal Cinema: The Spirit of Roslyn." *Film Culture* nos. 67/68/69 (1979a).
Kleinhans, Chuck. "Wanda: 'Marilyn Times Five': Seeing Through Cinema Verité." *Jump Cut* 1 (May-June 1974).
Koch, Stephen. " Performance, A Conversation." *Artforum* 11,4 (December 1972).
Krauss, Rosalind. "A View of Modernism." *Artforum* 11,1 (September 1972).
———. "Video: The Aesthetics of Narcissism." *October* 1 (Spring 1976).
Landow, George. "Notes on Film." *Canyon Cinema News* 2 (March-April 1977).
———. "George Landow." *Cinemanews* nos. 3/4 (1978).
LeGrice, Malcolm. "Thoughts on Recent 'Underground' Film." *Afterimage* 4 (Autumn 1972).
———. "Vision." *Studio International* 185 (March 1973).
Lehman, Peter. "For Whom Does the Light Shine?: Thoughts on the Avant-Garde" and "Michael Snow: The Nature of the Material." Parts 1 and 2. *Wide Angle* 7,1 (1985); 2 (1985).
Liebman, Stuart. "Apparent Motion and Structure: Paul Sharits' Shutter Interface." *Millennium Film Journal* nos. 1/2 (Spring/Summer 1978).
Lippard, Lucy. "10 Structurists in 20 Paragraphs." In Richard Kostelanetz, ed., *Esthetics Contemporary*. Buffalo: Prometheus Books, 1978.
Locke, John. "*La Région Centrale*." Parts 1 and 2. *Artforum* 12, 3 (November 1973); 4 (December 1973).
Lopate, Phillip. "The Films of Warren Sonbert." *Film Culture* nos. 70/71 (1983).
Lyotard, Jean-François. "Acinema." *Wide Angle* 2,3 (1978).
MacDonald, Scott. "Avant-Garde Films: Cinema as Discourse." *Journal of Film and Video* 40,2 (Spring 1988).
———. "Hollis Frampton's *Hapex Legomena*." *Afterimage* 5,7 (January 1978).
———. "Interview/Frampton." *Film Culture* nos. 67/68/69 (1979a).
———. "Interview: *Zorns Lemma*." *Quarterly Review of Film Studies* 4,1 (1979).
———. "Interview with Hollis Frampton: The Early Years." *October* 12 (Spring 1980).
———. "We Were Bent on Having a Good Time: An Interview with Robert Nelson." *Afterimage* 11,2 (Summer 1983).
———. "If the Vision is Intense Enough, Everything Is Grist for the Mill." *Afterimage* 11,3 (October 1983).
———. "Hollis Frampton, 1936–1984." *Afterimage* 11, no. 10 (May 1984).
———. "Text as Image in Some Recent North American Avant-Garde Films." *Afterimage* 13,8 (March 1986).
———. "Lost, Lost, Lost Over *Lost, Lost, Lost*." *Cinema Journal* 25,2 (1986).
———. "Putting All Your Eggs in One Basket: The Single Shot Films as Cinematic Meditation." *Afterimage* 16,8 (March 1989).
———. "From Zygote to Global Cinema via Su Friedrich's Films." *Journal of Film and Video* 44, nos. 1 and 2 (Spring/Summer 1992).

Martin, Katrina. "Marcel Duchamp and *Anemic Cinema*." *Studio International* 189,973 (January-February 1975).

Mekas, Jonas. "Aspects of the Avant-Garde: Independence for Independents." *American Film* 3,10 (September 1978).

———. "Interview." *Cinemanews* nos. 5/6 (Spring 1980).

Mellencamp, Patricia. "Academia Unbound: The Adventures of the Red-Hot Texts of Land, Nelson, and Snow." *Cinematograph* 1 (1985).

———. "Receivable Texts: U.S. Avant-Garde Cinema, 1960–80." *Wide Angle* 7,3 (1985).

Meyers, Ellen and Toni Arnstrong, Jr. "A Visionary Woman Creating Visions: Barbara Hammer." *Hot Wire* 7,2 (May 1991).

Michelson, Annette. "Toward Snow." *Artforum* 9,10 (June 1971a).

———. "Foreword in Three Letters." *Artforum* 10,1 (September 1971b).

———. "Screen/Surface: The Politics of Illusionism." *Artforum* 11,1 (September 1972a).

———. "The Man With the Movie Camera: From Magician to Epistemologist." *Artforum* 10,7 (March 1972b).

———. "Camera Lucida/Camera Obscura." *Artforum* 11,5 (January 1973).

———. "About Snow." *October* 8 (Spring 1979).

———. "Film and the Radical Aspiration." In Gerald Mast and Marshall Cohen, eds., *Film Theory and Criticism*, 2d ed. New York: Oxford University Press, 1979.

———. "Yvonne Rainer, Part 1: The Dancer and the Dance." *Artforum* 12,5 (January 1974).

———. "Yvonne Rainer, Part 2: Lives of Performers." *Artforum* 12,6 (February 1974).

———, et al. "Hollis Frampton Issue." *October* 32 (Spring 1985).

Moritz, William. "Non-Objective Film: the Second Generation." In *Film as Form: Formal Experiment in Film, 1910–1975*. London: Arts Council of Great Britain, 1979.

Morris, Robert. "Some Notes on the Phenomenology of Making." *Artforum* 8,8 (April 1970).

Mulvey, Laura. "Visual Pleasure and Narrative Cinema." *Screen* 16,3 (Autumn 1975).

O'Pray, M. "*Zorn's Lemma*." *Monthly Film Bulletin* 50 (September 1983).

Penley, Constance. "The Avant-Garde and Its Imaginary." *Camera Obscura* 2 (Summer 1976).

———, and Janet Bergstrom. "The Avant-Garde: Histories and Theories." *Screen* 19,3 (Autumn 1978).

Peterson, James. "The Artful Mathematicians of the Avant-Garde." *Wide Angle* 7,3 (1985).

Peterson, Vicki Z. "Two Films by Chick Strand." *Millennium Film Journal* nos. 1/2 (Spring/Summer 1978).

Pollock, Griselda. "What's Wrong With Images of Women?" *Screen Education* 24 (Autumn 1977).

Rainer, Yvonne. "A Quasi Survey of Some 'Minimalist' Tendencies in the Quantitatively Minimal Dance Activity Midst the Plethora, or an Analysis of Trio A." In Gregory Battcock, ed. *Minimal Art: A Critical Anthology*. New York: E. P. Dutton, 1968.

———. "The Performer as a Person: An Interview with Yvonne Rainer." *Avalanche* (Summer 1972).

———. "Film about a Woman Who . . . ." *October* 2 (Summer 1976).

———. "Yvonne Rainer: Interview." *Camera Obscura* 1 (Fall 1976).

———. "Working Title: Journeys from Berlin/1971." *October* 9 (Summer 1979).

———. "Looking Myself in the Mouth." *October* 17 (Summer 1981).

Ramoso, R. "A Serial for a Sentimental Scientist." *Cinematograph* 1 (1985).

Reisman, L. "Interview." *Camera Obscura* 11 (Fall 1983).

———. "Personal Film/Feminist Film." *Camera Obscura* 11 (Fall 1983).

Reynolds, M. "Bruce Baillie's *Quick Billy*." *Cinemanews* 3 (May–June 1975).

Rosenbaum, Jonathan. "Diaries . . . ." *Monthly Film Bulletin* 44 (January 1977).

———. "Aspects of the Avant-Garde: Three Innovators." *American Film* 3,10 (September 1978).

———. "Explorations: The Ambiguities of Yvonne Rainer." *American Film* 5,5 (March 1980).

Ruoff, Jeffrey K. "Movies of the Avant-Garde: Jonas Mekas and the New York Art World." *Cinema Journal* 30,3 (Spring 1991).

Schwartz, Therese. "The Politicization of the American Avant-Garde," Parts 1–4. *Art in America* (November 1971); (March 1972); (March 1973); (January 1974).

Segal, Mark. "Hollis Frampton's *Zorn's Lemma*." *Film Culture* no. 52 (Spring 1971).

Semkow, J. "Valse Triste." *Film Library Quarterly* 15, 2 and 3 (1982).

Sharits, Paul. "A Cinematics Model for Film Studies in Higher Education." *Film Culture* nos. 65/66 (1978).

————. "Words Per Page." *Afterimage* 4 (Autumn 1972).

Sheldon, M. "Marilyn." *Film Quarterly* 27, 3 (1974).

Simon, William. "A Completely Open Space: Michael Snow's *La Région Centrale*." *Millennium Film Journal* nos. 4/5 (Spring 1979b).

————. "Reading *Zorns Lemma*." *Millennium Film Journal* nos. 1/2 (Spring/Summer 1978).

————. "Talking About Magellan: An Interview with Hollis Frampton." *Millennium Film Journal* nos. 7/8/9 (Fall/Winter 1980–1981).

Sitney, P. Adams. "Structural Film." *Film Culture* no. 47 (Summer 1966).

————. "Interview with George Landow." *Film Culture* no. 47 (Summer 1966).

————. "The Avant-Garde Film : Kenneth Anger and George Landow." *Afterimage* 2 (1970).

————. "Notes on *Rameau's Nephew*." *October* 4 (Fall 1977).

————. "Autobiography in Avant-Garde Film." *Millennium Film Journal* no. 1 (Winter 1977).

Snow, Michael. "*La Région Centrale*." *Film Culture* no. 52 (Spring 1971).

————. "Passage." *Artforum* 10, 1 (September 1971).

————. "Pages From *Rameau's Nephew by Diderot (Thanx to Dennis Young) by Wilma Schoen*." *Afterimage* 7 (Summer 1978).

————. "A lot of Near Mrs." *Film Reader* 3 (1978).

Snyder, Joel. "Picturing Vision." *Critical Inquiry* 6 (1980).

Springer, P. G. "New Improved George Landow Interview." *Film Culture* nos. 67/68/69 (1979a).

Strand, Chick. "Notes on Ethnographic Film by a Film Artist." *Wide Angle* 2,3 (1978).

Taubin, Amy. "Doubled Visions." *October* 4 (Fall 1977).

————. "Robert Breer, Whitney Museum; Ernie Gehr, Anthology Film Archive." *Artforum* 19, 11 (September 1980).

Tuchman, M. "The Mekas Bros. Brakhage and Baillie Traveling Circus." *Film Comment* 14,2 (March–April 1978).

Vogel, Amos. "Independents: Smiles and Tears." *Film Comment* 12,1 (January–February 1976).

Weinbren, Grahame. "Six Filmmakers and an Ideal of Composition." *Millennium Film Journal* no. 3 (Winter 1979).

Wollen, Peter. "'Ontology' and Materialism in Film" *Screen* 17,1 (Spring 1976). (Republished in *Readings and Writings: Semiotic Counter-Strategies*. London: Verso, 1982.)

Zita, Jacqueline. "Counter Currencies of a Lesbian Iconography: The Films of Barbara Hammer." *Jump Cut* 24 (1981).

BOOKS

American Federation of the Arts. *A History of the American Avant-Garde Cinema*. New York: American Federation of the Arts, 1976.

Arts Council of Great Britain. *Film as Form: Formal Experiment in Film, 1910–1975*. London: Arts Council of Great Britain, 1979.

Barrett, Gerald, and Wendy Brabner. *Stan Brakhage: A Guide to References and Resources*. Boston: G.K. Hall, 1983.

Battcock, Gregory, ed. *Minimal Art: A Critical Anthology*. New York: E.P. Dutton, 1968.

Bourdon, David. *Warhol*. New York: Abrams, 1989.

Brakhage, Stan. *Metaphors on Vision*. New York: Film Culture, 1963.

————. *The Brakhage Lectures*. Chicago: The Good Lion Press, 1972.

————. *Brakhage Scrapbook*. Edited by Robert J. Haller. New Paltz, NY: Documentext, 1972.

————. *The Seen*. San Francisco: Zephyrus Image, 1975.

————. *Film Biographies*. Berkeley: Turtle Island, 1977.

————. *Film at Wit's End. Eight Avant-Garde Filmmakers*. Kingston, NY: Documentext-McPherson, 1989.

Broughton, James. *Seeing the Light*. San Francisco: City Lights, 1977.

Buchloh, Benjamin H. D. *Modernism and Modernity in the Arts*. Halifax: Press of the Nova Scotia College of Art and Design, 1983.

Burch, Noel. *A Theory of Film Practice*. Translated by Helen Lane. New York: Praeger, 1973.

Burger, Peter. *Theory of the Avant-Garde*. Translated by Michael Shaw. Minneapolis: University of Minnesota Press, 1984.

Caws, Mary Ann. *The Eye in the Text: Essays on Perception, Mannerist to Modern*. Princeton: Princeton University Press, 1981.

Cornwall, Regina. *Snow Seen*. Toronto: PMA Books, 1980.

Curtis, David. *Experimental Cinema: A Fifty Year Evolution*. New York: Delta, 1971.

Debord, Guy. *Society of the Spectacle*. Detroit: Black and Red, 1967.

Dixon, Wheeler Winston. *The Exploding Eye: A Re-Visionary History of 1960s American Experimental Cinema*. Albany, NY: SUNY Press, 1997.

Enzensberger, Hans Magnus. *The Consciousness Industry: On Literature, Politics and the Media*. New York: The Seabury Press, 1974.

Foster, Hal, ed. *Vision and Visuality*. Seattle: Bay Press, 1988.

Frampton, Hollis. *Circles of Confusion*. Rochester, NY: Visual Studies Workshop Press, 1983.

Garrels, Gary, ed. *The Work of Andy Warhol*. Seattle: Bay Press and the Dia Foundation, 1989.

Gidal, Peter, ed. *Structural Film Anthology*. London: British Film Institute, 1976.

———. *Materialist Film*. London: Routledge, 1989.

Greenberg, Clement. *Art and Culture*. Boston: Beacon, 1965.

Haskell, Barbara, and John G. Hanhardt. *Yoko Ono: Arias and Objects*. Layton, Utah: Peregrine Smith, 1991.

Heath, Stephen. *Questions of Cinema*. Bloomington: Indiana University Press, 1971.

James, David. *Allegories of Cinema: American Film in the Sixties*. Princeton: Princeton University Press, 1989.

Jameson, Fredric. *The Prison-House of Language: A Critical Account of Structuralism and Russian Formalism*. Princeton: Princeton University Press, 1972.

Jenkins, Bruce, and Susan Krane. *Hollis Frampton: Recollections/Recreations*. Cambridge, MA: MIT University Press, 1984.

Johnston, Claire, ed. *Notes on Women's Cinema*. London: Society for Education in Film and Television, 1973.

Kaplan, E. Ann. *Women and Film: Both Sides of the Camera*. New York: Methuen, 1983.

Keller, Marjorie. *Childhood in the Films of Cocteau, Cornell, and Brakhage*. Rutherford, NJ: Fairleigh Dickinson University Press, 1986.

Koch, Stephen. *Stargazer: Andy Warhol's World and His Films*. New York: Praeger, 1973.

Kostelanetz, Richard, ed. *Esthetics Contemporary*. Buffalo: Prometheus Books, 1978.

Lane, Michael, ed. *Introduction to Structuralism*. New York: Basic Books, 1970.

LeGrice, Malcolm. *Abstract Film and Beyond*. Boston: MIT Press, 1977.

MacCabe, Colin, ed. *Who Is Andy Warhol?* Bloomington: Indiana University Press, 1997.

MacDonald, Scott. *A Critical Cinema: Interviews with Independent Filmmakers*. Los Angeles: University of California Press, 1988.

———. *Avant-Garde Film: Motion Studies*. Cambridge: Cambridge University Press, 1993.

Mekas, Jonas. *Movie Journal: The Rise of American Cinema, 1959–71*. New York: Collier, 1972.

Mellencamp, Patricia. *Indiscretions: Avant-Garde Film, Video, and Feminism*. Bloomington: Indiana University Press, 1990.

Merleau-Ponty, Maurice. *The Phenomenology of Perception*. Translated by Colin Smith. London: Routledge & Kegan Paul, 1962.

Metz, Christian. *Language and Cinema*. Translated by Donna Jean Umiker-Sebeok. The Hague: Mouton, 1974.

Michelson, Annette, ed. *New Forms in Film*. Switzerland: Montreux Exhibition Catalog, 1974.

Nichols, Bill, ed. *Movies and Methods*. Berkeley: University of California Press, 1976.

Noguez, Dominique. *Eloge du cinéma expérimental*. Paris: Centre Georges Pompidou, 1979.

O'Pray, Michael, ed. *Andy Warhol, The Film Factory*. Bloomington: Indiana University Press, 1990.

Peterson, Sidney. *The Dark of the Screen*. New York: Anthology Film Archives and New York University Press, 1980.

Poggioli, Renato. *The Theory of the Avant-Garde*. New York: Harper and Row, 1968.

Polan, Dana. *The Political Language of Film and the Avant-Garde*. Ann Arbor: UMI Research Press, 1985.

Projected Images. Minneapolis: Walker Art Center, 1979.

Rainer, Yvonne. *Work 1961–1973*. New York and Halifax: Nova Scotia College of Art and Design and New York University Press, 1974.

Rich, B. Ruby. *Yvonne Rainer*. Minneapolis: Walker Art Gallery, 1981.

Rosen, Marjorie. *Popcorn Venus: Women, Movies and the American Dream*. New York: Avon, 1973.

Rosenbaum, Jonathan. *Film: The Front Line—1983*. Denver: Arden, 1983.

Rowe, Carel. *The Baudelairean Cinema: A Trend within the American Avant-Garde*. Ann Arbor: University of Michigan, 1982.

Schneemann, Carolee. *More Than Meat Joy*. New Paltz, NY: Documentext, 1979.

Sitney, P. Adams, ed. *Film Culture Reader*. New York: Praeger, 1970.

————, ed. *The Essential Cinema: Essays on Films in the Collection of Anthology Film Archives*. New York: New York University Press, 1975.

————, ed. *The Avant-Garde Film: A Reader of Theory and Criticism*. New York: New York University Press, 1978.

————. *Visionary Film: The American Avant-Garde*. 2nd ed. New York: Oxford, 1979.

Turim, Maureen. *Abstraction in Avant-Garde Films*. Ann Arbor: UMI Research Press, 1985.

Vogel, Amos. *Film as a Subversive Art*. New York: Random House, 1974.

Warhol, Andy. *The Philosophy of Andy Warhol*. New York: Harcourt Brace Jovanovich, 1975.

————. *Portraits of the Seventies*. New York: Random House, 1979.

Wees, William C. *Light Moving in Time: Studies in the Visual Aesthetics of Avant-Garde Film*. Berkeley: University of California Press, 1992.

Wheeler, Dennis, ed. *Form and Structure in Recent Film*. Vancouver: Talon Books, 1972.

Youngblood, Gene. *Expanded Cinema*. New York: E. P. Dutton, 1970.

Picture Sources

All of the photographs in this volume are from Photofest, with the following exceptions:

Museum of Modern Art Film Stills Archive. Pages: 8, 10, 11, 12, 13, 24, 32 (top), 47, 48, 61, 63, 64, 72, 73, 75, 80 (top), 82, 86, 87 (bottom), 88, 92, 97, 114, 120, 123 (top), 132, 148, 150, 160, 162, 169 (bottom), 170, 179 (bottom), 186 (bottom), 189, 191, 213, 215, 221, 225 (bottom), 228, 245, 277, 286, 296, 297, 329, 365, 380, 456, 459, 466, 468, 469, 471.

Jerry Ohlinger's Movie Material Store. Pages: 81, 91.

William H. Phillips (private collection). Pages: 38, 42, 53 (top), 78, 94, 117 (bottom), 121, 123 (bottom), 124 (top), 125, 126, 127, 134, 143, 181, 186 (top), 187, 208, 211 (bottom), 214, 240, 249, 298, 368, 369, 370, 376, 377, 378.

Cinema Products Corporation. Page: 375.

Solid State Logic. Page: 388.

Sound One Corporation. Page: 393.

Douglas Gomery (private collection). Page: 408.

Jill Godmilow. Page: 423.

William Rothman (private collection). Pages: 429, 431, 441, 449.

Zipporah Films. Page: 437.

Amalie Rothschild. Page: 446.

Zeitgeist Films. Page 475.

All poster art, publicity materials, and memorabilia are from the Reel Poster Gallery, London, or the author's private collection.

General Index

Italic numerals signify illustration captions.

Index of Films

Italic numerals signify illustrations.